HAUSA-ENGLISH
ENGLISH-HAUSA
DICTIONARY

by

NICHOLAS AWDE

HIPPOCRENE BOOKS

New York

For information, address:
Hippocrene Books, Inc.
171 Madison Avenue
New York, NY 10016

ISBN 0-7818-0426-4 (pbk.)

Typesetting and font design by Nicholas Awde / Desert♥Hearts

Printed in the United States of America

CONTENTS

Acknowledgements   iii
Abbreviations   v
Notes on use   vi

HAUSA-ENGLISH DICTIONARY   1

ENGLISH-HAUSA DICTIONARY   181

Appendix 1: English irregular verbs   430
Appendix 2: Hausa verbs   434
Appendix 3: Hausa pronouns   442
Appendix 4: Useful phrases and vocabulary   446
Appendix 5: Ajami   452

Introduction

I hope this new dictionary will be a useful resource to all those speakers of English and Hausa who wish to deepen their knowledge and use of these languages. The dictionary is intended to cover their needs with the most up-to-date entries in a handy reference form, and it should especially prove to be an aid in navigating the growing global vocabulary of politics, telecommunications, computers, business and travel.

I would like to thank Malami Buba for his invaluable editorial contributions and suggestions in the final stages of completing this volume.

I would also like to thank the following for their contributions and encouragement over the years: Graham Furniss, Barry Burgess, Jack Carnochan, Tom Shea, Phil Sawyer, Hakim Baba-Ahmed, Sa'idu Ɓaɓura Ahmad, Sani Yusuf Sada, Tukur Ingawa, Sambo Junaidu, Ahmad Amfani, Mary MacIntosh, Flavia Grassi, Mzekala Shanidze, Martin Orwin, Bayero University Kano, Ahmadu Bello University Zaria, the School of Oriental and African Studies, the Hausa Section of the BBC World Service, and all those who made a childhood in Zaria so memorable.

Special thanks go to Fred Hill (whose first sentences were in Hausa) and Emma Hill, Michael Wylde, Emanuela Losi (who helped typeset), Evie Arup, Laurence Chabert, Peter Davies, Kevin Smith, Andrew Honey, Ian Carnochan, John Wright, Imad Al-Assir, Hugh Mulcahey, Jan Barrington, Richard Brow, Saidi el-Gheithy, Farouque Abdillah, Bruce Ingham, Anne Raufaste, and most of all George Blagowidow, Paula Redes and all at Hippocrene.

This dictionary is dedicated to Neil Skinner, in honour of a lifetime's work for the Hausa people and their language.

Nicholas Awde
London

Gabatarwa

Ina fatar wannan sabon ƙamus zai yi amfani ga dukan jama'ar da ke magana da Hausa ko Turanci, waɗanda kuma ke bukatar zurfafa iliminsu cikin waɗannan harsuna. An ƙuduri cewa sabon ƙamus ɗin zai biya bukatunsu ta hanyar ba da sabbin ma'anoni da aka gabatar ta hanya mafi sauƙi. Haka kuma zai zama jagora ne wajen fahimtar tarin kalmomin siyasa, na sadarwa, na kwamfuta, na cinikayya, da na yawon shaƙatawa dake ta turarowa cikin rayuwar jama'ar duniya.

Wannan ƙamus ɗin an buga shi ne da anniyar girmama Neil Skinner, saboda tarin gudummawar da ya bayar wajen haɓaka harshen Hausa da al'adun Hausawan.

Introduction

J'espère que ce nouveau dictionnaire constituera un instrument de travail utile pour tous ceux qui pratiquent l'anglais et le haoussa et qui souhaitent approfondir leur connaissance et leur maîtrise de ces langues. Ce dictionnaire cherche à répondre à leurs besoins sous une forme pratique et en incluant les définitions les plus modernes. Il devrait en particulier permettre de mieux ulitiser le vocabulaire sans cesse croissant dans les domaines de la politique, des télécommunications, de l'informatique, des affaires ou des voyages.

Ce dictionnaire est dédié à Neil Skinner, qui a consacré toute sa vie au peuple haoussa et à sa langue.

Abbreviations

acad.	academic / *na jami'a*
adj	adjective / *siffa*
adv	adverb / *bayanau*
conj	conjunction / *harafin haɗau*
Chr.	Christian / *na Kirista*
ec.	economic / *na tattalin arziki*
ed.	education / *na ilimi*
f	feminine / *tamata*
fin.	finance / *sha'anin kudî*
gen	genitive / *nasaba*
Isl.	Islamic / *na Musulunci*
leg.	legal / *na shari'a*
m	masculine / *namiji*
med.	medical / *na aikin likita*
mil.	military / *na soja*
mus.	music / *na kiɗa*
n	noun / *suna*
Nr	Niger Hausa / *Hausar Nijar*
pl	plural / *jam'i*
pol.	political / *na siyasa*
prep	preposition / *harafin bigire*
rel.	religious / *na addini*
sl.	slang / *sara*
s.o.	someone / *wani*
spor.	sporsts / *wasanni*
tel.	telecommunications / *sadarwa ta wayar iska*
UK	British English / *Ingilishi*
US	American English / *Turancin Amirka*
v	verb / *fi'ili*

Notes

1. Brackets following an English verb contain its past tense and past participle.

2. Brackets following a Hausa verb contain other verbal forms and/or its verbal noun.

3. *v1-7* indicates a Hausa verb's grade (see Appendix).

4. The asterisk in *v2** is put there as a reminder that these are 'changing' or 'variable vowel' verbs.

5. Brackets following a noun contain other noun forms and/or its plural

6. Long vowels in Hausa are marked with a macron: ā, ē, ī, ō, ū.

7. Low tone is marked with a grave accent: à, ā̀, è, ḕ, ì, ī̀, ò, ṑ, ù, ū̀. Falling tone by a circumflex: â, ê, î, ô, û. High tone is unmarked.

8. A tilde over an r indicates that it is rolled/trilled, not flapped: r̃, R̃.

9. *duba wajen* indicates *see* another word.

HARUFFAN TURANCI

a	[ei]	**n**	[en]
b	[biː]	**o**	[əu]
c	[siː]	**p**	[piː]
d	[diː]	**q**	[kjuː]
e	[iː]	**r**	[aː]
f	[ef]	**s**	[es]
g	[dʒiː]	**t**	[tiː]
h	[eitʃ]	**u**	[juː]
i	[aːi]	**v**	[viː]
j	[jei]	**w**	[dʌbljuː]
k	[kei]	**x**	[eks]
l	[el]	**y**	[wai]
m	[em]	**z**	[zed; ziː]

THE HAUSA ALPHABET

Hausa letter	Hausa name of letter	Approximate English equivalent
'	[hamzà]	*glottal stop*
a	[à]	*short:* fat *long:* father
b	[bā]	box
ɓ	[ɓā]	—
c	[cā]	church
d	[dā]	dog
ɗ	[ɗà]	—
e	[ē]	*short:* pet *long: like the* a *in* paid
f	[fā]	fat
g	[gā]	get
h	[hā]	hat
i	[ì]	*short:* sit *long:* seat
j	[jā]	jet
k	[kā]	kick
ƙ	[ƙā]	—
l	[lā]	let
m	[mā]	mat
n	[nā]	net
o	[ō]	*short:* cot *long:* coat
r	[rā]	*either 'flapped', or 'rolled' as in Scots English*
s	[sā]	sit
sh	[shā]	shut
t	[tā]	ten
ts	[tsā]	—
u	[ū]	*short:* put *long:* shoot
w	[wā; wō]	win
y	[yā]	yes
'y	['yā]	—
z	[zā]	zebra

Notes on the Hausa alphabet

1. **ɓ, ɗ, ƙ, ts** and **'y** represent the glottalised forms of **b, d, k, s** and **y** respectively. Capitals of these letters are **Ɓ, Ɗ, Ƙ, Ts** and **'Y**.

2. Any consonant may be doubled/geminate.

3. For **p** see **h** or **f**.

4. **sh** and **ts** are listed under **s** and **t** respectively.

5. Doubled **sh** and **ts** are written **ssh** and **tts** respectively.

6. In Niger **yˁ** may be found for **'y**.

7. The letter **'** is ignored when putting words in alphabetical order.

8. The short vowels **i** and **u** are frequently interchangeable.

HAUSA-ENGLISH

Aa

à *prep* 1. at 2. in
a, à, ā, â 1. one 2. they
ā'à no
à'àlā *f* 1. importance 2. crucial
àbā *f see* àbù
àbàdâ, haŕ àbàdâ *adv*
   1. forever 2. eternity 3. haŕ
   àbàdâ dundùndun forever
   and ever
àbā'isì *see* ummàl àbā'isì
ābàn *m* oven
àbàrbā *f* pineapple
àbàsiyà *m* overseer
àbàtayà *m/f* overtime
àbin *see* àbù
àbin baƙin cikì *adv* unfortunately
àbîn dà 1. what 2. which
àbin dà zâi jē yà zō *m* current
   affairs
àbin ɗanà wutā *m* light switch
àbinci *m* food
àbincin darē *m* supper
àbincin rānā *m* lunch
àbin hannū *m* material wealth
àbin shâ *m* drink
àbin tāyaŕ dà bôm *m* detonator
àbiyansō *f*, (Nr) àbìyàsō *m*
   aerodrome
àbìyàtâr *f* (Nr) tee-shirt
àbìyô *m* (Nr) aeroplane
àbòkâ *m* (Nr) lawyer
àbòkantakà *f* friendship
àbōkī *m* (*f* àbōkìyā, *pl* àbòkai)
   1. friend 2. companion 3. client
   4. partner
àbōkin àdāwà *m* member of
   the opposition

àbōkin aikì *m* work colleague
àbōkin cìnikī *m* trading partner
àbōkin gàbā *m* enemy
àbōkin gàsā *m* opponent
àbōkin hàmayyà *m* 1. rival 2.
   member of the opposition
àbōkin huldâ *m* 1. accomplice
   2. (pol.) friend
àbōkin shàŕi'à *m* (leg.) party
àbòtā *f* friendship
àbù *m* (*gen* àbin, *pl* abūbuwà)
   thing
àbùtā *f* 1. friendship 2.
   yàŕjējēnìyaŕ àbùtā treaty of
   friendship
adàbī *m* literature
adàbin gaŕgājiyā *m* traditional
   literature
adàbô! goodbye!
adàdī *m* (*pl* àdàdai) 1. number
   2. numeral 3. total 4. rate
adàdin mutànē *m* population
àdakà *m* (*pl* àdàkū, adakōkī)
   1. box 2. dane gun
ādalcì *m* justice
ādàlī *m* (*f* ādàlā, *pl* àdàlai)
   honest
ādànà *vl* (*m* ādànì) 1. to look
   after 2. to maintain
àdànà *m* inferior
ādànà kāyàyyakin àbinci
   1. to store food 2. to hoard
ādànì *m* maintenance
àdāwà *f* 1. hatred 2. opposition
   3. jàm'iyyàŕ àdāwà (pol.)
   opposition party 4. nūnà
   àdāwà gà to oppose 5. sàmi

àdāwà to be challenged

àddā f (pl addunà) matchet

àddabà 1. f harassing 2. v2* to harass 2. to cause suffering to

àddīnì m (pl àddìnai) 1. religion 2. ilìmin àddīnì theology

àddu'à f (pl addu'ō'ì) 1. prayer 2. (rel.) tàron àddu'à retreat

àdìbâs m 1. cash advance 2. down payment

àdikô m head-tie

àdìre m tie-dye

àdìrēshì m (pl àdìr̃ìsai, adir̃isōshì) address

adō m 1. decoration 2. mài iyà adō smart 2. fashionable 4. yi adō to be dressed up

aduwà f (pl aduwōyi) desert date tree

afà v1 (m afî) to pop into one's mouth

àfàrētà m/f 1. operator 2. projectionist

àfil m legal appeal

Afir̃kà f Africa

Afir̃kà à kudù dà Sàhār̃à f sub-Saharan Africa

afkà wà v1 1. to happen to 2. to hit

Afrìl, Àfrìlù m April

aftò m yārinyàr̃ aftò actress

àfu v7 to be eager

afūwā f forgiveness

agà f fashion

àgàdè m/pl plantain

āgàjī m 1. assistance 2. relief aid

āgàjin kâi tsàye m direct aid

agânā f smallpox

àgazà v2* (-ji/jē, m āgàjī) to assist

àgōgo m (pl àgògai, agōgunà) 1. watch 2. clock

agòlà m (f agōlìyā, pl àgòlai) stepchild

àgushī m/pl melon seeds

Àgustà m August

àgwàgwa f (pl àgwàgī) duck

àhìr...! don't you dare...!

ahuwà f leniency

aibàtā v1 to blame

aibì, aibù m (pl aibōbī) 1. blame 2. mark 3. stain

àidîn m iodine

àikā v2* (m aikì) 1. to send someone 2. to depute

aikàcē v4 to work out

àikàce adv à aikàce in practice

àikàce-àikàce pl 1. activities 2. see aikì

aikà dà v1 1. to send something 2. to supply

aikà dà kāyā to ship

aikàtā v1 to do

àikē m (pl àike-àike) errand

aikì m (pl ayyukà, àikàce-àikàce) 1. work 2. employment 3. action 4. (med.) surgery 5. bā dà aikì to employ

aikìn bàban gīwā m (pol/ec.) white elephant

aikìn cùdê-ni-ìn-cùdê-kà m cooperation

aikìn gwamnatì, (Nr) aikìn sàr̃ūshì m civil service

aikìn kùlā m maintenance

aikìn nâs m nursing

aikìn nōmā m agriculture

aikìn sābìs, (Nr) aikìn sàr̃bîs m restaurant service

aikìn sōjà m military service

aikìn yî m 1. employment 2.

rashìn aikìn yî unemployment
3. adàdin maràsà aikìn yî unemployment rate
Ailàn *f* Ireland
ainihi *m* **1.** reality **2. na ainihi** real
ainihin *adv* exact
ainùn *adv* **1.** very much **2.** too
aiwatař da *v5* **1.** to go ahead with **2.** to operate **3.** to carry out
ajàlī *m* **1.** period **2.** fate
àjàmi *m* Hausa written in Arabic script
àjandà *f* (*pl* **àjàndū**) agenda
ajì *m* (*pl* **azūzuwà**) **1.** (school) class **2.** heap
àjiyà 1. *f* (*pl* **àjìye-àjìye**) deposit **2.** (fin.) savings **3.** *v2** to deposit
àjiyàř zūcìyā *f* yi **àjiyàř zūcìyā** to sigh
ajìyē *v4* **1.** to put **2.** to put down **3.** to park
ajìyè aikì 1. *m* retirement **2.** *v4* to retire
ajìyè dàngàntakà to break off relations
ājizancì *m* **1.** weakness **2.** shortcoming
ājìzī *m* mortal
akà *relative completive* **1.** one **2.** they
akaifā *f* (*pl* **àkàifū**) **1.** fingernail **2.** toenail **3.** claw
akàlà *f* jā **akàlà** to control
akalà *f* trough
akàn, a kàn *habitual* **1.** one **2.** they
àkantà *m* (*pl* **akantōcī**) accountant
àkàsarà *adv* at most

akasàrī *m* maximum
akàsī *m* opposite
akasìdân, (Nr) **àkàsìdân** *m* car accident
àkàwu *m* (*pl* **akāwunà, àkàwu-àkàwu**) clerk
akè *relative completive* **1.** one **2.** they
akiřka *f* second-hand
ākìtâ *m* architect
à-kòri-kūrā *f* van
àku *m/f* parrot
àkul *conj* whenever
àkwiyà *f* (*pl* **awākì**) goat
àkwai there is, there are
àkwàtì *m* (*pl* **akwātunà**) **1.** box **2.** case
àkwàtìn gidan wayà *m* P.O. box
aƙàlī *m* covenant
àƙallà *adv* at least
àƙallà àkàsarà *adv* more or less
àƙīdà *f* **1.** belief **2.** ideal **3.** ideology **4. maràs àƙīdà** unprincipled
àlàbō *m* yam flour
alà cùtā alà māgànī *adv* **1.** intermittent **2.** haphazard
àl'ādà *f* (*pl* **àl'àdū**) **1.** custom **2.** menstruation **3. à bisà àl'ādà** normally
àladè *m* (*pl* **àlàdai**) pig
àl'àdū *pl* fannìn àl'àdū culture
àlaikà, àlaikùn Sàlāmù àlaikà/ àlaikùn! Peace be upon you! (*response:* **Àlaikà/ àlaikùn sàlâm!** And upon you!)
àl'ajàbī *m* (*pl* **al'ajubà**) **1.** miracle **2.** wonder
alà kullà hālìn *adv* at any time
àlāƙà *f* **1.** relationship **2.** links
àlaƙaƙài *adv* in utter frustration

alal mìsālì, alàl mìsālì *adv* for example

àlāmà *f* (*pl* **àlàmū**) **1.** sign **2.** label **3.** (med.) symptom

àlāmàř hanyà *f* road sign

àl'amàrī *m* (*pl* **al'amurà**) **1.** matter **2.** trend **3.** ƙanānàn al'amuřà minor issues **4.** hanyàř al'amuřà course of events

àlāmàř karìn sautì *f* tone mark

àlāmàř mòtsin râi *m* exclamation mark

àlāmàř tàmbayì *m* question mark

àlāmàř zàncen wani *m* quotation mark

alàmtā *v1* to indicate

àlamtà *v3* to be indicated

al'amuřàn gidā *pl* internal affairs

ālātù *m* **1.** luxury **2.** mài ālātù luxurious

àlàtūřè *m* yi àlàtūřè to protest

àlāwà *f/pl* sweet(s)

àlāwùs *m* cash allowance

àlayyàhō *m* spinach

àlbařàs *m* leprosy

àlbařkà *f* **1.** prosperity **2.** fertility **3.** mài àlbařkà fertile **4.** maràs àlbařkà infertile **5.** Àlbařkà! No sale! **6.** Congratulations!

àlbařkàcin bàkī *m* **1.** opinion **2.** fàɗì àlbařkàcin bàkī to have a say (gàmè dà in)

àlbařkàř gōnā *f* agricultural products

àlbařkàtā *v2** (**-ci/cē**) to ratify

àlbařkàtū *pl* **1.** resources **2.** mineral wealth **3.** *see* àlbařkàcī

àlbàřkàtun ƙasā *pl* **1.** minerals **2.** raw materials

àlbàřùsai *pl* ammunition

àlbàřūshì *m* gunpowder

àlbasà *f/pl* onion

àlbâshi *m* **1.** wages **2.** hanà tāshìn àlbâshī wage restraint

àlbishìř *m* good news

àlbīûř *m* (Nr) referee

àlēwà *f/pl* sweet(s)

àlfadařī *m* (*f* **àlfadařā,** *pl* **àlfàdàřai**) mule

àlfahàřī *m* **1.** boasting **2.** yi àlfahàři dà to acclaim (tàmkař as)

àlfařmā *f* mài àlfařmā His Excellency

àlfijìř *m* dawn

àlfyan *f* two thousand

àlgaitā *f* (*pl* **àlgàitū**) shawm

algàshī *m* (*f* **algàsā,** *pl* **àlgàsai**) green

àlgûs *m* malpractice

àlhajì *m* (*f* **àlhajìyā,** *pl* **àlhàzai**) pilgrim (to Mecca)

àlhakī *m* **1.** sin **2.** revenge **3.** guilt **4.** responsibility **5.** mutànē dà bâ su dà àlhakī innocent people

àlhakin bā dà shaidà *m* (leg.) burden of proof

àlhālī *conj* in fact

àlhālī kùwa... *conj* whereas in fact...

àlhamdùlìllāhì! praise be to God!

Àlhàmîs *f* Thursday

àlhēřì *m* **1.** Sai alhērì! Only good news! (reply to ìnā làbàrì? *etc.*) **2.** hangō àbin àlhēřì to be optimistic

àlhudàhudà *f* hoopoe crane

alìf *f* thousand
àlìlô *m/f* nylon garment
àlìmètì *m* (Nr) match
àljabařà *f* algebra
àljan *m* (*f* àljanā, *pl* àljànū) jinn
àljannà, àljannà *f* 1. heaven 2. paradise
àljìhù *m* (*pl* aljìhunà) pocket
àlkadàřī *m* 1. value 2. strength
alkàhôn *m* alcohol
àlkāhùřā *f* somersault
àlkālì *m* (*pl* àlkàlai) judge
alkamà *f* wheat
àlkařyà *f* (*pl* àlkàřyū) 1. town 2. city
àlkawàřī *m* (*pl* alkawařà) 1. promise 2. yì àlkawàřī to promise 3. takàřdař àlkawàřī I.O.U. 4. mài àlkawàřī reliable
àlkawàřī na fātář bakà *m* empty promise
àlkūkì *m* (*pl* àlkùkai) niche
àlkwâl *m/f* (Nr) alcohol
àlkyabbà *f* (*pl* àlkyàbbū) burnous
àlƙadàřī *see* àlkadàřī
àlƙalàmì *m* (*pl* alƙalumà) 1. pen 2. numeral
àlƙālì *m* judge
àlƙàlin àlƙàlai *m* chief judge
àlƙàlin wàsà *m* referee
alƙalumà *pl* statistics
Àlƙùř'ànì *m* Koran
allà *f* (*pl* allôlì) a god
allà-allà *f* 1. eagerness 2. likelihood
Allàh *m* 1. God 2. *see* wadai
allàzì *m* 1. who 2. which
âllì *m* chalk
àllō *m* (*pl* allunà) blackboard
àllūřà *f* (*pl* àllùřai) 1. pin

2. needle 3. syringe 4. injection 5. yì àllūřà to inject
àllūřař barcī *f* anaesthetic
àllūřař rìgàkafì *f* vaccination
àlmājìřī *m* (*f* àlmājìřā, *pl* àlmàjìřai) 1. beggar 2. Koranic student 3. disciple
àlmakàshì *m* (*pl* àlmàkàsai) scissors
àlmàřā *f* 1. fiction 2. fantasy 3. illusions
Àlmàsīhù *m* Messiah
almìnjîř *m* rat-trap
almubazzařancì *m* 1. extravagance 2. waste of money
àlmūřù *m* dusk
à lōkàcin bāya *adv* in the past
àl'ummà *f* (*pl* al'ummômì) 1. nation 2. community
àlwàlā *f* religious ablutions
àlwāshì *m* 1. cì àlwāshin... to pledge to...
àlwàtìkà *f* triangle
amai *m* (*gen* aman) 1. vomit 2. yì amai to vomit
amakù *m* stretcher
àmàlālô *m* flood water
aman wutà *m* eruption
àmānà *f* 1. trust 2. peace 3. honesty 4. treaty 5. mài cîn àmānà traitor 6. *see* bā dà àmānà
āmànū *m* niche
àmàrtùsâr *m* (Nr) shock absorber
amaryà *f* (*pl* amàrē) bride
ambàliyà *f* 1. flood 2. congestion 3. yì ambàliyà to flood 4. yì ambàliyà à kàsuwà to flood the market
ambàliyař jàma'à *f* population explosion

àmbàsàdâr *m* (Nr) ambassador
àmbatà *v2* * (-cì/-cē, *m*
   ambatō) 1. to mention 2. to
   quote 3. to state
ambatō *m* 1. mention 2. quote
àmbìr̃ìyājì *m* (Nr) clutch
àmbìtê *m* (Nr) reception
àmbōlà *f* abusive gesture
ambùlàn *m* (*pl* **ambulōlì**) 1.
   ambulance 2. envelope
àmbùryājè *m* car clutch
àmfàgâi *adv* in large amounts
àmfân *m* (Nr) breakdown
àmfānà *v2* * (*m* **àmfànī**) 1. to
   benefit from 2. to benefit
àmfānà *v3* to benefit
àmfànī *m* 1. benefit 2. **yanà dà**
   àmfànì it is useful 3. produce
àmfànin dà akà sāmù à
   shèkarà *m* gross national
   product (GNP)
àmfànin gōnā *m* crops
àmfànin ƙasā *m* national
   interest
àmfûl *m* (Nr) lightbulb
àmin! amen!
amìncē dà *v4* 1. to accept 2. to
   trust 3. to agree on 4. to
   recognise 5. to approve 6. to
   ratify
amìncêwā *f* 1. approval 2.
   recognition 3. **nūnà amìncêwā**
   dà to welcome 4. **ƙi amìncêwā**
   dà to reject
amìncì *m* 1. trust 2. friendship 3.
   reliability
àmìntà dà *v3* to trust
àmmā *conj* but
amō *m* 1. sound 2. recording
amon kàɗe-kàɗe *m* 1. noise 2.
   sound 3. (mus.) recording
amon wutā *m* tsagàità amon

wutā cease-fire
amōsànin gàɓɓai *m* arthritis
àmōsànin ƙashì *m* rheumatism
amsà 1. *f* (*pl* **amsōshì**) answer 2.
   plea 3. **bìsà amsà rôƙon...** at
   the express request of... 4. *v1*
   to answer 5. to reflect
àmsā *v2* * (-shì/shē) 1. to accept
   2. to assume
àmsà-kàma, àmsà-muryà *f*
   onomatopoeia
àmsà-kuwwà *m* 1. echo 2.
   loudspeaker
amsàr̃ fātàr̃ bakà *f* empty reply
amshì *m* 1. chorus 2. ɗan
   amshìn Shātā (pol.) puppet
amukù *m* stretcher
amyà *f* (*pl* **amyōyì**) beehive
an *completive* 1. one 2. they
anà *continuous* 1. one 2. they
àndîr *m* (Nr) building
angà *f* anchor
angàzā *v1* 1. to pressurise
àngazà *v2* * (-jì/jē, *f* **àngazà**)
   1. to push 2. **kai àngazà** to
   attack
angìzā *v1* to pressurise
angizō *m* influence
angò *m* (*pl* **angwàyē**) bridegroom
ànīnì *m* (*pl* **ànnìnai**) button
àniyà *f* 1. determination 2.
   ambition
ànkarà *v3* 1. to notice 2. to pay
   attention
ankwà *f* handcuffs
ànnabì *m* (*pl* **annabāwā**) 1.
   prophet. 2. **Ànnabì** the Prophet
   Muhammad
annē *m* (Nr) fertilizer
ànnōbā *f* epidemic
ànnòbā dàgà aindàllāhì *f*
   natural disaster

ànnòbaɍ tattalin aɍzìkì *f* economic sanctions

ànnūɍì *m* 1. light 2. brightness

antamfarētì *m* (Nr) interpreter

antarē, antarētì *m* (Nr) 1. retirement 2. pension 3. ɗan antaɍee pensioner

anyà anyà hakà nē? really?

àrā *v2** (*m* arō) to borrow

arà *vl* to lend

àɍādù *f* thunder

àɍàhā *f* 1. Yanà dà àɍàhā. It is cheap. 2. Nā sàmē shì àɍàhā. I got it it easily.

aràngamà *f* 1. clash 2. yi aràngamà to clash (dà with)

aɍanjì *m* orange

aɍas *adv* kāyan aɍas 1. fragile goods 2. dowry

àràzùwâr *m* (Nr) razor

aɍbà *f* 1. four thousand 2. yi aɍbà to meet by chance

àɍbà'in *f* forty

àɍbàminyà *f* four hundred

àrēbuwâl! (Nr) goodbye!

arèwa *f* 1. north 2. jihar arèwa the northern region 3. na arèwa northern

arèwa masò gabàs northeast

arèwa masò yâmba northwest

arèwa sak due north

arēwacin north of

àrèzùwâr *m* (Nr) watering can

àri bàkin... to quote... (dà cêwā as saying)

àɍiyà *f* arrears

aɍmashì *m* yi aɍmashì to be rewarding

aɍnè *m* (*f* aɍnìyā, *pl* aɍnā) pagan

arō *m* loan

àɍu-àɍu *adv* long ago

aɍzìkì *m* (*pl* aɍzukà) 1. wealth

2. prosperity 3. resources

aɍzìkin ƙasā *m* natural resources

aɍzùtā *vl* to make wealthy

àɍzutà *v3* to prosper

Àsabàɍ *f* Saturday

asalì *m* (*pl* àsàlai) 1. origin 2. reason 3. principle 4. lineage 5. yiwō asalì to originate (dàgà from)

àsāɍà *f* 1. yi àsāɍà to suffer casualties 2. yi àsāɍàɍ kudì to make a financial loss 3. *see* hàsāɍà

àsawàkì *m* 1. toothbrush 2. chewing stick

asfiɍìn *m* aspirin

àshānā *f* match(es)

àshē 1. Is that so? 2. of course

àshìɍin *f* twenty

asìbitì *f* (*pl* asibitōcì) 1. hospital 2. clinic

asìbitin dabbōbì *f* veterinary clinic

asìbitìn haifùwā *f* maternity clinic

àsìɍce *adv* à àsìɍce secretly

àsìɍì *m* (*pl* àsìɍai) secret

asìɍtā *vl* 1. to confide 2. to keep secret

Àsìyà *f* Asia

askā *f* (*pl* asàkē) 1. razor 2. scalpel 3. tribal marks

àskàliyè *m* (Nr) stairs

askaɍāwā *see* bà'askaɍè

askè *v4* to shave

askì *m* 1. shaving 2. haircut

àskìlâtâr *m* (Nr) accelerator, throttle

àstìlô *m* (Nr) pen

àsùbâ *f* 1. morning 2. first Islamic prayer of the day

asūsù *m* 1. cash box 2. safe

3. Treasury 4. funds
asūsùn āgàji *m* relief fund
Asūsùn IMF *m* International
Monetary Fund (IMF)
**Asūsùn Tàimakon Yârā na
MDD** *m* United Nations
International Children's
Emergency Fund (UNICEF)
atalàs *m* atlas
atasāyè *m* 1. physical exercises
2. exercising horses
atìbau...! it's not possible that...!
atìnī *m* dysentery
atìshāwà *f* sneeze
atòm *m* atom
àtōnè-janàr̃ *m* attorney-general.
àttājìr̃i *m* (*f* **àttājìr̃ā**, *pl*
àttàjìr̃ai) 1. rich person 2.
businessman 3. ƙàramin
àttājìr̃i bourgeois
Àttaur̃ā *f* Old Testament
au... au *conj* either... or
audùgā *f* 1. cotton 2. cotton wool
aukà wà *vl* 1. to attack 2. to
happen to
aukà wà... dà yāƙì to wage
war on
àuku *v7* to happen
àunā *v2** to buy by the measure
aunà *vl* (*m* **awò**) 1. to weigh 2.
to measure 3. to test
aunà hanyà to survey
àunē *v4* realization
àurā *v2** (*m* **aurē**) to marry
aurà *vl* Yā aurà wà ɗansà
Kànde. He arranged for his
son to marry Kande.
àuràtayyà *f* intermarriage
aurē *m* (*pl* **àure-àure**) 1.
marriage 2. kisàn aurē divorce
àutā *m/f* youngest child

awà *f* (*pl* **awōyī**) hour
àwā *conj* as if
awākī *pl see* àkwiya
àwazà *m* (*pl* **àwàzū**) rib
awò *m* (*pl* **àune-àune**) 1.
measure (of weight) 2. pound
(weight) 3. weight 4. *see* aunà
awòn gàba *m* yi awòn gàba to
do away (dà with)
āyà *f* (*pl* **āyōyī**) 1. full stop 2.
(Islam) Koranic verse
āyàr̃ tàmbayà *f* question mark
àyàbà *f* banana(s)
āyàn *m* 1. an iron 2. ironing
āyàr̃i *m* (*pl* **āyar̃ōr̃i**) caravan
āyìs *f* ice
ayyukà *pl* 1. activities 2. *see*
aikì
ayyukàn kētà dōkōkī *pl*
criminal activities
azà *vl* 1. to put on top 2. to
impose 3. to think
àzābà *f* (*pl* **àzàbū, azābōbī**) 1.
torture 2. torment
azabtar̃ dà *v5* to torture
àzahàr̃ *f* 1. mid afternoon 2.
Muslim second prayer of the day
àzal *adv* tun fìl àzal always
azancì *m* 1. sense 2. intelligence
azàr̃ā *f* (*pl* **àzàr̃ū**) 1. timber 2.
beam
à zō à ganì *adv* na à zō à ganì
1. tangible 2. exemplary
azùmī *m* 1. fasting 2. Ramadan
azùr̃fā *f* silver
azūzuwà *pl see* ajì
àzzakàr̃i *m* penis
àzzālùmī *m* (*f* **àzzālùmā**, *pl*
àzzàlùmai) 1. bully 2.
oppressor
azzìkī *m* (*pl* **azzukà**) *see* ar̃zìkì

Bb

Bà'àmiřkè *m* (*f* **Bà'àmiřkìyā,** *pl* **Amiřkāwā**) American
ba'àsī *m* investigation
Bà'āsìyē *m* (*f* **Bà'āsiyìyā,** *pl* **Āsiyāwā**) Asian
bà... ba not
bâ, bābu **1.** there is not / there are not **2.** without **3.** ƙarfe biyu bâ kwatà a quarter to two **4. Bâ kōmē!** It doesn't matter!
bā, bà not
bà... ba not, is not, are not
bā (**bâ** + *noun*) *v* **1.** to give (to someone) **2.** to cause **3.** *see* **bā dà, ban**
ba'à *f* **1.** joke **2. yi bā'à** to make fun (**wà** of)
bà'arè *m* northerner
bà'askařè *m* (*pl* **askařāwā**) soldier
bàba *m* father
bābà *f* **1.** aunt **2.** mother
bābā *m* indigo
bàbàkērē *m* **1.** monopoly **2.** blockade **3. yi bàbàkērē** to monopolise **4. yi bàbàkērē** to take control (**à/dà** of)
bàbba *m/f* (*pl* **mànyā**) **1.** big **2.** important **3.** senior
bàbbakà *f* **yi bàbbakà** to char
bàbban bankìn jihà *m* federal state bank
bàbban bankìn ƙasā *m* central bank
bàbban baƙī *m* capital letter
bàbban kwàmandàn rundunōnin mayàƙā *m* commander-in-chief of the armed forces
bàbban kwàmandàn sōjì *m* (mil.) supreme commander
bàbban kwàmishinà *m* high commissioner
bàbban lìmân *m* (Chr.) bishop
bàbbař bindigà *f* cannon
bàbbař mōtà *f* (*pl* **mânyan mōtōcī**) truck
Bàbbař Yàřjējēnìyař Hàřājì dà Cìnikī *f* General Agreement on Tariffs and Trade (GATT)
bābì *m* **1.** chapter **2.** category
bābù **1. Àkwai nāmà? – Bābù.** Is there any meat? – No, there isn't. **2.** *see* **bâ**
bàbuř, bàbûř *m* (*pl* **bāburà**) motor scooter
bā dà *v* **1.** to give something **2.** to supply **3.** to betray
bādà *v1* to give away
bā dà aikì *v* **1.** to employ **2. mài bā dà aikì** employer
bā dà àmānà *v* **1.** to entrust **2.** to mandate
bā dà bàyānì *v* to make a statement
bā dà hannū *v* **mài bā dà hannū** traffic policeman
bā dà làbāřì *v* to tell a story
bādàwā *f* **yi bādàwā** to give (**gà** to)
baddàlā *v1* to alter
badò *m* water-lily
bàdūkù *m* (*pl* **dùkàwā**) leatherworker

bàdî f/adv next year
bādînī m na bādînī covert
bàdî waccàn f/adv the year after next.
bàfādà m (pl **fàdàwā**) courtier
Bàfàr̃anshè m (f **Bàfàr̃anshìyā**, pl **Fàr̃ànsâi**) French
baffà m (pl **bàffànnī**) uncle
Bàfilācè m (f **Bàfilātà**, pl **Filànī**) Fulani
bāgarâr̃wā f not serious
bàgàruwā f acacia tree
bàgàtatàn adv unexpectedly
bàgidâjè m 1. naive 2. unsophisticated
bahā f sea
bàhagò m (f **bàhagùwā**, pl **bàhàgwai**) 1. someone left-handed 2. someone/ something difficult
bahàsī m 1. investigation 2. inquiry.
Bàhaushè m (f **Bàhaushìyā**, pl **Hàusàwā**) Hausa
bahò m 1. basin 2. bathtub 3. pushcart
bai v to hand over (**wà** to)
bài... ba he did not...
bâi ɗaya adv 1. **mài bâi ɗaya** uniform 2. **na bâi ɗaya** common
bainà-bainà adv neither one nor the other
bainar̃ jàma'à adv in the public eye
baitakin à baitakin wannàn as well as this
Bà'itāliyè m (f **Bà'itāliyìyā**, pl **Ītāliyāwā**) Italian
baitì m stanza
bai wà v to give to
bàibâi adv 1. inside-out 2. back-to-front

baibàyē v4 (f **bàibayà**) to thatch
baikō m **An yi manà baikō dà ità. I** have become engaged to her.
baitì m (pl **baitōcī**) line of poetry
bàiùlmālì m 1. treasury 2. central bank
baiwā f (pl **bàye-bàye**) 1. gift 2. generosity 3. engagement (to be married)
Bàjafanè m (f **Bàjafanìyā**, pl **Jafanāwā**) Japanese
bajè v4 1. to level 2. to spread out
bajì m badge
bājì m barge
bàjintà f **nūnà bàjintà** to claim credit (**wajen sāmùn** for)
bàjintar̃ dūniyà f (spor.) 1. world title 2. world record
bājò m badge
bakà adv in the mouth
bàkā m (pl **bakunkunà**) 1. bow 2. **bàkan gizo** rainbow
bā kâi to give in (**gà** to)
bàkanikè m mechanic
bàkâns f (Nr) holidays
bàkī m (pl **bākunà**) 1. mouth 2. opening 3. entrance 4. **sâ bàkī** to interfere 5. **yi bàkī** to swear at 6. **iyà bàkī** to be quick-witted
bàkī dà bàkī adv face-to-face
bàkin dāgā m front-line
bàkī dà hancì adv in/at close quarters
bàkī ɗaya, gà bàkī ɗaya adv 1. total 2. unanimously
bàkin 1. in exchange for 2. on the verge of 3. at the limit of

bàkin àlƙalàmì *m* nib
bàkin būtà *m* spout
bàkin ƙōfà *m* threshold
bàkin kogi *m* river bank
bàkin tèku *m* coast
bàkin titì *m* verge
bàkudù *m* southerner
bakwài *f* 1. seven 2. na bakwài seventh 3. bakwài biyu fortnight
bàkwàinì *m/f* premature baby
baƙàntā *vl* 1. to slander
baƙàntà rân... to prove embarrassing for...
baƙař dūniyà *f* criminal underworld
baƙař hājà *f* stock
baƙař kàsuwā *f* blackmarket
bàƙauyē *m* unsophisticated
baƙī *m* 1. (*f* baƙā, *pl* baƙàƙē) black 2. dark 3. bad 4. mài baƙin cikì unhappy 5. (*pl* babbaƙū) letter 6. consonant
baƙī ƙirin jet black
baƙin cikì 1. unhappiness 2. àbin baƙin cikì unfortunately
baƙin dājì *m* forest
baƙin jinī *m* unpopularity
baƙin ƙarfè *m* steel
baƙin mâi *m* (petroleum) oil
baƙin ruwā *m* clear water
bàƙō *m* (*f* bàƙuwā, *pl* bàƙī) 1. stranger 2. visitor 3. immigrant 4. Mun yi bàƙō. We have a guest
bàƙon darē *m* burglar
bàƙon dàurō *m* 1. measles 2. german measles
bàƙon hàurē *m* illegal immigrant
bàƙùncì Lāhiřà to die
bâl *f* ball

bàlagà *v3* to reach puberty
bàlāgà *f* rhetoric
bàlāguřō *m* 1. trip 2. yi bàlāguřō to go on a trip
bàlā'ì *m* disaster
bàlā'ì dàgà indàllāhì *m* natural disaster
bàlā'ìn dà kè saukař wà ƙanānàn yârā *m* (med.) polio
bàlā'ìn farì *m* drought
bàlā'ìn gurɓàcêwař yanàyī *m* ecological disaster
bàlā'ìn yunwà *m* famine
bàlànshâř *m* washerman
Bàlārabè *m* (*f* Bàlārabà, *pl* Lārabāwā) Arab
balàs *m* 1. (financial) balance 2. yi balàs settle the score.
bàl-bàl *adv* yi bàl-bàl to flicker, to flutter
bālìgī *m* (*f* bālìgā, *pl* bàlìgai) adult
bàlîs *m/f* (Nr) suitcase
bàllè *adv* 1. certainly 2. let alone
bàlô *m/f* 1. balloon 2. football
balō-balō *m* balloon
balshē *m* (Nr) 1. wound 2. scar
bâm *m* (*pl* bàmàbàmai) *see* bôm
bàmāgujè *m* (*f* bàmāgujìyā, *pl* māguzāwā) non-Muslim Hausa
bambam *adv* different
bambancì *m* 1. difference 2. nūnà bambancì to discriminate (wà against)
bambancìn launì *m* racism
bambàntā *vl* 1. to distinguish 2. to separate
bàmbantà *v3* to be different
bāmì *m* (*pl* bāmàyē) novice

bâmmī *m* palm wine

bana *f/adv* **1.** this year **2.** age

bana-bâ-haŕkằ *f* pickup truck

bànasāŕề *m* (*f* **bànasāŕìyā**, *pl* **nàsầŕa**) Christian

banatì *m* bayonet

bàn... ba I did not...

bandà *prep* **1.** apart from **2.** except **3.** without

ban dằriyā *m* **1.** humour **2.** ban dằriyā humorous

bandējì *m* bandage

bandìŕ *m* (*pl* **bandiŕōŕì**) bundle

bân dằkì *m* toilet

bàngā *f* dan bàngā hooligan

bangàjē *v4* to shove

ban gàskiyā *m* reliability

ban girmā *m* respect

bangō *m* (*pl* **bangwầyē**) **1.** wall **2.** book cover

ban haushī *m* annoyance

bànī... people of...

bànkā *v2** **1.** to patch up **2.** to break down **3.** to collide **4.** to use a lot of **5.** Yā bànki kuɗì. He embezzled.

bankằ wà *vl* to set ablaze

bankàɗà *vl*, **bànkaɗà** *v2** to reveal

bankàɗề *v4* to push aside

bankề *v4* to knock down

bankì *m* **1.** (*pl* **bankunằ**) bank **2.** (*pl* **bànke-bànke**) patch **3.** see bàbban bankìn...

bankìn àjiyàŕ kuɗì *m* savings bank

Bankìn Dūniyằ *m* World Bank

bankìn tsimī dà tānàdī *m* reserve bank

bankìn tsimī dà tānàdī reserve bank

ban kwānā *m* goodbye

banƙàrē *v4* to tie up

bân ƙasā *m* surface of the earth

ban màmākì *m* mài ban màmākì wonderful

ban ruwā *m* irrigation

bansìŕ! (Nr) good evening!

bàntē *m* (*pl* **bantunằ**) **1.** loincloth. **2.** underpants **3.** yi bàntē to circumcise

ban tsòrō *m* mài ban tsòrō frightening

banzā *f* **1.** stupid **2.** na banzā useless **3.** à banza in vain **4.** Tā sằmē shì à banza. She bought it cheap.

baŕ *see* barì

barà *m* (*f* **baranyằ**, *pl* **barōrì**) servant

baŕằ *f* begging

bàra *f/adv* last year

bàŕā *f* abin bàŕā target

bàrà-gurbì irresponsible

baram-bàràm *adv* Mun ràbu baram-bàràm We are on bad terms.

bàrằmū *m* mineral

bàràncē *m* bondage

baràndà *m/f* **1.** veranda **2.** patio **3.** (fin.) speculation **4.** ɗan baràndà middleman

bàŕàsā *f* liquor

Bàŕāshè *m* (*f* **Bàŕāshìyà**, *pl* **Ŕāshāwā**) Russian

bàra waccàn *f* the year before last

baŕāzànā wà *vl* to threaten

bàŕằzanā *f* **1.** threat **2.** kāwō bàŕằzanā to pose a threat (kân/gà to)

baŕbàɗằ *vl* to spread

barbarā *f* yi barbarā to mate

barci *m* 1. sleep 2. **Inà jîn barci.** I am sleepy. 3. **yi barci** to curdle

barcin rāna *m* siesta

bar̃dē *m* (*pl* **bar̃àdē**) 1. knight 2. brave person

bàr̃ē *m/f* stranger

bàrēwā *f* (*pl* **bàrēyī**) gazelle

bàr̃gā *f* 1. stable 2. ɗan **bàr̃gā** stablehand

bàr̃gō *m* (*pl* **bar̃gunà**) blanket

barì (**bar̃** + *noun/pronoun*) 1. to leave 2. to stop 3. **Bàri mù tàfi!** Let's go! 4. to resign

barì *m* 1. **mài barì** outgoing 2. *see* **barì**

bār̃ikì *f* 1. barracks 2. urban area

bàr̃imà *f* (*pl* **bàr̃imū**) corkscrew

bar̃jì *m* barge

bar̃kà! greetings!

bàr̃kàtài *adv* disorderly

bàr̃kònō *m* pepper

bàr̃kònon tsōhuwā *m* tear gas

barō *v6* to leave (then return)

bar̃kwancì *m* 1. wit 2. **yi bar̃wancì** to joke

bâ-ruwanmù *adv* na 'yan **bâ-ruwanmù** (pol.) 1. neutral 2. non-aligned

bāsāsā *f* **yāƙìn bāsāsà** civil war

bàsamāwī *m* destined

bàsambò *m* nephew

bàsarākè *m* (*pl* **sarākunà**) member of royalty

basàwājà *f* Volkswagen

basfà, (Nr) **bàsfâ** *m* motor scooter

bāshi *m* stink

bāshì *m* (*pl* **bāsussukà**) 1. debt 2. credit 3. **ci bāshì** to be in debt 4. **ci bāshì à bankì** (fin.)

to be overdrawn 5. *see* **ƙasàshē**...

bāshì wajen tafiyar̃ dà ayyukà *m* overheads

bāsikèl *m* prison cell

bàsīr̃à *f* 1. intelligence 2. understanding 3. **dà idòn bàsīr̃à** realistically

bāsukùr̃ *m* (*pl* **bāsukur̃ōr̃ī**) bicycle

bà-ta-kāshī 1. coming to blows 2. struggle

bàtāliyà *f* (*pl* **batāliyōyì**) 1. battalion 2. (Nr) regiment

ɓātancì *m* slander

bàtī *m* second rate

bātìr̃ *m* (*pl* **bātur̃à**) 1. battery 2. police baton

bātìsìm *m* baptism

bàtònè *m* ɗan **bàtònè** baton

bātsa *f* crude talk

bàtū *m* (*pl* **batūtuwà**) 1. speech 2. conversation 3. matter 4. (pol.) proposal, motion 5. **bàtun dūniyà** chatting 6. **kāwō bàtū** to table a motion

bàtun *prep* concerning

bàtun yankì-yankì *m* regionalism

Bàtūr̃ē *m* (*f* **Bàtūr̃ìyā**, *pl* **Tùr̃àwā**). 1. European 2. British, Briton 3. senior government official

bàtūr̃èn Dutch *m* Dutchman

bàtūr̃èn Ingìlà 1. Englishman 2. Briton

baucà *f* (*pl* **baucōcì**) voucher

baudè *v4* to swerve

bâutā wà *v1* 1. to worship 2. to serve

bàutā *f* slavery

bāwà *m* (*f* **bâiwā**, *pl* **bāyī**) slave

bawàlī m 1. urine 2. **yi bawàlì** to urinate

bāwùl m (pl **bāwulōlī**) valve

bāya adv 1. behind 2. backwards 3. **dàgà bāya** afterwards 4. **na bāya** previous 5. **na dàgà bāyan nàn** the latest

bāyā m 1. back 2. **gòyi bāyā** to support

bāya-bāya adv 1. recently 2. **ta bāya-bāya** in reverse order 3. **yi bāya-bāya** to reverse

bāya-bāyan nàn adv 1. just recently 2. **na bāya-bāyan nàn** the latest

bāya gà hakà, à bāya gà hakà as well as this

Bàyahūdè m (f **Bàyahūdìyā**, pl **Yahudāwā**) Jew

bāyan prep 1. after 2. behind

bāyan gidā, bāyan ɗàkì m 1. toilet 2. **na bāyan gidā** secret 3. illicit 4. blackmarket

bāyan hakà adv afterwards

bāyân dà prep after

bāyan fagē m na bāyan fagē 1. private 2. personal 3. unofficial 4. **kàsuwāɼ bàyan fagē** blackmarket 5. **ɗan kàsuwā na bàyan fagē** blackmarketeer

bāyan haihùwaɼ (Ànnabì) Īsā A.D.

bàyānì m (pl **bàyànai**) 1. explanation 2. information

bàyànai pl data

bāyan wannàn kuma conj moreover

bayaɼ dà v5 1. to give away 2. to hand over 3. to supply 4. to betray

Bàyarabè m (f **Bàyarabìyā**,

pl **Yarabāwā, Yaràbā**) Yoruba

bāyâɼwā f (ec.) supply

bāyì see **bāwà**

bayyànā v1 1. to explain 2. to reveal

bàyyanà v3 to appear

bàyyànannē m (f **bàyànanniyā**, pl **bàyyànū**) 1. public 2. **bā bàyyànannē ba** (pol.) underground

bàyyanàɼ cùtā f (med.) symptom

bazà v1 to spread out

bàzā f fringed dance costume

bazà jìta-jìta v **mài bazà jìta-jìta** rumourmonger

bazà làbāɼì v to spread the news

bazà lābulē v to draw the curtains

bàzamà v3 to run away

bazarā f hot season before the rains

bà-zàta adv 1. surprise 2. unexpectedly 3. **na bà-zàta** unexpected

bâ zàtō bâ tsàmmānì adv suddenly

bēbē m (f **bēbiyā**, pl **bēbàyē**) deaf mute

bēdì m (pl **bēdūdukà**) 1. flower bed 2. stable bedding

bègē m 1. desire 2. nostalgia 3. **yi bègen wani** to miss someone

bēguwā f porcupine

bêl m 1. belt 2. seatbelt

bēlì m bail

bēlô m bicycle

bencì m (pl **bencunà**) bench

bēnē m (pl **bēnàyē**) 1. storey 2. apartment

bêr *m* (Nr) drinking glass
bèrê *f* beret
bi *v* (*m* bî) 1. to follow 2. to obey
3. to go by 4. to be owed
bibbiyu kàrɓā dà hannū
bibbiyu to receive well
bìbìlòtêk *m* (Nr) library
bī dà *v* 1. to subdue 2. to tame 3.
to lead along
bî dà bî *adv* one after the other
bìdanjì *m* (Nr) engine oil change
bidi'ā *f* (*pl* bidi'ō'ī) 1. festivity
2. heresy
bìdô *m* (Nr) oil can
bìdā *v2** to look for
bîf *adv* thud
biji-biji *adv* 1. havoc 2. yi biji-
biji to wreak havoc
bijìrē wà *v4* 1. to revolt against
2. to abandon 3. to cold-
shoulder
bijìrêwā *f* desertion
bîk *m* biro
bìkā m baboon
bìkì *m* (*pl* bukūkuwà) 1.
celebration 2. party 3. festival
4. ceremony 5. (spor.)
competition 6. bìkin aurè
wedding
Bìkin Kōfìn Dūniyà na
Kwallon Kafā *m* World Cup
Soccer Competition
bìkin sâ hannū *m* signing
ceremony
bìkin tunàwā *m* remembrance
ceremony
bîl *m* 1. bill 2. invoice
bìl'adamà *m* (*pl* bànī ādamà)
1. human being 2. hakkìn
bìl'adamà human rights
bìla haddìn *adv* 1. many 2.
without limit

bìlā adàdin *adv* countless
bìlètân *f* (Nr) bulletin
bîllāyì *m* queue
bincìkā *v1* (*m* bìncìkē),
bincìkē *v4* 1. to research
2. to investigate
bìncìkē *m* (*pl* bìncìke-
bìncìke) 1. research
2. investigation 3. evaluation
4. (mil.) reconnaissance 5. yi
bìncìkē to reconnoitre
bìncìkē dà bà zâi mārà wà
kōwā bāyā ba *m* independent
inquiry
bindìgà *f* (*pl* bindigōgī) 1. gun
2. bàbbař bindìgà cannon 3.
ɗan bindìgà gunman 4. Tàyàř
mōtà tā yi bindìgà. The car
has blown a tyre.
bindìgà-dādî *adv* ɗan bindìgà-
dādî trigger-happy
bindìgà mài hàřsāshì / jìgìdā
f machine gun, automatic rifle
binì-binì *adv* repeatedly
bîn lāyì *m* queue
binnè *v4* to bury
binnè rāmì *v* to fill in a hole
bintà Sùdân *f* fashion model
bìřgêd *m* brigade
bìřgēdiyà *m* 1. brigadier 2.
brigadier-general
birì *m* (*pl* birai) monkey
biřì-bōkò *m* superficiality
bìřìkê *m* (Nr) lighter
biřis *adv* Nā yi biřis dà shì. I
ignored him.
bìřjik *adv* in large numbers
biřkì *m* (*pl* birkunà, biràkā)
1. brake(s) 2. jā biřkì to brake
birkìcē *v4* to overturn
bìrkìce *adv* à bìrkìce upside-
down

biřkìlà *m (pl* biřkilōlī) bricklayer

biřnī *m (pl* biřânē) 1. town 2. city 3. bàbban biřnī capital city 4. na biřnī urban

biřò *m* biro

bìřô *m* (Nr) office

Bìřtāniyà *f* Great Britain

bîs *f* (Nr) screw

bisà *adv/prep* 1. on (top of) 2. above 3. concerning 4. according to 4. ukù bisà huɗu three quarters

bisà gà, bisà kân, bisà lafàzin *prep* according to

bisà *f* (pl bisàshē) pack animal

bìsà *f* visa

bìsānī *adv* 1. finally 2. dàgà bìsānī afterwards

bìshàf *m* bishop

bìshāřà *f* good news

bishiyà *f* (pl bishiyōyī) tree

bìshôn *m* cork

bìskîn, bìskît *m* biscuit

bît *m* police beat

bìtà *f* 1. revision 2. course 3. seminar 4. training workshop 5. na bìtà follow-up 6. yi bìtàř... to review

bìtàmîn, (Nr) bìtàmîn *m* vitamin

bìtìnāřè *m* veterinary surgeon

bìtìnāřiyà *f* veterinary clinic

bìtôn *m* (Nr) button

biyā *v* (*m/f* biyà) 1. to pay 2. to grant

biyà 1. *m/f* payment 2. *v/* to pass by 3. to call at 4. to read aloud

bìyà *f* 1. short trip 2. obedience

bìyař *f* 1. five 2. na bìyař fifth

bìyayyà *f* 1. obedience 2. loyalty (gà to)

bìye *adv* à bìye in succession

bìyê *m/f* (Nr) 1. banknote 2. five francs

bìyêř *f* (Nr) beer

biyè wà *v4* to follow

biyu *f* 1. two. 2. double 3. na biyu second 4. na-biyu runner-up 5. 'yan biyu twins

bizò *m* rubbish heap

bōbuwā *f* horsefly

bōcà *f* (pl bōcōcī) voucher

bōdì *m* (pl bōdōjī) vehicle body

bōgà *m/f* burger

bōgì *m* na bōgì bogus

bōkā *m* (f bōkanyà, pl bōkàyē) traditional healer

bōkìtì *m* (pl bòkìtai) bucket

bōkò *m* 1. Roman script 2. education 3 trick 4. manoeuvre 5. na bōkò secular

bōkùl *m* (pl bōkulōlī) buckle

bôl *m* 1. metal bolt 2. *see* bâl

bōlà *f* (pl bōlōlī) 1. rubbish heap 2. rubbish container 3. incinerator

bòlân *m* (Nr) steering wheel

bôm *m* (pl bôm-bôm, bàmàbàmai) 1. bomb 2. ɗan bôm bomber plane 3. jēfà bôm to drop bombs

bòmbô *m* (Nr) sweets

bonêl *m* car bonnet, (US) hood

bòřē *m* 1. riot 2. ɗan bòřē rioter 3. tsai dà bòřē to quell a riot 4. Mun yi musù bòře. We rebelled against them.

bòrī *m* Bori cult

bōřìs *m* 'ya'yan bōřìs ball bearings

bòrōrò *m* blister

bôs *f* (pl bôs-bôs) bus

bōtà *m* margarine

bōtì *m* (Nr) 1. boots 2. tin can

bòyi, (Nr) bōyì *m* (*pl* bòyi-bòyi, (Nr) bōyì-bōyì) house-servant

būdà *f* harmattan haze

bùdurwā *f* (*pl* buduwōyì) 1. unmarried teenage girl 2. girlfriend

būdà *vl* 1. to open slightly 2. to reveal

bùdà-bàki *m* first daily meal (in Ramadan)

būdè *v4* 1. to open 2. būdè famfò to turn on a faucet

bùdè *adv* open

būdî *m* 1. opportunity 2. progress

bugà *vl* 1. to hit 2. to kick 3. to fire (a gun) 4. to print

bùgā *v2** (*m* bugù) 1. to strike 2. to afflict

bugà dà tàfìrētà to type

bùgaggē *m* (*f* bùgaggiyā, *pl* bùgàggū) drunk

bugà hātìmì/tambàrī to stamp

bugà sìlìmâ (Nr) màì bugà sìlìmâ projectionist

bugà wāyà to telephone

bugè *v4* to knock over

bugè har̃ ƙasā (spor.) to knock out

bùgu *v7* 1. to be beaten 2. to be drunk

bugù dà ƙārì kuma *conj* moreover

bugùn dūtsè *m* na bugùn dūtsè printed

bùhū *m* (*pl* buhunhunà) 1. bag 2. sack

bùjî *m* (Nr) sparkplug

būjwà *m* ɗan būjwà bourgeois

bùkārī *m* compasses

bùkātà *f* (*pl* bùkàtū) 1. need 2. requirement

bùkātà dà bāyâr̃wā *f* supply and demand

bùkàtū *pl* 1. (pol.) demands 2. *see* bùkātà

būkè *m* helmet

bukkâ *f* (*pl* bukkōkī) hut

bùƙātà *see* bùkātà

bûl *m/f* (Nr) boule, bowls

bulà *f* washing powder

bùlāgur̃ō *m* 1. journey 2. yi bùlāgur̃ō to go on tour

būlālà *f* whip

būlālìyā *f* (med.) shingles

bùlbît *m* (Nr) mineral water

bulbùlā *vl* to pour

bùlô *m* 1. block 2. brick 3. (Nr) metal bolt

bunƙàsā *vl* to develop

bùnƙàsà *v3* 1. to develop 2. (ec.) to grow

bùnƙàsà *f* (ec.) growth

bùnƙàsàr̃ tattalin ar̃zìkī *f* economic growth

bùnsurū *m* (*pl* bùnsùrai) goat

buntsùrā *vl* 1. to stick out 2. Tā buntsùrà bàkì. She pursed her lips.

bùra *v3* to be ripe

bùrā *f* penis

bùr̃bùdî *m* 1. crumbs 2. trace 3. bùr̃bùdîn tāshìn hankàlī outbreak of rioting

bùr̃gā 1. *f* intimidation 2. *v2** to intimidate

bùr̃gā à bàkī *f* bluffing

bur̃gè *v4* to thrill

būrì *m* 1. ambition 2. objective

burjì *m* gravel

bur̃kì *m* 1. brick 2. *see* bir̃kì

bur̃mì *m* àbōkin bur̃mì associate

bùr̃ô *m* (Nr) office

bur̃ôdì *m* 1. bread 2. loaf

Bùrōkà *m/f* Pidgin English

bùrōshì *m* (*pl* burōsōshī) brush

bùrōshìn haƙōrī, bùrōshìn gōgè bàkī *m* toothbrush

bùr̄tū *m* 1. hornbill 2. shìgar̄ bur̄tū private investigation

būrù *m* (Nr) bread

burùjī *m* 1. galaxy 2. Na sàmi burùjī. I've had good luck

bùr̄ûs *f* (Nr) 1. scholarship 2. grant

burwàyā *v1* 1. to upset 2. to stir up

bùrwawayà *f* commotion

bùsā *v2** (-shi/shē) to winnow

būsâ 1. (*pl* bùshe-bùshe) music 2. *v1* to blow

būsar̄ dà *v5* to dry (something)

būshè *v4* 1. to blow out 2. to get dry 3. to run out

būshè dà dariya to burst out laughing

būshêwar̄ danshin ruwā *f* evaporation

bushiyā *f* hedgehog

bùshô *m* (Nr) cork

but *adv* suddenly

būtà *f* (*pl* būtōcī) 1. jug 2. kettle

būtàr̄ shāyì *f* teapot

bùtô *m* (Nr) button

būtsàrī *m* yi būtsàrī to buck

butùcē, butùlcē, butùr̄cē *v4* to be undecided (wà about)

būtūtū *m* 1. funnel 2. watering can 3. pipe 4. pipeline

būtūtun àmsà-kuwwà *m* microphone

būtūtun ƙārà màganà *m* megaphone

būtūtun mâi *m* oil pipe-line

buwātì *m* (Nr) tin can

bùwāyà *v2** to be impossible for

bùwāyà *v3* to be impossible

būyāgī *m* kindling

Būzancī *m* Tuareg language

būzāyè *m* bull's eye

būzū *m* (*f* būzuwā, *pl* būzàyē) 1. Tuareg 2. sheepskin rug

bùzūzù *m* stag beetle

bwàcîr̄ *m* (Nr) car

Ɓb

Ɓaɓɓàkē v4 1. to uproot 2. to be loose

Ɓāɓ̀ḕ v4 to break off relations

Ɓacề v4 1. Littāfī yā ɓacḕ minì. I have lost my book. 2. Hanyà tā ɓacḕ masà. He is lost.

Ɓācì v 1. to be damaged 2. to be ruined 3. to worsen 2. dòkař tā ɓācì emergency law 4. zaman dòkař tā ɓācì state of emergency

Ɓad dà v5 see ɓatař dà

Ɓagas, à ɓagas adv 1. with ease 2. at a bargain

Ɓāgurề m chip

Ɓakànē see ɓaunā

Ɓalākùcē v4 to diminish

Ɓalɓalcē v4 1. to waste 2. to get lazy

Ɓalgà v1 to burst out

Ɓallà v1 to fasten

Ɓallề v4 1. to unfasten 2. to break away 3. to burst 4. to secede

Ɓallèwā f 1. secession 2. ř'a'àyin ɓallèwā separatism

Ɓalō-ɓalō adv clearly

Ɓam adv pop

Ɓamɓarề v4 (f bàmɓarà) to strip

Ɓamɓarōkì m scab

Ɓangàlē v4 to break off

Ɓangarē m (pol.) 1. bloc 2. faction 3. side 4. à wannàn ɓangarè..., à ɗaya ɓangarèn kuma... on the one hand..., and on the other...

Ɓangarèn jàm'iyyà m faction

Ɓantarō v6 to detach

Ɓārà v1 to sit up

Ɓàrakà f 1. rip 2. rift 3. breach of trust 4. Yā yi minì ɓàrakà. He broke my trust.

Ɓàràmɓaràmā f extreme provocation

Ɓaràncē v4 to be adamant

Ɓarař dà v5 1. to spill 2. to drop 3. to damage

Ɓararràkā v1 to boil

Ɓàrāwồ m (f ɓàraunìyā, pl ɓàràyī) thief

Ɓàrāwòn zaunề m fence (of stolen goods)

Ɓàřɓàshī m 1. bits 2. crumbs 3. particle

Ɓārề v4 to peel

Ɓargō m bone marrow

Ɓàrī m 1. miscarriage 2. stillborn

Ɓarì m 1. shivering 2. trembling

Ɓārì m one (of two)

Ɓarkề v4 1. to break out 2. to burst

Ɓarkèwā f ɓarkèwař faɗà outbreak of fighting

Ɓàřnā f 1. damage 2. trouble 3. Yā cikà ɓàřnā. It's a waste. 4. yi wà... ɓàřnā to sabotage

Ɓařnatař dà v5 to sabotage

Ɓas adv crack

Ɓatà v (m ɓatà) 1. Littāfīnā yā ɓatà. I have lost my book. 2. Yā ɓatà hanyà. He is lost.

Ɓātà v1 1. to spoil 2. to damage 3. ɓātà râi to get angry 4. to insult

ɓàtà-gàri *m* na **ɓàtà-gàri** undesirable

ɓatař dà *v5* (**ɓad dà** + *direct object*) 1. to lose 2. to spend 3. to waste

ɓātà wà... řâi to anger

ɓaunā *f* (*pl* **ɓakànē**) bush-cow

ɓaurē *m* fig

ɓāwō *m* 1. bark 2. shell 3. peel

ɓēřā *m* (*pl* **ɓēřàyē**) 1. mouse 2. rat

ɓikī *m* (Nr) feces

ɓingìrē *v4* to topple

ɓoɓɓòyē *v4* to keep secret

ɓōshō *m* (Nr) second-hand

ɓōyè *v4* (*m* **ɓōyō**) to hide

ɓòye *adv* hidden

ɓūlà *v1* to bore a hole

ɓugè *v4* to idle about

ɓullō *v6* 1. to (suddenly) appear 2. to respond (**wà** to)

ɓullō dà to introduce (a law)

ɓuntù *m* husk

ɓùřɓushī *m* trace

ɓurmà *v1* to cave in

ɓusà *v1*, **ɓushè** *v4* to make a hole in

ɓūya *v* (*m* **ɓūyā**) to hide

ɓūyā *m* 1. hiding 2. **shìga ɓūyā** to go into hiding

Cc

câ *f* Câ nake Dauda ne. I thought it was Dauda.

càɓê *m* (*pl* **càɓê-càɓê**) lamp post

cāɓà *vl* 1. to mumble 2. An cāɓà màhāwaɍà. The discussions were inconclusive.

càɓi *m* muddy water

cāca *f* 1. gambling 2. yi cāca to gamble

cācar bakà *f* 1. recriminations 2. yāƙìn cācar bakà cold war

cācaɍ bàkī *f* yi cācaɍ bàkī to wrangle

cācaɍ ƙwallon ƙafà *f* football pools

càccakà *f* yi càccakà to rattle

Cādì *f* Chad

cafè *v4* to catch

caffà *f* allegiance

cafƙè *v4* to catch red-handed

cājè *v4* to search

cājì *m* 1. charge 2. fee 3. search 4. (spor.) yi cājì to dribble

cājì-ōfis *m* police station

cak *adv* completely

càkā *v2** to stab

caka *m* clubs

caka-caka *adv* in profusion

càkòlâ *m* (Nr) chocolate

càkùɗā *vl* to mix up

càkùɗē *v4* 1. to be mixed up 2. to be confused

cākùlàt, cākùlàn *m/f* 1. chocolate 2. toffee

càkulkùlī *m* tickling

càkumà *v2** to grab at

cākùsōɓà *f* shock-absorber

cāli *m* string bag

càli-càli *m* comedian

càmfā *v2** (*m* **camfì**) to be superstitious about

camfì *m* (*pl* **càmfe-càmfe**) superstition

cân 1. there (visible) 2. cân, càn that, those (visible)

can 1. there 2. cân, càn that, those

càncantà *v2** (-ci/-cē) 1. to deserve 2. to be eligible for

càncantà *v3* to be appropriate

canjà *vl* (*m* **canjì**) 1. to change 2. to transfer 3. to exchange

canjaɍàs, canjaɍas *m* Chelsea dà Manchester United sun yi canjaɍàs. Chelsea and Manchester United drew the match.

canjì *m* (*pl* **cànje-cànje**) 1. change 2. (money) change 3. transfer 4. gear

canjì mài tāsīɍì *m* dramatic change

cankàcakaɍè *adv* in short supply

canzà *see* **canjà**

caɍ *adv* 1. vertical 2. straight 3. severe

cāɍā *f* cock-crow

càɍbì *m* (*pl* **caɍbunà**) worry-beads

càɍkwai *adv* 1. very sweet 2. very severely

cas *adv* 1. tidily 2. completely

cāsà *v1* (*f* càsā) 1. to thresh 2. to beat up

càsà'in *f* ninety

cātầ *f* charter

càzā *v2** (-ji/jē) to charge

càzbi *m* worry-beads

cê *v* (*f* cêwā) 1. to say 2. Kà cê dà shi/ masà yà zō. Tell him to come. 3. to reckon 4. sai kà cê as if 5. ya cê zâi... he offered to...

cē, cè *see* nē

cē-cē-kù-cē *f* 1. angry exchange 2. infighting

cēdìyā *f* (*pl* cēdìyōyī) fig-tree

cêfànē *m* 1. shopping 2. groceries 3. yi cêfànē to shop

cêk, cēkì *m* cheque

cètā *v2** (-ci/cē, *m* cètō) to rescue

cêwā *f* 1. saying 2. statement 3. that 4. dà cêwā as soon as 5. màsu ta cêwā those with a say in the matter

ci *v* (*m* cî) 1. to eat 2. to win 3. to overcome 4. to betray

ci jaȓȓàbâwā to pass an exam

cî *see* ci, cîn

cibī *m* teaspoon

cibìyā *f* (*pl* cibiyōyī) 1. navel 2. centre

cibìyaȓ cìnikī *f* trading point

cibìyaȓ kāsuwancì *f* trade centre

Cibìyaȓ Nazàrin Haȓkōkin Tsàrō dà Màkầmai *f* Institute of Strategic Studies

cibìyaȓ sàyē dà sayâȓwā *f* trading point

cìccibầ *v2** to lift sth. heavy

ciccìjē *v4* to exert one's strength

ciccìrā *v1* to rip apart

cìccirầ *f* scorn

cidầ *f* thunder

cī dà *v* to feed

cī dà cètō yi wà... ci dà cètō to let off scot-free

cī dà gùmī to exploit

ci-dà-kâi *m* self-support

cī dà zūci 1. *m* overeagerness 2. *v* to be overeager

cìdầniyā *f* exertion

cif *adv* 1. exactly 2. fully 3. intact

cîf *m* chief

cîfjōjì *m* (leg.) judge

ci gàba *v* 1. to continue (dà with) 2. to progress 3. to develop 4. to promote

cî gàba *m* 1. progress 2. promotion

cigiyà *f* search

cigiyaȓ aikì *f* job search

cigìtā *v1* (*pl* cigiyằ) to look for

cìjē *v4* 1. to bite 2. to jam 3. to come to a halt

cik *adv* Yā tsayà cik. He came to a standstill.

cikằ *v1* 1. to fill 2. to carry out 3. to complete 4. to add 5. to crowd 6. Tā cikà kyâu. She's very pretty. 7. Yā cikà shèkarà gōmà. He's ten years old. 8. Yā cikà. He has died.

cìka *v3* 1. to be full 2. to be complete

cikà àlkawàri to keep a promise

cìkakkē *m* (*f* cìkakkiyā, *pl* cìkàkkū) 1. full 2. complete

cìkakken ìkò *m* 1. absolute power 2. shùgàba mài cìkakken ikò executive president

cìkàmakò *m* 1. fulfilment 2. final step

cīkàs *m* 1. obstacle 2. shortcoming 3. bà tàre dà wani cīkàs ba unhindered 4. jāwō cīkàs gà to obstruct 5. to wreck

cikàsā *v1* 1. to fulfil 2. to complete

ci kàsuwā to go shopping

cikè *v4* 1. to fill in 2. to be tired out 3. to run out

cikì *m* (*pl* cikkunà) 1. stomach 2. farin cikì happiness 3. baƙin cikì unhappiness 4. Tanà dà cikì. She is pregnant.

ciki *adv* inside

cikī-cikī *adv* yi cikī-cikī to be obsessed with

ciki dà bâi *adv* 1. inside out 2. back to front

cikin *prep* 1. in 2. among

cikò *m* 1. balance (outstanding) 2. tooth filling 3. kuɗin cikò subsidy

cìkōwà *f* 1. glut 2. overflowing

cikwīwìyā *v1* to crumple

cilàkōwà *f* hornbill

cìmā *f* (staple) food

cìmakà *f* 1. food 2. kàyàyyakin cìmakà foodstuff

cimà-zàune *m/f* parasite

cim ma *v* 1. to overtake 2. to catch up with 3. to achieve

cim mà yàřjējēnìyā to reach an agreement

cincìn *m* doughnut

cìncìrindò *m* congestion

cìncìrindòn jiràgen ruwā *m* fleet

cìncìrindòn mōtōcī *m* traffic jam

cindò *m* person with sixth finger

cìngâm *m* chewing-gum

cîn gashìn kâi *m* 1. autonomy 2. sovereignty

cîn hancì *m* bribery

cìnìkayyà *f* 1. trade 2. trade relations

cìnìkayyàř ƙasàshen dūniyà *f* international trade

cìnikī *m* 1. trade 2. business 3. offer 4. habit 7. àbin dà akè sàmù dàgà cìnikī na ƙētarè balance of trade 8. màtàkai na kāriyař cìnikī trade protectionism

cìnikin bà-ni-gishirī-na-bā-kà-mandā *m* barter trade

cìnikī bà tàre dà cīkàs ba *m* free trade

cìnikī na bāyan gidā *m* black market trade

cìnikī na fasà ƙwàuri *m* smuggling

cìnikin bāyī *m* slave trade

cìnikin ƙētarè *m* foreign trade

cìnkōsō *m* abundance

cìnkōson mōtōcī *m* traffic jam

cinnà *v1* Sun cinnà masà wutā. They set fire to it.

cìnnākà *f* (*pl* cìnnākū) biting ant

cîn râi *m* mài cîn râi 1. boring 2. monotonous

cîn rānī *see* cì rānī

cìntā *v2** (-ci/ē) to guess

cinyà *f* (*pl* cinyōyī) 1. thigh 2. leg

cînyē *v4* 1. to consume 2. to steal 3. to defeat

cîn zařàfī *m* slander

ciř *adv* 1. straight (up) 2. full

cirà *v1* 1. to raise 2. to rise 3. in kā cirè... with the exception of...

cìrā *v2** to extract

cirà muryà to raise one's voice

cì rānī, cîn rānī *m* 1. migration 2. ɗan cì rānī migrant

3. settler 4. temporary worker
cirè *v4* to extract
cirè tufāfī to undress
ciřòma *m* 1. heir apparent 2.
kiran ciřòma feeling hungry
cīshē *v5* 1. **Nā cishē shì.** I fed
him. 2. *see* **ciyař dà**
cìtā *v2** (**-ci/cē**) to guess
città *f/adv* 1. four days from now
2. **shèkaràn città** five days
from now
cìttař àhò *f* ginger
cīwò *m* (*pl* **cìwàce-cìwàce**) 1.
illness 2. disease 3. pain 4.
drawback
cīwòn būshiyā, cīwòn bauřù
m rinderpest
cīwòn dājì *m* tumour
cīwon dà kè gurgùntà yârā *m*
polio
cīwòn innà *m* polio
cīwòn màmā *m* (med.) mastitis
ciyàmàn *m* chairman
ciyař dà *v5* (**cì dà** + *direct object*) to feed
ciyař dà... gàba to further
cìyāwà *f* (*pl* **cìyàyī**) grass
cìzā *v2** (**-jì/jē**, *m* **cīzò**) to bite
cìzgā *v2** to wrench out
cizìl *m* (*pl* **cizilōlī**) chisel
cīzò *m* bite
cīzòn kùrân *m* electric shock
cōcìlàn, (Nr) **cōcìlà** *f* torch
cōgē *m* yi **cōgē** to cheat
cōkàlī *m* (*pl* **cōkulà**) spoon
cōkàlī mài yātsà *m* fork
cù *adv* sizzling
cūďà *v1*, **cùďà** *v2** 1. to knead
2. to massage
cùďanyà *v3* to mix together
cūďè *v4* 1. to mix 2. to be mixed
cùďè-ni-ìn-cùďè-kà 1. aikìn

cùďè-ni-ìn-cùďè-kà cooperation 2. **zaman cùďè-ni-ìn-cùďè-kà** integration
cukū *m* cheese
cùkù-cuku *adv* deviously
cuku-cùkù *adv* 1. tangled
2. tatters
cukwī *see* **cukū**
cukwikwìyā *v1* to be tangled
cul *adv* actually
cūnà 1. *f* (*pl* **cūnōni**) gusset 2. *v1*
Yā cūnà minì kàrē. He set the
dog on me.
cùnē *m* yi **cùnē** to inform (**wà**
on)
cùnkōsō *m* abundance
cùnkōson mōtōcì *m* traffic jam
cùnkus *adv* 1. many 2. **cikà**
cùnkus to be crowded
cunkùshē *v4* to be overcrowded
cuř *adv* exactly
cūrà *v1* (*m* **cūrì**) to knead into
balls
cūrì *m* ball of food
cūsà *v1* (*f* **cùsā**) 1. to stuff 2. to
impose (**wà** on) 3. **An cūsà**
masà řēdiyò. He's been forced
to accept the radio.
cùsàyī *m* syphilis
cūshē *v4* 1. to be stuffed up 2. to
be blocked 3. **Kàsuwā tā cūshè.**
The market has slumped.
cùtà 1. *f* (*pl* **cùce-cùce**) harm 2.
cheating 3. deception 4. (*pl*
cūtuttukà) illness 5. disease 6.
v2* (**-ci/ē**) to harm 7. to
deceive 8. to cheat
cùtař ajàlī *f* killer disease
cùtař dà kè yàďuwā ta
hanyàř gògayyàř jūnā *f*
contagious disease
cùtař kâi *f* self-deception

Dd

dà *prep/conj* 1. with 2. and 3. by
4. than 5. that, which, who 6.
when 7. since 8. there is/are 9.
dà ƙaffè huɗu at four o'clock
10. **Yanà dà kuɗî.** He has
money. 11. **Yanà dà nauyī.** It
is heavy. 12. **dà rāna** in the
daytime
dà... dà both... and
dâ *adv* 1. formerly 2. before 3.
just now 4. **na dâ** old-
fashioned 5. former 6. **tun dâ**
from earliest times 7. **zāmànin
dâ** formerly
dà... dà if... then
dà mā if only
dà'àwā *f* 1. legal position 2.
claim 3. **mài dà'àwā** claimant
dabà *f* **ɗan dabà** thug
dābà *f* durbar
dabaibàyē *v4* 1. to hobble 2. to
tangle 3. to get tangled
dàbam *adv* 1. different (**dà**
from) 2. separate (**dà** from)
dàbam dàbam *adv* 1.
completely different 2. distinct
types
dàbāɍà *f* (*pl* **dàbāɍū,
dàbàɍce-dàbàɍce**) 1. plan 2.
idea 3. plot 4. trick 5. **na
dàbāɍà** tactical 6. **Ìnā
dàbāɍà?** What's to be done?
dàbāɍàɍ warwàrè... (pol.) the
solution to...
dabàɍcē *v4* to cheat
dabbà *m/f* (*pl* **dabbōbī**) animal
dab dà *adv* 1. close to 2. next to

dab dab *adv* right next to each
other
dàbgē *m* 1. meat broth 2. **shân
dàbgē** the high life
dabīnò *m* 1. dates 2. (*f*
dabinùwā, *pl* **dàbìnai**) date
palm
dabò *m/pl* 1. trick 2. magic 3.
see **ƙasà**
dabùɍ *m* emergency parade
dābùɍcē *v4* to be stunned
dābùɍtā *v1* to stun
dāɓā *v1* (*f* **dāɓà**) 1. to do a lot
of 2. to stab
daɓà à ƙasà *v1* 1. to beat earth
2. to be ineffective
daɓa-daɓa *adv* in masses
dàɓaɍɓàshī *m* (*f* **dàɓaɍɓàsā,**
pl **dàɓàɍɓàsai**) stocky
dàɓàrō *m* 1. black soil 2. **zaman
dàɓàrō** sitdown protest
dàɓê *m* beaten floor
dācè *v4* 1. to be suitable 2. to
have success
dàcē *m* coincidence
dācèwaɍ bàkī à àsìrce *f* secret
deal
daddàgē wà *v4* to resist
dàddare *adv* **dà dàddare** at
night
dàddawā *f* locust-bean cakes
dādirō *f* lover
daɗā *v1* (*m* **daɗî**) 1. to add 2. to
increase 3. to do again
dāɗàɗā wà *v1* to please
dàɗai *adv* 1. always 2. never/
ever

dàɗau *m* 1. novelty 2. rarity
daɗè *v4* to last a long time
daɗèwā *f* (nân) bà dà daɗèwā
  ba 1. not long ago 2. soon
dāɗì *m* 1. pleasure 2. enjoyment
  3. ji dāɗìn to enjoy
dàɗu *v7* to increase
dafà *v1* to cook
dāfā wà *v1* 1. to press with the
  hand 2. to favour 3. to support
dàfà-dukà *m* jollof rice
daffò *m* 1. depot 2. warehouse
dafī *m* poison
dàfīfī *adv* in large numbers
daf dà *see* dab dà
dafkà *v1* An dafkà wà jàkī
  kāyā. The donkey's been given
  a heavy load.
daftàrī *m* (*pl* dàftàrai) 1.
  ledger 2. daftàrin hàrājì tax
  register 3. daftàrin àlƙàlī
  court records
dàgà *prep* 1. from 2. by 3. after
dagā *f* (*pl* dagàgē) lucky charm
  bangle
dāgā *f* 1. Sun jā dāgā. They
  prepared for battle. 2. fīlin
  dāgā battle field 3. Sunà
  bàkin dāgā. They are at the
  battle front. 4. yi dāgā to
  struggle (dà with)
dàgà bāya *adv* 1. next 2.
  afterwards
dagacì *m* (*pl* dàgàtai) village
  head
dagaргàzā *v1* to crush
dàgà yâu *adv* from now on
dāgè *v4* 1. to strive 2. to be
  obstinate
dāgèwā *f* insistence
dāgì *m* (*pl* dāgōgī) digging rod
dàgī *m* (*pl* dāgunà) 1. paw

2. emblem 3. trade-mark 4.
  logo
dāgiyā *f* resistance
dàgo-dàgo *m* left-overs
dāgùlā *v1* 1. to ruin 2. to disturb
  3. to mess up 4. to destabilise
  5. to deteriorate 6. to
  complicate
dàgulà *v3* 1. to be ruined 2. to
  be disturbed 3. to be messed up
dāgùlē *v4* 1. to become ruined
  2. to be disturbed
dāgùlêwā *f* crisis
dagwalgwàlā *v1* to dirty
dāhìr *m* 1. reality 2. undoubtedly
  3. definitely
dai 1. well 2. then 3. really
dā'ì *m* plaintiff
daidai *adv* 1. correct(ly) 2.
  exact(ly) 3. straight 4. equal 5.
  corresponding to 5. zō daidai
  to coincide (dà with) 6.
  Wannàn bài yi minì daidai
  ba. This doesn't suit/ fit me.
dàidaitā *v2* (-ci/cè) to go
  straight to
daidàitā *v1* 1. to straighten 2. to
  adjust
dàidaità *v3* 1. to be in order
  2. to be symmetrical
dàidàitaccē *m* (*f* dàidàitacciyā,
  pl dàidàitàttū) 1. standard
  2. correct
dàidàitakà *f* equality
dàidaitō *m* balance
dàidaiton bìyàce-bìyàce *m*
  balance of payments
dàidaiton cìnìkī na ƙètarè *m*
  balance of trade
dàidàituwā *f* 1. improvement 2.
  rashìn dàidàituwā discrepancy
dàidàituwaр yanàyin dōrōn

ƙasā *f* ecological balance

dā'imàn, dā'ìmī *adv* 1. eternal 2. always

daimòn *m* diamond

dainà *v1* 1. to stop (doing) 2. to give up

dainà hailà to reach menopause

dā'ìr̃ā, dā'ir̃à *f* (*pl* dā'i'r̃ōr̃ì) 1. circle 2. mài dā'ìr̃à round

dājè *v4* (*f* dājiyā) 1. to reinforce 2. to edge

dājì *m* (*pl* dāzuzzukà) 1. the 'bush' 2. uninhabited country 3. forest 4. jungle 5. tashàr̃ dājì rumour

dàjìnē *m* wiping one's nose

dājìn jikà *m* cancer

dakà *vl* 1. to pound 2. to beat 3. Tā dakà ƙōfà. She knocked at the door.

dàkàli *m* 1. platform 2. ledge

dàkārè *m* (*pl* dàkārū) infantryman

dàkàrū *pl* infantry

dàkatà *v2** (-ci/cē, *m* dākò) to wait for

dākatar̃ dà *v5* 1. to make wait 2. to postpone 3. to suspend

dākàta wà *vl* 1. to wait (for) 2. to pause

dakì-dakì *adv* 1. in order 2. one by one 3. step by step

dakō *m* ɗan dakō porter

dākò *m* yi dākò to wait for

dàkùlô *m/f* (Nr) typist

dàkusar̃ dà *v5* 1. to blunt 2. to retard 3. to cripple

dākùshē *v4* 1. to be blunt 3. to subside 3. to deteriorate

dākùshêwā *f* deterioration

dākùsā *vl* to blunt

dākùshē *v4* 1. to be blunt

2. Sūnansà yā dākùshē. He's lost his reputation.

daƙàshin ƙwai *m* scrambled eggs

daƙau *adv* dry and hard

dàkau *m* pounding corn for pay

dàƙìƙà *f* (*pl* dàƙìƙōƙì) second (of time)

dàƙìƙì *m* (*f* dàƙìƙìyā, *pl* dàƙìƙai) stupid

daƙìƙàncē *v4* to be stupid

dāƙùnā *vl* 1. to mess up 2. to dirty

dàƙunà *v3* 1. to be messed up 2. to get dirty

daƙuwà *f* 1. nut sweets 2. abusive gesture

daƙwā-dàƙwà *see* danƙwalēlè

daƙwalwā *f* (*pl* daƙwàlē) 1. laying-hen 2. curvaceous

dalà *f* (*pl* dalōlì) 1. dollar 2. twenty-five kobo

dàlā *f* pyramid

dàlàkī *m* sediment

dàlālà *v3* to dribble

dàlìlì *m* (*pl* dàlìlai) 1. reason 2. cause 3. excuse 4. means

dàlìlan sìyāsà *pl* political considerations

dallā-dallā *adv* 1. step by step 2. group by group

dallàr̃ā *vl* to dazzle

dālumā *adv* curvaceous

dam *adv* 1. shut tight 2. blocked up

dāma *f* 1. right (hand) 2. dà dāma to/ at/ with/ on the right 3. kwântā dāma to die

dāmā *f* 1. chance 2. opportunity 3. Bâ dāmā! No chance! 4. Bâ shi dà dāmā. He has no equal. 5. Yā ji dāmā. He is feeling

better. **6. dà dāmā** quite a few
7. sàu dà dāmā often
dāmà *vl* **1.** to mix **2.** to confuse
dàmā *v2** (*m* **dāmù**) **1.** to
worry **2.** to bother **3.** to irritate
dâ mā *adv* **1.** originally **2.** in the
first place **3.** already **4.** it has
always been the case that **5.** *see*
dâ
dāmacī *m* right-hand side
dāma-dāma *adv* slightly
Dàmāgàràm *f* Zinder
dāmājè *m* **1.** damaged **2.**
wrecked
dàmanā *f see* **dàmìnā**
dāmaŕ fadìn àlbaŕkàcin bàkī
f freedom of speech
dāmaŕ kā dà k̃ùŕi'à *f* right to
vote
dāmā ta dòkā *f* legal right
dàmbàŕwā *f* row (quarrel)
dambe *m* **1.** boxing **2.** ɗan
dambe boxer
dambū *m* dumplings
dāmè *v4* **1.** to be mixed into a
paste **2.** to be confused
dāmējì *m* damage
dàmfamī *m* grass fence
dàmfarà 1. *f* swindling **2.** ɗan
dàmfarà swindler **3.** *v2** to
swindle
damfàrā *vl* **1.** to stuff into **2.** to
collect **3.** to do a lot of
damì *m* (*f* **dammunà**, *pl*
dàmmai) bundle
dàmìnā *f* rainy season
dàmisà *m/f* (*pl* **dāmisōshī**,
dàmìsū) leopard
damō *m* (*pl* **damàmē**) land-
monitor lizard
damtsè *m* (*pl* **damàtsā**)
forearm

dàmu *v7* **1.** to be mixed into a
paste **2.** to be worried
dāmùk̃ā *vl* to grip with both
hands
dàmunā *f see* **dàmìnā**
dàmuwā *f* **1.** worry **2.** concern
3. strain **4.** stress
dà-nā-sanì, dà-nā-shinà
regret
dandàlī *m* **1.** town square
2. forum
dandàlin jìn ŕa'àyin jàma'à
m opinion poll
dandamàlī *m* **1.** stage
2. platform **3.** raised doorstep
dandan *adv* **1.** firmly **2.** solidly
dandàk̃ā *vl* **1.** to pound **2.** to
mistreat
dandàk̃è *v4* to castrate
dàndī *m* ɗan **dàndī** vagabond
dangā *f* (*pl* **dangōgī**) fence
dangàcē *v4* to put a fence
around
dànganà *f* **1. Yā ɗauki**
dànganà. He resigned himself
to his fate. **2.** pledge
dànganà *v3* **1.** to be resigned to
2. to steel oneself to
dangànà *vl* **1.** to pawn **2.** to
lean (**dà** against) **3.** to base (**dà**
on)
dangàne dà *prep* regarding
dàngantà *v2** (**-ci/cē**) **1.** to be
related to **2.** to correspond to
3. to suit
dangàntā *vl* **1.** to associate **2.** to
entrust **3.** to trace back
dàngantà dà *v3* **1.** to depend on
2. to be related to
dàngàntakà *f* **1.** relationship **2.**
relations **3. ajìyè dàngàntakà**
to break off relations

dàngàntakà dà jàma'à *f*
public relations

dangì *m* (*pl* dangōgī)
relative(s)/ relation(s)

danjà *f* 1. danger 2. (*pl* danjōjī)
red (traffic) light 3. taillight

dànkalì *m* sweet-potato(es)

dànkalìn tùřàwā *m* potato(es)

dànƙā *v2** to grip

dankà *v1* 1. to hand over 2. to
entrust

danƙàrē *v4* 1. to pack down 2.
to press down

danƙàri! what a lot!

danƙè *v4* to take prisoner

danƙarō *m* (Nr) jiřgin
danƙaroo tractor

danƙì *m* handful

danƙò *m* 1. rubber 2. gum 3.
stickiness 4. Zamansù yā yi
danƙò. They've been friends a
long time.

danƙòn... long-lasting...

danƙwàfē *v4* to come to a halt

danƙwalēlè *m* (*f*
danƙwalēlìyā, *pl* danƙwal-
dànƙwàl, daƙwā-dàkwà
large and round

dannà *v1* 1. to press on 2. to
force

dannè *v4* 1. to oppress 2. to
suppress

danniyā *f* 1. oppression
2. suppression 3. na danniyā
repressive 4. mulkìn danniyā
totalitarianism

danshi *m* 1. moisture
2. damp

darà *f* 1. board game 2. mài
gidan darà checked

dàřâ *f* (Nr) cloth

dara'à *f* shapely figure

dařajà *f* (*pl* dařajōjī) 1. value
2. worth 3. rank 4. position
5. respect 6. step 7. mài dařajà
valuable

dařajàř mùsāyař kudî *f* (fin.)
rate of exchange

dàřaktâř *m* (Nr) manager

dařam *adv* 1. stable 2. in perfect
condition

dařàsī *m* (*pl* dařussà) 1. study
2. lesson

darē *m* (*pl* daràrē) 1. night
2. àbincin darē supper 3.
daren Lahàdì Sunday night

dare *adv* 1. dà dare at night
2. Lahàdì dà dare on Sunday
night

dàre *adv* yâu dà dare tonight

dārē *v4* 1. to be cracked 2. to fall
apart

dàřēktà *m* (*pl* dařētōcī)
director

dārì *m* length

dàřìƙà see dàřìƙà

dàriyā *f* 1. laughter 2. yi dàriyā
to laugh

darjè *v4* 1. to graze oneself 2. to
pick the best of

dařmà *f* 1. tin 2. lead

dàřnī *m* (*pl* dařnukà) corn-
stalk fence

dasà *v1* (*m* dashì) 1. to
transplant 2. to add to

dāsàshī *m* gums

dàshē *m* (*pl* dàshē-dàshē)
1. seedling 2. transplanting

dāshì *m* tip, dash

dāskàrē *v4* 1. to coagulate 2. to
solidify 3. to condense

dàtsā *v2** 1. to intercept 2. to
dam 3. to block

dātsà *v1* to cut up

datsè *v4* 1. to intercept 2. to block 3. to dam
datsè tàkunkùmī to impose a blockade
datsiyā *f* **yi datsiyā** damming up water
dattakò *m* 1. respectability 2. dignity 3. gentlemanliness 4. hālin dattākò maturity
dàtti *m* 1. dirt 2. waste 3. Yā yi dàtti. It is dirty.
dattìjò *m* (*f* **dattìjìyā,** *pl* **dàttìjai, dàttàwā**) 1. gentleman 2. respectable person 3. senator
daudù *m* **ɗan daudù** 1. homosexual 2. transvestite
daudā *f* filth
daujè *v4* to graze (skin)
daulā *f* (*pl* **daulōlī**) 1. power 2. wealth 3. empire 4. political order 5. kāyan daulā luxury articles
daurà dà *prep* 1. right beside 2. à daurà dà compared with
daurè *v4* 1. to endure patiently 2. to bow to the inevitable
daurī *m* tonic
dàurī *adv* 1. formerly 2. in the olden days
dauriyā *f* endurance
dàurō *m* millet
dausàyī *m* pasture
dàtu *v5* to become an adult
dawà *m* 1. the 'bush' 2. forest
dāwā *f* guinea-corn
dàwaiwainìyā *f* going to and fro
dàwàmammē *m,* (*f* **dàwàmammiyā,** *pl* **dàwàmàmmū**) 1. lasting 2. permanent
dawākī *see* **dōkī**

dàwarā *f* 1. circling 2. aimless
dawò *m* (*pl* **dawâyyā**) milkless fura
dāwō *v6* to return (here)
dāwō dà to restore
dawwàmā *v1* 1. to make permanent 2. to entrust
dàwwamà *v3* 1. to last forever 2. to be permanent 3. aikì mài dàwwamà permanent work
dāzà *v1* 1. to arrange 2. to hit 3. to reinforce
dāzuzzukà *see* **dājì**
dēfilē *m* (Nr) 1. parade 2. yi dēfilē to march
dèftê *m* (Nr) (pol.) deputy
dēmòn *m* diamond
dìddigā *f* remainder
diddìgē *v4* to be ragged
diddigè *m* (*pl* **digàdìgai**) heel
diddigī *m* Mun bi diddigin màganàr̃. We investigated the matter.
difilē *m* (Nr) yi difilē to march
dìfìtê *m* (Nr) (pol.) 1. deputy 2. senator
dìflòmàsiyyà *f* diplomacy
digà *f* (*pl* **digōgī**) pickaxe
digàdìgai *see* **diddigè**
digir̃gir̃ *adv* very short
dìgir̃ī *m* (*pl* **digir̃ōr̃ī**) degree
dìlā *m* (*pl* **dilōlī**) jackal
dìllālì *m* (*f* **dìllālìyā,** *pl* **dìllàlai**) 1. broker 2. middleman
dillancì *m* brokerage
dìllālìn jār̃ì *m* stockbroker
dîm *m* dimmer
Dìmāshì *m/f* (Nr) Sunday
dìmòkùràdìyyà *f* democracy
dìmùn-dā'imàn *adv* without fail

dinà f dinner party

dìnàmô m (Nr) dynamo

dìndimī m 1. nightblindness 2. awkwardness

dindìndin adv 1. permanently 2. forever 3. bà na dindìndin ɗ̃a temporary 4. haƙ dindìndin forever

dingà vl Tã dingà ŕùbùtū. She kept on writing.

dìntsa datsiyā vl to take a handful of

dintsì m handful

dinyã f goose

dì'ò m (pl dì'ò-dì'ò) district officer

dìra v3 1. to leap down 2. to swoop down 3. to alight

dìŕàksô m (Nr) steering of car

dìŕàktâŕ m (Nr) headmaster

dìŕàktìŕîs f (Nr) headmistress

dìŕèbà m (pl dìŕèbōbī) 1. driver 2. chauffeur

dìŕì m reprimand

dìŕì m standing upright

dìŕkà f (pl dìŕkōkī) forked stick

dìrkākā v2* to do with a will

dìŕô m (spor.) draw

dìŕôm m oil drum

Dìsambà m December

dìsfensà f (pl disfensōshī) 1. dispenser 2. dispensary assistant

dishi-dishi adv dimly

dīwānì m (pl dìwànai) 1. anthology 2. register

diyyà f 1. compensation for homicide or injury 2. war-indemnity

dōdànà vl to apply

dōdò m Sun yi dōdò. They formed a long line.

dòdō m (f dòdannìyā, pl dòdànnī) 1. evil spirit 2. monster

dòdon hòtō m film negative

dòdon kōɗì m 1. snail 2. snail shell

dòdon kûnnē m eardrum

dōɗè v4 to plug

dōgàrā vl to lean on

dògarà v3 1. to lean (dà/gà on) 2. to rely (dà/gà on) 3. (fin.) to peg

dògarà f 1. endurance 2. stamina

dōgarì m (f dògàrai, pl dōgarāwā) armed escort

dògarō m dependence (kân on)

dògarō dà jūnā m interdependence

dōgō m (f dōguwā, pl dōgàyē) 1. tall 2. long 3. railway line

dōgon Tūŕancī m bureaucracy

dòkā 1. f (pl dōkōkī) order 2. rule 3. law(s) 4. shìrìn dòkā legislative bill 5. bà bisà dòkā ba unlawful 6. kētà dòkā to break the law 7. v2* (m dūkà) to beat up 8. to thrash 7. to hit

dòkà f hairpad

dòkaŕ kō-tā-kwàna, dōkàŕ sōjà f martial law

dòkaŕ-tā-ɓàcì f 1. zaman dòkaŕ-tā-ɓàcì state of emergency 2. kafà dòkaŕ-tā-ɓàcì to declaŕe a state of emergency

dōkì m (f gōɗìyā, pl dawākī) 1. horse 2. yì kûnnen dōkì to be identical

dōkìn Allàh m praying mantis

dōkìn cāca m dice

dōkìn ƙōfà m doorstep

dōkìn ruwā *m* irrigation channel

dōkìn wuyà *m* nape of the neck

dōkìn zūcìyā *m* rash act

dōkōkin hanyà *pl* highway code

dōlà *f* dollar

dōlè 1. must 2. necessary

dōlō *m* (*f* dōluwā, *pl* dōlàyē) idiot

dòmin, don *conj* 1. because 2. in order that/ to 3. because of 4. for the sake of

dòmin kàdà *conj* in case

don Allàh! 1. for God's sake! 2. please!

don mè? why?

dòrinā *f* 1. hippopotamus 2. whip

dōriyā *f* small market

dōrō *m* 1. hump 2. convex 3. **Yā yi dōrō.** He hunched his shoulders.

dōron Ƙasā *m* surface of the earth

dòsā *v2** (-shi/shē) 1. to set out for 2. to lead to 3. to go directly to 4. to face

dòsà *v1* 1. to haft 2. to carry on doing

dòsê *m* (Nr) office file

dòshē *m* short cut

dōyà *f* yam

dōzìn *m* 1. dozen 2. ten

dù'à'ì *m* 1. a prayer 2. (Chr.) service

dūbā *m* 1. fortune-telling 2. **màlàmin dūbā** fortune teller 3. *see* **dùbā**

dūbà *v1* 1. to look (at) 2. to inspect 3. to face 4. to look for 5. to pay attention (to) 6. to

supervise 7. to divine 8. to visit the sick

dùbā *v2** (*m* dūbā) 1. to look (at) 2. to inspect

dùbà-gàrì *m* health inspector

dùbân, dùbbân *f* (Nr) wine

dūbàwā *f* supervision

dubū *f* (*pl* dùbbai) thousand

dùbulê *m* (Nr) yi **dùbulê** to overtake

dubùřā *f* (*pl* duburōřī) anus

dū-dù-dū *adv* all in all

dugè *m* (Nr) news

dùgùnye *m* (Nr) customs official

dùgùnzumà *v3* to be serious

duguřgùjē *v4* to disintegrate

dùgùzùm *adv* 1. shaggy 2. in tatters

duhù *m* 1. dark(ness) 2. shadow 3. ignorance 4. **Ƙasā tā yi duhù.** The land is densely wooded.

duhùntā *v1* to darken

duhuwà *f* (*pl* duhuwōyì) thick woods

duk, dukà 1. all 2. every 3. completely 4. **àmmā duk** in spite of

dūkà *m* 1. punch 2. blow 3. *see* **dòkā**

dūkancī *m* leatherworking

dùkàwā *see* **bàdūkù**

duk dà *prep* in spite of, despite

duk dà hakà *adv* 1. nevertheless 2. still

duk indà wherever

dūkìyā *f* (*pl* dūkiyōyì) 1. wealth 2. asset 3. property

dukkà *see* **duk**

duku-duku *m* crack of dawn

dukuřkùcē *v4* to be ruined

duk wandà whoever

dūƙà *vl* 1. to bend down 2. to be determined

dùƙufà *v3* 1. to be determined (wajen to) 2. Tā dùƙufà kân aikîn. She put everything into the job.

dùƙùnƙùnē *m* deceit

duƙus *adv* very short

dùƙushī *m* (*f* dùƙusā, *pl* dùƙùsai) foal

dùlmuyà *v3* to be immersed

dumà *vl* to plunge

dumā *m* (*pl* dumàmē) gourd/ pumpkin

dùmāshì *m* (Nr) Sunday

dùmbuzà *v2** (-ji/jē) to take a handful/ mouthful of

dumɓū *m* (*pl* dumɓàyē) 1. old tool 2. idiot

dùmfarà *v2** to go up to

dumu-dùmù *adv* red-handed

dùndū *m* thump

dundunìyā *f* (*pl* dunduniyōyī) heel

dunɗè *v4* Gàrī yā dunɗè. The sky is overcast.

dùngū *m* 1. elusiveness 2. (*pl* dungunà) stub

dùngun ràsît *m* counterfoil

dùngurà *v2** 1. to bump into 2. to butt

dūniyà *f* 1. world 2. na dūniyà universal 3. international

dunƙùlà *vl* 1. to clench one's fist 2. to knead into balls

durƙùsā *vl* (*m* dùrƙusō) to kneel

durƙusař dà *v5* to bring to one's knees

durƙùsâwā *f* yi durƙùsâwā to kowtow (gàban to)

dùřô *m* 1. oil drum 2. betting draw 3. drawer 4. (spor.) draw

duřōbà *m* (*pl* duřōbōbī) prison warder

dùřôs *m* underpants

durùmī *m* (*pl* durumà) fig-tree

dùsà *m* 1. bran 2. filings 3. dùsař zīnàřìyā tinsel

dūsà *m* spades (in cards)

dùsař ƙànƙařā *f* 1. snow 2. snowflakes

dùsař makāmashin nūkìliyà *f* nuclear fall-out

dusàshē *v4* to tarnish

dushè *v4* 1. to grow dim/ dark 2. to fade

dushi-dushi *adv* barely visible

duskùrē *v4* to be blunt

dūtsè *m*(*pl* duwàtsū) 1. stone 2. hill 3. mountain

dùwân *m* (Nr) 1. *f* customs 2. *m* customs official

dùwànyê *m* (Nr) customs official

Ɗɗ

ɗã *m (pl* 'yā'yā) **1.** son **2.** fruit

ɗã·'à *f* **1.** good manners **2.** etiquette **3.** loyalty (gà to) **4.** rashìn ɗã'à indiscipline

ɗã'āmì *m* meal

ɗabbà'ā *vl (m* ɗab'ì) **1.** to print **2.** to publish

ɗabì'à *(pl* ɗabì'ū) **1.** character **2.** trait **3.** behaviour **4.** mannerism

ɗàcī *m* bitterness

ɗàɗà wà *vl* **1.** Yā ɗàɗà masà mārì. He slapped him. **2.** Yā ɗàɗà wà dawà wutā. He set fire to the bush. **3.** Tā ɗàɗà kwâllì à idò. She's put kohl on her eyes.

ɗaɗɗaf *adv* tightly

ɗàɗàrā wà *vl* to brand

ɗafà *vl* **1.** to stick onto/into **2.** Yā ɗafà matà sātà. He falsely accused her of theft.

ɗafè *v4* to stick to

ɗagà *vl* **1.** to raise **2.** to rise **3.** to postpone **4.** to budge

ɗàgā, ɗàgāwā *f* arrogance

ɗàgà-bodì *f* tipper truck

ɗàgaggē *m (f* ɗàgaggiyā, *pl* ɗàgàggū) raised

ɗagà wà... hankàlì to unsettle

ɗage *adv* yi ɗage to stand on tiptoe

ɗagè *v4* **1.** to lift **2.** to get smaller **3.** to suspend **4.** to postpone

ɗagō *v6* to raise a matter

ɗàgōgo *adv* **1.** shakily **2.** uncertain

ɗagwas *adv* well-formed

ɗai-ɗai *adv* **1.** one by one **2.** only a few

ɗai-ɗai dà ɗai-ɗai *adv* one after another

ɗaiɗàitā *vl* **1.** to lay out one by one **2.** to disperse

ɗàiɗàità *v3* to be dispersed

ɗakà *adv* **1.** in the house/ room **2.** indoors

ɗākì *m (pl* ɗākunà) **1.** room **2.** hut **3.** house **4.** building

ɗàkìn kàràtū *m* library

ɗàkìn kwānā *m* bedroom

ɗàkìn sayař dà lìttàttàfai *m* bookshop

ɗàlìbī *m (f* ɗàlìbā, *pl* ɗàlìbai) student

ɗàlibtà *f* being a student

ɗàmarà *(pl* ɗàmàrū) **1.** belt **2.** tails (of coin) **3.** ɗaurè ɗàmarà to arm oneself **4.** kwancè ɗàmarà to disarm

ɗàmbā *f* **1.** bog **2.** deception

ɗàmè *v4* **1.** to tighten **2.** to straighten out

ɗan *m (f* 'yař, *pl* 'yan) **1.** 'yař Sokoto a Sokoto woman **2.** ɗan kasuwa market trader **3.** 'yan kallo spectators **4.** young **5.** little **6.** a little (bit) of **7.** slightly **8.** *see* ɗã

ɗanà *vl* **1.** to set **2.** to adjust

ɗanà bindìgà to cock a gun

ɗanà tarkò to set a trap

ɗanà wutā *f* àbin ɗanà wutā light switch

ɗanà *vl* 1. to borrow 2. to apply to

ɗan Adàm *m* (*pl* 'yan Adàm) human being

ɗan bindigà *m* gunman

ɗan cì rānī, ɗan cîn rānī *m* 1. migrant 2. settler 3. temporary worker

ɗanɗanā *vl* 1. to taste 2. to feel 3. to experience

ɗànɗanà *f*, ɗanɗanō *m* (sense of) taste

ɗan dàndī *m* vagabond

ɗan daudù *m* transvestite

ɗan digà *m* roadworker

ɗan dòkā *m* local policeman

ɗan dàkì *m* steward

ɗan fashì *m* highway robber

ɗan fashìn jirgī *m* hijacker

ɗan gàngànimā *m* spy

ɗangō *m* newly hatched locust

ɗan gudùn hijiřā *m* refugee

ɗan haɗìn bàkī *m* collaborator

ɗan hàlâl *m* 1. honest person 2. legimately born person

ɗan harì *m* raider

ɗan hayà *m* tenant

ɗan Holland *m* Dutchman

ɗànì *m* 1. temporary loan 2. span 3. lift (in a car) 4. bā dà ɗànì to give a lift (wà/zuwà to)

ɗan jàřidà *m* (*f* 'yař jàřidà, *pl* 'yan jàřidū) journalist

ɗan jāři-hujjà *m* capitalist

ɗan jauřa *m* peddler

ɗankàɗafī *m* crab-louse

ɗan kallō *m* spectator

ɗankāma *m* comedian of 'yankamanci

ɗan kàřen *m* excessive

ɗan kàsuwā *m* market trader

ɗan kòkawà *m* wrestler

ɗan kûnnē *m* ear-ring

ɗankwālī *m* head-tie

ɗan kwamìnìs *m* communist

ɗan kwangilā *m* contractor

ɗan Ƙasā *m* citizen

ɗan makařantā *m* pupil

ɗan mishàn *m* missionary

ɗan sìyāsà *m* politician

ɗan ta'àdda *m* terrorist

ɗan tà kifè *m* 1. extremist 2. die-hard

ɗan tāwāyè *m* rebel

ɗan tîřēdà *m* trader

ɗan tsagèrā *m* (*pl* 'yan tsàgèrū) 1. extremist 2. radical

ɗan'uwā *m* (*pl* 'yan'uwā) 1. brother 2. colleague

ɗan wākē *m* bean flour dumplings

ɗanyàntakà *f* 1. rawness 2. freshness 3. inexperience 4. naivety

ɗanyē *m* (*f* ɗanyā, *pl* ɗànyū) 1. raw 2. fresh 3. uncooked 4. unripe 5. inexperienced

ɗanyen mâi *m* crude oil

ɗař-ɗař *adv* shaking with terror

ɗarà *vl* 1. to be a little more than 2. to supersede

ɗarè *v4* to leap onto

ɗàrī *m* cold

ɗàrī *m* (*pl* ɗarurruwà) hundred

ɗàri-ɗàri *adv* yi ɗàri-ɗàri to be reluctant (dà to)

ɗàřiƙà *f* (*pl* ɗařiƙōƙī) sect

ɗàtànniyā *f* gall bladder

ɗau *see* ɗaukà

ɗàu *adv* 1. hotly 2. painfully 3. intensely

ɗau àlkawàřī to promise

ɗau fansā to take revenge

ɗaukà v2* (ɗàuki/ɗàukē, m/f ɗaukà) 1. to take 2. to lift up 3. to carry 4. to overcome 5. to regard 6. to accept 7. to put up with 8. to adopt 9. to rate 10. to undertake

ɗaukà à r̃àkōɗà 1. to record 2. to tape

ɗàukacin the whole of

ɗaukàkā v1 1. to lift 2. to honour 3. to promote 4. to help

ɗàukakà f 1. honour 2. respect 3. glory 4. promotion

ɗaukàkà k̃ār̃ā (leg.) to appeal

ɗaukàr̃ mutànē à sōjà f (mil.) draft

ɗaukà wà... hankàlī to interest

ɗâukē v4 1. to remove 2. to relieve 3. to cease

ɗaukè ɗà to wean an infant

ɗaukē wà... idò to attract the attention of

ɗâukī m 1. (mil.) attack 2. assault 3. operation 4. shoot-out 5. yi wà... ɗâukī to storm

ɗàukī m ration

ɗâuki bâ daɗî m (mil.) 1. clash 2. major battle

ɗàuki fansā to take revenge

ɗàuki nauyī to take responsibility

ɗàuki wutā to catch fire

ɗâukī m (mil.) operation

ɗaukō mutuwà v6 1. to be dying 2. to wear out

ɗàuku v7 to be misunderstood

ɗaurà v1 1. to tie (gà on to) 2. to put on 3. to settle up

ɗaurà sir̃dì to saddle up

ɗaurà aurē to perform a marriage

ɗaurà k̃ūsà to screw (à jìkin into)

ɗauraỳa f 1. explanation 2. instructions

ɗauràyē v4 (f ɗàurayà) 1. to rinse 2. to plate

ɗaurè v4 (m ɗaurì) 1. to tie up 2. to put in prison

ɗaurè ɗàmarà 1. m armament 2. v4 to arm oneself

ɗaurè wà... gìndī to support

ɗaurì m 1. bundle 2. imprisonment 3. prison sentence 4. yi wà... ɗaurìn tālālā to put under house arrest 5. see ɗaurè

ɗaurìn gìndī m support

ɗaurìn gwar̃mai m puzzle

ɗàwāfî m circumambulation of the Ka'aba

ɗàwàiniyā f 1. task 2. effort

ɗàwīsù m peacock

ɗaya 1. one 2. other 3. only 4. duk ɗaya nè it doesn't matter

ɗaya... ɗayân... one... the other...

ɗâyā v2* (f ɗâyā) to strip away/off

ɗàzu adv just now

ɗêbè v4 1. to set aside 2. to remove 3. to give up

ɗêfî m 1. edge 2. tip

ɗìbà v2* (ɗèbi, ɗèbē) 1. to scoop out 2. to draw

ɗìbbù m magic

ɗìbgà v1 1. to experience a lot of 2. to suffer

ɗîf adv silently

ɗìgà v1 to pour in drops

ɗìga v3 to drip

ɗìgil adv very short

ɗìgìrgìrē m balancing load on head

ɗìgō m (pl ɗìge-ɗìge) 1. drop
2. point 3. decimal point

ɗîm adv thud

ɗìmā vl An ɗìmà masà sàndā.
He was beaten with a stick.

ɗìmàmā vl 1. to warm 2. to heat
up

ɗìmàucē v4 to get confused

ɗìmbī m 1. mass 2. ɗìmbin itàcē
a great deal of wood 3. yàkì
ɗìmbī a huge war

ɗìmī m warmth

ɗìmì adv in great amounts

ɗìmuwā f yi ɗìmuwā to get lost

ɗìn of

ɗìn 1. the 2. the one referred to 3.
this one exactly

ɗìngishī m 1. limping 2. lameness

ɗìnkà vl (m ɗìnkì) to sew

ɗìnkì m 1. sewing 2. embroidery
3. (med.) suture

ɗìřkà vl 1. to poke (cikin into)
2. to enter without warning
3. to thrust (à into) 4. to deploy
5. Nā ɗìřkà masà wukā.
I stabbed him. 6. Yā ɗìřkà
dūnìyà. He has vanished.

ɗis adv dripping

ɗìwā f pus

ɗìyā f daughter

ɗìyautař dà v5 to free from
slavery

ɗòfà vl to stick onto / into

ɗòkī m 1. eagerness 2. pain

ɗòrà vl (m ɗòrì) 1. to put (à
kân on) 2. to set (a broken
limb) 3. to add (wà to)

ɗòrawà f (pl ɗòràyī) locust-
bean tree

ɗòrawà-ɗòrawà light-yellow

ɗòrè v4 to last a long time

ɗòrē m missing Ramadan pre-
dawn meal

ɗòrì m 1. bone-setting 2. An yi
masà ɗòrì. They've extended
it. 3. see ɗòrà

ɗòriyā f 1. stacking 2. surplus

ɗòruwā f mài ɗòruwā long-
term

ɗòsànā vl to set fire to

ɗòyī m stench

ɗumàmā vl see ɗìmàmā

ɗumbū m see ɗìmbī

ɗùmī m 1. hubbub 2. see ɗìmī

ɗumì m see ɗìmì

ɗùmi-ɗùmi m làbàřì mai
ɗùmi-ɗùmi the latest news

ɗùngum adv completely

ɗùngumà v3 to move in a group

ɗùngùřùngum adv completely

ɗùngushē m 1. dishonest work
2. corruption

ɗùrà vl (m ɗùrì) 1. to load a
gun 2. Nā ɗùrà ruwā à būtà.
I poured water into the bottle.

ɗùrà jinī to give a blood
transfusion

ɗùrà kàrìn jinī to give blood
(wà to)

ɗùriyā f Kō ɗùriyàřsà bà à ji
ba... There has been no news
of him...

ɗuwàwū, ɗuwàiwai m
buttocks

Ee

ē 1. yes 2. well...
editā *m (pl* editōcī) editor
ēhò̩ *m* yi ēhò̩ to scream and shout
ēkà̩ *f (pl* ēkōkī, ēkà̩-ēkà̩) acre
ēkìs *m/f* cross, 'x'
è̩kuřû *m* (Nr) screw
è̩kwâl *f* (Nr) primary school
el'ê *f (pl* el'ê-el'ê) local
  authority

elèmantařè *f* elementary school
è̩lìbā̩jì *m* (Nr) veterinary clinic
emtì *m* 1. empty container 2.
  blank
ēriyà *f (pl* ēriyōyī) aerial
ēřiyà̩ř gidan řēdiyò̩ *f*
  transmission tower
è̩sanshì *m* (Nr) petrol, (US) gas
ēshàm, eshâm *m* stationmaster

Ff

fa certainly
fà what about...?
fā *f (pl* **fànnai)** outcrop
Fàbřairù *m* February
faca-faca *adv* **yi faca-faca** to scatter
fàcàkā *f* **yi fàcàkā** to squander
fàcè *v4* to blow your nose
fàcē *prep* except
fàcì *m* 1. patch 2. puncture
fādà *f* 1. royal court 2. approval
fàdā *m* priest
fàdamà *f (pl* **fadamōmi)** marsh
fādancì *m* 1. audience 2. flattery 3. insincerity 4. sycophancy 5. **ɗan fādancì** sycophant
fàdàwā *see* **bàfādà**
fadà *f (pl* **fàdàce-fàdàce)** 1. quarrel 2. dispute 3. fight
fàdà 1. *f* saying 2. *v2** *(m* **faɗì)** to say
fādà wà *v1* 1. to fall into/onto 2. to jump into 3. to attack
fadà dà màkàmai *f* battle
fādàɗà *v1* 1. to widen 2. to spread
fàdàɗà *v3* to be wide
fadakař dà *v5* 1. to teach 2. to inform
fàdà-wuta *m* moth
fadè *m* 1. sandals 2. slippers
fàdè *m* 1. rape 2. **yi wà... fàdè** to rape
fadì *v* to say
fāɗì *v (f* **fāɗùwā)** 1. to fall 2. to set 3. to fail 4. to lose 5. **Gàbantà yā fāɗì.** She was disappointed.

fāɗì *m* width
fàɗì-à-ji *m* **mài fàɗì-à-ji** influential
fàɗì-kà-mutù *m* crockery
fāɗìn řâi *m* conceit
fāɗùwā *f* 1. fall 2. setting 3. failure 4. loss
fāɗùwař fàřāshì *f* fall in prices
fāɗùwař gàbā *f* disappointment
fāɗùwař hařkōkin tattalin ařzìkì *f* economic collapse
fāɗùwař rānā *f* sunset
fāɗùwař tattalin ařzìkì *f* (ec.) negative growth
fāfà *v1* to split
fàfā *f* scraping out
fàfarà *v2** 1. to pursue 2. to chase off
fàfàřandà *f* veranda
fāfàtā *v1* to struggle with
fāfàtâwā *f* struggle
fàfè *v4* to scrape out
fàfùřàtan *adv* **ki fàfùřàtan** to refuse point-blank
fàfùtùtā *f* 1. trouble-making 2. effort
fagē *m (pl* **fagàgē)** 1. open space 2. area 3. arena 4. *see* **bāyan fagē**
fagen fāmā, fagen dāgā, fagen yāƙì *m* 1. battlefield 2. front-line
fahàmì *m* intelligence
fahàřì *m* pride
fàhìmì *m* 1. perception 2. intelligence
fāhìmì *m (pl* **fàhìmai)** perceptive

fàhintà 1. *f* understanding
2. intelligence 3. *v2** (**-cì/cē**) to
understand
fahintaȓ dà *v5* to make
someone understand
fā'idà *f (pl* **fā'idōjī)** 1. benefit
2. profit 3. gain 4. **mài fā'idà**
useful
faifā *f (pl* **faifōfī)** note (of
money)
faifai *m (pl* **fàyàfàyai)** 1. round
mat 2. disc 3. record
fàkā *2** *(m* **fàkō)** 1. to lie in wait
for 2. to eavesdrop
fàkàice *adv* à **fàkàice** 1.
cautiously 2. implicitly
fàkarā *f (pl* **fàkàrū)** bush-fowl
fakè *v4* 1. to take shelter 2. to
seek refuge
fakè dà *v4* to make an excuse
(**cêwā** that)
fàkê *m* (Nr) packet
fākìn *m* yi **fakìn** to park
fākìtì *m (pl* **fākitōcī)** packet
fàkō *m* 1. ambush 2. *see* **fàkā**
fàku *v7* to pass away/ die
fàkīȓī *m (f* **fàkīȓìyā**, *pl* **fàkìȓai)**
poor
fàkō *m* 1. semi-desert 2. **mài**
fakō infertile
fal *adv* full to capacity
fàlâ *f* (Nr) platter
falàkī *m* stars of the zodiac
falalā *f* 1. prosperity 2.
abundance
fàlale, fàlalè *m* 1. outcrop 2.
slab
fàlàntô *m* messenger
falē *m* saucer
fale-fale *adv* thin and flimsy
fàlîs mìlìtâȓ *f* (Nr) military
police

fallàsā *vl* 1. to embarrass 2. to
expose 3. to disclose
fàllasà *f* àbin **fàllasà** scandal
fallē *m* sheet of paper/cloth
fallè *v4* to hit hard
fallē-fallē *adv* bit by bit
falmàȓàn *f* waistcoat
fālō *m* 1. reception room 2.
sitting room, (US) lounge
falsafā *f* philosophy
fâlwayà *f* telegraph pole
fâm *f (pl* **fàmfàmai)** 1. pound 2.
two Naira
fāmā *f* 1. struggle 2. suffering
fāmà *vl (m* **fāmì)** to reopen a
matter thought closed
fambêl *m* fanbelt
famfàrā *vl* 1. to flee 2. to speed
off
fàmfarà *f* losing baby teeth
famfō *m (pl* **famfunà)** 1. pump
2. enema 3. **kân famfō** tap,
(US) faucet 4. **yi wà...famfō** to
pump 5. to incite
fāmì *m see* **fāmā**
fàmît, fàmêt *m* permit
fànāȓìtè, fànāȓētì *m/f* (spor.)
penalty
fancà *f* puncture
fandàrē *v4* to stray
fangalì *m (pl* **fangulà)** 1. open
plain 2. irrigated-farm bed(s)
fangìl *m (pl* **fangilōlī)** (Nr)
safety pin
fànjāmà *m* 1. pyjamas 2. loose
trousers
fankà *f (pl* **fankōkī)** 1. large fan
2. electric fan
fankamā *f* insolence
fankàshālì *m (f* **fankàshālìyā**,
pl **fànkàshàlai)** lacking in
common sense

fànkē *m* pancake
fankèkè *f* 1. pancake 2. make-up powder
fànkō *m* *(pl* fankunà) 1. something used 2. empty matchbox
fànkon àshānā *m* matchbox
fannì *m* *(pl* fannōnī) 1. type 2. category 3. subject 4. branch 5. science
fannìn àl'àdū *m* culture
fannìn mà'ànā *m* semantics
fannìn sōjà à fannìn sōjà military
fannìn tsārìn gìne-gìne *m* architecture
fànô *m* (Nr) road sign
fàns *f* (Nr) pliers
fansā *f* 1. revenge 2. ransom 3. redemption
fànsā *v2** (-shi/shē) 1. to ransom 2. to redeem 3. to purchase
fansaɍ dà *v5* to sell
fanshò *m* 1. pension 2. mài kàrɓaɍ fanshò pensioner
fàntìmōtì *m* suitcase
fàntîɍ *m* (Nr) 1. paint 2. painting
fantsàmā *v1* 1. to scatter 2. to spread 3. to disperse
fàntsamà *v3* 1. to be scattered 2. to be spread
fara *f* anaemia
fārà *v1* to begin to
fàrā *f (pl* fàrī) 1. grasshopper 2. locust
faɍa'à *f* cheerfulness
fārà aikì to come into force
fārà aikì dà to bring into force
faɍābitì *m* *(pl* faɍābitōcì) (mil.) private
fàɍāfagandà *see* fuɍōfàgandà

fàɍāgà *f* 1. leisure 2. opportunity
faɍàli *m* religious obligation
faɍam ministà *m* (Nr) prime minister
Fàɍansà *f* France
Faɍansancī *m* French language
Faɍansanshin tsōhon sōjì *m* Pidgin French
Fàɍanshì *m* 1. France 2. French language 3. ƙasaɍ Fàɍanshì francophone country
fàɍāshìn kàsùwànnin dūniyà *pl* international market prices
fàɍāshìn kāyàyyakī *m* commodity prices
faràntā *v1* 1. to whiten 2. to please 3. mài faràntà râi pleasing
faràntā wà... zūcìyā to make happy
fàɍantì *m* *(pl* fàɍàntai) 1. plate 2. tray
faraɍ-hùlā *m/f* civilian
faraɍ ƙasā *f* 1. whitewash 2. shāfà faraɍ ƙasā to whitewash
faraɍ-ƙayà *f* gum arabic tree
faraɍ tsūtsā *f* hookworm
faraɍ zūcìyā *f* good temper
fàɍāshì *m* 1. price 2. ƙàyyàdadden fàɍāshì fixed price
fàɍāshì mài ɍàhūsā *m* reduced price
faɍat *adv* suddenly
faɍat ɗaya *adv* immediately
faɍātì *m* parade
fārà tùnàni to contemplate
farau-farau *adv* openly
fàrautā *v2** (-ci/cē) 1. hunting 2. to hunt
farcè *m* *(pl* faràtā) 1. fingernail 2. toenail

fàr̃dā *m/f* unique
fàr̃dà *v2** to hoe up
far̃e *m* yi far̃e to bet (à kân on)
fàr̃êfê *m* (Nr) administrative prefect
far̃êtì *m* parade
far̃fādìyā *f* 1. epilepsy 2. mài far̃fādìyā epileptic
far̃fad̃ô *v6* (med.) to recover
far̃fad̃ô dà 1. to revive 2. to boost
far̃fad̃ôwā *f* (med/ec.) recovery
far̃fàgandà see fur̃ôfàgandà
fàr̃fājìyā *f* open space before compound
farfarā *f* early type of guinea-corn
fàr̃fê *m* see fàr̃êfê
fàr̃fēlà *f* (*pl* far̃fēlōlì) 1. propellor 2. motor fan
fàr̃fēsà, (Nr) fàr̃fàsâr̃ *m/f* professor
far̃fêsū *m* pepper soup
far̃ga *v* (*f* far̃ga) to realize
fàr̃gàbā *f* fear
fari *m* ((*f* farā, *pl* faràr̃ē) 1. white 2. fair 3. good 4. (*pl* farfarū) vowel sign in Ajami
farì *m* drought
fārì *m* 1. beginning 2. na fārì first 3. dà fārì in the first place
fari fat snow white
fàr̃illà *f* 1. certainty 2. (rel.) obligation
farin cikì *m* 1. happiness 2. mài farin cikì happy
farin jinì *m* 1. popularity 2. mài farin jinì popular
farin kāyā *m* 1. disguise 2. 'yan sàndan farin kāyā secret police
fàrin shìgā *m* 1. novice 2. newcomer

fārìn farkō *adv* right from the start
fàrì see fàrā
fàr̃illà *f* (*pl* fàr̃illai) religious obligation
fàr̃iyà *f* showing off
far̃jì *m* vagina
fàrkā *m/f* (*pl* farèkanì) lover
far̃kà *vl* to wake up
far̃kē *m* (*pl* fatàkē) travelling trader
far̃kè *v4* 1. to get even with 2. to rip open
farkō *m* 1. beginning 2. na farkō first 3. first of all 4. dà farkō at first 5. tun dàgà farkon fārāwā from the very start
fàr̃makì *m* 1. sudden attack 2. ambush 3. kai wà... fàr̃makì to attack
fàr̃mànkàlâsh *m* (Nr) (mil.) private
fàr̃màsî *f* (Nr) pharmacy
fàr̃mî *m* (Nr) 1. permit 2. driving licence
fàr̃nàtî *m* (spor.) penalty
farsā *f* (*pl* faràshē) split kolanut(s)
farsà *vl* to irradiate
fàr̃tàmànê, far̃tamāni *m* (Nr) purse
far̃tanyā *f* (*pl* far̃ètanì) short hoe
fàr̃tî *m* (Nr) (pol.) party
fàr̃zìdân *m* (Nr) president
fàru *v7* to happen
fâs *f* (Nr) 1. post office 2. *adv* yi fâs to come first
fasà *vl* (*m* fashì) 1. to shatter 2. to disperse
fāsà *vl* (*m* fāshì) 1. to postpone

2. to cancel 3. to be postponed
4. to be cancelled
fàsāhà *f* 1. art 2. skill 3.
technology 4. ƙàyyàtacciyaȓ
fàsāhà high technology
fàsàjê *m* (Nr) passenger
fàsà-ƙwàuri *m* 1. smuggling 2.
ɗan fàsà-ƙwàuri smuggler 3.
kāyan fàsà-ƙwàuri smuggled
goods 4. yi fàsà-ƙwàuri to
smuggle
fasàlī *m* (*pl* fasalōlī) 1. chapter
2. section 3. order 4. season 5.
structure
fasàl'ōdà *f* 1. postal order 2.
money order
fasà'ōfìs *m* (*pl* fas'ōfōfī) post
office
fas dà fàlîs *m* (Nr) police station
fāsē *m* (Nr) ironing
fàsè *v4* (Nr) to iron
fàsê *m* (Nr) 1. driving test 2. yi
fàsè to pass
fàsfâȓ *m* (Nr) passport
fàsfô *m* (*pl* fasfunà) 1. passport
2. bā dà fàsfô to issue a
passport
fashè *v4* 1. to be broken 2. to be
dispersed
fashè dà dàriyà to burst into
laughter
fashè dà kūkā to burst into tears
fashì *m* 1. highway robbery
2. ɗan fashì highway robber
3. ɗan fashì dà makāmī
armed robber 4. ɗan fashìn
jirgī hijacker
fāshì *m* 1. delay 2. yi fāshì to
omit 3. bābù fāshì without
interruption 4. *see* fàsà
fashìn jirgī *m* ɗan fashìn jirgī
hijacker

fāsìƙī *m* (*f* fāsìƙā, *pl* fàsìƙai)
1. flirt 2. immoral person
fàsìl *m* (*pl* fāsilōlī) parcel
fàsìn *m* yi fàsìn to pass
fāsinjà *m* (*pl* fāsinjōjī)
passenger
faskàrā 1. *f* parting in hair
2. *vl* (*m* fàskàrē) to be beyond
one's control
fàskarà *v2** to be impossible
fàskarà *v3* to split firewood
faskìlà *m* first-class
fàsō *m* chapping of skin
fâs-ōdà *f* 1. money order
2. postal order
fassaȓà *f* (*pl* fassaȓōȓī) 1.
translation 2. explanation
fassàȓā *vl* 1. to translate 2. to
explain
fastò *m* (*pl* fastōcī) pastor
fat *adv* farī fat snow white
fātā *m/f* 1. hope 2. yi fātā to
hope
fàtà *f* (*pl* fātū) 1. skin 2. leather
fata-fata *adv* An kòrē sù fata-
fata. They've been chased off
in all directions.
fata-fàtà *adv* broad
fatàkē *see* faȓkē
fatalà *f* (*pl* fàtàlū) head-tie
fàtàlī *adv* 1. disregard 2. yi fàtàlī
to throw to one side 3. yi fàtàlī
dà to flout
fatalwā *f* (*pl* fatalwōyī) ghost
fātā nagàrī *m* optimism
fàtantì *m* (Nr) trading licence
fatanyà *f* (*pl* fàtànyū) short hoe
fataȓā *f* 1. lack 2. Mun yi
fataȓaȓ ganintà. We haven't
seen her for a while.
fātàȓ bakà *f* na fātàȓ bakà
1. insincere 2. groundless

fataɍaɍ kuɗi f bankruptcy
fàtàri m 1. petticoat 2. skirt
fātàɍ kûnnē f earlobe
fàtàttakà v2* 1. f rout
  2. crackdown 3. v2* (-ci/cē) to
  rout
fatauci m travelling trade
fàtàwā f 1. request 2.
  explanation
fàtè-fate m flour and vegetables
  mush
fàtìrì m (Nr) 1. 'yan fàtìrì patrol
  2. yi fàtìrì to patrol
fatō-fàtò adv extremely wide
fatsa f 1. fishhook 2. angling
fàu adv brilliantly
faucè v4 1. to swoop on 2. to
  snatch away
fàufau adv 1. absolutely 2. never
fawà m butchery
fàyàfàyai see faifai
fayè v4 to be
fāyìl m (pl fāyilōlì) 1. file 2.
  folder
fāyìnt m pint
fayyàcè v4 to explain in detail
fàzgô m (Nr) passport
fēdà f (pl fēdōjì) pedal
fēdè v4 (f fidà) 1. to skin 2. to
  analyse
fēgì m (pl fēgunà) 1. stake
  2. plot of land
fēlì, fēlù m (Nr) shovel
fēɓè v4 to sharpen to a point
fēlēɓē m yi fēlēɓè to ogle
fēlù m (Nr) spade
fenshò m 1. pension 2. retirement
fensìr m (pl fensiɍōɍì) pencil
fentà m painter
fentì m 1. paint 2. shāfè bangō
  dà fentì to paint a wall
fèrân m (Nr) brake

fērè v4 (f fìrà) to cut down
fes adv 1. clean 2. neat
fēsà vl 1. to spray 2. to spread
fèshì m 1. spray 2. crop dusting
fētìkâsh m petty cash
fētò m 1. shorts 2. underpants
fētùr m petrol, (US) gas
fi v 1. to be more than 2. to be
  better than 3. Yā fi nì ƙarfì.
  He is stronger than I am. 4. Yā
  fi gàban màmākì. It's most
  extraordinary. 5. Iskà tā fi
  zuwà dàgà yâmma. The wind
  usually blows from the the the
  west. 6. Itàtuwàn Kanò sun fi
  girmā. Kano has the biggest
  trees. 7. Aikìn nân yā fi
  ƙarfīnā. This work is too
  much for me.
fi kyâu to be better
ficè v4 to go out and away
fìdā'ù m prayers for the dead
fid dà see fitaɍ dà
fìddau m reject
fìdà f 1. (med.) operation 2. see
  fēdè
fidìyē v4 (f fidìyà) to castrate
fìfà f (Nr) siren
fìffìkā f flapping
fìffìkè m (pl fìkàfìkai) wing
fìfìkò m 1. superiority 2. priority
fìfìtā vl (f fìfìtā) 1. to promote
  2. to cool food by fanning
fìfìtà v3 to excel
fìgā v2* to snatch (à from)
fìgè v4 1. to pluck out 2. to snatch
fì'ìli m (pl fì'ìlāi) verb
fìkàfìkai see fìffìkè
fiknìk m picnic
fìkò m superiority
fìƙà f (pl fìƙōƙì) canine tooth
fìƙè v4 to sharpen

fiƙihù *m* (Isl.) jurisprudence

fìl *m* 1. pin 2. (Nr) electric wire

filàfilī *m* (*pl* filàfilai) paddle

filākò *m* modesty

Fìlānī *see* Bàfilàcè

filankì *m* (*pl* filànkai) plank

filàntô *m* (Nr) 1. messenger 2. orderly

filâs *m* flask

filastà *f* 1. plaster 2. yì filastà to plaster

filāyà *f* (*pl* filāyōyī) pliers

fil àzal *adv* tun fil àzal ever since the beginning

filfilò *m* kite

filì *m* (*pl* filàyē) 1. field 2. open space 3. chance 4. yawàn fili area 5. à fili publicly 6. bai wà... fili to make way for

filìm *m* film

filin dāgā *m* 1. battle field 2. à filin dāgā tactical

filin fàdì sônkà *m* readers' page

filin jirgin samà *m* 1. airport 2. airfield

filin fẽdiyò *m* radio programme

filin wàsā *m* 1. playing field 2. court 3. stadium

fillā-fillā *adv* 1. detailed 2. step by step

fillè *v4* to chop off

filò *m* (*pl* filōlī) pillow

filtà *f* (*pl* filtōcī) filter

fîm *m* 1. film 2. transparency 3. cinema

fìn *m* pin

fincikà *v2** to yank out

fìnê *m* (Nr) tyre

fìnē sèkûf *m* (Nr) spare tyre

fìnjàlì *m* (*pl* fìnjàlai) (Nr) drinking glass

fìn ƙarfì *m* 1. duress 2. force

fifâm *m* 1. frame 2. door 3. pram

fifāmàfè *f* (*pl* fifāmafōfī) primary school

fir'aunà *m* 1. pharoah 2. mài hālin fir'aunà sadistic

fir'aunancì *m* sadism

fifāyìm ministà *m* prime minister

fifdausì *m* paradise

fifgàgī *m* uproar

firgigit *adv* Tā tāshì firgigit. She jumped up startled.

firgìtā *v1* 1. to scare 2. to startle

firgìtà *v3* 1. to be scared 2. to be startled

firgitâfwā *f* mài firgitâfwā shocking

fifî *f* (Nr) neutral

fifîjì *m* (*pl* fifîjōjī) refrigerator

fifîm *f* (Nr) retirement pay

fifìmâf (Nr) 1. *m* premier 2. *f* primary school

fifîmiyà *m* premier

fifintà *f* desktop printer

fifîs *f* (Nr) plug

fifshìdân *f* (Nr) fridge

fiftà *f* filter

fisà *f* 1. pizza 2. *see* bisà

fìsh *f* (Nr) electric plug

fisìks *m* physics

fi sô to prefer

fisshē *see* fitaf dà

fistìn, (Nr) fistân *m* piston

fistòlê *m* (Nr) pistol

fita *v3* 1. to go out 2. to appear 3. to succeed

fìtaccē *m* (*f* fìtacciyā, *pl* fitàttū) renowned

fitaf dà *v5* (fìd dà + *direct object*) 1. to take out 2. to get rid of

fitàfô *m* 1. kerosene 2. petrol

fitikì *m* grass cutting

fitilà *f (pl* fìtìlū) 1. lamp 2. light 3. electricity

fitilàr̃ ruwā *f* pressure lamp

fitinà *f (pl* fìtìnū) 1. trouble 2. dissent

fito m yi fito to ferry (across)

fito m palm wine

fito m yi fitò to whistle

fito-nā-fito m confrontation

fitôwar̃ rānā *f* sunrise

fitsārī m 1. urine 2. yi fitsārī to urinate

fîyayyē m *(f* fîyayyiyā, *pl* fîyàyyū) superior

fîye dà 1. more than 2. better than

fîye dà kōyàushè more than ever

fîzgā *v2** to wrench out/ away

fok m (*pl* fōkunà) fork

fòlîs 1. *f* police force 2. m policeman

fōlìyestā *f* polyester

fôskàd m postcard

fôtî m putty

fùkā *f* bronchitis

ful *adv* sābō ful brand new

fùlāwà *f* flour

fulōgì m (*pl* fulōgōgī) 1. plug 2. sparkplug

fulōtì m 1. plot of land 2. buying point

fùmfùnā *f* mildew

fùnkàsō m fried wheat-cake

furā *f* balls of cooked flour in sour milk

fùrē m (*pl* fùrànnī) flower

furfurā *f* grey hair

furfùrā *vl* to barter

fùrfurà *v3* to be bartered

fur̃ōfàgandà *f* propaganda

fùr̃ōfēsà *m/f* professor

fùr̃ōsashàn *f* procession

fur̃ōtìn m protein

fur̃sùnà m (*pl* fur̃sunōnī) prisoner

fur̃tà *vl* to mention

fur̃tùmì m (*pl* fur̃tumà) bullock

furùcī m yi furùcī to state

furzà *vl* to spit out

fusàtà *vl* to anger

fùsatà *v3* to get angry

fushī m 1. anger 2. mài fushī angry 3. yi fushī to be angry

fuskà *f (pl* fuskōkī) 1. face 2. surface 3. direction 4. ta fuskàr̃ tsàrō strategic

fuskà biyu *f* 1. hypocrisy 2. mài fuskà biyu hypocritical 3. two-edged 4. twofold

fùskantà *v2** (-ci/cē) 1. to face 2. to deal with

fuskàr̃ gàrī *f* traditional borough

fyācè *v4* to blow your nose

fyādì m 1. canteen 2. shop 3. kiosk

fyādà *vl* 1. to whip 2. to knock down

fyàdè m 1. rape 2. yi wà... fyàdè to rape

fyaucè *v4* 1. to swoop on 2. to snatch

Gg

ga *see* ganī

gà *prep* (gàrē + *possessive pronoun*) 1. in the presence of 2. at 3. to 4. on 5. regarding 6. for 7. against 8. from 9. against 10. on the side of

gā̀ 1. here is/ are 2. there is/ are

gàba *adv* 1. in front 2. nan gàba from now on

gàbā *m* 1. front 2. genitals 3. towards

gā̀bā *f* 1. hostility 2. àbōkin gā̀ba enemy

gàbā ɗaya *adv* all together

gàban *prep* 1. in front of 2. in the presence of 3. on the other side of 4. beyond

gàbànin, gàbànnin *prep* 1. just before 2. just about to 3. on the eve of

gàbàr̃dîn *m* (Nr) gabardine

gàbàruwā *f* acacia tree

gabàs *f* 1. east 2. eastwards 3. na gabàs eastern

gabashin *prep* east of

Gabàs ta Tsakiyà *f* Middle East

gàbātà *v3* to precede

gàbātà *v2** (-ci/cē) 1. to be leader (of) 2. to approach 3. to precede 4. to pass away (to die)

gabātar̃ dà *v5* 1. to introduce 2. to promote 3. to elect as leader 4. to nominate

gabātâr̃wā *f* 1. introduction 2. foreword

gabcè *v4* 1. to collapse 2. to run out 3. to deduct (a large amount of)

gàb-gàb-gàb *adv* hau gàb-gàb-gàb to start without thinking

gab dà *prep* 1. next to 2. near, nearby 3. about to

gabtà̀ wà *v1* to bite into

gàbtarà *v2** to break off (a large amount of)

gàbzā *v2** (-ji/jē) 1. to hit hard 2. to do a lot of

gabzà yā̀ƙì to wage war (dà on)

gaɓā̀ *f* (*pl* gaɓōɓī, gàɓɓai) 1. joint 2. limb 3. syllable

gā̄ɓà̀ *f* river bank

gā̄ɓò *m* (*f* gā̄ɓùwā) fool

gacī *m* 1. river bank 2. opposite shore

gadà̀ *f* (*pl* gadōjī) bridge

gàdà̀ *f* duiker

gàdā *v2** (-ji/jē, *m* gā̄dò) 1. to inherit 2. to succeed in office

gàdà̀-gadā *f* obtaining by deception

gàdār̃à̀ *f* yi gàdār̃à̀ to be arrogant (wà to)

gadar̃ dà *v5* 1. to bequeath 2. to cause

gā̄dī *m* 1. guarding 2. mài gā̄dī night-watchman

gā̄dìnà *m* (*pl* gā̄dinōnī) 1. garden 2. gardener

gadō *m* (*pl* gadaàjē) bed

gā̄dò *m* 1. inheritance 2. natural behaviour 3. country of origin 4. *see* gàdā

gàdō *m* (*pl* gadunà̀) weaverbird

gadon sàrautà *m* throne
gadon fîtò *m* raft
gàdū *m* (*pl* **gadōjī**) warthog
gafakā *f* satchel
gàfalà *v3* to act recklessly
gāfaɍā *f* 1. pardon 2. forgiveness
3. ròƙon gāfaɍā apology
gāfaɍā dai! 1. Excuse me!
2. Out of the way please! 3.
May I enter?
gāfàɍta wà *vl* 1. to pardon 2. to
forgive
gàfaɍtà *v2** (-ci/cē) 1. to
pardon 2. to forgive
gāfî *m* 1. prosperity 2. taste of
raw beans
gafîlî *m* (*f* **gāfîlā**) 1. careless
2. reckless
gafîyà *f* (*pl* **gafîyōyī**) bandicoot
gagài *m* aphrodisiac
gàgàniyā *f* yi gàgàniyā to
struggle
gàgarà *v2** 1. to be impossible
for 2. to be impossible to do
3. to be uncontrollable for
gàgarà *v3* 1. to be impossible
2. to be out of control
gàgàrarrē *m* (*f* **gàgàrarrîyā**,
pl **gàgàràrrū**) 1. hard to
control 2. unmanageable
gàgārùmī *m* (*f* **gàgārùmā**, *pl*
gàgàrùmai) 1. important 2.
massive
gâggā-gâggā *pl* 1. leading
figures 2. *see* **gāgò**
gaggàutā *vl* to hurry
gaggāwā *f* 1. haste 2. **mài
gaggāwā** quick 3. **na gaggāwā**
urgent 4. **cìkin gaggāwā**
swiftly
gàgijè *v4* to grow
gāgò *m* (*pl* **gâggā**) 1. mighty

person 2. large ladle
gaibì, gaibù *m* 1. the unknown
2. **na gaibù** supernatural
gai dà *see* **gayaɍ dà**
gàigayà *v2** (*m* **gàigàyē**) 1. to
gnaw 2. to nibble
gailō *m* 1. nomadic Fulani
2. country bumpkin
gaiɍà *f* 1. deficit 2. without
3. minus 4. less 5. **yì gaiɍà** to
be missing
gaisà dà *vl* to greet
gaishē *see* **gayaɍ dà**
gaisuwā *f* (*pl* **gàishe-gàishe**)
greeting(s)
gaisuwaɍ mutuwà *f* condolences
gâiwā *f* (*pl* **gaiwōyī**) lungfish
gajartā *f* shortness
gajàrtā *vl* to shorten
gàjērē *m* (*f* **gàjērìyā**, *pl*
gàjērū) short
gàjēren lōkàcī *m* **na** (**wani
ɗan**) **gàjēren lōkàcī** 1. short-
term 2. temporary
gàji *v* (*f* **gàjiyà**) to be tired
gàjìmàrē *m* cloud(s)
gàjiyà *f* 1. tiredness 2. **Ìnā
gàjiyà?** How are you? 3. *see*
gàji
gàjiyà *f* **cì gàjiyà** to benefit
gàjìyayyē *m* (*f* **gàjìyayyiyā**, *pl*
gàjìyàyyū) 1. tired 2.
destitute
gaƙè *v4* to hinder
galà *f* 1. (Nr) stripe 2. *see* **galàn**
galabà *f* 1. victory 2. **yì galabà**
to overcome
gàlàbaità *v3* 1. to deteriorate 2.
to suffer
gàlàbaità *f* wandering
gàlàdīmà *m* 1. top official 2.
mayor

galàn *m* 1. gallon 2. tin container
3. rut(s) 4. yì galàn to jolt
gàlâs *m* (Nr) ice
galàtsī *m* error
galaucì *m* lack of purpose
gàlgùlētù *m* cooling jar
gālibàn *adv* usually
gālìbī *m* 1. majority 2. usually
gālìbin adj. most of
gālīhù *m* 1. maràs gālīhù
dispossessed 2. Bâ shi dà
gālīhù. He has no means of
support.
gàllabâ *v2** to worry
gallàzā *v1* to force (wà onto)
gam *adv* firmly
gâm *m* gum
gamâ *v1* 1. to finish 2. to join
3. to share 4. to combine
gamà bàkì to collude
gàmà-gàrì *adv* universal
gàmàjìgô *m* 1. drill 2. drilling
gamà kâi to cooperate
gamà ƙarfī to join forces
gà-macìji *adv* hostile
gàmayyā *f* pooling resources
gàmayyàr̃ tattalin ar̃zìkī *f*
enterprise zone
gambâ *f* tall grass
gàmbarā *f* 1. satire 2. ɗan
gàmbarà comedian
gàmbīzā *f* 1. na gàmbīzà
incompetent 2. haɗin gàmbīzà
temporary coalition 3. alliance
gamè *v4* Sun gamè minì kâi.
They conspired against me.
game dà *prep* 1. (together) with
2. regarding
gamì *m* impurity
gàmje-gàmje *adv* greedy
gamjì *m* (*pl* gamuzzà) gutta-
percha tree

gammō *m* (*pl* gammàyē)
1. headpad 2. coil
gàmō *m* encounter
gàmon kàtar̃ī *m* 1. luck
2. chance
gamsar̃ dà *v5* to satisfy
gamsâr̃wā *f* mài gamsâr̃wā
satisfactory
gamshē *see* gamsar̃ dà
gàmshèƙā *f* cobra
gàmsu *v7* to get on well (dà
with)
gàmsuwā *f* 1. satisfaction 2.
rashìn gàmsuwā dissatisfaction
gàmu *v7* 1. to meet (dà with)
2. to be joined
gà-mu-dai depression
gamuzzà *see* gamjì
gàmzākì *m* the morning star
gan *see* gani
gānâ *v1* 1. to discuss privately
2. to confer 3. Sun gānâ musù
dàɗî. They treated us well.
gānâ wà to treat badly
gānàwā *f* private discussion
gàndā *f* beef stew
gândir̃ōbà *m* (*pl* gandir̃ōbōbī)
prison warder
gandū *m* (*pl* gandàyē) large farm
gandun dājì *m* forest reserve
gândur̃ōbà *m* (*pl* gandur̃ōbōbī)
warder
gàndā̃ *f* palate
gandô *m* dam
gānè *v4* 1. to understand 2. to
realise 3. to find
gàngā *f* (*pl* gangunà) 1.
(cylindrical) drum 2. cylinder
3. barrel
gàngàmau *m* turmeric
gangamī *m* 1. alarm 2. yì
gangamī to raise the alarm

gàngan *adv* **1.** na gàngan artificial **2.** dà gàngan deliberately

ganganci *m* yi ganganci to act recklessly

gàngànìmà *f* **1.** spying **2.** dan gàngànìmà spy

gangàrā *vl* **1.** to descend **2.** to flow down

gàngarà *f* slope

gangarè *m* downhill

gangàriyà *f* **1.** pure(ly) **2.** absolute(ly)

gàngaṟ jìkī *f* trunk of the body

gàngaṟ zōmō *f* helmet

ganī 1. *m* sight **2.** à ganinā in my opinion **3.** *v* (ga + *object noun*, gan + *object pronoun*; *m* ganì) to see **4.** to look at **5.** to consider

gà-ni-kàshè-ni 1. dan gà-ni-kàshè-ni militant **2.** dan gà-ni-kàshè-ni na jàm'iyyà party militant

gànìmà *f* loot

ganin cêwā considering that

gāniyà *f* **1.** prime **2.** peak,

gānō *vó* to learn of

gànsàkūkà *f* **1.** slime **2.** moss

gàntàlallē *m* (*f* gàntàlalliyā, *pl* gàntàlallū) tramp

gàntàli *m* yi gàntàli to wander

gantsàrā *vl* **1.** to curve **2.** to do in excess **3.** to renege on a debt/ deal

gàntsarà *f* curve

gānō *vó* **1.** to discover **2.** to devise

gānuwā, ganwā *f* **1.** rampart **2.** wall (of town/ compound)

ganyē *m* (*pl* ganyàyē) **1.** leaf, leaves **2.** shrub **3.** marijuana

gàrā *f* termite(s)

gāṟà *vl* **1.** to rush **2.** to roll **3.** to drive/ ride quickly

gāra, gàra it would be better to

gārā *f* wedding presents

gàrâd *m* (Nr) rank

garai-garai *adv* ruwā garai-garai sparkling water

gàràjē *m* **1.** haste **2.** yi gàràjē to be sloppy

gaṟàlī *m* Mun kashè gaṟàlinmù. We achieved our aim.

gaṟambāwùl *m* **1.** overhaul **2.** reorganisation **3.** reshuffle **4.** reform

gàràntī *m* guarantee

gàrārà *f* yi gàrārà to be partially sighted

gaṟàṟī *m* **1.** trouble **2.** *see* gaṟàlì

gàràrī *m* yi gàràrī to wander about

gàràtūtè, gàṟàtūtì *m* **1.** gratuity **2.** retirement pay **3.** golden handshake

garau *adv* clearly

gàrāyā *f* (*pl* gàràyū) two-stringed guitar

gàṟdàbû *m* (Nr) (mil.) **1.** salute **2.** yi wà... gàṟdàbû to salute

gaṟdamà *f* (*pl* gaṟdàndamī, gaṟdàddamī) **1.** dispute **2.** argument

gàṟdànyê, gaṟdì *m* (Nr) **1.** guard **2.** night watchman

gaṟdì *m* **1.** taste of cassava **2.** taste of roasted nuts

gàrē *see* ga

gàṟê *m* yi gàṟê to park

gàṟêfê *adv* (Nr) grafted

gàrèjì *m* garage

gaṟgadā *f* (*pl* gaṟgadōjì) **1.** ruts **2.** turbulence **3.** wash-out gàr̃gaɗà *v2** (*m* gàr̃gàɗì) to warn

gàr̃gàɗì *m* 1. warning 2. advice 3. *see* gàr̃gaɗà

gar̃gājiyā *f* 1. olden times 2. tradition 3. na gar̃gājiyā traditional

gàr̃gàliyyà *f* colloquial Arabic

gar̃gàzâwā *f* failure

gàrī *m* 1. sky 2. (*pl* garūruwà) town

gàrī *m* flour

gàrin *prep* 1. in order to 2. because of 3. while

gàrin... powdered...

gàrin kātākō *m* sawdust

gàrin sukàr̃ī *m* granulated sugar

garkā *f* (*pl* garàkē) fenced land

garkàmā *v1* to do a lot of

garkè *m* (*pl* garukkà) 1. herd 2. flock

gàrkuwā *f* (*pl* garkuwōyī) 1. shield 2. film (on liquid) 3. yi gàrkuwā dà to take as hostage

garƙà *v1* to do a lot of

garƙàmā *v1* 1. to do a lot of 2. to impose sanctions (wà on)

garƙàmè *v4* to confiscate (wà off)

gàr̃mā *f* (*pl* gar̃èmanī) 1. large hoe 2. plough

gàr̃màhô *m* record-player

gàr̃ū *f* (*pl* gàr̃ukà) wall (of town/ compound)

garwā *f* (*pl* garèwanī) 1. kerosene can 2. pot 3. used 4. dilapidated

garwar̃ jūjì *f* dustbin

garwar̃ mâi *f* oil barrel

garwar̃ shàr̃ā *f* waste container

garwāshī *m* hot embers

gâs *m* 1. diesel fuel 2. butane gas

gasà *v1* (*m* gashì) 1. to grill 2. to roast

gāsà! gosh!

gàsā *f* 1. rivalry 2. competition 3. tournament 4. ɗan gàsā competitor 4. yi gàsā to compete

gasà'ōyìl *m* diesel oil

gàsar̃ zūcī *f* ambition

gāsàyā *f* pot-herb

gāshì *m* (*pl* gāsū) 1. hair 2. feathers

gashì *m* physiotherapy

gāshìn bàkī *m* moustache

gashìn kâi *m* 1. cîn gashìn kâi autonomy 2. sovereignty 3. bāyar̃ dà gashìn kâi decentralisation

gaskàtā *v1* 1. to verify 2. to believe

gàskatā *v3* to be verified

gàske *adv* 1. na gàske real 2. dà gàske really 3. seriously

gàskiyā *f* 1. truth 2. ban gàskiya reliability

gâs kūkà *m* cooker

gâs mài gubà *m* poison gas

gà-su-gà-kàmar̃sù *adv* unreliable

gātā *m* 1. support 2. livelihood 3. privileged

gātà *f/adv* three days from now

gātancì *m* preferential treatment

gàtarī *m* (*pl* gāturà) axe

gatò *m* vagina

gàtô *m* cake

gatsà *v1* to bite (wà at)

gatsà màganà to make a gaffe

gàtsà *v2** to bite off

gàtsē *m* sarcasm

gàtsìnē *m* sneer

gàuƙā *f* eagerness

gaulā *m/f* (*pl* **gaulàyē**) fool

gaulancī *m* foolishness

gàurākà̀ *f* (*pl* **gàuràkī**) crownbird

gauràyā *v1* to mix

gàurayà *v3* to be mixed

gautsī *m* brittleness

gāwā *f* (*pl* **gāwàwwakī**) corpse

gawàyī *m* charcoal

gàwuřtà *v3* 1. to grow to full strength 2. to become important 3. to become serious

gayà̀ wà *v1* to tell

gāyà *adv* very much

gāyā *m* (*pl* **gāyàyyakī**) 1. lump 2. Watà yā yi gāyā. The moon is full. 3. gāyan furā plain furaa 4. Yā zō gāyansà. He came unaccompanied.

gāyà̀ *f* maximum

gayař dà *v5* (gai dà + *direct object*) to greet

gàyaunā *f* (*pl* **gàyàunī**) farm plot

gāyè̀ *m* ɗan gāyè̀ dude

gàyyā *f* 1. communal work 2. communal workers 3. aikìn gàyyā teamwork 4. rāmuwař gayyà̀ retaliation

gayyà̀ *f* malicious act

gàyyarà *v3* to suffer

gayyàrà *v1* to bring suffering to

gàyyatà *v2* (-ci/cē) to invite

gazā *v1* 1. to fail 2. to be unable (to) 3. to not be enough 4. to be less (than) 5. to lack

gàzêt *f* gazette

gàzùwâl *m* (Nr) diesel oil

gēfè̀ *m* (*pl* **gyâffā**) 1. edge 2. side 3. bâ gēfè̀ without exception

gèfen, gèfin *prep* just before

gègā *v2** to come close to

gējì̀ *m* gauge

gēmù̀ *m* (*pl* **gyâmmā, gēmunà̀**) 1. beard 2. kafà̀ gēmù̀ to grow a beard

gērō *m* millet

gēwàyā *v1* 1. to go round 2. to surround 3. to tour 4. to go to the toilet

gèwayà̀ *f* 1. circuit 2. inspection tour 3. cycle

gēwayè̀ *m* 1. enclosure 2. circumference 3. toilet

gēwàyē *v4* to surround

gèzā *f* (*pl* **gēzōjì**) 1. mane 2. fringe

gìɓī *m* (*pl* **giyāɓū**) 1. gap 2. shortage 3. deficit

gìɓìn cìnikī *m* 1. trade deficit 2. rufè gìɓìn cìnikī to balance a trade deficit

gìɓìn kasàfin kudî *m* budget deficit

gicìyā *v1* to place across

gidā *m* (*pl* **gidàjē**) 1. house 2. compound 3. home 4. household 5. building 6. container 7. portion 8. mài gidā householder 9. na gidā domestic

gidādancī *m* naivety

gidan àbinci *m* restaurant

gidan àshānā *m* matchbox

gidan gàjìyàyyū *m* shelter for the homeless

gidan mân gōgè haƙòrā *m* tube of toothpaste

gidan ruwā *m* radiator

gidan saurō *m* mosquito net

gidan waƙàfi *m* prison

gidan wayà̀ *m* post office

gidan wutā *m* power plant

gidan yārì *m* prison
gidan zumà *m* beehive
gidimō *m* goat pen
giftà *vl* to cross in front
gìggìwà *f* tantrum
gigìcē *v4* 1. to be upset 2. to be shocked
gìgin-tsūfā *m* senility
giginyà *f* (*pl* gìgìnyū) deleb palm
gīgìtà *vl* to upset
gīgìtâr̃wā *f* mài gīgìtâr̃wā shocking
gijì *adv* 1. to home 2. at home
gìjìgìm *adv* clumsy
gijiyà *f* 1. hometown 2. homeland
gìlâs, gìlāshì *m* glass
gillà, gīlà *f* kisàn gillà 1. murder 2. assassination 3. massacre
gilmà *vl* to cross in front
gīlō *m* wandering about
gimbìyā *f* (*pl* gimbiyōyī) princess
ginà *vl* (*m* ginì) to build
ginà tukwànē to make pottery
gìna *f* flying ant
gindī *m* (*pl* gindàyē) hobbling rope
gìndī *m* (*pl* gindinà) 1. base 2. bottom 3. genitals
gìndin *prep* at the base of
gìne-gìne *pl* 1. fannìn tsārìn gìne-gìne architecture 2. *see* ginì
gìngimārì *f* lorry
ginì *m* (*pl* gìne-gìne) 1. building 2. *see* ginà
ginìn jimlà *m* syntax
gìnsā *v2** (-shi/shē) to have had enough of
gìnshikì *m* (*pl* gìnshìk̃ai) 1. pillar 2. mainstay

girā *f* (*pl* giràrē/girōrī) eyebrow(s)
gìrâm *m* gramme, (US) gram
girbè *v4* (*m* girbì) to reap
gir̃bùnà *vl* to confuse
girè *m* flattery
gìr̃gam *m* (Nr) 1. official register 2. record
gir̃gìdē *v4* to dislodge
gir̃gìjē *v4* (*f* gìr̃gizà) to shake off
gir̃gijè *m* (*pl* gìzàgìzai) stormcloud
gir̃gizà *vl* to shake
gìr̃gizà *f* 1. shaking 2. tremor 3. shock
gìr̃gizàr̃ k̃asā *f* earthquake
girì *m* 1. trick 2. hoax 3. Yā yi manà girì. He's tricked us.
gìr̃îs *m* 1. grease 2. sâ wà... gìr̃îs to lubricate
girkà *vl* (*m* girkì) 1. to put on 2. to cook
gìrke-gìrke *pl* recipe
girma *v* 1. to grow up 2. to get big
girmā *m* 1. size 2. bigness 3. importance 4. ban girmā respect 5. yi girmā to grow
gìrmā *v2** to be older than
girmā dà af̃zìkī *m* zaman girmā dà af̃zìkī good relations (dà with)
girmàmâwā *f* 1. honours 2. respects
girman kâi *m* conceit
girmàmà *vl* 1. to honour 2. to promote
girōrī *see* girā
gìrsā *v2** to overstrain
gishìr̃ī *m* salt
gīwā *f* (*pl* gīwàyē) 1. elephant

2. **aikìn bàban gīwā** (pol/ec.)
white elephant
gīwař-ruwa *f* Nile perch
gīwař tattalin ařzìkī *f*
economic giant
giyà *f* 1. beer 2. wine 3. gear
gìzàgìzai *see* **gìřgijè**
gìzàgō *m* adze
gizò *m* 1. trickster (in folklore) 2.
bàkan gizò rainbow
gizò *m* **Sun ƙullà gizò**. They
hatched a plot.
gìzō *m* untidy hair
gizògizò *m* (*pl* **gìzàgìzai**) spider
gōbà *f* guava
gòbařā *f* blaze
gòbe *f/adv* 1. tomorrow 2. **Sai**
gòbe! See you tomorrow!
gōcè *v4* 1. to swerve 2. to
dislocate 3. to knock away
4. to get knocked away 5. to
compromise (**dàgà** on)
gōcèwař ƙasà *f* landslide
gōciyā *f* 1. swerving 2. dodging
gōdè *v4* 1. to thank 2. **Nā gōdè!**
Thank you!
gòdiyā *f* thanks
gōdō *m* **yi wà... gōdō** to urge
gōdìyā *f* (*pl* **gōdìyōyī**) mare
gōgà *vl* to rub (**wà** on)
gògaggē *m* (*f* **gògaggiyā**, *pl*
gògàggū) 1. experienced
2. skilled
gògayyà *f* 1. experience 2.
friction
gògayyàř kāsuwancì *f* market
competition
gògayyàř lùmānà *f* (ec.)
peaceful competition
gōgè *v4* (*f* **gūgà**) 1. to rub 2. to
polish 3. to scrape 4. to saw 5.
to iron

gògē *m* one-stringed violin
gōgè haƙòrā to brush one's
teeth
gōgè wajen 1. to specialise in
2. to be experienced in
gògu *v7* 1. to be experienced
2. to be accustomed
gòguwā *f* experience
gôl *m* (*pl* **gōlōlī**) (spor.) 1. goal
2. goalpost
gōlà *m* goalkeeper
gòlê *m* (Nr) goalkeeper
gōlō *m* (*pl* **gōlàyē**) testicle
gōmà *f* ten
gòmiyā *f* multiple of ten
gōnā *m* (*pl* **gònàkī**) farm
gōrà *f* (*pl* **gōrōrī**) 1. bamboo
2. cane 3. crease 4. **jā wà...**
gōrà to lead... along 5. *see* **jà-**
gōrà
gòrā *m* (*pl* **gōrunà**) gourd-
bottle
gōrì *m* **yi wà... gōrì** to mock
gòřiyā *f* largest and best kolanuts
gōřò *m* (*pl* **gwâřřā, gòřàřřakai**)
1. kolanut(s) 2. gift
gòrubà *f* (*pl* **gòrùbū**) dum-
palm
gòshì *m* 1. forehead 2. forefront
3. **gòshìn tudù** brow of hill 4.
Tā yi gòshi. She is lucky.
gòshin *prep* just before
gôsùlô *m* 1. traffic jam 2. work-
to-rule
gōtà *vl* to exceed slightly
gōyà *vl* to carry on the back
gòyā *v2** (*m* **gōyō**) 1. to care for
a child 2. to treat well
gòyi bāyā 1. to support 2. to
concur with
gòyi bāyan bàtū to second a
motion

gōyō, gòyō *m* 1. baby 2. load carried on back

gōyon bāyā *m* 1. support 2. backing 3. mài/ ɗan gōyon bāyā supporter 4. yi gōyon bāyā to support 5. to recommend

gû *m* (*pl* gurārē) place

gubà *f* (*pl* gubōbī) 1. poison 2. toxin 3. chemical 4. mài gubà poisonous 5. toxic

gùdā 1. *m* (*pl* gùdàjī) lump 2. (a single) one 3. Gùdā nawà? How many? Gùdā bakwài. Seven of them. 6. *v2* * (-jē/jì) to avoid

gùdānà *v3* 1. to flow 2. to happen 3. to progress

gudānaȓ dà *v5* to administer

gudānaȓ dà tārō to hold a meeting

gudānaȓ dà yāƙì to wage war (kân on)

gudānâȓwā *f* hùkūmàȓ gudānâȓwā governing body

gùdàȓô *m* road

gudàwā *f* diarrhoea

gùdùȓô *m* (Nr) tar

gudù *v* (*m* gudù) 1. to run 2. to flee

gudù *m* 1. flight 2. yi gudù to run 3. to flee

gùdumà *f* (*pl* gudumōmī) hammer

gudùmmawā, gudùmmowā *f* 1. aid 2. yi gudùmmawā to make a contribution (don in/ towards)

gudùn dōgon zangò *m* (spor.) marathon

gudùn gàske *m* dà gudùn gàske at top speed

gudun-gùdùn *adv* huge

gudùn hakà *conj* in order to avoid (that)

gudùn hijiȓā *m* ɗan gudùn hijiȓā refugee

gudùn-zūcìyā *m* tact

gùdushēdì *m* goods yard

gūdà *f* (*pl* gùɗe-gùɗe) ululation

gùgā *m* (*pl* gūgunà) bucket

gùguwà *f* (*pl* gùgùwai) whirlwind

guhuȓnamà *m* (Nr) governor

gujè wà *v4* to run away from

gujiyā *f* (*pl* guzàyē) Bambara groundnut(s)

gulbì *m* (*pl* gulàbē) 1. river 2. pond

gùlôb *m* lightbulb

gùhùȓnùmâ *f* (Nr) government

gulmà *f* (*pl* gùlmàce-gùlmàce) quarrel

gùlû *m* glue

gùmàgùmai *see* gungumè

gumàkā *see* gunkì

gùmāsà *v3* to go sour

gùmbā *f* pounded millet with water

gùmì *m* 1. sweat 2. hot weather 3. cì dà gùmì to exploit

gûn *prep* 1. at 2. with

gunàgunì *m* yi gunàgunì to grumble (gà about)

gundà *f* (*pl* gundōjì) young fruit

gundārī *m* gist

gundūdū *m* waist

gundùmā *v1* An gundùmā masà satà. He was badly robbed.

gùndumà *f* (*pl* gundumōmī) 1. administrative district 2. local council

gùndurà *v2** to bore
gùndurà *v3* to be bored
gunduwā *f* slice
gungù *m* 1. gang 2. yi gungù to form a crowd
gungumè *m* (*pl* gùmàgùmai) log
gùngùnī *m* 1. grumbling 2. growling
gunjì *m* roaring
gunkì *m* (*pl* gumàkā) 1. fetish 2. idol 3. dictator
gunsùr̃ *m* 1. abundance 2. importance
guntsìlē *v4* to behead
guntū *m* (*f* guntuwā, *pl* guntàyē) 1. short 2. fragment 3. stub
guntùlē *v4* 1. to break a piece off 2. to cut short 3. to be cut short
gùr̃āsà *f* wheat-cake(s)
gurbì *m* (*pl* guràbū, guràbā) 1. hole 2. indentation 3. socket 4. place 5. māyè gurbì to replace
gurbìn aikì *m* 1. job 2. workplace
gurbìn idò *m* eye socket
gurɓàcē *v4* to stir up sediment
gurɓàcêwā *f* pollution
gurɓàcêwar̃ yanàyī *f* environmental pollution
gur̃ɓàtā *v1* to stir up
gùrɓàtà *v3* to become cloudy (water)
gùrɓàtaccē *m* (*f* gùr̃ɓàtacciyā, *pl* gùr̃ɓàtàttū) turbulent
gùrɓàtaccen mâi *m* crude oil
gur̃dè *v4* 1. to sprain 2. to dislocate 3. to twist out of shape 4. to be sprained 5. to be

dislocated 6. to be twisted out of shape
gùrfā *f* yi gùrfā 1. to clear land 2. to uproot
gur̃fànā *v1* to kneel on all fours
gur̃fànar̃ dà *v5* to make kneel
gurgù *m* (*f* gurgùwā, *pl* guràgū) 1. limping 2. lame 3. cripple(d)
gurgùncē *v4* 1. to limp 2. to be lame 3. to ail
gurgùntā *v1* 1. to lame 2. to cripple 3. to subvert
gùrguntà *v3* 1. to limp 2. to be lame 3. to go badly
gùrgurà *v2** to gnaw at
gur̃guzancī *m* socialism
gur̃guzū *m* 1. (homogeneous) group 2. ɗan gur̃guzū socialist 3. r̃a'àyin gur̃guzū socialism
gurì *m* place
gurin *prep* 1. at 2. with
guringuntsī *m* cartilage
gurjè *v4* to gin cotton
gùr̃nànī *m* 1. purring 2. growling
gùr̃nât *m* grenade
gùr̃sìmētì *m* goldsmith
gur̃ū *m* (*pl* gūr̃àyē) large belt
gùrūrù *m* deception
gusà *v1* to shift slightly
gushè *v4* 1. to pass away to 2. become extinct
gushèwā *f* extinction
gusùm *m* south
gutsùrā *v1* to break a piece off
gutsurè *m* fragment
gutsùrē *v4* to break off
gūgūtū *m* enema
guzà *m* water monitor
guzumā *f* (*pl* gùzùmai) 1. old woman 2. old cow

gùzurī *m* 1. journey provisions 2. travel allowance

gwāɓà *v1* to haft

gwadà *v1* (*m* **gwajī**) 1. to measure 2. to test 3. to compare 4. to demonstrate 5. to inflict

gwadà ƙarfin īkò (mil/pol.) to confront

gwàdayyà *f* 1. testing 2. competition 3. comparison

gwādàrē *m* ostentatious

gwàfā *f* (*pl* **gwàfànnī**, **gwafōfī**) forked stick

gwàfaŕ danƙò *f* catapult

gwaggò 1. *f* paternal aunt 2. old woman 3. *m* (*pl* **gwaggunà**) babboon

gwāgwàgwā *f* grappling

gwagwarcì *m* wifeless

gwagwàrmayà *f* struggling (dà with)

gwàgwiyà *v2** to gnaw at

gwaibà *f* guava

gwaidùwā *f* yolk

gwaiwā *f* testicle(s)

gwajè *v4* 1. to test thoroughly 2. to measure thoroughly

gwajī *m* (*pl* **gwàje-gwàje**) 1. test 2. experiment 3. demonstration 4. na gwajī experimental

gwajìn nūkìliyà *m* nuclear test

gwâl *m* 1. gold 2. (spor.) goal

gwàlâf *m* (Nr) light bulb

gwalè *v4* 1. to ignore 2. to snub

gwalè fātā to dash hopes

gwālè-gwālè *m* 1. corporal punishment 2. (mil.) fatigues 3. sansànin gwālè-gwālè concentration camp

gwālè idò *v4* to open eyes wide

gwalì *m* strap

gwālō *m* grimace

gwambàzā *f* waterbuck

gwāmiyà *f* grafting

gwàmmà 1. rather (dà than) 2. it would be better if...

gwammàcē *v4* 1. to prefer 2. yā gwammàcē... it would be preferable if... (dà... than...)

gwamnà *m* (*pl* **gwamnōnī**) governor

gwamnà-janàŕ *m* governor-general

gwamnatì *f* (*pl* **gwamnatōcī**) 1. government 2. regime 3. aikìn gwamnatì civil service

gwamnatìn faraŕ hùlā *f* civilian government

gwamnatìn hadìn gàmbīzà *f* coalition government

gwamnatìn jihà *f* (federal) state government

gwamnatìn mulkìn sōjà *f* 1. military government 2. junta

gwamnatìn tàrayyà *f* federal government

gwamnatìn tsakiyà *f* central government

gwamnatìn wucìn gādì *f* temporary government

gwāmùtsā *v1* 1. to mix 2. to squash

gwàmutsà *v3* to be crowded together

gwanàncē *v4* to be expert (gà in)

gwandà *f* (*pl* **gwandōjī**) pawpaw

gwandàŕ dawà *f* wild custard apple

gwàndà 1. rather (dà than) 2. it would be better if...

gwangwanī *m* (*pl* **gwangwanàyē**) 1. tin-can 2. na gwangwanī tinned

gwangwanin baƙin mâi *m* oil can

gwangwanin fèshī *m* spray-gun

gwànī *m* (*f* **gwànā**, (*pl* **gwanàyē**) 1. expert 2. excellent

gwànjō *m* 1. auction 2. sale

gwankī *m* (*pl* **gwankàyē**) roan antelope

gwànō *m* 1. stink-ant 2. jērìn gwànō in single file

gwara-gwara *adv* clearly written

gwarai *adv* 1. only 2. sole

gwarè *v4* to collide

gwàr̄gwadō *m* 1. proportion 2. standard

gwàr̄gwadon *prep* 1. in proportion to 2. approximately

gwārī *m* shunting-engine

gwar̄zō *m* (*f* **gwar̄zuwā**, *pl* **gwar̄zàyē**) dynamic

gwàtsò *m* gyrating

gwaurō *m* (*f* **gwauruwā**, *pl* **gwāgwàrē**, **gwauràyē**) someone no longer married

gwāzā *f* koko-yam

gwīwà *f* (*pl* **gwīwōyī**) 1. knee 2. curve 3. ƙòƙon gwīwà knee-cap 4. *see* hadà gwīwà, haɗìn gwīwà

gyàɗà *f* groundnut(s)

gyaggyàrā *v1* to modify

gyàlè *m* (*pl* **gyalōlī**) shawl

gyàmbō *m* (*pl* **gyambunà**) 1. sore 2. ulcer

gyàngyaɗì *m* nodding off

gyangyàrē *v4* 1. to fall in a faint 2. to drop dead

gyārā *m* (*pl* **gyàre-gyàre**) 1. repair 2. amendment 3. shaving 4. reform 5. extra 6. kāyan gyārā spare parts

gyārà *v1* 1. to repair 2. to improve 3. to reform 4. to amend

gyàre-gyàre *pl* 1. repairs 2. modification 3. (pol.) reforms

gyârtā *v1* to repair

gyartai *m* calabash mender

gyàtsā *f* burp

gyàtumā *f* (*pl* **gyàtùmai**) old woman

gyàurō *m* plants left for second crop

gyautò *m* (*pl* **gyautunà**) woman's wrapper

Hh

habà 1. come on! 2. finally...
haba-haba *adv* yi haba-haba
  dà to look after
habaicī *m* 1. innuendo 2. hint
Habashà *f* Ethiopia
habzì *m* yi habzì to take
  possession
haɓà *f* (*pl* haɓōɓì) chin
haɓàkā *v1* to cause to expand
hàɓakà *v3* to expand
haɓàkà bùkàtū to fuel demand
haɓakař dà *v5* to expand
haɓàř kadà *f* cap with ear-flaps
hāɓè *m/pl* 1. indigenous
  person/people 2. Hausa with no
  Fulani ancestry 3. *see* kāɗò
haɓò *m* nose-bleed
hàdà-hada *f* 1. buying season
  2. yi hàdà-hada to be
  extremely busy
hàdà-hadař cìnikī à ɓòye *f*
  (fin.) racket
hàdà-hadař kudì *f* 1. finance
  2. na hàdà-hadař kudì
  financial
hadarì *m* storm
hadāyā *f* (rel.) 1. sacrifice 2.
  offering
haddà *f* memorization
haddàcē *v4* to memorize
haddàcē à kā to learn by heart
haddàsā *v1* 1. to cause 2. (leg.)
  to lay down
haddì *m* (*pl* haddōdì) 1. limit
  2. (Isl.) fixed punishment
hadirì *see* hadarì
hàdìsì *m* (*pl* hàdìsai) traditions

of the Prophet Muhammad
hadɗà *v1* 1. to join 2. to unite 3.
  to finish 4. to introduce (dà to)
hadɗà bàkī to conspire
hadɗà dà 1. to include 2. to
  comprise
hàdɗaddḕ *m* (*f* hàdɗadɗìyā, *pl*
  hàdɗadɗù) 1. joined 2. united
hàdɗadɗìyař tàrayyà *f*
  federation
hadɗà gwīwà 1. to work together
  2. to conspire 3. to join forces
  (dà with)
hadɗà jìkī to gather in a group
hadɗà kâi 1. to unite 2. to
  amalgamate 3. to conspire
hadɗà ƙarfī to join forces (dà
  with)
hàdɗàkā *m* communality
hàdɗamà *m* greed
hadɗař dà *v5* to include
hadɗař dà tàrō to hold a meeting
hadɗàřī *m* (*pl* hadɗařuřřukà) 1.
  danger 2. risk 3. accident
  4. disaster 5. hostility 6. mài
  hadɗàřī dangerous
hadɗàřin mōtà *m* car accident
hadɗàřin tashàř nūkìliyà *m*
  nuclear power station accident
hadɗì *m* fortune-telling
hàdɗe *adv* à hàdɗe jointly
hadɗì *m* 1. mixing 2. co-operation
  3. cikin hadɗì together
hadɗin bàkī *m* ɗan hadɗin bàkī
  collaborator
hadɗin bàkī *m* ɗan hadɗin bàkī
  collaborator

hadîn gàmbīzà *m* 1. temporary coalition 2. alliance
hadîn gwīwà *m* 1. co-operation 2. na hadîn gwīwà joint
hadîn kâi *m* 1. co-operation 2. unity 3. conspiracy
hadîyē *v4* (*m* hàdîyà) to swallow
hàdu *v7* 1. to be joined (dà to) 2. to be united 3. to be connected (dà with) 4. to be at maximum point
hàdu dà to join
hafsà *m* (*pl* hafsōshī) (mil.) 1. officer 2. ƙaramin hafsà non-commissioned officer
hafsàn hafsōshī *m* (mil.) chief of staff
hāfīzī *m* (*pl* hàfīzai) one who has memorised the Quran
hàgā *v2** borrow without meaning to pay back
hagu, hagun *f/adv* 1. left (-hand) 2. contrary to expectation
hai (Nr) *see* sai
haibà *f* awesome
hàifā *v2** 1. to give birth to 2. to reproduce
haifař dà *v5* 1. to produce 2. to bring about
hàifayyà *f* 1. birth 2. genealogy
haifù *v* (*f* haifùwā) to give birth
haifùwā, haihùwā *f* birth
haiƙàn *adv* extremely
haiƙàncē *v4* to keep to
hailà *f* 1. menstruation 2. Tanà hailà. She has her period. 3. dainà hailà to reach menopause
hā'incì *m* 1. treachery 2. fraud

hairàn *m* good deed
hājà *f* (*pl* hājōjī) 1. merchandise 2. goods 3. hājà làlàtàttū damaged goods 4. baƙař hājà unsaleable goods
hajì, hajjì *m* pilgrimage to Mecca
hàjījiyà *f* giddiness
hàjjàtū *m* learning to read in syllables
hajjì *see* hajì
hakà *adv* in this way
hakà dîn *adv* exactly so
hakà nan *adv* just like that
hakà nē *adv* 1. thus 2. dà hakà/kàmař hakà in this way 3. duk dà hakà nevertheless 4. sabòdà hakà therefore
hakà-hakà *adv* so-so
hakì *m* (*pl* hakūkuwà) grass
hàkī *m* yi hàkī to pant
hàkīkà *adv* 1. undoubtedly 2. true facts 3. bisà gà hàkīkà in actual fact
hakīkàncē *v4* 1. to be sure (that) 2. to verify
hākìmcē *v4* to be pretentious
hākìmī *m* (*pl* hàkìmai) 1. district head 2. traditional title-holder
hakiyà *f* leucoma
hakkàkē *v4 see* haƙƙàƙē
hakkàn *adv* 1. undoubtedly 2. na hakkàn certain
hakkì *m* (*pl* hakkōkī) 1. right, rights 2. due
hakkin dòkā *m* legal right
hakkin hàƙař mâi *m* oil rights
hakkin màllakàř dūkiyōyī *m* property rights
hakkin mawàllàfī *m* copyright

hakkìn tsārìn mulkì *m* consitutional rights

haƙà 1. *m* **wurin haƙà** mine **2. mài haƙàn mà'àdìnai** miner **3.** *vl* to dig **4.** to mine **5.** to excavate

hàƙā *f* **1.** digging **2.** boring **3.** drilling for oil

haƙàrƙarī *m* (*pl* **hàƙàrƙàrai**) rib(s)

hàƙaȓ mâi *f* **1. wurin hàƙaȓ mâi** oilfield **2. injìn hàƙaȓ mâi** oil rig **3. rìjìyaȓ hàƙaȓ mâi** oil well

hàƙīƙà *see* **hàkīkà**

hàƙīlō *m* wasted effort

haƙƙàƙē *v4* **1.** to confirm **2.** to prove **3.** to convince **4.** to be sure **5.** to assume (**cêwā** that)

haƙƙàn, haƙƙùn *adv* **1.** undoubtedly **2. na haƙƙàn** certain

haƙō *v6* **1.** to mine **2.** to drill for oil

haƙò *m* trap

haƙō kwâl 1. *m* coal mining **2.** *v6* to mine coal

hàƙon jūnā *m* deterrent

haƙōrī *m* (*pl* **haƙōrā**) tooth

haƙòran arō *m* false teeth

haƙōrin hankàlī *m* wisdom tooth

hàƙurà *v3* **1.** to be patient

hàƙurà dà to endure

hàƙurī *m* **1.** patience **2.** endurance **3. Ìnā hàƙurī?** How are you? **4. mài hàƙurī** patient

hàlâ *adv* possibly

hàlâk, hàlâl *m* **1.** honest act **2.** (Isl.) lawful act **3. na hàlâk** legitimate **4.** *see* **ɗan hàlâl**

halàkā *vl* to destroy

hàlakà *v3* to be destroyed

halàltā *vl* *see* **halàttā**

hàlâs *see* **hàlâk**

hàlatà *v3* **1.** to be legal **2.** (Isl.) to be lawful

halàttā *vl* **1.** to legalize **2.** (Isl.) to declare lawful

hàlāmà *adv* **1.** possibly **2.** *see* **àlāmà**

hàlaȓtà 1. *f* attendance **2.** *v2** (-ci/cē) **3.** to attend **4.** to visit

hàlayyà *f* **1.** nature **2.** state **3.** attitude

hàlayyàȓ zaman jàma'à *f* **1. ilìmin hàlayyàȓ zaman jàma'à** sociology **2. mài ilìmin hàlayyàȓ zaman jàma'à** sociologist

halī, hālī *m* (*pl* **hālàyē**) **1.** character **2.** attitude

hālī *m* **1.** state **2.** condition **3.** situation **4.** circumstances **5. na hālin yànzu** current **6. à hālin yànzu dai** at the present moment

hàlīlù *m* favourite

hālin dattākò *m* maturity

hālin kawaicì *m* solitude

hàlittà *f* (*pl* **hàlìttū, hàlìcce-hàlìcce**) **1.** creature **2.** shape

hàlittà mài bā dà nōnò *m* mammal

hàlìttū *pl* species

halƙà *f* **1.** circle **2.** encirclement

hàllaȓà *v3* to present oneself

hallâu *see* **haȓ ìllā yâu**

halwà *f* (rel.) retreat

hàm *m* **1.** car horn **2. yi hâm** to honk

hàmādà *f* desert

hamàtā *see* **hammàtā**

hàmayyà *f* **1.** rivalry **2.**

opposition 3. *see* **àbōkin**
hàmayyà
hàmɓarà *v2** 1. to kick 2. to
overthrow
hamɓaraɍ dà *v5* 1. to knock
over 2. to topple 3. to oust
hàmɓàrarrē *m* (*f*
hàmɓàrarriyā, *pl*
hàmɓàràrrū) ousted
hamdalà *f* praising God
hàmīlà *f* (*pl* **hàmìlū**) sword-
sling
hammà *f* 1. yawn 2. hammer
hammàtā *f* (*pl* **hammatōcī**)
armpit
hamsà *f* five thousand
hàmsàmiyà *f* five hundred
hàmsin *f* fifty
hanà *vl* 1. to prevent 2. to forbid
3. to consider illegal 4. to
refuse
hanà fītā *f* 1. curfew 2. ɗaurìn
dòkaɍ **hanà fītā** house arrest
hanà ruwā gudù to bring to a
standstill
hanà tāshìn àlbâshī *m/f* wage
restraint
hancì *adv* à **hancì** in/on the nose
hancì *m* (*pl* **hantunà**) 1. nose
2. bribe 3. cîn **hancì** bribery
hancìn jirgī *m* prow
hancìn àllūɍà *m* eye of needle
handasà *f* architecture
hàndumà *v2** to eat a lot of
hàndùmau *m/f* glutton(s)
hàngā *v2** (*m* **hàngē**) to see...
in the distance
hàngē *m* 1. observation 2.
prediction 3. mài **hàngen nēsà**
observer
hangō àbin àheɍì *v6* to be
optimistic

hàngum *m* mumps
hanì *m* 1. prohibition 2. yi wà
hanì to forbid
hàni'àn *adv* Yanà **hàni'àn.**
He's contented.
hànīniyà *f* yi **hànīniyà** to neigh
hanjī *m* intestines
hanjin fìtilà *m* wick
hankàɗà *vl* 1. to thrust forward
2. to lift up the edge of
hànkākà *f* (*pl* **hànkàkī**) crow
hankàlī *m* (*pl* **hankulà**) 1.
intelligence 2. sense 3. mind
4. **mài hankàlī** careful 5. **mài**
rashìn hankàlī careless
6. **Hankàlī sà yā tāshì.** He's
worried. 7. **Mài dà hankàlī!**
Pay attention! 8. à **hankàlī**
slowly 9. carefully 10.
gradually
hankicì *m* (*pl* **hankitōcī**) 1.
handkerchief 2. face towel
hànKōrō *m* 1. eagerness 2.
anticipation 3. impatience
hannū *m* (*pl* **hannàyē,**
hannuwà) 1. hand 2. control
3. **sà hannū** to sign
hannū bakà hannū Kwaryā
m subsistence
hannun gīwā *m* elephant's
trunk
hannun jāɍì *m* (fin.) 1. stock
2. share 3. **mài hannun jāɍì**
stockholder, shareholder
hannun rìgā *m* sleeve
hannun tèku *m* sea channel
hannū-yā-san-na-gidā *m*
hālin hannū-yā-san-na-gidā
nepotism
hantà *f* (*pl* **hantunà**) liver
hantsà *f* 1. udder 2. trouser
crotch

hàntsaki *m* (*pl* **hantsukà, hàntsàkai**) 1. tweezers 2. forceps 3. tongs

hàntsī *m* 7.00 a.m. to 11 a.m.

hanyà *f* (*pl* **hanyōyī**) 1. road 2. path 3. way 4. sect 5. method

hanyà mài kâi daya *f* (Nr) one-way street

hanyàr̃ bâs *m* bus route

hanyàr̃ dōgō *f* railway line

hanyàr̃ jirgī *m* train route

hanyàr̃ jirgin samà *m* air route

hanyàr̃ rānī dà dàminā *f* all-season road

hanyàr̃ ruwā *f* 1. channel of water 2. canal

hanyōyin kīwòn lāfiyà *pl* healthcare

hanzarī *m* 1. excuse 2. haste 3. **Inà hanzarī.** I'm in a hurry.

hanzùgā *vl* to incite

har̃ *conj* 1. till 2. up to 3. even 4. so much so that 5. in spite of

hàrā *v2** 1. to make for 2. to raid

hàrābà *f* (*pl* **har̃ābōbī**) 1. site 2. enclosure 3. premises 4. territory 5. area 6. locality

har̃afī *m* (*pl* **har̃ufà, hàr̃àfai, har̃afōfī**) 1. letter of alphabet 2. consonant

hàr̃ājì *m* 1. tax 2. **mài tārā/kàr̃6ar̃ hàr̃ājì** tax collector 3. **sâ hàr̃ājì** to tax

hàr̃ājìn kāyā *m* value added tax (VAT)

hàr̃âm *m* 1. dishonest act 2. (Isl.) unlawful act

har̃àmī *m* (Isl.) obligations for the hajj

har̃àmtā *vl* 1. to outlaw 2. (Isl.) to declare unlawful

hàr̃amtà *v3* (Isl.) to be unlawful

hàr̃àmtaccē *m* (*f* **hàr̃àmtacciyā**, *pl* **hàr̃àmtàttū**) (Isl.) unlawful

hàrārà *v2** (*f* **hàrārā**) to glare at

harāwà *f* fodder

har̃bà *vl* 1. to fire 2. to ripen 3. to ruin one's chances

hàr̃bā *v2** (*m* **har̃bì**) 1. to shoot 2. to sting 3. kick 4. to infect

har̃bè *v4* 1. to shoot down 2. to shoot dead

har̃ dà *prep* 1. including 2. even

har̃dà *vl* 1. to interlock 2. to cross... over

hàr̃de *adv* à **hàr̃de** cross-legged

har̃dè 6afā *v4* to sit cross-legged

hàrgàgī *m* 1. uproar 2. gunfire

hàrgitsī *m* 1. disagreement 2. argument 3. dissension 4. skirmish 5. dan **hàrgitsī** troublemaker

har̃hàdà *vl* to assemble

harì *m* (*pl* **hàre-hàre**) 1. raid 2. attack 3. **kai wà... harì** to raid 4. to attack

har̃ ìlā yâu *adv* furthermore

harìn bôm *m* 1. bombing raid 2. **kai harìn bôm** to carry out a bombing raid

harìn gàbā dà gàbā *m* frontal attack

harìn dàuki bâ dadî *m* (mil.) lightning attack

har̃kà *f* (*pl* **har̃kōkī**) 1. affair(s) 2. business 3. movement

har̃kàr̃ kudî *f* na **har̃kàr̃ kudî** monetary

har̃ kāwō yâu moreover

har̃kōkin cikin gidā *pl* internal affairs

haɍkōkin nōmā *pl* agriculture

haɍkōkin wàje *pl* foreign affairs

haɍkōkin yâu dà kullum *pl* current affairs

hàɍsāshì *m/pl* 1. bullet 2. shell 3. foundation (of building) 4. turning point

hàɍsāshì mài lìnzāmì *m* guided missile

hàɍsāshìn tòkā *m* tear gas

harshè *m* (*pl* harsunà, haràsā) 1. tongue 2. language 3. tip

harshèn gudānaɍ dà ayyukà official language

harshèn wutā *m* flame

harsunà *pl* ìlìmin harsunà linguistics

haɍ yànzu up till now

haɍ yâu kuma moreover

hàɍzuƙà *v3* to lose one's temper

hàsalà *f* anger

hàsalà *v3* to get angry

hāsàli (mā) 1. in fact 2. luckily 3. it would be better to...

hàsāɍà *f* (*pl* hasāɍōɍì) loss(es)

hàsàshē *m* 1. speculation 2. yi hàsàshē to speculate 3. to forecast

haskà *v1* 1. to light 2. to illuminate

haskè *m* (*pl* haskōkì) 1. light 2. quick intellect 3. hint 4. yi haskè to shine

hassadà *f* envy

hassàlā *v1* to achieve

hàssalà *v3* to be achieved

hàsūmìyà *f* 1. minaret 2. tower

hātìmì *m* (*pl* hàtìmai) 1. official seal 2. official stamp

hàtsàbìbì *m* (*f* hàtsàbībìyā,

pl hàtsàbìbai) 1. magician 2. extraordinary

hàtsàniyā *f* (*pl* hatsāniyōyì) bickering

hatsàɍì *m* (*pl* haɗaɍuɍɍukà) 1. danger 2. risk 3. accident 4. disaster 5. hostility

hatsī *m* (*pl* hatsàitsai) corn

hàttā *conj* even

hattaɍà *f* alertness

hau *v* (*m* hawā) 1. to rise 2. to increase 3. to climb 4. to mount 5. to ride 6. to begin 7. to attack 8. Kwabò naiɍà sun hau. There's ten naira too much.

haufì *m* doubt

hau gadō *v* 1. to get into bed 2. to succeed to the leadership

hàuhawā, hàuhawà *f* rise

hàuhawà *v3* (fin.) to rise

hàuhawaɍ fàɍāshì *f* (ec.) inflation

hàukā *m* 1. madness 2. ferocity

haukàcē *v4* to go mad

hàukan kàrē *m* rabies

hau kujèraɍ nā ƙi *v* to veto

hauni *m* 1. executioner 2. left (-hand)

hauɍà *v1* 1. to climb over 2. to exceed 3. to remain (over) 4. (fin.) to rise

haurè *m* 1. tusk 2. tooth

hausa *f* 1. the Hausa language 2. the Hausa people 3. (*pl* hausōshì) language 4. meaning

hàusànce *adv* à hàusànce clearly

hàusàntu *v7* to be well said

haushī *m* 1. annoyance 2. anger

haushì *m* barking

hautsùnā *v1* to mix

hàutsunà v3 to be mixed

hauyā f (pl hauyōyī) small hoe

hauzì m yi hauzì to take possession

hawā m 1. storey 2. see hau

hàwā'ī m/f irresponsible

hàwainìyā f 1.chameleon 2. tàfiyàr̃ hàwainìyā slow progress

hawan hawā m extremely serious

hawàyē pl 1. tears 2. zubar̃ dà hawàyē to cry

hayà 1. f ɗan hayà tenant 2. vl to cross 3. to rent

hayāƙi m smoke

hayāƙi mài gubà m toxic fumes

hàyànìyā f 1. hubbub 2. uproar

hàyàyyafà m yawàn hàyàyyafà birth rate

hayì m 1. side 2. thatched roof

hayìs f minibus

hāzā f Sun ga hāzā. They realised the situation was impossible.

hàzāƙà f 1. great intelligence 2. mài hàzāƙà gifted

hāzā wassàlam... Yours sincerely...

hazbiyā f 1. stye 2. (pl hazbiyōyī) pigeon

hāzìƙi m (f hāzìƙā, pl hàzìƙai) clever

hazō m 1. mist 2. haze

hazō-hazō m 1. dimness 2. indistinctness

heɗìmastà m headmaster

hêdkwatà m 1. headquarters 2. centre

hêdkwatàr̃ ƙasā f capital city

helikwàftà m helicopter

hēlùmà m (pl hēlumōmī) foreman

hidimā f (pl hidimōmī) service

hìjābì m 1. veil 2. screen 3. protection

hijìr̃ā f 1. mass flight 2. (Isl.) the Hijra 3. ɗan gudùn hijìr̃ā refugee 4. zaman hijìr̃ā exile

hijìr̃ar̃ ƙwàr̃àr̃r̃un ma'àikàtā f brain drain

hìkāyà f (pl hìkàyū) tale

hìkāyàr̃ mafār̃ī f myth

hikimà f (pl hikimōmī) 1. wisdom 2. experience

hìlâl m 1. new moon 2. crescent

hìlālainì pl brackets

himmà f (pl himmomī) determination

hìmmàtu v7 1. to strive 2. to put effort (wajen/à kân into)

hinjì, hinjìs m (pl hinjōjī, hinjishōshī) hinge(s)

hir̃! stop it!

hīr̃a f 1. conversation 2. interview

hìsābì m 1. analysis 2. (rel.) reckoning

hītà f heater

hìyâs f (Nr) minibus

hizìfī m (Isl.) section of the Koran

hôb m 1. hub 2. hub-cap

hoɓɓàsà! 1. lift! 2. rashìn hoɓɓàsàn shūgabancì lack of leadership

hōɗà m powder

hōɗàr̃ Iblîs f 1. cocaine 2. heroin

hōgè m (pl hôggā) clod of earth

hōhò! 1. condolences! 2. how unlucky!

hōkì m hockey

hōlè *v4* **1.** to have a good time **2.** to enjoy

hōlèwā *f* **1.** fun **2.** enjoyment

hōlò *m* polo

hòlô *f* (Nr) tee-shirt

hōlōkō *m* storm without rain

hōmà *f* boasting

hōmàn *m* (*pl* **hōmōmī**) foreman

hôn *m* horn

hòrā *v2** (*m* **hòrō**) **1.** to train **2.** to discipline **3.** to punish

hòrō *m* **1.** training **2.** discipline **3.** punishment **4. màtàkan hòrō** punitive measures

hòtêl *f* (*pl* **hòtêl-hòtêl, hōtelōlī**) **1.** hotel **2.** restaurant **3.** bar

hòtō *m* (*pl* **hōtunà**) **1.** photograph **2.** picture **3.** drawing **4.** illustration **5. ɗauki hòtō** to take a photo

hubbārè *m* saint's tomb

hūcè *v4* **1.** to cool (down) **2.** to calm (down)

hūdà 1. *f* (*pl* **hōdōji**) hole **2.** *v1* (*m* **hūjì**) to pierce

hùdā *f* **1.** bud **2.** blossom

hūɗà *v1* (*f* **hùɗà**) to make ridges

huɗu *f* **1.** four **2. na huɗu** fourth

huɗubà *f* (*pl* **huɗubōbī**) sermon

hùgū *m* **yi hùgu 1.** to cancel **2.** to fail to happen

hùhū *m* lung(s)

hūjì *m* **1.** hole **2.** inoculation (of livestock)

hujjà *f* (*pl* **hujjōjī**) **1.** reason **2.** excuse

hùkūmà *f* (*pl* **hukūmōmī**) **1.** authority **2.** governing body **3.** commission **4.** public board

5. corporation **6. na hùkūmà** official **7. na hùkūmà** official **8. bisà hùkūmà** officially

Hùkūmàr̃ Àbinci dà Ayyukàn Nōmā ta Màjàlisàr̃ 'Dinkìn Dūniyà *f* Food and Agricultural Organisation (FAO)

hùkūmàr̃ bìncìkē *f* committee of inquiry

hùkūmàr̃ gàrī *f* **1.** town council **2.** local authority

hùkūmàr̃ gudānâr̃wā *f* governing body

Hùkūmàr̃ Kìwòn Lāfiyà ta Dūniyà *f* World Health Organisation (WHO)

Hùkūmàr̃ Kuɗî ta Dūniyà *f* International Monetary Fund (IMF)

Hùkūmàr̃ Kwallon Kafā ta Dūniyà *f* Federation of International Football Associations (FIFA)

Hùkūmàr̃ Tàrayyàr̃ Tūrai *f* The European Commission

Hùkūmàr̃ Tsàrō *f* Security Council

hùkūmàr̃ zar̃târ̃wā *f* executive commission

hùkūmàr̃ zàɓē *f* electoral commission

hukūmōmī *see* **hùkūmà**

hukuncì *m* (*pl* **hùkùnce-hùkùnce**) **1.** authority **2.** regulation(s) **3.** (leg.) sentence

hukuncìn kisà *m* death sentence

hukuncìn ladabtâr̃wā *m* disciplinary action

hukùntā *v1* **1.** to pass judgement **2.** to sentence **3.** to administer

hùlā f (pl hūlunà) 1. cap
2. farar̃ hùlā civilian
hùlar̃ kwānô f helmet
hùlar̃ màzàkutà f condom
hùlar̃ sàrautà f crown
hùlātîr̃ m (Nr) plaster cast
huld̃à f (pl huld̃ôd̃ì) 1.
transactions 2. relations
3. affairs 4. àbōkin huld̃à
(pol.) friend 5. yankè huld̃à to
break off relations
huld̃ar̃ cìnikī f trade relations
huld̃ar̃ jakādancì, huld̃ar̃
dìflòmàsiyyà f diplomatic
relations
huld̃ôd̃in jirgin samà pl 1. air
flights 2. air routes
huld̃ôd̃in k̃asàshen dūniyà pl
international affairs
hulô m (pl hulōlī) (Nr) pillow
hultsà see huld̃à
hulu-hùlù adv swollen
humùsì, humùshi m one fifth
hùnhùnā f mould
huntū m (f huntuwā, pl
huntàyē) naked
hùntur̃ù m 1. harmattan 2.
winter

hūrà vl 1. to blow (on)
2. to inflate
huwàcē v4 1. to relieve 2. to
bestow
hūrà wà... kûnnē to incite
hūrà wutā to light a fire
hùr̃dē m dappled grey horse
hur̃tumāmì m (Nr) purse
hūr̃ù, hūr̃ù m (Nr) 1. oven
2. kiln
hur̃ùmī m common land
hùsūfì, hùsûf m eclipse
husūmà f (pl husūmōmī) 1.
bad-feeling 2. chaos
hūtà vl 1. to rest 2. to relax
3. to relieve (dà from) 4. to die
hūtsū m (f hūtsuwā, pl
hūtsàyē) bad-tempered
hutsubà see hud̃ubà
hūtū m 1. rest 2. school break
3. holiday
hwàkê m (Nr) packet
hwàlâ f (Nr) take-away food
hwàmât m (Nr) cosmetic cream
hwànàtîr̃ m (Nr) window
hwàr̃màshî m/f (Nr) chemist's,
(US) drugstore
hwàr̃màtûr̃'èkàlâr̃ f (Nr) zip

Ii

ī **1.** yes **2.** *see* **im mà, iyar̄ dà**
ìbādà *f* **1.** serving God **2.** **gidan ìbādà** house of worship
ìbār̄à *f* warning
ìblîs *m* Satan
icè, iccè *m* **1.** wood **2.** tree
icèn wutā *m* firewood
ī dà *v5* **1.** to convey **2.** to accomplish
ìdan *see* **in**
idar̄ dà *see* **ī dà**
iddā̀ *f* period during which a woman may not remarry
īdì *m* religious festival
ido *adv* à ido in/on the eye
idò *m* (*pl* idànū) **1.** eye **2.** kashè idò to wink
idòn bàsīr̄à *adv* dà idòn bàsīr̄à realistically
idòn kòg̀ī *m* **1.** spring **2.** river source
idòn sau *m* ankle
ìfīr̄itù *m* evil spirit
igiyà *f* (*pl* igiyōyī) rope
igiyar̄ lēgàs *f* (Nr) mosquito coil
igiyar̄ ruwā *f* water current
ìgwā *f* (*pl* igōgī, igwōyī) (artillery) gun
ìgwā mài ruwā *f* (mil.) tank
ihù *m* shouting
ihù bāyan harì *m* crying over spilt milk
ì'ìnā *f* stammering
ìjābà *f* success
ìjār̄à *f* **1.** wages **2.** commission **3.** fee **4.** wage level
ijè *v4* to put to one side

ìkìr̄ār̄ì *m* **1.** claim **2.** yi ìkìr̄ār̄ì to make a claim
īkò *m* **1.** power **2.** control **3.** authority **4.** mài ikò powerful **5.** sàmi ikòn... to have the right to... **6.** Tanà dà cìkakken ikòn... She is empowered to...
ìkwaità *f* equator
ìlāhìr̄i *m* entirety
ìlgāzì *m* allegory
ìlēr̄ì *f* (Nr) oil mill
ìlhāmì *m* (*f* ìlhāmà̀) **1.** instinct **2.** inspiration **3.** vision
illà *f* (*pl* illōlī) **1.** fault **2.** crime **3.** shàrā mài illà toxic waste **4.** yi illà to have a harmful effect (gà on) **5.** *see* ìllā
ìllā **1.** except **2.** yes **3.** sai ìllā mā shā Àllāhù indefinitely
ilìmī, ilmì *m* **1.** knowledge **2.** learning **3.** education **4.** science **5.** mài ilìmī scholar
ilìmin fir̄āmàr̄è *m* primary education
ilìmin harsunà̀ *m* linguistics
ilìmin mânyā *m* literacy campaign
ilìmin mandîkì *m* (acad.) logic
ilimintar̄ dà *v5* to educate
ìllòrì *m* yellow
im *see* in
ìm *see* ìn
īmānì *m* **1.** faith **2.** compassion **3.** yi ìmānì to believe (cêwā that) **4.** to be confident (dà about)
ìmmā... ìmmā/kō... either... or...

im mà v to overcome

in, ìdan conj 1. if 2. when 3. whether 4. in dai provided that 5. im bà hakà ba otherwise

ìn subjunctive I

inà continuous I

ìnā? 1. Where? 2. How is/are...? 3. Ìnā sūnankà? What's your name?

inàbī m grape(s)

ìnā mā... if only...

ìnàrjî f (Nr) 1. electricity 2. power supply 3. gidan ìnàrjî power plant

indarārō m spout

incì m inch

indà 1. where 2. duk indà wherever

ìndà-indā adv Yanà ìndà-indā. He can't make up his mind.

indàlāhì, indàllāhì adv ànnōbā dàgà ìndàllāhì natural disaster

ìndaīarō m (pl ìndàīaīai) roof gutter-pipe

ingancì m 1. validity 2. reliability 3. efficiency 4. quality 5. mài ingancì valid 6. efficient

ingàntā vl 1. to strengthen 2. to promote

ìngàntaccē m (f ìngàntacciyā, pl ìngàntàttū) suitable

ìngàntuwā f improvement

ingaīmā m (pl ìngàīmū) 1. stallion 2. thoroughbred

Ingìlà f 1. England 2. Great Britain

ingìlîs, ingìlīshì m/f/pl 1. Englishman, Englishwoman 2. the English language

ìngirìcì m hay

inifâm, inìfâm m uniform

injì m (gen injìn, injìmin, pl injunà) engine

ìn ji... according to...

injìmin see injì

injìniyà m (pl injiniyōyì) engineer

in kā cirè... with the exception of...

ìnkārì m 1. denial 2. yi wà... ìnkārì to doubt 3. to deny

ìnkiyà f 1. temporary address 2. ɗan ìnkiyà communal agent

innà f 1. mother 2. (maternal) aunt 3. paralysis

innānàhā f 1. na innānàhā utter 2. kai innānàha to become extreme

ìnnàtû m inner tube

in shā Àllāhù God willing...

ìnshōrà, ìnshuwārà f insurance

intàhā f 1. end 2. limit

inuwà f 1. shade 2. shadow 3. reflection 4. protection

ìnzālì m orgasm

ìrādà f will

ìrànìyân m (Nr) uranium

irì m 1. seed(s) 2. offspring 3. kind (of) 4. see irìn

irì-irì adv of different types

irìn prep like

ìsa v3 1. to be enough/ sufficient 2. to arrive (at)

ìsā v2* (-shì/shē) to be enough for

ìsanshì m (Nr) petrol, (US) gas

isaī dà v5 to deliver

ìsfàīàdàrâ f (Nr) plaster

ìshārà f (pl ishārōrì) 1. indication 2. omen

ishè v4 1. to overtake 2. to pursue 3. to find out (that)

ishìrìn f twenty

isìmì *m* noun

iskà *m/f* 1. wind 2. air 3. (*pl* iskōkī) spirit 4. ɗan iskà idle person 5. shā iskà to go for a walk

iskà mài gubà ta nūkìliyà *f* 1. radiation 2. radioactivity 3. nuclear fallout

iskancì *m* immoral living

iskè *v4 see* ishè

ìskwâc *m* sellotape

ìstājì *m* (Nr) 1. course 2. seminar 3. training workshop

ìstìlô *m* (Nr) pen

istìmàt *m* 1. estimate 2. budget

ìstìngìfāfì *m* prayer for forgiveness

ìsyānà *f* sedition

ita *f* 1. she 2. her

itàcē *m* (*pl* itātuwà) 1. tree 2. stick 3. wood

itācìyà *f* tree

Itālìyà *f* Italy

ìtinà *m* (Nr) lieutenant

ìwā *prep see* yà

iyā *prep* as far as

iyà *f* 1. mother 2. (maternal) aunt

iyà *v1* 1. to be able (to) 2. to know how (to)

iyā adàdin... the exact amount of...

iyàkā *f* (*pl* iyākōkī) 1. frontier 2. boundary 3. limit 4. yi iyàkā dà to share a border with

iyākàcē *v4* 1. to limit 2. to restrict

iyākacì *m* 1. all 2. each and every

iyākàncē *v4* to limit

iyàkwàndishàn *f* air-conditioner

ìyālì *m* 1. (immediate) family 2. dependants 3. ƙayyàdè ìyālì family planning

iyaf dà *v5* (ī dà + *direct object*) to accomplish

iyàwā *f* ability

iyàyē *pl* parents

iyò *m* swimming

izà *v1* 1. to push 2. to force 3. to persuade

izà wutā *v1* to stoke a fire

izà wutā à to intensify

izgā *f* 1. fly-switch 2. (metal) spring 3. (mus.) bow

izgìlī *m* 1. boasting 2. risk

izìfī *m* section of the Koran

izìnī, iznì *m* 1. permission 2. takàfdaf iznì permit

iznà *f* 1. example 2. standard 3. measure

izzà *f* contempt

Jj

jā 1. *m/f* (*pl* jàjầyē) red 2. severe
3. *v* (*m* jâ) to pull 4. to draw
5. to attract 6. to drag
jā akàlà 1. to control 2. to lead
jā dà to confront
jā dà bāya 1. to withdraw 2. to
retreat 3. to slow down 4. to
regress 5. (ec.) to stagnate 6. to
slump
jàbu *m* 1. ɗan jàbu counterfeit
2. fàsfô na jàbu forged
passport 3. kāyàyyakin jàbu
pirated goods
jāɓā *f* shrew-mouse
jàcē *m* second-hand
jà-cikì, jà-jìki *m* reptile
jadawàlī *m* (*pl* jàdàwàlai) 1.
schedule 2. timetable 3. table
jadawàlin sàu *m* multiplication
table
jaddàdā *vl* 1. to renew 2. to
reform 3. to emphasise
jaddàdā wà to reassure
jaddàdâwā *f* ƙārà jaddàdâwā
to reaffirm
jàfa'ì *m* 1. abuse 2. slander
Jàfân *f* Japan
jāfī *m* salute
jagab *adv* jiƙè jagab to saturate
jà-gàba *m/f* 1. guide 2. leader
3. intermediary
jàgirā *f* eye-shadow
jāgìrcē *v4* to be well established
jà-gōrà *m/f* 1. guide-book
2. guide 3. leader
jāgōrancì *m* 1. leadership
2. guidance

jahầ *f* 1. region 2. state
3. direction
jàhādì *m* holy war
jāhilcì *m* 1. ignorance 2.
illiteracy
jāhìlī *m* (*f* jāhìlā, *pl* jàhìlai)
1. ignorant 2. illiterate
jā'ibầ *f* misfortune
jàijaikō *m* condolences
jā'ìrī *m* (*f* jā'ìrā, *pl* jà'ìrai)
disrespectful
jàjē *m* sympathy
jàjibèr̃e *m* day before a festival,
eve
jâk *m* 1. car jack 2. bicycle stand
jàkā *f* (*pl* jakunkunầ) bag
jàkādầ *m* (*f* jàkādìyā, *pl*
jàkầdū) 1. ambassador 2. ɗan
ƙàramin jàkādầ consul
jakàdancì *m* 1. huldầr̃
jakàdancì diplomatic relations
2. ōfìshin jakàdancì embassy
jàkar̃ ƙwàlầtai *f* scrotum
jākèt *m* jacket
jàkī *f* (*f* jầkā, *pl* jàkai) 1. donkey
2. idiot
jàkulkul *adv* in large amounts
jàlàsin *m* window blinds
jàllàbiyầ *f* man's gown
jallầɓōyì *m* Sir
jallìnjal *adv* unique
jàllo *m* water-bottle
jàlôr̃ *m/f/pl* stationwagon
jâm *m* jam, (US) jelly
jàma'ầ *f* (*pl* jama'ō'ī) 1. the
public 2. crowd 3. community
4. inhabitants

jamalā f sentence
jàmbàkì m lipstick
jamfā f (pl **jamfōfī**) jumper
jàmhūřiyà f (pl **jamhūřiyōyì**)
1. republic 2. salon mulkìn
jàmhūřiyà republicanism
jàmhūřiyàř àl'ummà f
people's republic
jàmhūřiyàř tàrayyà f federal
republic
jàmhūřù m 1. empty talk 2. yi
wà... **jàmhūřù** to conspire
against
jam'ì m 1. plural 2. (rel.)
gathering
jāmi'à f (pl **jāmi'ō'ì**) university
jàmì'an dìflòmàsiyyà pl
diplomatic corps
jāmì'ì m 1. main mosque 2.
(f **jāmì'ā**, pl **jàmì'ai**) director
3. officer 4. official
jàmì'an dìflòmàsiyyà pl
diplomatic corps
jàmì'in ayyukàn jàma'à m
public officer
jàm'iyyà f (pl **jàm'ìyyū,
jam'iyyōyì**) 1. society 2. club
3. association 4. (pol.) party
5. ɗan **jàm'iyyà** party member
Jāmùs f Germany
jànabà f (rel.) state of impurity
Jànairù m January
jànā'izà f funeral
**jàn akàlàř manufōfin
hařkōkin wàje** m steering
committee
janàř m (pl **janàř-janàř**) (mil.)
general
jànàřàl m (Nr) (mil.) general
jànàřetò m generator
jànâs m (pol.) youth party
jàn-bàki m lipstick

jandařmà m (Nr) gendarme
jàndàřmàřì f (Nr) gendarmerie
jàn-farcè m nail varnish
jangàlì m cattle-tax
jàngwam m misfortune
jānàbì, jānìbì see **mùkāmì**
janjàmì m (pl **jànjàmai**)
1. strap 2. sash
jante m feverish cold
jânyē v4 1. to pull away 2. to
withdraw
jânyē dàgà tākařā (pol.) to
withdraw one's candidacy
jânyè kuɗìn cikò to lift
subsidies
janyō ta tìyyô v6 (Nr) to siphon
jàřabà f (pl **jařabōbì**) 1. desire
2. addiction 3. obsession
4. mania 5. calamity
jàřdân m (Nr) park
jàřfā f facial tattoo marks
jāřì m (fin.) capital
jàřīdà f (pl **jàřìdū**) 1.
newspaper 2. journal 3. ɗan
jàřīdà m (f **'yař jàřīdà**,
pl **'yan jàřìdū**) journalist 4.
mài kařàntà jàřīdà newspaper
reader
jāřì-hujjà m ɗan **jāřì-hujjà**
capitalist
jāřì-hujjà, tsārìn jāřì-hujjà
m 1. capitalism 2. kàsuwař
jāřì-hujjà capital market 3.
zubà **jāřì-hujjà** to invest (à in)
4. **mài zubà jāřì-hujjà**
investor
jàrīrì m (f **jàrīrìyā**, pl **jàrìrai**)
infant
jàřkâl m petrol can
jařřàbā v1 1. to try 2. to test
3. to examine
jařřàbâwā f 1. test 2.

examination 3. **ci jařřàbâwā**
to pass an examination 4. **fàɗì**
à jařřàbâwā to fail an
examination
jāřùmī *m* (*f* **jāřùmā**, *pl*
jàřùmai) brave
jāřumtakà, **jař zūcìyā** *f*
bravery
jàřun *m* (Nr) ɗan **jàřun** prisoner
jàstîs *f* (Nr) court of law
jàtan landè *m* shrimp
jauhàřī *m* jewel
jauřa *f* 1. petty trading 2. ɗan
jauřa peddler 3. kuɗìn **jauřa**
capital investment
jàwābì *m* (*pl* **jàwàbai**) 1. reply
2. speech 3. message 4. **mài**
jàwābì speaker 4. **mài dà**
jàwābì to reply
jàwābìn haɗìn gwīwà *m* joint
statement
jāwō *v6 see* **jā**
jāwō hankàlī 1. to cause 2. to
draw attention (**cêwā** to)
3. **mài jāwō** source of 4. *see* **jā**
jàyayyà *f* 1. dispute 2. hostility
jàzā'ì *m* retribution
jē v (*m* **zuwà**) 1. to go (to) 2. to
set out 3. to arrive (at)
jēfà *v1* 1. to throw 2. to post
jèfà *v2** (*m/f* **jifà**) 1. to throw at
2. to accuse
jēfè *v4* to stone
jēfì-jēfì *adv* often
jēgò *m* suckling (of baby)
jèjekō *m* condolences
jējì *m* (*pl* **jàzzā**) 1. the bush 2.
uninhabited land 3. forest
4. jungle
jè-ka-kà-dāwō *adv* **makařantař**
jè-ka-kà-dāwō day school
jèlā *f* tail

jēmà *v1* (*f* **jīmà**) to tan
jēmāgè *m* (*pl* **jèmàgū**) bat
jēřà *v1* 1. to arrange 2. to line up
jère *adv* **à jère** in sequence
jērì *m/pl* row
jērì-jērì *adv* in rows
jērìn gwànō *m* 1. procession 2.
queue
jērin gwànon mōtōcì *m*
convoy
jēsì *m* (*pl* **jēsunà**) (spor.) jersey
jēwā *f* 1. hovering 2. going to
and fro
ji v (*m* **jî**) 1. to hear 2. to listen
3. to understand 4. to feel 5. to
taste 6. to smell 7. to be
concerned about 8. **ìn ji**...
according to...
jî *see* **ji**
jibgà *v1* to pile up
jibgè *v4* 1. to load onto 2. to
offload
jìbi *f/adv* the day after tomorrow
jìbì *m* meal
jìɓì *m* sweat
jìdā *m* 1. rainclouds 2. *v2** to
transfer
jî dà kâi *m* 1. pride 2. self-
esteem
jìdālà, **jìdālì** *m* struggle
jìdò *m* judo
jîf *f* (Nr) skirt
jifà *m/f see* **jēfà**
jìga *f/pl* jigger
jìgāwā *f* soil
jìgìdā *f* (*pl* **jìgìdū**) hip-girdle
jigilā *f* 1. transport back and
forth 2. **jirgī mài jigilā**
transporter, shuttle
jigò *m* (*pl* **jigōgī**) 1. pole
2. theme 3. condition
jihà *f* (*pl* **jihōhī**) 1. region 2.

federal state 3. direction
4. point of the compass
jìhādì *m* (Isl.) 1. holy war 2.
crusade
jìjìyā *f* (*pl* **jìjiyōyī**) 1. vein
2. artery 3. muscle 4. nerve
jìjìyar̃ itàcē *f* tree-roots
jìjjìgā *vl* to shake around
jìjjìgè *m* (*pl* **jìgàjìgai**) 1. beam
2. pillar 3. basis 4. influential
jikà *adv* **à jikà** on/into the body
jikà *m/f* (*pl* **jikōkī**) grandchild
jìkī *m* (*pl* **jikunà**) 1. body 2. yi
jìkī to get fat 3. **ji jìkī** to feel
ill/tired 4. **mai dà jìkī** to
recover 5. **Yanà zamā jìkī**
gàr̃ē sù. They are becoming
addicted to it.
jìkin *prep* 1. onto 2. (fixed) in
jiƙà *vl* to wet
jìƙa *v3* to get wet
jiƙè *v4* (*m* **jiƙò**) to soak
jiƙè jagab to saturate
jiƙò *m* 1. **sai wani jiƙò** until
another time 2. *see* **jiƙè**
jimà *vl* 1. to spend some time
2. **Sai an jimà!** See you soon!
jìmà *see* **jēmà**
Jìmādā Lāhìr̃ *m* (Isl.) sixth
month
Jìmādā Lawwàl *m* (Isl.) fifth
month
jì mā dàɗì *m* favourite
jìmā'ì *m* 1. sexual intercourse
2. **yi jìmā'ì** to make love
jìmā'ìn rōbà *m* safe sex
jimàwā *f* **bà dà jimàwā ba** soon
jìmillà *f* (*pl* **jìmìllū**) 1. total
2. amount 3. gross
jìminā *f* (*pl* **jìmìnū**) ostrich
jìmir̃i *m* perseverence
jim kàɗan, jìm kàɗan *adv* 1.

after a while 2. **tun jìm kàɗan**
bāyan soon after
jimlà *f* (*pl* **jimlōlī**) 1. amount
2. total 3. gross 4. *see* **jumlà**
jimlàr̃ abūbuwàn dà ƙasā ta
sāmar̃ à shèkarà *f* gross
national product (GNP)
jimlàtā *vl* to total
jìngā *f* 1. wages 2. wage level
3. **yi jìngā** to negotiate
jìngim *adv* in abundance
jingìnā *vl* to lean against
jìnginà *v3* to lean (**dà/gà**
on/against)
jìnginà *f* (fin.) deposit
jìnginàr̃ gidā *f* mortgage
jìngìnē *v4* 1. to suspend 2. to
postpone
jinī *m* 1. blood 2. lineage 3. **farin**
jinī popularity 4. **baƙin jinī**
unpopularity 5. **ƙi jinī** to
dislike
jinijimī *m* ibis
jìniyà *f* siren
jîn jìkī *m* suffering
jinjìnā *vl* to test
jìnjinà *f* 1. salute with raised
fist/weapon 2. **yi wà... jìnjinà**
à kâi to single out for praise
jinjìri *m* (*f* **jinjinnìyā**, *pl*
jìràjìrai) infant
jinkā *f* 1. thatch 2. **yi wà... jinkā**
to thatch
jinkè *v4* to thatch
jìnkiri *m* 1. delay 2. **jā jìnkiri** to
delay
jinkìrtā *vl* 1. to delay 2. to
procrastinate
jinsì *m* (*pl* **jinsunà**) 1. race
2. gender 3. sex 4. species 5.
type
jinyà *f* *see* **jiyyà**

jirā v (m **jirà**) to wait for

jìrā f/pl weaverbird

jiràn kàntī m **mài jiràn kàntī** sales assistant, (US) salesclerk

jirgà v1 1. to move aside 2. to tilt

jirgī m (pl **jiràgē**) vehicle

jirgin dà kĕ tàfiyà ƙarƙashin ruwā m submarine

jirgin danƙarō m road-roller

jirgin ɗaukàr̃ kāyā m cargo vessel

jirgin jigilā m shuttle

jirgin ƙàr̃ƙashin ƙasā m underground train, (US) subway train

jirgin ƙasā m train

jirgī mài jigilā m transporter

jirgin ruwā m 1. boat 2. ship 3. canoe

jirgin ruwā na yāƙì m battleship

jirgin samà m aeroplane

jirgin samà mài sàukar̃ ùngùlu m helicopter

jirgin samàn lĕƙen àsīr̃ī m spy plane

jìrī m 1. neuralgia 2. dizziness

jìr̃kâl m (Nr) petrol can

jirkìcē v4 to tilt

jirkìtā v1 1. to turn around 2. to distort

jirkitâr̃wā f **mài jirkitâr̃wā** controversial

jìta-jìta f 1. rumour(s) 2. **mài bazà jìta-jìta** rumourmonger

jìtô, jìtôn m 1. coin 2. token

jìtu v7 to be on good terms (dà with)

jìtuwā f **rashìn jìtuwā** disagreement

**jiwō dàgà bàkin... ** v6 1. to hear

2. **jiwō dàgà bàkin... ** to quote...

jiyà f/adv 1. yesterday 2. **na jiyà** previous

jiyâr̃wā f announcement

jiyyà f (med.) 1. treatment 2. **yi wà... jiyyà** (med.) to treat 3. **Tā yi masà jiyyà.** She nursed the patient. 4. **Ya kwânta jiyyà.** He lay sick.

jiyyà ta far̃r̃aɗôwā f recuperation

jōjì m (pl **jōjì-jōjì**) 1. judge 2. magistrate

jōnì m 1. join 2. joint

jūjī m 1. rubbish 2. **garwan jūjī** dustbin

jūjì m (Nr) judge

jùjū m juju

jùmhūr̃iyà see **jàmhūr̃iyà**

jumlà f (pl **jumlōlī**) sentence

Jumma'à f Friday

jūnā m 1. each other 2. **na jūnā** mutual 3. **Tanà dà jūnā biyu.** She's pregnant.

jūrè wà v4 1. to endure 2. to tolerate

jūriyā f hardiness

jùwā f dizziness

jūyà 1. f (pl **jūyōcī**) sterile (woman) 2. v1 to turn 3. to rotate 4. to change 5. to translate 6. to transfer (**dàgà** from, **zuwà** to)

jūyā v2* to copy

jūyà wà... bāyā 1. to turn one's back on 2. to reject

jùyàyī m 1. anxiety 2. sympathy 3. **rānar̃ jùyàyī** day of remembrance

jùye adv à **jùye** the other way round

jùyen baƙin mâi *m* oil change

jūyì *m* change

jūyìn jūyà-hālī, jūyìn jùyà-hālī *m* 1. revolution 2. **na jūyìn jùyà-hālī** revolutionary 3. ɗan

jūyìn jūyà-hālī revolutionary

jūyìn mulkì *m* 1. coup d'etat 2. overthrow

jūyìn wàinā *m* (pol.) reversal

juzù'ì *m* section

Kk

ka 1. *m* you **2.** *adv* **dà ka** at random

kà *m* **1.** you **2.** your

kā 1. *m completive* you **2.** *adv* **à kā** on/in the head

kâ *m indefinite future* you

kabà *f* **1.** cover **2.** (*pl* **kabōbī**) palm fronds

kabàd *m see* **kabàt**

kabàřī *m* (*pl* **kabuřbuřà**) **1.** grave **2.** tomb

kabàt *m* cupboard

kābējì *m* cabbage

kàbēwà *f* (*pl* **kàbèyī**) pumpkin

kābìl *m* (Nr) cable

kàbīlà (*pl* **kàbìlū**) **1.** tribe **2.** ethnic origin **3.** race **4.** relatives

kàbīlà maràs yawà *f* ethnic minority

kabilancī *m* **1.** ethnicity **2.** tribalism

kàbîn *m* (Nr) lorry cab

kābòyi *m* cowboy

kābùl *m see* **kābìl**

kàbûs, kàbūshì *m* **1.** marrow **2.** pumpkin **3.** pawpaw

kābūsù *m* chain-smoker

kàbà *v2** to collide with

kàɓànce *adv* **à kàɓànce** upside-down

kaɓàttā *v1* **1.** to humiliate **2.** to frustrate

kaɓè *v4* to flick

kacà *f* chain

kaca-kaca *adv* **1.** messy **2.** mutilated

kacal *adv* mere

kacau *adv* uneven

ka-cè-na-cè *m* argument

kàciɓìs *adv* unexpectedly

kà-cīci-kà-cīci, kà-cinci-kà-cinci *m* riddle

kàciyà *f* **1.** circumcision **2.** yi wà... **kàciyà** to circumcise

kadà 1. do not **2.** (so) that not

kadà̃ *m* (*pl* **kàdànnī**) crocodile

kā dà *v5* **1.** to fell **2.** to knock down **3.** to defeat

kàdai *adv* **sànnu kàdai!, bařkà kàdai!** *etc.* very well, thank you!

kā dà ƙùři'à to cast a vote

kadařà *f* (*pl* **kadařōřī**) **1.** property **2.** assets **3.** goods **4.** **kàsuwař ta dařajàř kadařà** stock exchange

kadařàř gwamnatì *f* state property

kadàřī *m* **1.** value **2.** worth **3.** price

kàdarkò *m* (*pl* **kàdàrkī**) (temporary) bridge

kaddamař dà kàmfê to campaign

kaddamař dà *v5* **1.** to set up **2.** to undertake

kaddamař dà yāƙì to declare war (à kân on)

kadò *m* (*pl* **kàdànnī**) crocodile

kaɗà *v1* **1.** to beat a drum **2.** to stir **3.** to shake

kaɗà audùgā to spin cotton

kaɗà kâi 1. to nod one's head **2.** to shake one's head

kaɗai *adv* 1. only 2. alone
kaɗaicī *m* 1. solitude 2. **mài kaɗaicī** solitary 3. lonely
kaɗàitā *vl* to isolate
kàɗan *adv* 1. (a) few 2. (a) little 3. slight 4. slightly 5. **saurā kàɗan** almost
kàɗan-kàɗan *adv* very slightly
kaɗanyà *f* (*pl* **kaɗānē**) 1. shea tree 2. shea fruit
kaɗè *v4* 1. to knock over 2. to flick 3. to shed
kàɗe-kàɗe *pl see* **kiɗà**
kaɗī *m* spinning (cotton)
kāɗo *m* (*f* **kāɗùwā**, *pl* **hāɓè**) 1. original inhabitant 2. person of Hausa origin
kaf *adv* completely
kafā *f* (*pl* **kafōfī**) 1. hole 2. opening 3. chance 4. loophole
kafà *vl* 1. to erect 2. to build 3. to issue 4. to found 5. (leg/pol.) to enact
kàfaɗà *f* (*pl* **kàfàɗù**) shoulder
kàfaffē *m* (*f* **kàfaffiyā**, *pl* **kàfàffū**) 1. established 2. permanent
kafà huldàr cìnikī to establish trade links
kàfàrân *m* (Nr) corporal
kafaȓ hancì *f* nostril
kafaȓ làbàȓai *f* journalistic source
kafè *v4* 1. to stick (à to) 2. to persist
kàfe *m* (Nr) 1. cafè 2. coffee
kàffōtì *f* (Nr) overcoat
kàfin, kàfin *conj* before
kāfintà *m* (*pl* **kāfintōcī**) carpenter
kàfìȓētò *m* carburettor

kāfìȓi *m* (*f* **kafìȓā**, *pl* **kàfìȓai**) unbeliever
kaf-kaf *adv* **yi kaf-kaf** to be tactful (da with)
kafōfin kìmiyyà dà fàsāhà *pl* technical installations
kafōfin sìyāsà *pl* political institutions
kafōfin wātsà làbàȓai *pl* mass media
kafsà *vl* to whack
kaftà *vl* 1. to dig deep 2. to farm
kàftân *m* (Nr) captain
kàftānì *m* caftan
kàftū *m* **yi kàftū à gōnā** to plough
kàfu *v7* to be established
kāfùȓ *m* camphor
kagò *m* (*pl* **kàggā**) thatched hut
kàhô *m* (Nr) car bonnet
kàhòȓân, kàhwàȓân *m* (Nr) corporal
kai 1. *m* you 2. *v* to take 3. to reach 4. to arrive 5. to be enough
kâi *m* (*gen* **kân**, *pl* **kāwunà**) 1. head 2. top 3. tip 4. beginning 5. chief 6. self: **nì dà kâinā** myself *etc.* 7. unit 8. ahead 9. **sâ kâi** to volunteer 10. **à kâi à kâi** regularly 11. *see* **sôn kâi, zaman kâi**
kai dà kāwôwā *adv* **yi kai dà kāwôwā** to shuttle
kaidì *m* **bâ kaidì** unlimited
kaifàfā *vl* to sharpen
kaifi *m* 1. sharpness 2. **Yanà dà kaifì.** It's sharp. 3. cutting edge
kai harì 1. *m* attack 2. *v* to attack
kàikàice *adv* **à kàikàice** 1. indirectly 2. sideways

3. yi magànā à kàikàice to beat about the bush
kaikàità *vl* to turn on one side
kâi ƙārā to file a complaint
kaito! bad luck!
kâi tsàye *adv* **1.** directly **2.** categorically **3.** na kâi tsàye direct
kâiwà dà kōmôwā yi kâiwā dà kōmôwā to shuttle
kai wà... harì to attack
kai zuwà to last till
kàjī *see* kàzā
kàkā **1.** *f* harvest-time **2.** *m/f* (*pl* kàkànnī) grandparent
kàkābì *m* wonder
kàkà-gidā *see* ƙàƙà gidā
kàkàkī *m* **1.** ceremonial horn **2.** funnel **3.** spokesman/woman
kàkàkin gwamnatì *m/f* government spokesman/ woman
ka kàn, kakàn *m habitual* you
kàkànnī *see* kàkā
ka kè, kakè *m relative continuous* you
kākìn zumà *m* honeycomb
kàkī *m* **1.** khaki **2.** phlegm
kàkidè *m* meat dripping
kàkkāmà *see* kànkāmà
kàkkaƙai *adv* à kàkkaƙai without reason
kàkkèɓe *adv* à kàkkèɓe privately
kâl *f* (Nr) wedge
kāla, kālā *m* **1.** gleaning **2.** yi kālan faɗà to pick a fight/ argument
kalà *f* colour
kàlàcī *m* mealtime
kàlāmì *m* words
kàlandà *f* (*pl* kalandōjī) **1.** calendar **2.** almanac

kàlàndìr̂ê *m* (Nr) calendar
kàlàngū *m* (*pl* kalangunà) talking-drum
kàlàsòr̂ì *m* (Nr) coachwork
kàlātà *v2** (-ci/cē) to glean
kàlīlàn *see* ƙàlīlàn
kàlìsô *m* (Nr) **1.** slip **2.** underwear
kalkùlètà *f* calculator
kallàbī *m* (*pl* kallubà) head-tie
kallàfā *vl* to impose (wà on)
kàllatà *v2** (-ci/cē) to look at
kàllī *m* **1.** nuisance **2.** fishing float
kallō *m* **1.** looking (at) **2.** àbin kallō a sight, show **3.** ɗan kallō spectator **4.** 'yan kallō audience **5.** yi wà... kallō to regard as
kalmà *f* (*pl* kalmōmī) word
kalmàr̂ arō *f* loanword
kalmàsā *vl* to hem
kaltìbētà *f* (*pl* kaltibētōcī) tractor
kàlūluwà *f* swollen glands
kam **1.** *adv* securely **2.** *conj* if
kàm *adv* definitely
kàmā *m/f* (*pl* kàmànnī) **1.** similarity **2.** equivalent **3.** appearance
kàmā dà *prep* like
kāmà *vl* (kāmù) **1.** to catch **2.** to capture **3.** to arrest **4.** to include **5.** to begin **6.** to kidnap
kāmà aikì **1.** to take up a position **2.** (pol.) to assume office
kàma-kàryā *m/f* **1.** oppressive measures **2.** mulkìn kàma-kàryā totalitarianism **3.** dictatorship
kàman, kàmar̂ *prep* **1.** like **2.** as **3.** about **4.** that **5.** as if

kamàntā *vl* 1. to compare (dà with) 2. to describe 3. to imitate

kàmař *see* **kàman**

kàmař hakà *adv* like this

Kàmàřu *f* Cameroon

kàmashô *m* 1. sales commission 2. ɗan **kàmashô** salesman

kàmātà *v2** (-ci/cē) to suit

kàmātà *v3* Yā kàmātà kà yi shì. You ought to do it.

kàmàzūřū *m* reins

kambàmā *vl* to honour

kàmbamā *f* showing off

kàmbàmâwā *f* respect

kambàs *m* trainers

kambêd *m* bed

kambī *m* crown

kamɓōrī *m* 1. egg-shell 2. nut-shell

kamɓōrin kīfī *m* fish-scales

kāmè *v4* 1. to stick together 2. to sit to one side 3. to sew up 4. to capture

kamfai *m* underwear

kamfànī *m* (*pl* **kamfanōnī**) 1. company 2. ƙàramin **kamfànī** subsidiary company 3. mânyan **kamfanōnī** multi-nationals

kamfànin àbòkan zubà jāřihujjà *m* joint-venture company

kamfànin dillancìn làbàřai *m* news agency

kamfànin wātsà làbàřai *m* news agency

kamfanōnin ayyukàn dà bà na ƙère-ƙère ba *pl* service industries

kamfàs *m* compass

kàmfatà *v2** (-ci/cē) to take a lot of

kàmfāwùl *m* 1. compound 2. dormitory buildings

kàmfê *m* campaign

kāmilàn *adv* complete

kāmìlī *m* (*f* **kāmìlā**, *pl* **kàmìlai**) perfect

kàmin, kàmìn *conj* before

kam-kam *adv* securely

kammàlā *vl* to complete

kàmmalà *v3* to be completed

kāmù *m* 1. measure of 18 inches 2. *see* **kāmà**

kàmu *v7* Yā kàmu dà cùtâř. He has caught the disease.

kāmùn lūdàyī *m* stance

kāmùn ƙafà *m* yi kāmùn ƙafà gà to pressurise

kàmyô *m* (Nr) truck

kân, à kân *prep* 1. on 2. about 3. on account of 4. in order to 5. *see* **kâi**

kàn *habitual tense marker*

kanà *m continuous* you

kānà 1. then 2. in addition

kân àlƙalàmī *m* nib

kànànzîř *m* kerosene

kanàř *m* (*pl* **kanàř-kanàř**) colonel

kànàsòřī *see* **kàlàsòřī**

kàndàgàrki *m* yi wà... **kàndàgàrki** to protect

kàndīřī *m* (*pl* **kàndìřai**) sceptre

kanē-kànè *m* 1. monopoly 2. yi kanē-kànè wajen/ à kân/ à to monopolise

kân gadō *m* common sense

kangà *vl* to screen off

kàngarà *v3* to rebel

kàngàrarrē *m* (*f* **kàngàrarriyā**, *pl* **kàngàràrrū**) unmanageable

kangè *v4* to segregate

kangiyā f 1. blockade 2. rūshè kangiyā to break a blockade

kangō m (pl **kangàyē**) deserted building/place

kanhwama f (Nr) resthouse

kànkāmà 1. f taking root 2. v2*to take root 3. to be established 4. to grow important

kankanā f watermelon

kankare m 1. concrete 2. concrete well

kankàrē v4 to scrape away

kankì m hartebeeste

kân làntařkì m electric plug

kannè v4 1. to close one eye 2. to wink

kân nōnò m nipple

kân sarkī m 1. postage stamp 2. head (of coin)

kantā f callus

kantà f (pl **kantōcī**) 1. counter 2. ledge 3. shelf

kantàrē v4 1. to be crooked 2. to swing off

kân tàřhō m handset

kàntī m (pl **kantunà**) shop, (US) store

kàntin māgànī m pharmacist

kàntomà f (pl **kantōmōmī**) local administrator

kantù m (pl **kantunà**) block

kānun làbàřai pl 1. news headlines 2. topics

kànumfàřī m cloves

Kànūrī m Kanuri

kanwā f potash

kanyà f (pl **kanyōyī**) ebony

kanzagī m (pl **kànzàgai**) 1. small drum 2. ɗan kanzagī accomplice

kân zagì m ɗan kân zagì 1. yes-man 2. (pol.) puppet

kâř 1. f (Nr) bus 2. see **kadà**

karā m (pl **karàrē**) stalk

karà v1 (**karò**) 1. to collide (dà with) (spor.) 2. to play (dà against)

kārà v1 1. to screen 2. to put next (à to) 3. to go near (wà to)

karà dà jūnā (spor.) to meet

kařaf adv suddenly

kàřagà f (pl **kàřàgū**) 1. bed 2. throne

kàřāhiyà f (Isl.) disfavoured but not forbidden

kàřāmà f (pl **karāmōmī**) generosity

kàřàmbànī m interference

kařamgàlàsê m (Nr) ice-cream

karan hancì m bridge of the nose

kàřāniyò, kàřànyô m 1. pencil 2. pen

kařàntā v1 (f **kařàntâwā**, m **kàřàtū**) 1. to read 2. to study

kařantař dà v5 1. to teach 2. to educate

kàrantsàyī m 1. tear 2. setback

kařàs m carrot(s)

kàřàtū m (pl **kàřànce-kàřànce**) 1. reading 2. study 3. education 4. yì kàřàtū to study

kāřaukà f (pl **kàřàukū**) highway

karàwā f (spor.) 1. match 2. meet 3. round

kàřāyà f Yā yì kàřāyà. He gave up.

kàřāyař fàřāshì f low prices

kàřbū m 1. cloth-edge 2. seam

kàřbùtājè m (Nr) assembly

kàř6ā v2* (m/f **kàř6ā**) 1. to

receive 2. to take 3. to suit
kàrɓi bāƙuncìn tàrō to host a
meeting
karɓō kudì v6 to withdraw
money
kàrɓuwā f **sàmi kàrɓuwā** to be
well received (**dàgà** by)
kařcè v4 to scrape
kàřcê m (Nr) town ward
kàrē m (f **kàryā**, pl **kařnukà**)
dog
kàřē m ɗan **kàřen** excessive
kārè v4 1. to guard 2. to protect
3. to screen off
kâřê m (Nr) 1. town quarter
2. plot of land
karè mutuncìn... 1. to protect
the interests of... 2. to represent
kàren mōtà m driver's mate
kàren ruwā m otter
karfasā f Nile perch
karfàtā f (pl **kàrfàtū**) shoulder
of meat
karì m 1. palm frond 2. crease 3.
profit 4. word usage
kàrìkìtai m odds and ends
kařimcì, kařincì m generosity
kàřimì m (f **kàřimìyā**, pl
kàřimai) generous
karìn kùmallō m breakfast
karìn màganà m 1. proverb
2. idiom
karìn sautì m tone
karìn sautì mài fāɗuwā m
falling tone
karìn sautì mài hawā m high
tone
karìn sautì mài sàukā m low
tone
karìn wāƙà m song text and
rhythm
kāriyà f screen

kàriyà f carrier
kāriyàř cìnikī f 1. trade
barrier 2. protectionism
3. **màtàkai na kāriyař cìniki**
trade protectionism 4. **kawař
dà kāriyàř cìniki** to lower
trade barriers
kařkàcē v4 1. to swerve 2. to
turn off 3. to be crooked
kařkàɗā v1 1. to jolt 2. to jerk
kařkàndà m/f rhinoceros
kàrkarā m 1. farmland 2. rural
area 3. **na kàrkarā** rural
4. **rāyà kàrkarā** rural
development
kařkàshè v4 to massacre
kařkàsu v5 to be disunited
kařkàtā v1 1. to swerve 2. to
turn off 3. to be crooked 4. to
twist
kařkatař dà v5 to make swerve
karmàtsā v1 to do carelessly
kàrmàtsē m careless work
kařnukà see **kàrè**
kařnukàn fàrautà pl (pol.)
puppets
karò m 1. collision 2. occasion 3.
cì karò to collide (**dà** with) 4.
(spor.) leg 5. see **karà**
karōfi m (pl **kàròfai**) dye-pit
kàřō-kàřō m subsidy
kàřōtì m (Nr) carrot(s)
kàřsanā f (pl **kàřsànū**) heifer
kařtà 1. f card-playing 2. v1 to
scratch
kâř tà kwāna adv ɗan **kâř tà
kwāna** radical opponent
kàřte m/f (Nr) membership card
kařtì f (Nr) card
kàřtìdànditê m/f (Nr) identity
card
kàřtô m (Nr) box

kàrtūshì *m* 1. cartridge 2. (Nr) packet

kār̃ùwà *m/f* (*pl* **kàr̃ùwai**) 1. prostitute 2. thief

karyā *f* 1. bitch 2. prostitute

karyà *vl* 1. to break 2. to defeat

karyà harshè *f* **wàsan karyà harshè** tongue-twister

karyar̃ dà *v5* to break

karyar̃ dà dar̃ajà to devalue

karyè *v4* 1. to snap 2. **Jar̃ìnsù yā karyè.** They have gone bankrupt.

kasà *vl* to arrange

kāsā *f* puff-adder

kāsà *vl* 1. to be insufficient 2. to be unable to

kàsadà *f* 1. risk 2. adventure 3. **na kàsadà** daring 4. **yi kàsadà** to take a risk

kàsàfài *adv* **bà kàsàfài ba** seldom

kasàfī *m* 1. preoccupation 2. allocation

kasàfin kuɗì *m* 1. budget 2. **na kasàfin kuɗì** fiscal

kàsài *adv* **bà kàsài ba** seldom

kasà kûnnē to pay attention

kàsālā *f* 1. lethargy 2. **ji kàsālà** to be lethargic

kasàncē *v4* 1. to be 2. to become 3. to happen

kàsàr̃ōlì *m* (Nr) casserole

kàsêt *m* cassette

kash! 1. oh dear! 2. damn it!

kashè *v4* 1. to kill 2. to cancel 3. to abolish 4. to extinguish 5. to finish off 6. to defeat

kàshēdì *m* warning

kàshègàrī *f/adv* (on) the following day

kashè kuɗì 1. to spend money

(**wajen/à** on) 2. **mài kashè kuɗì** consumer

kashè ƙwāyōyī màsu sâ cùtā to sterilise

kashè wà... **aurē** to divorce

kashè wà... kàsuwā (fin.) to undercut

kashì *m* 1. pile 2. section 3. fraction 4. part 5. chapter

kashì-kashì *adv* in piles

kāshī *m* excrement

kàshìngiɗà *v3* to lie on one's side

kashin maƙērā *m* slag

kàshiyà *m/f* (*pl* **kāshiyōyī**) 1. cashier 2. bank teller

kaskà *f* tick

kaskō *m* (*pl* **kasàkē**) clay bowl

kasò *m* (Nr) 1. jail 2. **ɗan kasò** prisoner

kàsu *v5* to be divided

kàsuwā *f* (*pl* **kàsùwànnī, kāsuwōyī**) 1. market 2. **ɗan kàsuwā** market trader

kāsuwancì *m* 1. market trading 2. **har̃kōkin kāsuwancì** market competition

kàsùwànnin dūniyà *pl* world market

kàsùwànnin hàdà-hadar̃ kuɗì *pl* finance markets

kàsùwànnin kadar̃ōr̃ī *pl* stock exchange

kàsuwar̃ bāyan fagē/gidā, **kàsuwar̃ darē** *f* black market

kàsuwar̃ jar̃ì *f* stock exchange

kàsuwar̃ mùsāyar̃ kuɗàɗē *f* foreign exchange market

katāɓus, kàtàɓus *m* 1. dynamism 2. impetus

kàtàfilà *f* (*pl* **katafilōlì**) 1. caterpillar tractor 2. earth-mover

kātākō *m* (*pl* **kàtàkai**) 1. plank
2. **gàrin kātākō** sawdust
3. **ma'aikatar̃ kātākō** sawmill
kātàn *m* carton
katangā *f* (*pl* **kàtàngū**,
kàtàngī) outer wall
kàtangà *m/f* (*pl* **kàtàngū**)
potsherd
kàtantanwà *f* (*pl* **kàtàntànyī**)
snail shell
katarà *f* (*pl* **katarōrī**) outer
thigh
kàtàr̃fàlâ *f* (Nr) 1. caterpillar
tractor 2. earth-mover
kàtar̃ī *m* 1. **gàmon kàtar̃ī** luck
2. **Sun gàmu dà kàtar̃ī.**
They've had good luck.
kātì *m* (*pl* **kātunà**) 1. card
2. playing cards
kātìbī *m* (**kātìbā,** *pl* **kàtìbai**)
1. clerk 2. scribe
kàtīfà *f* (*pl* **kàtìfū, kàtìfai,**
katìfōfī) mattress
kàtīfar̃ iskà *f* air mattress
kàtīfar̃ r̃ōbà *f* rubber mattress
kātìn gàyyatà *m* invitation card
kàtōɓarā, kàtōɓarā *f* 1. slip of
the tongue 2. **yi kàtōɓara** to be
tactless
katsalandàn, katsarandàn *m*
1. interference 2. (mil.)
intervention 3. **yi katsalandàn**
to intervene
katsè *v4* 1. to interrupt (**wà** s.o.)
2. to run out 3. to snap
kātsè *v4* to scrape (clean/
smooth)
katsè hulɗar̃ dìflômàsiyyà
to break off diplomatic
relations
katsè hulɗōɗì to break off
relations

katsè shāwàr̃war̃ī to break off
negotiations
katsè wutā to cut off power
kau *v* to move away
kaucè wà/dàgà *v4* 1. to avoid
2. to sidestep 3. to evade
kaucè dàgà to compromise
kaucè wà tsārìn dōkōkin
ƙasā to be unconstitutional
kauciyā *f* evasion
kau dà *v5* (**kaushē** + *direct*
object) 1. to move 2. to abolish
3. to neutralise
kauɗì *m* 1. talkativeness 2.
uncomfortable experience
kaurà *v1* (*m* **karò**) 1. to collide
(**dà** with) 2. **Tā kaurà masà**
mārì. She slapped him hard.
kaurī *m* 1. thickness 2. fullness
kaushē *see* **kau dà**
kaushī *m* roughness
kàushû *m* (Nr) rubber
kawài *adv* 1. only 2. without
reason
kawaicì *m* reticence
kàwālì *m* (*f* **kàwālìyā,** *pl*
kàwàlai) pimp
kawar̃ dà *v5 see* **kau dà**
kāwō *v6* 1. to arrive (at) 2. to
bring
kàwō yànzu, kàwôwā yànzu
adv so far
kàwu *m.* (*pl* **kàwùnai**)
(maternal) uncle
kāwunà *see* **kâi**
kāwunàn màkàmai *pl* warheads
kāyā *m* (*pl* **kāyàyyakī**) 1. load
2. goods 3. stuff 4. property
5. clothes
kāyà *v1* to turn out
kāyan àbinci *m* 1. foodstuff
2. ingredient(s)

kāyan aikì *m* tools

kāyan ařas *m* 1. fragile goods 2. dowry

kāyan dà akà ƙērà *m* 1. industrial products 2. production

kāyan dà akè sayâřwā à ƙasàshen wàje *m* 1. export 2. exports

kāyan dà akè sayôwā dàgà ƙasàshen wàje *m* 1. import 2. imports

kāyan ɗākì *m* furniture

kāyan fadà *pl* war materiel

kāyan gyārā *m* spare part

kāyan làmbū *m* vegetables

kāyan màsàřūfì na yâu dà kullum *m* basic necessities

kāyan miyà *m* food ingredients

kāyan sōjà *m* military uniform

kāyan yājì *m* seasoning

kayař dà *see* kā dà

kāyàyyakì *pl* 1. commodities 2. *see* kāyā

kāyàyyakin cìmakà *f* foodstuff

kāyàyyakin gařgājiyā *pl* antiques

kāyàyyakin màsàřūfì *pl* consumer goods

kàyê *m* (Nr) 1. notebook 2. register

kāyè *m* shā kāyè to suffer a decisive defeat

kayya! I doubt it!

kayyà! hey you!

kàzā *adv* 1. such and such 2. so and so

kàzā *f* (*pl* kàjī) 1. chicken 2. hen

kazàf *m* false accusation

kàzālìka *adv* likewise

kazganyà *f* young sheep, teg

kē *f* you

kè 1. *relative continuous marker* 2. *see* kè nan

kèɓàɓɓun kalmōmī *pl* terminology

kēɓè *v4* to set aside

kēɓì *m* section

kēcè *v4* 1. to tear 2. to be torn 3. Naa kēcè dà dāriyà. I burst out laughing.

kējì *m* (*pl* kējōjì) cage

kek *m* cake

kèkè *m* (*pl* kēkunà) 1. bicycle 2. machine

kèkèn dìnkì *m* sewing-machine

kèkèn hannū *m* wheelchair

kellà *f* (*pl* kellōlī) goat

kè nan *used for emphasis*

kētà *v1* 1. to split 2. to tear 3. to disregard

kētà dōkā to break the law

kētùř *m* (*pl* kētuřà) kettle

kēwā *f* 1. grief 2. longing

kēwař gidà *f* home-sickness

kèwàyā *v1* to go around

kèwayà *f* màì kèwayā round

kèwàyayyē *m* (*f* kèwàyayyiyā, *pl* kèwàyàyyū) round

kēwayè *m* 1. enclosure 2. surrounding area

kēwàyē *v4* to surround

kēwayèn ɗan Adàm *m* the environment

kēwayō *v6* to come round again

ki, kì *f* 1. you 2. your

kibiyà *f* (*pl* kibiyōyī, kibau) arrow

kicì *see* kicìn

kìciɓìs *adv* unexpectedly

kicìn *m/pl* kitchen

kicìn-kicìn *adv* deeply involved

kiɗà *m* (*pl* kàɗe-kàde) 1. drumming 2. music

kiɗàn gaȓgājiyā *m* traditional music

kifā *vl* to invert

kifaȓ dà *v5* 1. to throw out 2. to spill

kifê *v4* 1. to overturn 2. ɗan tà kifè extremist 3. die-hard

kìfe *adv* à kìfe upside-down

kifī *f (pl* kìfàyē) fish

kìfīfiyà *f* turtle

kikà *f relative completive* you

kikàn, ki kàn *f habitual* you

kikè, ki kè *f relative continuous* you

kiki-kàkà *m* ì. row 2. yi wà... kiki-kàkà to unsettle

kiki-kàkàȓ dìflòmàsiyyà *m/f* diplomatic row

kilākì *m/f (pl* kilākāwā) call girl

kìlê *m* (Nr) ɗan kùlê key

kìlê àmùlât *m* (Nr) spanner

kìlìf *m* clip

kìlīsà *f* Yā hau kìlīsà. He went for a ride.

kìlìshê *m* (Nr) 1. film negative 2. transparency

kìlìshī *m* biltong

kìliyà *m* yi kìliyà 1. to park 2. to give way

kìlìyòtân *m* (Nr) indicator light

kìlô *m/pl* 1. kilogramme, (US) kilogram 2. kilometre, (US) kilometer

kìlògìȓâm *m/pl* kilogramme, (US) kilogram

kìlòmītà *f/pl* kilometre, (US) kilometer

kìm *adv* huge

kīmà *f* 1. a little 2. a few 3. moderately

kìmānìn 1. *adj* approximate 2. *prep* approximately

kìmàntā *vl* 1. to estimate 2. to assess

kìmiyyà, kìmiyyà *f* 1. science 2. chemistry 3. na kìmiyyà scientific 4. mài ilìmin kìmiyyà, masànin kìmiyyà scientist 5. ilìmin kìmiyyàȓ ƙère-ƙère physics 6. mài ilìmin kìmiyyàȓ ƙère-ƙère physicist

kìmmānìn *prep see* kìmānìn

kimmàntā *see* kimàntā

kimsà *vl* 1. to cram 2. to stab 3. *see* kintsà

kin *f completive* you

kîn (Nr) 1. the 2. the one referred to 3. this one exactly

kinà, ki nà *f continuous* you

kìndìȓmō *m* yoghurt

kinî *m* one like, those like

kìnîn *m* quinine

kìntâcē *m* 1. speculation 2. statistics 3. mài kìntàce statistician

kìntātà *v2** (-ci/cē) 1. to reckon 2. to estimate

kintsà *vl* 1. to pack 2. to tidy up

kìntsattsē *m (f* kìntsattsiyā, *pl* kìntsàttsū) 1. methodical 2. polite

kirā *v (m* kirà) 1. to call 2. to invite 3. to describe

kìȓâf *f* (Nr) trainers

kiràn kàsuwà *m* (ec.) yi kiràn kàsuwà to promote

kiràn sūnā *m* roll-call

kìȓâȓ *f* (Nr) trainers

kirārì *m* 1. praise epithet 2. reputation

kirāwō *v6* to summon

kirɓà *vl (m* kirɓì) to pound

kircī *m* eczema

kirī *m* 1. retail 2. ɗan kirī
retailer 3. peddler

kìřîk *m* (Nr) 1. car jack
2. bicycle stand

Kiřistà *m/f* (*pl* Kiřistōcì)
Christian

kiřkì *m* 1. excellence 2. kindness

Kiřsìmatù *m* Christmas

kìřtānì *m* 1. string 2. twine

kisà *m* 1. killing 2. defeat
3. cancellation

kisàn aurē *m* divorce

kisàn gillà *m* 1. murder 2.
assassination 3. massacre

kisàn kâi *m* murder

kisàn kâi dà gàngan *m*
premeditated murder

kīshì *m* 1. jealousy 2. rivalry 3. à
kīshìn hakà on the contrary

kīshìn ƙasā *m* patriotism

kīshìn zūci *m* ambition

kìshìngiɗà *v3* to lie on one's
side

kīshìyā *f* (*pl* kīshiyōyī) 1. co-
wife 2. rival 3. opposite

kissà *m* 1. tact 2. (*pl* kissōshì)
intrigue

kitsè *m* 1. (meat) fat 2. *v4* to plait
hair

kitsò *m* hair-do

kīwàtà *vl* (*m* kīwò) 1. to herd
animals 2. to feed an animal

kīwò *m* 1. herding 2. feeding
3. grazing

kīwòn lāfiyà *m* 1. hygiene
2. hanyōyin kiwòn lāfiyà
health care

kiyā-kiyā *f* minibus

kìyāmà *f* Ran Kìyāmà the Day
of Resurrection

kiyâs *m* kiosk

kìyāyà *v2** 1. to protect 2. to
beware of

kiyàyē *v4* 1. to protect 2. to pay
attention (dà to)

kìzìnyêř *f* (Nr) stove

kō *prep/conj* 1. or 2. whether
3. introduces question 4.
perhaps 5. even 6. even if

kō dà 1. even 2. even if 3. when

kō dà yakè although

kōɗà *vl* (*f* kūɗà) to sharpen

kōɗè *v4* to fade (colour)

kōɗì *m* dòdon kōɗì snail

kòfatò *m* (*pl* kòfàtai) 1. hoof
2. head of cattle

kofè *m* 1. copy 2. duplicate

kòfì *m* coffee

kōfùř *m* (*pl* kōfùř -kōfùř)
(mil.) corporal

kògī *m* (*pl* kōgunà) river

kògō *m* (*pl* kōgunà) 1. cavity
2. hollow 3. cave

kō'ìnā 1. everywhere 2. anywhere
3. nowhere 4. wherever

kòkawà *f* (*pl* kòkàwe-
kòkàwe) 1. wrestling 2.
struggling 3. ɗan kòkawà
wrestler

kōke-kōke *pl* 1. objections
2. complaints 3. *see* kūkā

kōko *m* gruel

kòkō *m* cocoa

kòkwàntā *vl* to be doubtful

kòkwantō *m* doubt

kōƙàƙà, kō ƙàƙà *adv* 1.
however 2. in every possible
way 3. in no way 4. no matter
how

kōlejì *f* college

kōlì *m* petty trading

kōmā *m/f* (*pl* kōmàyē) fishing
net

kōmā *vl* 1. to return 2. to become
kōmā bāya *v* 1. to retreat 2. to
regress
kòmà-bāya *m* 1. retreat
2. decline 3. (fin.) fall 4. ɗan
kòmà-bāya reactionary
kòmà-bāyan tattalin ařzìkī *m*
recession
kòmaɗà *v3* 1. to buckle up 2. to
crumple up
kòmaɗà *f* (ec.) slump
kòmaɗař tattalin ařzìkī *f*
economic slump
kòmbùkàsô *m* (Nr) summons
kōmē 1. everything 2. anything
3. nothing 4. whatever
kòmfanyò *f* (mil.) company
kōmī *m* (*pl* kōmàyē) 1. boat
2. trough
kòmitì *see* kwàmitì
kōmō *v6* to come back
kònònâl *m* colonel
kōrā *f* ringworm
kòrā *v2** to drive away (dàgà
from)
kòrā *f* 1. driving away 2. ɗan
kòrà (pol.) puppet
kòrarrē *m* (*f* kòrarriyā, *pl*
kòrarrū) fugitive
kòrau *m* negative
kōrē *m* 1. chasing 2. ɗan kōrē
(pol.) puppet
kōřè *m* (*f* kōřìyā, *pl* kwâřřā)
green
kôs *m* (*pl* kosōshī) 1. (ed.)
course 2. trumps
kōtù *m* (*pl* kōtunà) (leg.) court
Kōtùn Dūnìyà *m* International
Court of Justice
kōwā 1. everyone 2. anyone 3.
no one 4. whoever
kōwàccē *see* kōwànnē

kōwàcè *see* kōwànè
kōwàɗànnē *see* kōwànè
kōwàɗànnè *see* kōwànè
kōwànè *m* (*f* kōwàcè, *pl*
kōwàɗànnè) 1. every 2. each
3. any 4. whatever
kōwànnē *m* (*f* kōwàccē, *pl*
kōwàɗànnē) 1. everyone 2.
none 3. whoever/ whichever
one
kōyà 1. *f* red earth 2. *vl* to teach
(wà someone)
kòyā *v2** (*m* kòyō) to learn
kòyař dà *v5* to teach (a subject)
kòyàushè *adv* 1. always 2. never
3. whenever 4. no matter when
kōyàyà, kō yàyà *adv* 1.
however 2. in every possible
way 3. in no way 4. no matter
how
kōyì *m* 1. imitation 2. àbin kōyì
example
kòyō *see* kòyā
ku, kù *pl* 1. you 2. your
kū *pl* you
kūbà *m* (*pl* kūbōbī) lock
kubbì *m* hearts (in cards)
kubcē *v4* to escape (wà from)
kùbē *m* (*pl* kùbànnī) sheath
kùbōyì *m* (Nr) cowboy
Kubřùs *f* Cyprus
kùbūbuwà *f* viper
kuɓewā *f* (*pl* kùɓeyī) okra
kuɓùcē *v4* to escape (wà from)
kuɓutař dà *v5* to release
kudancin *prep* south of
kudù *m* 1. south 2. na kudù
southern
kudù masò gabàs *m* south-east
kudù masò yâmma *m* southwest
kudù sak *adv* due south

kūdù *m* (med.) boil

kūɗà *f see* kōɗà

kudàɗè *see* kuɗì

kudàɗen mùsāyā na ƙētarè *pl* foreign exchange

kuɗàɗen shìgā dàgà mâi *pl* oil revenue

kuɗàɗen shìgā *pl* revenue

kùɗai *pl* zunzùrūtùn kùɗai large amount of money

kuɗè *v4* to withdraw (cìkin into)

kuɗì *m/pl* (*pl* kuɗàɗè) 1. money 2. currency 3. price 4. fee

kuɗì hannu *m* cash payment

kuɗìn àjiyà *m* savings

kuɗìn cikò *m* subsidy

kuɗìn-cīzò *m* bedbug(s)

kuɗìn fitò *m* 1. customs duties, tariff 2. import duties

kuɗìn jauřa capital investment

kuɗìn ƙasā *m* currency

kuɗìn ruwā *m* (fin.) interest

kufai *m* (*gen* kufan) 1. ruins 2. abandoned site

kùffê *f* cooperative society

kūjè *v4* 1. to fray 2. to scrape

kujèrā, kùjèrā *f* (*pl* kùjèrū) 1. chair 2. seat

kujèrař-nā-ƙi 1. hawan kujèrař-nā-ƙi veto 2. hau kujèrař-nā-ƙi to veto

kukà, ku kà *pl relative completive* you

kūkā *m* (*pl* kòke-kòke) 1. cry 2. crying 3. complaint

kūkà 1. *m* stove 2. *f* (*pl* kūkōki) baobab

kūkā dà shàsshèƙā *m* yi kūkā dà shàsshèƙā to sob

kukàn, ku kàn *pl habitual* you

kūkan kūrā *m* 1. sudden attack

2. (pol.) coup d'etat

kukè, ku kè *pl relative continuous* you

kūkù *m* (*pl* kūkù-kūkù) cook

kulà *v1* 1. to pay attention (dà to) to care

kùlā *m* 1. attention 2. care

kùla dà *v3* to take seriously

kùlā dà aikì *m* mài kùlā dà aikìn... 1. the person in charge of... 2. co-ordinator of...

kulàwā *f* control

kulɓà *f* (*pl* kulɓōɓī) skink

kulkī *m* (*pl* kulằkē) cudgel

kullè *v4* 1. to lock 2. Yā kullè ta. He put her in purdah.

kullum, kullun *adv* 1. always 2. every 3. whenever 4. yâu dà kullum day-to-day

kullùyaumìn, kullùyōmìn *adv* always

kùlôb *m* (*pl* kùlôb-kùlôb) club

kulōcì *m* clutch

kuma also

kumà *v1* to do again

kùmallō *m* 1. karìn kùmallō breakfast 2. karyà kùmallō to have 3. ji kùmallō to feel nauseous

kùmāmā *m/f* (*pl* kùmàmai) feeble person

kùmàndân *m* (Nr) commandant

kumàntā *v1* to weaken

kùmantà *v3* to be weak

kumàtū *see* kuncì

kumbò *m* (*pl* kumbunà) 1. spaceship 2. satellite 3. flat bowl

kumbòn sādâřwā, kumbòn sàƙō *m* communications satellite

kumbùrā *v1* to make swell

kùmburà *v3* to swell
kùmburī *m* swelling
kumfā *m/f* foam
kùmurcī *m* cobra
kun *pl completive* you
kunā̀, ku nà̀ *pl continuous* you
kùnāmà̀ *m* (*pl* **kùnàmū**)
1. scorpion 2. trigger
kuncè̀ *v4* to untie
kuncì̀ *m* (*pl* **kumàtū**) 1. cheek
2. side of face
kundī *m* (*pl* **kundà̀yē**) 1.
dissertation 2. written source
kundin lìssāfì̀ *m* (Nr) accounts
register
kùnî *m* quinine
kùnkunnìyā *f* soot
kùnkurū *m* (*pl* **kùnkùrai**)
tortoise
kunnà̀ *v1* 1. to light 2. to switch
on
kunnà̀ kâi to enter without
permission
kunne *adv* à kunne in/on the ear
kûnnē *m* (*pl* **kunnuwà̀**) 1. ear
2. ɗan kûnnē ear-ring
kûnnen dōkì̀ *m* 1. (spor.) draw
2. yi kûnnen dōkì̀ to be
identical
kùntū *m* (*pl* **kuntunà̀**) army
blanket
kùnū *m* gruel
kunyā *f* (*pl* **kunyōyī**) ridge
kunyà̀ *f* 1. shame 2.
embarrassment 3. modesty
4. à̀bin kunyà̀ scandal
kunyàtà̀ *v1* to scandalise
kūrā *f* 1. hand cart 2. (*pl* **kūrà̀yē**)
hyena 3. ɗan kūrā ally 4.
rā̀mìn kūrā stronghold
kurà̀dā *f* hatchet
kùrân *m* (Nr) electric current

kùràrī *m* 1. intimidation
2. threat
kuřàtā *pl* 1. military reserves
2. *see* **kuřtù**
kùrɓā 1. *f* sip 2. *v2** to sip
kurciyā *f* (*pl* **kurciyōyī**) dove
kuřdàdī *m* (ed.) 1. adult course
2. literacy campaign
kuřɗà̀ *v1* to detour
kuřɗàɗā *v1* 1. to snake along
2. to infiltrate
kūrè̀ *m* (*pl* **kūrà̀yē**) hyena
kùrēgē *m* (*pl* **kùrègū**) squirrel
kùrfau *m/pl* military police
kūrī *m* empty threat
kûřkudù *m* sandhopper
kûřkukù *m* prison
kùřkunū *m* guinea-worm
kurkùrē *v4* (*f* **kùrkurà̀**) to
rinse out one's mouth
kuřkusa *adv* closely
kurmā *m/f* (*pl* **kurà̀mē**) deaf
person
kurmàmā *v1* to deafen
kurmì̀ (*pl* **kurà̀mē**) forest
kuřnà̀ *f* thorn tree
kuř nòmâl *f* (Nr) teacher
training college
kùrô *m* (Nr) mail
kurtsà̀ *v1* to spurt
kuřtù *m* (*pl* **kurà̀tā**) (mil.)
recruit
kùřtū *m* (*pl* **kuřtunà̀**) small
gourd container
kurùm 1. *f* silence 2. *adv* only
kurūrùtā *v1* 1. to exaggerate
2. to inflame
kùrūruwà̀ *f* shout(ing)
kùřûs *f* (Nr) race-course
kùrwā *f* 1. soul 2. ghost
kusa 1. *adv* near (dà to) 2. *v* to
be almost...

kusa-kusa *adv* in/at close quarters

kusan *adv* almost

kùsantàr̃ jūnā *f* rapprochement

kùsàntuwà *f* encroachment

kùsātà *v2** (**-ci/cē**) **1.** to approach **2.** to nearly do

kush *adv* thud

kūshè wà *v4* to criticise

kùshē *m* **1.** cricitism **2.** ɗan kùshē critic

kùshēwā *f* (*pl* **kùshèyī**) grave

kushilī *m* ɗan kushilī homosexual

kushìn *f* cushion

kùskurà *v3* **1.** to miss **2.** to misbehave

kuskurè *m* **1.** miss **2.** mistake

kuskùrē *v4* **1.** to miss **2.** to mistake

kūsù *m* (*pl* **kūsā, kūsàyē**) **1.** mouse **2.** rat

kusùrwā *f* (*pl* **kusurwōyī**) **1.** corner **2.** angle **3.** point of the compass

kūtsà *vl* **1.** to rush into **2.** to launch

kūtsà kâi 1. to interfere (**cikin** in) **2.** (mil.) to make an incursion (**cikin** into)

kùtsē *m* (mil.) **1.** incursion **2.** intervention

kùtùbâl *f* (Nr) football

kutuf *adv* aged

kùtùhôn *m* (Nr) kick

kutu-kutu *m* **1.** conspiring **2.** contrivance

kutùr̃ī *m* hindquarters

kuturtà *f* leprosy

kùturtà *v3* to be/become a leper

kuturū *m* (*f* **kuturwā,** *pl* **kutàrē**) leper

kùtutturè (*pl* **kùtùttùrai**) tree stump

kūwà, kuwwà *f* shout(ing)

kùwa indeed

kuwwà *see* **kūwà**

kùzà *m* tin

kūzà *vl* to pour (à into)

kùzārī *m* **1.** enthusiasm **2.** yi kùzārī to make a threat **3.** mài kùzārī activist

kwâ *pl indefinite future* you

kwâ *pl negative continous* bā kwà... you are not...

kwabô *m* (*pl* **kwabbunà, kwàbbai**) **1.** kwabo **2.** penny

kwaɓà *vl* to haft

kwàɓà *v2** **1.** to warn **2.** to knock (à from) **3.** to snub

kwāɓà *vl* (*f* **kwàɓā**) to mix into a paste

kwàɓà *f* slip of the tongue

kwaɓè *v4* **1.** to unhaft **2.** to knock away

kwāɓì *m* mortar

kwàddàr̃ût *f* (Nr) highway code

kwāɗà *vl* to do intensely

kwaɗàitā wà *vl* **1.** to stimulate **2.** to stimulate demand **3.** to push a product on

kwàɗaità *v3* to be eager

kwàɗaità *v2** (**-ci/cē**) to hanker after

kwàɗàyī *m* **1.** eagerness **2.** stimulation **3.** greed **4.** envy

kwàɗò *m* (*pl* **kwaɗunà, kwàdî**) **1.** frog **2.** padlock

kwâf *m* **1.** (*pl* **kwafōfī, kwāfunà**) cup **2.** (*pl* **kwâf-kwâf**) prize cup

kwàfsā *f* outer covering

kwàikwayà *v2** (*m* **kwakwaiyō**) to imitate

kwaikwayō *m* **1. wàsan kwaikwayō** (theatre) play **2.** *see* **kwàikwayà**

kwākī *m* cassava flour

kwākì *m* hooded cobra

kwakkwàfā *vl* to knock (cikin into)

kwàkkwàfā *f* **yi kwàkkwàfā** to canter

kwākwā *f* **1.** oil-palm **2.** coconut palm **3.** coconut

kwàkwāzò *m* loud fuss

kwal 1. *adv* spotlessly clean **2. Kwal lāfiyà?** Did you sleep well?

kwâl *m* coal

kwalā *f* (*pl* **kwalōlī**) collar

kwalabā *f* (*pl* **kwalābē**) bottle

kwalàshât *f* shirt and collar

kwalbatì *m* (*pl* **kwalbatōcī**) culvert

kwalējì *f* college

kwalējìn fàsāhà dà sànā'à *f* polytechnic college

kwàlekwàle *m* small canoe

kwàlekwàlen fadà *m* missile boat

kwàlgât *m* (Nr) toothpaste

kwālī *m* (*pl* **kwālàyē**) **1.** cardboard **2.** cardboard box **3.** carton

kwâllī *m* **1.** kohl **2.** galena

kwalliyā *f* **yi kwalliyā** to put on make-up

kwàlò-kwalō *m* **yi kwàlò-kwalō** to renege on a deal

kwàltâ *m* **1.** tar **2.** tarred road

kwàmandà *m* (*pl* **kwamandōjī**) **1.** commander **2. bàbban kwàmandàn sōjì** supreme commander **3. bàbban kwàmandàn rundunōnin**

mayàƙā commander-in-chief of the armed forces

kwàmashò *m* commission

kwàmbîn *m* (Nr) trick

kwàmbìtâr *m* potato

kwàmbùkàsô *f* (Nr) warrant

kwàmfīyūtà, kwàmfūtà *f* computer

kwàmî *m* (Nr) **1.** junior official **2.** sales assistant, (US) salesclerk

kwamìnìs *m* **1.** communism **2. ɗan kwamìnìs** communist

kwaminisancī *m* communism

kwàmishinà *m* (*pl* **kwamishinōnī**) **1.** commissioner **2. Bàbban Kwàmishinà** High Commissioner **3. Mùƙaddàshin Bàbban Kwàmishinà** Deputy High Commissioner

kwàmìtê *m* (Nr) (pol.) exeutive committee

kwàmìtì *m* (*pl* **kwamitōcī**) **1.** committee **2. ƙàramin kwàmitì** sub-committee

kwàmìtî na mùsammàn *m* ad hoc committee

Kwàmitìn Àbinci dà Al'amuràn Nōmā *m* Food and Agricultural Organisation (FAO)

kwàmitìn bā dà shāwarà *m* advisory committee

kwàmitìn gaggàwà *m* emergency committee

kwàmìtîn shiryà aikì *m* steering committee

Kwàmitìn Sulhù *m* Security Council

kwàmitìn tsakiyà *m* central committee

kwàmitìn tsārà manufōfī *m* drafting committee

kwàmitìn zařtâřwā *m* politburo
kwàmsàřiyà, kwàmsêřiyà *f*
(Nr) police headquarters
kwanà *f* corner
kwāna *v* 1. to spend the night
2. to spend a whole day
kwānā *m* (*pl* kwànàkī) 1. night
2. kwănă gōmà ten days
kwānā biyu *adv* a while
kwànàkī *adv* 1. lately 2. na
kwànàkin bāya current 3. *see*
kwānā
kwāna-kwāna *m* 1. fire-
fighting 2. ɗan kwāna-kwāna
fireman 3. mõtàř kwāna-
kwāna fire-engine 4.
ma'aikatař kwāna-kwāna
fire department
kwānan bāya *adv* recently
kwancè *v4* 1. to untie 2. to get
loose
kwànce *adv* 1. mài hankàlì
kwànce peaceful 2. na kwànce
horizontal
kwàncē *m* used
kwancè ɗamarà 1. *m*
disarmament 2. *v* to disarm 3.
shāwařwařin kwancè ɗamarà
disarmament talks
kwànciyā *f* 1. lying down 2.
layer
kwànciyař hankàlì *f* 1. peace
2. (pol.) stability
kwàndō *m* (*pl* kwandunà)
basket
kwànfītīř *m* jam, (US) jelly
kwangilā *f* 1. contract 2. ɗan
kwangilā building contractor
kwangwalā *f* pole
kwànjê *m* (Nr) vacation
kwankò *m* (*pl* kwankàyē) (Nr)
tin

kwànkwadà *v2** to drink down
kwankwanī *m* (Nr) tin
kwànkwasò *m* small of the back
kwānò *m* (*pl* kwānōnī,
kwānukà) 1. (metal) bowl
2. corrugated iron
kwànsànyê *m* (Nr) councillor
kwântā *v1* (*f* kwànciyā) 1. to
lie down 2. to subside
kwàntaccē *m* (*f* kwàntacciyā,
pl kwàntàttū) laid down
kwântà dāmā to die
kwantàfõyìl *m* (*pl* kwantafõyilõlī)
counterfoil
kwantai *m* (*gen* kwantan)
1. surplus 2. Fàřāshì yā yi
kwantai. Prices have fallen.
kwàntâř *m* (Nr) 1. meter
2. speedometer
kwantař dà *v5* 1. to relieve
2. to repress 3. to suppress
kwantař dà tsòràce-tsòràce
to allay fears
kwàntàřēgì *m* contract
kwàntîř-mētìř *m* (Nr) overseer
kwantō *m* 1. hiding 2. yi
kwantō to take up position
kwanyā *f* 1. brains 2. skull
kwànyâk *f* (Nr) cognac
kwāřà *v1* to do intensely
Kwārà, Kwârà *f* River Niger
kwàrā-kwàrà *f* stilts
kwaràm *adv* suddenly
kwàràmniyā *f* loud noise
kwàrangā *f* ladder
kwaràřā *v1* to pour down
kwàràrà *v3* to flow
kwàràrà *f* 1. flow 2. influx
3. spread
kwàràřàř làbàřai *f* freedom of
information
kwararō *m* alley

kwarārôwā *f* advance
kwarārôwař hàmādà *f* desertification
kwārè *v4* 1. to lift off 2. to expose 3. to clear
kwàrī *m* (*pl* kwarūruwà, kwarūrukà) quiver
kwarì *m* (*pl* kwarūruwà) valley
kwàrjinī *m* 1. prestige 2. mài kwàrjinī prestigious
kwařkwařō *m* (*pl* kwàřàkwàřai) spindle
kwàřkwasà *f* flirting
kwařkwàsā *f* driver ant(s)
kwàřkwàshī *m* dandruff
kwâřkwatà *m/f/pl* louse/lice
kwâřkwatàn idànū *m* 1. curiosity 2. kashè kwâřkwatàn idànū to satisfy one's curiosity
kwařtancì *m* adultery
kwařtō *m* (*f* kwařtuwā, *pl* kwařtàyē) lover
kwàsā *v2** (-shi/-shē) 1. to take 2. to extract
kwàsā-kwàsā *f* pelican
kwàsař mâi *f* oil production
kwàsfā *f* outer covering
kwāshè *v4* 1. to take out 2. to collect up 3. to extract
kwàskwàrīmà 1. restoration 2. refurbishment 3. superficial change
kwastàn *m* 1. customs 2. import/ custom duties
kwât *f* (*pl* kwât-kwât) coat
kwatā *f* 1. quarter 2. town 3. drain
kwàtā *f* 1. quay 2. slaughterhouse
kwata-kwata *adv* totally
kwàtami *m* cesspit
kwàtàncē *m* 1. description 2.

directions 3. yi wà... kwàtàncē to direct
kwatancì *m* 1. comparison 2. example
kwàtankwàcī *m* equivalent
kwatàntā *v1* 1. to compare 2. to give an example of
kwatàntâwā *f* comparison
kwàtàntu *v7* to be comparable
kwàtashì *m/pl* upper storey
kwatsàm *adv* suddenly
kwāzārī *m* first rains
kwàzazzabô *m* (*pl* kwàzàzzàbai) 1. gorge 2. gully
kwī6ì *m* (*pl* kwiyà6ā) side of body
kwīkwiyò *m* 1. puppy 2. cub
kyâ *f* indefinite future you
kyà *f* negative continuous you
kyaftìn *m* captain
kyâk *m* cake
kyàkkè6e *adv* à kyàkkè6e privately
kyàkkyāwā *m/f* (*pl* kyāwàwā) 1. good 2. beautiful 3. handsome
kyàkkyāwan fātā *m* optimism
kyamařà *f* (*pl* kyamařōřī) camera
kyamìs *m* 1. pharmacist 2. pharmacy
kyân *see* kyâu
kyandìř *m* (*pl* kyandiřōřī) 1. candle 2. light strip
kyànkyasò *m* (*pl* kyànkyàsai) cockroach
kyânwā *f* (*pl* kyanwōyī) cat
kyař dà kyař 1. hardly 2. almost 3. just
kyarmā *f* 1. favourite 2. shivering
kyařsē *m* (Nr) betting
kyâs *m* (Nr) box

kyàsìyê *m* 1. cashier 2. bank teller

kyât *m* cake

kyâu *m* (*gen* **kyân**) 1. good 2. beauty 3. **dà kyâu!** Okay!

kyaurō *m* (*pl* **kyauràyē**) arrow shaft

kyâutā *vl* 1. to do well 2. to be kind (**wà** to) 3. to be justified in doing 4. to lower price/increase amount

kyàutā *f* gift

kyautàtā *vl* 1. to improve 2. *see* **kyâutā**

kyàutatà *v3* to be improved

kyautàtà zàtō to be optimistic

kyàutàyuwā *f* improvement

kyàutu *v7* to be suitable

Ƙƙ

ƙà? how?

ƙābā 1. m pain 2. v (m ƙābā) to be angry 3. to be conceited

ƙàbalà v2* 1. to contest 2. to challenge

ƙāban ƙàshī m rheumatism

ƙàbīlà f (pl ƙàbīlū) see kàbīlà

ƙabīlancì see kabilancì

ƙàdangarè m (f ƙàdangarùwà, pl ƙàdàngàrū) lizard

ƙadàr̃ī see kadàr̃ī

ƙaddamar̃ dà see kaddamar̃ dà

ƙaddàr̃ā v1 1. to (pre)ordain 2. to estimate 3. to assume

ƙàddar̃à f fate

ƙafà f (pl ƙafàfū, ƙafāfuwà, ƙafōr̃ī) 1. foot 2. leg 3. wheel 4. pair 5. dà ƙafà on foot 6. jā ƙafar̃ wàndō to fight for

ƙafè v4 to dry up

ƙàfō m (pl ƙàhònī) horn

ƙāgà v1 to invent

ƙàgaggen làbār̃ī m novel

ƙàgautà v3 to be eager to

ƙagè v4 to stiffen

ƙàge adv à ƙàge eagerly

ƙāge m 1. lie 2. allegation

ƙàgè v4 to invent

ƙàhō m (pl ƙàhònī) horn

Kàhon Afìr̃kà m Horn of Africa

ƙai m (gen ƙan) Yā ji ƙansù. He had pity on them.

ƙā'idà f (pl ƙā'idōdī, ƙā'idōjī) 1. regulation 2. method 3. limit 4. law 5. standard 6. quota

ƙā'idar̃ bāshì f lending rate

ƙā'idōjin ɗòkā pl the letter of the law

ƙàilūlà f siesta

ƙaimī m 1. spur 2. yi wà... ƙaimī to spur on

ƙā'ìmī m (f ƙā'ìmā, pl ƙà'ìmai) 1. householder 2. leader 3. reliable

ƙàiƙàyī m 1. chaff 2. itch(ing)

ƙàƙà? how?

ƙàƙà gidā adv ɗan ƙàƙà gidā 1. migrant 2. emigrant 3. settler 4. ex-patriot

ƙàƙƙarfē m (f ƙàƙƙarfìyā, pl ƙàƙƙàrfū) strong

ƙaƙƙàutâwā f bâ ƙaƙƙàutâwā without a break

ƙàlà m 1. word 2. rasà ƙàlà to be speechless

ƙalau adv 1. very 2. absolutely

ƙàlīlàn adv 1. small 2. limited

ƙallà adv à ƙallà at least

ƙallàfā v1 1. to falsely accuse 2. ƙallàfà râi to be keen (à kân on)

ƙàlūbàlà f, ƙàlūbàlē m 1. dare 2. challenge

ƙàlùbàlantà v2* (-ci/cē) 1. to dare 2. to challenge 3. to provoke

ƙamè v4 1. to stiffen through drying 2. to be petrified

ƙamfā f 1. shortage 2. lack 3. failure

ƙan see ƙai

ƙamshī m (good) smell
ƙāmùs m dictionary
ƙanānā see ƙànƙanè, ƙàramī
ƙàndàrarrē m (f ƙandàrarriyā,
  pl ƙàndàràrrū) rigid
ƙandàrē v4 to be rigid
ƙandas adv dried out
ƙanè m (f ƙanwà, pl ƙânnē,
  ƙannuwà) younger brother/
  sister
ƙanƙàncē v4 to get small
ƙanƙancì m humiliation
ƙànƙanè m (f ƙànkanùwā, pl
  ƙanānà) 1. small 2. a little
  3. slightly
ƙanƙantà f smallness
ƙànƙarā f 1. ice 2. snow 3. hail
  4. flint 5. gravel
ƙanƙàrà v1 to craft finely
ƙânnē, ƙanwà see ƙanè
ƙanshī see ƙamshī
ƙāra v (f ƙārā) 1. to cry (out)
  2. make a noise
ƙārā f 1. noise 2. sound
  3. complaint 4. ɗaukàkà ƙārā
  (leg.) to appeal 5. see ƙāra
ƙārà v1 (m ƙàrì) 1. to increase
  2. to do more (of) 3. to carry
  on 4. to add to 5. to do again
  6. Yanà ƙàrà ƙibà. He is
  fatter.
ƙārà fàɗìn ƙasā f manufaɽ
  ƙārà fàɗìn ƙasā expansionism
ƙaràirai see ƙaryā
ƙārà izà wutā to exacerbate
ƙàrā-ƙàrā f snack
ƙārà ƙàruwā to escalate
ƙàramaɽ hùkāmà f local
  government
ƙàràmbau m chickenpox
ƙàramī m (f ƙàramā, pl
  ƙanānà) 1. small 2. young

ƙàramin ministà m minister of
  state
ƙarancī m 1. smallness 2.
  shortage
ƙàràngiyā f prickly grass
ƙarantà f being small-minded
ƙàrantà v3 to run out
ƙarara adv crystal clear
ƙàrarrawā f bell
ƙàrarrē m (f ƙàrarriyā, pl
  ƙàràrrū) 1. finished 2. worn-
  out
ƙāràsā v1 to finish
ƙarātō v6 to approach
ƙārè v4 1. to finish 2. to be ready
  3. to be worn out
ƙārē dangī m màkàman ƙàrē
  dangī nuclear weapons
ƙarfàfā v1 1. to strengthen 2. to
  encourage 3. to stress
ƙàrfafà v3 to get strong
ƙarfàfà màganà to reaffirm
ƙarfè m (pl ƙaràfā) 1. metal
  2. o'clock
ƙarfèn ƙafà m/f stumbling
  block
ƙarfī m 1. strength 2. force
  3. power 4. loudness 5. mài
  ƙarfī strong/powerful 6. dà
  ƙarfin sōjà by military means
ƙarfin bindigà m military
  might
ƙarfin gwīwà m 1. morale 2.
  support
ƙarfin hatsī m 1. vigour 2.
  violence
ƙarfin ƙàruwā m growth rate
ƙarfin tuwō m force of arms
ƙarì m 1. sting 2. benign tumour
ƙārì m 1. increase 2. book
  appendix 3. see ƙàrà
ƙàrìn additional

ƙārìn àlbâshì *m* salary increase

ƙārìn bàyānì *m* further explanation

ƙārìn jinì *m* blood transfusion

ƙàrƙashî 1. *m* underside 2. *adv* underneath

ƙàrƙashin *prep* underneath

ƙarƙō *m* 1. durability 2. mài ƙarƙō fixed 2. yi ƙarƙō to endure

ƙaɼnì *m* (*pl* ƙaɼnukà) century

ƙaɼnì gōmà *m* millennium

ƙārō *m* gum

ƙàrshē *m* 1. end 2. tip 3. na ƙàrshē final 4. à ƙàrshē finally 5. *see* wàsā

ƙàru *v7* 1. to increase 2. to make progress (dà with)

ƙāɼūɼà *f* (*pl* ƙāɼūɼōɼ̄ī, ƙàɼ̄ūɼai) flask

ƙàruwā *f* 1. increase 2. growth 3. m̀ài saurin ƙàruwā fast-growing

ƙàruwaɼ tattalin aɼzìkī *f* economic growth

ƙaryā *f* (*pl* ƙàryàce-ƙàryàce) 1. lie 2. yi ƙaryā to tell a lie 3. na ƙaryā false

ƙaryàtā *v1* to deny

ƙas, ƙasà *adv* 1. à ƙas on(to) the ground 2. yi ƙasà to fall 3. Àl'amàɼī yanà ƙasà yanà dabô. The matter is uncertain.

ƙasā *f* (*pl* ƙasàshē) 1. earth 2. ground 3. land 4. country 5. state 6. nationality 7. ɗan ƙasā citizen

ƙàsaità *v3* to develop

ƙàsaità *f* 1. development 2. na ƙàsaità prestigious

ƙasàn *prep* at the bottom of

ƙasaɼ gādò *f* country of origin

Ƙasàshē màsu Rènon Ingìlà *pl* the Commonwealth

ƙasàshē dà akè bî bâshì *pl* debtor nations

ƙasàshen dà bà sù sàmi cî gàba ba *pl* developing nations

ƙasàshen ƙētarè *see* ƙasàshen wàje

ƙasàshē màsu bîn bâshì *pl* creditor nations

ƙasàshen màsu cî gàban màsànà'àntū *pl* developed nations

ƙasàshen wàje *pl* 1. foreign countries 2. abroad 3. overseas 4. na ƙasàshen wàje foreign

ƙasàshen 'yan bâ-ruwanmù *pl* non-aligned nations

ƙàshī (*pl* ƙasūsuwà, ƙassà) 1. bone 2. summary 3. plot

ƙàshin bāyā *m* spine

ƙàshin kâi *m* na ƙàshin kâi unilateral

ƙashiyà *f* 1. bottom 2. origin

ƙàsìdà *f* (*pl* ƙàsìdū) 1. ode 2. leaflet 3. pamphlet

ƙàsìdaɼ manufōfin jàm'iyyà *f* election manifesto

ƙasƙàstà *v1* to undermine

ƙātò *m* (*f* ƙātùwā, *pl* ƙâttā) huge

ƙātùwaɼ gùdumà *f* sledgehammer

ƙaulìn bìla àmalìn *adv* yi ƙaulìn bìla àmalìn to break a promise

ƙàunā *f* love

ƙàunatà *v2** (-ci/cē) 1. to love 2. to plead with

ƙaura *v3* (*f* ƙaurā) 1. to migrate 2. to emigrate 3. to die

ƙaurā *f* 1. migration 2.

emigration 3. ɗan ƙaurā migrant 4. refugee

ƙauràcē wà v4, ƙauràtā wà vl 1. to boycott 2. to shun 3. to balk at

ƙauyè m (pl ƙauyukà) village

ƙawā f (pl ƙawàyē) 1. friend 2. ally

ƙāwā f desire

ƙàwàncē m alliance

ƙàwàntakà f 1. alliance 2. partnership

ƙawanyà f (pl ƙàwànyū) 1. ring 2. circuit

ƙawàtā vl to make beautiful

ƙàwātā v3 to be beautiful

ƙàwà-zuci m greed

ƙayà f (pl ƙayōyī) 1. thorn 2. spine

ƙayàr̃ kifī à wuyà f 1. threat 2. scourge 3. snag

ƙāyatar̃ dà v5 to make beautiful

ƙàyàtaccē m (f ƙàyàtacciyā, pl ƙàyàtàttū) 1. beautiful 2. sophisticated

ƙàyyàdadden m see ƙàyàdajjen

ƙàyyàdajjen aikì m yi ƙàyàdajjen aikì to work to rule

ƙàyyàdadden fàr̃āshì m fixed price

ƙàyyàdajjen yawàn gudù m speed limit

ƙayyàdē v4 1. to define 2. to fix 3. to restrict 4. to establish 5. to pass a law/order 6. to specify

ƙayyàdè ìyālì m family planning

ƙàyyàtacciyar̃ fàsāhà f high technology

ƙayyatâr̃wā f mài matuƙar̃ ƙayyatâr̃wā remarkable

ƙazàf m false accusation

ƙàzāmī m (f ƙàzāmā, pl ƙàzàmai) 1. dirty 2. Yanà dà ƙàzāmin tsàdā. It's extremely expensive.

ƙazàncē v4 see ƙàzantà

ƙàzântā f 1. filth 2. abundance

ƙàzantà v3 1. to be dirty 2. to be extremely

ƙazantar̃ dà v5 to dirty

ƙazwā f scabies

ƙēƙàsā vl 1. to dry 2. to cure (meat/fish)

ƙèƙasà v3 to get dry

ƙēmēmē adv absolutely

ƙērà vl (f ƙīrà) 1. to forge 2. to manufacture

ƙērà màkàmai to manufacture arms

ƙère-ƙère m/pl 1. manufacture 2. kamfanōnin ayyukàn dà bà na ƙère-ƙère ba service industries 3. see kìmiyyà

ƙètā f 1. evil 2. malice

ƙētàrā vl 1. to step over 2. to cross

ƙētarè m 1. river-bank 2. the other side 3. na ƙètarè foreign 4. à ƙètarè abroad

ƙētàrè v4 to cross over

ƙēyà f 1. nape of the neck 2. hindsight 3. tasà ƙēyà to arrest

ƙi v (m ƙî) 1. to refuse 2. to dislike 3. to be unwilling 4. hau kujèrar̃ nā ƙi to veto

ƙî m 1. dislike 2. hatred 3. unwillingness

ƙi jinī to hate

ƙibà f fat(ness)

ƙidàyā vl to count (up)

ƙìdāyā f 1. counting (up) 2. census

ƙidàyà kāyā to take stock
ƙidāyar̃ jàma'à f census
ƙidìddigà, ƙìdìddigà f
1. counting 2. statistics 3.
illìmin ƙìdìddigà (study of)
statistics
ƙidìddigar̃ mutànē f census
ƙifìfiyà f turtle
ƙiftà v1 to blink
ƙiftà idò to wink (wà at)
ƙiƙi-ƙàƙà see kiki-kàkà
ƙil adv 1. tiny 2. only
ƙilà adv perhaps
ƙīmà f value
ƙîn ƙāràwā m na ƙîn ƙāràwā
utter
ƙīrā f (pl ƙère-ƙère) 1. forging
2. manufacturing 3. type
4. model 5. see ƙērà
ƙiràr̃ē m/pl firewood
ƙirgà v1 to count (up)
ƙirgì m (pl ƙiràgā) cowhide
ƙirin adv baƙī ƙirin pitch black
ƙìrinjìjiyà f old bicycle
ƙiris adv a tiny bit
ƙìrji m chest
ƙìrƙâ f vervet monkey
ƙirƙìrā v1, ƙirƙirō v6 1. to
create 2. to invent
ƙishì m thirst
ƙishin-ƙishin m rumours
ƙishirwā f 1. thirst 2. need
3. scarcity
ƙissà f (pl ƙissōshī) story
ƙiyāsì m 1. analogy 2. à kân
ƙìyāsì by analogy
ƙiyàstā v1 1. to assume 2. to
consider 3. to assess
ƙìyayyà f hatred
ƙōdà m (pl ƙōdōjī) kidney
ƙōdagò m 1. paid work 2. 'yan
ƙōdagō workforce

ƙòdagò m (pl ƙòdàgai) palm
nut
ƙōfà f (pl ƙōfōfī) 1. doorway
2. door 3. gate 4. way out
ƙòƙarī m 1. effort 2. attempt
3. yi ƙòƙarī to try
ƙōkàrtā v1 to try
ƙōkìƙōƙì m praying mantis
ƙòƙō m (pl ƙōƙunà) small
calabash
ƙòƙon gwīwà m kneecap
ƙòƙon kâi m cranium
ƙōƙuwā, ƙōƙwā f 1. top 2. apex
3. maximum
ƙōlì m 1. top 2. na ƙōli summit
ƙōnè v4 1. to burn 2. to use up 3.
to be used up 4. to short-circuit
ƙōnèwā f short-circuit
ƙōràfī m yi ƙōràfī to make a
fuss
ƙôrai see ƙwaryā
ƙòramà f (pl ƙòràmū) large
stream
ƙōsà v1 1. to be fed up 2. to
ripen 3. to be eager
ƙōsai m/pl fried bean-cakes
ƙòshì v (m ƙòshī) 1. to be filled
up 2. to be enough 3. to do
constantly
ƙòshiyà f (pl ƙōshiyōyī) ladle
ƙòshiyar̃ sìmintì f (Nr) trowel
ƙōtà f (pl ƙōtōcī) long handle
ƙòtō m bait
ƙudà m (pl ƙudàjē) fly
ƙudàn tsandō m tsetse-fly
ƙudàn zumà m bee
ƙudìr̃i m 1. decision 2. ɗauki
ƙudìr̃i to take a decision 3.
gabàtar̃ dà to introduce a
motion 4. zar̃tar̃ dà to pass a
resolution
ƙudùrà v1, ƙùdurà v2* 1. to

knot 2. to decide to 3. to be determined to

ƙudùƙ̃i *see* ƙudìƙ̃i

ƙūgì *m* 1. sound 2. voice

ƙūgìyā *f* (*pl* ƙūgiyōyī) hook

ƙūgù *m* lower back

ƙuƙut *adv* 1. close 2. small

ƙūƙùtā *vl* to strive

ƙulè *v4* to lose one's temper

ƙulī-ƙulī *m* fried groundnut cakes

ƙullà *vl* 1. to knot 2. to plan 3. to conspire (wà against)

ƙullà dàbāƙ̃à/maƙaƙ̃ƙashìyā to conspire (wà against)

ƙullà yàƙ̃jējēnìyā to make a treaty

ƙùllēlēnìyā *f* plot

ƙùllī *m* punch(ing)

ƙùllūtù *m* (*pl* ƙùllùtai), ƙùlūlù 1. swelling 2. cyst

ƙūlumi *m* (*f* ƙūlumā, *pl* ƙùlùmai) miserly person

ƙùmā *m/pl* flea

ƙùmbā *f* 1. talon 2. mussel-shell

ƙùmbìyà-ƙumbiyā *f* avoiding the issue

ƙūnā *m* burn

ƙūnà *f* intense heat

ƙūnan baƙin wākē *m* 1. 'yan ƙūnan baƙin wākē commandos 2. na ƙūnan baƙin wākē daring

ƙuncī *m* 1. bad temper 2. narrow space

ƙùndùmbāla *f* 1. daring 2. sōjōjin ƙùndùmbāla commandos

ƙundùmē *v4* 1. to pollard 2. to lop off

ƙungìyā *f* (*pl* ƙungiyōyī) 1. group 2. union 3. society 4. association 5. ɗan ƙungìyā (spor.) teammate

ƙungìyā mài kùlā dà tsārìn ìyālì *f* family planning organisation

Kungìyaƙ̃ Āgàji ta Red Cross *f* Red Cross

ƙungìyaƙ̃ dāgaƙ̃ nēman 'yancì *f* liberation movement

Kungìyaƙ̃ Haɗà Kân Kasàshen Afìƙ̃kà *f* Organisation of African Unity (OAU)

Kungìyaƙ̃ Kàsuwaƙ̃ Tàrayyàƙ̃ Tūƙ̃ai *f* the European Community (EC)

Kungìyaƙ̃ Kìwòn Lāfiyà ta Dūniyà *f* World Health Organisation (WHO)

ƙungìyaƙ̃ ƙwādagō *f* trade union

Kungìyaƙ̃ Kyautàtà Ilìmī dà Kìmiyyà dà Àl'àdū ta MƊD *f* United Nations Educational, Scientific and Cultural Organisation (UNESCO)

ƙungìyaƙ̃ lèƙen àsìƙ̃ī *f* secret service

Kungìyaƙ̃ Ma'àikàtā ta Dūniyà *f* International Labour Organisation (ILO)

Kungìyaƙ̃ Mùsùlman Dūniyà *f* World Muslim Congress

Kungìyaƙ̃ Nēman Afuwā ta Dūniyà *f* Amnesty International

Kungìyaƙ̃ Tàimakon Gàjìyàyyū *f* Red Cross

Kungìyaƙ̃ Tattalin Aƙ̃zìkī ta Kasàshen Yammancin Afìƙ̃kà *f* Economic Community of West African States (ECOWAS)

ƙungurmin dājì *m* rain forest

ƙunƙà *adv* absolute

ƙùnƙuntā m/f (pl ƙuntàtā) limited

ƙunsà v1 (m ƙunshì) to wrap

ƙùnsā v2* (-shi/-shē) to contain

ƙunshì m (pl ƙùnshe-ƙùnshe) 1. bundle 2. parcel

ƙùntatà v3 to be restricted in size

ƙunzùgē v4 to tuck in

ƙurà idò v1 to stare (wà at)

ƙùrā f dust

ƙurè v4 to restrict

ƙùri'à f (pl ƙuri'ō'ī, ƙùrì'ū) 1. vote 2. ballot 3. jēfà ƙùri'à to cast a vote 4. mài jēfà ƙùri'à voter 5. rùmfàr jēfà ƙùri'à polling booth 6. yi rōwàr ƙùri'à to abstain

ƙùri'àr dàgà hannū f vote of hands

ƙurjì m (pl ƙuràjē) 1. pimple 2. boil 3. abcess

ƙùrmus adv Yā ƙōnè ƙùrmus. It has burned up completely.

ƙùru m risk-taking

ƙūrù m (f ƙūrùwā, pl ƙūrunà) pony

ƙùrùciyā f youthfulness

ƙùrungù m catfish

ƙūsà f (pl ƙūsōshī) 1. nail 2. senior official

ƙūsà mài tīrēdì f screw

ƙùsumbī m hump

ƙut adv 1. close 2. small

ƙutà v1 to tut

ƙwàcè v4 1. to snatch 2. to take by force

ƙwādagō m 1. paid work 2. 'yan ƙwādagō workforce

ƙwadò m draughts

ƙwaf m ganin ƙwaf curiosity

ƙwàfā f tut

ƙwāfà v1 to wedge

ƙwàfē m jealousy

ƙwai m (gen ƙwan, pl ƙwayàyē) 1. egg 2. light bulb

ƙwàƙƙwārā m/f (pl ƙwāràrā) firm

ƙwàƙulà v2* to pick on

ƙwàƙwā f curiosity

ƙwaƙwalwā f brain

ƙwal adv alone

ƙwālà v1 to fling

ƙwallō m (pl ƙwallàyē) 1. fruit stone 2. ball

ƙwallon ƙafà m 1. football 2. maì wàsan ƙwallon ƙafà footballer

ƙwallon rāgā m basketball

ƙwallon tēbùr m table-tennis

ƙwallon zàri-rùgā, ƙwallon zàrūrùgā m rugby

ƙwam m ganin ƙwam curiosity

ƙwambò m showing off

ƙwan see ƙwai

ƙwanƙwàsā v1 1. to knock on 2. to tap on

ƙwànƙwasà v2* to question (gamè dà on/ about)

ƙwànsō m 1. shell 2. case 3. pod

ƙwārà f (pl ƙwārōrī) shea-nuts

ƙwàrà v2* 1. to overload 2. to overcharge, to short-change 3. to overcome 4. to exploit

Kwàrâ m/f/pl Lebanese

ƙwarài adv very much

ƙwarài dà gàske adv definitely

ƙwàràrrē m (f ƙwàràrrìyā, pl ƙwàràrrū) expert

ƙwarbai m (gen kwarban) trouble

ƙwàrè v4 1. to be expert (dà at/in) 2. to specialise (dà in)

ƙwārè *v4* to choke (dà on)
ƙwārī *m* 1. soundness 2.
firmness 3. spell 4. yi wà...
ƙwārin gwīwà to encourage
ƙwārin kâi *m* stubbornness
ƙwâřƙwatà *m/f/pl* louse, lice
ƙwàřnàfi *m* flatulence
ƙwàrō *m* (*pl* ƙwàrī) 1. insect
2. thief
ƙwàru *v7* to choke
ƙwaryā *f* (*pl* ƙôrai, ƙôrē) 1.
calabash 2. strip
ƙwàryà-ƙwaryà *f* not serious
ƙwaryař kâi *f* skull
ƙwaryař kògī *f* river bed
ƙwàřzabà *v2** to annoy
ƙwàřzanà *v2** to scratch
ƙwasai-ƙwasai *adv* spick and span
ƙwayàyē *see* ƙwai
ƙwàurī *m* (*pl* ƙwaurukà) 1.
shin 2. calf (of leg) 3. *see* fàsà-
ƙwàurì
ƙwaurò *m* insufficient
ƙwàyā *f* (*pl* ƙwāyōyī) 1. grain
2. tuber 3. pill 4. shân ƙwàyā
drug-taking 5. shā ƙwàyā to
take a pill 6. to take drugs
ƙwàyař cùtà *f* virus
ƙwàyař idò *f* 1. eyeball 2. pupil
of eye
ƙwàyař sukàřī *m* sugar cube
ƙwāyōyin dà kè gàrkuwā dà
jìkī dàgà cūtuttukà *pl* the
body's immune system
ƙwàzō *m* 1. diligence 2. good

performance
ƙyāfè *v4* 1. to grill 2. to smoke
meat/fish
ƙyālè *v4* to ignore
ƙyalì *m* make-up
ƙyal-ƙyal *adv* exactly
ƙyàl-ƙyàl *adv* brightly
ƙyalƙyàlā *v4* Sun ƙyalƙyàlā dà
dàriyā. They burst out
laughing.
ƙyàlƙyàlī *m* 1. shining
2. twinkling
ƙyallà *v1* 1. to glimpse 2. to
light
ƙyallē *m* (*pl* ƙyallàyē) piece of
cloth
ƙyallen takàřdā *m* tissue paper
ƙyàllī *m* shining
ƙyàmā *f* 1. aversion 2. mài
ƙyàmař... opponent of...
ƙyândā *f* measles
ƙyànƙyasà *v2** (-shi/shē) to
hatch
ƙyanƙyàshē *v4* to hatch
ƙyař dà ƙyař *adv* 1. hardly 2.
almost 3. just
ƙyas *adv* nothing at all
ƙyāsà *v1* to admire
ƙyàshī *m* jealousy
ƙyastà *v1* 1. to strike a match
2. to light
ƙyàstū *m* flint
ƙyaurē *m* (*pl* ƙyamàrē) door
ƙyēyà *see* ƙēyà
ƙyûyā *f* laziness

Ll

lā! no, really!

là'adà f sales commission

là'akàřī m 1. care 2. yi là'akàřī to consider

là'allà adv perhaps

là'anà f 1. crime 2. curse

là'antà v2* (-ci/cē) 1. to curse 2. to shame

là'àntaccē m (f là'àntacciyā, là'àntàttū) cursed

là'asàř f 1. (Isl.) third prayer of the day 2. late afternoon

lābà f pound (weight)

làbàřī m (pl làbàřū, làbàřai) 1. story 2. news 3. report 4. information 5. Ìnā làbàřì? How are you? 6. mài nazàřin làbàřai newsreader 7. bā dà làbàřī to inform

làbàřìn ƙasā m geography

labtà v1 to (over)load

làbuddà adv definitely

lābulē m curtain

lābùřàřē m (pl lābuřôřī) library

laƁàƁà v1 to sneak

laƁè v4 to lurk

laccà f (pl laccōcī) 1. lecture 2. public address 3. cross-examination 4. bā dà laccà to lecture

lādā m 1. wages 2. reward

ladàbī m good manners

ladàbtā v1 to discipline

ladabtâřwā f na ladabtâřwā disciplinary

làdân, làdànì m (pl làdànai) muezzin

Lādì f Sunday

lafà v1 1. to die down 2. to decrease

làfàfā f shroud

lāfař dà v5 to ease

lafàzī m 1. pronounciation 2. bìsà lafàzin... according to

lāfiyà 1. f good health 2. safety 3. zaman lāfiyà peace 4. ilìmin kùlà dà lāfiyàř mātā gynaecology 5. adv safely

laftanà-kanàř m lieutenant-colonel

làftanàn m (pl laftanōnī) lieutenant

lagà f accounts register

lagwadà f pleasantness

Lahàdì f Sunday

lahàntā v1 1. to harm 2. to maim

Lāhiřà f (rel.) the Hereafter

lâifī m (pl laifuffukà, laifukà) 1. crime 2. fault 3. blame 4. sâ wà... lâifī to accuse

làgìřētò m car radiator

laimà f 1. umbrella 2. sunshade 3. parachute 4. tent 5. damp

laimōtà f (mil.) mortar

lakā f spinal cord

lākā m mud

lakànī m (pl lakanōnī) nickname

làkilê m (Nr) key

lākin conj but

lakkànā v1 to prompt

làkkwâl f (Nr) primary school

làkuřù m (Nr) recruit

làkwàf *adv* floppily
lakwàtar̀ò *m* (Nr) hospital aide
lak̃àbā *vl* 1. to impose (wà on)
2. to give a nickname (wà to)
lak̃àbī *m* nickname
lak̃àbtā wà *vl* 1. to label 2. to
nickname
làk̃antà *v2** to master
lālàcē *v4* 1. to deteriorate 2. to
go wrong
làlàce *adv* à làlàce in ruins
lālàcêwar̀ tattalin arzìkī *f*
economic woes
lālācì *m* laziness
lalai *adv* without effort
lallakkuwà *f* (Nr) armpit
lālàtā *vl* 1. to ruin 2. to explode
lālè *v4* to shuffle
làlītà *f* 1. money bag 2. tsūkè
làlītà to introduce austerity
measures
lallàbā *vl* 1. to soothe 2. to
repair 3. to woo
làllamà 1. *f* lobbying 2. *v2** to
lobby
lallàsā *vl* 1. to persuade 2. to
lobby
làllāsà *v2** (-shi/shē) to
persuade
lallāshī *m* persuasion
lallē *adv* 1. certainly 2. it is
essential that/to...
lallè *m* henna
làlùbī *m* guesswork
lâm *f* (Nr) razor blade
lamàr̄ī see àl'amàr̄ī
lambà *f* (*pl* lambōbī) 1. sign
2. trademark 3. licence plate
4. vaccination 5. immunisation
6. size 7. yi wà mōtà lambà to
get a car licence 8. matsà wà...
lambà to pressurise

lambàr̄ girmā *f* decoration
lambàr̄ mōtà *f* licence plate
làmbàtû *m* 1. second (place)
2. drain
làmbàwân *m* 1. first (place)
2. poison
làmbū (*pl* lambunà) 1. irrigated
field 2. meadow 3. garden
lamfà *f* 1. waiting in ambush
2. lying low
làmfêdà *f* (Nr) pressure lamp
lāmì *m* tastelessness
lāmì lāfiyà! in good health!
làmīr̀ì *m* 1. intention 2. personal
pronoun
lāmùnī *m* 1. guarantee 2. credit
3. mài lāmùnī guarantor
4. sàssauk̃an lāmùnī soft loan
làmuntà *v2** (-ci/cē) 1. to
guarantee 2. to give credit
lāmùshē *v4* to devour
landir̀òbà *f* four-wheel drive
làngā *f* (*pl* langunà) lidded pot
làngàɓaɓɓe *m* (*f* làngàɓaɓɓiyà,
pl làngàɓaɓɓū) 1. droopy
2. soggy
langàɓē *v4* 1. to droop 2. to go
soggy
langàcē *v4* to interplant
langaciyà *f* interplanting
lanhò, lanhù *m* (Nr) tax
lank̃àyā wà *vl* 1. to falsely
accuse 2. *see* lak̃àbtā
lank̃wàmē *v4* to gobble up
lank̃wàsā *vl* to bend
làngà-làngà *m* 1. grass-cutter
2. batten
làntar̀kì, làntir̀kì *m* 1.
electricity 2. light
Làr̀àbā *f* Wednesday
lar̀dì *m* 1. district 2. province 3.
area

làr̄ūr̄à f (pl lar̄ūr̄ōr̄ì) need
làr̄ūr̄ì m just before sunset
làsā v2* (-shi/shē) 1. to lick
2. (spor.) to beat
lāsàfīkā f 1. loudspeaker
2. megaphone
lāsàftā vl to calculate
làshi takòbin... to pledge to...
lāsìfīkà f see lāsàfīkà
lāsìn m licence
lâskōfùr̄ m lance-corporal
latàs m lettuce
làtir̄ì m (Nr) 1. electricity
2. electric light
làtir̄ik, làtr̄îk m 1. electricity
2. lighting equipment
lātsà vl to squeeze
lattù m lateness
lau adv Lāfiyà lau! In the best of
health!
làujē m (pl laujunà) sickle
laulàyin cikì m morning
sickness
launì m (pl launukà) 1. colour
2. style
launìn wāk̄à m tune
laushī m 1. softness 2. tenderness
3. fineness 4. flexibility
lauyà 1. m/f (pl lauyōyì) lawyer
2. vl to turn back
lauyàn gwamnatì m
prosecuting lawyer
lauyà mài karè wândà akè
tùhumà m defence lawyer
lāwàlī m (pl làwàlai) path
làwùr̄jē m trouser-string
lāyà (pl lāyū) talisman
lāyì (pl lāyukà) line
lāyìn mōtōcì m (Nr) traffic jam
layya f sallàr̄ layya Id el-Kabir
lazzà f flavour
lēbùr̄ m Yā yi lēbùr̄. It is level.

lēbùr̄à m (pl lēbur̄ōr̄ì) labourer
lēɓè m (lēɓunà, lâ66ā) lip
lēdà f 1. carrier bag 2. lino
leftanà m see làftanàn
lēk̄à vl to peek
lèk̄ē m peeping
lèk̄en àsir̄ì m 1. spying 2. ɗan
lèk̄en àsir̄ì spy 3. ɗan lèk̄en
àsir̄in màsànà'àntū industrial
spy 4. kungìyar̄ lèk̄en àsir̄ì
secret service
lèmō, lèmū m (pl lēmunà) 1.
orange 2. soft drink
lèmō mài tsāmī m 1. lemon
2. lime
lèmon zāk̄ī, (Nr) lèmon Kanò
m orange
lēnàn m nylon
lētàr̄ m (Nr) 1. litre 2. letter
letàs m lettuce
lētìr̄, lētùr̄ m see lētàr̄
lībà m (pl lībōbì) lever
lībar̄à m (Nr) (mil.) service book
lìbar̄bà m pistol
lìfāfà m shroud
lîf, lìfì m leave
lifìdì m quilted armour
lîg-lîg m (spor.) division, league
likità m/f (pl likitōcì) doctor
likitàn mātā m/f gynaecologist
likìtàyà f tie, (US) neck-tie
lìkkāfà f (pl lìkkàfū) stirrup
lìkkafànī m (pl lìkkàfànai)
shroud
līk̄à vl to stick
lilimàn, lilimantì m ointment
lilìn m linen
lilò m swinging
lìlō, (Nr) lìlô m nylon thread
lìmāmì, lìmân m (pl lìmàmai)
imam
lìmānà f goodwill

limār̃on mōtā (Nr) licence
plate
lìmònât *m/f* (Nr) lemonade
limar̃ō *m* number
Lìnjīlā *f* 1. New Testament
2. the Gospels
lintì *m* lint
lìnzāmì *m* (*pl* lìnzàmai) 1.
bridle 2. rein(s) 3. **hàr̃sāshì**
maì lìnzāmì guided missile
lis *f* late afternoon
lìsê *f* (Nr) upper secondary school
lìsē tàknîk *f* polytechnic college
lìshā *f* 1. (Isl.) fifth prayer of the
day 2. evening
lìshìdân *m* (Nr) adjutant
lìssāfì *m* 1. calculation 2. bill
3. **ilìmin lìssāfì** mathematics
4. **littāfìn lìssāfì** account book
lìssāfìn kudì *m* accounting
lìtā, (Nr) **lìtàr** *m* litre, (US) liter
Lìtìnîn *f* Monday
lìtìr̃ *m see* **lētàr̃**
littāfì *m* (*pl* **lìttàttàfai,**
lìttàfai) book
lìyāfā *f* 1. hospitality 2. reception
lìyāfàr̃ àlfar̃mā *f* state
reception
lìyàfàr̃ cîn àbincin darē *f*
dinner party
lōdì *m* 1. load 2. **yi lōdì** to load
(**wà** onto)
lōfè *m* pipe (for smoking)
lōkàcì *m* (*pl* **lòkàtai**) 1. time
2. period 3. **na ɗan lōkàcì**
temporary 4. **na gàjēren**
lōkàcì short-term 5. **na dōgon**
lōkàcì long-term 6. **ɗau wani**

lōkàcì to defer
lōkàcì ƙanƙanè bāyan *prep*
soon after
lōkàcì-lōkàcì *adv* sometimes
lōkàcin dà when
lòkòtorò *m* (Nr) 1. hospital aide
2. doctor
lōmà *f* (*pl* **lōmōmī**) 1. mouthful
2. piece of food
lōtàr̃è *f* (Nr) lottery
lōtò *m* time
lōtò-lōtò *adv* from time to time
lōtsà *vl* to sag
lūdàyī *m* 1. small gourd
2. **kāmùn lūdàyī** stance
lūɗù *m* 1. homosexuality 2. **ɗan**
lūɗù homosexual
lùgùdē *m* pounding in rhythm
lùgùden igwōyī *m* artillery fire
lūlà 1. *f* ruler 2. *vl* to flee
3. to shoot far
lùlētì *m* (Nr) spectacles
lùmānà *f* 1. goodwill 2.
tranquillity 3. **zaman lùmānà**
peace
lumshè *v4* to cloud over
lùmshì *m* **yi lùmshì** to be cloudy
lungù *m* (*pl* **lungunà**) corner
lùr̃ā *f* 1. care 2. **àbin lùr̃ā**
something remarkable 3. **mài**
lùr̃ā dà... someone in charge
of... 4. **mài lùr̃ā dà har̃kōkin**
sìyāsà political observer
lùr̃a dà *v3* 1. to pay attention
2. to notice
lūtsù, luwādì *see* **lūɗù**
luwul, luwuldàmòtâr̃ *m* (Nr)
engine oil

Mm

mà *prep* 1. to 2. for
mā 1. in fact 2. **dâ mā** already
3. **dà mā** if only
mâ *pl indefinite future* we
mǎ *pl negative continuous* **bā**
mǎ... we are not...
ma'àbùcì *m* (*f* **ma'abūcìyā**, *pl*
ma'àbùtā) 1. remarkable
2. user 3. dealer
ma'ādinī *m* (*pl* **mà'àdìnai**)
safe-box
mà'àdìnì *m* (*pl* **mà'àdìnai**)
mineral
mà'àdìnai *pl* mineral resources
ma'ahàdī *m* (*pl* **mà'àhàdai**)
institute
ma'àikàcì *m* (*f* **ma'aikacìyā**,
pl **ma'àikàtā**) worker
ma'aikatā *f* (*pl* **mà'àikàtū**)
1. workplace 2. factory
3. ministry
mà'àikàtan dìflòmàsiyyà *pl*
diplomatic staff
ma'àikàtan jirgī *pl* crew
ma'aikataɽ kātākō *f* sawmill
ma'aikataɽ magàjin gàrī *f*
town hall
ma'aikataɽ mulmùlà ƙarfè *f*
steelmill
ma'àikàtà-talakāwā *pl*
proletariat
ma'àikī *m* messenger
ma'aji, ma'àjī *m* 1. treasurer 2.
Chancellor of the Exchequer,
(US) Treasury Secretary 3.
gidan ma'aji treasury
ma'ajī, ma'ajiyī *m* (*pl*

mà'àjìyai) storeroom
mà'āmalà *f* (*pl* **ma'āmalōlì**)
1. transaction 2. business
3. (ec.) co-operation
mà'ànā *f* (*pl* **ma'anōnī**)
1. meaning 2. **mài mà'ànā**
concrete 3. constructive
ma'aunī *m* (*pl* **mà'àunai**)
scales
ma'aunin tàswīɽā *m* map scale
ma'aunin zāfī dà sanyī *m*
thermometer
mabǎ *m/f/pl* giver of (**dà** of)
mabàɽcī *m* (*f* **mabaɽcìyā**, *pl*
mabàɽcā) 1. creditor 2.
debtor
mabì *m/f/pl* follower of
màbîl *m* (Nr) caterpillar tractor
mabìyā *pl* retinue
mabìyī *m* (*f* **mabiyìyā**, *pl*
mabìyā) 1. younger brother,
younger sister 2. follower
3. servant
mabūdî *m* (*pl* **màbùɗai**) key
mabùkàcì *m* (*f* **mabukācìyā**,
pl **mabùkàtā**) someone in
need
mabùnƙùsà ƙasā *m* rootcrop(s)
mabùshī *m* (*f* **mabūshìyā**, *pl*
mabùsā) trumpeter
maɓallī *m* (*pl* **màɓàllai**) button
maɓàɽnàcī *m* (*f* **maɓaɽnacìyā**,
pl **maɓàɽnàtā**) saboteur
maɓōyā *f* hiding place
màce *adv* **à màce** dead
màcè *f* (*pl* **mātā**) 1. woman
2. wife 3. female

macè *v4* to die
macèci *m* (*f* macēcìyā, *pl* macètā) rescuer
màce-màce *pl* 1. the dead 2. yawàn màce-màce mortality rate
macì àmānàr̃ ƙasā *m* traitor
mācì *m* yi mācì to march
macìjī *m* (*f* macijìyā, *pl* màcìzai) 1. snake 2. gà-macìjī hostile
macìjin cikì *m* roundworm
maciyā *f* (*pl* màcìyai) roadside market
macùcī *m* (*f* macūcìyā, *pl* macùtā) cheat
madàdin *prep* instead of
madafā *f* (*pl* màdàfai) kitchen
madāfā *f* (*pl* màdàfai) support
madàidàicī *m* (*f* madaidaicìyā, *pl* madàidàitā) 1. medium 2. exact 3. certain 4. corresponding (dà to)
mādàllā! 1. thank you! 2. excellent!
màdân *f* (Nr) modern girl
madar̃ā *f* milk
madatsā *f* (*m* màdàtsai) dam
madatsar̃ ruwā ta sàmar̃ dà wutar̃ làntar̃kì *f* hydroelectric dam
madàwwàmì *m* (*f* madawwamìyā, *pl* madàwwàmā) permanent
madōgarā *f*, madōgari *m* (*pl* màdògàrai) support
madūbī *m* (*pl* màdùbai) mirror
madūbin hàngen-nēsà *m* telescope
madūbin likità *m* microscope
màdugū *m* (*f* màdugā, *pl* màdùgai) 1. convoy leader 2. leader

madaba'ā *f* (*pl* madaba'ō'ī) 1. (printing) press 2. publisher
madācī *m* (*pl* màdàtai) mahogany tree
màdaukai *m* pleurisy
madaukàkī *m* (*f* madaukakìyā, *pl* madaukàkā) 1. highest 2. intense
madaurī *m* (*pl* màdaurai) 1. seatbelt 2. anything used for tying
madaurin r̃ōbà *m* rubber band
madebī *m* (*pl* màdebai) ladle
mādìgō *m* 'yar̃ mādìgō lesbian
madìnkī *m* (*pl* madìnkā) tailor
madìnkìyā *f* (*pl* madìnkā) seamstress
madōrī *m* (*pl* màdōrai) splint
mādugō *m* see mādìgō
mâf *m* map
mafakā *f* (màfàkai) shelter
mafakar̃ sìyāsà *f* 1. political asylum 2. bā dà mafakar̃ sìyāsà to grant political asylum (wà to)
mafàràucī *m* (*f* mafaraucìyā, *pl* mafàràutā) hunter
mafārī *m* (*pl* màfàrai) 1. start 2. reason
mafar̃kī *m* (*f* màfàr̃kai, *pl* màfàr̃ke-màfàr̃ke) dream
mafàshī *m* (*pl* mafàsā) highwayman
mafī *m/f/pl* 1. mafī yawànsù most of them 2. Wannàn mafī tsàdā. This is more/the most expensive.
mafìcī *m* (*pl* màfìtai) ford
mafìcī *m* (*f* maficìyā, *pl* mafītā) temporary
mafìfìcī *m* (*pl* màfìfìtai) hand-held fan

mafìfìci *m* (*f* **mafìfìcìyā**, *pl* **mafìfìtā**) superior

mafìtā *f* 1. exit 2. outlet

mafìtar̃ làbàr̃ai *f* news outlet

mafìtsār̃ā *f* bladder

magàbci *m* (*f* **magabcìyā**, *pl* **magàbtā**) enemy

magàji *m* (*f* **magājìyā**, *pl* **magàdā**) heir

magàjin gàrī *m* mayor

magamī *m* (*pl* **màgàmai**) meeting point

màganà *f* (*pl* **màgàngànū**) 1. word 2. speech 3. matter(s) 4. yi **màganà** to talk (wà to)

màgànādìsò *m* magnet

māgàncē *v4* to resolve

māgàni *m* (*pl* **māgungunà**) 1. medicine 2. treatment 3. cure 4. chemical

māgànin kashè kwàrī *m* insecticide

māgànin saurō *m* mosquito coil

māgànin shāfàwā *m* ointment

màgàr̃ibà *f* 1. (Isl.) fourth prayer of the day 2. sunset

màge *f* (*pl* **māgunà**) cat

maginī *m* (*f* **maginìyā**, *pl* **maginà**) 1. builder 2. potter

magōgī *m* (*pl* **màgògai**) eraser

magōgin hakōr̃ā *m* (Nr) toothbrush

magòyin bāyā *m* (*pl* **magòyā bāyā**) (pol.) supporter

magudā *f* (*pl* **màgùdai**) refuge

magudānā *f* water channel

màgudī *m* 1. sloppy work 2. malpractice 3. manipulation 4. fraud 5. racketeering 6. yi **màgudī à zàɓē** to rig an election

magūdìyā *f* (*pl* **magùdā**) woman who ululates

magùji *m* (*f* **magujìyā**, *pl* **magùdā**) fugitive

màgwài-māgwai *m* fraud

magwajī *m* (*pl* **màgwàdai**) measure

mahadî *m* (*pl* **màhàɗai**) 1. join 2. chemical compound

mahaifā *f* 1. womb 2. placenta 3. birthplace

mahàifī *m* (*f* **mahaifìyā**, *pl* **mahàifā**) parent

mahàjjàcī *m* (*f* **mahajjacìyā**, *pl* **mahàjjàtā**) hajj pilgrim

mahaƙā *f* (*pl* **màhàƙai**) mine

mahaƙar̃ kwâl *f* coal mine

mahaƙar̃ mâi *f* oil well

màhâlli *m* (*pl* **màhàllai**) 1. place 2. context 3. housing 4. ghetto

màhâllin ɗan Adàm *m* environment

mahàr̃bī *m* (*f* **mahar̃bìyā**, *pl* **mahàr̃bā**) 1. shooter 2. hunter

mahàssàdī *m* (*f* **mahassadìyā**, *pl* **mahàssàdā**) jealous

mahàucī *m* (*pl* **mahàutā**) 1. butcher 2. meatseller

mahàukàci *m* (*f* **mahaukacìyā**, *pl* **mahàukàtā**) mad (person)

mahautā *f* 1. slaughterhouse 2. butcher's

màhāwar̃à *f* (formal) discussion

mahàyī *m* (*f* **mahayìyā**, *pl* **mahàyā**) rider

mahàyin bàbûr̃ *m* (*pl* **mahàyan bàbûr̃**) motorcycle rider

mahùkùncī *m* (*f* **mahukuncìyā**, *pl* **mahùkùntā**) 1. administrator 2. judge

mahukuntā f (leg.) court
mâi m (gen **mân**) 1. oil 2. fat
3. petrol 4. ɓaƙin mâi
(petroleum) oil
mài m/f (pl **màsu**) 1. possessor
of 2. doer of
ma'ibādā f (pl **mà'ìbàdai**)
temple
mài bugà sìlìmâ m/f (Nr)
projectionist
mai dà v5 see **mayař dà**
mài dà jàwābì to reply
maidō dà v6 to restore
mài ɗàkì f housewife
mài ɗòrì m/f bone-setter
mài fařfāɗìyā m/f epileptic
mài gādì m night-watchman
mài gidā, màigidā m
1. householder 2. head of the
house
mài haƙàn mà'àdìnai m miner
maiƙò m 1. greasiness 2. nāmà
mài maiƙò juicy meat 3.
màƙāmì mài maiƙò highly-
paid position
maimàitā v1 to repeat
màimakō m substitute
màimakon prep instead of
mài mōtà m motorist
mâitā f witchcraft
màiwā f millet
màjàlisâ f (pl **màjàlìsū**)
1. assembly 2. council
3. legislative body
Màjàlisař Dàttìjai f 1. Upper
House 2. (UK) House of Lords
3. (US) Senate 4. ɗan
màjàlisař dàttìjai senator
Màjàlisař Dinkìn Dūniyà f
United Nations (UN)
Màjàlisař Dōkōkì f 1.
parliament 2. Lower House 3.

(UK) House of Commons 4.
(US) House of Representatives
Màjàlisař Ƙōlōluwā ta Sōjà f
Supreme Military Council
màjàlisař ministōcì f (pol.)
1. cabinet 2. mânyan 'yan
màjàlisař ministōcì inner
cabinet
màjàlisař tūrū ta àl'ummà f
people's revolutionary council
màjàlisař wucìn-gādì f interim
national assembly
màjàlisař zařtařwā f executive
council
Màjàlìsun Dōkōkì pl (US)
Congress
màjàmi'à f (pl **màjàmì'ū**)
church
màjâř m (Nr) (mil.) major
màjànūnì m (f **màjànūnìyā**, pl
màjànùnai) mad person
majè... m/f someone who died
at...
majēmā f tannery
majèmì m (f **majēmìyā**, pl
majēmā) tanner
majìgì m 1. film, (US) movie
2. film show
màjinā f mucus
majinācìyā f (pl **màjìnàtai**)
1. vein 2. artery
màjistàřè m (pl **màjistařōřì**)
magistrate
majiyā f (pl **màjìyai**) source of
information
majiyā tagàri f news source
majìyyàcì m (f **majiyyacìyā**,
pl **majìyyàtā**) 1. nurse
2. patient
màjōřatè m majority
makà to/for you masculine
singular

mākà vl to beat down

màkàbūlì m religious souvenir

makàɗî m (f makaɗìyā, pl
makàɗā) 1. drummer
2. musician

màkāhò, màkāhò m (f
makaunìyā, pl màkàfī)
blind

màkàlūtū m shìga màkàlūtū to
become embroiled (wajen in)

makāmā f (pl màkàmai)
handle

màkàman àl'àdà pl conventional
weapons

makàmànci m (f makamancìyā,
pl makàmàntā) 1. replica
2. similar

màkàman gubà pl chemical
weapons

màkàman ƙàrē dangì/
nūkìliyà pl 1. nuclear
weapons 2. yawàn màkàman
nūkìliyà ƙàrìn zaman lāfiyà
nuclear deterrent

makāmashī m 1. fuel 2. energy

makāmashin nūkìliyà m
nuclear energy

makāmashin zāfin rānā m
solar energy

makāmī m (pl màkàmai)
weapon

màkāmì m 1. position 2. status

makāmī mài lìnzāmì m guided
missile

makàncē v4 to go blind

màkanikè m (pl màkànìkai)
mechanic

makankarī m (pl màkànkàrai)
scraper

makantà f blindness

màkarà v3 1. to be late 2. to be
delayed

màkàrā f 1. funeral bier
2. coffin 3. zaman màkàrā
period of mourning

makàrànci m (f makaràncìyā,
pl makàràntā) well-read

makaȓantā f (pl màkàȓàntū)
1. school 2. ɗan makaȓantā
pupil

makaȓantaȓ hòron màlàmai
f teacher training college

makaȓantaȓ jè-ka-kà-dāwō f
day school

makaȓantaȓ kwānā f boarding
school

makaȓantā ta ƙanānàn yârā
f nursery school

makarī m (pl màkàrai)
antidote

makaȓɗàɗà f 1. peninsula
2. straits

màkàȓùfô m microphone

makashī m (pl màkàsai)
weapon

makàshī m (f makashìyā, pl
makàsā) killer

màkassàȓi m (f màkassàȓa, pl
màkàssàȓai) cripple

makaunìyā see màkàfô

makawā f bâ makawā it's
unavoidable

mākēkè m (f makēkìyā)
1. vast 2. large-scale

màkērò m ringworm

makēwayī m (f makēwayā, pl
màkèwàyai) toilet

mākì m 1. mark 2. school marks

màkìlîn m toothpaste

mākìn Jāmùs m deutschmark

mākiȓcì m cunning

mākìȓi m (f mākìȓā, pl
màkìȓai) sly

Mākisancì m Marxism

makitsìyā *f* (*pl* makìtsā) hairdresser

makiyāyā *f* (*pl* màkìyâyai) pasture(land)

makìyàyī *m* (*f* makiyāyìyā, *pl* makìyâyā) herdsman

mākò *m* (*pl* mākò-mākò) week

mākò biyu *m* fortnight

makōkī *m* mourning

makòkī *m* (*f* makōkìyā, *pl* makòkā) mourners

makōmā *f* future

makullī *m* (*pl* màkùllai) 1. key 2. lock

makuɽɗā *f* (*pl* màkùɽɗai) 1. hill pass 2. river narrows

makuɽɗàɗā *f see* makaɽɗàɗā

makūsā *f* (*pl* màkùsai) 1. mark 2. fault

makùsàcī *m* (*f* makusacìyā, *pl* makùsàtā) 1. near 2. similar

makuwā *f* yi makuwā to stray

makwàɗaicī *m* (*f* makwaɗaicìyā, *pl* makwàɗaitā) greedy

makwafin *prep* in the place of

makwarārā *f* (*pl* màkwàràrai) channel

makwarwā *f* (*pl* makwàrē) bushfowl

makà *vl* to fix (à into)

màƙàƙī *m* tickle in throat

maƙàlā *vl* to attach (à into/ onto)

màƙàlà *f* 1. newspaper article 2. (acad.) paper 3. lecture

maƙàlē *v4* 1. to get stuck 2. to staple

màƙàlūtū *m* shìga màƙàlūtū to become embroiled (wajen in)

màƙàmì *m* position (of authority)

maƙàrā *vl* 1. to fill up 2. to monopolize

maƙaɽƙashìyā *f* 1. betrayal 2. conspiracy 3. sabotage 4. na maƙaɽƙashìyā subversive

maƙaɽƙashìyaɽ maɓàɽnàtā *f* sabotage

màƙàɽɽàbai *pl* retinue

maƙàryàcī *m* (*f* maƙaryacìyā, *pl* maƙàryàtā) liar

màƙàsūdī *m* (*pl* màƙàsùdai) 1. aim 2. meaning

maƙàuràcī *m* (*f* maƙauracìyā, *pl* maƙàuràtā) migrant

maƙè *v4* to hide away

maƙērā *f* (*pl* màƙèrai) smithy

maƙèrī *m* (*pl* maƙèrā) smith

màƙèrò *m* ringworm

màƙèsu *m* firefly

maƙètàcī *m* (*f* maƙètacìyā, *pl* maƙètàtā) malicious

maƙètarā *f* ford

maƙì *m/f/pl* 1. hater of 2. refuser of

màƙil *adv* in abundance

maƙìyī *m* (*f* maƙiyìyā, *pl* maƙìyā) enemy

màƙōgwàrò *m* throat

màƙùdan a large amount of

màƙùrè *v4* to choke

maƙwàbcī *m* (*f* maƙwabcìyā, *pl* maƙwàbtā) neighbour

màƙwàbtakà *f* adjacency (dà to)

maƙwàrwā *f* gulp

maƙyùyàcī *m* (*f* maƙyùyacìyā, *pl* maƙyùyàtā) lazy

mālā *f* sâ à mālā 1. to put to one side 2. to postpone

malahà *f* (*pl* malahōhī) sole

màlā'ikà *m* (*pl* màlà'ìkū) angel

malàlā *vl* to pour (kân onto/ over)

màlàlà *v3* to flow (cikin into)

malàlàcī *m* (*f* malālācìyā, *pl* malàlàtā) lazy

malallautā *f* (*pl* màlàllàutai) (Isl.) place for religious ablutions

mālàm *m* 1. Mr 2. *see* mālàmī

mālàmā *f see* mālàmī

mālàm-bùɗe-littāfī *m* butterfly

mālàmī *m* (*f* mālàmā, *pl* mālàmai) 1. teacher 2. learned person 3. supervisor

mālantà *f* teaching

malāsā *f* usefulness

màlātì *m* (Nr) (med.) 1. disease 2. ɗan màlātì patient

mālējì *m* speedometer

mal-gàřê (Nr) yi mal-gàřê to park badly

malittāfā *f* (*pl* màlìttàfai) (Nr) library

malƙwàsā *vl* to bend

mallàkā *vl* to manipulate

màllakā 1. *f* colonialism 2. imperialism 3. colony 4. ownership 5. *v2** to own 6. to govern 7. *see* mulkìn màllakà

màllakàř tàjìřai *f* private ownership

mallàkī *m* property

màlô *m* (Nr) melon

màma *m* 1. (female) breast 2. mother

mamàcī *m* (*f* mamacìyā, *pl* mamàtā) 1. deceased 2. mortal

màmākì *m* 1. surprise 2. àbin màmākì wonderful 3. ironic

màmayà *v2** (mil.) 1. to invade 2. to occupy

mâmayē *m* sōjōjin màmayē (mil.) occupying forces

mâmàyē *v4* (mil.) 1. to conquer 2. to occupy

mâmàyè shāwàřwařī to dominate a discussion

mambà *see* membà

mamōrā *f* use

mamuřɗì *m* (*pl* màmùřɗai) knob

mân *see* mâi

manà *pl* to/for us

màna 1. for sure! 2. come on!

manajà *m* (*pl* manajōjì) manager

manajàn dàřaktà *m* managing director

mànāřà *f* minaret

manàzàřcī *m* (*pl* manàzàřtā) observer

mâncē *v4* to forget

màndâ *f* (Nr) 1. warrant 2. money/ postal order

màndā dàhô *m* (Nr) warrant

màndūlà *f* (Nr) marijuana

mân fētùř *m* petroleum

màngarà *v2** 1. to kick 2. to lash out at

màngàzâ *f* (Nr) 1. storeroom 2. warehouse

mân gōgè haƙòrā *m* toothpaste

mangwàrò *m* (*pl* mangwarōřì) mango

mân gyàɗà *m* groundnut oil

manhajà *f* (*pl* manhajōjì) syllabus

mànî, màniyyì *m* 1. semen 2. sperm

manì'ōɗà *f* money/ postal order

mân jā *m* palm oil

manjàgarà *f* (*pl* mànjàgàrū) rake

manjò *m* (*pl* manjōjī) (mil.)
major

mân kātākō *m* 1. varnish 2.
shāfà mân kātākō to varnish

mànƙùdan a large amount of

mân màsâj *m* ointment

mannà *v1* to glue (à onto)

mannàwā *f* takàrdar mannàwā
poster

mannè *v4* to be stuck (à to)

manòmī *m* (*f* manōmìyā, *pl*
manòmā) farmer

mân shānū *m* butter

mântā (dà) *v1* to forget

mantuwā *f* forgetfulness

manufā *f* 1. intention 2. policy
3. thesis

manufaȓ ƙàrà fādìn ƙasā *f*
expansionism

manufōfī *pl* 1. manifesto 2. *see*
manufā

manūnìyā *f* sign

mânyā *see* bàbba

mânya-mânya *pl* 1. the rich
2. VIPs

mânyan bindigōgī *pl* artillery

mânyan kamfanōnī *pl* multi-
nationals

mânyan ƙasàshen dūniyà *pl*
(pol.) major powers

mànyètô *m* tape recorder

mân zàitûn *m* olive oil

manzancì *m* 1. message
2. (pol/mil.) mission 3. ī dà
manzancì to carry out a
mission

manzìlī *m* place of arrival

mànzō *m* (*pl* mànzànnī)
messenger

marà *m/f see* maràs

mārà *f* abdomen

màrā *v2** (*m* mārì) to slap

marabā *f* (*pl* màràbai) difference

mařàba! 1. welcome! 2. yi wà...
mařàba to welcome

mařàbcē *v4* to welcome

màràicē *m* 1. late afternoon
2. evening

màraƙī *m* (*f* màraƙā, *pl*
maruƙà) calf

mararrabā *f* (*pl* màràrràbai)
crossroads

maràs, marà *m/f* (*pl* maràsā)
1. not having 2. without, -less

marātayī *m* (*pl* màràtàyī) peg

màřawwà *f* respect

marāyā *f* (*pl* màràyai) 1.
unwalled town 2. suburb 3. na
yankunàn marāyā urban

màràyà *m* (*f* màrainìyā, *pl*
màràyū) orphan

màrì *m* (*pl* marūruwà) shackle

mārì *m* slap

mařìdī *m* (*pl* màřìdai) (rel.)
follower

mariƙī *m* (*pl* màrìƙai) handle

marìgàyī *m* 1. deceased 2. the
late...

màřìlì *m* (*f* mařīlìyā, *pl*
màřìlai) sick

marinā *f* (*pl* màrìnai) dye-pit

marìnī *m* (*f* marinìyā, *pl*
marìnā) dyer

Māřìs *m* March

màřkā *f* 1. wettest part of the
rainy season 2. wet day

markàdà *v1* to mash

màřmàř *adv* fluttering

marmarā *f* (*pl* màràmàrai)
laterite

marmarī *m* desire

maròƙī *m* (*f* maròƙìyā, *pl*
maròƙā) 1. praise-singer
2. professional beggar

maròwàci *m* (*f* marōwacìyā,
pl maròwàtā) miser
mařsandî *f* Mercedes Benz
mařtabà *f* (*pl* mařtabōbī)
1. status 2. rank 3. prestige 4.
mài mařtabà His Excellency
mařtànī *m* mai dà mařtànī to
respond in kind (gamè dà to)
màrtô *m* (Nr) hammer
mařùbùcī *m* (*f* mařubūcìyā,
pl mařùbùtā) 1. writer
2. author
màrūrù *m* boil
mâs *m/f* (Nr) 1. mallet 2.
sledgehammer
masà *m* to/for him
masai *m/f* cesspit
masakī *m* (*pl* màsàkai) large
calabash
màsākī *m* (*pl* màsàkai) leper
masāƙā *f* (*pl* màsàƙū) 1.
weaver's workshop 2. textile
factory
masàƙī *m* (*f* masāƙìyā, *pl*
masàƙā) weaver
masalàn *adv* for example
masallācī *m* (*pl* màsàllàtai)
mosque
màsammàn *see* mùsammàn
masana'antā *f* (*pl* màsànà'àntū)
factory
masana'antař sařřàfà
màkàmai *f* arms factory
màsànà'àntū *pl* 1. industry
2. na màsànà'àntū industrial
masànī *m* (*f* masanìyā, *pl*
masànā) 1. someone who
knows 2. knowledgeable
masànin ilìmin sìyāsà *m*
political scientist
Masàř *f* Egypt
masàřā *f* maize

masàràucī *m* (*pl* masàràutā)
official
masarautā *f* (*pl* màsàràutai)
administrative area
màsàřūfì *m* kāyan màsàřūfì
1. staple 2. basic commodity
màsàřūfì *m* kāyàyyakin
màsàřūfì consumer goods
masassaƙā *f* carpenter's shop
masàssàƙī *m* (*pl* masàssàƙā)
carpenter
masaukī *m* (*pl* màsàukai)
1. place to stay 2. mài
masaukī host
māshā'à *f* desire
mà shā Àllāhù! 1. as God
wills! 2. wonderful!
màshàhūřì *m* (*f* màshàhūřìyā,
pl màshàhùřai) famous
màshāƙò *m* bronchitis
màshasshařā *f* (*pl* màshàsshàrū)
fever
mashàwàřcī *m* (*f* mashāwařcìyā,
pl mashàwàřtā) 1. adviser
2. consultant
mashāwařtā *f* (pol.) assembly
mashāyā *f* (*pl* màshàyai)
watering place
mashàyī *m* (*f* mashāyìyā, *pl*
mashàyā) 1. drinker 2.
smoker
māshì *m* (*pl* māsū) 1. spear
2. shooting star
mashigi *m* (*pl* màshìgai)
1. opening 2. ford
màshîn *f* (Nr) typewriter
màshîn *m/f* (*pl* màshîn-
màshîn) 1. machine 2.
motorbike
màshingàn, màshingàn *m/f*
machine-gun
màsīfà (*pl* màsìfū) misfortune

māsinjà *m* (*pl* māsinjōjī)
1. messenger 2. courier
màslahâ *f* (pol.) interest
màslahàr̄ kasā *f* national
interest
masò *m/f/pl* 1. someone who
likes/loves 2. arèwa masò
yâmma north-west
masōkìyā *f* pleurisy
masōmī *m* (*pl* màsòmai) 1.
beginning 2. place of origin
3. cause
màsôn *m* (Nr) mason
màsōr̄o *m* black pepper
masòyī *m* (*pl* masōyìyā, *pl*
masòyā) 1. someone who
likes/loves 2. lover
masùncī *m* (*pl* masùntā)
fisherman
matà to/for her
mâtā *f* (*pl* mātā) 1. wife
2. woman
matàbbàcī *m* (*f* matabbacìyā,
pl matàbbàtā) 1. certain
2. permanent
màtacce *m* (*f* màtacciyā, *pl*
màtàttū) 1. dead 2. (mil.)
casualty
matàfìyī *m* (*f* matafìyìyā, *pl*
matàfìyā) 1. traveller
2. pedestrian
matàimàkī *m* (*f* mataimakìyā,
pl matàimàkā) 1. helper
2. assistant 3. deputy 4. vice-
5. (spor.) runner-up
matàimàkin shùgàba *m* vice-
president
màtàkai *pl* 1. measures
2. zâfàfan màtàkai drastic
measures 3. *see* matàkī
matākalā *f* (*pl* màtàkàlū)
stairs

màtàkan hòrō *pl* punitive
measures
màtàkan kāriyàr̄ cìnikī *pl*
trade protectionism
màtàkan tsìmī *pl* (ec.) cuts
màtàkan tsūkè bàkin àljīhū
pl austerity measures
matākī *m* (*pl* màtàkai) 1. step
2. stage
matàk̄àicī *m* (*f* matak̄aicìyā,
pl matàk̄àitā) restricted
màtàlâ *f* (Nr) mattress
matàlàucī *m* (*f* matalaucìyā,
pl matàlàutā) poor
matàmbàyī *m* (*f* matambayìyā,
pl matàmbàyā) questioner
màtàr̄nâl *f* (Nr) 1. kindergarten
2. nursery school
matāshī *m* (*pl* màtàsai)
1. cushion 2. pillow
matàshī *m* (*f* matāshìyā, *pl*
matàsā) 1. teenager
2. developing
matāshìyā *f* 1. reminder 2.
reference
matātar̄ mâi, matātar̄ mân
fētùr̄ *f* oil refinery
mataunī *m* (*pl* màtàunai)
molar tooth
màtìr̄yāshì *m* (Nr) machine-gun
matōshī *m* (*pl* màtòsai) stopper
matsà *vl* 1. to pinch 2. to worry
3. to force (dà against) 4. to
approach
mātsà *vl* to squeeze out
matsàkàicī *m* (*f* matsakaicìyā,
pl matsàkàitā) 1. medium
2. average
matsàkàicin r̄a'àyī *m* màì
matsàkàicin r̄a'àyī liberal
màtsalà *f* (*pl* matsalōlī)
1. matter 2. problem

màtsalàr̃ taɓarɓàrêwar̃ tattalin ar̃zìkì *f* economic crisis

matsànàncī *m* (*f* **matsananciyā,** *pl* **matsànàntā**) 1. serious 2. severe

matsànàncin r̃a'àyī *m* **mài matsànàncin r̃a'àyī** extremist

matsàrkàkī *m* (*f* **matsarkakìyā,** *pl* **matsàrkàkà**) 1. clean 2. pure

matsayī *m* (*pl* **màtsàyai**) 1. position 2. status

mātsè *v4* to squeeze out

màtsèfatà *f* (*pl* **màtsèfàtai**) tweezers

matsēfī *m* (*pl* **màtsèfai**) comb

matsègùncī *m* (*f* **matsēguncìyā,** *pl* **matsègùntā**) gossip

matsì *m* 1. shortage 2. overcrowding 3. crowded 4. narrow 5. **cikin hālin matsì** in a crisis

matsìn tattalin ar̃zìkì *m* economic mess

matsìyàcī *m* (*f* **matsiyācìyā,** *pl* **matsìyàtā**) poor

matsalōlin dūniyà *pl* international affairs

matsòràcī *m* (*f* **matsōracìyā,** *pl* **matsòràtā**) 1. afraid 2. coward

matsùbbàcī *m* (*f* **matsubbacìyā,** *pl* **matsùbbàtā**) magician

matsugunā *f* 1. residence 2. dwelling

mātūcì *m* femininity

matuƙā 1. *f* limit 2. *adv* extremely

matuƙar̃ *conj* as long as

matùƙī *m* (*f* **matūƙìyā,** *pl* **matùƙā**) 1. driver 2. pilot

màulūdì *m* the Prophet's birthday

mawàdācī *m* (*f* **mawadācìyā,** *pl* **mawàdàtā**) wealthy

màwāfakà *f* 1. good luck 2. **cim mà màwāfakà** to strike a deal

mawàƙī *m* (*f* **mawāƙìyā,** *pl* **mawāƙā**) 1. singer 2. poet

mawàllàfī *m* (*f* **mawallafìyā,** *pl* **mawàllàfā**) author

mawùyàcī *m* (*f* **mawuyacìyā,** *pl* **mawùyàtā**) difficult

màyā *v2** 1. to take the place of 2. to succeed

màyā *m* weevil

mayāfī *m* (*pl* **màyàfai**) shoulder wrap

mayàƙī *m* (*f* **mayāƙìyā,** *pl* **mayàƙā**) 1. soldier 2. warrior

mayankā *f* (*pl* **màyànkai**) slaughterhouse

mayar̃ dà *v5* 1. to put back 2. to give back 3. to restore 4. to get back 5. to transfer 6. to convert (into) 7. to exert 8. to repatriate 9. (leg.) to commute

mayàudàrī *m* (*f* **mayaudarìyā,** *pl* **mayàudàrā**) 1. swindler 2. deceiver

mayè *v4* to succeed (à as)

māyè *m* (*f* **mâyyā,** *pl* **māyū**) witch

màyē *m* drunkenness

māyè gurbin... *v4* to take the place of....

Māyù *m* May

mayùnwàcī *m* (*f* **mayunwacìyā,** *pl* **mayùnwàtā**) hungry

mâyyā *see* **māyè**

maza *adv* quickly

mazà *see* **mijì**

mazābā *f* (*pl* **màzàɓai**) 1. polling station 2. constituency mazàjē *see* mijì

maza-maza *adv* extremely quickly

màzàkutà *f* 1. virility 2. hùlař màzàkutà condom

mazàmbàcì *m* (*f* mazambacìyā, *pl* mazàmbàtā) 1. cheat 2. corrupt

mazarī *m* spindle

màzàrƙwailà *f* brown sugar

mazaunī *m* (*pl* màzàunai) 1. seat 2. abode

mazàunī *m* (*f* mazaunìyā, *pl* mazàunā) 1. resident 2. inhabitant

mazhàbī *m* (*pl* màzhàbai) (rel.) 1. sect 2. school of thought

maziyařtā *f* 1. shrine 2. mausoleum

M'DD *see* Màjàlisař 'Dinkìn Dūniyà

mè? *m/f* (*pl* su mè?) 1. what? 2. don mè? why?

mècē cè? *see* mènē nè?

mêl *m* mail

membà *m/f* (*pl* membōbī) 1. member 2. subscriber

mènē nè *m* (*f* mècē cè, *pl* su mènē nè) what is (it)?

mêř *m* (Nr) mayor

mēřî *m/f* (Nr) 1. mayor's office 2. town hall

mēsà *f* (*pl* mēsōshī) 1. hose 2. python

mēsàř ruwā *f* water cannon

mēsìn *m* (*pl* mēsìn-mēsìn) mason

mètan, mètin *f* two hundred

mētìř, mèzîř *m* (Nr) 1. tape-measure 2. dàuki mèzîř to measure

mìdî *f* noon

midìl *f* middle school, lower secondary school

mijì *m* (*pl* mazā, mazàjē) husband

mikì to/for you *feminine singular*

mikì *m* (*pl* mīyākū) 1. sore 2. ulcer

mìkùřô *m* (Nr) microphone

miƙà *vl* 1. to stretch 2. to hand over (wà to)

mìƙaƙƙē *m* (*f* mìƙaƙƙiyā, *pl* mìƙàƙƙū) straight

miƙà wuyà to surrender

miƙè *v4* to stretch out

mîl *m* (*pl* mīlōlī) mile

mìla *v3* to be strongly inclined (à kân to)

milìmītà *f* millimetre

miliyàn, milyàn, (Nr) miliyò *m/f* (*pl* miliyōyī) million

mìlōniyà *m/f* millionaire

minì to/for me

ministà, (Nr) mìnistìř *m* (*pl* ministōcī) 1. minister 2. ƙàramin ministà minister of state

ministàn kārè kēwayèn dan Adàm *m* minister for the environment

minìt *m* minutes of a meeting

mìnìzê *m* (Nr) carpenter

minjiryā *f* pins and needles

minshārī *m* snoring

mintì *m* 1. mint 2. (*pl* mintōcī) minute (of time)

minzìlī *m* point in time

mirgìnā *vl* to roll along

mirgìnē *v4* to roll over

mìsālì 1. *m* (*pl* mìsàlai, màsàlce-màsàlce) example 2. something similar 3. *adv* for example mìsālìn *adv* 1. like 2. approximately

misàltā, misìltā *vl* 1. to compare (dà with) 2. to estimate 3. to hail (tàmkaȓ as)

mishàn *m* 1. (Christian) mission 2. ɗan mishàn missionary

miskìlī *m* (*f* miskìlā, *pl* mìskìlai) 1. puzzling 2. unpredictable

mìskìnì *m* (*f* mìskìnìyā, *pl* mìskìnai) destitute

mìstîn *m* mistake

mītà *f* (*pl* mītōcī) 1. meter 2. metre 3. (radio) wavelength

mītà mài gàjēren zangò *f* short-wave radio

mìtìn *m* meeting

mitsilī *m* (*f* mìtsilā, *pl* mitsil-mitsil) minute

miyà *f* 1. soup 2. sauce

miyàgū *see* mūgù

miyàgun màkàmai *pl* nuclear arms

miyau *m* 1. saliva 2. mài màganà dà miyan gwamnatì government spokesman 3. mùsāyaȓ miyau exchange of ideas

mizānì *m* (*pl* mìzànai) 1. scales 2. indication

mizānìn zīnāȓìyā *m* gold standard

mòbîl *m see* màbîl

mòbìlât *m* (Nr) motor scooter

mòdâl *m* (Nr) 1. pattern 2. model

mōdà *f* (*pl* mōdàyē) ladle

mōlō *m* (*pl* mōlàyē) three-stringed guitar

mòlò *m* (Nr) brick mould

moni'ōdà *f* 1. money order 2. postal order

mòrā *v2** (*m* mòrō) to utilize

mōrè *v4* to enjoy

mōrì *m* ɗan mōrì favourite

mòriyā *f* 1. use(fulness) 2. ci mòriyā to exploit

mòrō *see* mòlō

mōshàn *m* (pol.) motion

mōtà *f* (*pl* mōtōcī) 1. car 2. bàbbaȓ mōtà lorry 3. à mōtà by car/road

mōtàȓ mâi *f* tanker lorry

mòtô *m* (Nr) moped

mōtōcī *pl*, yawàn mōtòcī *pl* traffic

mōtsà *vl* to move

mòtsattsē *m* (*f* mòtsattsìyā, *pl* mòtsàttsū) mad

mōtsì *m* movement

mōwà *f* favourite wife

mu, mù *pl* 1. we 2. us

mū, mù *pl* we

mù'āmalà *f* (*pl* ma'āmalōlī) 1. transactions 2. business

mù'annàsā *f* feminine gender

muddà *f* period

muddàȓ, muddìn *conj* 1. when 2. if 3. provided that 4. so long as

muddì *m* period

muddìn *conj see* muddàȓ

mudàba'à *f see* madàba'ā

mufuȓàdì *m* singular

mùfùtī (*pl* mùfùtai) judicial assessor

mūgù *m* (*f* mūgùwā, mūgunyà, *pl* māgàyē, miyàgū) 1. bad 2. evil

mūgùn dawà *m* warthog

mùguntà *v3* to be evil

mùgùntā *f* 1. evil 2. (*pl* mùgùnce-mùgùnce) evil act

Mùhaȓȓàm *m* (Isl.) first month

mùhaɍɍàmì *m* (*f* mùhaɍɍàmā, *pl* mùhàɍɍàmai) (Isl.)
1. someone you cannot marry because of close blood relationship 2. forbidden 3. holy place

mùhāwaɍā̀, mùhawwaɍā̀ *f* 1. argument 2. debate

mùhibbā̀ *f* popularity

muhìmmancì *m* 1. importance 2. mài muhìmmancì significant

mùhìmmì *m* (*f* mùhimmìyā, *pl* mùhìmmai) important

mùjādalā̀ *f* 1. argument 2. dispute

mùjādàlī *m* (pol.) opponent

mùjaddàdì *m* (*pl* mùjàddàdai) (Isl.) reformer

mùjallà̀ *f* (*pl* mujallōlì) 1. magazine 2. mùjallàɍ watà-watà monthly magazine

mùjaɍɍàbì *m* (*f* mùjaɍɍàbā) well-tried

mùjāzà̀ *f* means

mūjìyā *f* (*pl* mūjiyōyì) owl

mukà, mu kà *pl relative completive* we

mùkā'àbì *m* 1. square 2. rectangle

mukàn, mu kàn *pl habitual* we

mukè̀, mu kè̀ *pl relative continuous* we

mukù to/for you

mùƙaddàs, mùƙaddàshì *m* (*pl* mùƙàddàsai) 1. deputy 2. representative

Mùƙaddàshin Bàbban Kwàmishìnà̀ *m* Deputy High Commissioner

mùƙaddàmā *f* introduction

mùƙāmì *m* 1. position 2. status

muƙāmuƙì *m* (*pl* mùƙàmùƙai) jaw

mùƙāɍàbì, mùƙaɍɍàbì *m* crony

mūƙèwā *m* shā mūƙèwā to decline

mùƙù-muƙū *m* acting covertly

mûl *m* (Nr) mould

mùlkā *v2** to rule

mulkì 1. rule 2. government 3. authority 4. regime 5. control 6. power 7. tsārìn mulkì constitution

mulkìn danniyā *m* totalitarianism

mulkìn kâi *m* 1. independence 2. self-government

mulkìn kàmā kàryā *m* 1. totalitarianism 2. dictatorship

mulkìn màllakā *m* 1. colonialism 2. colonial rule 3. imperialism

mulkìn rinjāyè̀ *m* majority rule

mulkìn sōjà *m* military regime

mulmùlā *v1* 1. to knead 2. ma'aikataɍ mulmùlà ƙarfè steelmill

mulmùlà ƙaràfā *m* steelmaking

mulūkiyà̀ *f* monarchy

mumbàɍì *m* (Isl.) pulpit

mūmìnì *m* (*f* mūmìnā, *pl* mùmìnai) (Isl.) believer

mummuƙè̀ *m* jaw

mùmmūnā *m/f* (*pl* mūnànā) 1. bad 2. evil 3. ugly

mùmmūnàɍ màtsalā̀ *f* crisis

mummunancì *m* niceness

mummūnancì *m* 1. ugliness 2. evil

mun *pl completive* we

munà̀, mu nà̀ *pl continuous* we

munāfùkì *m* (*f* munāfùkā, *pl* mùnàfùkai) 1. hypocrite 2. traitor

munāfuncì *m* 1. hypocrisy 2. backbiting

mùnàfuntà *v2** (**-ci/cē**) to betray

mūnànà *see* **mùmānā**

munduwā *f* (*pl* **mundàyē**) bracelet

mùnēgàř *m* (Nr) vinegar

mūnì *m* 1. evil 2. ugliness

mùnùwî *m/f* (Nr) midnight

muntàƙā *f* 1. peak 2. extreme

muřà *f* **Muřà yā kāmà ni.** I have caught a cold.

mùřabbà'ī *m* (*f* **mùřabbà'ā**, *pl* **mùřàbbà'ai**) square

mùřabbà'ī mài dārì *m* oblong

mùřabbà'in kìlòmìtà *m/f* square kilometre

mùřābùs *m* 1. retirement 2. resignation 3. abdication (**dàgà** from)

mùřādì *m* 1. desire 2. requirement

muřďà *vI*, **muřďē** *v4* to twist

muřďēďè *m* (*f* **muřďēďìyā**, *pl* **muřďà-muřďà**) 1. muscular 2. burly

murfì *m* (*pl* **mùrfai**) cover

murfù, murhù *m* (*pl* **muràfū**) 1. stove 2. fire for cooking

mùřjānì *m* coral

murƙushē *v4* to crush

mùřmùshì *m* 1. smile 2. **yi mùřmùshì** to smile

muřnà 1. happiness 2. pleasure 3. **yi wà... muřnà** to congratulate

murtsùkē *v4* to squash

muřtùkē *v4* to stir up

muryà *f* (*pl* **muryōyì**) 1. voice 2. sound 3. tune

murzà *vI* 1. to rub 2. to massage

mùrzā *f* massage

musà *vI* to deny

mùsabbàbì *m* reason

mùsāfahà *f* **Yā yi mùsāfahà dà ni.** He shook hands with me.

mùsākì *m* (*pl* **mùsàkai**) leper

mùsammàn *adv* 1. especially 2. in one's own right 3. **na mùsammàn** special 4. **ƙasā ta mùsammàn** a sovereign state

mùsanyā *see* **mùsāyā**

mùsāyā *f* exchange

mùsāyà *v2** to exchange

mùsāyař àlbàřkàtū *f* 1. barter 2. **kuďàďen mùsāyā na ƙètarè** foreign exchange

mùsāyař cî gàban fàsāhà *m* technology transfer

mùsāyař řa'ayōyì *f* exchange of opinion

mùshe, mùshe *m* (Nr) 1. educated person 2. official 3. **Mùshe** Mr.

mùshen fàřmàsî *m* (Nr) pharmacist

mushiřìkì *m* (*f* **mushiřìkā**, *pl* **mùshìřìkai**) (Isl.) polytheist

mussà *f* cat

mùsshuwàř *m* (Nr) handkerchief

mùstaƙabùlì *m* future

musù *pl* to/for them

musù *pl* 1. contradiction 2. **yi musùn cêwā** to deny that

mùsùlmi *m* (*f* **mùsùlmā**, *pl* **mùsùlmai**) 1. Muslim 2. **ƙasař mùsùlmi** the Islamic world 3. **wandà bà mùsùlmi ba** non-Muslim

Musulunci *m* Islam

mùsùluntà *v3* to convert to Islam

mutàgādì *m* bumper

mutànē *pl* 1. people 2. *see* **mùtûm**

mutànē dà bâ su dà àlhakī *pl* innocent people
mutù *v* (*f* **mutuwà**) to die
mùtûm *m* (*pl* **mutànē**) 1. man 2. male 3. person 4. (*f* **mùtūnìyā**) native (of)
mùtum-mùtumī *m* effigy
mutuncì *m* 1. decency 2. reputation 3. **ci mutuncì** to betray 4. **kārè mutuncìn...** to defend the interests of... 5. **mayař dà mutuncì** to restore credibility
mutùntā *vl* 1. to treat with respect 2. to evaluate

mùtùntakà *f* human nature
mutuwà *f* death
mutuwàř ajàlī *f* manslaughter
mù'ùjizà *f* (*pl* **mu'ujizōjī**) (Isl.) miracle of the Prophet
mùwāfakà *f* 1. luck 2. **cim mà mùwāfakà** to strike a deal
mùzakkàřī *m* 1. masculine 2. (*f* **mùzakkàřā**, *pl* **mùzàkkàřai**) energetic
muzgùnâwā *f* **mulkìn muzgùnâwā** iron rule
mùzūrū *m* (*pl* **mùzùrai**) cat
mwâ *pl* indefinite future we
mwi-mwi *adv* twitching of mouth

Nn

na **1.** *relative completive* I
2. (*f* ta, *pl* na) of
nā *completive* I
nâ *indefinite future* I
nā **1.** *negative continuous* I
2. *continuous tense marker*
na'àm! of course!
nà'am! yes!
na-biyu *m* runner-up
nadàkamà *m* very deaf
nàdāmà *f* **1.** regret **2.** worry
nādiřàn *adv* **1.** uncommon
2. rarely
nādìřī *m* (*f* nādìřā, *pl* nàdìřai)
1. rare **2.** rarety
naɗà *v1* **1.** to wrap around **2.** to
appoint
naɗē *v4* **1.** to roll up **2.** to fold **3.**
to turn
naɗēwā *f* summary
naɗì *m* (*pl* nàɗe-nàɗe) **1.**
rolling up **2.** appointing
nāfilà *f* (*pl* nāfilōlī, nāfilfilī)
optional prayers
nagàri *m* (*f* tagàri, *pl*
nagàrgàrū) good
nàgàřtā *f* goodness
nahawù *m* grammar
nàhīsā *f* bad luck
nāhiyà *f* (*pl* nāhiyōyī) **1.**
district **2.** continent
nai = na yi, nā yi
nā'ìbì *m* (*pl* nà'ìbai) deputy
nailàn *m* nylon
naiřà *f* (*pl* naiřōřī) naira
nàjasà *f* **1.** excrement **2.** (Isl.)
unclean

Nàjēřiyà *f* Nigeria
nākà *m* yours
nakàn, na kàn habitual I
nakè, na kè *continuous* I
nākì *f* yours
nàkìyà *f* (*pl* nākiyōyī)
explosives
nàkìyàř dà akà dasà à tèku *f*
sea mine
nàkìyàř dà kè hàɗe dà wayà
f (mil.) mine
nākù *pl* yours
nàƙaltà *v2** (-ci/-cē) to learn
nàƙaltà dà idòn bàsīřà to
view realistically
naƙàsā *v1* to harm
nàƙasà *v3* to be harmed
nàƙasàř ƙwāyōyin jinī *f* sickle
cell anaemia
nàƙàsasshē *m* (*f* nàƙàsasshiyā,
pl nàƙàsàssū) **1.** crippled
2. handicapped **3.** injured
nākudā *f* Tanà nākudà. She is
in labour.
nāmà *m* (*pl* nāmū, nāmōmī)
1. meat **2.** flesh **3.** wild animal
namijì *m* (*f* mazā, *pl* mazàjē)
1. male **2.** masculine **3.** brave
nàmōnìyā *f* pneumonia
nāmù *pl* ours
nan, nàn *adv* **1.** there **2.** that,
those
nân *adv* **1.** here **2.** nân, nàn this,
these
nānàtā *v1* to reiterate
nan dà nan *adv* immediately
nānè *v4* **1.** to seal up **2.** to stick

nan gàba kàɗan *adv* in the near future

nàrkakkē *m* (*f* narkakkìyā, *pl* nàrkàkkū) 1. melted 2. liquid

nàrkakken dàtti *m* liquid waste

narkè *v4* 1. to melt 2. to dissolve

nâs *f* (*pl* nâs-nâs) 1. nurse 2. aikìn nâs nursing

nasà *m* his

nasabà *f* 1. (family) relationship 2. genitive

nasařẽà *f* (*pl* nasařẽōřī) 1. success 2. victory 3. cì nasařà to be victorious/successful

nàsāřa, nàsàřū *pl* Christians

nāsàřè *f* 1. kindergarten 2. nursery school

nàsīhà *f* (*pl* nasīhōhī) advice

nāsù *pl* theirs

nātà *f* hers

nàtìjà *f* result

nàtse *adv* à nàtse calmly

nàtsuwā *f* calmness

nau'ì̃ *m* (*pl* nau'ō'ī) type

nau'ìn hàlittà *m* species

nà'ūřà *f* (*pl* nā'ūřōřī) machine

nā'ūřař aunà sautìn jìkī *f* stethoscope

nà'ūřař tācè hayāƙī exhaust

nausà *v1* 1. to punch 2. to flee

nàusà *v2** (*m* naushì) to punch

naushì *m* blow

nauyī *m* 1. weight 2. heaviness 3. responsibility 4. strain

nawà? 1. how much? 2. how many?

nàwā *f* reluctance

nà̃wa *pro* mine

nawà nawà? how much each?

nazàřī *m* 1. study 2. research 3. investigation 4. mài

nazàřin làbàřai newsreader

nàzàřiyyà *f* theory

nàzařtà *v2** (-ci/-cē) 1. to study 2. to analyse

nē, nè *m* (*f* cē, cè, *pl* nē, nè) am, is, are

nèmā *v2** (*m* nēmā) to look for

nēmā *m* 1. seeking to 2. *see* nèmā

nēsà *adv* far (dà from)

nìsà *see* nēsà

ni, nì *pro* me

nī *pro* I

nìfāƙà *f* evil intent

ni'imà *f* (*pl* ni'imōmī, nì'ìmū) 1. prosperity 2. fertility

Nìjâř *f* Jùmhūřiyàř Nìjiař republic of Niger

Nìjēřiyà *f* Nigeria

Nìjēřiyà, Nìjēřiyà *f* 1. Nigeria 2. ɗan Nìjēřiyà a Nigerian

nìƙà *v1* to grind

ninkà *v1* 1. to fold 2. to multiply

ninkà sàu biyu to double

ninkà sàu huɗu to quadruple

ninkà sàu ukù to triple

ninkì *m* increased amount

nìnƙāyà *f* 1. swimming 2. mài nìnƙāyà swimmer

nīsà *m* 1. distance 2. mài nīsā distant

nìsà *see* nēsà

nìsan mīlōlī *m* mileage

nìsantà *v2** (-ci/-cē) to distance oneself from

nìshāɗì *m* pleasure

nishì *m* yi nishì to moan

nīsō *v6* to approach

nitsař dà *v5* to sink

nitsè *v4* 1. to settle 2. to sink 3. to drown

nitsò *m* swimming underwater

niyyà *f* aim
nōƙè *v4* to draw back
nōmā *m* farming
nōmà *v1* to farm
nōman ban ruwā *m* irrigation farming
nōman rānī *m* dry season farming
nōmè *v4* 1. to farm 2. to weed
nōnò *m* 1. milk 2. female breast
nōnòn gwangwanī *m* dried baby's milk
nōtì *m* (*pl* **nōtōcī**) metal nut
nōtìs *m* notice
nùfā *v2** (*m* **nufì**) 1. to mean 2. to intend 3. to head for
nufì *m* 1. intention 2. **dà nufì** purposely
nukà *v1* to ripen by storing
nūkìliyà *m* 1. nuclear power 2. **na nūkìliyà** nuclear 3. **gwajìn nūkìliyà** nuclear test 4. **tashàr̃ nūkìliyà** nuclear power station

nukur̃à *f* hostility (**dà** to)
numfāshī *m* (*pl* **numfàr̃fashī**)
1. breathing 2. breath 3. **dàukè numfāshī** to hold one's breath
nūnà *v1* (*m* **nūnì**) 1. to show 2. to pretend
nùna *v3* to ripen
nūnì *m* (*pl* **nùne-nùne**) 1. demonstration 2. show 3. exhibition, expo
nūnà baƙin cikì to regret
nūnà bambancì 1. discrimination 2. to discriminate (**wà** against)
nūnà bambancìn launìn fātā *m/f* racial discrimination
nūnà shàkkū to be pessimistic
nūnìn kāyan màsànà'àntū *m* industrial exhibition
nūnìn sōjà *m* show of force
nūnìn sanā'ō'ī *m* trade fair
nutsè *v4* 1. to settle 2. to sink 3. to drown
Nùwambà *m* November

Oo

ōbà *f* 1. excess amount 2. yì ōbà to be in excess

òbàkwât *f* overcoat

ōbà-ōbà *f* 1. walkman 2. walkie-talkie 3. mobile phone

ōbàtayà *f* overtime

ōbìn *m* oven

ōdà *f* (*pl* ōdōjì) 1. order 2. prison sentence

òdàjàbît *m* bleach

ōdàlè *m* (*pl* ōdalōlì) (mil.) aide (de camp)

ōdità *m* (*pl* ōditōcì) auditor

ōdōjì *see* ōdà

ōfàr̃làr̃ *m* (Nr) loudspeaker

òfèr̃ê *m* (Nr) (med.) 1. operation 2. surgery

ōfìs *m* (*gen* ōfìshin, *pl* ōfisōshì) office

ōfìsà, ōfusà *m* (mil.) officer

ōfìshin bā dà làbār̃ì *m* information office

ōfìshin dillancìn aikì *m* employment agency

ōfìshin dillancìn làbàr̃ai *m* news agency

ōfìshin jākadancì *m* embassy

ōfìshin k̃àramar̃ hùkumà *m* town hall

ogànēzà *m/f* (*pl* oganēzōjì) organizer

òho!, òho'o'o! what do I care? òhô! I see!

Òktōbà *m* October

ōmò̀, (Nr) ò̂mô *m* washing powder

òpìtâl *m* (Nr) hospital

ōr̃anjì, or̃anjì *m* (Nr) orange

òtêl *see* hòtêl

ōzà *m* (*pl* ōzōjì) ounce

Rr

ř̃a'àyī *m* (*pl* řa'ayōyī) 1. opinion 2. idea 3. editorial

ř̃a'àyin ɓallèwā *m* separatism

ř̃a'àyin guř̃guzū 1. socialism 2. mài ř̃a'àyin guř̃guzū socialist

ř̃a'àyin rìƙau *m* (pol.) mài ř̃a'àyin rìƙau 1. conservative 2. fundamentalist

ř̃a'àyin sassaucì mài ř̃a'àyin sassaucì (pol.) liberal

rabà *v1* 1. to divide 2. to separate 3. to share out 4. to settle

ràba gař̃damà *f* 1. settlement of a dispute 2. zàɓen ràba gař̃damà referendum

rabè *v4* to distinguish

ràbe *adv* apart

rabì *m* 1. half 2. part

rabì dà rabì *adv* 1. unfinished 2. semi

rabìn *prep* between

Ř̃abī'ù Lāhìř̃ *m* (Isl.) fourth month

Ř̃abī'ù Lawwàl *m* (Isl.) fifth month

ràbō *m* (*pl* ràbe-ràbe) 1. division 2. sharing (out) 3. share 4. separation 5. settlement 6. luck

ràbu *v7* 1. to part (dà from) 2. Mun ràbu. We are divorced.

rāɓā *f* dew

ràɓā *v2** to go close to

rāɓè *v4* to hide behind

ràɓe *adv* hidden

rāɓùkē *v4* to hide oneself

ř̃àdà, (Nr) ř̃àdâř̃ *f* radar

radà *v1* to whisper

ř̃àdàdì *m* agony

radè-radì *m* 1. rumour 2. speculation

ř̃àdì *see* ř̃ā'ì

ř̃àdìyô *m* (Nr) radio

ř̃af *adv* Tā kāmà shi ř̃af. She snatched it up.

ř̃afàlì, ř̃àfàlì *m* referee

ř̃āfànī *m* (*pl* ř̃àfànai) (maternal) uncle

ràfī (*pl* rāfukà, rāfuffukà) 1. stream 2. irrigated field 3. valley

ř̃affō *m* (Nr) 1. rest 2. holiday

ř̃afƙà *v1* to hit (wà s.o.)

ř̃àfkanà *v3* to make a mistake

ř̃afkanà *f* mistake

ř̃afƙè *v4* to deteriorate

ř̃àf-ř̃àf *adv* clapping

ragà *v1* to reduce

ràgā *v2** to decrease

rāgā *f* (*pl* rāgōgī) 1. net 2. netting

ragàmā *f* (*pl* ragamōmì) halter

ragàmař̃ mulkì *f* reins of power

ř̃aga-ř̃aga *adv* yì wà... ř̃aga-ř̃aga 1. to demolish 2. to blow up

ř̃agař̃gàjē *v4* 1. to destroy 2. to be destroyed

ř̃agař̃gàzā *v1* to destroy

ř̃àgàř̃gazà *f* yi ř̃àgàř̃gazà dà to raze to the ground

rāgař tanìs ƒ tennis net

ràgayà ƒ (pl ràgàyū, rāgayōyī) hanger

řàgayyà ƒ respect

ragè v4 1. to reduce 2. to shorten 3. to leave over 4. to be left over 5. to fall short 6. to be outstanding

ragè dařajař kudì (fin.) to devalue

ragè yawàn màkàmai m arms reduction

ragì m (pl ràge-ràge) 1. reduction 2. discount

ragō m (ƒ raguwā, pl ragwàyē) lazy

ràgō m (pl rāgunà) ram

ràgōwà ƒ remainder

ràguwā ƒ 1. reduction 2. loss

ràguwař àmānà ƒ loss of trust (gà in)

řahà ƒ chatting

řahamà ƒ mercy

řahōtò m 1. report 2. ɗan řahōtò informant 3. spy

řàhūsā ƒ 1. cheapness 2. sale 3. mài řàhūsā cheap

rài m (gen rân, pl rāyukà) 1. life 2. spirit 3. mài rài alive 4. ɓàcìn rài disappointment

řā'ì m 1. theory 2. yì řā'ì to be willing

řā'ìn kâi m na řā'ìn kâi personal

rainà v1 1. to despise 2. to underestimate

ràinā v2* (m ràinō) to look after

rainì m contempt

ràinō see ràinā

ràirayà ƒ tànkàɗē dà ràirayà shake-up

rairàyē v4 1. to sift 2. to screen

ràiràyī m sand

Řajàb m (Isl.) seventh month

rājè v4 to erode

řajimantù m regiment

řajistà ƒ 1. official register 2. record 3. registration 4. yi řajistà to register 5. wàsìkà ta řajistà registered letter

řajistařà m/ƒ registrar

řak adv 1. precisely 2. extremely

rakà v1 1. to accompany 2. to see off 3. to last

řaka'à ƒ (pl řaka'ō'ì) (Isl.) prostration in prayers

řākāɗì m raising one's voice

ràkē m sugar cane

řākèt m (spor.) racket

rākì m cowardice

rakiyà ƒ escorting

řàkōdà ƒ tape recorder

řaƙas adv crack!

raƙe-raƙe adv bulging

ràƙumi m (ƒ ràƙumā, pl rāƙumà) camel

ràƙumin ruwā m wave

ràƙumin dawà m giraffe

řaƙwas adv crack!

řam adv firmly

ramà ƒ hemp

rāmà v1 1. to retaliate 2. to take revenge (wà on)

Řàmàlân m (Isl.) Ramadan (ninth month)

ràmammē m (ƒ ràmammiyā, pl ràmàmmū) skinny

řàmârk ƒ (Nr) lorry

rāmè v4 to become emaciated

řamfùwân m (Nr) roundabout

rāmì m (pl rāmukà) hole

rāmìn kūrā m stronghold

rāmuwā ƒ 1. retaliation 2. revenge

rāmuwaṙ gayyà f retaliation
ran see **rānā**
rân see **râi**
rāna adv dà rāna in/by the day
rānā f (gen **rānaṙ, ran,** pl **rànàikū**) 1. sun 2. day 3. date 4. sâ rānā to make an appointment
rānā-rānā adv from time to time
rānaṙ haihùwā f birthday
rānaṙ jùyàyī f day of remembrance
ràncē m 1. borrowing 2. loan
ràndā f (pl **randunà**) water pot
ṙângādì m 1. official tour 2. sentry duty 3. **mài ṙângādì** sentry
rangamaṙ dà v5 to pay in kind
ràngwadà f swaying
rangwamè m 1. reduction 2. bargain 3. clemency
ran hūtū f holiday
rānī m dry season
ṙanjì m (mil.) range
ṙankì m rank
ràntā v2* (-ci/cē) to borrow
rântā v1 to lend
rantsaṙ dà v5 1. to put under oath 2. to swear into office
rantsè v4 to swear (dà by)
rantsùwā f 1. oath 2. affidavit
rantsùwā bisà (kân) ƙaryā f perjury
ṙànyô m (Nr) meeting
ṙārā f surplus
ṙāraṙ àmfànin gōnā f agricultural surplus
ṙāraṙ cìnikī f 1. trade surplus 2. balance of trade
ràrakà v2* to rout
rāriyā f (pl **rāriyōyī**) 1. drain 2. sieve

rarràbā v1 to share out
rarràbē v4 1. to distinguish 2. to recognize (dà s.o.)
ràrràbu v7 to be divided
rarràfā v1 to crawl
ràrràfē m crawling
rarrāshì m persuasion
ràrraunā m/f (pl **raunànā**) 1. weak 2. injured
ràrumà v2* to snatch
ṙas adv completely
rasà̀ v1 (m **rashì**) 1. to lack 2. to be unable to
rasà rậi to lose one's life
rasà yaddà to not know what to do
Ṙāshà f Russia
ṙashawā f bribe
ṙāshè v4 to linger
rashì m 1. lack 2. shortage 3. loss 4. An yi rashì. There's been a death.
rashìn àbinci mài àmfànī à jikà m malnutrition
rashìn aikì, rashìn aikìn yî m unemployment
rashìn cîn nasaṙà m failure
rashìn dàidàituwā m discrepancy
rashìn dằ'à m indiscipline
rashìn kunyà m impudence
rashìn ƙarfī m weakness
rashìn lāfìyà m illness
rashìn zaman lāfiyà m discontent
ṙashô m cooker
ṙàsît, ṙàsīdì m/f (pl **ṙàsìtai**) receipt, (US) sales slip
rậssā see **rēshè**
ràsu v7 to die
Ṙàsūlùllāhì m the Messenger of God, Muhammad

ràsuwā *m* death

rātā *f* 1. advantage 2. (spor.) headstart

r̃atata *adv* scattered about

rātàyā *vl* to hang

ràtayà *v3* to depend (dà on)

rātàyē *v4* to hang a criminal

rātsǎ *vl* 1. to pass through 2. to insult

rātsè *v4* 1. to stray 2. to divert

rātsì *m* stripe

r̃attàbā *vl* 1. to organise 2. to put in order 3. to report fully

r̃attàbà hannū kân yàr̃jējēnìyā to sign a treaty

r̃au *adv* perfectly

rau dà *see* rawar̃ dà

r̃auji *m* clapping

raunànā *vl* to weaken

raunǎnā *see* ràrraunā

ràunanà *v3* to get weak

raunī *m* 1. weakness 2. suppleness

ràunī *m* (*pl* raunukà) 1. injury 2. mài ràunī casualty 3. yi/ji wà... ràunī to injure

raushì *m* slapping hands

rawā *f* (*pl* ràye-ràye) 1. dance 2. dancing 3. shaking 4. wobbling

rawar̃ dājì *f* (mil.) manoeuvres

rawar̃ dājì à tèku *f* naval manoeuvres

rawar̃ ganì *f* yi rawar̃ ganì to set a good example

rawar̃ jìkī *f* 1. trembling 2. shivering

rawar̃ sōjà *f* (mil.) drill

rawànī *m* (*pl* rawunà) turban

rawar̃ dà *v5* to shake

ràwayà *m/f* (*pl* ràwàyū) yellow

r̃awùll *m* roundabout

rayà *vl* to tempt

rāyà *vl* to revive

rāyà bir̃ânē urban development

rāyà kàrkarā *f* rural development

rāyà k̃asā (ec.) 1. *f* development 2. *vl* to develop a country

ràye-ràye *see* rawā

ràye *adv* à ràye 1. alive 2. live

ràyu *v7* to prosper

rāyukà *see* râi

ràyuwā *f* 1. life 2. existence 3. à fannìn sha'ànin ràyuwā social

ràyuwar̃ jàma'à *f* ilìmin ràyuwar̃ jàma'à social science

rāzànā *vl* to terrify

ràzanà *v3* to be terrified

r̃azdàn *m* (*pl* r̃azdōdī) (administrative) resident

razgè *v4* 1. to snap off 2. to burn up

r̃àzùwâr̃ *m* (Nr) razor

r̃ēdiyò *m/f* (*pl* r̃ēdiyōyī) radio

r̃ēdiyò mài hòtō *m/f* television

r̃ēɗè *v4* to slice up

r̃ēgìl *f* (Nr) ruler

r̃ēhùl *m* 1. raffle 2. gidan r̃ēhùl gambling house

r̃ektà *m* (*pl* rektōcī) rector

r̃ēlùwè, r̃ēlùwài *f* railway

rēmā *m* (*pl* rēmàyē) hyrax

rēnà *vl* 1. to despise 2. to underestimate

rènā *v2** (*m* rènō) to look after

rēnì *m* contempt

rènō *m* 1. k̃asā rènon Ingìlà anglophone country 2. k̃asā rènon Fàr̃ansà francophone country 2. *see* rènā

rēr̃à *vl* to sing

rēshè *m* (*pl* ràssā) 1. branch 2. section

r̄esh̄ô *m* (Nr) cooker

r̄esî *m* (Nr) 1. ticket 2. receipt, (US) sales slip

r̄esuwâl *m* (Nr) metal spring

r̄etô *m* yi r̄etô to hang down

r̄ezà *f* (*pl* r̄ezōji) 1. razor 2. razor blade

r̄ibà *f* (*pl* r̄ibàce-r̄ibàce) 1. profit 2. ci r̄ibà to profit (dàgà from) 3. kāwō r̄ibà gà to benefit

r̄ibâs *m* 1. reverse gear 2. yi r̄ibâs to reverse

ribɗà *v1* 1. to do a lot of 2. to collapse

rìbìbî *m* 1. clamour 2. scramble

r̄ibô *m* rivet

ribà, ribànyā *v1* 1. to multiply 2. to be more than

rìbanyà *v3* 1. to be multiplied 2. to escalate

rìbanyà sàu biyu to be doubled

rìbanyà sàu huɗu to be quadrupled

rìbanyà sàu ukù to be tripled

r̄iddā *f* (Isl.) 1. blasphemy 2. apostasy

r̄ìdô *m* (Nr) door curtain

r̄idî *m* beniseed

r̄if *adv* shut tight

rigā, rìgāyà *v* 1. Sun rigā mù tàfiyà. They went before we did. 2. Sun rigā sun tàfi. They have already gone.

rìgā *f* (*pl* r̄igunà) gown

rìgàkafî *m* 1. prevention 2. precaution 3. àllūr̄ar̄ rìgàkafî vaccination

rìgar̄ mātā *f* dress

rìgar̄ ruwa *f* raincoat

rìgāyà *see* rigā

rige *m* yi rige to compete

rìgimà *f* (*pl* rìgìngìmū, rigimōmī) 1. uproar 2. noisiness 3. quarrelling

rigunà *see* rìgā

rijìyā *f* (*pl* rijiyōyī) well

rijìyar̄ gwajìn nēman mâi *f* test well

rijìyar̄ hàƙar̄ mâi *f* oil well

rikìcē *v4* to get tangled

rìkicî *m* 1. intrigue 2. conflict 3. dispute

rikìɗā *v1* to confuse

rìkiɗà *v3* to be transformed

rìkìr̄kiɗà *f* transformation

rikitâr̄wā *f* mài rikitâr̄wā conflicting

rikitō *v6* to plunge (dàgà from)

r̄ikùmàndê *m* 1. yi r̄ikùmàndê to register 2. lētìr̄ r̄ikùmàndê registered letter

rikà *v1* to keep on doing

rìka *v3* 1. to ripen 2. to prosper

rìƙā *v2** (*m* rìƙò) to look after well

rìƙaƙƙē *m* (*f* rìƙaƙƙiyā, *pl* rìƙàƙƙū) 1. established 2. notorious

rìƙau *adv* (pol.) 1. manufar̄ rìƙau conservatism 2. mài r̄a'àyin rìƙau reactionary 3. right-wing 4. conservative

rìƙē *v4* (*m* rìƙò) 1. to hold 2. to keep 3. to maintain

rìƙe dà *adv* in possession of

rìƙò *m* ɗan rìƙò, 'yar̄ rìƙò adopted child

r̄im *adv* crash!

rimî *m* (*pl* rimàyē) kapok tree

r̄imìs-r̄imìs *adv* crunch!

rinà *v1* (*m* rinì) to dye

rinā *f/pl* hornet

r̄ingì *m* piston ring

rìnjāyà *v3* to predominate
rìnjāyà *v2** 1. to overcome
2. to convince
rinjāyè *m* 1. dominance 2. (pol.)
màsu rìnjāyè majority
3. maràs rinjāyè minority
4. mulkìin rinjāyè majority
rule 5. àl'ummà maràs
rinjāyè ethnic minority
rintṑ *m* cheating
rintsà *vl* to nap
rintsà idṑ to squint
rìskā *v2** to catch hold of
r̄ìtāyà *f* 1. retirement 2. mài
r̄ìtāyà pensioner 3. yi r̄ìtāyà to
retire
r̄ìtāyàr̄ dōlè *f* compulsory
retirement
ritsà *vl* to surround
r̄iyà *vl* 1. to conclude 2. to tempt
(wà s.o.)
r̄ìyā *f* deceit
r̄ôb *f* (Nr) dress
rōbà *f* (*pl* rōbōbī) 1. plastic
2. rubber 3. condom
rōgò *m* cassava
r̄ōkà *m/f* (*pl* r̄ōkōkī) 1. rocket
2. missile
r̄ṑk̄ā *v2** (*m* r̄ṑk̄ō) 1. to request
2. to beg
r̄ṑk̄on gàfar̄à *m* apology
r̄ôm *m* (Nr) rum
rōmō *m* broth
rōmon bakà *m* 1. empty words
2. insincerity
r̄ṑrā *v2** (*m* rōrṑ) 1. to harvest
2. to collect
r̄ṑtī *m* (Nr) roast
rōtsà *vl* to smash
rōwà *f* 1. being miserly 2. yi
rōwàr̄ k̄ùr̄ī'à (pol.) to abstain
r̄ūbà *f* boasting

r̄ùb-dà-cikì *adv* face down
r̄ùbùce *adv* à r̄ùbùce 1. written
2. in theory
r̄ubù'ī *m* one quarter
r̄ubùtā *vl* to write
r̄ùbùtū *m* (*pl* r̄ùbùce-r̄ùbùce)
1. writing 2. handwriting
ru6à *vl* to ferment
rù6a *v3* to become fermented
ru6è *v4* to be rotten
rūd̄à *vl* (*m* rùd̄è) 1. to confuse
2. to stir
rùd̄à *v2** (*m* rūd̄ì) to mislead
rùd̄āmī, rùd̄ānī *m* 1. hubbub
2. confusion 3. hālin rùd̄āmī
chaos 4. jāwō rùd̄āmī gà to
endanger
rūd̄àr̄wā *f* mài rūd̄àr̄wā
confusing
rūd̄è *v4* to get confused
rūd̄èwar̄ tsūfā *f* senility
r̄ud̄ù-r̄ùd̄ù *adv* swollen
ru6à *vl* 1. to cover 2. to roof
3. to conceal
rù6a *v3* to be wrapped (dà in)
rù6ā *v2** to hoodwink
rù6ā-rù6ā *f* secrecy
ru6è *v4* (*m* ru6ī) 1. to cover 2. to
close
ru6ī *m* roof
rugā *f* (*pl* rugōgī, rugàgē)
Fulani settlement
rūgà *vl* to rush
r̄ùgùbî *m* (Nr) rugby
rùgùgī *m* 1. rumbling 2. noise
r̄ùgùm *adv* boom!
r̄ùhì, r̄ūhù *m* spirit
r̄ùhūsā *f* cheapness
r̄ukùnī *m* (*pl* r̄ùkùnai) 1. group
2. section 3. share 4. (pol.) bloc
r̄ūlà *f* (*pl* r̄ūlōlī) ruler
R̄ūm *f* Bahàr̄ R̄ūm Mediterranean

rùmbū *m* (*pl* **rumbunà**) corn bin

rùmbun ādànī *m* silo

rùmbun ajìyè mân fētùř *m* oil storage tank

rùmbuzà *v2** (**-ji/ē**) to clutch

rùmfā *f* (*pl* **rumfunà**) 1. shed 2. shelter

rùndunā *f* (*pl* **rundunōnī**) 1. army 2. crowd

rùndunař jiràgen ruwa *f* 1. fleet 2. navy

rùndunař sōjà *f* army

rùngumà 1. *f* embrace 2. community 3. partnership 4. *v2** to embrace 5. to embark on

rungùmē *v4* 1. to embrace 2. to clutch

runtsè *v4* to clench

řuntùmā *v1* to leave together

rūrì *m* 1. roaring 2. wailing

řùřùmā *f* noisy crowd

rūshè *v4* 1. to collapse 2. to demolish 3. to dissolve 4. (fin.) to plummet

rūshè kangiyā to break a blockade

rùshe-rùshe *pl* 1. destruction 2. demolition

rusùnā *v1* to bow

řututu *adv* in abundance

řù'ùyā *f* a vision

ruwa *adv* à ruwa in/into the water

ruwā *m* (*pl* **ruwàyē**) 1. water 2. juice 3. colour 4. blade 5. baƙin ruwā clear/drinking water 6. yi ruwa to rain 7. rìgař ruwa raincoat 8. Bâ ruwānā! It's none of my business! 9. *see* bâ-ruwanmù

řuwàitā *v1* Sun řuwàità làbàřì. They spread the news.

řuwaitō *v6* to carry a report

ruwan dare *adv* universal

ruwan famfò *m* running water

ruwan kudî *m* (fin.) interest

ruwan samà *m* rain

ruwan shâ *m* drinking water

ruwa-ruwa *adv* watery

Ss

sa *m* him

sà *m* 1. his 2. him

sằ *pl negative continuous* they

sâ 1. *pl indefinite future* they 2. *m* (*pl* shānū) bull 3. *v* to put 4. to cause 5. to fix 6. to appoint 7. to wear

sa'ằ *m/f* (*pl* sa'ō'ī) contemporary

sā'ằ *f* (*pl* sā'ō'ī) 1. hour 2. time 3. clock 4. watch 5. luck

sā'ằ-sā'ằ *adv* occasionally

sa'àd dà when

sā'àn nan *conj* 1. then 2. when 3. so 4. in addition

sābằ *vl* 1. to be used to 2. to be in the habit (dà of)

sabàbī *m* reason

sabàbin *prep* on account of

sàbà'in *f* seventy

sâ bàkī to interfere

sabgằ *f* (*pl* sabgōgī) business affairs

sàbìlì dà *conj* on account of

sābìs 1. *m* waiter 2. *f* waitress

sābō *m* (*f* sābuwā, *pl* sàbàbbī, sàbbī) new

sàbō *m* familiarity

sabò dà, sabòdà 1. *conj* because 2. *prep* because of

sābon fasàlin mulkìn màllakằ *m* neo-colonialism

sābon shìgā *m* newcomer

sàbulù, (Nr) sàbulì, sàbunì *m* (*pl* sàbùlai) soap

sābùntā *vl* 1. to renew 2. to modernise

sabằ *vl* 1. to swear by 2. to sling over the shoulder

sāɓà *vl* 1. to miss 2. to vary (wà from) 3. to argue 3. to contravene

sàɓānī *m* disagreement

saɓàttā, saɓàutā *vl* 1. to frustrate 2. to humilate

sāɓà wà *vl* to contravene

sāɓè *v4* to scrape

sàɓō *m* 1. wrongdoing 2. sin

sāɓùlē *v4* to take off

sācè *v4* to steal

sādà *vl* 1. to deliver 2. to introduce (dà to)

sadakằ *f* (*pl* sadakōkī) 1. charity 2. bā dà sadakằ to give alms

sādâr̃wā *f* 1. communications 2. sādâr̃wā ta wayàr̃ iskằ telecommunications 3. kumbòn sādâr̃wā communications satellite

sadâr̃war̃ bāyan tàr̃ō *f* final statement

sadaukar̃ dà *v5* 1. to volunteer 2. to sacrifice

sadaukī *m* (*pl* sàdàukai) courageous

sādà-zùmùntā *f* yi tàron sādà-zùmùntā to have a reunion

saddà *conj* when

saddaƙar̃ cêwā *v5* to believe strongly that

sàdîn *m* sardine

sàdishàn *m* bullshit

sàdu dà *v7* 1. to meet 2. to suit 3. to reach 4. to receive

sàdūdà *v3* to give up
sàduwā *f* sexual relations
sàdãr̃à *f* (*pl* sàdãr̃ū) line (of text)
sàfâ *f* (*pl* sàfâ-sàfâ) bus
sàfā *f* (*pl* sāfōfī) sock
sàfài *adv* bà sàfài ba seldom
sàfar̃ hannū *f* glove
Safar̃ *m* (Isl.) second month
safar̃ā *f* travelling trade
sàfasa *f* stockings
sàfayà *f* 1. spare 2. spare tyre
sāfe *adv* dà sāfe in the morning
sāfir̃ullà! May God forgive me!
sāfiyā *f* morning
sàfiyà *f* *see* sàfayà
sàfiyò *m* surveying
sàgìmâ *m* piston ring
sàhānì *m* (*pl* sàhànai) kettle
Sàhār̃à *f* 1. Sahara Desert 2. à kudù dà Sàhār̃à sub-Saharan
sāhìbī *m* (*f* sāhìbā, *pl* sàhìbai) close companion
sàhīhì *m* (*f* sàhīhìyā, *pl* sàhìhai) 1. honest 2. real 3. healthy
sahū *m* (*pl* sahū-sahū) row
sahū-sahū *adv* in rows
sai 1. then 2. if 3. until 4. unless 5. except (for) 6. than 7. only 8. but (merely) 9. before 10. nevertheless 11. no matter what/how 12. should 13. must
sā'ì *m* 1. time 2. wani sā'ì sometimes
sai dà 1. when 2. not until 3. *see* sayar̃ dà
sà'ìdà *f* 1. luck 2. success
sâ idò to supervise
sàidu *v7* to be sold out
saifā *f* (*pl* saifōfī) 1. spleen 2. cìwòn saifā anthrax

saimō *m* barren land
sā'ì-sā'ì *adv* occasionally
saisàyē *v4* to shear
saisùwā *see* sayâr̃wā
sâiwā (*pl* saiwōyī) root
sājà *m* (*pl* sājōjī) sergeant
sājè dà *v4* 1. to imitate 2. to resemble
sàjē *m* sideburns
sak *adv* straight
sâk *m/f* (Nr) sack
sakà *v1* to lay
sàkā *v2** *see* sakì
sākà *v1* to compensate
sàkàcē *m* tsìnin sàkàcē toothpick
sakacī *m* carelessness
sàkainar̃ kāshì *f* potty
sakà jirgī à ruwā to launch a boat
sâ kâi *v* to volunteer
sàkàmakō *m* 1. compensation 2. result
sakàn *m/pl* second (of time)
sakandàr̃è *f* secondary school, upper secondary school
sàkatà *f* (*pl* sàkàtū) latch
sakatar̃è *m* (*f* sakatar̃ìyā, *pl* sakatar̃ōr̃ì) 1. secretary 2. bàbban sakatar̃è (pol.) permanent secretary
Sakatar̃èn Baitulmālì *m* (US) Treasury Secretary
sakatar̃èn zar̃târ̃wā *f* executive secretary
sàkàtēr̃ìyà, (Nr) sàkàtàr̃ìyâ *f* secretariat
sàkayyà *f* 1. retaliation 2. compensation
sākè *v4* 1. to change 2. to do again
sàke *adv* à sàke released

sākè lāsìn to renew a licence
sākè fařfad̂ôwā *m/f* (ec.)
rebirth
sakì 1. *m* release 2. *v2** (sàki/kē,
m sakì) to release 3. to divorce
4. to fire (wà at) 5. to give up
sakìn jìkì *m* detente
sakìn lāyì *m* paragraph
sākiyā *f* 1. alteration 2.
amendment
sakkò *m/f* (Nr) sack
sako-sako *adv* 1. loosely 2. na
sako-sako loose
sàkôt *f* (Nr) bag
sàkwàf *adv* flapping
sàkwàrā *f* pounded yam
sakwařkwàcē *v4* to slacken
sāƙà *v1* to weave
saƙàmêmař jìkī *f* rigor mortis
sāƙò *m* 1. niche 2. hiding place
sàƙō *m* (*pl* sàƙwànnī) message
sàƙon tayà mufnà *m* message
of congratulation
sal *adv* farī sal snow white
sālà *f* slice
sàlâk *m* salad
sàlāmà *f* 1. relief 2. peace
sàlāmù àlaikùm! peace be
upon you! (*response:* àlaikùm
sàlâm! and upon you!)
sàlansà *f* (*pl* sàlànsū) silencer
sàlātì *m* (Isl.) invoking God's
name
salàtîf *m* sellotape
sālè *v4* to peel
salfà *f* tākìn salfà chemical
fertilizer
sālìhi *m* (*f* sālìhā, *pl* sàlìhai)
honest
sālin-ālin *adv* Mun ràbu sālin-
ālin. We left on good terms.
Sàlìyô *f* Sierra Leone

sàlkā *f* (*pl* salèkanī) water
bottle
sallà *f* 1. (Isl.) one of the five
daily prayers 2. religious
festival 3. Bàbbař Sallà Id al-
Kabir 4. Kàramař Sallà Id al-
Fitr 5. yi sallà to pray
sàllahù *m* message
sallamà *f* greeting
sallàmā *v1* 1. to agree 2. to a
price to give way 3. to
surrender
sàllamà *v2** to dismiss (from
work)
sallatař dà *v5* 1. to lead in
prayer 2. to circumcise
salō *m* 1. style 2. pattern
salon mulkìn jàmhūřiyà *m*
republicanism
salō-salō *adv* of different kinds
salsalà *f* genealogy
sālùɓē *m* to peel
saltē *m* (Nr) filth
sàlûn *f* saloon car
salwàncē *v4*, sàlwantà *v3* to
get lost
sam 1. *v* to give (mà to) 2. *adv*
completely
samà 1. *m* (*pl* sàmmai) sky
2. heaven 3. *adv* up 4. yi samà
to go up
samācì *m* summons
samà dà *prep* 1. above 2. more
than
samà jànnàtî *m* d̂an samà
jànnàtî astronaut
sàmàmē *m* 1. raid 2. d̂an
sàmàmē raider
sàmāniyà *f* sky
sàmanjà *m* (*pl* sāmanjōjī) 1.
sergeant-major 2. non-
commissioned officer (NCO)

sàmàr̃â f (Nr) sandals

sāmar̃ dà v5 1. to produce 2. to provide (gà for) 3. to supply

sàmàr̃ī see sauràyī

samà-samà adv 1. scarcely 2. superficial

sàmà wà vl to provide

sàmbàlmâ m (Nr) (mil.) assembly

sàmbàtū m 1. chit-chat 2. yi sàmbàtū to rave

Sàmdî f (Nr) Saturday

sàmfēfā f sandpaper

samfùr̃ m (pl samfur̃ōr̃ī) 1. model 2. sample 3. pattern

sàmî f (Nr) lorry

sammācì m summons

sàmmakō m early start

samnà m/f (pl samnōnī) incompetent

sāmù v2* (sàmi, sàmi, m sāmù) 1. to get 2. to earn 3. to happen to

sāmù dà lâifī to convict

san see sau, sanì

sànā'à f (pl sanā'ō'ī) 1. profession 2. trade 3. na sànā'à technical

sanàdī m (pl sànàdai) cause

sànàdiyyà f 1. cause 2. à sànàdiyyàr̃ as a result of

sanar̃ dà v5 to inform

sanâr̃wā f 1. announcement 2. notice

sànayyà f knowledge

sàndā f (pl sandunà) 1. stick 2. bar 3. force 4. ɗan sàndā policeman 5. 'yan sàndan kwantar̃ dà tàr̃zòmā riot police

sandà conj when

sandàl m sandals

sàndìkâ f (Nr) trade union

sandâ f stealth

sàne adv aware (dà of)

sànē m experience

sangalī m (pl sàngàlai) shin

sànhû m (Nr) indifference

sanì 1. m knowledge 2. v (san + object) to know

sanìn Allàh m ilìmin sanìn Allàh theology

sanìn gaibì m the unknown

sanìn kōwà nè... it is common knowledge that...

sanìn madafā m know-how

sānìyā f (pl shānū) cow

sànkàrau m meningitis

sanƙè v4 to tuck

sanƙō m baldness

sânnan conj 1. then 2. when 3. so 4. in addition

sànnu f 1. hello! 2. sorry to hear that! 3. slowly please! 4. carefully!

sànnu-sànnu adv slowly

sansàn m census

sansànā vl to smell

sànsanà f (sense of) smell

sànsanī m (pl sansanōnī) military camp

sànsanin gwajìn nūkìliyà m nuclear test site

sànsanin gwālè-gwālè m concentration camp

santàr̃ī, sàntîr̃ m (Nr) belt

santilità f centilitre

santìmītà f centimetre

sàntìnâl m (Nr) sentry

santsī m 1. smoothness 2. slipperiness

sanwicì, (Nr) sànwîc m sandwich

sânyā vl 1. to put 2. to cause 3.

to fix 4. to appoint 5. to wear 6.
to impose (wà on)
sanyàyā *vl* to cool
sanyī *m* 1. cold, coldness 2. **mài**
sanyī cold
sanyin jìkī *m* 1. laziness 2.
slowness
sanyin ƙàshī *m* rheumatism
sanyi-sanyi *adv* lukewarm
sārā *m* (mil.) salute
sārà *vl* (*m* **sārā**) 1. to cut (out)
2. (mil.) to salute (wà s.o.)
sàrā 1. *f* custom 2. slang 3. *v2**
(*m* **sārā**) to chop 4. to bite 5. to
clear 6. to buy wholesale
saɍai *adv* perfectly well
sâ râi 1. *m* hope 2. commitment
3. *v* to be optimistic (à/ à kân
about)
sàràkī *m* (*pl* **sàràkai**) member
of royalty
sarākunà *see* **sarkī**
sàràkuwā *f* (*pl* **sùrùkai**) 1.
mother-in-law 2. daughter-in-
law 3. sister-in-law
sâ rānā to fix a date
sāraɍ dà *v5* to sell wholesale
sararī *m* 1. open space 2. clear
sky
sararin samà, **sararin**
sàmāniyà *m/f* outer space
sàràrraƙà *vl* to be interlinked
saraunìyā *f* (*pl* **sarākunà**)
queen
saraunìyaɍ kyâu *f* beauty queen
sàrautà *f* (*pl* **sàràutū**) 1.
kingship 2. position of emir
3. official position 4. reign
sàɍbētì *m* (Nr) towel
sàɍbîs (Nr) 1. *m* waiter 2. *f*
waitress
sàɍbìyât *see* **sàɍbētì**

sàɍdauna *m* 1. chief prince
2. top official
sàɍdîn *m* (Nr) sardine
sārè *v4* 1. to slash at 2. to run out
3. to give up
sārè dāzuzzukà *f* deforestation
sàrēwà *f* flute
sārì *m* 1. wholesale trade 2. ɗan
sārì wholesaler
sàɍjân *m* (Nr) sergeant
sàɍjan-màjâɍ *m* (Nr) sergeant-
major
sàri-kà-nōƙè *m* ɗan **sàri-kà-**
nōƙè guerrilla
saɍƙè *m/f* (Nr) administrative
district
sarkī *m* (*f* **saraunìyā**, *pl*
sarākunà, **sàràkai**) 1. king
2. emir 3. head 4. ace
sarƙà 1. *f* (*pl* **sarƙōƙī**) chain
2. *vl* to twist
sarƙàfā *vl* to hook (wà onto)
sarƙàfè *v4* to get hooked
sàrƙaƙƙiyā *f* undergrowth
sarƙèwaɍ hakōrā *f* tetanus
saɍɍàfā *vl* 1. to control 2. to rule
3. to process 4. to produce 5. to
manufacture 6. to manipulate
sàɍɍàfaffē *m* (*f* **sàɍɍàfaffiyā**, *pl*
sàɍɍàfàffū) manufactured
sàɍɍàfàffun kāyàyyakī *pl*
manufactured products
sàɍsân *m* (Nr) sergeant
sàɍtìfìkâ *f* (Nr) school certificate
sartsè *m* (*pl* **sarutsà**) splinter
sàɍūshè, **sàɍūshì** *m* (Nr) 1.
military service 2. department
3. aikìn **sàɍūshì** civil service
sāsàntā *vl* 1. to reconcile 2. to
be reconciled
sāsàntâwà *f* 1. reconcilation
2. **mài sāsàntâwà** mediator

sāshè, sāshì *m* (*pl* **sâssā**) 1.
section 2. department 3. sector
4. district

sassàbē *v4* (*m* **sàssàbē**) to clear
(land)

sàssàbē *m* land clearance

sassàƙā *v1* to do carpentry

sassàucē *v4* to become loose

sassaucì *m* (pol.) **mài ɍa'àyin
sassaucì** liberal

sàssauƙā *m/f* (*pl* **sauƙàƙā**) 1.
cheap 2. easy-going

sàssauƙan lāmùnì *m* soft loan

sassàutā *v1* 1. to loosen 2. to
ease

sàtā *v2** (**sàci/ē**, *f* **sātà**) to steal

sātà *f* stealing

sāti *m* 1. Saturday 2. week

sàtifikèt *f* (*pl* **sàtìfìkai,
sātifikōkì**) certificate

sàtôf *m* (Nr) 1. stop sign 2. that's
all!

Sàtumbà *m* September

sau *m* (*gen* **san**, *pl* **sāwàyē**) 1.
footprint 2. trace 3. times

sàu *m* multiplied by

sàu ɗaya *adv* once

sàu biyu *adv* twice

sàukā 1. *f* graduation 2. *v2** to
give lodgings to

sàuka *v3* 1. to descend (à/dàgà
from) 2. to subside 3. to fall
4. to arrive 5. to lodge 6. to
register at a hotel

saukaɍ dà *v5* to welcome

saukè *v4* to complete one's
studies

sauƙàƙā *v1* 1. to reduce 2. to
relieve

sàuƙaƙà *v3* to diminish

sauƙì *m* 1. easiness 2. relief
3. scarcity

saunà *m/f* (*pl* **saunōnì**)
incompetent

saura *v* to be left over

saurā *m* 1. remainder 2. other
3. **dà saurā?** is/are there any
left? 4. **ƙarfè huɗu saurā
mintì gōmà** ten minutes to
four o'clock

saurā kàɗan *adv* almost

sauràrā *v1* 1. to listen carefully
2. to wait a while

sàurārà *v2** (*m* **sàuràrē**) 1. to
listen carefully to 2. to wait a
while for 3. (pol.) to hear a bill

sàurārō *m* **màsu sàurārō**
listeners

sauràyī *m* (*pl* **sàmàrī**) young
man

saurī *m* 1. speed 2. **dà saurī**
quickly 3. **yi saurī** to hurry
(up)

saurō *m/pl* 1. mosquito 2. **gidan
saurō** mosquito net

sautì *m* 1. sound 2. **ɗaukàn sautì**
recording

sauyà *v1* 1. to change 2. to
exchange 3. to rotate 4. to
alternate

sauyà rawā to rethink

sauyì *m* 1. change 2. exchange 3.
rotation 4. alternation 5. **mài
nēman sauyì** progressive

sàwābà *f* 1. cheapness 2. relief
3. better days

sàwaɍwàɍì *m* 1. carelessness
2. bad luck

sàwayà *f* transformation

sāwàyē, sāwū *see* **sau**

sàyā *v2** (*m* **sàyē**) to buy

sayaɍ dà *v5* to sell

sàyayyà *f* 1. purchase 2. shopping
3. **yi sàyayyà** to go shopping

sàyē *m* (*pl* sàye-sàye) 1. shopping 2. purchase

sāyè *v4* to cover

sāyì *m* size

sayō à ƙasàshen wàje to import

sayôwā à ƙasàshen wàje *f* import

sàyyê! (Nr) okay!

sè'êjê *f* (Nr) lower secondary school

sêf *m* safe box

shā *v* (*m* shâ) 1. to drink 2. to smoke 3. to eat 4. to experience 5. to suffer 6. to do often

shâ 1. (gōmà) shâ ɗaya... (gōmà) shâ taƙà eleven... nineteen 2. *see* shā

Shà'àbân *m* (Isl.) eighth month

sha'ànī *m* (*pl* sha'anōnī) 1. matter 2. affair 3. dealings

sha'ànin gidā *m* internal affairs

sha'ànin sōjà *m* military affairs

shà'awā *f* (*pl* shà'àwàce-shà'àwàce) 1. interest 2. liking 3. mài ban shà'awā interesting

shācì *m* 1. plan 2. sketch 3. blueprint 4. zone

shàci-fàdì *m* mere speculation

shā dà *see* shayaƙ dà

shâddā *f* (*pl* shaddōdī) cesspit

shàddadà *v3* to be severe

shaɗaƙà *f* sentence

shaf *adv* completely

shāfà *v1* to rub (à on)

shâfà 1. *f* concern 2. *v2** to wipe 3. to coax 4. to affect

shāfà faraƙ ƙasā to whitewash

shāfanà *f* pencil sharpener

shāfè *v4* 1. to paint 2. to plaster 3. to wipe out

shàfē *m* 1. painting 2. plastering

shàfe-shàfe *pl* making oneself up

shāfì *m* (*pl* shāfuffukà) 1. page 2. coat of paint

shàfô *m* (Nr) hat

shàgālà *v3* to be occupied (dà with)

shagalaƙ dà *v5* to distract (dàgà from)

shagàlī *m* (*pl* shagulgulà) 1. party 2. festivity 3. ceremonial occasion

shàgàltu *v7* to be preoccupied (dà with)

shāgìɗē *v4* to be crooked

shāgò *m* 1. workshop 2. shop 3. kiosk 4. showroom

shāgòn canzà kuɗî *m* bureau de change

shàgùɓē *m* 1. innuendo 2. hint

shagwàɓā *v1* to spoil

shàhādà *f* (*pl* shahādōdī) 1. certificate 2. (Isl.) martyrdom 3. kalmàƙ shàhādà Muslim creed

shàhaƙà *v3* to be famous

shàhīdì *m* (*f* shàhīdà, *pl* shàhìdai) (Isl.) martyr

shāhò *m* (*pl* shāhunà) hawk

shai'àn *adv* (not) a word

shaidà *m/f* (*pl* shàidū) 1. witness 2. evidence 3. sign

shâidā *v1* 1. to give evidence 2. to inform (wà s.o.)

shaidàƙ biyà *f* receipt

shaidàƙ zûƙ *f* perjury

shàidân *m* (*f* shàidānìyā, *pl* shàidānū) 1. devil 2. Satan

shaihù *m see* shēhù

shaihùn màlàmī *m* professor

shakàsōɓà *f* shock absorber

shakkà *f* (*pl* **shàkkū**) 1. doubt
2. **bâ shakkà** without doubt 3.
nūnà shàkkū to be pessimistic
shâƙā *v2** to smell
shāƙaƀ dà *v5* to breathe
shāƙàtā *vl* to rest
shāƙàtâwā *f* **yâwòn shāƙàtâwā**
tour
shāƙè *v4* 1. to cram 2. to choke
shàƙīƙì *m* (*f* **shàƙīƙìyā**, *pl*
shàƙìƙai) 1. full brother, full
sister 2. crony
shàƙiyyì *m* (*f* **shàƙiyyìyā**, *pl*
shàƙìyyai) rogue
shâƙu *v7* to be fond (**dà** of)
shaƙuwà *f* **yi shaƙuwà** to
hiccough
shàmakì *m* (*pl* **shàmàkai**) 1.
stables 2. tethering post
shàmbûƀ *m* (Nr) inner tube
shàmfâmâ *f* (Nr) silencer
shā mūƙèwā *m* decline
shàmfû *m* shampoo
shàmmatà *v2** (**-ci/cē**) 1. to
trick 2. to catch unawares
shàmuwā *f* stork
shā iskà to take a stroll
shantàkē *v4* 1. to stall 2. to
dawdle 3. to procrastinate
shānū *see* **sâ, sānìyā**
shanyà *f* (Nr) **yi shanyà** to glide
shânyà *vl* (*f* **shanyà**) to leave
out to dry
shânyē *v4* 1. to drink up 2. to
endure
shânyêwaƀ jìkī *f* (med.) stroke
shārà *vl* to do a lot of
shàrā *f* 1. rubbish 2. waste 3.
kwàndon shàrā rubbish bin 4.
zubaƀ dà shàrā to dump waste
shafàdì *m* (*pl* **shaƀudà̀,**
shaƀudɗà̀) 1. agreement

2. condition 3. stipulation 4. **bâ
shaƀàdì** unconditional
shafaf *adv* drenched
**shàrā mài gubà̀, shàrā mài
illà̀** *f* 1. toxic waste 2.
chemical waste
shàraƀ màsànà'àntū mài illà̀
f industrial waste
shàraƀ nūkìliyà̀ *f* nuclear waste
shaƀ dà kwàmbâ *m* (Nr) (mil.)
tank
shārè *v4* (*f* **shàrā**) 1. to sweep
2. to clear away
shaƀhàntā *vl* 1. to explain 2. to
comment on
shaƀhì *m* (*pl* **shaƀhōhī**) written
commentary
shàri'à̀ *f* (*pl* **shari'ō'ī**) (Isl.)
law
shàrīf, shàrīfì *m* (*f* **shàrīfìyā**,
pl **shàrìfai**) (Isl.) descendant
of the Prophet
shàrjê *m* (Nr) charge
shaƀrì *m* evil
shartù *m* close friend
shaƀuɗɗà̀ *pl* terms
shaƀuɗɗàn sìyāsà̀ *pl* political
considerations
shaƀuɗɗàn yàrjējēnìyā terms
of agreement
shāshàcē *v4* to disappear
shāshancì stupidity
shāshàshā *m/f* (*pl* **shàshàshai**)
stupid
shâsshāwà̀ *f* (Nr) 1.
immunisation 2. vaccination 3.
yi wa.. shâsshāwà̀ to vaccinate
shatà̀ *f* **yi shatà̀** to charter
shātà̀ *vl* (*m* **shācì**) 1. to mark
out 2. to sketch 3. to plan out
4. to outline 5. to reconnoitre
6. to orbit

shāwà *f* shower

shàwāgì *m* yi shàwāgì to hover

shāwarà *f* (*pl* shāwàŕwaŕī, shàwàŕce-shàwàŕce) 1. advice 2. decision 3. recommendation 4. (med.) jaundice 5. yellow fever 6. yi shāwarà à kân 7. yankè shāwarà to discuss to resolve

shāwàrākì *m* (*pl* shàwàràkai) irresponsible

shāwàŕwaŕī *pl* 1. talks 2. negotiations 3. katsè shāwàŕwaŕī to break off discussions

shāwàŕwaŕin kwancè dàmarà *pl* disarmament talks

shāwàŕwaŕin sulhù *pl* peace talks

shāwàŕwaŕī na shārè fagē *pl* preparatory talks

shàwaŕtà *v2** (-ci/cē) 1. to advise 2. to consult

shāwàŕwaŕī *pl* yi shāwàŕwaŕī to negotiate

shāwō kâi *v6* 1. to convince 2. to resolve

Shàwwâl *m* (Isl.) tenth month

shayaŕ dà *v5* 1. to water 2. to irrigate 3. to suckle

shàye-shàye *m/pl* drinks

shāyì *m* tea

shēbùŕ *m* (*pl* shēbuŕōŕī) shovel

shēdì *m* goods-shed

shègàntakà *f* 1. obstinacy 2. rudeness

shēgè *m* (*f* shēgìyā, *pl* shēgū) 1. illegimate child, bastard 2. rude

shēhù *m* (*f* shēhùwā, *pl* shēhùnnai) 1. religious scholar 2. professor

shèkarà *f* (*pl* shèkàrū) 1. year 2. age

shēkaranjiyà *f/adv* day before yesterday

shèkaràŕ kasàfin kudî *f* fiscal year

shèkarà-shèkarà *adv* 1. annually 2. na shèkarà-shèkarà annual

shēƙà *v1* 1. to winnow 2. to pour 3. to do well

shèƙā 1. *f* (*pl* shēƙunà) nest 2. canzà shèƙā to defect 3. *v2** to inhale

shēƙà Lāhiŕà to die

shèƙè ayā to have a good time

shèƙèƙē *adv* contemptuously

shèlà *f* 1. proclamation 2. yi shèlà to make a proclamation (à kân/wai that)

shērà ƙaryā *v1* to tell a lie

shèrā *v2** (*f* shèrā), shērè *v4* to be attractive to

shi, shì *m* him

shī *m* he

shibtà *f* dictation

shidà *f* 1. six 2. na shidà sixth

shìftamā *f* drivel

shìga *v3* 1. to enter 2. to put on 3. to reach 4. to start

shìgā *f* 1. entry 2. opportunity

shìga mutànē to mingle

shìgaŕ buŕtū *f* private investigation

shigè *v4* 1. to pass by 2. to exceed 3. to enter

shìgē *m* resemblance

shigēgè *m* 1. intervention 2. yi shigēgè to intervene

shìgi dà fici *m* restlessness

shigō dà *v6* 1. to introduce 2. to import

shikà *see* sakì
shìkàshìkai *see* shisshikè
shi kè nan okay
shíƙà *see* shéƙà
shillò *m* swinging
shimfìɗà *v1* 1. to spread 2. to establish
shìmfìɗà *f* introduction
shìmî *m* 1. slip 2. blouse
shin...? I wonder whether...?
shinà *v1* Ĩ, nā shinà! Yes, I know!
shingē *m* (*pl* shingàyē) 1. fence 2. yankìn cìnìkayyà marà shingē free trade zone 3. yi bàbban shingē to form a united front 4. à bāyan shingē behind the scenes
shingì *m* remainder
shìnkāfà *f* rice
shinkù *m* (Nr) five franc coin
shirgà *v1* to overdo
shirgì *m* pile
shirì *m* (*pl* shìrye-shìrye) 1. preparation 2. plan 3. settlement 4. project 5. draft 6. yi shirì to make preparations 7. *see* shiryà
shirìn bìncìkē *m* research programme
shirìn dòkā *m* parliamentary bill
shirìn faɍfaɗò dà ƙasā *m* national recovery programme
shirìn faɍfaɗò dà tattalin aɍzìkì structural adjustment programme (SAP)
shirìn tsārìn mulkì *m* draft constitution
shirìn ɍēdiyò *m* radio programme
shìrìrìtà *f* yi shìrìrìtà 1. to stall 2. to procrastinate

shiɍkà *f* partnership
shirū *m* silence
shiryà *v1* (*m* shirì) 1. to prepare 2. to arrange 3. to settle
shìryayyē *m* (*f* shìryayyiyā, *pl* shìryàyyū) arranged
shìrye-shìrye *pl* 1. plans 2. preparations 3. *see* shirì
shìrye-shìryen gaggāwā *pl* contingency plans
shisshigī *m* 1. intervention 2. yi shisshigī to intervene
shisshikè *m* (*pl* shìkàshìkai) pillar
shiyyà *f* 1. direction 2. sector 3. region
shòlishò *m* (liquid) solution
shôt *m* yi shôt to fall short
shūcì *m* thatch
shūɗè *v4* to pass by
shūɗì *m* (*f* shūɗìyā, *pl* shûɗɗà) blue
shùgàbā *m/f* (*pl* shùgàbànnī) 1. leader 2. head 3. president 4. chairman, chairwoman 5. yi shùgàban tàrō to chair a meeting
shùgàba mài cìkakken ìkò *m* executive president
shūgabancì *m* leadership
shùgàban gwamnatì *m* leader of the government
shùgàban màjàlisà *m* speaker (of parliament)
Shùgàban Màjàlisàɍ 'Dinkìn Dūniyà *m* Secretary General of the United Nations
shùgàbantà *v2* 1. to lead 2. to preside over
shùgàban tàrō *m* chairman
shūkà 1. *f* (*pl* shùke-shùke) sowing 2. crop(s) 3. *v1* to sow

shûmēkà *m* (*pl* shūmēkōkī)
shoemaker
shūni *m* 1. indigo 2. màì hannū
dà shūni bourgeois
shunkù *m* (Nr) five franc coin
shūrà *vl* (*m* shūrì) to kick
shūrè *v4* to kick over
shūrì *m* kick
shûshainà *m* shoeshiner
shûshāyè, shûshāyì *m*
shoeshine
shu'ùmī *m* (*f* shu'ùmā, *pl*
shù'ùmai) haunted
sī'aidî *m* secret police
sìddabaﬁù *m* conjuring
sidìk *adv* baﬁi sidìk jet black
siffà, sifà *f* (*pl* siﬀōfī) 1. form
2. description 3. adjective
sifētô *m* (*pl* sifētōcī) police
inspector
sìﬁkà *m* speaker of parliament
sìfīkìn *m* ɗan sìfīkìn 1. neat
2. fashionable
sìﬁlì *m* gears
sifìﬁ *m* zero
sìﬁﬁn *m* 1. metal spring 2. hire
sìfīﬁtà *v2** (-ci/ē) to hire
sīgà *f* (*pl* sīgōgì) 1. shape
2. version 3. structure 4. clause
5. proviso
sìgāﬁ *m*, (Nr) sìgàﬁatì *f*
cigarette
siginà, sìgìnà *f* 1. signal 2. sign
3. indicator light
sihìﬁi *m* (*pl* sìhìﬁce-sìhìﬁce)
magic
sīhulē *m* (Nr) whistle
sìkāwùt, ɗan sìkāwùt *m* (*pl*
'yan sìkāwùt) boy scout
sìkēlì *m* (*pl* sikēlōlì) scales
sìkêt *m* skirt
sikinkìlà *m* second class

sìkōsè *see* sìkwāsè
Sìkotlàn *f* Scotland
sìkwāsè *m* (spor.) squash
silà *f* immediate cause
silifà *m* slippers
sìlikì *m* (*pl* sìlìkai) silk
sìlìmân *m* cinema
sìlìn *m* ceiling
sìlô *m* 1. slow 2. slowness
sìmﬂô *m* semaphor
sìmintì, (Nr) sìmâ *m* 1. cement
2. concrete
sìmōgà *see* sùmōgà
Sin *m* China
sìnādàﬁ *m* 1. solder 2. chemical
singa *f* saloon car
singìlà *m* signaller
singìlētì *m* (*pl* singilētōcī) 1.
vest 2. tee-shirt
sinìmà *f* cinema
sintàlì *m* (*pl* sìntulà) kettle
sintìﬁ, sintìﬁ *m* 1. sentry duty
2. ɗan sintìﬁ sentry 3. 'yan
sintìﬁ patrol 4. yi sintìﬁ to
patrol
sìnyê *m* (Nr) 1. signature
2. signing
sìﬁàﬁà *see* sìﬁﬁ
sìﬁdì *m* (*pl* sìﬁàdā) saddle
sìﬁnjì *m* syringe
sìﬁﬁ *m* (*f* sìﬁﬁìyā, *pl* sìﬁàﬁā)
slender
sìﬁô *m* (Nr) syrup
sìﬁﬁ *m* secret
sisì *m* five kobo
sistà *f* (*pl* sìstōcī) nurse
sìtâm *m* stamp
sìtansìl *m* stencil
sìtâﬁ *f* (Nr) tanker lorry
sìtātà *f* car starter
sìtātì *m* yi sìtātì to be neat
sìtēfìlà *f* stapler

sìtēmàn *m* (fin.) statement
sìtìr̃à *f* (*pl* sìtìr̃ū) clothing
sìtìr̃iyò *m* stereo
sìtìyār̃ì *m* steering wheel
sìtô *m* (*pl* sìtô-sìtô) storeroom
sittà *f* 1. six thousand 2. *see* sistà
sìttìn *f* sixty
sìyāsà *f* 1. politics 2. na sìyāsà political 3. ɗan sìyāsà politician 4. masànin ilìmin sìyāsà political scientist
so *v* (*m* sô) 1. to like 2. to love
sô *m* 1. liking 2. love 3. àbin sô ·something loved 4. (Nr) bucket
sōcì *f* 1. socks 2. stockings 3. tee-shirt 4. jersey
sōdà *f* 1. soda 2. mineral water 3. soap 4. solder
sōdè *v4* (Nr) to solder
sòdê *m* (Nr) solder
sōjà *m* (*pl* sōjōjì) 1. soldier 2. army 3. military training 4. na sōjà military
sōjàn gōnā *m* impostor
sōjàn hayà *m* mercenary
sōjì *m/pl* 1. soldier 2. army 3. *see* sōjōji
sōjōjì *pl* 1. troops 2. forces 3. militia 4. guard 5. *see* sōjà
sōjōjin māmayē *pl* occupying forces
sōkà wà *v1* to stab
sòkà *v2** (*m* sūkà) 1. to pierce 2. to criticise 3. to disqualify 4. to cancel 5. to revoke
sōkè *v4* (*m* sūkà) 1. to pierce 2. to contradict 3. to delete
sòke-sòke *see* sūkà
sōkō *v6* to sprout
sōmà *v1* to begin
sōmì *m* beginning
sònê *m* (Nr) ringing

sôn kâi *m* 1. selfishness 2. self interest 3. màì nūnà sôn kâi individualist
sōr̃ō *m* (*pl* sōr̃àyē) 1. storey 2. upstairs 3. apex
sōsà *v1* (*f* sūsà) to scratch an itch
sòsai *adv* 1. well 2. straight
sòsatì *m* (Nr) socks
sòsō *m* sponge
sòtôf *see* sàtôf
sōyà *v1* (*f* sūyà) 1. to fry 2. to roast
sòyayyà *f* love
sôyē *m* roast meat
su *pl* 1. them 2. such as
sù *pl* 1. them 2. their
sū *pl* they
sû *m* 1. fishing 2. (Nr) drunkenness 3. cabbage
Subdù *f* (Nr) Saturday
sùbhānàllāhì! good heavens!
suɓùcē *v4* to slip away
suɗè *v4* 1. to wear out 2. to use up
sudì *m* leftovers
sūfà, (Nr) sùfâr̃ *m* 1. super (petrol) 2. tākìn sūfà superphosphate fertilizer
sùfâf *m* (Nr) valve
sùfānà *f* (*pl* sufānōnì, sàfānū) spanner
sùfàntakà *f* 1. sufism 2. monasticism
sūfàr̃èfê *m* (Nr) sub-prefect
sùfētò *m* (*pl* sufētōcì) police inspector
sūfì *m* (*pl* sūfàyē) 1. sufi 2. monk
sùfô *m* (Nr) spoke
sufùr̃ì *m* 1. transport 2. freight 3. cost of transport 4. *see* sifìr̃i

sufùřin jirgin samà *m* 1. air flights 2. air routes

suhulē *m* (Nr) whistle

sukà, su kà *pl relative completive* they

sūkà *m* (*pl* **sòke-sòke**) 1. criticism 2. *see* **sòka, sōkè**

sukàn, su kàn *pl habitual* they

sukàři *m* sugar

sukè, su kè *pl relative continuous* they

sùkōlà *f* 1. neatness 2. cleanliness

sùkōlàshîf *m* 1. scholarship 2. grant

sùkùndiřēbà *f* (*pl* **sukundiřēbōbī**) screwdriver

sùkūnì *m* 1. leisure 2. opportunity 3. means of living 4. **mài sùkūnì** of independent means

sùkûř *m* (*pl* **sukuřōřì**) screw

sukuřkùcē *v4* 1. to slacken 2. to stale

sùkût *m* (Nr) boy scout

sukùwā *f* galloping

sukwànē *v4* to loot

sulàlē *v4* 1. to slide along 2. to slip (**zuwà** into)

sūlàncē *v4* to come to nothing

sùlâř *m* (Nr) cocky

sùdê *m* (Nr) **yi wa...** **sùdê** to weld

sulè *m* (*pl* **sulūluwà**) ten kobo

sulhù *m* 1. peace 2. treaty 3. arbitration 4. reconciliation

sùlkē *m* 1. armour 2. **mài sùlkē** armoured

sullùɓē *v4* to slip away

sùlmiyà *v3* to slip

sùlùlù *adv* stealthily

sùlùsānì *pl* two thirds

sulùsī *m* one third

sūma *v* to faint

sùmā *f* hair (on head)

sumbā *f* kiss

sumbàcē *v4* to kiss

sumbai *m* **shìnkāfā sumbai** wild rice

sùmōgà, sùmōgàl *m* 1. smuggling 2. **ɗan sùmōgà** smuggler 3. **kāyan sùmōgà** contraband

sùmōgàř màkàmai *f* 1. gunrunning 2. **ɗan sùmōgàř màkàmai** gunrunner

sumùnī *m* one eighth

sumùnin galàn *m* pint

sùmuntì *m* 1. cement 2. concrete

sun *pl completive* they

sunà, su nà *pl continuous* they

sūnā *m* (*pl* **sūnàyē**) 1. name 2. reputation 3. price 4. **Ìnā sūnankà?** What is your name? 5. **sâ wà... sūnā** to name 6. **ran sūnā** naming day

sūnan mahàifī *m* surname

sùndūƙì *m* (*pl* **sùndùƙai**) box

sùnkutà *v2** (**-ci/cē**) to heave up

sunkùyā, sunkwìyā *v1* to bend down

sunkuyè *m* opposite

sùnƙūrù *m* 1. uncultivated land 2. **sōjàn sùnƙūrù** guerrilla 3. **yāƙìn sùnƙūrù** guerrilla warfare

sunnà 1. *f* (Isl.) orthodox Islam 2. *v1* to pass on (**wà** to)

sùntā *v2** (**-ci/ē**) to fish

sùntum *adv* **Yā yi sùntum.** He is fat.

sunù *m* depression

sūr̃à *f* (*pl* **sūr̃ōr̃ì**) **1.** appearance **2.** picture **3.** (Isl.) chapter of the Quran

sur̃è *v4* to snatch up

sūr̃ì *m* anthill

sùrkē *see* **sùlkē**

sur̃k̃àk̃ā *v1* to hide oneself

sur̃k̃ūk̃ì *m* thicket

sùrukì *m* (*pl* **sùr̃ùkai**) **1.** father-in-law **2.** son-in-law **3.** brother-in-law

sùr̃ūtù *m* (*pl* **sùr̃ùtai**) chatter

sūsà *see* **sōsà**

sūsancì *m* stupidity

sùsatì, sùsātì *m see* **sòsatì**

sussùkā *v1* to thresh

sūsùcē *v4* to fail

sūsùsū *m* (*f* **sūsūsùwā**, *pl* **sùsùsai**) idiot

sùtùwâr̃ *m* (Nr) **1.** palaver **2.** talk

sùwaità *f* (*pl* **suwaitōci**) **1.** sweater **2.** (spor.) vest

sūyà *f* **1.** fried meat **2.** *see* **sōyà**

su wà *see* **wà**

su wànē nè *see* **wànē nè**

su wānè, wancè *see* **wānè**

swâ *pl indefinite future* they

Tt

ta 1. *f* of **2.** she **3.** her **4.** *prep* via
4. Tanà ta dàriyā. She keeps
on laughing. **5. Tā yi ta
dàriyā.** She started laughing.
tà *f* **1.** *subjunctive* she **2.** her
tā *f completive* she
tà *f negative continuous* she
tâ *f indefinite future* she
ta'àdda *f* **1.** act of terrorism
2. vandalism **3.** ɗan ta'àdda
terrorist **4.** vandal
ta'addancì *m* terrorism
tà'ajjàbī, tà'ajjùbī *m* wonder
tà'ammàlī *m* **1.** trade **2.** yi
tà'ammàlī dà to put into
practice
tà'annàtī *m* cross-questioning
tà'àsā *f* massacre
tà'āsā *f* **1.** contemptible
behaviour **2.** atrocities
ta'asìrì *see* tàsìrì
tà'àzzaɍà *v3* **1.** to worsen **2.** to
escalate
tà'àziyyà *f* condolences
tābà *f* **1.** tobacco **2.** shā tābà to
smoke
tàbā *f* fraud
tābābà *f* **1.** scepticism **2.** yi
tābābà to be sceptical (kō
whether)
tàbàrau *m* **1.** spectacles **2.**
sunglasses
tàbarmā *f* (*pl* tàbàrmī) mat
tabbàcī *m* **1.** confirmation
2. certainty
tabbàs *adv* **1.** for sure **2.** rashìn
sanìn tabbàs volatility **3.** na
rashìn sanìn tabbàs volatile
tabbàtā *v1* **1.** to be sure that
2. to make sure (dà of) **3.** to
confirm (cêwā that)
tàbbatā *v3* **1.** to be certain **2.** to
be permanent
tàbbàtaccē *m* (*f* tàbbàtacciyā,
pl tàbbàtàttū) **1.** certain
2. outstanding **3.** genuine
tabbataɍ dà *v5* **1.** to ensure
2. to ratify
tabdî! imagine!
tābìlì, tābùl *m* (Nr) table
tabkà *v1* to do a lot of
tabō *m* (*pl* tâbbā, tabbunà,
tàbbai) scar
tabà *v1* **1.** to touch **2.** to taste
3. to take **4.** to affect **5.** to do a
little of **6.** to have done before
tàɓaɓɓē *m* (*f* tàɓaɓɓiyā, *pl*
tàɓàɓɓū) mentally ill
tàɓà-kunne *m/f* **1.** great-
grandchild **2.** great-grandparent
taɓarɓàrā *v1* (fin.) to ruin
taɓarɓàrē *v4* (ec.) to stagnate
taɓarɓàrêwā *f* **1.** deterioration
2. ills
taɓaɍgazā *f* **1.** scandal **2.** affair
taɓaryā *m* (*pl* taɓàrē) pestle
tāɓè *v4* **1.** to rip **2.** to fail
tàɓō *m* **1.** mud **2.** clay
tàɓū *v7* to be mentally ill
tāɓùkā *v1* to make a little
progress
tācè *v4* (*f* tàtā) **1.** to filter **2.** to
strain **3.** to refine **4.** to
investigate

tācè làbàřai 1. *f* censorship of the press **2.** *v* to censor the press

tā dà *v* **1. tā dà zàune tsàye** destabilise **2. manufař tā dà zàune tsàye** destabilisation **3.** *see* **tayar dà**

tādfà *vl* to chat

tādfè, tādìyē *v4* to trip up

tādfì *m* **1.** chat **2.** converssation

taf *adv* full (up)

tāfà *vl* **1.** to clap **2.** to slap hands **3.** to hand (wà to)

tàfannuwā *f* garlic

tafarkì *m* (*pl* **tàfàrkū**) **1.** road **2.** path **3.** ideology

tàfařnuwā *f* garlic

tafàsā *vl* to boil

tàfasà *v3* to be boiled

tàfe *adv* **1.** coming **2.** underway

tàfi *v* (*f* **tàfiyà**) **1.** to go **2.** to walk **3.** to travel

tàfī *m* (*pl* **tāfukà**) **1.** palm of hand **2.** sole of foot **3.** clap **4.** (ban) **tàfī** applause

tafī dà *see* **tafiyař dà**

tàfi-dà-gidankà 1. mobility **2. na tàfi-dà-gidankà** mobile

tāfintà *m* (*pl* **tāfintōcī**) **1.** interpreter **2.** translator **3.** translating

tàfīřētà *f* (*pl* **tāfīřētōcī**) typewriter

tàfiyà *f* (*pl* **tàfīye-tàfīye**) **1.** walking **2.** journey **3.** travel **4.** *see* **tàfī**

tàfiyà-dà-dāwôwā *f* **tikitìn tàfiyà-dà-dāwôwā** return ticket

tafiyař dà *v5* **1.** to move **2.** to manage **3.** to administer

tafiyař dà cìnikī to run a business

tàfiyà zuwà dà dāwôwā *f* return trip

tafkì *m* (*pl* **tafkunà**) **1.** pond **2.** lake

tafō *v6* to come

tàfsīřì *m* (*pl* **tàfsìřai**) (Isl.) commentary

tāgà *f* (*pl* **tāgōgī**) window

tagàri *see* **nagàri**

tagayyàrā *vl* to bring suffering to

tàgàyyarà *v3* to suffer

tàgazà *v2* * (-ji/jē) **1.** to aid **2.** to shore up **3.** to attempt

tàgiyà *f* (*pl* **tàgìyū**) cap

tagōmàshì *m* popularity

tagùllā *f* (*pl* **tagullōlī**) **1.** copper **2.** bronze

tàgumì *m* **1.** deep thought **2.** distress

taguwà *f* (*pl* **taguwōyī**) (man's) gown

tàguwà *f* (*pl* **tàgùwai**) camel

tagwai *m* **dan tagwai, 'yař tagwai** twin

tagwàyē *pl* **1.** twins **2.** pair **3.** dan tagwàyē , 'yař tagwàyē twin

tahō *v6* to come

tai = ta yi, tā yi

tàibà *f* paunch

tàifìs *m/f* typist

taikì *m* (*pl* **taikunà**) pannier

tàimakà *v2* * (*m* **tàimakō**) to help

tàimakō *m* **1.** help **2.** charity

tàimakon āgàjī *m* relief aid

tàimakon farkō *m* first aid

tàitayà *v2* * to encourage

tàjàdīdì *m* (rel.) reform

tājè *v4* to comb out

ta-jikà *f* jaundice

tàjìn-tàjìn *adv* Mun yi tàjìn-tàjìn. We were at a loss.

tājìrī *see* àttājìrī

tājìrtā *v1* to become rich

tàjìrtà *v3* to make rich

tak *adv* (daya) tak one only

tākà yours + *feminine noun*

tākà *v1* 1. to step 2. to pace

tàkā *v2** 1. to step onto 2. to rely on

takabà *f* widow's mourning

tàkaddàmā *f* 1. introduction 2. *see* tàkàddamà

tàkàdīrì *adv* approximately

tākà dòkā to disobey the law

tàkā hàyē *adv* yi tàkā hàyē to lord it (wà over)

tàkâicī *m* 1. indignation 2. frustration 3. nūnà tàkâicī to deplore 4. bā dà tàkâicī to frustrate 5. Yā ji musù tàkâicī. He riled them.

tàkalà *v2** to provoke

tàkàlmī *m* (*pl* tākalmà) shoe

tākalō *v6* to bring up

tàkàmaimai *adv* for certain

takàn, ta kàn *f* habitual she

tàkànas *adv* 1. especially 2. directly

tākà ōdà to disobey a command

tākarā *f* 1. competition 2. contest

tākarar harkōkin kāsuwancì *f* free market competition

takàrdā *f* (*pl* tàkàrdū) 1. paper 2. letter 3. certificate 4. dan takàrdā intellectual 5. ƙyallen takàrdā tissue paper

takàrdar iznì *f* 1. permit 2. warrant

takàrdar kafà... *f* charter of...

takàrdar kāmù *f* warrant

takàrdar makaranta *f* school certificate

takàrdar nēman aikì *f* job application form

takàrdar shaidà *f* certificate

takàrdar shaidà ta kammàlà kàrātū *f* school-leaving certificate

tàkàrdun aikì *pl* credentials

tàkàrìmì *m* respect

tàkarkàrī *m* (*pl* tàkàrkàrai) pack-ox

tàkàsî *m/f* (*pl* takasòshī) taxi

tàkà-tsantsan *f* yi tàkà-tsantsan to act with caution

takè, ta kè *f* continuous she

tākē *m* 1. heading 2. designation 3. national anthem

tākè *v4* 1. to tread on 2. to pass 3. to disobey

tàke *adv* suddenly

tākì yours + *feminine noun*

tākì *m* 1. manure 2. step 3. pace 4. pair

tākìn lākā *m* marking time

tākìn zāmànì *m* chemical fertiliser

tàki sā'à to strike it lucky

tàkō *m* hoof

takòbī *m* (*pl* takubbà) sword

tàksî *m* (*pl* taksòshī) taxi

tākù yours + *feminine noun*

tākù *m see* tākì

tākùn tàkàlmī *m* footprint

tàkunkùmī *m* (*pl* tākunkumà) 1. muzzle 2. embargo 3. blockade 4. sanction

tàkunkùmin tattalin arzìkī *m* 1. trade embargo 2. trade sanctions

tākùrā *v1* 1. to cause to huddle up 2. to restrict

tàkurà *v3* 1. to crouch 2. to huddle

takwalā *f* thread

tàkwàřā *m/f* 1. namesake 2. counterpart

takwàs *f* eight

taƙà *vl* to measure out

tàƙā *m* pace

tàƙàddamà *f* 1. discussion 2. argument 3. progress 4. *see* tàkaddàmā

tàƙàdīřì *adv* approximately

tàƙàice *adv* à tàƙàice briefly

taƙàitā *vl* 1. to reduce 2. to summarize

tàƙamā *f* yi tàƙamā 1. to rely 2. to show off

taƙì *m* span

tàƙiyì *m* pious

talàbijìn *f* 1. television 2. yi kallon talàbijìn to watch television

tàlàhō *m* telephone

talàkà *m/f* (*pl* talakāwā) commoner

talakāwā *pl* the common people

tālālā *f* 1. long tethering rope 2. yi wà... ɗaurìn tālālā to put under house arrest

tàlâm *f* (Nr) lorry

tàlātà *f* 1. Tuesday 2. three thousand

tàlàtin *f* thirty

talàucē *v4* to be poor

talaucì *m* poverty

talàutā *vl* to impoverish

tâlbōdì *f* lorry

tālè *v4* to open wide

talèbijìn *f* television

talgìřàm, (Nr) tàlgàřâm *m* telegram

tàlìbambam *m/pl* tadpole

tālìfì *m* (*pl* tālìfōfì, tàlìfai) literary work

talihôn *m* telephone

tālìkī *m* (*f* tālìkā, *pl* tàlìkai) creature

tàliyà *f* pasta

tàllā *f* (Nr) container

tàllà *m* (*pl* tàllàce-tàllàce) 1. displaying for sale 2. advertisement 3. advertising 4. yi tàllà to advertise

tàllàce-tàllàce *pl* 1. advertising 2. publicity

tallàfā wà *vl* 1. to support 2. to sponsor 3. to carry by hand

tàllafà *v2** 1. to provide for 2. to relieve

tallàfâwā *f* 1. support 2. sponsorship

tallàtā *vl* 1. to display for sale 2. to advertise 3. to publicise

tàlô *m* (Nr) shoe heel

tàlo-tàlo *m/f/pl* turkey

tam *adv* firmly

tamā *m* 1. ore 2. iron ore

tamànī *m* 1. price 2. value

tàmànin *f* eighty

tamàta *f* (*pl* mātā) 1. female 2. feminine

tambàrī *m* (*pl* tamburà) 1. drum 2. seal 3. official stamp

tambàřin kamfànī *m* trademark

tambàtsā *vl* to fill up

tàmbatsà *v2** to splash over

tàmbayà 1. *f* (*pl* tambayōyì) question 2. *v2** to ask

tàmbōlà, (Nr) tàmbòlâ *f* 1. bingo 2. lottery

tambùlàn *m* (*pl* tambulōlì, tambulà) drinking glass

tambùř *m* (Nr) postage stamp

tàmfâl *m* canvas
tàmfô *m* (Nr) rubber stamp
tàmkař *prep* as
tàmê *m* (Nr) metal sieve
tàmfô *m* (Nr) rubber stamp
tàmfôl *m* tarpaulin
tāmōjī *pl* wrinkles
tamtèbùl *m* timetable
tāmù ours + *feminine noun*
tân *m* ton
tanà, ta nà *f continuous* she
tānā *f/pl* worm
tànadà *v2** (*m* tānàdī) 1. to
  prepare 2. to protect
tānadař dà *v5* to establish
tānàdī *m* 1. preparation
  2. foresight 3. protection 4.
  see tànadà
tandà *f* (*pl* tandōjī) tender
tandàrā *v1* to knock down
tàndèřū *m* oven
tandū *m* (*pl* tandàyē) small
  container
tandà *v1*, tàndà *v2** to lick
tàngadì *m* rocking
tangàřāhò, tangàřāhù *m* 1.
  telegraph pole 2. wayàř
  tangàřāhò telegram
tangařam, tangařan 1. *m*
  crockery 2. *adv* clearly
tangařďà *f* 1. difficulty 2. bâ
  tangařďà without a hitch
tanhwarāshì *see* antamfařētì
tanìs, wàsan tanìs *m* tennis
tànjàřīn *m* tangerine
tankà *v1* to answer back (wà to)
tankàďē *v4* 1. to winnow 2. to
  knock over
tànkàďē dà ràirayà *m* 1.
  reshuffle 2. reorganisation
  3. shake-up
tànkař *prep* like

tankì *m* (*pl* tankunà, tankōkī)
  1. tank 2. tanker
tankìfà, tânkìfà *m/f* (*pl*
  tankifōfì) timekeeper
tankiyā *m* arguing
tanƙwàrā *v1* to bend
tàntabàřā *m/f* (*pl* tàntàbàřai)
  pigeon
tantàlā *v1* to rush off
tantamā *f* doubt
tantàncē *v4* 1. to waste 2. to
  analyse 3. to evaluate
tantàncē dà to be certain of
tantì *m* (*pl* tantōcī, tantunà)
  1. tent 2. canvas
tàntīřì *m* (*f* tàntīřìyā, *pl*
  tàntìřai) poor
tařà *f* 1. nine 2. na tařà ninth
tàrā *v2** to go to meet
tārà *v1* 1. to collect 2. to add up
  3. to stock 4. to do in unison
tàrā *f* 1. fine 2. yì tàrā to care
  about
tàřaddàdi *m* Munà cikin
  tàřaddàdin... We are anxious
  to...
tařafìs, tařāfìs *m* 1. traffic
  police 2. traffic policeman
tàřagù *m* (*pl* tàřàgwai) 1.
  railway coach 2. railway truck
tàřaktà *f* (*pl* tařaktōcī) tractor
tararř dà *v5* 1. to find 2. to
  overtake
tàrayyà *f* 1. federation 2.
  partnership 3. àbōkin tàrayyà
  partner 4. gwamnatìn tàrayyà
  federal government
Tàrayyàř Soviet *f* Soviet
  Union
Tàrayyàř Tūřai *f* European
  Union (EU)
tàrbā *v2** *see* tàrā

tàr̃biyyà *f* 1. education 2. upbringing

tare *v4* to block

tàre *adv* together (dà with)

tarfà *v1* to pour out drop by drop

tarfî *m* small amount

targad̃ê *m* yi targad̃ê to sprain

tàr̃gâl *m* (Nr) nylon

tàr̃hô *m* 1. telephone 2. kân tàr̃hō handset

tārì 1. *m* heap 2. collection 3. large amount 4. *adv* a lot

tàrī *m* 1. cough 2. coughing

tār̃ihì *m*, tār̃ihà *f* 1. history 2. date 3. biography 4. na tār̃ihì record

tār̃ihìn kâi *m* autobiography

tàr̃iƙà see d̃ar̃iƙà

tārìn àlbàr̃kàtun mâi *m* oil reserves

tàrkàcē *pl* 1. belongings 2. debris

tarkàtā *v1* 1. to collect up 2. to go about one's business

tarkō, tarkò *m* (*pl* tarkunà) trap

tar̃nàƙē *v4* 1. to hobble 2. to disable

tar̃natsà! I swear!

tar̃ō *m* (*pl* tar̃àr̃ē) two and a half kobo

tàr̃ō *m* 1. meeting 2. crowd 3. conference 4. bàbban tàr̃ō congress

tàron bìtà *m* follow-up conference

tàron jàma'à *m* crowd

tàron ƙoli *m* summit conference

tàron manèmā làbàr̃ai *m* press conference

tàr̃sàshì *m* tàr̃sàshinsù all of them

tàr̃tsatsī *m* sparks

tar̃tsō *v6* to spurt out

tārū *m* (*pl* tārunà) fishing-net

tàru *v7* to assemble

tar̃wad̃à *f* (*pl* tar̃èwad̃î) catfish

tar̃wàtsā *v1* to scatter

tar̃wàtsē *v4* 1. to disperse 2. to break up

tar̃wàtsêwā *f* collapse

tàryā *v2** to go to meet

tàr̃zòmā *f* 1. struggle 2. dispute 3. violence 4. riot 5. revolt 6. d̃an tàr̃zòmā rioter 7. 'yan sàndan kwantar̃ dà tàr̃zòmā riot police 8. kashè tàr̃zòmā to quell a riot

tāsà his + *feminine noun*

tāsà 1. *f* (*pl* tāsōshì) basin 2. plate 3. *v1* to rise up

tàsā *v2** (-shi/ē, *m* tāshì) 1. to raise 2. to start up 3. to restore 4. to send out 5. to move 6. to proceed to

tasà ƙēyà 1. to arrest 2. to round up

tasam mà *v* 1. to attack 2. to head for

tàsau *m* disrespect

tashà *f* (*pl* tashōshì) 1. station 2. television channel

tashàr̃ har̃bà r̃ōkà *f* launch pad

tashàr̃ mōtà *f* lorry park

tashàr̃ nūkìliyà *f* nuclear power station

tāshē *m* popularity

tàshē *m* holiday

tāshì *v* (*m* tāshì) 1. to stand 2. to rise 3. to go up 4. to fly 5. to set out 6. to reach 7. to recur 8. to proceed to 9. to become 10. to break out 11. to get serious

tāshì *m* yi tāshì to rise
tāshìn hankàlī *m* 1. unrest
2. anger 3. tension
tàshìntāshinā *f* 1. disturbance
2. riot
tāshìn zūcìyā *m* nausea
tàsī *f* taxi
tāsīrì *m* 1. influence 2. yi tāsīrì
to make progress 3. effect
4. power 5. benefit 6. màì
tāsīrì influential 7. maràs
tāsīrì discredited
taskà *f* (*pl* taskōkī) 1. safe box
2. storeroom
taskìlà *m* third class
taskù *m* gwadà wà... taskù to
oppress
tāsō dà *v6* 1. to introduce 2. to
set in motion
tasō ƙeyàr... 1. arrest 2. to
round up
tāsù their + *feminine noun*
tàswīrà *f* (*pl* taswīrōrī) 1. map
2. plan
tātà hers + *feminine noun*
tàtā *see* tācè
tàtaccē *m* (*f* tàtacciyā, *pl*
tàtàttū) 1. filtered 2. refined
3. sound
tàtaccen mâi *m* refined oil
tātìkē *v4* to impoverish
tàtil *adv* full up
tàtsā *v1* to squeeze (à into)
tàtsā *v2* to milk
tàtsìtsì *m* (*f* tàtsìtsìyā, *pl*
tàtsìtsai) tiny
tàtsùlē *v4* to squash flat
tàtsūnìyā *f* (*pl* tātsūniyōyī)
story
tàttàbà-kunne *m/f* 1. great-
grandchild 2. great-grandparent
tàttabàrā *f* pigeon

tàttagà *v2** to make an attempt
at
tattàkā *v1* to trample
tattàkī *m* 1. trip 2. tour
tattàkin būɗe idò *m* sight-
seeing trip
tàttalà 1. *f* economising 2. *v2**
to do carefully
tattalī *m* preparation
tattalin ařzìkī *m* 1. economy
2. economics
tattàrā *v1* to collect up
tattàrā *v1* to assemble
tattàrà bàyànai to gather data
tàttàre dà *adv* connected with
tattàunā *v1* 1. to discuss 2. to
negotiate
tattàunâwā *f* discussion
tattàunâwā ta mùsammàn *f*
official talks
tàttaurā *m/f* (*pl* tauràrā) tough
tàuhīdì *m* belief in one god
tàulā *f* water carrier
taunà *v1* to chew
taurā *f* (*pl* tauràyē) plait(s)
tàurārò *m* (*f* tàurārùwā, *pl*
tàurārī) 1. star 2. planet
tàurārùwā màì wutsiyà *f*
comet
taurī *m* 1. hardness 2. toughness
3. resilience 4. tenacity
taurin kâi *m* stubbornness
tausà *v1* 1. to force 2. to massage
tàusā 1. *f* massage 2. *v2**
(-shi/shē) to coax
tausàsā *v1* to soften
tàusasà *v3* to become reconciled
tàusàyī *m* 1. pity 2. ji tàusàyī to
pity
taushī *m* softness
tauyè *v4* 1. to shrink 2. to hinder
3. trip to restrict

tàwa mine + *feminine noun*
tàwadà *f* (*pl* tàwàdū) ink
tàwagà *f* delegation
tàwāli'ù *m* 1. humility 2. mài
 tàwāli'ù humble
tàwayà *v3* to decrease
tāwāyè *m* 1. rebellion 2. ɗan
 tāwāyè rebel
tāwùl *m/pl* towel
tayà *v1* 1. to make an offer of
 2. to help
tāyà *f* (*pl* tāyōyī) tyre, (US) tire
tàyā *v2** to strip off
tāyar̃ dà *v5* 1. to raise 2. to erect
 3. to rebel 4. to attack 5. to
 terminate 6. to straighten out
 7. to start 8. to set in motion 9.
 to wake up
tāyar̃ dà bôm *f* àbin tāyar̃ dà
 bôm detonator
tayà wà... mur̃nà to
 congratulate
tāyè *m* tie, (US) necktie
tāyì *m* (spor.) draw
tàyī, ɗan tàyī *m* foetus, (US)
 fetus
tazar̃ā *f* 1. distance 2. dà tazar̃ā
 some distance away
tēbùr̃ *m* (*pl* tēbur̃à) 1. table
 2. shovel 3. trailer
tēbùr̃in shāwàr̃war̃ī *m*
 negotiating table
têf *m* tape
tèku *f* (*pl* tēkunà) 1. sea
 2. ocean 3. hannun tèku sea
 channel
tēlà *m* (*pl* tēlōlī) tailor
tèlâm *f* (Nr) lorry
telèks *m* telex
telìbijìn *f/pl* television
tènîs *m* (Nr) tennis
tèstàmōnìyà *f* certificate

tî *m* tea
tîb *m* inner-tube
tìbì *m* tuberculosis
tîf *m see* tîb
tifà *f* (*pl* tifōfī) tipper truck
tìjār̃à *f* trading
tik *adv* stark naked
tìk! *adv* bang!
tìkê *m* (Nr) ticket
tikis *adv* Yā gàji tikis. He is
 tired out.
tikitì *m* (*pl* tikitōcī) ticket
tikitìn shìgā *m* admission ticket
tìƙā *v3* to chew the cud
tìƙā *v2** to beat down
tilà *v1* to pile up
tīlàs 1. *f* necessity 2. *adv* definitely
tīlàstā wà *v1* to compel
tìlō *m* 1. sole 2. ɗan tìlō an only
 child
tîm *m* team
timbà *f* timber
tìnjim *adv* in large amounts
tìnkār̃à *v2** 1. to go towards
 2. to confront 3. to tackle
tìnƙāhò *m* yi tìnƙāhò to show
 off
tinkìyā *f* sheep
tìntiris *adv* abruptly
tir̃ *adv* yi tir̃ to be annoyed (dà
 with)
tirà *see* turà
tirè *v4* to provoke
tìrê *m* tray
tìr̃ēdà *m* 1. selling 2. ɗan tìr̃ēdà
 trader
tìr̃ēdì *m* ƙūsà mài tìr̃ēdì screw
tìr̃ēlà *f* (*pl* tìr̃ēlōlī) 1. trailer
 2. child carried on back
tìrìrì *m* steam
tìrìrin makāmashin nūkìliyà
 m nuclear radiation

tìrjè *v4* 1. to resist 2. to slide 3. to halt 4. to trample

tìr̃sàsā *v1* to humiliate

tìsà'in, tìs'in *f* ninety

tî-shât *f* tee-shirt

tìsī, tìsî *m* (Nr) material

tìtì *m* (*pl* tìtunà, tìyàtā) street

tìtisì, tìtisî 1. *f* teacher training college 2. *m* ticket collector

tìyà *f* 1. tare 2. container

tìyàgâs *m* tear gas

tìyàtā *see* tìtì

tìyātà *f/pl* 1. theatre 2. (med.) operation theatre 3. surgery

tìyàtì *m* public humiliation

tìyàtîr̃ *m* 1. show 2. entertainment

tìyō, (Nr) tìyô, tìyyô *m* (*pl* tìyōyī) 1. hose 2. tube

tìzgā *v2** to pluck

tô 1. okay! 2. well then...

tōcìlàn *m/f/pl* torch, (US) flashlight

tōfā *f* elephant grass

tōfà *v1* to spit (wà at)

tòfī *m* spitting

tòfî *m* (Nr) toffee

tòfin Allàh tsinè *m* condemnation

tōge *m* cheating

tōgè *v4* 1. to withdraw 2. to hesitate 3. to exclude 4. to exempt

tōgèwà *f* exemption

tōgiyā *f*, tògō *m* 1. excuse 2. exception 3. yi wà... tògō to exclude

tōhō *v6* to bud

tòhō *m/pl* bud

tòkā *f* ashes

tōkàrā *v1* 1. to use as a prop 2. to assist (wà s.o.)

tōkàre *v4* 1. to prop up (dà with) 2. to support 3. to be stuck

tòka-tòka *m/f* grey

tōliyā *f* crest

tôn *m* ton

tōnà *v1* (*m* tònō) 1. to dig up 2. to investigate 3. to reveal

tònā *v2** (*m* tònō) to taunt

tōnè *v4* to dig out

tōnìk, tònîk, tònîs *m* 1. tonic water 2. grapefruit

tònō *see* tōnà, tònā

tòr̃on gīwā *m* bull elephant

tōshè *v4* 1. to stop up 2. to block 3. to stymie

tòshi *m*, tōshìyā *f* bribe

tōtùr̃ *m* accelerator

tōtùwā *f* pulp

tōyà *v1* (*f* tūyà) 1. to fry 2. to burn

tòye-tòye *m* fried food

tòyī *m* burning

tōzàlī *m* kohl

tōzàr̃tā *v1* to despise

tòzar̃tà *v3* to be despised

tōzō *m* (*pl* tōzàyē) 1. hump 2. mound

tsābà *f* small change

tsābàr̃ kudî *f* cash

tsàbì'à *f* (*pl* tsabī'ō'ī) 1. character 2. trait

tsabtà *f* cleanliness

tsabtàcè *v4* to clean

tsàdā *f* expensiveness

tsàdar̃ r̃àyuwā *f* cost of living

tsāfà *v1* to squeeze a way

tsāfî *m* juju

tsāgā *f* 1. tribal marks 2. split

tsāgà *v1* 1. to split 2. to make an incision (wà in)

tsagagī *m* ibis

tsagàitā *v1* to reduce

tsagàità wutā, tsagàità amon wutā *f* cease-fire

tsāgè *v4* to be split
tsagèrā *m/f* (*pl* **tsàgèrū**)
1. irritable 2. **ɗan tsagèrā**
extremist
tsagì *m* revolt
tsāgì *m* portion
tsagiyā *f* (med.) bilharzia
tsai *adv* **Tā tsayà tsai.** She stood
still.
tsai dà *see* **tsayaɍ dà**
tsaikŏ *m* frame
tsaiwā *see* **tsayà**
tsâiwā *f* door curtain
tsakā *f* (*pl* **tsakàkē**) gecko
tsakà *adv* 1. in the middle (of)
2. **ɗan tsakà** clitoris
tsàkānī *adv* (in) between
tsàkānin *prep* between
tsakaɍ, tsakàɍ *f* **à tsakaɍ, à
tsakàɍ** in the middle of
tsakaɍ darē *adv* midnight
tsakaɍ rānā *adv* midday
tsakaɍ tsakà, tsakà-tsakà *adv*
right in the middle
tsakà-tsakancì *m* (pol.)
1. neutrality 2. non-alignment
tsàkà-tsakī *adv* **na tsàkà-tsakī**
medium-sized
tsàkī *m* flour
tsàkī *m* 1. tut 2. *see* **tsàkŏ**
tsakiyà *f* (*gen* **tsakiyàɍ,
tsakaɍ**) 1. centre 2. **na
tsakiyà** central
Tsakiyàɍ Afiɍkà *f* Central
Africa
tsàkŏ *m* (*f* **tsàkuwā**, *pl* **tsàkī**)
chick
tsakuwà *f* (*pl* **tsakuwōyī**)
gravel
tsalà *m* buttermilk
tsālà 1. *f* crust 2. *vl* to do a lot of
tsālàɍ dūniyà *f* earth's crust

tsallàkā *vl* to cross
tsallàkē *v4* 1. to jump 2. to omit
tsallē *m* (*pl* **tsàlle-tsàlle**)
jumping
tsam *adv* **Yā tāshì tsam.** He
stood up abruptly.
tsāmārī *m* **yi tsāmārì** to turn
serious
tsāmè *v4* to withdraw
tsāmī *m* 1. sourness 2. soreness
tsāmin bàkī *m* speech defect
tsāmiyā *f* (*pl* **tsàmàikū,
tsāmiyōyī**) tamarind
tsàmmānì *m* 1. thought
2. opinion 3. **yi tsàmmānì**
to think 4. **fid dà tsàmmānì**
to give up hope
tsàmmātà *v2** (**-ci/ē**) to think
that
tsamō-tsàmŏ *adv* soaked
tsana *f* '**yaɍ tsana** doll
tsànā 1. *f* disapproval 2. *v2** to
detest
tsànàke *adv* **à tsànàke** carefully
tsananī *m* 1. severity
2. **tsananin yunwà** extreme
hunger 3. **màì tsananī** serious
4. severe 5. violent
tsanàntā *vl* 1. to urge 2. to
harass (**wà** s.o.)
tsànantà *v3* 1. to be severe 2. to
be extreme
tsanàntà dòkā to tighten up a
law
tsandaurī *m* infertile land
tsandŏ *m* **ƙudan tsandŏ** tsetse
fly
tsanè *v4* to dry up
tsangwàmā wà *vl*, **tsàngwamà**
*v2** 1. to ill-treat 2. to harass
tsānì *m* (*pl* **tsānukà**) 1. ladder
2. scaffold

tsantsā 1. *f* purity **2.** *adv* pure(ly)
3. sole(ly)
tsantsan *adv* **1.** firmly **2. yi tàkà
tsantsan** to act with caution
tsanwā *f* green
tsanyà *f* (*pl* **tsanyōyī**) cricket
tsārā *m/f* (*pl* **tsāràrrakī**) **1.**
contemporary **2.** generation
tsārà *vl* (*m* **tsārì**) **1.** to arrange
2. to draft
tsàrabà *f* (*pl* **tsarabōbī**)
souvenir
tsarè *v4* **1.** to guard **2.** to protect
3. to block **4.** to detain
tsaṙgà *vl* to spit
tsàṙgā *v2* * **1.** to ostracise **2.** to
dicriminate against
tsaṙgè *v4* to slit
tsàṙguwā *f* discrimination
tsarì *m* **1.** guarding **2.**
imprisonment **3.** prohibition
4. purdah
tsārì *m* (*pl* **tsàre-tsàre**) **1.**
arrangement **2.** scale **3.** plan
4. system **5.** infrastructure
6. mài tsārì organised **7.** *see*
tsārà
tsàṙīkà *see* **d'àṙīkà**
tsārìn àlbâshī *m* salary scale
tsārìn dōkōkī *m* charter
tsàron kasā *m* state security
tsārìn mulkì *m* **1.** constitution
2. shirìn tsārìn mulkì draft
constitution
tsārìn sūnā *m* trademark
tsarkàkā *vl* **1.** to cleanse **2.** to
purify
tsarkī *m* **1.** purity **2.** cleanliness
3. Littāfì Mài Tsarkī the
Bible
tsàrō *m* **1.** protection **2.** defence
tsaṙtà *vl* to spit

tsaṙtō *v6* to spurt out
tsàru *v7* to be practical
tsātsà *f* rust
tsatsò *m* waist
tsàtsò *m* earwig
tsattsafī *m* drizzle
tsàttsagà *v2* * to jeer at
tsattsàgē *v4* to ram
tsàttsaurā *m* (*f* **tsàttsauriyā**,
pl **tsàttsàurū**) stringent
tsàttsauran ṙa'àyī *m* **mài
tsàttsauran ṙa'àyī** rigid
tsâttsēwà *f* **1.** swallow, swift
2. (med.) thrush
tsaunì *m* (*pl* **tsaunukà**) hill
tsauràrā *vl* to pull tight
tsauràrā 1. *vl* to harden **2.** *see*
tsàttsaurā
tsaurī *m* **1.** hardness **2.** stiffness
3. tightness
tsaurin idò *m* insolence
tsàutsàyī *m* accident
tsāwā *f* thunder
tsawàitā *vl* **1.** to lengthen **2.** to
prolong
tsàwaità *v3* to be long
tsāwatâṙwā *f* warning
tsawō *m* **1.** length **2.** height
tsawwàlā *vl* **1.** to get serious
2. (fin.) to rise high
tsayà *vl* (*f* **tsaiwā**) **1.** to stand
2. to wait **3.** to stop **4.** to insist
5. to resist **6.** to be restricted **7.**
to persevere (**dà/kân** at)
tsayà kân cêwā 1. to insist that
2. to maintain that
tsayaṙ dà *v5* **1.** to stop **2.** to
delay **3.** to set up
tsayà tsayèn dakà to support
strongly
tsayàwà *f* **1.** halt **2.** stand
tsàyayyà *f* perseverance

tsàyayyē *m* (*f* **tsàyayyìyā**, *pl* **tsàyàyyū**) 1. stable 2. reliable
tsàye *adv* 1. standing 2. stopped 3. à tsàye lengthways 4. na tsàye vertical 5. yi tsàye to persevere
tsayì *m* 1. length 2. height
tsēfè *v4* (*f* tsīfà) to comb
tsēgùmì *m* gossip
tsēraȓ dà *v5* to rescue
tsēre *m/pl* 1. competition 2. race
tsērè *v4* 1. to escape 2. to surpass
tsēren gudù *m* mai tsēren gudù (spor.) runner
tsērērēnìyaȓ ƙērà màkàmai *f* arms race
tsibì *m* pile
tsibìrcē *v4* to sit alone
tsìbiri *m* (*pl* tsìbìrai) island
tsidik *adv* suddenly
tsifà *see* tsēfè
tsìgā *v2** to pull out
tsigè *v4* to swear (wà at)
tsigigi *adv* tiny
tsila *f* 1. tapeworm 2. (med.) kwashiorkor
tsimà *v1* (*m* tsimì) 1. to soak 2. to infuse
tsìma *v3* to be soaked
tsimi *m* 1. infusion 2. storage 3. economising 4. stocking up 5. yi tsimi to economise 6. bankìn tsimi dà tānàdi reserve bank
tsimì *m* infusion
tsìnā *v2** to select
tsīnànā *v1* to point
tsīnè *v4* to select
tsìni *m* (*pl* tsīninnukà) point
tsìnin sàkàcē *m* toothpick
tsinkà *v1* to snap
tsinkā *v2** to pick

tsìnkāyā *f* 1. prediction 2. foresight
tsìnkāyà *v2** (*f* tsìnkāyā) 1. to see in the distance 2. to predict
tsinkē *m* (*pl* tsinkàyē) skewer
tsinken àshānā *m* matchstick
tsinkè *v4* 1. to snap 2. to break away
tsìntā *v2** (-ci/cē) 1. to pick out 2. to find
tsìntaccē *m* (*f* tsìntacciyā, *pl* tsìntàttū) something picked up by chance
tsintsiyā *f* (*pl* tsintsiyōyī) broom
tsìra *v3* 1. to sprout 2. to grow
tsìrā *v2** 1. to be the first to 2. to pretend to
tsìra *v* to escape
tsīrā *f* 1. escape 2. salvation
tsīrà *v1* 1. to pile up 2. to prosper
tsiràità *v1* 1. to strip 2. to expose
tsirārà 1. *f* nudity 2. *adv* nude
tsīraȓ dà *v5* to rescue
tsìràri *m* 1. small amount 2. minority 3. Sun zo tsìràri. Only a few came.
tsīrè *v4* 1. to pierce 2. to skewer
tsìrē *m* kebab
tsìre-tsìre *pl* 1. plants 2. *see* tsirò
tsīri *m* 1. strip of land 2. yi tsīri to rise high
tsīrì *m* pile
tsiȓit *adv* tiny
tsirkìyā *f* (*pl* tsirkiyōyī) string
tsirò *m* (*pl* tsìre-tsìre) 1. (plant) shoot 2. plant
tsit *adv* yi tsit to be silent
tsittsigè *m* (*pl* tsìgàtsìgai) stump

tsĩwà *f* (*pl* **tsìwàce-tsìwàce**) insolence

tsìyā *f* 1. poverty 2. bad-temperedness

tsiyàcē *v4* 1. to become poor 2. to go bankrupt

tsiyàtā *vl* to impoverish

tsiyā-tsìyà *f* yi tsiyā-tsìyà to dispute (**dà** with)

tsìyāyà *v3* to stream out

tsōhō *m* (*f* **tsōhuwā**, *pl* **tsòfàffī**, **tsòffī**) 1. old 2. parent

tsōkà *f* (*pl* **tsōkōkī**) 1. muscle 2. **mài tsōkà** substantial

tsōkàcī *m* 1. scrutiny 2. analysis 3. yi tsōkàcī to draw attention (**gà** to)

tsōkànā *vl* to poke

tsōkanà *v2*, **tsōkanō** *v6* to provoke

tsōkànē *v4* to poke

tsòlōlò *m* (*f* **tsòlōlùwā**) tall and thin

tsòlōlò *adv* very tall and thin

tsōmà *vl* to dip

tsōmà bàkī to interfere (**cikin** in)

tsōnē *v4* 1. to poke 2. to select

tsòràce-tsòràce *see* **tsòrō**

tsòràtā *vl* to frighten

tsòratà *v3* to be afraid

tsòratà *v2* (-ci/cē) to be afraid of

tsòrō *m* (*pl* **tsòrāyē**) 1. plait 2. crest

tsòrō *m* (*pl* **tsòràce-tsòràce**) fear

tsòrōruwā *f* 1. top 2. summit

tsōtsà *vl*, **tsòtsā** *v2* to suck

tsōtsè *v4* 1. to absorb 2. to be emaciated

tsubbù *m* magic

tsūfa *v* to get old

tsūgà *vl* to pour heavily

tsugul *adv* very short

tsugùnā *vl* to squat

tsugunaɽ dà *v5* 1. to settle 2. (mil.) to station to deploy

tsūkè *v4* to tighten up

tsukù *m* pangs

tsūlà *f* moped

tsūlìyā *f* (*pl* **tsūliyōyī**) anus

tsumāgìyā *m* (*f* **tsumangìyā**, *pl* **tsumāgiyōyī**) cane

tsùmammìyā *f* loathing

tsùmāyà *v2* to wait for

tsumbùrē *v4* 1. to be badly developed 2. to be stunted

tsùmbùrarrē *m* (*f* **tsùmbùrarriyā**, *pl* **tsùmbùràrrū**) stunted

tsûmmā *m* (*pl* **tsummōkī**) rag(s)

tsumulmulā *f* stinginess

tsunàmī *m* tidal wave

tsuntsū *m* (*f* **tsuntuwā**, *pl* **tsuntsàyē**) bird

tsuntsun Makà *m* peacock

tsūɽā *m* blade

tsurū-tsùrù *adv* yi tsurū-tsùrù to be unsettled

tsūtsà *f* (*pl* **tsūtsōtsī**) worm

tsūtsàɽ cikì *f* roundworm

tù'ammàlī *see* **tà'ammàlī**

tūba *v* 1. to be sorry 2. to repent

tūbā *m* 1. being sorry 2. repentance

tūbàlī *m* (*pl* **tūbalà**) brick

tùbaɽkallà *f* bravo!

tuburàn *adv* absolute(ly)

tūɓè *v4* 1. to depose 2. to impeach

tudù *m* (*pl* **tùddai**) 1. high ground 2. hill

tudùn dàfàwā *m* 1. compromise 2. basis

tufã f (pl **tufāfī**) 1. garment 2. clothes

tufāfin ƙasā pl national dress

tufkà vl 1. to twist 2. to plait

tùfkā f strand

tūgè v4 1. to uproot 2. to depose

tùhumà f (pl **tùhùmce-tùhùmce**) 1. suspicion 2. interrogation

tùhùmammē m (f **tùhùmammiyā**, pl **tùhùmàmmū**) (leg.) 1. suspect 2. the accused

tùhumtà v2* (-cē/ci) 1. to suspect 2. to interrogate (à kân about)

tūjè 1. m bustard 2. v4 to scrape off

tūkà vl 1. to twist 2. to plait

tùkā f strand

tukkū m (pl **tukkàyē**) 1. plait 2. crest

tukùbā f (pl **tukubōbī**) mound

tukuf-tukuf adv aged

tùkùn, tùkùna adv 1. (not) yet 2. until 3. only when 4. only after 5. first

tukunyà f (pl **tukwànē**) cooking pot

tukunyař jirgī f locomotive

tukurwā f (pl **tukurwōyī**) raffia palm

tūƙà vl (m **tūƙì**) 1. to stir 2. to drive 3. to steer

tùƙā f yi **tùƙā** to feel a pain

tùƙàddamà see **tàƙàddamà**

tūƙè v4 to stir up

tūƙì m 1. driving 2. **canjà tūƙì** to change course

tuƙuƙī m 1. anger 2. density

tuƙùru adv 1. greatly 2. **mài aikì tuƙùru** hard-working

tulà vl to pile up

tulì m 1. heap 2. crowd

tulluwā f summit

tùlū m (pl **tūlunà**) 1. jar 2. bottle

tum adv entirely

tùma v3 to jump

tumāki see **tunkìyā**

tumàƙasà m jug cover

tumāmì m jumping

tùmātìř, (Nr) tùmātì m tomato(es)

tumbàtsē v4 1. to overflow 2. to be crowded

tùmbī m (pl **tumbunà**) stomach

tùmbuřkùmā f pancreas

tumɓùkē v4 1. to uproot 2. to depose 3. to overthrow

tùntùm m/pl pouf

tumuř adv firm

tun 1. prep/conj since 2. ever since 3. ago 4. after 5. during 6. while 7. before 8. adv especially

tunà dà vl 1. to remember 2. to remind (wà s.o.)

tùnànī m 1. thought 2. **sākè tùnànī** to change one's mind

tunātař dà, tunāsař dà v5 to remind someone of

tunàwā f 1. remembering 2. memory

tun bà mā... bâ adv particularly

tun dà prep 1. after 2. since

tun dàgà prep after

tun dà yakè conj in view of the fact that

tun fil àzal adv ever since the beginning

tungùltā vl to impoverish

tungùmē v4 to secure

tùni, tun tùni adv long ago

tunì *m* reminder
tùnjērē *m* syphilis
tunkìyā *f* (*pl* tumākī) sheep
tùnkū *m* (*pl* tunkunà) mongoose
tunkùɗā *v1* to knock to one side
tunkurō *v6* (Nr) to be vexed
tùnkuyā *v2** to butt
tùnkùyau *m/pl* flea(s)
tunnuƙū *m* dense smoke
tuntsùrā *v1* 1. to roll 2. to topple
tuntsùrē *v4* to topple
tuntuɓà *f* 1. dialogue 2. contact
tùntuɓà 1. *f* riƙà tùntuɓà to keep in contact 2. *v2** to contact
tuntuɓàr̃ jūnā à fannìn àl'àdū *f* cultural contact
tuntuɓè *m* stumble
tuntumi *m* ibis
tun tùni *adv* long ago
tùntuzù *m* cluster
tun yànzu *adv* by now
tunzùrā *v1* to incite
tùnzurà *v3* 1. to be afraid 2. to get angry
tùnzùrarrē *m* (*f* tùnzùrarriyā, *pl* tùnzùràrrū) bad-tempered
turà *f* ci turà to fail in an undertaking
tūrà *v1* 1. to push 2. to shove 3. to incite 4. to be advanced 5. to accredit
Tūr̃ai *f* Europe
tūr̃ancī *m* English (language)
tùrārà *v3* to flow
tùràrē *m* perfume
turārō *m* flow
tùrarre *m* (*f* tùrarriyā, *pl* tùrarrū) 1. mad 2.

contentious 3. difficult
Tūr̃āwā, Tùr̃àwā *see* Bàtūr̃è
tūràwā *f* ƙārà tūràwā to take one step forward
turɓà *f* (*pl* turbōbī) 1. road 2. path
tùr̃ɓāyā *f* sandy soil
tur̃da'anshè *m* (Nr) hip measurement
tur̃dàfàtìr̃în *m* (Nr) chest measurement
tur̃dàtāyè *m* (Nr) waist measurement
tūrè *v4* 1. to knock down 2. to depose
turkè 1. *m* (*pl* turàkā) stake 2. *v4* to tether 3. to hamper
turmī *m* (*pl* turàmē) mortar
turmùsā *v1* to force down
tùr̃nàbîs *m* (Nr) screwdriver
tùr̃ōzà *m* trousers
tur̃sàsā *v1* to humiliate
tūrū *m* 1. opposition 2. revolt
tūrù *m* (*pl* tūrunà) stocks
tùrumbà *f* (*pl* turumbōbī) oil can
tùrùrī *m* 1. steam 2. vapour
tùrūruwā *f/pl* ant
turzà *v1* to try hard
tūsa *f* fart
tūshè *m* 1. plant 2. base 3. basis 4. origin 5. mài tūshè reliable 6. maràs tūshè baseless
tūtà *f* (*pl* tūtōcī) 1. flag 2. banner
tūtiyà *f* zinc
tūtù *m* excrement
tùtur̃ *adv* forever
tuwō *m* 1. porridge, mash 2. ƙarfin tuwō force of arms
tūyà *see* tōyà
tùzūrū *m* (*pl* tùzùrai) bachelor

Uu

ùbā *m* (*pl* ùbànnī) **1.** father **2.** head **3.** specialist

Ùbangijì *m* God

ūfè *v4* to run off

uffàn *adv* Bài cê dà sū uffàn ba. He didn't say a word to them.

ujilā *f* **1.** haste **2.** price **3.** wages

ujìlì *m* price

ujiřā *f* **1.** legal fees **2.** *see* ujilā

ukù *f* three

ùkùnnī *pl* triplets

ùƙūbà *f* anguish

ūlù *m* wool

ùmařtà *v2** (-ci/cē) to order

ummàl àbā'isì *m* the real reason

umřā *f* the Lesser Hajj

ùmùřnī *m* command

ùngo! here you are, take it!

ungōzancì *m* midwifery

ùngōzòmà *f* (*pl* ùngòzòmai) midwife

ùngùlu *f* (*pl* ùngùlàyē) vulture

ùnguwā, ungwà *f* (*pl* unguwōyī) **1.** borough **2.** district **3.** quarter

ùnguwař talakāwā *f* **1.** ghetto **2.** inner city

ushiřā *see* ujiřā, ushìřī

ushìřī *m* one tenth

usùř *m* (*pl* usuřōřī) whistle

Ût *m* (Nr) August

uwā *f* (*pl* iyàyē) mother

uwař bāshì *f* credit

uwařgidā *f* mistress of the house

uwař hanjì *f* (med.) appendix

uwā-ùbā *m* umbrella organisation

uwař yāƙì *f* commander-in-chief

uzùřī *m* excuse

Ww

wà 1. *prep* to 2. for 3. *conj* and
wâ *m* (*pl* yayyē, yāyū) elder
  brother
wà? (*pl* su wà?) who?
wa'àdī *m* (*pl* wa'adōdī)
  1. appointment 2. pledge
  3. time limit 4. ultimatum
  5. yankè wà... wa'àdī to set a
  time limit
wa'àzī *m* (*pl* wà'àzai) 1.
  sermon 2. warning
waccàn *see* wancàn
wàccan *see* wàncan
waccè *see* wandà
wàccē *see* wànnē
wàcè *see* wànè
wàcēcè *see* wànēnè
wàdā *f* wealth
wàdā *m/f* (*pl* wàdànnī) dwarf
wadai, wadan *m* 1. curse 2. yi
  Allàh wadai dà to condemn
waddà *see* wandà
wadàtā *v1* to make wealthy
wàdàtā *v3* to have enough (dà
  of)
wàdātà *v2* (-ci/cē) 1. to make
  wealthy 2. to be enough for
wadàncân *see* wancàn
wàdàncan *see* wàncan
wadàndà *see* wandà
wadànnân *see* wannàn
wàdànnē *see* wànnē
wàdànnè *see* wànè
wadànsu *see* wani
wāgā *m* (*pl* wāgàgē) pannier
wāgùnù *m* (*pl* wāgunōnī)
  goods wagon

wahà *f* wurin wahà swimming
  pool
wàhalà *f* (*pl* wahalōlī) trouble
wahàmī *m* 1. doubts 2. delusions
wahàyī *m* vision
wai 1. look out! 2. that 3. it is
  said that 4. in order that 5.
  named 6. kō wai in the hope
  that 7. bâ wai no doubt!
wai don *prep* because of
wai don kō *conj* in the hope that
  that
waifà *f* (*pl* waifōfī) windscreen
  wiper
waigà *v1* to swing round
waigì, waijì *m* 1. wedge
  2. chock
wàinā *f* fried cakes
wai-wai *m* rumour
waiwàyā *v1* 1. to turn to look
  (kân at) 2. to consider
wàiwayà *v2* 1. to turn to 2. to
  refer to (dà about)
wàiwàyē *m* 1. allusion 2. Yā
  mai dà wàiwàyē. He made
  reference to it again.
waiwayō *v6* 1. to turn back (dà
  to) 2. to refer back 3. to return
  unexpectedly
wàjabà *v3* to be compulsory
wajàbtā *v1* to make compulsory
  (wà to)
wajē *m* (*pl* wajèjē) 1. direction
  2. area 3. place 4. side
wàje *adv* outside
wajen *prep* 1. to 2. towards
  3. at 4. with 5. during 6. in the

region of **7.** approximately **8.** as regards

wàjen *prep* outside of

wājìbī *m* (*f* **wājìbā,** *pl* **wàjìbai, wājibōbī**) compulsory

wājòkō *f* lover

wakàɓī *see* **waɓàɓī**

wākē *m* (*pl* **wākàikai**) bean(s)

wāken tùřāwā *m* pea(s)

wakilcì *m* **1.** representation **2.** mandate

wàkìlì *m* (*pl* **wàkīlìyā,** *pl* **wàkìlai**) **1.** representative **2.** delegate **3.** member of legislature

wakìltā *v1* **1.** to appoint as representative **2.** to delegate

wàkiltā 1. *f* representation **2.** *v2** to represent

wakiltař dà *v5* to appoint as representative

wāɓà *f* (*pl* **wāɓōɓī, wàɓe-wàɓe**) **1.** song **2.** poem

waɓàfī *m* **1.** detention **2.** comma **3.** gidan waɓàfī prison

waɓàfī mài ruwā *m* semicolon

waɓàftā *v1* (leg.) **1.** to bequeath **2.** to put in trust

wàɓē *m* (*pl* **wāɓōɓī**) religious song

wāɓōɓī *see* **wāɓà, wàɓē**

wālà *v1* to relax

walà'allà *adv* maybe

wàlāgīgī *m* **1.** negligence **2.** irresponsibility

wàlàhā *f* mid-morning

wàlā-wàlā, wàlà-walā *f* ɗan wàlā-wàlā **1.** double-dealer **2.** black marketeer

waldà *f* **1.** mai waldà welder **2.** yi waldà to weld

waldì *m* welding

wàlî, wàliyì *m* (*pl* **wàlìyai**) (Isl.) saint

wàlīmà *f* (*pl* **walimōmì**) wedding banquet

wàliyì *m see* **wàlî**

wàlɓiyā *f* **1.** lightning **2.** shininess

wallà! by God!

wàllafà *v2** **1.** to write **2.** to compose

wàllāhì! by God!

wallē *m* weak spot

Waluhù *m* Wolof

wānà *v1* (*m* **wānì**) **1.** to wind **2.** to crank **3.** to turn

wancàn (*f* **waccàn,** *pl* **waɗancân**) that

wàncan (*f* **wàccan,** *pl* **wàɗancan**) **1.** that over there **2.** the one mentioned

wancè *see* **wānè**

wandà (*f* **waddà, waccè,** *pl* **waɗàndà**) **1.** who **2.** which **3.** the one who **4.** that which

wandàrā *v1* to bend

wàndàř-wandař *adv* zigzag

wàndō *m* (*pl* **wandunà**) trousers

wànè? *m* (*f* **wàcè?,** *pl* **wàɗannè?**) which?

wānè *m* (*f* **wancè,** *pl m* **su wānè,** *pl f* **su wancè**) so-and-so

wànē? who do you think...?

wànēnè? *m* (*f* **wàcēcè?,** *pl* **su wànēnè?**) who?

wàngan *adv* wide open

wani *m* (*f* **wata,** *pl* **wasu, waɗansu**) **1.** a, an **2.** some **3.** someone **4.** something **5.** any **6.** anyone **7.** anything **8.** many **9.** another **10.** other than

wani... **wani** one... the other
wānì *see* **wanà**
wankā *m* washing oneself
wankè *v4* (*m* **wankì**) 1. to wash
2. to absolve
wànke-wànke *m* washing up
wankì *m* washing
wannàn *m/f* (*pl* **waɗànnân**)
this
wannàn... **wannàn** one.. the
other
wànnan *m/f* (*pl* **wàɗànnan**)
that
wànnē? *m* (*f* **wàccē?**, *pl*
wàɗànnē?) which one?
wân shēkarè *adv* (on) the day
after tomorrow
wànwâi, wanwê *f* one-way
street
wânyē *v4* to end
wànzāmì *m* (*pl* **wànzàmai**)
barber
wanzancì *m* barbering
wanzaɽ dà *v5* 1. to bring into
existence 2. to bring into force
wànzu *v7* 1. to happen 2. to
remain (over)
wànzuwā *f* 1. existence 2.
presence
waɽ *see* **wàɽ hakà**
warakà *see* **waɽƙà**
waɽantì *m* (*pl* **wàɽàntai,**
waɽantōcì) warrant
wàràrì *m* perfume
wara-wara *adv* spaced out
wàɽdì *m* rosewater
wāɽè *v4* 1. to separate 2. to
allocate 3. to earmark
wàrē *m* yi **wà... sānìyaɽ wàrē** to
ostracise
wargàjē *v4* 1. to be scattered
2. to fail 3. (fin.) to collapse

wargàzā *v1* 1. to scatter 2. to
make fail
wargī *m* (*pl* **wàrgàce-**
wàrgàce) playing
wàɽ hakà *adv* gòbe **wàɽ hakà** at
the same time tomorrow
wārī *m* stink
wārì *m* one (of two)
wāriyā *f* 1. isolation 2. segregation
wāriyaɽ àl'ummà *f* racial
segregation, apartheid
warkâ *f see* **waɽƙà**
warkè *v4* 1. to revover from an
illness 2. to be cured
wàɽkī *m* (*pl* **waɽkunà**)
loincloth
waɽƙà *f* (*pl* **waɽƙōƙì**) 1. leaf
2. sheet (of paper) 3. note (of
money)
wartsàkē *v4* 1. to recover 2. to
be alert 3. to clear up
warwàrē *v4* 1. to unfold 2. to
cancel 3. to dissolve 4. to
exercise
warwàrè màtsalà to solve a
problem
wàrwàtsu *v5* to spread
wàsā *v2** (-shi/ē, *m* **wàshī**)
1. to infect 2. to affect 3. to
dislike
wāsà *v1* (*m* **wāshì**) 1. to sharpen
2. to speed up
wāsà ƙwaƙwalwā *f* quiz
wàsā *m* (*pl* **wàsànnī**) 1. game
2. sport 3. fīlin **wàsā** playing
field 4. stadium
wasàlī *m* (*pl* **wasulà**) vowel
wàsan kusà dà ƙàrshē *m*
(spor.) semi-final
wàsan ƙàrshē *m* (spor.) final
wàsan ƙwallon ƙafà *m*
1. football game 2. **maì**

wàsan ƙwallon ƙafà footballer
wāsàshē v4 1. to quickly clear
  2. to quickly finish
wàsa-wàsa adv gradually
wàsan kwaikwayō m (theatre)
  play
Wàsànnin Olympics pl
  Olympic Games
wâsh! oh no!
wāshā f (pl wāshōshī) washer
wāshè v4 1. to improve 2. to
  clear up 3. to settle 4. to raid
wàshègarī f/adv (on) the
  following day
wāshì m 1. praise 2. see wāsà
wàsīƙà f (pl wàsìƙū,
  wasìƙōƙī) letter
wàsīƙàr tunì f 1. reminder
  2. memo
wàsìƙū ta ƙasà/jirgin ruwā
  pl surface mail
wàsìƙū ta samà pl airmail
wàsiyyà f (pl wasiyyōyī) will
wàsōsò m yi wàsōsò to scramble
wassàlam hāzā wassàlam...
  Yours sincerely...
wasu see wani
wàswāsì m 1. deep thought 2. yi
  wàswāsì to be undecided
wata see wani
watā m (pl wàtànnī) 1. moon
  2. month 3. Watā yā tsayà.
  There's a new moon tonight.
wataƙīlà, ƙīlà adv perhaps
watàn ɗan Adàm m satellite
wàtàu, wàtò 1. that is to say...
  2. so,...
wàtàu kā ga... in fact...
wata-wata adv 1. hesitantly
  2. yi wata-wata to hesitate
wātàyâwā f 1. hovering 2.
  orbiting

wātsà vl (m wātsì) 1. to scatter
  2. to disperse 3. to broadcast
  4. to televise
wātsà làbàrai to broadcast
  news
wàtsàlniyā f struggle
wàtsàl-watsal adv yi wàtsàl-
  watsal to wriggle
wātsè v4 to be dispersed
wātsì, wàtsī m 1. broadcast
  2. yi wātsì dà to reject 3. yi
  wātsì dà bùkātà to drop a
  demand 4. see wātsà
wàtsu v7 1. to spread 2. to be
  distributed
wâutā f senselesnes
wāwā m/f (pl wāwàyē) 1. fool
  2. jester
wāwilō m/f toothless
wàwurà v2* to snatch
wayà f 1. wire 2. spoke 3. pound
  (weight) 4. scales 5. telegraph
  6. telephone 7. gidan wayà
  post office 8. bugà wà... wayà
  to telephone
wayam adv deserted
wāyè v4 1. to clarify 2. Gàrī yā
  wāyè. It dawned.
wàyè? who?
wàyō m cunning
wâyyō! oh dear!
wazanà f (Isl.) call to prayer
wàzīrì m (pl wàzìrai) 1. vizier
  2. top minister
wējì m 1. wedge 2. chock
weldà see waldà
wīlì m (pl wīlōlī) wheel
windò m/f (pl windōjī) window
Wìskindiyà f West Indies
wî-wî m marijuana
wòfì m/f (pl wōfàyē) 1. useless
  2. à wòfì uselessly

wōhò *m* booing
wōkàcì *m* 1. time 2. period
wòshè? when?
wucè *v4* 1. to pass 2. to surpass
3. to elapse 4. to die
wucì *m* wani wucì occasionally
wucìn gàdì *m* 1. reserve 2. na
wucìn gàdì temporary 3.
interim 4. short-term 5. acting
wuf *adv* yi wuf to move suddenly
wuffì *m* slipper(s)
wuƙā *f (pl* wuƙàƙē) 1. knife
2. trowel
wuƙař sìmintì *f* trowel
wuƙì-wùƙì *m* shame
wul *adv* baƙi wul pitch black
wùl *adv* at great speed
wulākàntā *see* wulāƙàntā
wùlàƙài *adv* with contempt
wulāƙàntā *vI* to treat badly
wulgà *vI* to pass
wundò *m (pl* wundunà) 1.
window 2. gìlāshìn wundò
windowpane
wunì *v* to spend a day
wunì *m* 1. day 2. daytime
wuř *adv* jā wuř bright red
wuřgà *vI* 1. to throw 2. to jerk

wuri *adv* dà wuri early
wurì *m (pl* wuràrē) place
wurì *m (pl* kuɗì) cowrie
wuri dà wuri *adv* openly
wurin *prep* 1. to 2. at 3. near
4. with
wurin haƙà *m* mine
wurin hàƙař mâi *m* oilfield
wurin zamā *m* place of residence
wuri-wuri *adv* dà wuri-wuri
very early
wurƙi *m* severity
wùrù-wurū *m* not being
straightforward
wùskî *f* (Nr) whisky
wuta *adv* à wuta in the fire
wutā *f (pl* wutàcē, wutōcì) 1.
fire 2. electricity
wutař làntařkì *f* electric shock
wutař 'Yōlà *f* glow-worm
wutsiyà *f (pl* wutsiyōyì) tail
wuyà *m (pl* wuyōyì) neck
wuyàn hannū *m* wrist
wùyā *f* 1. difficulty 2. trouble
wùyàce *adv* à wùyàce with
difficulty
wuyàtā *vI* to make difficult
wùyatà *v3* to be difficult

Yy

ya 1. *relative completive* he **2.**
see **shi**

yà 1. *subjunctive* he **2.** *prep* (just)
like **3.** amongst

yā *completive* he

yâ 1. *indefinite future* he **2.** *f* (*pl*
yayyē, yāyū) elder sister

yà *negative continuous* he

yabà *v1* to praise

yàbā *v2** (*m* **yàbō**) **1.** to praise
2. to eulogise **3.** tɔ approve of
4. to recommend

yabanyà *f* young corn

yabà wà to recommend

yàbirbìrā *f* fruit bat

yàbō *m* **1.** praise **2.** eulogy
3. approval **4.** recommendation

yàɓā *v2** (*m* **yàɓē**) to plaster

yācè *v4* **1.** to wipe off **2.** to cold-
shoulder **3.** (Nr) to open

yā dà *v* **1.** to throw away **2.** to
abandon

yaddà how

yādì *m* (*pl* **yāduddukà**) **1.** yard
2. depot **3.** cloth

yādā *v1* to spread

yàdā *v2** to skim

yàdu *v7* to be spread

yàɗuwā *f* **1.** spread **2.** advance
3. cùtā mài yàɗuwā infectious

yàɗuwař cùtā *f* epidemic

yāfà *v1* **1.** to put around
shoulders **2.** to sprinkle

yàfā *v2** to forgive

yàfatā *v2** (**-ci/cē**) to beckon to

yāfè *v4* **1.** to forgive **2.** to
renounce

yāgè *v4* to rip

yai = ya yi, yā yi

yājì *m* (*pl* **yāzūzukà**) **1.** hot
spice **2.** strike **3.** boycott

yājìn aikì *m* strike

yak *adv* exactly

yakàn, ya kàn *m habitual* he

yakê, ya kê *m continuous* he

yàkusà *v2** (**-shi/ē**) to claw at

yàƙā *v2** **1.** to wage war on
2. to tackle

yàƙadò *m* **yi wà... yàƙadò** to
scold

yàƙayyà *f* warfare

yāƙè *v4* to grimace

yāƙì *m* (*pl* **yàƙe-yàƙe**) war

yāƙì dà jāhilcì *m* campaign for
literacy

yāƙìn cācař bakà *m* cold war

yàƙinì *m* **yi yàƙinì** to be certain

yallàɓai *m* Sir

yàlwā *f* **1.** abundance **2.** yi yàlwā
to flourish

yàlwàce *adv* à yàlwàce in
abundance

yalwàtā *v1* to increase the size
of

yàlwatà *v3* to be ample

yàlwatà *v2** (**-ci/cē**) to be
ample for

yāmī *m* sourness

yâmma 1. *f* west **2.** na yâmma
western **3.** *adv* dà yâmma
in/during the afternoon

yâmmā *f* afternoon

yammacin *prep* **1.** west of
2. western

yāmùtsā *v1* **1.** to stir in **2.** to muddle up **3.** to quarrel

yamùtsē *v4* **1.** to be stirred in **2.** to be muddled up

yàmutsī *m* **1.** confusion **2.** quarrel

yanà, ya nà *m continuous* he

yanàyī *m* **1.** weather **2.** climate **3.** atmosphere **4.** temperament **5.** na yanàyī environmental **6.** ecological

yanàyin shigèwā *m* vulnerability

yandà how

yangàrā *v1* to grind coarsely

yankā *m see* **yankà, yànkā**

yankà *v1* (*m* **yankā**) **1.** to slaughter **2.** to execute **3.** to cut up **4.** to fix

yànkā *v2** (*m* **yankā**) **1.** to cut off **2.** to sever **3.** to slit **4.** to take a short cut

yankā-yankā *adv* **mài yankā-yankā** sliced

yanke 1. *m* lie **2.** *adv* cut (off) **3.** slaughtered

yankè *v4* **1.** to cut off **2.** to decide on **3.** to be in short supply

yànkē *m* short cut

yankè hukuncì to pass sentence

yankè shāwařà to come to a decision

yankì *m* (*pl* **yankunà**) **1.** piece **2.** section **3.** district

yankìn cìnìkayyà marà shingē *m* free trade zone

yankì-yankì *m* **bàtun yankì-yankì** regionalism

yanyànā *v1* to cut into strips

yânyāwà *f* (*pl* **yànyàyī**) fennec

yànzu *adv* **1.** now **2.** hař yànzu up till now

yař dà *v* **1.** to throw away **2.** to abandon

yârā *see* **yàrò**

Yaràbā, Yarabāwā *see* **Bàyarabè**

Yarabancī *m* Yoruba language

yàràntakà *f* childhood

yařɓà *v1* to fling

yařɓař dà *v5* to cold-shoulder

yařɓè *v4* to splash

yàřda *v3* **1.** to agree **2.** to consent **3.** to approve (**dà/à kân** of)

yàřdā *f* consent

yàřē *m* mother tongue

yařɓè *v4* to splash

yārì *m* **1.** chief warder **2.** gidan yārì prison

yàřimà *m* prince

yārinyà *f* (*pl* **'yammātā**) girl

yařjè *v4* **1.** to permit (**wà** s.o.) **2.** to agree (**à kân** on)

yàřjējēnìyā *f* **1.** consent **2.** agreement **3.** treaty

yàřjējēnìyař àbùtā *f* **1.** alliance **2.** treaty of friendship

yārò *m* (*pl* **yârā**) **1.** boy **2.** servant

yāsà *v1* to clean out

yàshī *m* **1.** sand **2.** soil

yātsà *m/f* (*pl* **yātsū**) **1.** finger **2.** toe

yātsàn ƙafà *m* toe

yàtsinà *f* grimace

yau *m* (*gen* **yan**) saliva

yâu *f/adv* today

yâu dà dare *adv* tonight

yâu dà gòbe *adv* **1.** gradually **2.** sooner or later

yâu dà kullum *adv* **1.** day-to-day **2.** basic **3.** hařkōkin yâu dà kullum current affairs

yaucī *m* lateness
yàudařà 1. *f* (*pl* **yaudařōřī**) trick 2. *v2** to trick
yàuƙaƙà *v3* to last long
yauƙī *m* sliminess
yausàsā *v1* 1. to make wither 2. to weaken
yàusasà *v3* 1. to wither 2. to feel weak
yàushè? when?
yaushī *m* weakness
yawā̀ *m* 1. amount 2. quantity 3. **dà yawā̀** much, many
yawaicī *m* majority
yawàitā *v1* 1. to increase 2. to produce in quantity 3. to overdo
yawancī 1. *m* majority 2. most 3. *adv* mostly
yawàn hàyàyyafā̀ *m* birth rate
yawàn ìsa shāwarā̀ *m* quorum
yawàn laifuffukā̀ *m* crime rate
yawà-yawancī *m* majority
yawà-yawancin most of
yāwṑ *m* (*pl* **yàwàce-yàwàce**) 1. walk 2. journey on foot 3. tour 4. fluctuation
yāwòn bùɗe idò *m* sight-seeing tour
yāwòn shāƙàtâwā *m* 1. tour 2. sightseeing
yāwū *m* 1. saliva 2. permission 3. **mài màganà dà yāwū** spokesman
yàyā *m/f* (*pl* **yayyē**, **yāyū**) 1. elder brother 2. elder sister
yàyà? 1. how? 2. **Yàyà sūnankì?** What is your name?

yāyàtā *v1* 1. to shout about 2. to gossip
yāyè *v4* 1. to wean 2. to remove 3. to disappear
yàyī *m* 1. time 2. fashion
yàyin dà when
yàyin makařantā *m* school uniform
yāyū *see* **wâ, yâ, yàyā**
yayyàfā *v1* to sprinkle
yayyafī *m* drizzle
yayyàgā *v1* to tear up
yayyē *see* **wâ, yâ, yàyā**
yayyè *v4* to leak
yàyyō *m* leaking
yēkùwā *f* proclamation
yi *v* (*m* **yî**) 1. to do 2. to make 3. to be 4. to happen 5. to succeed 6. to be done 7. to spend (time) 8. **yi ta** to keep on doing
yì *prep* 1. (just) like 2. amongst
yî *see* **yi**
yifā *v1* to cover over
yinì *v* to spend a day
yinì *m* 1. day 2. daytime
yînyē *v4* to complete
yiwṑ *v6 see* **yi**
yìwu *v7* to be possible
yìwuwā *f* possibility
Yūlì *m* July
yumɓū *m* clay
Yūnì *m* June
yunƙùrā *v1* to take every effort
yùnƙurī *m* attempt
yunwā̀ *f* 1. hunger 2. famine 3. **ji yunwā̀** to feel hungry
yùnwatà *v3* to feel hungry
yùřēniyàm *m* uranium

’Y ’y

’yā *f* (*pl* ’yā’yā) daughter
’yammātā, ’yam mātā *pl*
1. girls 2. young women
’yan *pl see* ɗan
’yancì *m* 1. freedom 2. self-
respect 3. right 4. yāƙìn nēman
’yancì freedom struggle
’yancìn faɗìn àlbařkàcin
bàkī *m* freedom of speech
’yancìn dà dòkā ta tānadař
m civil rights
’yancìn jàřìdū *m* freedom of
the press
’yancìn kā dà ƙùři’à *m*
1. right to vote 2. suffrage

’yancìn kâi *m* independence
’yan kâi *m* 1. extra 2. tàlàtin dà
’yan kâi thirty and a bit
’yankāmancì *m* street comedy
’yântā *v1*, ’yantař dà *v5* 1. to
free 2. to liberate
’yàntaccē *m* (*f* ’yàntacciyā, *pl*
’yàntàttū) 1. free 2.
independent
’yan’uwā *pl* 1. colleagues
2. fellow
’yař *m see* ’yā, ɗan
’yař’uwā (*pl* ’yan’uwā) sister
’yā’yā *pl* 1. children 2. sons
3. daughters 4. fruit

Zz

zā *future marker*

zâ to be going to + *subject pronoun*

zàbgā *v2** to do a lot of

zabgē *v4* 1. to remove a lot of 2. to stab 3. to erode

zābì *m* choice

zàbī *see* **zàbō**

zàbîb *m* raisin(s)

zàbīr̃à *f* (*pl* **zàbìr̃ū**) wallet

zàbiyā *mf* albino

zābìyà *f* (*pl* **zābiyōyī**) lead-singer

zàbō *m* (*f* **zàbuwā**, *pl* **zàbī**) 1. guinea-fowl 2. **yi tāshìn zàbō** to make rapid progress

zabtàrē *v4* to take a lot of

zàbur̃à *v3* 1. to leap up 2. to rush away

zàbūr̃ā *f* psalms

zàɓā *v2** (*m* **zàɓē**) 1. to select 2. to elect

zàɓaɓɓē *m* (*f* **zàɓaɓɓiyā**, *pl* **zàɓaɓɓū**) chosen

zàɓē *m* 1. choice 2. election 3. **'yàntaccen zàɓē** free elections 4. **rùmfar̃ zàɓē** polling booth

zàɓen cikè gurbìn kujèrar̃ màjàlisà *m* by-election

zàɓen jĩn r̃a'àyin jàma'à *m*, **zàɓen rabà gar̃damà** *m* referendum

zāɓì *m* 1. choice 2. alternative

zāɓukà *pl* elections

zāfàfā *v1* to heat up

zàfafà *v3* to become heated up

zāfàfà *see* **zàzzāfā**

zāfàfan màtàkai na danniyā *pl* repressive measures

zāfàfà wà to anger

zāfĩ *m* 1. heat 2. pain 3. intensity

zāgà *v1* 1. to go round 2. to follow closely 3. to move on to 4. to tour

zàgā *v2** (*m* **zāgì**) 1. to insult 2. to swear at 3. to draw (sword/water)

zāgàyā *v1*, **zàgayà** *v2**, **zāgàyē** *v4 see* **zāgà**, **r̃ājè**

zāgayè *m* 1. round 2. (spor.) leg

zāgayôwar̃ r̃ānā *f* anniversary

zagē *v4* to be in the middle of

zāgè *v4* 1. to erode 2. to undress

zāgè damtsè to set to work

zāgī *m* (*pl* **zagàgē**) escort

zagì *m* (*pl* **zagàgē**) 1. escort 2. **ɗan kân zagì** (pol.) yes-man

zāgì *m* (*pl* **zàge-zàge**) 1. insult(s) 2. *see* **zàgā**

zagō *m* termite

zagon k̃âs *m* sabotage

zàgwàɗì *m* eagerness

zāhìr̃ĩ *m* (*f* **zāhìr̃ā**, *pl* **zàhìr̃ai**) 1. clear 2. obvious 3. **à zāhìr̃ĩ** obviously 4. in reality

zâi *m future* he will

zaibà *f* mercury

zā'idà *f* exaggeration

zàikē *m* spirit possession

zaitì *m* eucalyptus oil

zàitûn, zàitūnì *m* 1. olive 2. **mân zàitûn** olive oil

zaizàyē *v4* 1. to erode 2. to collapse

zaizàyêwā *f* erosion

zàkā *f* 1. (Isl.) religious tax
2. alms

zàkarà *m* (*pl* zàkàrū) 1. cock
2. hero

zākì *m* (*f* zākanyà, *pl* zākōkì)
lion

zàkkā *f* 1. (Isl.) religious tax
2. alms

zàƙā *v2** to eat a lot of

zāƙàƙā *v1* to sweeten

zāƙī *m* sweetness

zàlāƙà *f* eloquence

zalɓè *m see* zarɓè

zālì *m* cîn zāli oppression

zallā 1. *f* purity 2. *adv* purely
3. in essence

zàluncì *m* 1. tyranny 2. cruelty
3. oppression 4. yi zàluncì à
zàɓè to rig an election

zàluntà *v2** (-ci/cē) to oppress

zalzalà *f* earthquake

zama *v*, zàmanà *v3* 1. to be
2. to become 3. to settle 4. to
happen (wà to)

zamā *m* 1. being 2. staying
3. state 4. living 5. wurin
zamā residence

zaman dàɓàrō *m* sitdown
protest

zaman dòkaȓ tā ɓācì *f* state of
emergency

zāmànī, zàmānì *m* (*pl*
zàmànai, zàmànū) 1. time
2. period 3. na zàmànì modern

zaman hijiȓā *m* exile

zaman kâi *m* mài zaman kâi
1. independent 2. private
3. personal

zaman kashè-wàndō *m* 1.
unemployment 2. mài zaman
kashè-wàndō unemployed

zaman lāfiyà dà lùmānà
peace and tranquillity

zàmanà tīlàs *v3* to become
necessary

zamantō *v6* to turn out to be

zamantôwā *f* becoming

zāmà-zāmà *adv* sometimes

zàmba *f* (*pl* zàmbàce-
zàmbàce) 1. fraud 2.
corruption

zambàȓ *m* one thousand

zàmbatà 1. *f* fraud 2. *v2**
(-ci/cē) to mock 3. to cheat

zàmbō *m* 1. satire 2. ridicule

zāmè *v4* 1. to slip 2. to slide
3. to rein in sharply 4. to
backslide

zāmiyā *f* wajen zāmiyā
playground

zân *future* I will

zānā *f* (*pl* zànàkū) mat

zānà *v1* 1. to draw 2. to mark

zàncē *m* (*pl* zantukà) 1.
conversation 2. topic 3. matter
4. mài iyà zàncē witty

zanè *m* (*pl* zannuwà) body
cloth

zànē *m* (*pl* zàne-zàne) 1. line
2. mark 3. drawing

zànen tambàȓi *m* coat of arms

zànen tāyà *m* tyre tread

zangarnìyā *f* head of corn

zàngà-zangà *f* 1. protest
demonstration 2. mài zàngà-
zàngà demonstrator

zàngà-zangà ta nūnà àdāwà
f protest march

zangò *m* (*pl* zangunà) 1. camp
2. range 3. stop-over

zàngū *f* hundred

zannì *m* 1. conjecture 2.
presumption

zântā *vl* 1. to converse (dà with)
2. to talk about
zanzanā *f* smallpox
zàrā *v2** to snatch
zar̃àf̃ī *m* (*pl* **zar̃afōf̃ī**) 1.
opportunity 2. wealth 3. leisure
4. **cîn zar̃àfī** slander
zārar̃ dà zārar̃ as soon as
zara-zara *adv* long and thin
zarɓê *m* heron
zar̃cè *v4* 1. to exceed 2. to go
beyond 3. to protrude
zàrē *m* (*pl* **zarūruwà**) 1. string
2. thread 3. ribbon
zārè *v4* 1. to unsheath 2. to
withdraw
zàrē *m* 1. reject 2. outcast
zàrgā *v2** 1. to accuse 2. to
blame
zàrgē *m* noose
zàrgī *m* 1. accusation 2. blame
zàrī *m* greed
zàri-rùgā *m* ƙwallon zàri-rùgā
rugby
zar̃tà *vl* 1. to bore into 2. to
permeate
zar̃tar̃ dà *v5* to carry out
zar̃tar̃ dà dōkā to pass a law
zar̃tar̃ dà hukuncì to deliver a
verdict
zar̃târ̃wā *f* 1. na zar̃târ̃wā
executive 2. kwàmitìn
zar̃târ̃wā politburo 3.
màjàlisàr̃ zar̃târ̃wā executive
council
zar̃tò *m* (*pl* **zar̃àtā, zar̃tunà**)
saw
zar̃tsī *m* ruwan zar̃tsī brackish
water
zār̃untakà *f see* **jār̃umtakà**
zàr̃ūr̃ùgā *f* ƙwallon zàr̃ūr̃ùgā
rugby

zàtā *v2** (-ci/cē, *m* zàtō) to
expect (that)
zàtō *m* 1. thought 2. expectation
zaunà *vl* 1. to sit (down)
2. to settle 3. to remain in
zàunà-gàrī-banzā *m/f*
unemployed
zàunannē *m* (*f* zàunanniyā, *pl*
zàunànnū) permanent
zàunannen wàkīlì *m*
permanent delegate
zàunanniyar̃ kujèrā (pol.)
permanent seat
zàune *adv* seated
zàune-tsàye *m* 1. riot 2. unrest
zaurè *m* (*pl* **zaurukà**) entrance
room
zàuzautà *v2** (-ci/ē) to pester
zāwàyī, zāwò *m* diarrhoea
zayyànā *vl* 1. to adorn
2. to improve 3. to describe
zàyyàne *adv* à zàyyàne in
theory
zàzū *m* (Nr) the latest fashion
zàzzàɓī *m* fever
zàzzàɓin cīzòn saurō, (Nr)
zàzzàɓin dàminā *m* malaria
zàzzāfā *m/f* (*pl* **zāfàfā**) 1. hot
2. drastic
zî *m* diamonds (in cards)
zîk *m* zip
zikìr̃ī *m* masculine
zìnā *f* (*pl* **zìnàce-zìnàce**)
adultery
zīnār̃ī, zīnār̃ìyā *f* gold
zìndīƙì *m* (*f* **zìndīƙìyā,** *pl*
zìndìƙai) 1. destitute 2.
heretic
zìr̃gà-zir̃gā *f* movement to and
fro
zīr̃ī *m* narrow place
zīr̃in gāɓà *m* strip of land

zìyārà *f* (*pl* zìyàr̃ce-zìyàr̃ce) 1. visit 2. (Chris.) pilgrimage

zìyār̃àr̃ aikì *f* 1. official visit 2. state visit

zìyār̃àr̃ ban girmā *f* courtesy call

zìyar̃tà *v2** (-cì/cē) to visit

zō *v* (*m* zuwà) 1. to come 2. na à-zō-à-ganì tangible

zobè 1. *m* (*f* zōbanyà, *pl* zôbbā) ring 2. *v4* to take back

zō6à *vl* to overlap

zògī *m* pain

zòlayà *v2** 1. to interrogate 2. to taunt

zòlōlò *m* (*f* zòlōlùwā) lofty

zōmō *m* (*pl* zōmàyē) rabbit

zōzàyē *v4* 1. to wear away 2. to erode

zû *m* gidan zû zoo

zubà *vl* 1. to pour 2. to put (à into) 3. to do a lot of

zùba *v3* 1. to leak 2. to collapse

zubà jār̃ì-hujjà 1. to invest (à in) 2. mài zubà jār̃ì-hujjà investor

zubar̃ dà *v5* to pour out

zubar̃ dà shàr̃ā to dump waste

zub dà *see* zubar̃ dà

zubè *v4* 1. to pour away 2. to collapse completely

zubèwar̃ mân fētùr̃ *f* oil spill

zūcì *adv* 1. à zūcì in the heart 2. kìshìn zūcì ambition

zūcìyā *f* (*pl* zukàtā) 1. heart 2. spirit 3. 6àcìn zūcìyā irritability 4. far̃ar̃ zūcìyā happiness 5. jar̃ zūcìyā courage 6. rìkè à zūcìyā to keep in mind

zufà, zuffà *f* 1. sweating 2. hot weather

zugà *vl* 1. to blow 2. to incite

zùgūgù *m* exaggeration

zuhudù *m* (Isl.) 1. abstinence 2. asceticism

zù6ā *v2** to inhale

zù6ā ta mēsà to siphon

zū6è *v4* 1. to suck in 2. to dodge

zù6e-zù6e *m* hesitation

zulai *m* (Nr) sallàr̃ zulai Bastille Day (14th July)

zùlāmà *f* 1. tyranny 2. cruelty

zùlāyà *v2** to cross-question

Zulhajjì *m* (Isl.) twelfth month

Zùlk̃idà *m* (Isl.) eleventh month

zulùmì *m* deep thought

zumà *m* 1. honey 2. k̃udan zumà bee

zummà *f* intention

zumù *m* (*f* zunìyā, *pl* zumai) 1. close friend 2. mak̃ì zumù elbow

zumuncì, zùmùntā *f* 1. (blood) relationship 2. good relations 3. friendship 4. solidarity

zùndum *adv* full up

zùndùm *adv* splash

zùndā *v2** (*m* zùndē) to point out (with lips)

zungùrā *vl* (*m* zungùrī) to poke

zùngurà *v2** to provoke

zungùrē *v4* to poke

zungùrī *m* 1. provocation 2. *see* zungùrā

zunguro bàkì *v6* to pout

zunkùdà *vl* to hitch up

zùnubì *m* (*pl* zùnùbai) 1. sin 2. yi zùnubì to sin

zunzùrūtù *m* a great deal

zunzùrūtùn kùɗai *m* large amount of money

zûr̃ *m* shaidàr̃ zûr̃ perjury

zurà *vl* to insert
zùràrà *v3* **1.** to slide down **2.** to drop (à into)
zurfàfà *vl* to deepen
zurfī *m* depth
zùr̃iyà *f* (*pl* **zur̃iyōyī**) descendant(s)
zurmà *vl* **1.** to put (cikin/à into) **2.** to collapse

zùrū *m* staring
zuwà **1.** *prep* to **2.** towards **3.** up till **4.** *m* arrival **5.** **mài zuwà** next **6.** *see* **zō**
zuwà gà... Dear...
zuwà gàba *adv* in the future
zuwà-zuwà *adv* from time to time
zuzù *m* (Nr) judge
zùzzurfà *m/f* (*pl* **zurfàfà**) deep

ENGLISH-HAUSA

Aa

a, an [ə, ei; ən, æn] **1.** wani **2.** ɗaya

abandon [ə·bændən] *v* bari

abate [ə·beit] *v* lafa

abattoir [ˈæbətwaː] *n* mahauta

abbey [ˈæbi] *n* gidan halwa

abbreviate [ə·briːvieit] *v* gajarta

abbreviation [əˌbriːviˈeiʃn] *n* gajartacciyar kalma

ABC [eibiˈsiː] *n* abacada

abdicate [ˈæbdikeit] *v* yi murabus

abdication [ˌæbdiˈkeiʃn] *n* murabus

abdomen [ˌæbdəmən] *n* ciki

abduct [æbˈdʌkt] *v* sace

abeyance [əˈbeijəns] *n* to fall into abeyance zama tsōhon yàyī

abhor [æbˈhoː] *v* yi ƙyama

abide [æˌbaid] *v* yarda (by da)

ability [əˈbiliti] *n* iyawa

able [ˈeibl] *adj* to be able iya

aboard [əˈbɔːd] *adv* **1.** a kan **2.** cikin da

abode [əˈbəud] *n* mazauni

abolish [əˈbɔliʃ] *v* **1.** kashe **2.** kawar da

abortion [əˈbɔːʃn] *n* zub da ciki

about [əˈbaut] *prep* **1.** a kan **2.** kamar **3.** wajen **4.** I am about to go. Yanzu zan tafi.

above [əˈbʌv] *prep* **1.** sama **2.** bisa **3.** fiye da

above all *adv* fiye da kome

abreast [əˈbrest] *adj* to keep abreast yi daidai (of da)

abroad [əˈbrɔːd] *adv* ƙasashen waje

abrogate [ˈæbrəugeit] *v* to abrogate a treaty soke yarjejeniya

abruptly [əˈbrʌpt] *adv* tintiřis

abscess [ˈæbses] *n* gyambo

absence [ˈæbsəns] *n* fāshì

absent [ˈæbsənt] *adj* ba nan ba

absolute [ˈæbsəluːt] *adj* na innanaha

absolutely [ˈæbsəluːtli; æbsəˈluːtli] *adv* kwata-kwata

absolve [əbˈzɔlv] *v* yafa wa... laifi

absorb [əbˈsɔːb] *v* sha

abstain [əbˈstein] *v* to abstain in voting ƙi jefa ƙuri'a

abstinence [ˈæbstinəns] *n* zuhudu

abstract [ˈabstrækt] *adj* mai zurfi

absurd [əbˈsəːd] *adj* na shirme

abundance [əˈbʌndəns] *n* **1.** yalwa **2.** in abundance cunkus

abundant [əˈbʌndənt] *adj* mai albarka

abundantly [əˈbʌndəntli] *adv* maƙil

abuse [əˈbjus] *n* **1.** azar **2.** azaba

abuse [əˈbjuːz] *v* **1.** zàgā **2.** azabta

academic [ˌækəˈdemik] **1.** *adj* na jami'a **2.** boko **3.** *n* furofesa

academy [əˈkædəmi] *n* kwalejin horawa

accelerate [əkˈseləreit] *v* ƙara wuta

accelerator [əkˈseləreitə] *n* totur, (Nr) askilatar

accent [ˈæksənt] *n* karin harshe

accept [ək'sept] v **1.** karɓa
2. yarda da **3. to accept
leadership** amshi shugabanci
access ['ækses] n **1.** shiga **2.** dāmā
accessible [ək'sesəbl] adj saukin
kai
accessory [ək'sesəri] n **1.** kayan
aiki **2.** (leg.) abokin hulɗa
accident ['æksidənt] n haɗari
accidental [,æksi'dentl] adj ba da
gangan ba
accidentally [,æksi'dentli] adv ba
da gangan ba
acclaimed [ə'kleimd] **it is
acclaimed** ana alfahari da shi
(as tamkar)
accommodate [ə'kɔmədeit] v
saukar da
accommodation [ə,kɔmə'deiʃn]
n masauki
accompany [ə'kʌmpəni] v raka
accomplice [ə'kʌmplis] n abokin
hulɗa
accomplish [ə'kʌmpliʃ] v **1.** cim
ma **2.** kammala
accomplishment [ə'kʌmpliʃmənt]
n abin yabawa
according to [ə'kɔ:diŋ] prep
1. gwargwadon **2.** bisa lafazin
account [ə'kaunt] n **1.** labari
2. lissafin kuɗi **3. bank
account** ajiyar banki **4. on
account of** saboda
accountancy [ə'kauntənsi] n
ilimin akanta
accountant [ə'kauntənt] n
akanta, (Nr) kwantabil
account book n littafin fasalin
kuɗi
accounting [ə'kauntiŋ] n **1.**
lissafin kuɗi, ƙidaya **2.** ilimin
akanta

accumulate [ə'kju:muleit] v tara
accumulation [ə,kju:mu'leiʃn] n
tarawa
accuracy ['ækjərəsi] n daidaito
accurate ['ækjərət] adv daidai
accusation [,ækju:'zeiʃn] n **1.**
tuhuma **2. false accusation**
ƙage
accuse [ə'kju:z] v **1.** tuhuma **2. to
accuse falsely** yi wa... ƙage
accused [ə'kju:zd] adj
tuhumamme
accustomed [ə'kʌstəmd] adj **to
be accustomed** saba (to da)
ache [eik] **1.** n ciwo **2.** v yi wa...
ciwo
achieve [ə'tʃi:v] v samu
achievement [ə'tʃi:vmənt] n **1.**
nasara **2.** abin yabo
acid [æsid] n ruwan batir
acid rain n gurɓataccen ruwan
sama
acknowledge [ək'nɔlidʒ] v **1.**
yarda da **2.** amsa
acknowledgement [ək'nɔlidʒmənt]
n **1.** amsa **2.** godiya
acquaintance [ə'kweintəns] n
idon sani
acquire [ə'kwaiə] v samu
acquit [ə'kwit] v sàkā
acquittal [ə'kwitl] n saki
acre ['eikə] n eka
across [ə'krɔs] prep/adv **a house
across the road** gida wanda ke
wancan gefen hanya
act [ækt] **1.** n aiki **2.** doka
3. kashi **4.** v aikata **5.** yi wasan
kwaikwayo
acting ['æktiŋ] **1.** adj na zaman
wucin gadi **2.** n yin wasan
kwaikwayo, cālì
action ['ækʃn] n **1.** aiki **2.** motsi

active [ˈæktiv] *adj* 1. mai ƙoƙari
2. rayayye

activist [ˈæktivist] *n* mai kuzari,
ɗan gwagwarmaya

activity [ækˈtivəti] *n* 1. motsi
2. aikace-aikace

actor [ˈæktə] *n* ɗan wasan
kwaikwayo

actress [ˈæktris] *n* 'yar wasan
kwaikwayo

actual [ˈæktʃuəl] *adj* ainihin

actually [ˈæktʃuli] 1. *adv* da
gaske 2. *conj* a gaskiya

acute [əˈkjuːt] *adj* mai tsanani

A.D. (**Anno Domini**) bayan
haihuwar Annabi Isa

adapt [əˈdæpt] *v* 1. daidaita
2. saje (to da)

adamant [ˈædəmənt] *adj* cul

adaptor [əˈdæptə] *n* macanjin
wutā

add [æd] *v* 1. ƙara 2. tara

added [ˈædid] *adj* 1. added risks
ƙarin haɗari 2. added to this...
a baitakin wannan...

addict [ˈædikt] *n* ɗan ƙwaya

addicted [əˈdiktid] *adj* to be
addicted kamu (to da)

addiction [əˈdikʃn] *n* jaraba

addition [əˈdiʃn] *n* 1. tarawa
2. lissafi 3. in addition bayan
wannan kuma 4. in addition to
ban da

additional [əˈdiʃənl] *adj* ƙarin

address [əˈdres] 1. *n* adireshi
2. *v* yi wa... jawabi

adequate [ˈædikwət] *adj*
mayalwaci

adhere [ədˈhiə] *v* 1. manne (to
wa) 2. bi

adherent [ədˈhiərənt] *n* maridi

adhesive [ədˈhiːsiv] *n* gulu

ad hoc committee *n* kwamiti
na musamman

adjacent [əˈdʒeisnt] *adj* dab (to
da)

adjective [ˈædʒiktiv] *n* siffa (ta
nahawu)

adjourn [æˈdʒəːn] *v* dakatar da

adjournment [æˈdʒəːnmənt] *n*
dakatarwa

adjust [əˈdʒʌst] *v* daidaita

adjustment [əˈdʒʌstmənt] *n*
daidaito

administer [ədˈministə] *v*
gudanar da

administration [əd,miniˈstreiʃn]
n hukuma

administrative [ədˈministrətiv]
adj na gudanarwa

administrator [ədˈministreitə] *n*
1. ma'aikaci 2. kantoma

admiral [ˈædmərəl] *n* admiřàn
sōjìn ruwā

admire [ədˈmaiə] *v* 1. yi sha'awa
2. yaba

admission [ədˈmiʃn] *n* 1. shiga
2. amshi

admit [ədˈmit] *v* 1. yarda da
2. shigar da

adolescence [,ædəˈlesns] *n*
balaga

adolescent [,ædəˈlesnt] *n* matashi

adopt [əˈdɔpt] *v* ɗauka

adoption [əˈdɔpʃn] *n* 1. ɗaukar
riƙo 2. reno

adoration [,ædəˈreiʃn] *n* ƙauna

adore [əˈdɔː] *v* yi ƙauna

adornment [əˈdɔːnmənt] *n*
kwalliya

adult [ˈædʌlt; əˈdʌlt] 1. *adj* na
manya 2. *n* baligi

adultery [əˈdʌltəri] *n* zina

advance [ədˈvaːns] 1. *n* ci-gaba

2. adibas 3. in advance a gaba
4. *v* ci gaba

advantage [əd·va:ntidʒ] *n* **1.**
amfani **2.** riba **3.** galaba

adventure [əd·ventʃə] *n* **1.** tafiya
mai ban mamaki **2.** labari mai
ban mamaki, buɗe ido

adverb [·ædvə:b] *n* hali (na
nahawu)

adverse [·ædvə:s] *adj* adverse
effect illa

advert [·ædvə:t] *n* talla

advertise [·ædvətaiz] *v* yi talla

advertisement [æd·və:tismənt] *n*
talla

advertising [,ædvə·taiziŋ] *n* talla

advice [əd·vais] *n* **1.** shawara
2. to give advice ba da shawara

advisable [əd·vaizəbl] *adj* It
would be advisable... Zai
kyautu...

advise [əd·vaiz] *v* ba da shawara

advisor [əd·vaizə] *n* mashawarci

advisory [əd·vaizəri] *adj* mai ba
da shawara

advisory committee *n*
kwamitin ba da shawara

advocate [·ædvəkeit] **1.** *n* lauya,
(Nr) aboka **2.** *v* shawarta

aerial [·eəriəl] **1.** *adj* na iska **2.** *n*
eriya, (Nr) antan

aeroplane [·eərəplein] *n* jirgin
sama, (Nr) abiyo

affair [ə·feə] *n* **1.** al'amari **2.**
harka **3.** sha'ani **4.** love affair
kwartanci **5.** international
affairs matsalolin duniya

affect [ə·fekt] *v* shafa

affection [ə·fekʃn] *n* soyaya

affectionate [ə·fekʃənət] *adj* mai
soyayya

affidavit [,æfi·deivit] *n* rantsuwa

affirmative [ə·fə:mətiv] *adj* to
take affirmative action ba da
dama

affluent [·æfluənt] *adj* mai dukiya

afford [ə·fɔ:d] *v* He cannot
afford a house. Ba shi da
ƙarfin mallakar gida.

afraid [ə·freid] *adj* **1.** mai tsoro
2. I'm afraid that... Ina
shakka ko...

Africa [·æfrikə] *n* Afirka

African [·æfrikən] **1.** *adj* na
Afirka **2.** *n* ɗan Afirka

after [·a:ftə] **1.** *prep/conj* bayan
2. only after sai da **3.** *adv* daga
baya

afterbirth [·a:ftə,bə:θ] *n* mahaifa

afternoon [,a:ftə·nu:n] *n* **1.**
yamma (maraice) **2.** good
afternoon! barka da rana!

aftershave [·a:ftəʃeiv] *n* turare
hana ƙuraje

afterwards [·a:ftəwədz] *adv* daga
baya

again [ə·gen] *adv* We want to go
to London again. Muna son
mu sake komawa London.

against [ə·genst] *prep* **1.** to fight
against yi yaƙi da **2.** Chelsea
played against Liverpool.
Chelsea sun yi wasa da
Liverpool. **3.** He put the
bicycle against the wall. Ya
jingina basukur a bango.

age [eidʒ] *n* **1.** shekara **2.** shekaru
3. zamani **4.** tsufa

agency [·eidʒənsi] *n* **1.** reshe
2. hukuma **3.** news agency
ofishin dillancin labari

agenda [ə·dʒendə] *n* ajanda

agent [·eidʒənt] *n* **1.** wakili
2. commercial agent ɗan

baranda 3. **secret agent** ɗan leƙen asiri

aggravate [ˈægrəveit] v tsananta

aggravating [ˈægrə,veitiŋ] adj mai tsanani

aggravation [ˌægrəˈveiʃn] n abin fitina

aggression [əˈgreʃn] n cin zali

aggressive [əˈgresiv] adj mai cin zali

agility [əˈdʒiləti] n zafin nama

agitate [ˈædʒiteit] v 1. dàmā 2. nema

agitation [ˌædʒiˈteiʃn] n tashin hankali

agitator [ˌædʒiˈteitə] n ɗan ta da zaune-tsaye

ago [əˈgəu] adv 1. **two years ago** ya yi shekara biyu 2. **many years ago** tun shekaru aru-aru

agony [ˈægəni] n raɗaɗi

agree [əˈgriː] v yarda (**with** da)

agreed [əˈgriːd] adj mai yarda

agreement [əˈgriːmənt] n 1. sharaɗi 2. yarjejeniya 3. **to reach an agrement** yanke shawara 4. **to enter into an agreement** ƙulla alkawari (**with** da)

agricultural [ˌægriˈkʌltʃərəl] adj na gona

agriculture [ˈægrikʌltʃə] n aikin noma

ahead [əˈhed] adv 1. a gaba 2. **to get ahead** ci gaba

aid [eid] 1. n taimako 2. v taimaka

aide [eid] n 1. mataimaki 2. **medical aide** ma'aikacin asibiti, (Nr) lakwataro

AIDS [eidz] n cuta mai karya garkuwar jiki, (Nr) tsîdà

ail [eil] v gurgunce

aim [eim] 1. n nufi 2. maƙasudi 3. v nufa 4. yi saitin

air [eə] n iska

air-conditioning n iyakwandishan, (Nr) kilimatizar

aircraft [ˈeəkraːft] n (pl **aircraft**) jirgin sama

aircraft-carrier n jirgin ruwa ɗaukar jiragen sama

airfield [ˈeəfiːld] n filin jirgin sama

airforce [ˈeəfɔːs] n sojin mayaƙan sama

air hostess [ˈeə,həustis] n mai tuwo

airline, airways [ˈeəlain; ˈeəweiz] n kamfanin jiragen sama

airlinks [ˈeəliŋks] pl hulɗoɗin zirga-zirga na sufurin jirgin sama

airmail [ˈeəmeil] n wasiƙun waje

airplane [ˈeəplein] n jirgin sama, (Nr) abiyo

airport [ˈeəpɔːt] n filin jirgin sama, (Nr) abiyaso

air-raid n samamen jirgin sama

air route n hanyar jirgin sama

alarm [əˈlaːm] 1. n alamar a yi sauri 2. v ta da hankali 3. **to give/raise the alarm** yi gangami 4. **alarm procedures** matakai na gargaɗi

alarm clock n agogo mai ƙararrawa

alarmed [əˈlaːmd] adj **He is alarmed.** Hankalinsa ya tashi.

alas! [əˈlæs] assha!

alcohol [ˈælkəhɔl] n sifirit, (Nr) alkwal

alcoholic [ˌælkəˈhɔlik] 1. n ɗan giya 2. adj na sifirit

ale [eil] n giya

alert [əlǝːt] **1.** *adj* mai hanzari
2. *v* faɗakar da
algebra [ˈæljibrə] *n* aljabara
alias [ˈeiliəs] *n* laƙabi
alien [ˈeiliən] *adj/n* **1.** baƙo
2. illegal alien baƙon haure
align [əˈlain] *v* daidaita
aligned [əˈlaind] *adj* **non-aligned
nations** ƙasashen 'yan-ba-
ruwanmu
alight [əˈlait] **1.** *adj* a haskake
2. *v* sauka (**from** daga)
alike [əˈlaik] *adj* **to be alike** yi
daidai
alive [əˈlaiv] *adj* a raye
all [ɔːl] *adj/adv* duk
all at once *adv* gaba ɗaya
allay [əˈlei] *v* kwantar da
allegation [ˌæliˈgeiʃn] *n* ƙage
allege [əˈledʒ] *v* zarga
allegiance [əˈliːdʒəns] *n* biyayya
allergy [ˈælədʒi] *n* rashin lafiyar
cin wani abu ko taɓa shi
alley [ˈæli] *n* lungu
alliance [əˈlaiəns] *n* ƙawance
all over *adv* It's all over.
Ya ƙare kakaf.
allocate [ˈælǝkeit] *v* kasafta
allocation [ˌælǝˈkeiʃn] *n* kasafi
allow [əˈlau] *v* **1.** bari **2.** yarda
allowance [əˈlauəns] *n* alawas,
(Nr) burs
alloy [ˈælɔi] *n* gami
all right [ˌɔːlˈrait] **1.** daidai **2.** shi
ke nan **3.** ba kome
all-season *adj* **all-season road**
hanyar rani da damina
all the same duk da haka
ally [ˈælai] *n* ƙawa
ally [əˈlai] *v* haɗa kai
almost [ˈɔːlmǝust] **1.** *prep* gab da
2. kusan **3.** *adv* saura kaɗan

alone [əˈləun] *adv* kaɗai
along [əˈlɔŋ] *prep* **1.** ta **2.** a bakin
3. along with tare da
alongside [əˌlɔŋˈsaid] *prep* dab da
aloud [əˈlaud] *adv* da murya mai
ƙarfi
alphabet [ˈælfəbet] *n* abjadi
already [ɔːlˈredi] *adv* **I have
already eaten.** Na riga na ci
abinci.
alright [ɔːlˈrait] **1.** daidai **2.** shi
ke nan **3.** ba kome
also [ˈɔːlsǝu] **1.** kuma **2.** har **3.** ma
alter [ˈɔːltə] *v* **1.** canja **2.** gyara
alteration [ˌɔːltəˈreiʃn] *n* **1.** canji
2. gyara
alternate [ˈɔːltəneit] *v* juya
alternation [ˌɔːltəˈneiʃn] *n* juyi
alternative [ɔːlˈtəːnətiv] *n* **We
have no alternative.** Ba zaɓi.
although [ɔːlˈðǝu] *conj* ko da
yake
altitude [ˈæltitʃuːd] *n* tsawo
altogether [ˌɔːltəˈgeðə] *adv* baki
ɗaya
aluminium [ˌaljuˈminjəm] *n* sanholo
always [ˈɔːlweiz] *adv* kullum
am [æm] *duba* wajen **be**
a.m. *adv* da safe
amalgamation [əˌmælgəˈmeiʃn] *n*
tarayya
amass [əˈmæs] *v* tara da
amateur [ˈæmətjəː] *adj/n* **1.** ɗan
koyo **2. amateur sportsman**
matashin ɗan wasa
amaze [əˈmeiz] *v* ba da mamaki
amazement [əˈmeizmənt] *n*
mamaki
amazing [əˈmeiziŋ] *adj* mai ban
mamaki
ambassador [æmˈbæsədə] *n*
jakada, (Nr) ambasadar

ambiguity [,æmbi·gju:əti] *n* baki biyu

ambiguous [,æm·bigjuəs] *adj* na baki biyu

ambition [æm·biʃn] *n* kishin zuci

ambulance [·æmbjuləns] *n* motar asibiti, (Nr) ambulans

ambush [·æmbuʃ] **1.** *n* haƙo **2.** *v* yi wa... kwanton-ɓauna

amends [æ·mendz] *pl* **to make amends** yi gyaran fuska (**to** wa)

America [ə·merikə] *n* Amirka, (Nr) Amirik

American [ə·merikən] **1.** *adj* na Amirka **2.** *n* Ba'amirke, (Nr) Amirkan

ammunition [,æmju·niʃn] *n* harsashi, (Nr) kartushi

amnesty [·æmnəsti] *n* afuwa

Amnesty International *n* Kungiyar Neman Afuwa ta Duniya

among, amongst [ə·mʌŋ; ə·mʌŋst] *prep* **1.** tsakanin **2.** cikin

amount [ə·maunt] *n* **1.** yawa **2.** jimla

amount to *v* kai

amplify [·æmplifai] *v* ƙara ƙarfin sauti

amputate [·æmpjuteit] *v* (med.) yanke

amuse [ə·mju:z] *v* sa wa... dariya

an [æn] *duba wajen* **a**

anaemia [ə·ni:mia] *n* ƙarancin jini

anaesthetic [,ænis·θetik] *n* maganin sa barci

analogy [ə·nælədʒi] *n* **1.** ƙiyasi **2. by analogy** a kan ƙiyasi (**with** da)

analyse [·ænəlaiz] *v* **1.** nazarta **2.** feɗe

analysis [ə·næləsis] *n* nazari

analyst [·ænəlist] *n* manàzàřci

anarchy [·ænəki] *n* mulkin ruɗu

anatomy [ə·nætəmi] *n* ilimin halittar jiki

ancestor [·ænsestə] *n* kakan kaka

anchor [·æŋkə] *n* anga

anchor-man [·æŋkəmæn] *n* mai ba da labarai

ancient [·einʃənt] *adj* **1.** tsoho **2.** na da **3.** dàɗaɗɗè

and [ən; ænd] *conj* **1.** da **2.** kuma

angel [·eindʒl] *n* mala'ika

anger [·æŋgə] **1.** *n* fushi **2.** *v* sa wa... fushi

angle [·æŋgl] *n* kusurwa

Anglo-Saxon [·æŋgləu·sæksən] *adj/n* **1.** Bature ɗan asali **2.** mai jan kunne

anglophone [·æŋgləufəun] *adj* **anglophone countries** ƙasashen renon Ingila

angry [·æŋgri] *adj* mai fushi

anguish [·æŋgwiʃ] *n* tagayyara

animal [·æniml] *n* **1.** dabba **2. wild animal** naman daji

animate [·ænimeit] **1.** *adj* mai rai **2.** *v* rayar da

animosity [,æni·mositi] *n* ƙiyayya

ankle [·æŋkl] *n* idon sau

annex [ə·neks] *v* kama

annexation [,ænek·seiʃn] *n* kamawa

annexe [·æneks] *n* ƙarin gida

annihilate [ə·naiəleit] *v* rushe

anniversary [,æni·və:səri] *n* ranar tunawa

announce [ə·nauns] *v* yi sanarwa

announcement [ə·naunsmənt] *n* sanarwa

announcer [əˈnaunsə] *n* mai ba da labari

annoy [əˈnɔi] *v* ba wa... haushi

annoyed [əˈnɔid] *adj* to be annoyed ji haushi

annual [ˈænjuəl] *adj* na shekara-shekara

annually [ˈænjuəli] *adv* shekara-shekara

annul [əˈnʌl] *v* 1. kashe 2. soke 3. warware

anonymous [əˈnɔniməs] *adj* baƙo

another [əˈnʌðə] *adj* 1. wani 2. wani dabam

answer [ˈaːnsə] 1. *n* jawabi 2. *v* amsa

answer back *v* tanka (to wa)

ant [ænt] *n* tururuwa

antagonistic [æntægəˈnistik] *adj* mai jidali

anteater [æntˈiːtə] *n* dabgi

antelope [ˈæntiləup] *n* gwanki

antenna [ænˈtenə] *n* eriya, (Nr) antan

anthem [ˈænθəm] *n* take

anthology [ˌænθˈɔlodʒi] *n* diwani

anthropology [ˌænθroˈpolodʒi] *n* ilimin halayya da al'adun ɗan Adam

anti-aircraft gun [ˌæntiˈeəkraːft ˌgʌn] *n* bindigar kaɓo jirgi

anti-apartheid [ˌæntiəˈpaːtait] *n* kawar da wariyar al'umma

antibiotics [ˌæntibaiˈɔtiks] *pl* maganin rigakafi

anticipate [ænˈtisipeit] *v* 1. yi tsammani 2. ƙaddara

anticipation [æn,tisiˈpeiʃn] *n* hango

antidote [ˈæntidəut] *n* makari

antique [ænˈtiːk] *adj* na gargajiya

antiques [ænˈtiːks] *pl* kayayyakin gargajiya

antiquity [ænˈtikwəti] *n* gargajiya

anus [ˈeinəs] *n* dubura

anxiety [ˈæŋˈzaiəti] *n* juyayi

anxious [ˈæŋkʃəs] *adj* damamme

any [ˈeni] *adj* 1. wani 2. kowanne

anybody [ˈenibɔdi] 1. kowa 2. kowanne 3. wani

anyday [ˈenidei] *adv* 1. da wuri 2. ko ta yaushe

anyhow [ˈenihau] ko ta yaya

anyone [ˈeniwʌn] 1. kowa 2. kowanne 3. wani

anything [ˈeniθiŋ] 1. kome 2. wani abu

anytime [ˈenitaim] kowane lokaci

anyway [ˈeniwei] ko ta yaya

anywhere [ˈeniweə] 1. ko'ina 2. duk inda 3. a wani wuri

apart [əˈpaːt] 1. a rabe

apart from *prep* ban da

apartheid [əˈpaːthait] *n* wariyar launin fata

apartment [əˈpaːtmənt] *n* gida

apathy [ˈæpəθi] *n* kasala

ape [eip] *n* biri ba ta da wutsiya

apex [ˈeipeks] *n* ƙoƙuwa

apiece [əˈpiːs] *adv* five naira apiece naira biyar biyar

apologise [əˈpɔlədʒaiz] *v* roƙi gafara

apology [əˈpɔlədʒi] *n* roƙon gafara

apostrophe [əˈpɔstrəfi] *n* baƙin ɓoye

appalled [əˈpɔːld] *adj* I'm appalled. Ya ƙona mini zuciya.

appalling [əˌpɔːliŋ] *adj* 1. abin takaici 2. tir 3. abin kunya

apparatus [ˌæpəˈreitəs] *n* na'ura

apparent [əˈpærənt] *adj* mai ƙanshin gaskiya

apparently [ə'pærəntli] *adv* ga
alama

appeal [ə'piːl] 1. *n* afil 2. roƙo
3. *v* ɗaukaka ƙara 4. kira

appealing [ə'piːliŋ] *adj* mai ban
daɗi

appear [ə'piə] *v* 1. ɓullo 2. fito
3. ba da alama

appearance [ə'piərəns] *n* 1. sura
2. shìgà

appease [ə'piːz] *v* lallasa

append [ə'pend] *v* maƙala

appendicitis [,əpendi'saitis] *n*
tsiro a uwar hanji

appendix [ə'pendiks] *n* rataye

appetite ['æpitait] *n* son cin
abinci

applaud [ə'plɔːd] *v* yi tafi

applause [ə'plɔːz] *n* ban tafi

apple ['æpl] *n* tuffa

appliance [ə'plaiəns] *n* kayan
aiki

applicant ['æplikənt] *n* mai nema

application form *n* takardar
neman aiki

apply [ə'plai] *v* 1. nema 2. shàfà

appoint [ə'pɔint] *v* 1. naɗa
2. wakiltar da

appointment [ə'pɔintmənt] *n*
1. alkawari 2. magama 3. naɗi

apportion [ə'pɔːʃn] *v* rarraba

appraisal [ə'preiʃl] *n* ƙima

appreciate [ə'priːʃieit] *v* yaba da

apprehend [æpri'hend] *v* kama

apprehension [,æpri'henʃn] *n*
1. juyayi 2. kamu

apprentice [ə'prentis] *n* ɗan koyo

approach [ə'prəutʃ] *v* kusata

appropriate [ə'prəupriət] *adj* to
be appropriate dace

appropriation [ə'prəuprieiʃn] *n*
kasafi

approve [ə'pruːv] *v* 1. yarda
2. to approve of yarda da 3. to
approve a resolution amince
da ƙudiri

approximate [ə'prɔksimət] *adj*
kimanin

approximately [ə'prɔksimətli]
adv misalin

April ['eiprəl] *n* Afrilu

aquatic [ə'kwætik] *adj* na ruwa

Arab ['ærəb] *adj/n* Balarabe

Arabic ['ærəbik] *n* Larabci

arbitrate ['aːbitreit] *v* yi sulhu
(**between** wa)

arbitration [,aːbi'treiʃn] *n* sulhu

arcade [aː'keid] *n* **shopping
arcade** gidan kashe ahu

arch [aːtʃ] *n* baka

architect ['aːkitekt] *n* mai zanen
gine-gine

architecture ['aːkitektʃə] *n*
fannin tsarin gine-gine

archives ['aːkaivz] *n* gidan ajiya

arduous ['aːdjuəs] *adj* mai
tsanani

are [aː] *duba wajen* **be**

area ['eəriə] *n* 1. yanki 2. fili
3. yawan fili

arena [ə'riːnə] *n* fage

argue ['aːgjuː] *v* yi jayayya

arguing ['aːgjuːiŋ] *n* jayayya

argument ['aːgjumənt] *n* 1.
gardama 2. muhawara

arid ['ærid] *adj* mai rashin ruwa,
faƙo

arise [ə'raiz] *v* tashi

aristocracy [,æris'tɔkrəsi] *n*
sarakai

arithmetic [ə'riθmətik] *n* lissafi

ark [aːk] *n* jirgin Annabi Nuhu

arm [aːm] 1. *n* hannu 2. *v* ba da
makamai 3. *duba wajen* **arms**

armada [aːˈmaːdə] *n* cincirindon
jiragen ruwa na yaƙi

armament(s) [ˈaːməmənts] *pl*
ɗaure ɗamara

armchair [ˈaːmtʃeə] *n* babbar
kujera

armed [aːmd] *adj* **1. armed
robbery** fashi da makami
2. armed struggle ƙarfin tuwo

armistice [ˈaːmistis] *n* sulhu

armour [ˈaːmə] *n* sulke

armoured car *n* mota mai
sulke

armpit [ˈaːmpit] *n* hamata, (Nr)
lallaƙƙuwa

arms [aːmz] *pl* makamai

arms race *n* yaƙin rigen tara
makamai

arms reduction *n* rage
makamai

army [ˈaːmi] *n* rundunar soja

aroma [əˈrəumə] *n* ƙamshi

aromatic [ˌærəuˈmætik] *adj* mai
ƙamshi

around [əˈraund] *adv/prep* **1.** a
kewaye **2.** ko'ina **3.** wajen

arouse [əˈrauz] *v* ta da

arrange [əˈreindʒ] *v* **1.** shirya
2. jera

arrangement [əˈreindʒmənt] *n*
1. shiri **2.** jeri

arrears [əˈriːəs] *n* ariya

arrest [əˈrest] **1.** *n* kamu
2. *v* kama

arrival [əˈraivl] *n* isowa

arrive [əˈraiv] *v* **1.** isa **2.** sauka

arrogance [ˈærəgəns] *n* girman
kai

arrogant [ˈærəgənt] *adj* mai
girman kai

arrow [ˈærəu] *n* kibiya

arsenal [ˈaːsinl] *n* gidan makamai

art [aːt] *n* **1.** fannin zare **2.** fasaha

artery [ˈaːtiəri] *n* jijiya

arthritis [aːˈθraitis] *n* amosanin
gaɓɓai

article [ˈaːtikl] *n* **1.** abu **2.** labarin
jarida

artificial [ˌaːtiˈfiʃl] *adj* abin da
ɗan Adam ya yi

artillery [aːˈtiləri] *n* igwa

artisan [ˈaːtizæn] *n* ɗan sana'a

artist [ˈaːtist] *n* mai aikin zane-
zane

artistic [aːˈtistik] *adj* mai fasaha

artistry [ˈaːtistri] *n* fasaha

as [əz; æz] **1. They arrived as
we were leaving.** Lokacin da
suka zo, muka tashi. **2. As he
was late, we went without
him.** Tun da yake makara,
muka bar shi baya. **3. Amina is
as tall as Audu.** Audu da
Amina tsawonsu ɗaya ne.
4. Do as I do. Ka yi kamar ni
na yi. **5. The dog acted as if it
were mad.** Kare ya yi kamar
ya haukata. **6. His brother
came as well.** Har wansa ya
zo.

as soon as possible da wuri-
wuri

ascend [əˈsend] *v* tashi

as far as har iyakacin

ash, ashes [æʃ; -iz] *n* toka

ashamed [əˈʃeimd] *adj* mai jin
kunya

ashtray [ˈæʃtrei] *n* tiren kashe
taba

Asia [ˈeiʒə] *n* Asiya

Asian [ˈeiʒn] *adj* Ba'asiye

aside [əˈsaid] *adv* a gefe

aside from *prep* ban da

ask [aːsk] *v* tambaya

ask for v roƙa

asleep [əˈsliːp] adj to be asleep yi barci

as long as muddin

aspect [ˈæspekt] n kama

aspiration [ˌæspəˈreiʃn] n kishin zuci

aspirin [ˈæsprin] n asfirin, (Nr) asfiro

assassin [əˈsæsin] n mai kisan kai

assassinate [əˈsæsineit] v kashe

assassination [əˌsæsiˈneiʃn] n kisan gilla

assault [əˈsɔːlt] 1. n farmaki 2. v kai wa... farmaki

assemble [əˈsembl] v 1. harhaɗa 2. tattara 3. taru

assembly [əˈsembli] n 1. taro 2. House of Assembly Majalisar Wakilai, (Nr) Gidan Shawara

assembly plant n maˈaikatar harhaɗa

assent [əˈsent] v yi naˈam (to da)

assert [əˈsəːt] v furta (cewa that)

assess [əˈses] v ƙiyasta

assessment [əˈsesmənt] n ƙima

assessor [əˈsesə] n muhuti

assets [ˈæsets] pl kadara

assign [əˈsain] v ba da aiki

assignment [əˈsainmənt] n aiki

assist [əˈsist] v taimaka

assistance [əˈsistəns] n taimako

assistant [əˈsistənt] n mataimaki

associate [əˈsəuʃiət] n abokin aiki

associate [əˈsəuʃieit] v danganta

association [əˌsəusiˈeiʃn] n 1. ƙungiya 2. in association with tare da

assorted [əˈsɔːtid] adj iri-iri

assume [əˈsjuːm] v 1. ɗauka (that cewa) 2. to assume office kama mulki

assurance [əˈʃɔːrəns] n tabbaci

assure [əˈʃɔː] v tabbatar wa

asthma [ˈæsmə] n fuka

as though [æzˈðəu] tamkar dai

astonish [əˈstɔniʃ] v ba da mamaki

astonishing [əˈstɔniʃ] adj mai ban mamaki

astonishment [əˈstɔniʃmənt] n ban mamaki

astray [əˈstrei] adv to go astray ɓata

astrology [əˈstrɔlədʒi] n hisabi

astronaut [ˈæstrənɔːt] n ɗan sama-jannati

astronomer [əˈstrɔnəmə] n mai ilimin taurari

astronomy [əˈstrɔnəmi] n ilimin taurari

as well as baitakin

asylum [əˈsailəm] n 1. gidan mahaukata 2. political asylum mafakar siyasa

at [ət; æt] prep 1. at school a makaranta 2. at Tukur's wurin Tukur 3. at two o'clock da ƙarfe biyu

ate [eit] duba wajen eat

at first adv da farko

athlete [ˈæθliːt] n ɗan wasa

athletic [æθˈletik] adj mai ƙira

athletics [æθˈletiks] pl wasanni

atlas [ˈætləs] n atalas

atmosphere [ˈætməsfiə] n yanayi

atom [ˈætəm] n atom

atom bomb n atom bom

at once adv nan da nan

atrocities pl taˈasa

atrocity [əˈtrɔsəti] n aikin mashaˈa

attach [əˈtætʃ] v haɗa
attack [əˈtæk] **1.** n hari **2. heart attack** ciwon zuciya **3. sudden attack** farmaki **4. surprise attack** samame **5.** v kai wa hari
attain [əˈtein] v samu
attempt [əˈtempt] v **1.** ƙoƙari **2.** yi ƙoƙari
attend [əˈtend] v **1.** zo **2.** halarta
attendance [əˈtendəns] n zuwa
attention [əˈtenʃn] n **1.** hankali **2. to attract attention of** ɗauke wa ido **3. to pay attention** kula (to da) **4. to turn attention** mai da hankali (**to** a kan)
attentive [əˈtentiv] adj mai kula
attic [ˈætik] n kwazago, kursali
attitude [ˈætitʃuːd] n **1.** hali **2.** ra'ayi
attorney [əˈtəːni] n lauya, aboka (Nr)
attorney-general n babban lauyan gwamnati
attract [əˈtrækt] v jawo
attractive [əˈtræktiv] adj **1.** mai jawo hankali **2.** kyakkyawa
aubergine [ˈəubəʒiːn] n gauta
auction [ˈɔːkʃn] n gwanjo
audible [ˈɔːkʃn] adj mai jiyuwa
audience [ˈɔːdiəns] n **1.** alkawari **2.** masu sauraro **3.** 'yan kallo
audit [ˈɔːdit] v bincika kuɗi
auditor [ˈɔːditə] n odita
auditorium [ˌɔːdiˈtɔːriəm] n babban ɗakin taro
August [ˈɔːgəst] n Agusta, (Nr) Ut
aunt [aːnt] n inna, baba
austerity [ɔˈsterəti] n tsuke bakin aljihu
austerity measures pl matakai na tsuke bakin aljihu

austerity programme n shirin tsuke bakin aljihu
Australia [ɔsˈtreilyə] n Ostireliya
authentic [ɔːˈθentik] adj na ainihi
author [ˈɔːθə] n marubuci
authorise [ˈɔːθəraiz] v ba da izini
authorisation [ˌɔːθəraiˈzeiʃn] n izini
authorities [ɔːˈθɔrətiːz] pl masu mulki
authority [ɔːˈθɔrəti] n **1.** hukuma **2.** iko **3. to have authority over** mallaka
auto [ˈɔːtəu] n mota
autobiography [ˌɔːtəbaiˈɔgrəfi] n tarihin kai
automatic [ˌɔːtəˈmætik] adj **1.** otomatik **2.** da kai
automatic rifle n bindiga mai jigida
automobile [ˈɔːtəməbiːl] n mota, (Nr) bwacir
autonomous [ɔːˈtɔnəməs] adj na gashin kai
autonomy [ɔːˈtɔnəmi] n cin gashin kai
autumn [ˈɔːtəm] n bazara
available [əˈveiləbl] adj **When will you be available?** Yaushe kake da lokaci?
avenge [əˈvendʒ] v rāmā
avenue [ˈævənjuː] n babban titi
average [ˈævəridʒ] adj **1.** matsakaici **2.** tsaka-tsaki **3. on average** a ƙaddarance
aversion [əˈvəːʃn] n ƙyama
avert [əˈvəːt] v kawar da
aviation [ˌeiviˈeiʃn] n **civil aviation** sufurin jirgin sama
avoid [əˈvɔid] v kauce wa
await [əˈweit] v jira
awake [əˈweik] adj a farke

award [əˈwɔːd] **1.** *n* lamba **2.** *v*
  ba da lamba
aware [əˈweə] *adj* **1.** a sane
  2. to be aware lura **(of** da) **3.**
  to become aware farga
away [əˈweɪ] *adv* **1. Go away!** Tafi!
  2. My mother is away. Uwata
  ba ta nan. **3. far away** da nisa

awe [ˈɔː] *n* al'ajabi
awful [ˈɔːfl] *adj* **1.** ba daɗi **2.** mai
  rashin kunya
awfully [ˈɔːflɪ] *adv* ainun
awkward [ˈɔːkwəd] *adj* maras
  kintsi
axe [æks] *n* gatari
axle [ˈæksl] *n* gindin mota

Bb

B.A. (**bachelor's degree**) *n* digiri na farko

babboon [ˈbæbuːn] *n* gwaggon biri

babe [beib] *n* jinjiri

baby [ˈbeibi] *n* jariri

babysit [ˈbeibisit] *v* (**babysat**) yi reno

babysitter [ˈbeibisitə] *n* mai reno

bachelor [ˈbætʃələ] *n* tuzuru

back [bæk] **1.** *n* baya **2.** *v* goyi baya **3. He came back.** Ya komo. **4. Give it back to me!** Maido mini da shi!

back ache *n* ciwon baya

backbiter [ˈbækbaitə] *n* munafuki

backbone [ˈbækbəun] *n* **1.** ƙashin baya **2.** ginshiƙi

backing [ˈbækiŋ] *n* goyon baya

backward [ˈbækwəd] **1.** *adj* wanda bai ci gaba ba **2.** *adv* baya

backwards [ˈbækwədz] *adv* da baya

bacon [ˈbeikən] *n* naman alade

bacteria [bækˈtiəriə] *pl* ƙwayoyin cuta

bad [bæd] **1.** *adj* maras kyau **2.** mugu **3.** *n* mugunta

bade [bæd; beid] *duba wajen* **bid**

badge [bædʒ] *n* bajo, (Nr) galo

badly [ˈbædli] *adv* ba sosai ba

badminton [ˈbædmintən] *n* ƙwallon gashi

badness [ˈbædnis] *n* mugunta

bad-tempered [ˌbædˈtempəd] *adj* mai baƙin rai

baffle [ˈbæfl] *v* rikita

bag [bæg] *n* jaka

baggage [ˈbægidʒ] *n* kaya

bail [beil] *n* beli

bail out *v* yi beli

bait [beit] *n* ƙoto

bake [beik] *v* gasa

baker [ˈbeikə] *n* mai yin burodi

bakery [ˈbeikəri] *n* gidan burodi

balance [ˈbæləns] **1.** *n* sikeli **2.** balas **3.** ciko **4. ecological balance** daidaituwar yanayin doron ƙasa **5.** *v* daidaita **6.** yi balas

balance of payments *n* daidaiton biyace-biyace

balance of trade *n* daidaiton ciniki na ƙetare

balcony [ˈbælkəni] *n* baranda

bald [bɔːld] *adj* mai sanƙo

balk [bɔːk] *v* ƙaurace (**at** wa)

ball [bɔːl] *n* ƙwallo, (Nr) bal

ball-bearings [ˌbɔːlˈbeəriŋ] *pl* 'ya'yan boris

ballet [ˈbælei] *n* rawa

balloon [bəˈluːn] *n* balan-balan, (Nr) bata

ballot [ˈbælət] *n* ƙuri'a

ballot-box *n* akwatin jefa ƙuri'a

ballpoint [ˈbɔːlpoint] *n* biro, (Nr) bik

bamboo [bæmˈbuː] *n* gora

ban [bæn] **1.** *n* hani **2.** *v* hana

banana [bəˈnaːnə] *n* ayaba

band [bænd] *n* **1.** ƙungiya **2.** makaɗa **3.** ɗauri **4. rubber band** maɗaurin roba

bandage [ˈbændidʒ] *n* bandeji
bandaid [ˈbændeid] *n* filasta, (Nr) isparadara
bandit [ˈbændit] *n* ɗan fashi
bang [bæŋ] **1.** *n* ƙara **2.** *v* buge **3. to start with a bang** fara da annashuwa
banish [ˈbæniʃ] *v* kòrā
bank [bæŋk] *n* **1.** banki **2.** gaɓa **3. federal state bank** babban bankin jiha **4. federal reserve bank** bankin ajiya na tarayya **5. World Bank** Bankin Duniya
banker [ˈbænkə] *n* ma'aikacin banki
bank fraud *n* laifin zambatar banki
banknote, (US) **bankbill** [ˈbæŋknəut; -bil] *n* takardar kuɗi, (Nr) biye
bankrupt [ˈbæŋkrʌpt] *adj* **1. to go bankrupt** yi fatarar kuɗi **2. They have gone bankrupt.** Jarinsu ya karye.
bankruptcy [ˈbæŋkrəpsi] *n* fatarar kuɗi
banner [ˈbænə] *n* tuta
banquet [ˈbæŋkwit] *n* walima
baptism [ˈbæptizəm] *n* baftizma
bar [baː] *n* **1.** hotel, (Nr) bar **2. a bar of soap** sandar sabulu **3. behind bars** a kurkuku
bar code [ˈbaːˌkəud] *n* lambar fakiti
barbecue [ˈbaːbikjuː] *v* gasa
barbed wire [ˌbaːbdˈwaiə] *n* waya mai ƙaya
bare [beə] *adj* **1.** huntu **2. to make bare** tsiraita
barefoot [ˈbeəfut] *adj/adv* ba takalmi
barely [ˈbeəli] *adv* da ƙyar

bargain [ˈbaːgin] **1.** *n* **I got a bargain.** Na sami rangwame. **2.** *v* yi ciniki
barge [bɔːdʒ] *n* baji
bark [baːk] **1.** *n* ɓawon itace **2.** *v* yi haushi
barley [ˈbaːli] *n* sha'ir
barn [baːn] *n* sito
barracks [ˈbærəks] *pl* bariki
barrel [ˈbærəl] *n* ganga
barren [ˈbærən] *adj* faƙo
barrier [ˈbæriə] *n* abin toshewa
barrister [ˈbæristə] *n* lauya, (Nr) aboka
barter [ˈbaːtə] *v* yi furfure
barter trade *n* musayar albarkatu
base [beis] **1.** *n* gindi **2.** sansani **3.** *v* dogara **4. to base opinion** dangana ra'ayi (**on** da)
baseball [ˈbeisbɔːl] *n* ƙwallon gora ta 'baseball'
baseless [ˈbeislis] *adj* maras tushe
basement [ˈbeismənt] *n* gidan ƙasa
basic [ˈbeisik] *adj* na yau da kullum
basic necessities *pl* kayan masarufi na yau da kullum
basin [ˈbeisn] *n* kwano
basis [ˈbeisis] *n* tushe
basket [ˈbaːskit] *n* kwando
basketball [ˈbaːskitbɔːl] *n* ƙwallon kwando, (Nr) basket
bastard [ˈbaːstəd] *n* **1.** shege **2.** (sl.) ɗan iksa
bat [bæt] *n* **1.** jemage **2.** kulki
bath [baːθ] *n* **1.** baho **2.** wanka
bathe [beið] *v* yi wanka
bathing costume *n* banten iyo
bathroom [ˈbaːθrum] *n* gidan wanka

battalion [bəˈtæliən] *n* bataliya
battery [ˈbætəri] *n* batir, (Nr) pil
battle [ˈbætl] **1.** *n* faɗa da makamai **2.** *v* sha daga
battlefield [ˈbatlfiːld] *n* filin daga
battleship [ˈbætlʃip] *n* jirgin mai ruwa na yaƙi
bay [bei] *n* sashen bakin teku
bayonet [ˈbeiənit] *n* banati
bazaar [bəˈzaː] *n* kasuwa
B.C. (before Christ) kafin haihuwar Annabi Isa
be [biː] *v* **1.** zama **2.** kasance
beach [biːtʃ] *n* rairayin bakin teku
beads [biːdz] *pl* dutsen ado
beak [biːk] *n* bakin tsuntsu
beam [biːm] *n* bim
beans [biːnz] *pl* wake
bear [beə] *v* (**bore, borne**) **1.** ɗauka **2.** jure **3.** haifa
beard [biəd] *n* gemu
beast [biːst] *n* **1.** dabba **2. wild beast** naman daji
beat [biːt] *v* (**beat, beaten**) **1.** buga **2.** ci **3.** lashe
beating [ˈbiːtiŋ] *n* duka
beautiful [ˈbjuːtifl] *adj* kyakkyawa
beauty [ˈbjuːti] *n* kyan gani
beauty queen *n* sarauniyar kyau
became [biˈkeim] *duba wajen* become
because [biˈkɔz] *pl* don
because of *prep* saboda
beckon [ˈbekən] *v* yafuta
become [biˈkʌm] *v* (**became, become**) **1.** zama **2.** kasance
bed [bed] *n* **1.** gado **2. river bed** ƙwaryar kogi **3. to go to bed** kwanta

bedroom [ˈbedrum] *n* ɗakin kwana
bee [biː] *n* ƙudan zuma
beef [biːf] *n* naman sa
beehive [ˈbiːhaiv] *n* amya
beer [biə] *n* giya, (Nr) biyer
befall [biˈfɔːl] *v* afka wa
before [biˈfɔː] **1.** *prep/conj* gaban **2.** kafin **2. just before** dab da **3.** *adv* **I have seen this film before.** Na taɓa ganin wannan fim.
beg [beg] *v* **1.** nema **2.** roƙa
began [biˈgæn] *duba wajen* begin
beggar [ˈbegə] *n* **1.** almajiri **2.** fakiri
begging [ˈbegiŋ] *n* bara
begin [biˈgin] *v* (**began, begun**) fara
beginner [biˈginə] *n* ɗan koyo
beginning [biˈginiŋ] *n* farko
begun [biˈgʌn] *duba wajen* begin
behalf [bəˈhaːf] *n* **on behalf of** a madadin
behave [biˈheiv] *v* **1.** nuna hali **2.** yi ladabi
behaviour [biˈheivjə] *n* hali
behind [biˈhaind] *prep* **1.** baya **2. behind the door** bayan ƙofa **3. to be behind** yi latti
behind the scenes *adv* a bayan shinge
being [ˈbiːiŋ] *n* **1.** kasancewa **2. human being** ɗan adam
belief [biˈliːf] *n* imani
believe [biˈliːv] *v* **1.** yarda da **2.** yi imani
believer [biˈliːvə] *n* mumini
belittle [biˈlitl] *v* wulakanta
bell [bel] *n* ƙararrawa
belly [ˈbeli] *n* ciki
belong [biˈlɔŋ] *v* **1. The book**

belongs to me. Littafin nawa ne. 2. **I belong to the sports club.** Ina cikin 'yan wannan kulob na wasanni. 3. **Put it back where it belongs.** Mai da shi wurinsa.

below [bɪˈləu] 1. *adv* a ƙasa 2. *prep* ƙarƙashin

belt [belt] *n* bel, (Nr) santir

bench [bentʃ] *n* benci

bend [bend] 1. *n* kwana 2. *v* (bent) lanƙwasa

bend down *v* duƙa

beneath [bɪˈniːθ] *prep* ƙarƙashin

beneficial [ˌbeniˈfiʃl] *adj* **to be beneficial** kawo riba (**to/for** ga)

benefit [ˈbenifit] 1. *n* riba 2. amfani 3. *v* ci riba

bent [bent] *duba wajen* **bend**

bereaved [bɪˈriːvd] *adj* **the bereaved** waɗanda aka yi wa rashi

bereavement [bɪˈriːvmənt] *n* rashi

beside [bɪˈsaid] *adv* a gefen

besides [bɪˈsaidz] 1. *prep* ban da 2. *adv* bayan wannan

besiege [bɪˈsiːdʒ] *v* yi ƙofar rago ga

best [best] *adj* mafi kyau duka

best man [ˌbestˈmæn] *n* abokin ango

bestseller [ˌbestˈselə] *n* fitaccen littafi

bet [bet] 1. *n* kasada 2. *v* (bet) yi fare (**on a kan**)

betray [bɪˈtrei] *v* ci amana

betrayal [bɪˈtreiəl] *n* maƙarƙashiya

better [ˈbetə] *adj* 1. mafi kyau 2. **to feel better** ji sauƙi 3. **We'd better go.** Gwamma mu tafi.

betting [ˈbetiŋ] *n* yin fare, (Nr) kyarse

between [bɪˈtwiːn] *prep* tsakanin

beverage [ˈbevəridʒ] *n* abin sha

beware [bɪˈweə] *v* yi hankali (**of da**)

beyond [bɪˈjɔnd] *prep/adv* 1. gaban 2. bayan

Bible [ˈbaibl] *n* Littafi mai Tsarki

bibliography [ˌbibliˈogrəfi] *n* jerin littattafai

bicycle [ˈbaisikl] *n* basukur, (Nr) belo

bid [bid] *v* (**bid**) sa kuɗi/suna

big [big] *adj* babba

bigot [ˈbigət] *n* mai faɗin rai

bigoted [ˈbigətid] *adj* mai faɗin rai

bike [baik] *n* basukur

bilharzia [bilˈhaːtsia] *n* tsagiya

bilingual [baiˈlingwəl] *adj* mai iya harshe biyu

bilingualism [baiˈlingwəlizm] *n* iya harshe biyu

bill [bil] *n* 1. lissafi 2. shirin doka 3. *duba wajen* **banknote**

billboard [ˈbilbɔːd] *n* allon talla

billion [ˈbiliən] *n* milyan dubu

bind [baind] *v* (**bound**) ɗaure

binoculars [bɪˈnɔkjuləz] *pl* tabaran hangen nesa

biography [baiˈɔgrəfi] *n* tarihi

biology [baiˈɔlədʒi] *n* ilimin halittu

biomass fuels [ˈbaiəuˌmæsˈfjuːəlz] *pl* makamashin da a ke samu a doron ƙasa

bird [bəːd] *n* tsuntsu

biro [ˈbaiərəu] *n* biro, (Nr) bik

birth [bəːθ] *n* 1. haihuwa 2. **to give birth to** hàifā

birth-rate [ˈbəːθreit] *n* yawan hayayyafa

birthday [ˈbəːθdei] *n* ranar haihuwa

birthplace [ˈbəːθpleis] *n* **1.** mahaifata **2.** garinmu

biscuit [ˈbiskit] *n* biskit

bisexual [ˌbaiˈsekʃuəl] *adj/n* maso maza da mata duk

bishop [ˈbiʃəp] *n* babban limamin Kirista

bit [bit] *n* **1.** kaɗan **2.** guntu **3.** linzami **4.** *duba wajen* **bite**

bite [bait] **1.** *n* mosquito bite cizon sauro **2.** *v* (**bit, bitten**) ciza

bitter [ˈbitə] *adj* mai ɗaci

bitterness [ˈbitənis] *n* ɗaci

black [blæk] *adj* baƙi

blackboard [ˈblækbɔːd] *n* allo

blacken [ˈblækən] *v* baƙanta

blackmail [ˈblækmeil] *v* yi wa... sharri

black market *n* kasuwar dare

black marketeer *n* ɗan walawala

black market goods *pl* kayan sari

blackout [ˈblækaut] *n/v* **1.** suma **2.** ɗauke wuta

bladder [ˈblædə] *n* mafitsara

blade [ˈbleid] *n* ruwan wuƙa

blame [bleim] **1.** *n* laifi **2.** *v* zarga

bland [blænd] *adj* mai lami

blank [blæŋk] *adj* emti

blanket [ˈblæŋkit] *n* bargo

blasphemy [ˈblæsfəmi] *n* saɓo

blast [blaːst] *n* fashe-fashe

blaze [bleiz] **1.** *n* gobara **2.** *v* ƙuna

bleach [bliːtʃ] *n* bilic, (Nr) odajabit

bleed [bliːd] *v* (**bled**) yi jini

blemish [ˈblemiʃ] *n* illa

blend [blend] *v* saje (**into** da)

bless [bles] *v* albarkata

blew [bluː] *duba wajen* **blow**

blind [blaind] *adj* **1.** makaho **2. to turn a blind eye** kau da kai (**to** daga)

blindness [ˈblaindnis] *n* makanta

blink [bliŋk] *v* yi ƙifce

blister [ˈblistə] *n* bororo

bloc [blɔk] *n* ɓangare

block [blɔk] **1.** *n* bulo **2.** gungume **3. block of flats** sashen gidaje **4.** *v* yi wa... babakere **5.** toshe

blockade [blɔˈkeid] *n* **1.** takunkuni **2. to impose a blockade** datse takunkumi **3. to break a blockade** rushe kangiya

blockage [ˈblɔkidʒ] *n* toshewa

blond, blonde [blɔnd] *adj* mai farin gashi

blood [blʌd] *n* **1.** jini **2. blood group** irin jini

blood bank *n* ma'ajiyar jini

bloody [ˈblʌdi] *adj* jina-jina

bloom [bluːm] **1.** *n* furen itace **2.** *v* fid da fure

blouse [blauz] *n* rigar mata

blow [bləu] **1.** *n* naushi **2.** *v* (**blew, blown**) hura **3.** busa

blow-out *n* fanca

blow up *v* **1.** yi kaca-kaca da **2.** yi wa... famfo

blue [bluː] *adj/n* shuɗi

blueprint [ˈbluːprint] *n* shaci

blues [bluːz] *n* **1.** rangajin soyayya **2.** (mus.) kiɗan 'blues'

blunder [ˈblʌndə] *n* kuskure

blunt [blʌnt] **1.** *adj* maras kaifi **2.** *v* dakusar da

bluntly [ˈblʌntli] *adv* baro-baro

blush [blʌʃ] v ji kunya, soke kai
board [bɔːd] **1.** n allo **2.** katako
3. v sauka **4.** shiga
boast [bəust] **1.** n da'awa **2.** to
boast cika bakin (that cewa)
boat [bəut] n jirgin ruwa
bodily [ˈbɔdili] adj na jiki
body [ˈbɔdi] n **1.** jiki **2.** gawa
body-cloth [ˈbɔdiklɔθ] n zanè
bodyguard [ˈbɔdigaːd] n mai
kare lafiya, ɗan banga
bogus [ˈbəugəs] adj jabu
boil [bɔil] **1.** n maruru **2.** v tafasa
bold [bəuld] adj **1.** mai ƙarfin
zuciya **2.** gagarumi
bolt [bəult] n **1.** sakata **2.** ƙusa,
(Nr) bis
bomb [bɔm] **1.** n bom **2.** v jefa
bom
bomb-proof [ˈbɔmpruːf] adj mai
maganin bindiga
bombard [bɔmˈbaːd] v yi ruwan
bom
bombardment [bɔmˈbaːdmənt] n
ruwan bom
bond [bɔnd] n **1.** maɗauri **2.** (fin.)
shaida
bondage [ˈbɔndidʒ] n barance
bonds of friendship pl danƙon
zumunci
bone [bəun] n ƙashi
bonfire [ˈbɔnfaiə] n gobara
bonnet [ˈbɔnit] n car bonnet
bonel, (Nr) kaho
bonus [ˈbəunəs] n **1.** daɗi **2.** ƙari
boo [buː] v yi ihu
booby-trap [ˈbuːbitræp] n haƙon
bam
book [buk] **1.** n littafi **2.** v to
book a room ajiye ɗaki
bookkeeper [ˈbukˌkiːpə] n akanta,
(Nr) kwantabil

booklet [ˈbuklət] n ƙasida
bookseller [ˈbukˌselə] n mai
sayar da littattafai
bookshop, bookstore [ˈbukʃɔp
ˈbukstɔː] n kantin sayar da
littattafai
boom [buːm] n **1.** tattalin arzikin
ƙasa ya ƙara bunƙasa
2. hargagin bindiga
boost [buːst] v farfaɗo da
boot [buːt] n **1.** takalmi, (Nr) boti
2. car boot but, (Nr) kyas
booth [buːð; buːθ] n polling
booth rumfar jefa ƙuri'a
booty [ˈbuːti] n ganima
border [ˈbɔːdə] n **1.** baki **2.** iyaka
border dispute n rikicin kan
iyaka
bore [bɔː] v **1.** ɓusa **2.** gundura
bored [bɔːd] adj I'm bored of this
job. Aikin nan ya gundure ni.
boring [ˈbɔːriŋ] adj mai gundura
born [bɔːn] adj to be born haifu
borough [ˈbʌrə] n ƙaramar
hukuma
borrow [ˈbɔrəu] v àrā
borrower [ˈbɔrəuə] adj mai aro
boss [bɔs] n shugaba
botany [ˈbɔtəni] n ilimin tsirrai
both [bəuθ] adj duk biyu
bother [ˈbɔðə] v dama
bothered [ˈbɔðəd] adj I couldn't
be bothered to visit them. Ban
yi ƙoƙari na ziyarce su ba.
both... and conj da... da
bottle [ˈbɔtl] n kwalba, (Nr)
butali
bottle-opener [ˈbɔtlˌəupnə] n
ɓfanà
bottom [ˈbɔtəm] n **1.** gindi
2. ƙarƙashi
bought [bɔːt] duba wajen **buy**

bounce [bauns] *v* 1. buga
2. rawar da
bound [baund] *adj* 1. a daure
2. lalle 3. **to be bound for** nufa
4. **to be bound to** ala tilas
boundary ['baundri] *n* iyaka
bourgeois ['bɔ:ʒwa:] *adj* mai
hannu da shuni
bourgeoisie ['bɔ:ʒwa:zi] *pl* masu
hannu da shuni
bow [bəu] *n* 1. baka 2. izga
bow [bau] *v* duka
bowl [bəul] *n* kwano
box [bɔks] 1. *n* akwati, (Nr) kyas
2. **a box of matches** fankon
ashana 3. *v* yi dambe
boxer ['bɔksə] *n* dan dambe
box office *n* tagar tikiti
boxing [bɔksiŋ] *n* dambe
boy [bɔi] *n* yaro
boycott ['bɔikɔt] 1. *n* yaji 2. *v*
kaurace wa
boyfriend ['bɔifrend] *n* saurayi
2. aboki
boyhood ['bɔihud] *n* kuruciya
boy scout *n* dan sikawut, (Nr)
sukut
bra [bra:] *n* rigar nono
bracelet ['breislit] *n* munduwa
bracket ['brækit] *n* 1. sashi
2. **brackets** marufai
brain [brein] *n* kwakwalwa
brain drain *n* hijirar kwararrun
ma'aikata
brake, brakes [breik; breiks] 1.
n birki, (Nr) feran 2. *v* ja birki
bran [bræn] *n* dusa
branch [bra:ntʃ] *n* 1. reshe
2. fanni
branch office *n* reshen kamfani
brand-name ['brændneim] *n*
alama

brand new *adj* sabo ful
brandy ['brændi] *n* giyar birandi
brass [bra:s] *n* farin karfe
brassiere ['bræsiə] *n* rigar nono
brave [breiv] *adj* jarumi
bravery ['breivəri] *n* jaruntaka
brawl [brɔ:l] *n* rikici
breach [bri:tʃ] *v* **to breach a**
contract saba yarjejeniya
breach of trust *n* cin amana
bread [bred] *n* burodi, (Nr) buru
breadth [bretθ] *n* fadi
break [breik] 1. *n* dan hutu, (Nr)
raffo 2. **without a break** ba
kakkautawa 3. *v* (**broke,**
broken) karye 4. **to break the**
law yi laifi
break away *v* balle
break-down ['breikdaun] *n*
fanca, (Nr) amfan
break in ['breikin] *v* 1. yi fashi
2. hori doki
break off *v* yanke
break out *v* tashi
breakable ['breikəbl] *adj*
breakable goods kayan aras
breakfast [brekfəst] *n* karin
kumallo
breast [brest] *n* 1. nono 2. kirji
breast-feed ['brestfi:d] *v* shayar
da
breasts [brests] *duba wajen*
breast
breath [breθ] *n* numfashi
breathe [bri:ð] *v* yi numfashi
breathing ['bri:ðiŋ] *n* numfashi
breed [bri:d] *v* yi kiwo
breeze [bri:z] *n* dan iska
brew [bru:] *v* dafa
brewery ['bruəri] *n* gidan yin giya
bribe [braib] 1. *n* hanci 2. *v* ba
da hanci

bribery [ˈbraɪbəri] *n* cin hanci
brick [brɪk] *n* bulo, (Nr) birgi
bride [braɪd] *n* amarya
bridegroom [ˈbraɪdɡruːm] *n* ango
bridge [brɪdʒ] *n* gada
bridle [ˈbraɪdl] *n* kayan linzami
brief [briːf] 1. *adj* ba daɗewa
2. *v* sanar da
briefcase [ˈbriːfkeɪs] *n* jakar
hannu
briefly [ˈbriːfli] *adv* a taƙaice
brigade [brɪˈɡeɪd] *n* birged
brigadier [ˌbrɪɡəˈdɪə] *n* birgediya
bright [braɪt] *adj* 1. mai haske
2. gwani
brighten [ˈbraɪtn] *v* haska
brightness [ˈbraɪtnɪs] *n* haske
brilliant [ˈbrɪliənt] *adj* 1. mai
walƙiya 2. mai hàzāƙà
brim [brɪm] *n* baki
bring [brɪŋ] *v* kawo
bring about *v* jawo
bring down *v* hamɓarar da
bring out *v* fito
bring to mind *v* tuna wa
bring up *v* 1. tayar da 2. rena
brink [brɪŋk] *n* baki
brisk [brɪsk] *adj* da ɗan hanzari
Britain [ˈbrɪtn] *n* Birtaniya
British [ˈbrɪtɪʃ] *adj* na Ingila
Briton [ˈbrɪtn] *n* Ba'ingilishi
brittle [ˈbrɪtl] *adj* mai gautsi
broad [brɔːd] *adj* mai faɗi
broadcast [ˈbrɔːdkɑːst] *n* 1.
watsin labari 2. *v* (**broadcast**)
watsa labari
broad-minded [ˌbrɔːdˈmaɪndɪd]
adj mai saukin kai
broadness [ˈbrɔːdnɪs] *n* faɗi
brochure [ˈbrəʊʃə] *n* ƙasida
broke, broken [brəʊk; ˈbrəʊkən]
duba wajen **break**

broker [ˈbrəʊkə] *n* dillali
brokerage [ˈbrəʊkərɪdʒ] *n* dillanci
bronchitis [brɒnˈkaɪtəs] *n*
mashaƙo
bronze [brɒnz] *n* tagulla
broom [bruːm] *n* tsintsiya
broth [brɒθ] *n* romo
brother [ˈbrʌðə] *n* ɗan'uwa
brother-in-law [ˈbrʌðərɪnlɔː] *n*
ƙane
brotherhood [ˈbrʌðəhuːd] *n* (rel.)
ɗariƙa
brought [brɔːt] *duba wajen*
bring
brow [braʊ] *n* goshi
brown [braʊn] *adj* mai ruwan
ƙasa
bruise [bruːz] 1. *n* ƙurma
2. *v* ƙuje
brush [brʌʃ] 1. *n* buroshi 2. *v*
goge
brutal [ˈbruːtl] *adj* maras imani
brutality [bruːˈtæləti] *n* rashin
imani
bubble, bubbles [ˈbʌbl; -z] *n*
kumfa
bucket [ˈbʌkɪt] *n* bokiti, (Nr) so
buckle [ˈbʌkl] *n* bokul
buckle up *v* komaɗa
bud [bʌd] *n* toho
budge [bʌdʒ] *n* motsa
budget [ˈbʌdʒɪt] *n* kasafin kuɗi
buffalo [ˈbʌfələʊ] *n* ɓauna
buffet [buˈfeɪ] *n* abinci zaɓi da
kanka
bug [bʌɡ] *n* ƙwaro
build [bɪld] *v* (**built**) gina
builder [ˈbɪldə] *n* magini
building [ˈbɪldɪŋ] *n* 1. gini 2. gida
built [bɪlt] *duba wajen* **build**
bulb [bʌlb] *n* 1. guda 2. **light**
bulb ƙwan fitila, (Nr) ampul

bulge [bʌldʒ] *v* taso
bulk [bʌlk] *n* girma
bulky [ˈbʌlki] *adj* mai girma
bull [bul] *n* sa
bullet [ˈbulit] *n* harsashi, (Nr) kartushi
bulletin [ˈbulətin] *n* mujalla, (Nr) biletan
bullet-proof [ˈbulitpruːf] *adj* mai maganin bindiga
bull's eye [ˈbulzai] *n* buzaye
bully [ˈbuli] *v* ci zali
bump [bʌmp] **1.** *n* kumburi **2.** galan **3.** *v* yi karo
bumper [ˈbʌmpə] *n* bamfa, (Nr) farshak
bumpy [ˈbʌmpi] *adj* mai galan
bunch [bʌntʃ] *n* ɗauri
bundle [ˈbʌndl] *n* dami
bungle [ˈbʌŋgl] *v* kuskure
burden [ˈbəːdn] *n* **1.** kaya **2.** nauyi
burden of proof *n* (leg.) alhakin ba da shaida
burdensome [ˈbəːdnsəm] *n* mai nauyi
bureau [ˈbjuːrəu] *n* ofis, (Nr) buro
bureau de change [ˈbjuːrəu də ʃɔːndʒ] *n* shagon canza kuɗi
bureaucrat [ˈbjuərəkræt] *n* ma'aikacin gwamnati, (Nr) ɗan sarushi
bureaucratic [ˌbjuərəˈkrætik] *adj* **bureaucratic language** dogon Turanci
burger *n* gurasa da nama, boga
burglar [ˈbəːglə] *n* ɓarawo
burglary [ˈbəːgləri] *n* sata
burial [ˈberiəl] *n* binnewa
burn [bəːn] **1.** *n* kuna **2.** *v* (burnt) kone **3.** kona

burp [bəːp] **1.** *n* gyatsa **2.** *v* yi gyatsa
burst [bəːst] *v* (burst) **1.** fashe **2.** ɓarke
bury [ˈberi] *v* binne
bus [bʌs] *n* **1.** bos, (Nr) kar **2. minibus** hayis, (Nr) hiyas
bush [buʃ] *n* **1.** karamar bishiya **2. the bush** daji
business [ˈbiznis] *n* **1.** ciniki **2.** kasuwa **3.** harka **4. to run a business** tafi da ciniki
business card *n* katin kasuwanci
businessman [ˈbiznismən] *n* ɗan ciniki
bus route *n* hanyar bas
bus-stop *n* mashigar bas, tashar bas
bust [bʌst] **1.** *n* nono **2.** *v* (bust) fasa
busy [ˈbizi] *adj* **1.** mai yin aiki **2.** mai motsi **3. The line is busy.** Ana waya.
but [bʌt] *conj* **1.** amma **2.** sai
butane [ˈbəutein] *n* gas
butcher [ˈbutʃə] *n* mahauci
butt [bʌt] **1.** *n* guntuwa **2.** *v* tunkuɗa
butter [ˈbʌtə] *n* man shanu
butterfly [ˈbʌtəflai] *n* malam-buɗe-littafi
buttermilk [ˈbʌtəmilk] *n* tsala
buttocks [ˈbʌtəks] *pl* ɗuwawu
button [ˈbʌtn] *n* maɓalli, (Nr) buto
button-hole [ˈbʌtnhəul] *n* kofar maɓalli
buy [bai] *v* sàyā
buyer [ˈbaiə] *n* mai saye
buzz [bʌz] *v* yi ziza
buzzer [ˈbʌzə] *n* kararrawa

by [bai] *prep* **1. by the house** dab da gidan **2. by train** cikin jirgin ƙasa **3. by day** da rana **4. by tomorrow** kafin gobe **5. a book by Charles Dickens** wani littafi wanda Charles Dickens ya rubuta

bye-bye! sai an jima!

by-election [ˈbai-eˌlekʃn] *n* zaɓen cike gurɓin kujerar majalisa

by-product [ˈbaiprɔdʌkt] *n* **petroleum by-product** abin da a ke samu bayan tacewar mai

bypass [ˈbaipaːs] *v* kewaya

bystander [ˈbaistændə] *n* ɗan kallo

Cc

cab [kæb] *n* tasi, (Nr) takasi

cabaret [ˈkæbərei] *n* rawar 'yammata

cabbage [ˈkæbidʒ] *n* kabeji, (Nr) shu

cabin [ˈkæbin] *n* bukka

cabinet [ˈkæbinit] *n* 1. kabad, (Nr) kwaba 2. the Cabinet majalisar ministoci

cable [ˈkeibl] *n* 1. waya 2. electric cable igiyar lantarki

cable television *n* talabijin unguwa

cadet [kəˈdet] *n* kurtu

Caesarean [səˈzeərijən] *n* haihuwar asibiti

cafe [kæˈfei] *n* gidan gahawa, (Nr) kafe

cage [keidʒ] *n* keji

cake [keik] *n* kyat, (Nr) gato

calabash [ˈkæləbæʃ] *n* ƙwarya

calamity [kəˈlæməti] *n* bala'i

calcium [ˈkælsiəm] *n* alli

calculate [ˈkælkjuleit] *n* lasafta

calculation [ˌkælkjuˈleiʃn] *n* lissafi

calculator [ˈkælkjuleitə] *n* injin lissafi

calendar [ˈkælində] *n* kalanda, (Nr) kalandire

calf [caːf] *n* (*pl* calves) 1. maraƙi 2. sha-raɓa

call [kɔːl] *v* 1. kira 2. buga waya 3. *duba wajen* **called**, **telephone call**

call-box [ˈkɔːlbɔks] *n* gidan wayar kwabbai

called [kɔːld] *adj* She is called Zainabu. Sunanta Zainabu ne.

calm [kaːm] 1. *adj* mai hankalin kwance 2. *n* shiru

calm down *v* huce

calmly [ˈkaːmli] *adv* da nitsuwa

calmness [ˈkaːmnis] *n* nitsuwa

calves [kaːvz] *duba wajen* calf

camcorder [ˈkæmkɔːdə] *n* kyamarar majigi

came [keim] *duba wajen* come

camel [ˈkæml] *n* raƙumi

camera [ˈkæmərə] *n* kyamara

camouflage [ˈkæməflaːʒ] *v* sake kamanni

camp [kæmp] *n* 1. zango 2. sansani 3. to set up camp ya da zango 4. concentration camp sansanin gwale-gwale

campaign [kæmˈpein] 1. *n* kamfe 2. *v* yi kamfe

campaigner [kæmˈpeinə] civil rights campaigner mai yaƙin neman hakkin ɗan Adam

camp site *n* zango

campus [ˈkaːmpəs] *n* harabar jami'a

can [kæn; kən] 1. *n* gwangwani, (Nr) kwankwani 2. *v* (could) iya

Canadian [kəˈneidiən] 1. *adj* na Kanada 2. *n* ɗan Kanada

canal [kəˈnæl] *n* hanyar ruwa

cancel [ˈkænsl] *v* (cancelled) soke

cancellation [ˌkænsəˈleiʃn] *n* suka

cancer [ˈkænsə] *n* ciwon kansa
candidate [ˈkændidət] *n* ɗan takara
candle [ˈkændl] *n* kyandir, (Nr) buji
candy [ˈkændi] *n* alewa, (Nr) bambo
cane [kein] *n* gora
canister [ˈkænistə] *n* gwangwani
cannabis [ˈkænibis] *n* wiwi, (Nr) mandula
canned food *n* abincin gwangwani
cannon [ˈkænən] *n* igwa
can-opener [ˈkænəupnə] *n* mabuɗin gwangwani, (Nr) ubirbwat
canteen [kænˈtiːn] *n* gidan abinci
canter [ˈkæntə] *v* yi rishi
cap [kæp] *n* hula
capability [ˌkeipəˈbiləti] *n* iyawa
capable [ˈkeipəbl] *adj* mai iyawa
capacity [kəˈpæsəti] *n* The tanks have been filled to capacity. Rumbuna sun cika maƙil.
cape [keip] *n* hancin ƙasa
capital [ˈkæpitl] *n* 1. hedkwatar ƙasa 2. jari hujja
capital letter *n* babban baƙi
capital market *n* kasuwar jari
capital punishment *n* hukuncin kisa
capitalism [ˈkæpitəlizəm] *n* tsarin jari-hujja
capitalist [ˈkæpitəlist] *n* ɗan jari-hujja
capsize [kæpˈsaiz] *v* kife
captain [ˈkæptin] *n* kyaftin, (Nr) kaftan
caption [ˈkæpʃn] *n* bayani
captive [ˈkæptiv] *n* fursuna
captivity [kæpˈtivəti] *n* ɗauri

capture [ˈkæptʃə] *v* kama
car [kaː] *n* mota, (Nr) bwacir
car accident *n* haɗarin mota
carbon [ˈkaːbən] *n* gawayi
card [kaːd] *n* 1. kati 2. game of cards karta 3. *duba wajen* I.D. card
cardboard [ˈkaːdbɔːd] *n* kwali
cardboard box *n* kwali, (Nr) karto
care [keə] *n* 1. hankali 2. to take care yi hankali (of da)
care about *v* kula da
career [kəˈriə] *n* aikin dindindin
care for *v* kiwata
careful [ˈkeəfl] *adj* mai hankali
carefully [ˈkeəfəli] *adv* da idon basira
careless [ˈkeəlis] *adj* maras hankali
carelessness [ˈkeələsnis] *n* sakaci
caretaker [ˈkeəteikə] *n* sarkin gida, kyātèkà
cargo [ˈkaːgəu] *n* kaya
cargo vessel *n* jirgin ɗaukar kaya
caricature [ˈkærikətjuə] *n* muzantawa, mutum-mutumi
carnival [ˈkaːnivl] *n* hawa
carol [ˈkærəl] Christmas carol wakan Kirsimeti
car park [ˈkaːpaːk] *n* filin mota
carpenter [ˈkaːpintə] *n* kafinta, (Nr) minize
carpet [ˈkaːpit] *n* kafet, (Nr) tầfî
carphone [ˈkaːfəun] *n* tarhon mota
carriage [ˈkæridʒ] *n* 1. keken doki 2. wagunu na fasinja
carrier [ˈkæriə] *n* 1. ɗan dako 2. kariya 3. (med.) mai ɗauke da...

carrier bag *n* lẽdằ

carrot [ˈkærət] *n* karas, (Nr) karoti

carry [ˈkæri] *v* 1. ɗauka 2. **to carry a report** ruwaito

carry on *v* ci gaba

carry out *v* zartar da

cart [kaːt] *n* kura

carton [kaːtn] *n* katan

cartoon [kaːˈtuːn] *n* 1. zane 2. majigin yara

cartridge [ˈkaːtridʒ] *n* 1. harsashi 2. **printer cartridge** faifan inki

carve [kaːv] *v* sassaƙa

case [keis] *n* 1. adaka, (Nr) kyas 2. magana 3. hali 4. (leg.) ƙara 5. **The lawyer took up my case.** Lauya ya ɗauki nauyina. 6. **in any case** ko da wane hali

cash [kæʃ] *n* tsabar kuɗi

cash a cheque *v* 1. amso kuɗi 2. shigar da cak

cash-card *n* katin banki

cashier [kæˈʃiə] *n* kashiya, (Nr) kyasiye

cash payment *n* kuɗi hannu

cash-point *n* injimin kuɗi

cash register *n* injimin buga boca

casino [kəˈsiːnəu] *n* gidan caca

cassava [kəˈsaːvə] *n* rogo

cassette [kəˈset] *n* kasat

cassette recorder *n* rakoda, (Nr) manyeto

cast [kaːst] 1. *n* ’yan wasa 2. *v* jefa

cast a vote *v* jefa ƙuri’a

castle [ˈkaːsl] *n* babbar fada

casual [ˈkæʒuəl] *adj* sakai-sakai

casualty [ˈkæʒuəlti] *n* mai rauni

cat [kæt] *n* kyanwa

catalogue [ˈkætəlɔg] *n* littafi

cataract *n* (med.) yanar ido

catastrophe [kəˈtæstrəfi] *n* bala’i

catch [kætʃ] *v* (**caught**) 1. kama 2. **I caught a cold.** Mura ta kama ni.

catch up *v* cim (**with** ma)

categorically [ˌkætəˈgɔrikli] *adv* a kai tsaye

category [ˈkætəgəri] *n* fanni

caterpillar [ˈkætəpilə] *n* 1. tsutsa 2. katafila, (Nr) katarfila

cathedral [kəˈθiːdrəl] *n* babban coci

Catholic [ˈkæθəlik] *adj/n* ɗan Katolika

cattle [ˈkætl] *n* shanu

caught [kɔːt] *duba wajen* catch

cauliflower [ˈkɔliflauə] *n* farin kabeji

cause [kɔːz] 1. *n* sanadi 2. *v* jawo

caution [ˈkɔːʃn] *n* tsanaki

cautious [ˈkɔːʃəs] *adj* mai tsanaki

cautiously [ˈkɔːʃəsli] *adv* a fakaice

cave [keiv] *n* kogon dutse

cave in *v* ribɗa

cavity [ˈkæviti] *n* rami

c.d. (**compact disc**) [siːˈdiː] *n* sidî

cease [siːs] *v* daina

cease-fire [ˌsiːsˈfaiə] *n* tsagaita amon wuta

ceaseless [ˈsiːslis] *adj* ba tsayawa

ceiling [ˈsiːliŋ] *n* silin

celebrate [ˈselibreit] *v* yi shagali

celebration [ˌseliˈbreiʃn] *n* shagali

celebrity [siˈlebrəti] *n* tauraro, shahararre

cell [sel] *n* 1. ɗakin kurkuku, (Nr) sulluru 2. ƙwaya

cellar [ˈselə] *n* gidan ƙasa

cement [si·ment] *n* siminti, (Nr) siman

cemetery [·semətri] *n* maƙabarta

censor [·sensə] *v* yi wa... takunkumi

censorship [·sensəʃip] *n* takunkumi

census [·sensəs] *n* ƙidayar jama'a

cent [sent] *n* 1. anini 2. ten per cent kashi goma cikin ɗari

centimetre [·sentimiːtə] *n* santimita, (Nr) santimetir

central [·sentrəl] *adj* 1. na tsakiya 2. babba

Central Africa *n* Tsakiyar Afirka

central bank *n* babban bankin ƙasa

central committee *n* babban kwamiti

central government *n* gwamnatin tsakiya

central heating *n* madimin gida

central office *n* hedkwata

centre [·sentə] *n* 1. tsakiya 2. cibiya 3. right in the centre tsaka-tsaka

centre-right *n* (pol.) mai ra'ayin riƙau

century [·sentʃəri] *n* ƙarni

CEO (chief executive officer) *n* (US) shugaba

cereal [·siəriəl] *n* hatsi

ceremony [·serimɔni] *n* biki

certain [·səːtn] *adj* 1. tabbatacce 2. na musamman 3. wani 4. to be certain tabbàtà (of da)

certainly [·səːtnli] *adv* lalle

certainty [·səːtnti] *n* tabbaci

certificate [sə·tifikət] *n* takardar shaida

certification [sətifiˈkeiʃn] *n* tabbatarwa

certify [·səːtifai] *v* tabbatar da

chain [tʃein] *n* sarƙa

chair [tʃeə] *n* kujera

chair a meeting *v* yi shugaban taro

chairman [tʃeəmən] *n* shugaban taro

chalk [tʃɔːk] *n* alli

challenge [·tʃælindʒ] 1. *n* ƙalubale 2. *v* ƙalubalanta

challenged [·tʃælindʒd] *adj* to be challenged sàmi adawa

chamber [·tʃeimbə] *n* 1. ɗaki 2. jam'iyya

chamber of commerce *n* jam'iyyar kasuwanci

chameleon [kəˈmiːliən] *n* hawainiya

champagne [ʃæmˈpein] *n* giyar shàmfê

champion [·tʃæmpiən] *n* zakara

championship [·tʃæmpiənʃip] *n* gàsã

chance [tʃaːns] *n* 1. dama 2. sa'a 3. kasada 4. by chance ƙaddara ce

chancellor [·tʃaːnsələ] *n* 1. shugaban jami'a 2. waziri

Chancellor of the Exchequer *n* ministan harkokin kuɗi

change [tʃeindʒ] 1. *n* canji 2. tsabar kuɗi 3. juyi 4. *v* sake 5. juya 6. I have changed my mind. Na sake shawara.

channel [·tʃænl] *n* 1. hannun teku 2. hanya ta talibijin

chaos [·keiɔs] *n* halin ruɗami

chaotic [keiˈɔtik] *adj* to be chaotic yamutse

chapel [·tʃæpl] *n* ƙaramin coci

chapter [ˈtʃæptə] *n* 1. babi
2. (Islam.) sura

character [ˈkærɪktə] *n* 1. hali
2. baƙi 3. tauraron labari
4. **of good character** nagari

characterise [ˈkærɪktəraɪz] *v*
faye hali

characteristic [ˌkærɪktəˈrɪstɪk] *n*
hali

charge [tʃaːdʒ] 1. *n* caji 2. kudi
3. shugabanci 4. **free of charge**
a kyauta 5. *v* yi caji 6. **The bull
charged at us.** Sa ya tasam
mana.

charity [ˈtʃærəti] *n* 1. sadaka
2. ƙungiyar taimako

charm [tʃaːm] *n* fara'a

chart [tʃaːt] *n* jadawali

charter [ˈtʃaːtə] 1. *n* usula 2. *v* yi
shata

charter flight *n* jirgin shata

chase [tʃeɪs] *v* bi wa... da gudu

chassis [ˈʃæsi] *n* firam, (Nr) shasi

chat [tʃæt] *v* yi taɗi

chatter [ˈtʃætə] *v* yi surutu

chauffeur [ˈʃəufə] *n* direba

cheap [tʃiːp] *adj* mai rahusa

cheaply [ˈtʃiːpli] *adv* a banza

cheat [tʃiːt] *v* 1. yi cuta 2. yi
magudi

cheating [ˈtʃiːtɪŋ] *n* magudi

check [tʃek] *v* 1. duba 2. tabbata
3. *duba wajen* **cheque**

checking account *n* (US) ajiyar
banki

check-up [ˈtʃekʌp] (med.) duba
lafiya

cheek [tʃiːk] *n* 1. kunci 2. shiga
hanci

cheeky [ˈtʃiːki] *adj* mai raini

cheer [tʃɪə] *v* yi shewa

cheer up *v* yi farin ciki

cheerful [ˈtʃɪəfl] *adj* mai farin
ciki

cheese [tʃiːz] *n* cuku

chemical [ˈkemɪkl] 1. *adj* na
kimiyya 2. *n* kimiyya

chemical factory *n* masana'antar
sarrafa magunguna

chemical warfare *n* yaƙin
amfani da guba

chemical waste *n* shara mai illa

chemical weapons *pl*
makaman guba

chemist [ˈkemɪst] *n* 1. ɗan
kimiyya 2. mai sayar da
magani

chemistry [ˈkemɪstri] *n* kimiyya

chemist's [ˈkemɪsts] *n* kyamis,
(Nr) mushen farmasi

cheque [tʃek] *n* caki, (Nr) shek

cheque-book *n* bandurin cak

cheque card *n* kati mai kama da
cak

cheque stub *n* dungun cak

cherish [ˈtʃerɪʃ] *v* yi ƙauna

chess [tʃes] *n* dara, shaɗaranji

chest [tʃest] *n* 1. ƙirji 2. gidan
aljihun tebur

chew [tʃuː] *v* tauna

chewing-gum [ˈtʃuːɪŋɡʌm] *n*
cingam, (Nr) shingwam

chick [tʃɪk] *n* ɗan tsako

chicken [ˈtʃɪkɪn] *n* kaza

chickenpox [ˈtʃɪkɪnpɒks] *n*
ƙarambau

chief [tʃiːf] 1. *adj* babba
2. *n* shugaba 3. sarki

chiefly [ˈtʃiːfli] *adv* musamman

chief of staff *n* hafsan hafsoshi

child [tʃaɪld] *n* (*pl* **children**)
yaro, yarinya

childbirth [ˈtʃaɪldbəːθ] *n*
haihuwa

childhood [ˈtʃaildhud] *n* yarantaka

childless [ˈtʃaildlis] *adj* mai rashin haihuwa

children [ˈtʃildrən] *duba wajen* child

children's [ˈtʃildrənz] *adj* na yara

chilly [ˈtʃili] *adj* mai sanyi

chimney [ˈtʃimni] *n* (*pl* chimneys) mafitar hayaƙi

chin [tʃin] *n* haɓa

china, chinaware [ˈtʃainə] *n* faɗi-ka-mutu

chip [tʃip] *n* 1. ɓagure 2. chips soyayyen dankali 3. microchip ƙwaƙwalwar kwamfuta

chocolate [ˈtʃɔklət] *n* cakulan, (Nr) cakola

choice [tʃɔis] *n* zaɓi

choir [ˈkwaiə] *n* mawaƙa

choke [tʃəuk] *v* ƙwaru

cholera [ˈkɔlərə] *n* kwalara

choose [tʃuːz] *v* (chose, chosen) zaɓa

chop [tʃɔp] 1. *n* yankakken nama 2. *v* (chopped) yanka, sare

chord [kɔːd] *n* (mus.) gambarar kiɗa

chorus [ˈkɔːrəs] *n* 'yan amshi

chose, chosen [tʃuːz; ˈtʃəuzən] *duba wajen* choose

Christian [ˈkristʃən] *adj/n* Kirista, (Nr) ɗan almasihu

christian name *n* sunan yanka

Christianity [ˌkristiˈænəti] *n* addinin Kirista

Christmas [ˈkrisməs] 1. *adj* na Kirsimati 2. *n* Kirsimati, (Nr) Nòwâl

chunk [tʃʌŋk] *n* ɓangare

church [tʃəːtʃ] *n* coci, (Nr) gidan almasihu

CIA *n* Kungiyar Leƙen Asiri ta Amirka ta CIA

cider [ˈsaidə] *n* giyar tuffa

cigarette [ˌsigəˈret] *n* sigari, (Nr) sigarati

cinema [ˈsinəmə] *n* siliman

circle [ˈsəːkl] *n* 1. da'ira 2. zobe

circuit [ˈsəːkit] *n* 1. keweye 2. short circuit tangarɗar wuta

circular [ˈsəːkjulə] *adj* mai siffar zobe

circulate [ˈsəːkjuleit] *v* 1. baza 2. zagaya

circulation [ˈsəːkjuˈleiʃn] *n* bugun jini

circumcision [ˌsəːkəmˈsiʒn] *n* kaciya

circumcize [ˈsəːkəmsaiz] *v* yi wa... kaciya

circumference [səːˈkʌmfərəns] *n* keweye

circumstances [ˈsəːkəmstənsiz] *pl* 1. hali 2. under the present circumstances a halin yanzu dai

circus [ˈsəːkəs] *n* gidan wasa da dabbobi

cistern [ˈsistən] *n* tanki

citizen [ˈsitizn] *n* ɗan ƙasa

citizenship [ˈsitiznʃip] *n* zama ɗan ƙasa

citrus [ˈsitrəs] *adj* na lemo

city [ˈsiti] *n* 1. birni 2. inner city cikin gari

city council *n* hukumar gari

city square *n* dandali, kanwuri

civic duty *n* kishin gari

civil aviation *n* sufurin jirgin sama

civil engineer *n* injiniyan gine-gine

civil rights *pl* 'yancin da doka ta tanadar

civil servant *n* ma'aikacin gwamnati, (Nr) ɗan sarushi

civil service *n* aikin gwamnati, (Nr) sarushi

civil war *n* yaƙin basasa

civilian [si·vilіən] *adj/n* farar hula

civilian government *n* gwamnatin farar hula

civilisation [ˌsivəlai·zeiʃn] *n* wayewar kai

civilised [ˈsivəlaizd] *adj* na wayewar kai

claim [kleim] **1.** *n* da'awa **2.** *v* yi da'awa

claimant [ˈkleimənt] *n* mai da'awa

clap [klæp] *v* (**clapped**) yi tafi

clapping [ˈklæpiŋ] *n* ban tafi

clarification [ˌklærifi·keiʃn] *n* bayani

clarify [ˈklærifai] *n* bayyana

clarity [ˈklærəti] *n* zahiri

clash [klæʃ] *v* **1.** ɗauki ba daɗi **2.** yi arangama (**with** da)

class [klaːs] *v* **1.** aji **2.** nau'i

classical [ˈklæsikl] *adj* na gargajiya

classify [ˈklæsifai] *v* karkasa

classmate [ˈklaːsmeit] *n* ɗan aji

classroom [ˈklaːsrum] *n* (Nr) ɗakin aji, kalas

clause [klɔːz] *n* **1.** sharaɗi **2.** (leg.) kashi

claw [klɔː] *n* akaifa

clay [klei] *n* yumɓu

clean [kliːn] **1.** *adj* mai tsabta **2.** *v* share

cleanse [klenz] *v* tsabtace

cleansing [ˈklenziŋ] *n* **ethnic cleansing** kisan rairayar al'umma

clear [ˈkliə] **1.** *adj* zahiri **2.** clear

water baƙin ruwa **3.** *v* kwashe **4.** yi kiliya **5.** **to clear land** sassabe

clearly [ˈkliəli] *adv* a zahiri

clemency [ˈklemənsi] *n* ahuwa

clench [klentʃ] *v* runtse

clergy [ˈklɔːdʒi] *n* **1.** (Isl.) malamai **2.** (Chr.) fada

clerk [klaːk] *n* akawu

clever [ˈklevə] *adj* mai fasaha

click [klik] *n* ƙararrawa

client [ˈklaiənt] *n* abokin ciniki

cliff [klif] *n* hayi

climate [ˈklaimit] *n* yanayi

climb [klaim] *v* hau

climb down *v* sauka

climb over *v* haura

climber [ˈklaimə] *n* ɗan hawa

clinch a deal [klintʃ] *v* sami kwangila

cling [kliŋ] *v* (**clung**) ɗafe (**to** wa)

clinic [ˈklinik] *n* **1.** asibiti **2.** **maternity clinic** asibitin haihuwa

clinical [ˈklinikl] *adj* na asibiti

clip [klip] **1.** *n* kilif, (Nr) taramban **3.** *v* datse

clitoris [ˈklitəris] *n* ɗan tsaka

clock [klɔk] *n* **1.** agogo **2.** **alarm clock** agogo mai ƙararrawa

close [kləus] *adj* kusa (**to** da)

close [kləuz] *v* rufe

closed [kləuzd] *adj* a rufe

closely [ˈkləusli] *adv* da hankali

closet [ˈklɔzit] *n* ɗan kabad, (Nr) almuwar

cloth [klɔθ] *n* **1.** zane, (Nr) tisi **2.** ɗan tsumma

clothe [kləuð] *v* tufantar da

clothes, clothing [kləuðz; ˈkləuðiŋ] *pl* tufafi

cloud [klaud] *n* gajimare

clown [klaun] *n* ta-banjama
club [klʌb] *n* 1. kulob 2. ƙungiya 3. kulki
clue [klu:] *n* alama
clumsiness [ˈklʌmsinəs] *n* rashin kintsi
clumsy [ˈklʌmsi] *adj* maras kintsi
clung [klʌŋ] *duba wajen* **cling**
clutch [klʌtʃ] 1. *n* kuloci, (Nr) amburyaje 2. *v* riƙa
co. *duba wajen* **company**
coach [kəutʃ] 1. *n* bas, (Nr) kar 2. kociya, (Nr) antirenar 3. *v* koya wa
coal [kəul] *n* kwal
coal-mine [ˈkəulmain] *n* mahaƙar kwal
coal-mining [ˈkəulmainiŋ] *n* haƙo kwal
coalition [ˌkəuəˈliʃn] *n* 1. haɗin gwiwa 2. **temporary coalition** haɗin gambiza
coalition government *n* gwamnatin haɗin gwiwa
coarse [kɔ:s] *adj* 1. mai kaushi 2. tsàki
coast [kəust] *n* gaɓar teku
coastal [ˈkəustl] *adj* na gaɓar teku
coat [kəut] *n* kwat, (Nr) manto
coat of arms *n* zanen tambari
coax [kəuks] *v* lallasa
cobra [ˈkəubrə; kɔbrə] *n* gamsheƙa
cocaine [kəuˈkein] *n* hodar Iblis
cock, cockerel [kɔk; ˈkɔkərəl] *n* zakara
cockroach [ˈkɔkrəutʃ] *n* kyankyaso
cocoa [ˈkəukəu] *n* koko
coconut [ˈkəukənʌt] *n* kwakwa
cod [kɔd] *n* gàrgazã
code [kəud] *n* 1. **highway code**

dokar hanya 2. **legal code** tsarin dokoki 3. **penal code** tsarin laifuffuka
coerce [kəuˈə:s] *v* tilasta wa
coffee [ˈkɔfi] *n* kofi, (Nr) kafe
coffin [ˈkɔfin] *n* akwatin jana'iza
coil [kɔil] *v* naɗa
coin, coins [kɔin; -z] *n* tsabar kuɗi
coincide [ˌkəuinˈsaid] *v* zo daidai (**with** da)
coincidence [kəuˈinsidəns] *n* **What a coincidence!** Faɗuwa ta zo daidai da zama!
cold [kəuld] 1. *adj* mai sanyi 2. *n* sanyi 3. **cold season** hunturu 4. **I caught a cold.** Mura ta kama ni.
cold-blooded *adj* maƙetaci
coldness [ˈkəuldnis] *n* sanyi
cold war *n* yaƙin cacar baka
collaborate [kəˈlæbəreit] *v* haɗa baki
collaborator [kəˈlæbəreitə] *n* ɗan haɗin baki
collapse [kəˈlæps] *v* 1. rushe 2. tarwatse 3. (ec.) wargaje
collar [ˈkɔlə] *n* kwala, (Nr) kwal
colleague [ˈkɔli:g] *n* abokin aiki
collect [kəˈlekt] *v* 1. kawo 2. tara 3. karɓa
collection [kəˈlekʃn] *n* tari
collective [kəˈlektiv] *adj* 1. na gama kai 2. **to take collective action** ɗauki mataki tare
college [ˈkɔlidʒ] *n* kwaleji
collide [kəˈlaid] *v* yi karo (**with** da)
collision [kəˈliʒn] *n* karo
colloquial [kəˈləukwiəl] *adj* na yaren gida
collusion [kəˈlu:ʒn] *n* gama baki

colonel [ˈkəːnl] *n* kanar, (Nr) kononal

colonial rule [kəˈləuniəl] *n* mulkin mallaka

colonialism [kəˈləuniəlizəm] *n* mulkin mallaka

colonization [ˌkɔlənaiˈzeiʃn] *n* mulkin mallaka

colonize [ˈkɔlənaiz] *v* yi wa... mulkin mallaka

colony [ˈkɔləni] *n* mallaka

colour [ˈkʌlə] *n* launi

column [ˈkɔləm] *n* 1. ginshiƙi 2. sashi

coma [ˈkəumə] *n* He is in a coma. Ransa ga Allah.

comb [kəum] *n* matsefi

combat [ˈkɔmbæt] 1. *n* jidali 2. *v* sha jidali

combination [ˌkɔmbiˈneiʃn] *n* haɗuwa

combine [kəmˈbain] *v* haɗa

come [kʌm] *v* (came, come) zo

come across *v* ci karo da

come apart *v* ɓarke

come back *v* dawo

come close *v* kusanta

comedian [kəˈmiːdiən] *n* cali-cali

come off *v* ɓalle

come out *v* fito

come up *v* auku

comedy [ˈkɔmədi] *n* wasan ban dariya

comet [ˈkɔmet] *n* tauraruwa mai wutsiya

comfort [ˈkʌmfət] 1. *n* haƙuri 2. ba wa... haƙuri

comfortable [ˈkʌmftəbl] *adj* 1. mai jin daɗi 2. mai sauƙi

comic [ˈkɔmik] 1. *adj* mai ban dariya 2. *n* cali-cali 3. jarida mai zane-zane masu ban dariya

coming [ˈkʌmiŋ] 1. *n* zuwa 2. *adj* mai zuwa

comma [ˈkɔmə] *n* waƙafi

command [kəˈmaːnd] 1. *n* umurni 2. shugabanci 3. *v* umurta

commander [kəˈmaːndə] *n* kwamanda, (Nr) kumandan

Commander-in-Chief of the Armed Forces *n* babban kwamandan rundunonin mayaƙa

commandos [kəˈmaːndəuz] *pl* sojojin ƙundumbala

commemoration [kəˌmemɔˈreiʃn] *n* bikin tunawa

commend [kəˈmend] *v* yaba

commence [kəˈmens] *v* fara

comment [ˈkɔment] *v* bayyana

comment on *v* sharhanta

commentary [ˈkɔməntri] *n* 1. sharhi 2. (Islam.) tafsiri

commerce [ˈkɔməːs] *n* ciniki

commercial [kəˈməːʃl] *adj* na ciniki

commercial agent *n* ɗan baranda

commercial centre *n* cibiyar kasuwanci

commercial law *n* dokokin cinikayya

commission [kəˈmiʃn] *n* 1. hukuma 2. kamasho

commissioner [kəˈmiʃənə] *n* kwamishina, (Nr) kwamsar

commit [kəˈmit] *v* (committed) 1. aikata 2. to commit a crime yi laifi

commitment [kəˈmitmənt] *n* alkawari

committee [kəˈmitiː] *n* 1. kwamiti, (Nr) kwamite 2. steering committee kwamitin shirya aiki

committee of inquiry *n* hukumar bincike

commodity, commodities [kəˈmɔdəti] *n* kayayyaki

commodity prices *pl* farashin kayayyaki,

common [ˈkɔmən] *adj* **1.** gamagari **2.** na yau da kullum **3.** na kowa

Common Market *n* Kasuwar Tarayyar Turai

commonplace [ˈkɔmənpleis] *adj* na yau da kullum

common sense [ˌkɔmənˈsens] *n* He has common sense. Yana da tunani da kuma sanin ya kamata.

Commonwealth [ˈkɔmənwelθ] *n* Kungiyar Commonwealth

Commonwealth nations *pl* Ƙasashe masu zumunci da Ingila

commotion [kəˈmeuʃn] *n* hadahada

communal [ˈkɔmjunl] *adj* na jama'a

communicate [kəˈmjuːnikeit] *v* sadar da

communication [kəˌmjuːniˈkeiʃn] *n* **1.** sadarwa **2.** magana

communications [kəˈmjuːniˈkeiʃnz] *pl* harkokin sadarwa

communications network *n* hanyoyin sadarwa

communications satellite *n* kumbon sadarwa

communique [kəˈmjuːnikei] *n* **1.** sanarwa **2.** joint communique sanarwa ta haɗin gwiwa

communism [ˈkɔmjunizm] *n* kwaminisanci

communist [ˈkɔmjunist] *n* **1.** ɗan kwaminis **2.** na kwaminis

community [kəˈmjuːnəti] *n* al'umma

commute [kəˈmjuːt] *v* **1.** yi tafiya ofis, yi ujula **2.** (leg.) mayar da

commuter [kəˈmjuːtə] *n* mai yin tafiya ofis, ɗan ujula

compact [kəmˈpækt] *adj* buzuzu

compact disc *n* sidî

companion [kəmˈpæniən] *n* aboki

company [ˈkʌmpəni] *n* **1.** ƙungiya **2.** kamfani, (Nr) komfanyo

comparable [ˈkɔmpərəbl] *adj* to be comparable yi daidai (to da)

comparatively [kəmˈpærətivli] *adv* a kwatance

compare [kəmˈpeə] *v* kwatanta

compared with [kəmˈpeəd] *adj* daura da

comparison [kəmˈpærisn] *n* **1.** kwatanci **2.** in comparison a kwatance

compartment [kəmˈpaːtmənt] *n* ɗaki

compass [ˈkʌmpəs] *n* **1.** kamfas **2.** bukari

compassion [kəmˈpæʃn] *n* tausayi

compatible [kəmˈpætəbl] *adj* to be compatible zo daidai

compel [kəmˈpel] *v* tilasta wa

compensate [ˈkɔmpənseit] *v* **1,** saka wa **2.** biya diyya

compensation [ˌkɔmpənˈseiʃn] *n* ramuwar diyya

compete [kəmˈpiːt] *v* yi gasa

competence [ˈkɔmpitəns] *n* gwaninta

competent [ˈkɔmpitənt] *adj* gwani

competition [ˌkɔmpeˈtiʃn] *n* **1.** gasa **2.** economic competition gasar ciniki **3.** peaceful

competition gogayya ta lumana

competitor [kɔmˈpetitə] n ɗan gasa

complain [kəmˈplein] v yi kuka

complaining [kəmˈpleiniŋ] n gunaguni

complaint [kəmˈpleint] n 1. kuka 2. ciwo 3. (leg.) **to lodge a complaint** yi ƙara

complement [ˈkɔmplimənt] v dace da

complete [kəmˈpliːt] 1. adj cikakke 2. v cika 3. kammala

completely [kəmˈpliːtli] adv sarai

complex [ˈkɔmpleks] adj rikitacce

complexion [kəmˈplekʃn] n launin fuska

complicate [ˈkɔmplikeit] v rikita

complicated [ˈkɔmplikeitid] adj mai wuya

compliment [ˈkɔmplimənt] 1. n yabo 2. v yàbā

comply with [kəmˈplai] v bi

component [kəmˈpəunənt] n ɓangare

compose [kəmˈpəuz] v 1. ƙage 2. shirya

composed [kəmˈpəuzd] adj **to be composed of** haɗa da

composer [kəmˈpəuzə] n mawaƙi

composition [ˌkɔmpəˈziʃn] n 1. talifi 2. waƙa

compound [ˈkɔmpaund] n 1. gida 2. **chemical compound** mahaɗi

comprehend [ˌkɔmpriˈhend] v fahimta

comprehension [ˌkɔmpriˈhenʃn] n fahimta

compress [kəmˈpres] v matsa

comprise [kəmˈpraiz] v haɗa da

compromise [ˈkɔmprəmaiz] 1. n sulhu 2. v daidaita

compulsory [kəmˈpʌlsəri] adj na dole

compute [kəmˈpjuːt] v lissafta

computer [kəmˈpjuːtə] n na'urar kwamfuta

computing [kəmˈpjuːtiŋ] n sarrafa kwamfuta

comrade [ˈkɔmræd] n aboki

concave [ˈkɔnkeiv] adj komaɗaɗɗe

conceal [kənˈsiːl] v ɓoye

concealment [kənˈsiːlmənt] n ɓuya

concede [kənˈsiːd] v ba da gari

conceited [kənˈsiːtid] adj **to be conceited** ɗaga hanci

conceive [kənˈsiːv] v 1. ɗau ciki 2. tuno

concentrate [ˈkɔnsntreit] v mai da hankali (**on** kan)

concentration [ˌkɔnsnˈtreiʃn] n natsuwa

concentration camp n sansanin gwale-gwale

concept [ˈkɔnsept] n tunani

concern [kənˈsəːn] 1. n damuwa 2. **business concern** kamfani 3. **causing concern** mai damuwa 4. v shafa

concerned [kənˈsəːnd] adj **to be concerned** damu (**da about**)

concerned with prep game da

concerning [kənˈsəːniŋ] prep bisa kan

concert [ˈkɔnsət] n kiɗa da wake-waƙe

concession [kənˈseʃn] n 1. sassauci 2. hakki

concise [kənˈsais] adj taƙaitacce

conclude [kənˈkluːd] v kammala

conclusion [kənˈkluːʃn] *n* **1.**
ƙarshe **2.** hukunci **3. in
conclusion** daga ƙarshe
concrete [ˈkɔnkriːt] **1.** *adj* mai
ma'ana **2.** *n* kankare, (Nr)
betan
condemn [kənˈdem] *v* **1.** yi Allah
wadai da **2.** (leg.) yanke wa...
hukunci
condemnation [ˌkɔndemˈneiʃn] *n*
tofin Allah tsine
condition [kənˈdiʃn] *n* **1.** halin
zama **2.** sharaɗi **3. good
condition** lafiya **4. on
condition that** matuƙar
condo [ˈkɔndəu] *n* (US) gida
condolences [kənˈdəulənsis] *pl*
jaijaiko
condom [ˈkɔndəm] *n* robar hana
ɗaukar ciki
condone *v* ɗaure wa... gindi
conduct [ˈkɔndʌkt] *n* hali
conduct [kənˈdʌkt] *v* **1.** ja wa...
gora **2.** shugabanta
conductor [kənˈdʌktə] *n* **1.**
kwandasta, ɗan kamasho (Nr)
2. (mus.) madugun makaɗa
cone [kəun] *n* mazugi
confectionery [kənˈfekʃəneri] *n*
alewa, (Nr) bambo
confederation [kənˌfedeˈreiʃn] *n*
tarayya
confer [kənˈfəː] *v* gana
conference [ˈkɔnfərəns] *n* **1.** taro
2. follow-up conference taron
bita **3. press conference** taron
manema labarai **4. summit
conference** taron ƙoli
confess [kənˈfes] *v* amsa laifi
confession [kənˈfʃnl] *n* iƙirari da
laifi
confidence [ˈkɔnfidəns] *n* tabbaci

confident [ˈkɔnfidəns] *adj* **1.** mai
rashin tsoro **2.** tabbatacce **3. to
be confident** yi limani (about
da)
confidential [ˌkɔnfiˈdənʃəl] *adj*
asirtacce
confine [kənˈfain] *v* tsare
confirm [kənˈfəːm] *v* tabbatar da
confirmation [ˌkɔnfəˈmeiʃn] *n*
tabbaci
confirmed [kənˈfəːmd] *adj*
tabbatacce
confiscate [ˈkɔnfiskeit] *v* garƙame
wa
conflagration [ˌkɔnfləˈgreiʃn] *n*
gobara
conflict [ˈkɔnflikt] *n* rikici
conflict [kənˈflikt] *v* saɓa
conflicting [kənˈfliktiŋ] *adj* mai
ruɗarwa
conflict resolution *n* warware
rikici
conform [kənˈfɔːm] *v* bi
conformist [kənˈfɔːmist] *adj/n*
ɗan amshin shata
confront [kənˈfrʌnt] *v* yi arangama
confrontation [ˌkɔnfrʌnˈteiʃn] *n*
arangama
confuse [kənˈfjuːz] *v* ruɗa
confused [kənˈfjuːzd] *adj* **to be
confused** ruɗe
confusing *adj* mai ruɗarwa
confusion [kənˈfjuːʒn] *n* rikici
congestion [kənˈdʒestʃən] *n*
cunkoso
congratulate [kənˈgrætʃuleit] *v* yi
wa... murna (**on** kan)
congratulations [kənˌgrætʃuˈleiʃnz]
pl **1.** yin murna **2.
congratulations!** albarka!
congregation [ˌkɔŋgriˈgeiʃn] *n*
masallata

congress [ˈkɔŋgres] *n* **1.** babban taro **2.** majalisa **3.** jam'iyya **4.** (US) **Congress** Majalisun Dokoki

congressman [ˈkɔŋgresmən] *n* ɗan Majalisun Dokokin Amirka

conjure [ˈkʌndʒə] *v* yi dabo

conjuring [ˈkʌndʒəriŋ] *n* dabo

connect [kəˈnekt] *v* haɗa

connected [kəˈnektid] *adj* well connected

connection, connexion [kəˈnekʃn] *n* **1.** haɗi **2.** in connection with dangane da

conquer [ˈkɔŋkə] *v* ci nasara

conqueror [ˈkɔŋkərə] *n* mai nasara

conquest [ˈkɔŋkwest] *n* nasara

conscience [ˈkɔnʃəns] *n* ganin bambancin kyau da sharri

conscientious [ˌkɔnʃiˈenʃəs] *adj* mai ƙoƙari

conscious [ˈkɔnʃəs] *adj* **1.** mai sani **2.** mai farka

conscript [ˈkɔnskript] *n* (mil.) shigar da

conscription [kənˈskripʃn] *n* ɗaukar mutane a soja

consecutive [kənˈsekjutiv] *adj* a jere

consecutively [kənˈsekjutivli] *adv* bi da bi

consensus [kənˈsensəs] *n* They have reached a consensus. An cimma ra'ayi ɗaya.

consent [kənˈsent] **1.** *n* yarda **2.** *v* yarda da

consequence [ˈkɔnsikwens] *n* **1.** sakomako **2.** of no consequence ba magana **3.** in consequence of saboda wannan

consequently [ˈkɔnsikwentli] *conj* saboda haka

conservation [ˌkɔnsəˈveiʃn] *n* kiyayewa

conservative [kənˈsɔːvətiv] *adj/n* (pol.) mai ra'ayin 'yan mazan jiya

conservative states *pl* ƙasashe masu bin manufar riƙau

consider [kənˈsidə] *v* **1.** yi zato **2.** yi la'akari

considerable [kənˈsidərəbl] *adj* mai yawa

considerate [kənˈsidərət] *adj* mai sanin ya kamata

consideration [kənˌsidəˈreiʃn] *n* **1.** la'akari **2.** political considerations sharuɗɗan siyasa

considering that [kənˈsidəriŋ] *conj* ganin cewa

consignment [kənˈsainmənt] *n* kaya

consist [kənˈsist] *v* ƙunsā

consistent [kənˈsistənt] *adj* to be consistent tashi tsaya (on/about a kan)

consolation [ˌkɔnsəˈleiʃn] *n* sauƙi

consolidate [kənˈsɔlideit] *v* ƙarfafa

consonant [ˈkɔnsənənt] *n* baƙi

conspicuous [kənˈspikjuəs] *adj* **1.** a fili **2.** a bayyane

conspiracy [kənˈspirəsi] *n* haɗin kai

conspire [kənˈspaiə] *v* haɗa kai

constable [ˈkʌnstəbl] *n* ɗan sanda, (Nr) falis

constant [ˈkɔnstənt] *adj* maras sauyawa

constantly [ˈkɔnstəntli] *adv* kullum

constituency [kən·stitjuənsi] *n* (pol.) mazaɓa
constituent [kən·stitjuənt] *n* (pol.) ɗan mazaɓa
constitute [·kɔnstitju:t] *v* tsara
constitution [,kɔnsti:tju:ʃn] *n* 1. halin jiki 2. (pol.) tsarin mulki
constitutional [,kɔnsti·tju:ʃənl] *adj* na doka
constraint [kən·streint] *n* tauyewa
construct [kən·strʌkt] *v* gina
construction [kən·strʌkʃn] *n* gini
construction industry *n* 'yan kwangila
constructive [kən·strʌktiv] *adj* mai amfani
constructor [kən·strʌktə] *n* magini
consul [·kɔnsl] *n* ɗan ƙaramin jakada
consult [kən·sʌlt] *v* shawarta
consultation [,kɔnsʌl·teiʃn] *n* shawara
consume [kən·sju:m] *v* cinye
consumer [kən·sju:mə] *n* mai kashe kuɗi
consumer goods *pl* kayayyakin masarufi
consumption [kən·sʌmpʃn] *n* ci
contact [·kɔntækt] *n* 1. hulɗa 2. **cultural contact** tuntuɓar juna a fannin al'adu 3. **to get in contact** haɗu (**with** da) 4. *v* taɓa
contagious [kən·teidʒəs] *adj* mai yaɗuwa
contain [kən·tein] *v* ƙunsa
container [kən·teinə] *n* 1. akwati 2. **freight container** kwàntēnà
contemplate [·kɔntempleit] *v* yi tunani

contemplation [,kɔntem·pleiʃn] *n* tunani
contemporary [kən·tempəreri] 1. *adj* na zamani 2. *n* sa'à
contemptible [kən·temptəbl] *adj* **contemptible behaviour** ta'asa
contempt [kən·tempt] *n* wulaƙanci
contemptuous [kən·temptʃuəs] *adj* na wulaƙanci
contend [kən·tend] *v* yi hamayya
content [kən·tent] *adj* mai farin ciki
contents [·kɔntents] *pl* abin da ke ciki
contest [kən·test] *n* gasa
contestant [kən·testənt] *n* ɗan gasa
context [·kɔntekst] *n* mahalli
continent [·kɔntinənt] *n* 1. ɓangaren duniya 2. **the Continent** Turai
continental [,kɔnti·nentl] *adj* na ɓaɓgaren duniya
contingency [kən·tindʒənsi] *n* **as a contingency** sabo da ɓacin rana
contingency plans *pl* shirye-shiryen gaggawa
continual [kən·tinjuəl] *adj* na kullum
continually [kən·tinjuəl] *adv* kullum
continue [kən·tinju:] *v* 1. ci gaba 2. yi ta
continued [kən·tinju:d] *adj* **to be continued...** â ci gàba...
continuous [kən·tinjuəs] *adj* ba iyaka
continuously [kən·tinjuəsli] *adv* ba tsayawa

contour [ˈkɔntuə] *n* kwane-
kwane

contraband [ˈkɔntrəbænd] *adj/n*
kayan sumoga

contraceptive [ˌkɔntrəˈseptiv] *n*
maganin hana haihuwa

contract [ˈkɔntrækt] *n* kwangila,
(Nr) kwantara

contractor [kənˈtræktə] *n* ɗan
kwangila

contractual [kənˈtræktʃuəl] *adj*
na kwangila

contradict [ˌkɔntrəˈdikt] *v*
ƙaryata

contradiction [ˌkɔntrəˈdikʃn] *n*
baki biyu

contrary [ˈkɔntrəri] *adj* on the
contrary a kishin haka

contrast [ˈkɔntraːst] 1. *n*
bambanci 2. *v* kwatanta

contravene [ˌkɔntrəˈviːn] *v* saɓa
wa

contribute [kənˈtribjuːt] *v* ba da
gudummawa

contribution [ˌkɔntriˈbjuːʃn] *n*
gudummawa

contributor [kənˈtribjutə] *n* mai
ban gudummawa

contrive [kənˈtraiv] *v* yi kutu-
kutu

control [kənˈtrəul] 1. *n* iko
2. remote control macanjin
tasha 3. self-control kama kai
4. *v* sarrafa

controller [kənˈtrəulə] *n* mai kula

controversial [ˌkɔntrəˈvəːʃl] *adj*
mai kawo rigima

controversy [kənˈtrɔvəsi] *n*
jayayya

convalesce [ˌkɔnvəˈles] *v* ji sauƙi

convene [kənˈviːn] *v* ƙaddamar da
taro

convenience [kənˈviːniəns] *n* at
your convenience lokacin da
ya dace maka

convenient [kənˈviːniənt] *adj* to
be convenient dace

convent [ˈkɔnvənt] *n* gidan sista

convention [kənˈvenʃn] *n* 1.
babban taro 2. al'ada

conventional [kənˈvenʃənl] *adj*
na al'ada

conversation [ˌkɔnvəˈseiʃn] *n*
magana

converse [kənˈvəːs] *v* yi magana

convert [kɔnˈvəːt] *v* 1. mayar da
2. (Isl.) musulantar (from da)
3. (Chr.) nasarantar (from da)

convex [ˈkɔnveks] *adj* mai doro

convey [kənˈvei] *v* 1. kai 2. to
convey a message i da manzanci

convict [ˈkɔnvikt] *n* fursuna, (Nr)
ɗan kaso

convict [kənˈvikt] *v* sami... da laifi

convince [kənˈvins] *v* shawo kai

convoy [ˈkɔnvɔi] *n* jerin gwanon
motoci

convulsion [kənˈvʌlʃn] *n*
farfaɗiya

cook [kuk] 1. *n* kuku, (Nr)
kuzinye 2. *v* dafa

cooker [ˈkukə] *n* kuka, (Nr)
kizinyer

cool [kuːl] 1. *adj* da ɗan sanyi 2. *v*
sanyaya

cool down *v* 1. huce 2. kwantar
da hankali

cooperate [kəuˈɔpəreit] *v* haɗa
kai

cooperation [kəuˌɔpəˈreiʃn] *n* 1.
haɗin kai 2. (ec.) ma'ammala

cooperative [kəuˈɔpərətiv] 1. *adj*
na haɗa kai 2. *n* ƙungiyar haɗa
kai

coordinator [kəuˈɔːdineitə] *n* mai kula (of da)

cop [kɔp] *n* (sl.) ɗan sanda, (Nr) falis

cope [kəup] *v* **They can't cope with it.** Ya fi ƙarfinsu.

copier [ˈkɔpiə] *duba wajen* **photocopier**

copper [ˈkɔpə] *n* jan ƙarfe

copulation [kɔpjuˈleiʃn] *n* **1.** jima'i **2.** barbara

copy [ˈkɔpi] **1.** *n* kwafi, (Nr) kopi **2.** *v* juya **3.** kwaikwaya

copyright [ˈkɔpirait] *n* hakkin mallaka, hakkin mawallafi

coral [ˈkɔrəl] *n* murjani

cord [kɔːd] *n* igiya

cordless phone *n* oba-oba

core [kɔː] *n* tsakiya

cork [kɔːk] *n* matoshi, (Nr) busho

corkscrew [ˈkɔːkskruː] *n* barima

corn [kɔːn] *n* masara

corn-bin [ˈkɔːnbin] *n* rumbu

corner [ˈkɔːnə] *n* **1.** kwana **2.** kusurwa

coronation [ˌkɔrəˈneiʃn] *n* naɗin sarki

coroner [ˈkɔrənə] *n* jam'in kula da mutuwar kwatsam

corporal [ˈkɔːpərəl] *n* kofur, (Nr) kafaran

corporal punishment *n* **1.** gwale-gwale **2.** hukuncin dukan bulala

corporation [ˌkɔːpəˈreiʃn] *n* **1.** hukuma **2.** kamfani mai rajista

corps [kɔː] *n* ƙungiyar soja

corpse [kɔːps] *n* gawa

correct [kəˈrekt] **1.** *adj* madaidaici **2.** *v* gyara wa

correction [kəˈrekʃn] *n* gyara

correctly [kəˈrektli] *adv* daidai

correspond [ˌkɔriˈspɔnd] *v* **1.** dace (to da) **2.** rubuta (with wa)

correspondence [ˌkɔriˈspɔndəns] *n* rubutu

correspondent [ˌkɔriˈspɔndənt] *n* **1.** ɗan jarida **2.** mai ba da rahoto

corresponding to [ˌkɔriˈspɔndiŋ] *adj* daidai da

corridor [ˈkɔridɔː] *n* hanya cikin gida

corrode [kəˈrəud] *v* lalata

corrugated iron [ˈkɔrəgeitidˈaiən] *n* kwanon rufi

corrupt [kəˈrʌpt] *adj* mazambaci

corruption [kəˈrʌpʃn] *n* rashawa

cosmetic [kɔzˈmetik] **1.** *adj* na kwaskwarima **2.** *n* kayan shafa

cost [kɔst] **1.** *n* kuɗi **2. the cost of living** tsadar rayuwa **3.** *v* **What does this cost?** Nawa ne kuɗinsa?

costly [ˈkɔstli] *adj* mai tsada

costume [ˈkɔstjuːm] *n* kaya

cottage [ˈkɔtidʒ] *n* gidan daji

cotton [ˈkɔtn] *n* **1.** auduga **2.** zare

cotton wool *n* auduga

couch [kautʃ] *n* babban kujera

cough [kɔf] **1.** *n* tari **2.** *v* yi tari

could [kəd; kud] *duba wajen* **can**

council [ˈkaunsl] *n* **1.** majalisa **2.** hukuma **3. local council** gunduma

councillor [ˈkaunsələ] *n* kansila, (Nr) kwansanye

Council of Europe *n* Ƙungiyar Kasashen Turai

counsel [ˈkaunsəl] *n* shawara

counsellor [ˈkaunsələ] *n* mashawarci

count [kaunt] *v* ƙidaya

count on *v* dogara da

counter ['kauntə] 1. *n* kanta 2. *v* mayar da martani

counteract [ˌkauntəˈrækt] *v* mai da hari

counterfeit ['kauntəfit] *adj* na jabu

counterfoil ['kauntəfɔil] *n* kwantafoyil

counterpart ['kauntəpa:t] *n* takwara

countless ['kauntlis] *adj* bila adadin

country ['kʌntri] *n* 1. ƙasa 2. ƙauye

countryside ['kʌntrisaid] *n* karkara

county ['kaunti] *n* ƙaramar hukuma

coup, coup d'etat [ku:, ku:deiˈta:] *n* juyin mulki

couple ['kʌpl] *n* 1. guda biyu 2. mata da miji

courage ['kʌridʒ] *n* jaruntaka

courageous [kəˈreidʒəs] *adj* jarumi

courier ['kuriyə] *n* mācinzà

course [kɔ:s] *n* 1. hanya 2. kos, (Nr) kur 3. **in due course** nan ba da daɗewa ba 4. **of course!** i mana! 5. **in the course of** a cikin 6. *duba* wajen **racecourse**

court [kɔ:t] *n* 1. fada 2. fili 3. (leg.) kotu, (Nr) jastis 4. **high court** babbar kotu 5. **supreme court** kotun ƙoli

courtesy ['kə:təsi] *n* ladabi

courtesy call *n* ziyarar ban girma

court-martial [ˌkɔ:tˈma:ʃl] *n* kotun soji

courtyard ['kɔ:tja:d] *n* tsakar gida

cousin ['kʌsin] *n* ɗan uwa, 'yar uwa

covenant ['kʌvənənt] *n* aƙali

cover ['kʌvə] 1. *n* murfi 2. **insurance cover** 3. *v* rufe 4. **to cover a deficit** cike giɓin kasafin kuɗi

covering ['kʌvəriŋ] *n* rufi

covert ['kəuvə:t] *adj* a asirce

cow [kau] *n* saniya

coward ['kauəd] *n* matsoraci

cowardice ['kauədis] *n* raki

cowboy ['kaubɔi] *n* kaboyi, (Nr) kuboyi

co-wife ['kəuˈwaif] *n* kishiya

co-worker ['kəuwə:kə] *n* abokin aiki

cowry ['kauri] *n* wurî

crab [kræb] *n* ƙaguwa

crack [kræk] *v* fasa

crackdown ['krækdaun] *n* fatattaka

crack troops *pl* sōjōjin à yi tà tà ƙàrè

cradle ['kreidl] *n* gadon jinjiri

craft [kra:ft] *n* (*pl* **craft**) 1. jirgi 2. sana'a

craftsman ['kra:ftsmən] *n* ɗan sana'a

craftsmanship ['kra:ftsmənʃip] *n* fasaha

crafty ['kra:fti] *adj* mai wayo

crane [krein] *n* 1. gauraka 2. injin ɗaga kaya

crank [kræŋk] *v* wana

crap [kræp] *n* (sl.) kāshī

crash [kræʃ] 1. *n* haɗari 2. faɗuwa 3. *v* faɗi 4. yi karo (into da)

crash-helmet ['kræʃˌhelmit] *n* hular kwano

crate [kreit] *n* akwati

cross

crawl [krɔːl] v rarrafa

crayon [ˈkreiən] n fensir mai launi

crazy [ˈkreizi] adj mahaukaci

cream [kriːm] n 1. kirim 2. man shafawa

crease [kriːs] v yamutsa

create [kriːˈeit] v 1. yi 2. ƙirƙira 3. halitta

creation [kriːˈeiʃn] n 1. ƙira 2. halitta

creative [kriːˈeitiv] adj mai fasaha

creator [kriːˈeitə] n mahalicci

creature [ˈkriːtʃə] n 1. halitta 2. dabba

credentials [kriˈdenʃlz] pl takardun aiki

credibility [ˌkredəˈbiləti] n mutunci

credible [ˈkredəbl] adj mai hujja

credit [ˈkredit] 1. n bashi 2. extension of credit lamuni 3. to buy on credit ci bashi 4. to claim credit nuna bajinta (for wajen) 5. to extend credit lamunta 6. to raise a credit limit ƙara kuɗin rance na asusun bayar da rance 7. to deserve credit isa yabo (for ga)

credit card n katin bashi

creditor [ˈkreditə] n mai bin bashi

creditor nation n ƙasa mai bin bashi

crematorium, (US) crematory [ˌkreməˈtɔːriəm; kremətəri] n maƙunar mamata

crescent [ˈkresnt] n hilali

crest [krest] n kan tudu

crew [kruː] n ƙungiyar ma'aikatan jirgi

cricket [ˈkrikit] n 1. tsanya 2. (spor.) wasan kurket

crime [kraim] n 1. laifi 2. to commit a crime yi laifi

criminal [ˈkriminl] n 1. mai laifi 2. criminal activities ayyukan keta dokoki

criminality [ˌkrimiˈnæləti] n yawan laifuffuka

crimson [ˈkrimzn] adj/n ja wur

cripple [ˈkripl] 1. n gurgu 2. v gurgunta

crippled [ˈkripld] adj naƙasasshe

crisis [ˈkraisis] n (pl **crises**) taɓarɓara

crisis point n magaryar taƙewa

crisps [krisps] pl ƙwalama

critic [ˈkritik] n mai sukar lamiri

critical [ˈkritikl] adj 1. mai suka 2. ba wasa 3. mai muhimmanci

critically [ˈkritikli] adv He is critically injured. Ya yi rauni, kuma yana nan rai hannun Allah.

criticise [ˈkritisaiz] v 1. ci gyara 2. sôkã

criticism [ˈkritisizəm] n 1. cin gyara 2. suka 3. to attract criticism kama kururuwa

critique [kriˈtiːk] n sharhi

croak [krəuk] v yi ƙugi

crockery [ˈkrɔkəri] n faɗi-ka-mutu

crocodile [ˈkrɔkədail] n kadã

crony [ˈkrəuni] n muƙarrabi

crook [kruk] n mai laifi

crooked [ˈkrukid] adj 1. ba daidai ba 2. abin da karkace 3. mai laifi

crops [krɔps] pl amfanin gona

cross [krɔs] 1. adj mai fushi 2. n kuros 3. ƙetare

cross out v kashe
cross examination n ta'annati
cross-examine v yi wa... ta'annati
crossing [ˈkrɔsiŋ] n maƙetara
crosslegged adj a harɗe
cross-question v zulaya
cross-section n sashi
crossword puzzle [ˈkrɔswəːd] n bini-binin kalmomi, kacici-kacici
crouch [krautʃ] v laɓe
crow [kreu] 1. n hankaka 2. v yi cara
crowd [kraud] n taron mutane
crowded [ˈkraudid] adj **to be crowded** cika cunkus
crowds [kraudz] pl ɗimbin mutane
crown [kraun] n kambi
crucial [ˈkruːʃl] adj mafi a'ala
crucify [ˈkruːsifai] v tsire
crude [kruːd] adj ɗanye
crude oil n ɗanyen mai
cruel [kruəl] adj mai zalunci
cruelty [ˈkruəti] n zalunci
cruise [kruːz] 1. n yawon duniya ta ruwa 2. v yi yawon duniya ta ruwa/sama
cruiser [kruːz] n jirgin ruwan yawo
crumb, crumbs [krʌm; -z] n ɓarɓashi
crumble [ˈkrʌmbl] v marmashe
crumple [ˈkrʌmpl] v yamutsa
crusade [kruːseid] n 1. yaƙi 2. (Isl.) jihadi
crush [krʌʃ] v murƙushe
crust [krʌst] n 1. **bread crust** ɓawon burodi 2. **crust of earth** tsalar duniya
crutch [krʌtʃ] n sanda

cry [krai] 1. n ƙara 2. v yi kuka
crying [ˈkrajiŋ] n kuka
crystal [ˈkristl] n lu'ulu'u
cube [kjuːb] n **sugar cube** shigen sukari
cucumber [ˈkjukʌmbə] n kokwamba
cue [kjuː] n matashiya
cuisine [kwiˈziːn] n abinci
cul-de-sac [ˌkʌldiˈsæk] n (UK) lungù
culprit [ˈkʌlprit] adj mai laifi
cult [kʌlt] n 1. daba 2. **followers of a cult** 'yan daba
cultivate [ˈkʌltiveit] v yi noma
cultivation [ˌkʌltiˈveiʃn] n noma
cultivator [ˈkʌltiveitə] n kaltibeta, (Nr) injin noma
cultural [ˈkʌltʃərəl] adj na al'adun gargajiya
cultural contact n tuntuɓar juna a fannin al'adu
culture [ˈkʌltʃə] n al'adun gargajiya
cultured [ˈkʌltʃəd] adj mai ladabi
cunning [ˈkʌniŋ] adj mai wayo
cup [kʌp] n 1. kofi, (Nr) bwal 2. (spor.) kwaf, (Nr) kuf
cupboard [ˈkʌbəd] n kabad, (Nr) kwaba
curable [ˈkjuərəbl] adj **The disease is curable.** Cutar tana magantuwa.
cure [kjuə] 1. n magani 2. v warkar da 3. shânyā
curfew [ˈkəːfjuː] n dokar hana fitar dare, (Nr) kūbìř fê
curiosity [ˌkjuəriˈɔsəti] n son neman sani
curious [ˈkjuəriəs] adj 1. mai ban mamaki 2. mai son neman sani
curl [kəːl] adj nannaɗe

currency [ˈkʌrənsi] *n* 1. kuɗin
ƙasa 2. **foreign currency**
kuɗin ƙasashen waje
current [ˈkʌrənt] 1. *adj* na halin
yanzu 2. *n* ƙarfin lantarki, (Nr)
kuran 3. igiyar ruwa
current affairs *pl* harkokin yau
da kullum
curry [ˈkʌri] *n* kori
curse [kəːs] *v* 1. yi tir 2. zàgā
curtain [ˈkəˑtn] *n* labule, (Nr)
rido
curve [kəːv] 1. *n* kwana
2. *v* karkace
curved [kəːvd] *adj* mai lanƙwasa
cushion [ˈkuʃn] *n* kushin, (Nr)
kusan
custody [ˈkʌstədi] *n* **in custody**
a bayan kanta
custom [ˈkʌstəm] *n* al'ada
customary [ˈkʌstəməri] *adj* na
al'ada
customer [ˈkʌstəmə] *n* ɗan ciniki

customs [ˈkʌstəmz] *pl* kwastan,
(Nr) duwan
customs duties *pl* kuɗin
kwastan
customs officer/official *n* ɗan
kwastan (Nr), duwanye
cut [kʌt] 1. *n* yanka 2. (ec.) ragi
3. **short cut** yanke 4. *v* (**cut**)
yanka
cut down *v* sassare
cute [kjuˑt] *adj* 1. daɓarɓashi
2. (sl.) mai wayo
cut off *v* yanke
cutlery [ˈkʌtləri] *n* wuƙaƙe da
cokula da cokula masu yatsu
duk
cuts [kʌts] *pl* (ec.) matakan tsimi
cycle [ˈsaikl] 1. *n* keke 2. *v* hau
keke
cylinder [ˈsilində] *n* silinda, (Nr)
silandir
cynical [ˈsinikl] *adj* mai zura ido
cyst [sist] *n* ƙari

Dd

dad, daddy [dæd; ˈdædi] *n* bàba
daft [dæft] *adj* daƙiƙi
dagger [ˈdægə] *n* wuƙa
daily [ˈdeili] **1.** *n* jarida **2.** *adj* na
kullum **3.** *adv* kullum
dairy [ˈdeəri] *n* gidan sarrafin
madara
dale [deil] *n* kari
dalek [ˈdaːlik] *n* mutum-
mutumin inji
dam [dæm] *n* madatsar ruwa
dam up *v* datse
damage [ˈdæmidʒ] **1.** *n* ɓarna
2. (leg.) lahani **3.** *duba wajen*
damages 4. *v* yi wa... ɓarna
damaged [ˈdæmidʒd] *adj* **to be
damaged** ɓaci
damages [ˈdæmidʒiz] *pl* (leg.)
diyya
damn [dæm] *v* **1.** tsine wa
2. damn! tir!
damp [dæmp] **1.** *adj* mai laima
2. *n* danshi
dampness [ˈdæmpnis] *n* danshi
dance [daːns] **1.** *n* rawa **2.** *v* yi rawa
dancer [ˈdaːnsə] *n* mai rawa
dancing [ˈdaːnsiŋ] *n* rawa
danger [ˈdeindʒə] *n* haɗari
danger sign *n* danja
dangerous [ˈdeindʒərəs] *adj* mai
kawo haɗari
dangle [ˈdæŋgl] *v* yi reto
dare [deə] *v* ƙalubalanta
daring [ˈdeəriŋ] *adj* na ƙunan
baƙin wake
dark [daːk] **1.** *adj* mai duhu
2. *n* duhu

darken [ˈdaːkən] *v* dakushe
darkness [ˈdaːknis] *n* duhu
darling [ˈdaːliŋ] *adj/n* masoyi,
masoyiya
dash [dæʃ] **1.** *n* dashi, (Nr) kàdô
2. *v* zabura **3. to dash hopes**
gwale
data [ˈdeitə] *n* bayanai
date [deit] *n* **1.** kwanan rana
2. hira, (Nr) randebu **3.** dabino
4. out of date na dâ **5. up to
date** na yanzu **6. to date** har
yanzu **7. to fix a date** sa rana
date of birth *n* ranar haihuwa
daughter [ˈdɔːtə] *n* 'ya mace
daughter-in-law [ˈdɔːtərinlɔː] *n*
sarakuwa
dawdle [ˈdɔːdl] *v* shantake
dawn [dɔːn] **1.** *n* wayewar gari
2. *v* **The day dawned.** Gari ya
waye.
day [dei] *n* **1.** rana **2.** kwana
3. yini
day after tomorrow *n/adv* jibi
day before yesterday *n/adv*
shekaranjiya
daybreak [ˈdeibreik] *n* wayewar gari
daydream [ˈdeidriːm] *n* mafarki
day in, day out *adv* kulluyaumin
daylight [ˈdeilait] *n* wayewar
safiya
day of remembrance *n* ranar
juyayi
daytime [ˈdeitaim] *n* rana
dazed [deizd] *adj* **to be dazed**
yi ɗimuwa
dazzle [ˈdæzl] *v* kashe wa... ido

dead [ded] *adj* 1. matacce 2. the dead mace-mace

dead-end *n* ba mafita

deadline [ˈdedlaɪn] *n* wa'adi

deadlock [ˈdedlɔk] *n* abin da ya hana ruwa gudu

deadly [ˈdedlɪ] *adj* 1. mai kisa 2. a deadly disease cutar ajali

deaf [def] *adj* kurma

deaf and dumb, deaf-mute *n* bebe

deafen [ˈdefən] *v* kashe wa... kunne

deafness [ˈdefnɪs] *n* bebantaka

deal [diːl] 1. *n* ma'amala 2. ciniki 3. yarjejeniya 4. a great deal da yawa sosai 5. *v* raba 6. yi hulɗa (with da) 7. yi ciniki (with da) 8. to deal in drugs yi fataucin ƙwayoyi

dealer [ˈdiːlə] *n* 1. dillali 2. drugs dealer mai fataucin ƙwayoyi

dealership [ˈdiːləʃip] *n* dillanci

dealings [ˈdiːlɪŋz] *pl* 1. ma'amala 2. ciniki

dear [dɪə] *adj* 1. na ƙwarai 2. mai tsada

death [deθ] *n* mutuwa

death sentence *n* hukuncin kisa

death-rate *n* yawan mutuwa

debate [dɪˈbeit] 1. *n* mahawara 2. *v* yi mahawara (on a kan)

debit [ˈdebit] 1. *n* bashi 2. *v* zare kuɗi

debris [ˈdeɪbriː] *n* tarkace

debt [det] *n* 1. bashi 2. to be in debt ci bashi 3. national debt bashin ƙasa

debtor [ˈdetə] *n* mai cin bashi

debtor nation *n* ƙasar da ake bi

bashi

decade [ˈdekeid] *n* shekaru goma

decadence [ˈdekədəns] *n* lalacewa

decapitate [diˈkæpiteit] *v* fille kai

decay [dɪˈkei] *v* ruɓe

deceased [dɪˈsiːsd] *adj* marigayi

deceit [dɪˈsiːt] *n* cuta

deceitful [dɪˈsiːtfl] *adj* mai cuta

deceive [dɪˈsiːv] *v* 1. cuta 2. (leg.) yaudara

deceiver [dɪˈsiːvə] *n* mayaudari

December [dɪˈsembə] *n* Disamba

decency [ˈdiːsnsi] *n* 1. nagarta 2. mutunci

decent [ˈdiːsnt] *adj* nagari, tagari

decentralization [diˌsentrəlaɪˈzeiʃn] *n* bayar da gashin kai

deception [dɪˈsepʃn] *n* cuta

decide [dɪˈsaid] *v* yanke shawara

decipher [dɪˈsaifə] *v* kwance

decision [dɪˈsiʒn] *n* 1. shawara 2. to take a decision tsai da shawara (about a kan)

decisively [dɪˈsaisivli] *adv* tare da cikakkiyar azama

declaration [ˌdekləˈreiʃn] *n* bayyanawa

declare [dɪˈkleə] *n* 1. faɗi 2. to declare war kaddamar da yaƙi (on a kan) 3. to declare independence bayyana 'yancin kai

decline [dɪˈklain] 1. *n* raunana 2. *v* ƙi 3. raunana

decode [ˌdiːˈkəud] *v* warware

decompose [ˌdiːkəmˈpəuz] *v* ruɓe

decomposition [ˌdikɔmpəˈziʃn] *n* ruɓewa

decorate [ˈdekəreit] *v* 1. yi wa... ado 2. ba da lambar girma

decoration [ˌdekəˈreiʃn] *n* 1. kayan ado 2. lambar girma

decorator [ˈdekəˌreitə] *n* mai shafe, mai filasta

decrease [diˈkriːs] 1. *n* ragi 2. rage

decree [diˈkriː] *n* (pol.) doka

decry [diˈkrai] *v* ƙi

dedicate [ˈdedikeit] *v* sadaukar da (to ga)

dedication [ˌdediˈkeiʃn] *n* sadaukarwa

deduce [diˈdʒuːs] *v* warware

deduct [diˈdʌkt] *v* ɗiba

deduction [diˈdʌkʃn] *n* ɗebe-ɗebe

deed [diːd] *n* aiki

deem [diːm] *v* ɗauka (that cewa)

deep [diːp] *adj* 1. mai zurfi 2. **a deep voice** babbar murya

deepen [ˈdiːpən] *v* zurfafa

deepness [ˈdiːpnis] *n* zurfi

deer [diə] *n* barewa

deface [diˈfeis] *v* ɓata

defame [diˈfeim] *v* ɓata suna

defeat [diˈfiːt] 1. *n* kayarwa 2. *v* kayar da 3. (spor.) ci 4. (pol.) to **defeat a proposal** shure shiri

defecate [ˈdefəkeit] *v* yi kashi

defect [ˈdiːfekt] *n* illa

defect [diˈfekt] *v* canza sheƙa

defection [diˈfekʃn] *n* canza sheƙa

defective [diˈfektiv] *adj* mai dameji

defence [diˈfens] *n* 1. tsaro 2. **self-defence** tsaron kai 3. **national defence** tsaron ƙasa

defenceless [diˈfenslis] *adj* gajiyayye

defend [diˈfend] *v* tsare

defend the interests of *v* kare mutuncin...

defendant [diˈfendənt] *n* (leg.) wanda ake ƙara

defender [diˈfendə] *n* mai tsaro

defensive [diˈfensiv] *adj* na noƙe-noƙe

defer [diˈfəː] *v* ɗage

deference [ˈdefərəns] *n* alkunya

deferment [diˈfeːmənt] *n* fāshì

defiance [diˈfaiəns] *n* kangara

defiant [diˈfaiənt] *adj* **to be defiant** kangara

deficiency [diˈfiʃnsi] *n* 1. cikàs 2. ƙaranci

deficit [ˈdefisit] *n* 1. kasawar kuɗi 2. **trade deficit** giɓin ciniki 3. **budget deficit** giɓin kasafin kuɗi

defile [diˈfail] *v* ƙazantar da

define [diˈfain] *v* 1. bayyana ma'ana 2. ƙayyade

definite [ˈdefinət] *adj* tabbatacce

definitely [ˈdefinətli] *adv* ba shakka

deflate [diˈfleit] *v* sacè

deflect [diˈflekt] *v* kare

deforestation [diːˌtɔrisˈteiʃn] *n* sare dazuzzuka

deform [diˈfɔːm] *v* naƙasa

deformed [diˈfɔːmd] *adj* naƙasasshe

deformity [diˈfɔːməti] *n* naƙasa

defraud [diˈfrɔːd] *v* zamabata

deft [deft] *adj* mai fasaha

defy [diˈfai] *v* 1. ƙi bi 2. kangare wa 3. **to defy solution** gagara

degenerate [diˈdʒenəreit] *v* lalace

degeneration [diˌdʒenəˈreiʃn] *n* lalacewa

degradation [ˌdegrəˈdeiʃn] *n* ƙanƙantarwa

degrade [diˈgreid] *v* ƙanƙantar da

degree [diˈgriː] *n* 1. zafi 2. yawa 3. (acad.) digiri, (Nr) difilam 4. **to a degree** da

dama-dama 5. *duba wajen*
B.A., M.A.
delay [diˈlei] 1. *n* jinkiri
2. *v* jinkirtar da
delayed [diˈleid] *adj* to be
delayed yi jinkiri
delegate [ˈdeligət] 1. *n* wakili
2. *v* wakiltar da
delegation [ˌdeliˈgeiʃn] *n* wakilai
delete [diˈliːt] *v* shafe
deliberate [diˈlibərət] *adj* da
niyya
deliberately [diˈlibərətli] *adv* da
gangan
delicate [ˈdelikət] *adj* 1. na aras
2. mai nauyi
delicious [diˈliʃəs] *adj* mai daɗi
delight [diˈlait] *adj* murna
delightful [diˈlaitfl] *adj* mai ban
murna
delinquent [diˈliŋkwənt] *adj*
fanɗararre
deliver [diˈlivə] *v* 1. kai 2. isar da
3. (med.) saukar da 4. to
deliver a speech yi jawabi
deliverance [diˈlivərəns] *n* ceto
delivery [diˈlivəri] *n* 1. bayarwa
2. (med.) haihuwa
delude [diˈluːd] *v* cuta
deluge [ˈdeljuːʒ] *n* ambaliya
delusion [diˈluːʒn] *n* wahami
demand [diˈmaːnd] 1. *n* bukata 2.
supply and demand bayarwa da
bukata 3. to fuel demand haɓaka
bukata 4. *v* nema 5. bukata
demarcation line [ˌdiˈmaːˈkeisnlain]
n layin da ya raba
demean [diˈmiːn] *v* wulaƙanta
demilitarization [ˈdiːmilitəreiˈzeiʃn]
n kwance ɗamara
demilitarize [diːˈmilitəraiz] *v*
kwance ɗamara

demobilization [ˈdiːmobileiˈzeiʃn]
n ajiye makamai
demobilize [diːˈməubəlaiz] *v* ajiye
makamai
democracy [diˈmɔkrəsi] *n*
dimokuraɗiyya
democrat [ˈdeməkræt] *adj/n* 1.
ɗan siyasa adili 2. (US) ɗan
jam'iyyar Democrat
democratic [ˌdeməˈkrætik] *adj*
mai adalci
democratization
[ˈdiːmɔcrateiˈzeiʃn] *n* shirin kawo
mulkin dimokuraɗiyya
democratize [diˈmɔkrətaiz] *v*
kafa dimokuraɗiyya
demolish [diˈmɔliʃ] *v* rushe
demolition [ˌdeməˈliʃn] *n* rushe-
rushe
demon [ˈdiːmən] *n* shaiɗan
demonstrate [ˈdemənstreit] *v* 1.
nuna 2. (pol.) yi zanga-zanga
demonstration [ˌdemənˈstreiʃn]
n 1. nuni 2. (pol.) zanga-zanga
demonstrator [ˈdemənstreitə] *n*
(pol.) mai zanga-zanga
demoralized [diˈmɔrəlaizd] *adj*
They were demoralized.
Gwiwarsu ta yi sanyi.
demote [diˈməut] *v* rage wa...
muƙami
den [den] *n* kogo
denial [diˈnaiəl] *n* inkari
denomination [diˌnɔmiˈneiʃn] *n*
iri
denote [diˈnəut] *v* nuna a fakaice
denounce [diˈnauns] *v* yi Allah
wadai da
dense [dens] *adj* mai yawa
density [ˈdensəti] *n* yawa
dent [dent] *v* komaɗa
dental [ˈdentl] *adj* na haƙori

dentifrice [ˈdentifris] *n* man goge haƙora

dentist [ˈdentist] *n* likitan haƙora

dentures [ˈdentʃə] *pl* haƙoran roba

denude [diˈnjuːd] *v* tsiraita

deny [diˈnai] *v* yi musu

depart [diˈpaːt] *v* tashi

department [diˈpaːtmənt] *n* 1. ma'aikata 2. (acad.) sashe 3. (pol.) ma'aikatar gwamnati

department store *n* babban shago

departure [diˈpaːtʃə] *n* tashi

depend [diˈpend] *v* dogara (**on** da)

dependence [diˈpendəns] *n* 1. dogaro 2. **economic dependence** ta'allakar tattalin arziki

dependent [diˈpendənt] *adj* mai dogara

depict [diˈpikt] *v* nuna

deplore [diˈplɔː] *v* nuna takaici

deploy [diˈplɔi] *v* ɗirka

depopulate [diːˈpɔpjuleit] *v* rage yawan jama'a

deport [diˈpɔːt] *v* kōrè daga ƙasa

deportation [ˌdiːpɔːˈteiʃn] *n* korewa daga ƙasa

depose [diˈpəuz] *v* tumɓuke

deposit [diˈpɔzit] 1. *n* adibas, (Nr) abans 2. zuba

depot [ˈdepəu] *n* daffo, (Nr) difo

depreciate [diˈpriːʃieit] *v* rage kadari

depreciation [diˌpriːʃiˈeiʃn] *n* rage kadari

depress [diˈpres] *v* 1. danne 2. ɓata rai

depressed [diˈprest] *adj* He is depressed. Ransa a ɓace yake.

depression [diˈpreʃn] *n* 1. (med.)

baƙin ciki 2. (ec.) tawayar tattalin arziki

deprive [diˈpraiv] *v* hana

depth [depθ] *n* zurfi

deputy [ˈdepjuti] *n* wakili

derail [diˈreil] *v* goce

derision [diˈriʒn] *n* ba'a

derive [diˈraiv] *v* samu

descend [diˈsend] *v* 1. gangara 2. sauka

descendants [diˈsendənts] *pl* zuriya

descent [diˈsent] *n* 1. gangare 2. sauka 3. jini

describe [diˈskraib] *v* siffanta

description [diˈskripʃn] *n* sifa

desert [ˈdezət] *n* hamada

desert [diˈzəːt] *v* 1. bijire wa 2. (mil.) gudu daga soja

desertification [diˌzəːtifiˈkeiʃn] *n* kwararowar hamada

desertion [diˈzəːʃn] *n* (mil.) gudu daga soja

deserve [diˈzəːv] *v* 1. cancanta 2. They deserved it. Abu ne da ke tafe gare su.

design [diˈzain] 1. *n* zane 2. *v* shirya 3. zana

designate [ˈdezigneit] *v* zàɓà

designer [diˈzainə] *n* mai zane

desirable [diˈzaiərəbl] *adj* abin ƙauna

desire [diˈzaiə] *v* 1. bege 2. yi bege

desist [diˈzist] *v* daina

desk [desk] *n* tebur, (Nr) buro

desktop [ˈdesktɔp] 1. *adj* na aiki kan tebur 2. *n* kan tebur

desolation [ˌdesəˈleiʃn] *n* karaya

despair [diˈspeə] 1. *n* karaya 2. *v* fid da rai

despatch [disˈpætʃ] *duba wajen* dispatch

desperate ['despərət] *adj* He is desperate. Yana cikin wani hali.

desperately ['despərətli] *adv* ruwa a jallo

despise [di'spaiz] *v* raina

despite [di'spait] *prep* duk da

despondency [di'spɔndənsi] *n* baƙin ciki

despotic [des'pɔtik] *adj* **despotic rule** mulkin kama karya

dessert [di'zə:t] *n* kayan zaƙi

destabilisation [di:,steibilai'zeiʃn] *n* manufar ta da zaune tsaye

destabilise [di:'steibilaiz] *v* ta da zaune tsaye

destination ['desti'neiʃn] *n* inda ake nufi

destine ['destin] *v* ƙaddara wa

destiny ['destini] *n* ƙaddara

destitute ['destitju:t] *adj* miskini

destroy [di'strɔi] *v* halàkã

destroyer [dis'trɔiə] *n* mai halaka

destruction [di'strʌkʃn] *n* hàlakà

destructive [di'strʌktiv] *adj* mai halaka

detach [di'tætʃ] *v* kwance

detail ['di:teil] *n* 1. sashe 2. in detail filla-filla

detailed ['di:teild] *adj* cikakke

details ['di:teilz] *pl* 1. bayani 2. further details ƙarin bayani

detain [di'tein] *v* tsare

detain indefinitely *v* tsarà haɗ sai illã mã shã Àllãhù

detect [di'tekt] *v* samu

detective [di'tektiv] *n* ɗan sandan ciki

detector [di'tektə] *n* 1. ƙanshin gari 2. injimin gano illa

detente [,dei'ta:nt] *n* sakin jiki

detention [di'tenʃn] *n* 1. tsari 2. **detention on remand** waƙafi

deter [di'tə:] *v* hana

detergent [di'tə:dʒənt] *n* õmõ

deteriorate [di'tiəriəreit] *v* taɓarɓare

deterioration [di,tiəriə'reiʃn] *n* taɓarɓarewa

determination [di,tə:mi'neiʃn] *n* aniya

determine [di'tə:min] *v* ƙayyade

determined [di'tə:mind] *adj* 1. a tsaitsaye 2. **to be determined to** lashi takobin

deterrent [di'terənt] *n* haƙon juna

detest [di'test] *v* tsànã

detonate ['detəneit] *v* fasa

detonator ['detəneitə] *n* abin da tayad da bom

detour ['di:tuə] *v* rãtsē

detrimental [,detri'mentl] *adj* **to be detrimental** shafa kashin kaza (to wa)

deutschmark ['dɔitʃma:k] *n* makin Jamus

devalue ['di:'vælju:] *v* karyar da darajar kuɗi

devastate ['devəsteit] *v* yi kaca-kaca da

devastation [,devəs'teiʃn] *n* 1. bala'i 2. muguwar ɓarna

develop [di'veləp] *v* 1. ci gaba 2. wanke hoto 3. (ec.) raya

developed [di'veləpt] *adj* 1. **developed nations** ƙasashe masu ci gaban masana'antu 2. **to be incompletely developed** tsumbure

developer [di'veləpə] *n* maginin gidaje

developing [di'veləpiŋ] *adj* 1. mai

tasowa **2. developing nations**
ƙasashe masu tasowa
development [di'veləpmənt] *n*
1. ci-gaba **2.** (ec.) raya ƙasa
development project *n*
ayyukan raya ƙasa
development worker *n*
ma'aikacin raya ƙasa
deviate ['di:vieit] *v* saɓa (**from**
da)
deviation [di:vi'eiʃn] *n* saɓawa
device [di'vais] *n* na'ura
devil ['devl] *n* shaiɗan
devious ['di:viəs] *adj* na cuku-
cuku
devise [di'vaiz] *v* ƙaga
devote [di'vəut] *v* dage
devotion [di'vəuʃn] *n* so
devour [di'vauə] *v* lamushe
devout [di'vaut] *adj* mumini
dew [dju:] *n* raɓa
dexterity [deks'terəti] *n* fasaha
diabetes [,daiə'bi:ti:z] *n* ciwon
sukari
diabetic [,daiə'betic] *n* mai ciwon
sukari
diagnose ['daiəgnəuz] *v* gano
diagnosis [,daiəg'nəusis] *n* (*pl*
diagnoses) (med.) bincikar
lafiya
diagram ['daiəgræm] *n* zane
dial [daiəl] **1.** *n* (tel.) fuska
2. buga lamba
dialect ['daiəlekt] *n* yare
dialogue ['daiələɔg] *n* zance
diamond ['daiəmənd] *n* daimun,
(Nr) deman
diaper ['daiəpə] *n* banten jinjiri
diaphragm ['daiəfræm] *n* tantani
diarrhoea [,daiə'ri:ə] *n* zawo
diary ['daiəri] *n* littafin tsarin
lokaci

dice [dais] *n* (*pl* **dice**) ɗan lido
dictate [dik'teit] *v* ba da shifta
dictation [dik'teiʃn] *n* shifta
dictator [dik'teitə] *n* mai mulkin
kama karya
dictatorial [,diktə'tɔ:riəl] *adj* na
mulkin kama karya
dictatorship [dik'teitəʃip] *n*
mulkin kama karya
dictionary ['dikʃənri] *n* ƙamus
did [did] *duba wajen* **do**
didactic [di'dæktik] *adj* na wa'azi
die [dai] *v* mutu
die down *v* kwanta
die-hard ['daiha:d] *adj* ɗan ta
kife
die out *v* shuɗe
diesel ['di:zl] *n* dizal
diet ['daiət] **1.** *v* abin da ake ci **2.**
to go on a diet rage shan miya
differ ['difə] *v* **1.** bambanta
2. yi dabam (**from** da)
difference ['difrəns] *n* **1.**
bambanci **2.** saɓani
different ['difrənt] *adj* dabam-
dabam
differentiate [,difə'rəntʃieit] *v*
bambanta
difficult ['difikəlt] *adj* mai wuya
difficulty ['difikəlti] *n* **1.** wuya
2. wahala **3. financial**
difficulties matsi **4. with**
difficulty da kyar
diffuse [di'fju:s] *v* yaɗa
dig [dig] *v* (**dug**) haƙa
dig up *v* tônā
digest [di'dʒest; dai'dʒest] *v*
haɗiye
digestible [di'dʒestəbl; dai'dʒestəbl]
adj **to be digestible** haɗiyu
digestion [dai'dʒestʃən; dai'dʒestʃən]
n lafiyar ciki

digit [ˈdidʒit] *n* 1. lamba 2. yatsa

dignified [ˈdignifaid] *adj* mai daraja

dignity [ˈdignəti] *n* mutunci

digress [daiˈgres] *v* shiga daji

dike [daik] *n* madatsa

dilate [daiˈleit] *v* yi ƙwala-ƙwàlà

dilemma [diˈlemə; daiˈlemə] *n* to be in a dilemma shiga uku

diligence [ˈdilidʒəns] *n* ƙwazo

diligent [ˈdilidʒənt] *adj* mai ƙwazo

dilute [daiˈljuːt] *v* surka

dim [dim] 1. *adj* mai dushewa 2. *v* yi dim

dimension [diˈmenʃn] *n* girma

diminish [diˈminiʃ] *v* ragu

diminutive [diˈminjutiv] *adj* ɗan ƙarami

dimly [ˈdimli] *adv* dishi-dishi

din [din] *n* ruruma

dine [dain] *v* ci

dining-room [ˈdainiŋrum] *n* ɗakin cin abinci

dinner [ˈdinə] *n* abincin dare

dinner-party *n* dina

dip [dip] *v* tsoma

diphtheria [dipˈθiəriə] *n* maƙarau

dimploma [diˈpləumə] *n* satifikat, (Nr) difilam

diplomacy [diˈpləuməsi] *n* diplomasiyya

diplomat [ˈdipləmæt] *n* ma'aikacin huldar jakadanci

diplomatic [ˌdipləˈmætik] *adj* na jakadanci

diplomatic corps *n* jami'an diplomasiyya

diplomatic relations *pl* huldar jakadanci

diplomatic row *n* kiki-kakar diplomasiyya

direct [diˈrekt; daiˈrekt] 1. *adj* kai tsaye 2. *v* ba da umurni 3. yi wa... kwatance

direct aid *n* agajin kai tsaye

direction [diˈrekʃn; daiˈrekʃn] *n* 1. shiyya 2. manufa

directions [diˈrekʃnz; daiˈrekʃnz] *pl* kwatance

directly [diˈrektli; daiˈrektli] *adv* kai tsaye

director [diˈrektə; daiˈrektə] *n* 1. darekta, (Nr) dirkitar 2. managing director manajan darakta 3. board of directors 'yan kwamitin gudanarwa

directory [diˈrektəri; daiˈrektəri] *n* kundin adireshi

dirt [dəːt] *n* dauɗa

dirty [ˈdəːti] 1. *n* mai dauɗa 2. *v* ƙazantar da

disability [ˌdisəˈbiləti] *n* rashin lafiya, nakkasar jiki

disable [disˈeibl] *v* gurgunta

disabled [disˈeibld] *adj* naƙasasshe

disadvantage [ˌdisədˈvaːntidʒ] *n* ƙwara

disagree [ˌdisəˈgriː] *v* saɓa (with da)

disagreeable [ˌdisəˈgriːəbl] *adj* mai tsamin rai

disagreement [ˌdisəˈgriːmənt] *n* 1. saɓani 2. to cause disagreement kawo rashin jituwa

disappear [ˌdisəˈpiə] *v* ɓace

disappearance [ˌdisəˈpiərəns] *n* ɓacewa

disappoint [ˌdisəˈpɔint] *v* ɓata wa... rai

disappointed [ˌdisəˈpɔintid] **Mari was disappointed.** Mari ba ta cim ma burinta ba.

disappointment [,disəˈpɔintmənt] *n* faɗuwar gaba

disapproval [,disəˈpruːvl] *n* 1. rashin yarda 2. to show disapproval tsana

disapprove [,disəˈpruːv] *v* ƙi jini

disarm [disˈaːm] *v* kwance ɗamara

disarmament [disˈaːməmənt] *n* kwance ɗamarar yaƙi

disarmament talks *pl* shawarwarin kwance ɗamara

disarranged [,disəˈreindʒd] *adj* a wargaje

disaster [diˈzaːstə] *n* 1. haɗari 2. masifa 3. ecological disaster bala'in gurɓacewar yanayi

disastrous [diˈzaːstrəs] *adj* mai masifa

disbelief [,disbiˈliːf] *n* rashin imani

disc [disk] *n* faifai, (Nr) dis

discard [diˈskaːd] *v* ya da

discharge [ˈdistʃaːdʒ] *n* 1. kòrā 2. mūgunyà

discharge [disˈtʃaːdʒ] *v* 1. sàllamà 2. harba

disciplinary measures [ˈdisiplinəri] *pl* matakan horo

discipline [ˈdisiplin] 1. *n* horo 2. tarbiyya 3. (acad.) fanni 4. *v* hòrā

disclose [disˈkləuz] *v* fallasa

disclosure [disˈkləuʒə] *n* fallasawa

discoloured [disˈkʌləd] *adj* to be discoloured koɗe

discomfort [disˈkʌmfət] *n* rashin jin daɗi

disconnect [,diskəˈnekt] *v* yanke

discontent [,diskənˈtent] *n* rashin zaman lafiya

discontented [,diskənˈtentid] *adj* mai rashin zaman lafiya

discontinue [,diskənˈtinjuː] *v* katse

discord [ˈdiskɔːd] *n* jayayya

discount [ˈdiskaunt] *n* rangwamen kuɗi

discourage [diˈskʌridʒ] *v* sage wa... gwiwa

discourse [ˈdiskɔːs] *n* jawabi

discover [disˈkʌvə] *v* gano

discoverer [disˈkʌvərə] *n* mai ganowa

discovery [disˈkʌvəri] *n* ganowa

discredited [disˈkreditid] *adj* maras tasiri

discreet [disˈkriːt] *adj* mai hankali

discrepancy [diˈskrepənsi] *n* rashin daidaituwa

discretion [diˈskreʃn] *n* hankali

discriminate [diˈskrimineit] *v* nuna bambanci (against wa)

discrimination [di,skrimiˈneiʃn] *n* 1. nuna bambanci 2. racial discrimination wariyar launin fata 3. ethnic discrimination kabilanci 4. sexual discrimination wariyar jinsi

discuss [diˈskʌs] *v* tattauna

discussion [diˈskʌʃn] *n* 1. magana 2. formal discussion mahawara

discussions [diˈskʌʃnz] *pl* 1. shawarwari 2. private discussions ganawa

disdain [disˈdein] *n* raini

disease [diˈziːz] *n* cuta

diseased [diˈziːzd] *adj* mai cuta

disembark [,disimˈbaːk] *v* sàuka

disengage [,disin'geidʒ] v zame jiki

disentangle [,disin'tæŋgl] v warware

disfigure [dis'figə] v nakasa

disgrace [dis'greis] 1. n abin kunya 2. v kunyata

disgraceful [dis'greisfl] adj mai ban kunya

disguise [dis'gaiz] n farin kaya

disgust [dis'gʌst] n kyama

disgusted [dis'gʌstid] adj mai jin kyama

disgusting [dis'gʌstiŋ] adj mai kyama

dish [diʃ] n tasa

dishearten [dis'ha:tn] v ɓata wa... rai

dishonest [dis'ɔnist] adj mai magudi

dishonesty [dis'ɔnisti] n magudi

dishonour [dis'ɔnə] n ci mutunci

dishonourable [dis'ɔnərəbl] adj mai ban kunya

disillusion [,disi'lu:ʒn] n ɓata wa... rai

disinfect [,disin'fekt] v kashe kwayoyin cuta

disinfectant [,disin'fektənt] n maganin kashe kwayoyin cuta

disinfection [,disin'fekʃn] n kashe kwayoyin cuta

disintegrate [dis'intigreit] v ragaragaje

disk [disk] n faifai, (Nr) dis

dislike [dis'laik] v wàsä

dislocate ['disləkeit] v (med.) gurɗe

dislocation [,dislə'keiʃn] n (med.) gocewa

dislodge [dis'lɔdʒ] v sàkatà

dismal ['dizməl] adj to be dismal lalace

dismantle [dis'mæntl] v wargaza

dismay [dis'mei] n faɗuwar gaba

dismiss [dis'mis] v 1. fitar da 2. (leg.) kòrä

dismissal [dis'misl] n 1. sallama 2. (leg.) kora

dismount [dis'maunt] v sàuka

disobedience [,disə'bi:diəns] n rashin biyayya

disobedient [,disə'bi:diənt] adj mai rashin biyayya

disobey [,disə'bei] v ki bi

disorder [dis'ɔ:də] n 1. hargitsi 2. in disorder a barkatai

disordered [dis'ɔ:dəd] adj a barkatai

disorderly [dis'ɔ:dəli] adj to be disorderly wargaje

disorganized [dis'ɔ:gənaizd] adj a birkice

disown [dis'əun] v kora

disparage [dis'pæridʒ] v yi wa.. kankancì

dispatch, despatch [di'spætʃ] v aika da

dispel [dis'pel] v kore

dispensable [di'spensəbl] adj to be dispensable yi ba da shi ba

dispensary [di'spensəri] n ɗakin magani, (Nr) gidan likita

dispenser [di'spensər] n disfensa

disperse [di'spə:s] v watsa

dispersed [di'spə:st] adj to be dispersed watse

displace [dis'pleis] v kawar da

displaced person [dis'pleist] n mutumin da aka raba da mahallinsa

display [di'splei] 1. n nuni 2. talla 3. v nuna 4. barbaza

displease [dis'pli:z] v ɓata wa... rai

displeasure [dis·pleʒə] *n* ɓacin rai

disposal [dis·pəusl] *n* 1. kwandon shara 2. 'yāřwā

dispose [dis·pəuz] *v* ya (of da)

disposition [,dispə·ziʃn] *n* hali

dispossessed [,dispə·zest] *adj* maras galihu

dispute [di·spju:t; ·dispju:t] *n* 1. gardama 2. rikici 3. border dispute rikicin kan iyaka

dispute [di·spju:t] *v* 1. yi wa... gardama 2. yi wa... musu

disqualify [dis·kwɔlifai] *v* sòkā

disregard [,disri·ga:d] *v* 1. ƙyale 2. to disregard the rules keta dokoki

disrespect [,disri·spekt] *n* rashin kunya

disrupt [dis·rʌpt] *v* katse

disruption [dis·rʌptʃn] *n* katsewa

dissatisfaction [,di,sætis·fækʃn] *n* rashin gamsuwa

dissect [di·sekt] *v* yanke

disseminate [di·semineit] *v* yaɗa

dissension [di·senʃn] *n* hargitsi

dissent [di·sent] 1. *n* hargitsi 2. *v* ƙi

dissertation [,disə·teiʃn] *n* kundi

dissident [·disidənt] *n* ɗan tawaye

dissimilar [di·similə] *adj* dabam

dissipate [·disipeit] *v* watse

dissociate [di·səuʃieitid] *v* ware kai

dissolve [di·zɔlv] *v* 1. narkar da 2. (pol.) rushe

distance [·distəns] 1. *n* nisa 2. some distance away tazara 3. from a distance daga nesa 4. *v* to distance oneself nisanta

distant [·distənt] *adj* mai nisa

distaste [dis·teist] *n* to have a distaste for wàsā

distend [dis·tend] *v* kumbura

distil [di·stil] *v* tankaɗa

distilled water *n* ruwan batir

distillery [dis·tiləri] *n* gidan dafa giya

distinct [di·stiŋkt] *adj* mai cikakken bambanci

distinction [di·stiŋkʃn] *n* 1. bambanci 2. daraja

distinctly [di·stiŋktli] *adv* a haƙiƙa

distinctive [di·stiŋktiv] *adj* mai cikakken bambanci

distinguish [di·stiŋgwiʃ] *v* bambanta

distinguished [di·stiŋgwiʃt] *adj* mashahuri

distort [di·stɔ:t] *v* murɗe

distortion [di·stɔ:ʃn] *n* murɗiya

distract [di·strækt] *v* ɗauke hankali

distracted [di·stræktid] *adj* mai ɗaukar hankali

distraction [di·strækʃn] *n* ɗaukuwar hankali

distress [di·stres] *n* 1. faɗuwar gaba 2. ɓacin rai

distressful [di·stresfl] *adj* 1. mai faɗuwar gaba 2. mai ɓacin rai

distressing [di·stresiŋ] *adj* how distressing! assha!

distribute [di·strɪbju:t] *v* rarraba

distribution [,distrɪbju:ʃn] *n* rabawa

distributive trades [di·strɪbjutiv] *pl* harkokin rarraba kayayyakin ciniki

distributor [dis·trɪbjutə] *n* ejan

district [·distrikt] *n* 1. gunduma 2. sashi

district council *n* majalisar lardi

distrust [dis·trʌst] *n* rashin amana

disturb [di·stə:b] *v* 1. ta da 2. dầmā

disturbance [di·stə:bəns] *n* tashin hankali

disturbed [di·stə:bəns] *adj* 1. mentally disturbed taɓaɓɓe 2. to be disturbed ɗagule

disunion [dis·ju:niən] *n* rashin haɗin kai

disunited [ˌdisju·naitid] *adj* to be disunited karkasu

disuse [dis·ju:s] *n* rashin amfani

ditch [ditʃ] *n* kwalbati, (Nr) gwalalō

dive [daiv] *v* 1. faɗi 2. nutse

diver [·daivə] *n* mai àlkāhùřā

diverge [dai·vədʒ] *v* rabu (**from** da)

diverse [dai·və:s] *adj* dabam-dabam

diversion [dai·və:ʃn] *n* 1. kwana 2. tiyata

diversity [dai·və:səti] *n* rabe-rabe

divert [dai·və:t] *v* rabu da

divide [di·vaid] *v* raba

divide and rule *n* manufar raba kan al'umma sa'an nan a mallake su

dividend [·dividend] *n* (fin.) rara

divine [di·vain] *adj* na Allah

diving [·daiviŋ] *n* àlkāhùřā

division [di·viʒn] *n* 1. reshe 2. rabawa 3. (mil.) ɓangare 4. (spor.) lig-lig

divorce [di·vɔ:s] 1. *n* kisan aure 2. *v* kashe aure

dizzy [·dizi] *adj* to feel dizzy yi jùwā

do [du:] *v* (**did, done**) 1. yi 2. aikata

dock, docks [dɔk; dɔks] *n* matsayar jirgin ruwa

docker [·dɔkə] *n* leburan tashar jirgin ruwa

dockyard [·dɔkja:d] *n* tashar jirgin ruwa

doctor [·dɔktə] *n* 1. (med.) likita, (Nr) lokotoro 2. (acad.) dakta, (Nr) daktar

document [·dɔkjumənt] *n* takarda

documentary film [ˌdɔkju·mentrî] *n* shirin gaskiya

dodge [dɔdʒ] *v* kauce wa

dodger [·dɔdʒə] *n* **tax dodger** mazambacin haraji

dog [dɔg] *n* kare

dole [dəul] *n* **to be on the dole** yi zaman kashe-wando

doll [dɔl] *n* 'yar tsana

dollar [·dɔlə] *n* dalar Amirka

dolphin [·dɔlfin] *n* dabbar ruwa

dome [dəum] *n* kubba

domestic [də·mestik] 1. *adj* na gida 2. *n* boyi

domestic affairs *pl* sha'anin cikin gida

domicile [·dɔmisail] *n* gida

dominant [·dɔminənt] *adj* mai mulki

dominate [·dɔmineit] *v* mamaye

domination [ˌdɔmi·neiʃn] *n* mulki

domineer [ˌdɔmi·niə] *v* sha kai

domineering [ˌdɔmi·niəriŋ] *adj* mai shan kai

dominion [də·miniən] *n* mallaka

don [dɔn] *v* sa

donate [dəu·neit] *v* ba da

donation [dəu·neiʃn] *n* abin taimako

done [dʌn] *duba wajen* **do**

donkey [ˈdɔŋki] *n* (*pl* **donkeys**) jaki

donor [ˈdəunə] *n* **blood donor** mai ba da jini

doom [duːm] *n* ƙaddara

door [dɔː] *n* 1. ƙofa 2. ƙyaure 3. **indoors** a ciki 4. **out of doors** waje

doorbell [ˈdɔːbel] *n* ƙararrawar ƙofa

doorman [ˈdɔːmən] *n* ƙofa, sabis

doorway [ˈdɔːwei] *n* ƙofa

dope [dəup] 1. *n* ƙwaya 2. (sl.) wagili 3. *v* bugar da... da ƙwaya

dormant [ˈdɔːmənt] *adj* 1. mai lafiya 2. maras ƙarfi

dormitory [ˈdɔːmitri] *n* mazaunin ɗalibai

dose [dəus] *n* awon magani

dossier [ˈdɔsijə] *n* fayil, (Nr) dôsê

dot [dɔt] *n* ɗigo

double [ˈdʌbl] 1. *adj* dobul, (Nr) dûbùl 2. *v* riɓanya sau biyu

doubt [daut] 1. *n* shakka 2. **without doubt** ba shakka 3. *v* yi shakka

doubtful [ˈdautfl] *adj* mai shakka

doubtless [ˈdautlis] *adv* ba shakka

dough [dəu] *n* ƙullu

doughnut [ˈdəunʌt] *n* cin-cin

dove [dʌv] *n* kurciya

down [daun] *adv* a ƙasa

downhill [ˌdaunˈhil] *adj/adv* ta gangara

download [ˌdaunˈləud] *v* shigar da

down payment *n* adibas, (Nr) abans

downpour [ˈdaunpɔː] *n* ruwan sama

downstairs [ˌdaunˈsteəz] *adj/adv* a ƙasa

downward, downwards [ˈdaunwəd; -z] *adj/adv* 1. zuwa ƙasa 2. (ec.) **downward movement** koma-baya

dowry [ˈdauəri] *n* kayan aras

dozen [ˈdʌzn] *n* dozin

Dr [ˈdɔktə] *duba wajen* **doctor**

draft [draːft] 1. *n* shiri 2. (mil.) ɗaukar mutane a soja 3. *v* tsara 4. *duba wajen* **draught**

draft constitution *n* shirin tsarin mulki

drafting committee [ˈdraːftiŋ] *n* kwamitin tsara manufofi

drag [dræg] *v* ja

drag away *v* janye

dragon [ˈdrægən] *n* dodo

dragonfly [ˈdrægən,flai] *n* ɗan mazarin-iyà

drain [drein] 1. *n* magudana 2. *v* malale

drainage [ˈdreinidʒ] *n* malalewa

drainpipe *n* ìndaɍaɍõ

drama [ˈdraːmə] *n* wasan kwaikwayo

dramatic [drəˈmætik] *adj* 1. na wasan kwaikwayo 2. tsattsaura

dramatist [ˈdræmətist] *n* mawallafin wasan kwaikwayo

drank [dræŋk] *duba wajen* **drink**

drape [dreip] *n* zane, (Nr) rido

drastic [ˈdræstik] *adj* tsattsaura

draught [draːft] *n* 1. ɗan iska 2. *duba wajen* **draft**

draughtsman [ˈdraːftsmən] *n* mai zane

draw [drɔː] 1. *n* zana 2. (spor.) duro 3. *v* (**drew, drawn**) ja 4. (spor.) yi duro 5. **to draw attention** jawo hankali

draw up *v* tsara

drawback [ˈdrɔːbæk] *n* ƙayar kifi a wuya

drawer [drɔ:] *n* aljihun tebur

drawing [ˈdrɔːɪŋ] *n* 1. zane 2. zanawa

drawn [drɔ:n] *duba wajen* **draw**

dread [dred] *n* fargaba

dreadful [ˈdredfl] *adj* mummuna

dream [driːm] 1. *n* mafarki 2. *v* (**dreamed/dreamt**) yi mafarki

drench [drentʃ] *v* jiƙe

dress [dres] 1. *n* rigar mata, (Nr) rob 2. kaya 3. *v* sa tufafi

dressmaker [ˈdresmeikə] *n* madinki

dried [draid] *adj* 1. busasshe 2. *duba wajen* **dry**

dried milk *n* madarar gwangwani

drift [drift] *v* yi gantali

drill [dril] 1. *n* mahuji 2. (mil.) rawar soja 3. *v* haƙo

drink [ˈdriŋk] 1. *n* abin sha 2. *v* (**drank, drunk**) sha

drinkable [ˈdriŋkəbl] *adj* **The water is drinkable.** Ruwan sha ne.

drip [drip] 1. *n* digo 2. *v* diga

drive [draiv] *v* (**drove, driven**) tuƙa

drive away *v* kòrā

drive on *v* ƙarfafa wa

drive out *v* kòrā

driver [ˈdraivə] *n* direba

driving [ˈdraiviŋ] *n* tuƙi

driving school *n* makarantar koyon mota

drizzle [ˈdrizl] 1. *n* yayyafi 2. *v* yi yayyafi

droop [druːp] *v* yi yaushi

drop [drɔp] 1. *n* digo 2. (ec.) faduwa 3. *v* (**dropped**) fadi 4. bar abu ya fadi

drop a demand *v* yi watsi da bukata

drop in *v* bàƙuntà

drought [draut] *n* farì

drove [drəuv] *duba wajen* **drive**

drown [draun] *v* nitse har mutuwa

drowsy [ˈdrauzi] *adj* mai jin mutuwar jiki

drug [drʌgz] *n* 1. magani 2. **dangerous drugs** ƙwaya

drugstore [ˈdrʌgstɔː] *n* (US) kanti

drum [drʌm] *n* 1. ganga 2. **oil drum** duro

drummer [ˈdrʌmə] *n* makadi

drunk [drʌŋk] *adj* 1. bugagge 2. *duba wajen* **drink**

drunkard [ˈdrʌŋkəd] *n* dan giya

dry [drai] 1. *adj* maras laima 2. *v* bushe

dryclean [draiˈkliːn] *v* dauraya ta injimi

dryness [ˈdrainəs] *n* bushewa

dry season *n* rāni

dry up *v* jânyē

dual carriage-way [ˈdjuːəl] *n* babbar hanyar mota

dubious [ˈdjuːbiəs] *adj* dan wàlā-wàlā

duck [dʌk] 1. *n* agwagwa 2. *v* kauce wa

due [djuː] 1. *adj* **due south** kudu sak 2. **The rent is due.** Lokacin biyan kudin haya ya zo. 3. **Due to her hard work, she passed the examination.** Saboda jan aikin da ta yi, ta ci jarrabawar. 4. *n* hakki

dues [djuːz] *pl* hakki

dug [dʌg] *duba wajen* **dig**
dull [dʌl] *adj* **1.** maras walƙiya
2. maras ban sha'awa
dumb [dʌmb] *adj* **1.** bebe **2.** (sl.)
shashasha
dummy [ˈdʌmi] *n* **1.** ɗan roba
2. mutum-mutumi **3.** (sl.) wawa
dump [dʌmp] **1.** *n* **rubbish**
dump juji **2.** *v* jagwaɓar da
dumpster [ˈdʌmpstə] *n* (US) bola
dump waste *v* zubar da shara
dung [dʌŋ] *n* tāƙì
dupe [djuːp] *v* yaudara
duplicate [ˈdʒuːplikeit] **1.** *n* kwafi,
(Nr) kofi **2. in duplicate** kwafi
biyu **3.** *v* yi kwafi
durability [ˌdʒuərəˈbiləti] *n* ƙarƙo
durable [ˈdʒuːərəbl] *adj* **1.** mai
ƙarƙo **2. to make durable**
inganta
duration [djuˈreiʃn] *n* tsawo
duress [djuˈres] *n* fin ƙarfi
during [ˈdjuəriŋ] *prep* **1.** dà
2. cikin lokacin

dusk [dʌsk] *n* magariba
dust [dʌst] *n* ƙurar ƙasa
dustbin [ˈdʌstbin] *n* kwandon
shara
dusty [ˈdʌsti] *adj* mai ƙura
duty [ˈdjuːti] *n* **1.** aiki **2.** wajibi
3. (ec.) haraji **4. customs duty**
kuɗin kwastan
duty-free *adj* ba haraji
dwarf [dwɔːf] *n* **(dwarves)** wada
dwell [dwel] *v* zauna
dwell on *v* mai da hankali
dweller [ˈdwelə] *n* mazàuni
dwelling [ˈdweliŋ] *n* mazauni
dye [dai] **1.** *n* rini **2.** *v* rina
dyeing [ˈdaːjiŋ] *n* rini
dying [ˈdaːjiŋ] *duba wajen* **die**
dyke [daik] *n* madatsa
dynamic [daiˈnæmik] *adj* mai
kuzari
dynamite [ˈdainəmait] *n* nakiya
dynamo [ˈdainəməu] *n* dinamo
dynasty [ˈdinəsti] *n* daula
dysentery [ˈdisəntri] *n* atùni

Ee

each [iːtʃ] *adj/adv* **1.** kowane
2. kowanne **3.** five naira each
naira biyar biyar
each other *n/adv* juna
eager [ˈiːgə] *adj* to be eager yi
alla-alla
eagerly [ˈiːgəli] *adv* alla-alla
eagerness [ˈiːgənis] *n* dŏki
eagle [ˈiːgl] *n* juhurma
ear [iːə] *n* kunne
earache [ˈiːəreik] *n* ciwon kunne
early [ˈəːli] *adj/adv* **1.** da wuri
2. na dâ
earmark [ˈiːə,maːk] *v* ware
earn [əːn] *v* **1.** sami albashi
2. to earn a living sami abinci
earnings [ˈəːniŋz] *pl* **1.** albashi
2. gross earnings albashi kafin
debe-debe
earphones [ˈiːə,fəunz] *pl* belun
kunne
earring [ˈiːəriŋ] *n* dan kunne
earth [əːθ] *n* **1.** duniya **2.** ƙasa
earthmover [ˈəːθmuːvə] *n* katafila
earth station *n* tashar tauraron
dan Adam
earthquake [ˈəːθkweik] *n* girgizar
ƙasa
earthworm [ˈəːθwəːm] *n* tsatso
ease [iːz] **1.** *n* sauƙi **2.** *v* sawwaƙa
easily [ˈiːzili] *adv* **1.** da sauƙi
2. da wuri
easiness [ˈiːzinis] *n* sauƙi
east [iːst] **1.** *adj* na gabas
2. *n* gabas
East Africa [ˌiːstˈafrikə] *n* Afirka
ta Gabas

Easter [ˈiːstə] *n* Ista
eastern [ˈiːstən] *adj* na gabas
easterner [ˈiːstənə] *n* bàgabàshi
eastwards [ˈiːstwədz] *adv* zuwa
gabas
easy [ˈiːzi] *adj* mai sauƙi
easy-going *adj* mai sauƙin kai
eat [iːt] *v* (ate, eaten) ci
ebony [ˈebɔni] *n* kanyà
eccentric [ikˈsentrik] *adj* He is
eccentric. Dabam yake.
echo [ˈekəu] *n* amsa kuwwa
eclipse [iˈklips] *n* husufi
ecological [ˌiːkəˈlɔdʒikl] *adj* **1.** na
yanayi **2.** na lafiyar yanayin
ƙasa
ecological balance *n*
daidaituwar yanayin ƙasa
ecological disaster *n* bala'in
gurɓacewar yanayi
ecology [iˈkɔlɔdʒi] *n* nazarin
lafiyar yanayin ƙasa
economic [ˌiːkəˈnɔmik; ˌekəˈnɔmik]
adj na tattalin arziki
economic crisis *n* bala'in
tattalin arziki
economic depression *n*
tawayar tattalin arziki
economic growth *n* bunƙasar
tattalin arziki
economic mess *n* matsin tattalin
arziki
economic recovery *n* farfado
da tattalin arziki
**Economic Commission for
Africa** *n* Hukumar Tattali da
Raya Arzikin Afirka

economical [ˌiːkəˈnɔmikl; ˌekəˈnɔmikl] *adj* mai tattali

economics [ˌiːkəˈnɔmiks; ˌekəˈnɔmiks] *n* 1. tattalin arziki 2. ilimin tattalin arziki

economise [iˈkɔnəmaiz] *v* yi tanadi

economizing [iˈkɔnəmaiziŋ] *n* tanadi

economy [iˈkɔnəmi] *n* 1. tanadi 2. tattalin arziki 2. mixed market economy tsarin harkokin kasuwanci na cakuɗa salon guguzu da na jari-hujja

ECOWAS (**Economic Community of West African States**) *n* Kungiyar Tattalin Arziki ta Kasashen Yammacin Afirka

ecu [ˈekju] *n* kuɗin Tarayyar Turai

eczema [ˈeksmə] *n* kirci

edge [edʒ] *n* 1. baki 2. gefe 3. kaifi

edible [ˈedibl] *adj* mai ciwuwa

edit [ˈedit] *v* shirya

edition [iˈdiʃn] *n* bugu

editor [ˈeditə] *n* 1. edita, (Nr) editar 2. mai shiri

editorial [ˌediˈtɔːriəl] 1. *adj* na edita 2. *n* shafin ra'ayi

educate [ˈedʒukeit] *v* ilimintar da (in a kan)

educated [ˌedʒuˈkeitid] *adj* mai ilimi

education [ˌedʒuˈkeiʃn] *n* 1. ilimi 2. aikin koyarwa

educational [ˌedʒuˈkeiʃnl] *adj* na aikin koyarwa

eel [iːl] *n* gwando

effect [iˈfekt] *n* 1. to put into effect aiwatar da 2. The law is in effect. Dokar ta yi aiki. 3. This has had an adverse effect. Wannan ya haddasa wani sakamako mai illa 4. Our action has had no effect. Mun daɓa a ƙasa. 5. to take effect fara ci 6. in effect a taƙaice

effective [iˈfektiv] *adj* 1. mai amfani 2. mai ci

effectively [iˈfektivli] *adv* a taƙaice

efficiency [iˈfiʃnsi] *n* inganci

efficient [iˈfiʃnt] *adj* mai inganci

effort [ˈefət] *n* 1. ƙoƙari 2. concerted effort namijin ƙoƙari 3. to combine efforts haɗa ƙarfi 4. to exert great effort tayar haiƙan

effortless [ˈefətlis] *adj* ba wahala

e.g. (**for example**) misalin

egg [eg] *n* ƙwai

eggplant [ˈegplaːnt] *n* gauta

egotism [ˈegəuizm] *n* son kai

egotistical [ˌegəuˈtistikl] *adj* mai son kai

eight [eit] *n/adj* takwas

eighteen [eiˈtiːn] *n/adj* goma sha takwas

eighteenth [ˌeiˈtiːnθ] *adj* na goma sha takwas

eighth [eitθ] *adj* 1. na takwas 2. one eighth sumuni

eightieth [ˈeitiəθ] *adj* na tamanin

eighty [ˈeiti] *n/adj* tamanin

either [ˈaiðə; ˈiːðə] *conj* 1. kowanne 2. ko 3. kuma

either...or *conj* ko...ko

ejaculate [iˈdʒækjuleit] *v* kawo

ejaculation [iˌdʒækjuˈleiʃn] *n* kawowa

eject [iˈdʒekt] *v* fitar da

elaborate [iˈlæbəreit] *adj* rikitacce

elapse [iˈlæps] *v* wuce

elastic [iˈlæstik] 1. *adj* na roba,

(Nr) na kaushu **2.** *n* roba, (Nr) kaushu

elbow [ˈelbəu] *n* gwiwar hannu

elder [ˈeldə] **1.** *adj* mafi girma **2.** *n* dattijo

elderly [ˈeldəli] *adj* tsoho

eldest [ˈeldist] *adj* eldest child babban ɗa

elect [ɪˈlekt] *v* **1.** zàɓà **2.** to elect as leader gabatar da

election [ɪˈlekʃn] *n* **1.** zaɓe **2. by-election** zaɓen cike gurbin kujerar majalisa **3. primary election** zaɓen shiga takara **4. general election** babban zaɓe **5. free elections** 'yantaccen zaɓe

election campaign *n* yaƙin neman zaɓe

election manifesto *n* ƙasidar manufofin jam'iyya

elections [ɪˈlekʃnz] *pl* zaɓe

elector [ɪˈlektə] *n* mai jefa ƙuri'a

electoral [ɪˈlektərəl] *adj* na zaɓe

electoral commission *n* hukumar zaɓe

electric [ɪˈlektrɪk] *adj* na lantarki

electrical engineer *n* injiniyan lantarki

electrician [ˌɪlekˈtrɪʃn] *n* mai aikin lantarki

electricity [ˌɪlekˈtrɪsəti] *n* **1.** lantarki, (Nr) latirik **2. to connect electricity** sa wuta **3. to interrupt electricity** katse wuta **4. to cut off electricity** yanke wuta **5. The electricity supply has failed.** An ɗàukè wuta.

electrify [ɪˈlektrɪfaɪ] *v* sa wuta

electrocute [ɪˌlektrəˈkjuːt] *v* kashe da wutar lantarki

elegance [ˈeligəns] *n* gwanin sa sitira

elegant [ˈeligəns] *adj* tsaf-tsaf

element [ˈelimənt] *n* abin sarrafawa

elementary [ˌeliˈmentri] *adj* **1.** mai sauƙi **2.** na farko

elementary school *n* firamire, (Nr) lakkwal

elephant [ˈelifənt] *n* giwa

elevate [ˈeliveit] *v* ɗaga

elevation [ˌeliˈveiʃn] *n* tsayi

elevator [ˈeliveitə] *n* lif

eleven [ɪˈlevn] *n/adj* goma sha ɗaya

eleventh [ɪˈlevnθ] *adj* na goma sha ɗaya

eligible [ˈelidʒəbl] *adj* to be eligible for càncantà

eliminate [ɪˈlimineit] *v* **1.** kashe **2.** (spor.) fitar da

eloquent [ˈeləkwənt] *adj* mai fasahar magana

else [els] *adv* **1.** dabam **2.** saura **3. Someone else will bring the books.** Wani kuma zai kawo littattafan. **4. or else** in ba haka ba

elsewhere [ˌelsˈweə] *adv* a wani wuri dabam

e-mail [ˈiːmeil] *n* saƙon 'e-mail'

emancipate [ɪˈmænsipeit] *v* 'yànta

embargo [imˈbaːgəu] *n* takunkumi

embark [imˈbaːk] *v* shiga

embark upon *v* kama aiki

embarrass [imˈbærəs] *v* **1.** kunyata **2.** gwale

embarrassing [imˈbærəsiŋ] *adj* mai ban kunya

embarrassment [imˈbærəsmənt] *n* kunya

embassy [ˈembəsi] *n* ofishin jakadanci, (Nr) ambasad

embezzle [im'bezl] v yi wa...
zamba
embezzlement [im'bezlmənt] n
zamba
emblem ['embləm] n dagi
embrace [im'breis] v rùngumà
embroidery [im'brɔidəri] n ado
embryo ['embrijəu] n tàyi
emerge [i'mə:dʒd] v fito (**from**
daga)
emergency [i'mə:dʒənsi] n 1.
gaggawa 2. **state** **of**
emergency zaman dokar ta
ɓaci
emergency aid n taimakon
gaggawa
emergency committee n
kwamitin gaggawa
emergency exit n mafitar
gaggawa
emergency landing n saukar
ƙundumbala
emergency law n dokar ta ɓaci
emergency session n taron
gaggawa
emigrant ['emigrənt] n ɗan ƙaura,
mai barin ƙasa
emigrate ['emigreit] v yi ƙaura,
bar ƙasa
emigration [,emi'greiʃn] n ƙaura,
barin ƙasa
emigre ['emigrei] n ɗan ƙaura,
mai barin ƙasa
eminent ['eminənt] adj mashahuri
emir [e'mi:ə] n sarki
emissary ['emi,seri] n ɗan àikē
emit [i'mit] v fitar da
emotion [i'məuʃn] n motsin rai
emotional [i'məuʃənl] adj mai
motsa rai
emperor ['empərə] n sarkin
sarakuna

emphasis ['emfəsis] n ƙarfafawa
emphasise ['emfəsaiz] v ƙarfafa
empire ['empaiə] n daula
employ [im'plɔi] v 1. ba da aiki
2. yi amfani
employee [em'plɔi:] n ma'aikaci
employer [im'plɔiə] n mai ba da
aiki
employment [im'plɔimənt] n
aikin yi
employment agency n ofishin
dillancin aiki
empowered [im'pauəd] adj We
are now empowered. Muna da
cikakken iko yanzu.
empress ['empris] n sarauniyar
sarakuna
empty ['empti] 1. adj ba kome a
ciki 2. **empty promise**
alkawari na fatar baka
3. v zubar da
empty-handed adj hannu banza
enable [i'neibl] v ba da ƙarfi
enact [i'nækt] v (leg.) kafa
enchanting [in'tʃa:ntiŋ] adj mai
ban sha'awa
encircle ['ensə:kl] v kewaye
enclose [in'kləuz] v saka
encore! ['ɔnkɔ:] mu ji! mu ji!
encounter [in'kauntə] v ci karo da
encourage [in'kʌridʒ] v 1.
They've encouraged doing
this. Sun ƙarfafa zuciyar yinsa.
2. **We were encouraged.** An
yi mana ƙwarin gwiwa.
encouragement [in'kʌridʒmənt]
n ƙwarin gwiwa
encouraging [in'kʌridʒiŋ] adj da
dama
encroach [in'krəutʃ] v kwararo
encroachment [in'krəutʃiŋ] n
kusantuwa

encyclopaedia [in,saiklə'pi:diə] *n* kundin sani

end [end] 1. *n* ƙarshe 2. maƙura 3. The End. Tàmat. 4. in the end a ƙarshe 5. *v* ƙare 6. kammala

endanger [in'deindʒə] *v* jawo ruɗami ga

endangered species [in'deindʒəd] *n* halittun da aka jefa su cikin haɗari

endeavour [in'devə] *v* yi ƙoƙari

ending ['endiŋ] *n* ƙarshe

endless ['endlis] *adj* ba iyaka

endorse [in'dɔ:s] *v* goyi baya

endurance [in'dʒuərəns] *n* daurewa

endure [in'dʒuə] *v* daure

enduring [in'dʒuəriŋ] *adj* dawwamamme

enema ['enəmə] *n* gūgūtū

enemy ['enəmi] *n* abokin gaba

energetic ['enədʒetik] *adj* mai kuzari

energy ['enədʒi] *n* 1. kuzari 2. ƙarfi 3. solar energy makamashin zafin rana

energy minister *n* ministan makamashi

enforce [in'fɔ:s] *v* zartar da

engage [in'geidʒ] *v* 1. jìngatà 2. haɗa

engaged [in'geidʒd] *adj* 1. cikin aiki 2. to be engaged yi baiwa

engagement [in'geidʒmənt] *n* 1. alkawari 2. baiwa

engine ['endʒin] *n* 1. inji, (Nr) motar 2. *duba wajen* locomotive

engineer [,endʒi'niə] *n* injiniya, (Nr) injinar

engineering [,endʒi'niəriŋ] *n* ilimin aikin inijiniya

England ['iŋglənd] *n* Ingila

English ['iŋgliʃ] 1. *adj* na Ingila 2. *n* Turanci, (Nr) Ingilishi

Englishman *adj* Ba'ingilishi

Englishwoman *adj* Ba'ingilishiya

engulf [in'gʌlf] *v* rufe da

enhance [in'ha:ns] *v* ƙara haɓaka

enjoy [in'dʒɔi] *v* ji daɗi

enjoyable [in'dʒɔiəbl] *adj* mai daɗi

enjoyment [in'dʒɔimənt] *n* jin daɗi

enlarge [in'la:dʒ] *v* ƙara girma

enlist [in'list] *v* shiga soja

enmity ['enmiti] *n* gàbā

enormous [i'nɔ:məs] *adj* ƙato

enough [i'nʌf] *adv* isasshe

enquire [in'kwaiə] *v* yi tambaya

enrich [in'ritʃ] *v* ƙarfafa

enrol [in'rəul] *v* sa suna

en route [ɔn'ru:t] *adv* a kan hanya

ensure [in'ʃɔ:] *v* tabbatar da

entangled [in'tæŋgəld] *adj* to be entangled harɗe

enter ['entə] *v* 1. shiga 2. shigar da

enterprise ['entəpraiz] *n* 1. ciniki 2. aniya

entertain [,entə'tein] *v* bayar da nishaɗi

entertainment [,entə'teinmənt] *n* abin ba da nishaɗi

enthusiasm [in'θju:ziæzm] *n* sha'awa

enthusiastic [in,θju:zi'æstik] *adj* mai ɗoki

entire [in'taiə] *adj* gaba ɗaya

entirely [in'taiəli] *adv* sarai

entrance ['entrəns] *n* mashiga

entrust [in'trʌst] *v* ba da amana

entry ['entri] *n* 1. mashiga 2. shigowa 3. (fin.) shigarwa

envelope [ˈenvələup] *n* ambulan, (Nr) ambulaf

envious [ˈenviəs] *adj* mai hassada

environment [inˈvaiərənmənt] *n* 1. mahalli 2. kewayen ɗan Adam

environmental [ˌinvaiərənˈmentl] *adj* na yanayi

environmental pollution *n* gurɓacewar yanayi

environment minister *n* ministan kare kewayen ɗan Adam

environs [ˈɔnvirɔnz] *pl* kewaye

envoy [ˈɔnvɔi] *n* ɗan àikē

envy [ˈenvi] *n* 1. *n* hassada 2. *v* yi hassada

epidemic [ˌepiˈdemik] *n* annoba

epilepsy [ˈepilepsi] *n* farfaɗiya

episode [ˈepisəud] *n* karo

epitaph [ˈepitaːf] *n* taken tunawa

epoch [ˈiːpɔk] *n* zamani

equal [ˈiːkwəl] *adj/n* 1. daidai 2. **to be equal** yi ɗaya

equality [iˈkwɔləti] *n* daidaitaka

equation [iˈkweiʒn] *n* lissafi

equator [iˈkweitə] *n* ikwaita

equilibrium [ˌiːkwiˈlibriəm] *n* ɗìgìrgìrē

equip [iˈkwip] *v* sanya

equipment [iˈkwipmənt] *n* 1. na'ura 2. kayan aiki

equivalent [iˈkwivələnt] *adj/n* makwatanci

era [ˈiərə] *n* zamani

eradicate [iˈrædikeit] *v* kawar da

eradication [iˌrædiˈkeiʃn] *n* kawarwa

erase [iˈreiz] *v* goge

eraser [iˈreizə] *n* roba, (Nr) gwam

erect [iˈrekt] 1. *adj* sak 2. *v* kafa

erection [iˈrekʃn] *n* 1. kafawa 2. tashi

erode [iˈrəud] *v* zaizaye

erosion [iˈrəuʒn] *n* zaizayewar ƙasa

err [əː] *v* yi kuskure

errand [ˈerənd] *n* hidima

error [ˈerə] *n* kuskure

erupt [iˈrʌpt] *v* ɓarke

eruption [iˈrʌpʃn] *n* ɓarkewa

escalate [ˈeskəleit] *v* ƙara ƙaruwa

escalator [ˈeskəleitə] *n* matakin inji

escape [iˈskeip] 1. *n* tsira 2. *v* tsira 3. **to have a narrow escape** tsallake rijiya da baya

escort [ˈeskɔːt] 1. *n* ɗan rakiya 2. *v* raka

especially [isˈpeʃəli] *adv* musamman

espionage [ˈespiənaːʒ] *n* aikin leƙen asiri

essay [ˈesei] *n* maƙala

essence [ˈesns] *n* ainihi

essential [iˈsenʃl] *adj* 1. muhimmi 2. na ainihi

establish [iˈstæbliʃ] *v* 1. kafa 2. **to establish ties** ƙulla zumunci

established [iˈstæbliʃt] *adj* kafaffe

establishment [iˈstæbliʃmənt] *n* 1. kafawa 2. kamfani 3. (UK) **the Establishment** masu jan ragamar mulki

estate [iˈsteit] *n* 1. kadara 2. gado 3. **real estate** ƙasa

estate agent *n* mai sayar ƙasa

esteemed [iˈstiːmd] *adj* dattijo

estimate [ˈestimət] 1. *n* istimat 2. *v* ƙiyasta 3. kimanta

estimation [ˌestiˈmeiʃn] *n* kìntàcē

etc. (= **et cetera**) [etˈsetərə] da sauransu

eternal [iˈtəːnl] *adj* na dàwwamằ

eternity [iˈtəːnəti] *n* 1. (tun fil) azal 2. (har) abada

ethical [ˈeθikl] *adj* mai ɗa'a

ethics [ˈeθiks] *pl* ɗa'a

ethnic [ˈeθnik] *adj* na kabila

ethnic cleansing *n* kisan taciyar ƙabila

ethnic minority *n* kabila maras yawa

ethnic origin *n* kabila

ethnicity [eθˈnisəti] *n* kabilanci

etiquette [ˈetiket] *n* ladabi

eucalyptus [ˌjuːkəˈliptəs] *n* tùrằrē

euro [ˈjuərəp] *n* 1. na Turai 2. kuɗin Tarayyar Turai

Europe [ˈjuərəp] *n* Turai

European [ˌjuərəˈpiːən] 1. *adj* na Turai 2. *n* Bature

European Commission *n* Hukumar Tarayyar Turai

European Community (EC) *n* Kungiyar Kasuwar Tarayyar Turai

European Union (EU) *n* Tarayyar Turai

evacuate [iˈvækjueit] *v* kwashe

evade [iˈveid] *v* guje wa

evaluate [iˈvæljueit] *v* kimanta

evaluation [iˈvæljueiʃn] *n* kimantawa

evaporate [iˈvæpəreit] *v* bushe

evaporation [iˌvæpəˈreiʃn] *n* bushewar danshin ruwa

eve [iːv] *n* 1. dare 2. (rel.) jajibere

even [ˈiːvn] 1. *adj* daidai 2. bai ɗaya 3. even number cìkā 4. *prep* har 5. *adv* ko

even if *conj* kō dà

evening [ˈiːvniŋ] 1. yamma 2. Good evening! Barka da yamma!

event [iˈvent] *n* 1. abin da ya faru

2. social event shagali 3. in any event ko ta yaya 4. in the event that/of idan

eventful [iˈventfl] *adj* abin tunawa

even though duk dà

eventually [iˈventʃuəli] *adv* 1. daga baya 2. yau da gobe

ever [ˈevə] *adv* 1. a kowane lokaci 2. Have you ever seen it? Ka taɓa ganinsa? 3. more than ever fiye da koyaushe 4. Don't ever...! Kada ka kuskura...!

ever since *conj* tun

ever so *adj/adv* ƙwarai

everlasting [ˌevəˈlaːstiŋ] *adj* na dàwwamằ

evermore [ˈevəmɔː] *adv* har abada

every [ˈevri] *adj* 1. kōwànè 2. duk 3. every day kullum

everybody, everyone [ˈevribɔdi; ˈevriwʌn] 1. kowa 2. duk wanda

every day *adv* kullum

everyday [ˈevridei] *adj* na yau da kullum

everything [ˈevriθiŋ] 1. kome 2. duk abin da

everywhere [ˈevriweə] 1. ko'ina 2. duk inda

evict [eˈvikt] *v* kōrā

evidence [ˈevidəns] *n* 1. alamu 2. (leg.) shaida

evident [ˈevidənt] *adj* to be evident tabbata

evidently [ˈevidəntli] *adv* 1. ga alama 2. ba shakka

evil [ˈiːvl] 1. *adj* mugu 2. *n* sharri

evolve [iˈvɔlv] *v* samo asali da

evolution [ˌiːvəˈluːʃn] *n* rikiɗar halitta

ewe [jəu] *n* tunkiya

exacerbate [eks·æsəbeit] v ƙara iza wuta

exact [ig·zækt] adj 1. daidai 2. ainihin 3. the exact figure ainihin jimla 4. the exact amount of iya adadin 5. to make exact daidaita

exactly [ig·zæktli] adv 1. daidai 2. cur

exaggerate [ig·zædʒəreit] v yi zùgūgù

exaggeration [ig·zædʒəreiʃn] n zùgūgù

exam, examination [ig·zæm; ig,zæmi·neiʃn] n 1. jarrabawa 2. (med.) duba lafiya

examine [ig·zæmin] v 1. duba 2. ba da jarrabawa

examiner [ig·zæminə] n malamin duba

example [ig·za:mpl] n 1. misali 2. for example misalin 3. to give an example buga misala (of da) 4. to set an example yi rawar gani

excavate [·ekskəveit] v haƙa

excavation [,ekskə·veiʃn] n haƙa

exceed [ik·si:d] v 1. fi 2. wuce

exceedingly [k·si:diŋli] adv haiƙan

excel [ik·sel] v fìfìtà

excellence [·eksələns] n ƙwari

excellency [,eksələnsi] n His Excellency Muƙaddashinsa

excellent [·eksələnt] adj da kyau ƙwarai

except [ik·sept] prep 1. ban da 2. sai

except for prep ban da

exception [ik·sepʃn] n 1. togiya 2. to make an exception keɓe 3. with the exception of ban da

exceptional [ik·sepʃənl] adj na ƙwarai

excess [ik·ses] adj/n oba

excessive [ik·sesiv] adj wuce-wuri

excessive force [ik·sesiv] n ƙarfin gaske

exchange [iks·tʃeindʒ] 1. n musaya 2. foreign exchange kuɗaɗen musaya 3. stock exchange kasuwar jari 4. telephone exchange gidan waya 5. exchange of opinion musayar ra'ayoyi 6. v mùsāyà

exchange-rate n darajàr mùsāyar kuɗi

Exchequer [iks·tʃekə] n (UK) Baitulmali

excite [ik·sait] v ba da sha'awa

excited [ik·saitid] to be excited yi zùmūdi

excitement [ik·saitmənt] n zùmūdi

exclaim [ik·skleim] v buɗe baki

exclamation [,ekslə·meiʃn] n buɗe baki

exclamation mark n alamar motsin rai

exclude [ik·sklu:d] v ware

exclusive [ik·sklu:siv] adj 1. keɓaɓɓe 2. na musamman

exclusion [ik·sklu:ʒn] n wariya

exclusive [ik·sklu:siv] adj 1. na musamman 2. keɓaɓɓe

excrement [·ekskrimənt] n kāshī

excursion [ik·skə:ʒn] n bàlāguřŏ

excuse [ik·skju:s] n 1. hujja 2. dalili 3. to make an excuse fake (that cɛ·ʋa)

excuse [ik·skju:ʾ] v yı wa. ahuwa

excuse me! gafara dai!

execute [·eksikju:t] v 1. zartar da 2. (leg.) yi wa... hukuncin kisa

execution [ˌeksɪˈkjuːʃn] *n* 1. zartarwa 2. (leg.) hukuncin kisa

executioner [ˌeksɪˈkjuːʃənə] *n* hauni

executive [ɪɡˈzekjutɪv] *adj/n* mai zartarwa

executive commission *n* hukumar zartarwa

executive council *n* majalisar zartarwa

executive power *n* ikon aiwatarwa

executive president *n* shugaba mai cikakken iko

executive secretary *n* sakataren zartarwa

exemplary [ɪɡˈzemplərɪ] *adj* na a-zo-a-gani

exempt [ɪɡˈzempt] *adj* We are exempt from... An keɓe mu daga...

exemption [ɪɡˈzempʃn] *n* keɓewa (from daga)

exercise [ˈeksəsaɪz] 1. *n* motsa jiki 2. aiki 3. *v* motsa jiki

exercise book *n* littafin aiki

exert [ɪɡˈzəːt] *v* mai da ƙoƙari

exertion [ɪɡˈzəːʃn] *n* ƙoƙari

exhale [eksˈheɪl] *v* hūrō

exhaust [ɪɡˈzɔːst] 1. *n* hayaƙi 2. *v* gajiyar da... tiƙis 3. ƙarasar da 4. *duba wajen* silencer

exhausted [ɪɡˈzɔːstɪd] *adj* 1. gaji tiƙis 2. Their supplies are exhausted. Kayansu sun ƙare.

exhaustion [ɪɡˈzɔːstʃən] *n* gajiya tiɓis

exhibit [ɪɡˈzɪbɪt] *v* nuna

exhibition [ˌeksɪˈbɪʃn] *n* 1. nuni 2. industrial exhibition nunin kayan masana'antu

exhibitor [ɪɡˈzɪbɪtə] *n* mabajin ƙoli

exhilarate [ɪɡˈzɪləreɪt] *v* ba da zùmūɗi

exhort [ɪɡˈzɔːt] *v* gàřgaɗà

exhortation [ˌeɡzɔːˈteɪʃn] *n* gargaɗi

exile [ˈeksaɪl] 1. *n* gudun hijira 2. *v* kòřà (from daga)

exist [ɪɡˈzɪst] *v* kasance

existence [ɪɡˈzɪstəns] *n* 1. rayuwa 2. kasancewa 2. to bring into existence wanzar da

existent [ɪɡˈzɪstənt] *adj* na yanzu

existing [ɪɡˈzɪstɪŋ] *adj* mai ci

exit [ˈeksɪt; ˈeɡzɪt] 1. *n* mafita 2. *v* fita

expand [ɪkˈspænd] *v* 1. haɓaka 2. haɓakar da

expanse [ɪkˈspæns] *n* fili

expansion [ɪkˈspænʃn] *n* faɗaɗa

expansionism [ɪkˈspænʃnɪzəm] *n* manufar ƙara faɗin ƙasa

expansive [ɪkˈspænsɪv] *adj* mai fili

expatriate [ɪkˈspætrɪət] *adj* bàƙō

expect [ɪkˈspekt] *v* 1. yi tsammani 2. sàurarà 3. *duba wajen* expecting

expectant [ɪkˈspektənt] *adj* mai sauraro

expectation [ˌekspekˈteɪʃn] *n* tsammani

expecting [ɪkˈspektɪŋ] *adj* mai ciki

expedition [ˌekspɪˈdɪʃn] *n* yawon ganin ƙwaf

expel [ɪkˈspel] *v* kore (from daga)

expenditure [ɪkˈspendɪtʃə] *n* kàsàssun kuɗi

expense, expenses [ɪkˈspens; -ɪz] *n* kuɗi

expensive [ik·spensiv] *adj* mai tsada

expensiveness [ik·spensivnəs] *n* tsada

experience [ik·spiəriəns] 1. *n* sani 2. gȍguwā 3. *v* sha

experienced [ik·spiəriənst] *adj* 1. gȍgagge 2. **to be experienced** gȍgè (in wajen)

experiment [ik·sperimənt] *n* gwaji

experimental [,iksperi·mentl] *adj* na gwaji

expert [·ekspə:t] *n* gwani

expertise [,ekspə:·ti:z] *n* gwaninta

expire [ik·spaiə] *v* 1. mutu 2. **My driving licence has expired.** Lasin dina ya ƙare.

explain [ik·splein] *v* bayyana

explanation [,eksplə·neiʃn] *n* bayani

explicit [ik·splisit] *adj* filla-filla

explicitly [ik·splisitli] *adv* ɓarō-ɓàrȍ

explode [ik·spləud] *v* 1. fasà 2. fashe

exploit [ik·splɔit] *v* 1. yi amfani da 2. **to exploit the people** ci da gumin jama'a

exploitation [,eksplɔi·teiʃn] *n* 1. amfani 2. ci da gumi

exploration [,eksplə·reiʃn] *n* bincike

explore [ik·splɔ:] *v* bincika

explorer [ik·splɔ:rə] *n* matafiyin ruwa

explosion [ik·spləuʒn] *n* fàshe-fàshe

explosive [ik·spləusiv] *adj* 1. na nakiya 2. mai ta da hankali 3. mai haɗari

explosives [ik·spləusivz] *pl* nakiya

expo [·ekspəu] *n* nuni

export [ik·spɔ:t] 1. *n* aikawa a ƙasashen waje 2. kayan da aka aikawa ƙasashen waje 3. *v* aika... ƙasashen waje

exportation [,ekspɔ:·teiʃn] *n* aikawa ƙasashen waje

exporter [ik·spɔ:tə] *n* mai aikawa ƙasashen waje

exports [·ekspɔ:ts] *pl* kayan da ake aika ƙasashen waje

expose [ik·spəuz] *v* fàllasà

exposé [ik·spəuzei] *n* àbin fàllasà

exposure [ik·spəuʒə] *n* fàllasà

express [ik·spres] 1. *adj* na ujilā 2. *v* nuna

express train *n* jirgin ujilā

express mail *n* **by express mail** dà ƙār̃-tà-kwāna

expression [ik·spreʃn] *n* 1. motsin rai 2. salon magana

expressly [ik·spresli] *adv* musamman

expressway [ik·spreswei] *n* babban titin mota

exquisite [·ekskwizit; ik·skwizit] *adj* ɗan karen kyau

extend [ik·stend] *v* 1. ƙara 2. miƙa

extension [ik·stenʃn] *n* ƙari

extensive [ik·stensiv] *adj* 1. mai yawa 2. mai tsanani

extent [ik·stent] *n* 1. iyākacī 2. **to a certain extent** dà dāmadāma

exterior [ik·stiəriə] *adj* na waje

exterminate [ik·stə:mineit] *v* ƙār̃è

external [ik·stə:nl] *adj* 1. na waje 2. na ƙetare

extinct [ik·stiŋkt] *adj* **to become extinct** ƙare gaba ɗaya

extinction [ik·stiŋkʃn] *n* ƙarewa gaba ɗaya, gushewa

extinguish [ɪkˈstɪŋgwɪʃ] v kashe wuta
extinguisher [ɪkˈstɪŋgwɪʃə] n randar kashe wuta
extort [ɪkˈstɔːt] v yi wa... sharri
extortion [ɪkˈstɔːʃn] n sharri
extra [ˈekstrə] adj fiye da
extract [ˈekstrækt] v 1. cire 2. tsame
extradite [ˈekstrədeit] v mai da mai kaifi ƙasarsu
extraordinary [ɪkˈstrɔːdnrɪ] adj mai ban mamaki
extravagance [ɪkˈstrævəgəns] n almubazzaranci
extravagant [ɪkˈstrævəgənt] adj almubazzari
extreme [ɪkˈstriːm] adj 1. matsananci 2. mai nesa da yawa

extremely [ɪkˈstriːmlɪ] adv 1. ƙwarai 2. mai tsanani
extremist [ɪkˈstriːmist] n mai matsanancin ra'ayi
extremity [ɪkˈstreməti] n matuƙa
eye [ai] n 1. ido 2. **in the public eye** a idon jama'a 3. **to keep an eye on** sa wa... ido 4. **They don't see eye to eye.** Bà sù jìtu ba.
eyebrow [ˈaibrau] n gira
eyeglasses [ˈaiglaːsiz] pl (US) tabarau, (Nr) lùlēù
eyelash [ˈailæʃ] n gashin ido
eyelid [ˈailid] n fatar ido
eyeshadow [ˈailʃadəu] n jagira
eyewitness [ˈai,witnis] n wanda aka yi a idonsa

Ff

fable [ˈfeibl] *n* hikaya
fabric [ˈfæbrik] *n* yadi
fabricate [ˈfæbrikeit] *v* 1. ƙera
  2. **to fabricate a lie** ƙaga ƙarya
fabulous [ˈfæbjuləs] *adj* bâ dāmā
facade [fəˈsaːd] *n* fuskar gida
face [feis] 1. *n* fuska 2. *v* fuskanta
  3. **He has lost face.** Martabarsa
  ta zube. 4. **to meet face to face**
  yi arba
face-lift *n* **to have a face-lift** ta
  da komaɗa
facet [ˈfæset] *n* ɓangare
facial [ˈfeiʃl] *adj* na fuska
facility [fəˈsiləti] *n* 1. sauƙi 2. aiki
facing [ˈfeisiŋ] *adj* daurà dà
fact [fækt] *n* 1. abin gaskiya 2. **in
  fact** a zahiri
faction [ˈfækʃn] *n* ɓangare
factor [ˈfæktə] *n* sanadi
factory [ˈfæktəri] *n* masana'anta
faculty [ˈfæklti] *n* 1. iyawa
  2. (*acad.*) sashen jami'a
fade [feid] *v* koɗe
fail [feil] *v* 1. kasa 2. faɗi 3. ƙi
  4. **to fail an exam** faɗi a
  jarrabawa 5. **without fail** bâ
  makawā
failure [ˈfeiljə] *n* 1. kasawa 2.
  faɗuwa
faint [feint] 1. *adj* maras ƙarfi
  2. *v* suma
fair [feə] *adj* 1. mai adalci 2. fari
  3. **trade fair** nuni sana'o'i
fairly [ˈfeəli] *adv* dà dāma-dāma
fairness [ˈfeənis] *n* adalci
fairy-tale [ˈfeəri,teil] *n* hikaya

faith [feiθ] *n* 1. imani
  2. amincewa 3. **to have faith**
  amince (**in** da)
faithful [ˈfeiθfl] *adj* amintacce
faithfully [ˈfeiθfəli] *adv* **Yours
  faithfully...** Hāzā wassàlàm...
faithfulness [ˈfeiθfəlnis] *n*
  amincewa
faithless [ˈfeiθlis] *adj* rashin
  aminci
fake [feik] *adj/n* 1. jabu
  2. na ƙarya
fall [fɔːl] 1. *n* faɗuwa 2. (*ec.*)
  sàukā 3. (*US*) bazara 4. *v* (**fell,
  fallen**) faɗi 5. (*ec.*) sàuka
  6. **to fall sharply** rushe
fall asleep *v* yi barci
fall ill *v* ji ciwo
fall in love *v* **I've fallen in love.**
  Na kamu.
fall on *v* kama rana
fall-out [ˈfɔːlaut] *n* **nuclear fall-
  out** dùsař makamashin nukiliya
fall short of *v* kāsà
false [fɔːls] *adj* na ƙarya
falsehood [ˈfɔːlshud] *n* ƙarya
false teeth *pl* haƙoran roba
fame [feim] *n* mashahurantaka
fame and fortune *n* sa'a da rabo
famed [feimd] *adj* mai suna
familiar [fəˈmiliə] *adj* mai
  sabawa (**with** da)
familiarity [,fəmiliˈærəti] *n* sàbō
family [ˈfæməli] *n* 1. iyali
  2. dangi
family planning *n* ƙayyade
  iyali

family planning organization
n ƙungiya mai kula da tsarin iyali

famine [ˈfæmin] *n* bala'in yunwa

famous [ˈfeiməs] *adj* mashahuri

fan [fæn] *n* 1. maficici 2. fanka, (Nr) bantilatar

fanatic [fəˈnætik] *n* mai matsanancin ra'ayi

fanbelt [ˈfænbelt] *n* fambel

fancy [ˈfænsi] 1. *n* na ado 2. *v* so

fantastic [fænˈtæstik] *adj* bâ dāma

fantasy [ˈfæntəsi] *n* almara

FAO (**Food and Agriculture Organization**) *n* Hukumar Abinci da Ayyukan Noma ta Duniya

far [faː] *adj/adv* 1. mai nisa (from daga) 2. **as far as** har

far away *adj/adv* mai nisa (from daga)

fare [feə] *n* kuɗin tafiya

farewell [ˌfeəˈwel] *n* ban kwana

farm [faːm] 1. *n* gona 2. *v* yi noma

farmer [ˈfaːmə] *n* manomi

farming [ˈfaːmiŋ] *n* noma

farm produce *n* amfanin gona

far-sighted *adj* mai hangen nesa

fart [faːt] 1. *n* tusa 2. *v* yi tusa

farther [ˈfaːðə] *adj/adv* mafi nesa

fascinate [ˈfæsineit] *v* ba da sha'awa

fascism [ˈfæʃism] *n* baƙin mulki

fascist [ˈfæʃist] *n* mai baƙin mulki

fashion [ˈfæʃn] *n* salo

fashionable [ˈfæʃnəbl] *adj* ɗan gāyè

fast [faːst] 1. *adj* mai sauri 2. tsantsan 3. **fast growing** mai

saurin ƙaruwa 4. *n* azumi 5. *v* yi azumi 6. **The clock is fast.** Agogon ya yi gudu.

fast asleep *adj* mai sharar barci

fast forward *n* gaba

fasten [ˈfaːsn] *v* 1. ɓalla 2. ɗaura

fastener [ˈfaːsnə] *n* maɓalli

fasting [ˈfaːstiŋ] *n* azumi

fat [fæt] 1. *adj* mai ƙiba 2. mài mâi 3. *n* ƙiba 4. mâi

fatal [ˈfeitl] *adj* na ajali

fatal illness *n* ciwon da ke sanadiyyar mutuwa

fatality [fəˈtæləti] *n* mutuwa

fate [feit] *n* ƙaddara

father [ˈfaːðə] *n* uba

father-in-law [ˈfaðərinlɔː] *n* suruki

fatigue [fəˈtiːg] *n* gajiya

fatigue duties *pl* (mil.) gwālè-gwālè

fatness [ˈfætnis] *n* ƙiba

fatty [ˈfæti] *n* mài mâi

faucet [ˈfɔːset] *n* (US) famfo

fault [fɔːlt] *n* 1. laifi 2. aibu 3. **to find find fault** kushe (with wa)

faultless [ˈfɔːltləs] *adj* maras laifi

faulty [ˈfɔːlti] *adj* mai illa

favour [ˈfeivə] 1. *n* taimako 2. farin jini 3. **to be in favour of** gòyi bāyan 4. *v* ɗaukaka

favourite [ˈfeivərit] *n/adj* mafi so

fax [fæks] 1. *n* wayar faks 2. *v* buga wa... wayar faks

fax-modem [ˈfæksˈməudem] *n* wayar faks ta kwafuta

fear [fiə] 1. *n* tsoro 2. *v* ji tsoro

fearless [ˈfiəlis] *adj* mai rashin tsoro

feasible [ˈfiːzəbl] *adj* mai yiwuwa

feast [fiːst] *n* 1. walima 2. biki

feat [fi:t] *n* aiki
feather [ˈfeðə] *n* gashin tsuntsu
feature [ˈfiːtʃə] *n* alama
feature film *n* majigin silima
featuring [ˈfiːtʃəriŋ] *adj* masu wasa...
February [ˈfebruəri] *n* Fabrairu
fed [ˈfedərəl] *duba wajen* **feed**
federal [ˈfedərəl] *adj* na tarayya
federal government *n* gwamnatìn tarayya
Federal Labour Exchange *n* Hukumar Kwadago ta Tarayya
federal republic *n* jamhuriyar tarayya
federation [ˌfedəreiʃn] *n* tarayya
Federation of International Football Associations (FIFA) *n* Hukumar Kwallon Kafa ta Duniya
fed up [ˈfedərəl] *adj* **to be fed up** ƙosa (**with** da)
fee [fi:] *n* kuɗi
feeble [ˈfiːbl] *adj* mai rauni
feebleness [ˈfiːblnis] *n* rauni
feed [fiːd] *v* (**fed**) 1. ciyar da 2. ci
feel [fiːl] *v* (**felt**) 1. taɓa 2. ji
feeling [ˈfiːliŋ] *n* abin da ake ji a rai
feel like *v* ji yin...
feet [fiːt] *duba wajen* **foot**
fell [fel] *duba wajen* **fall**
fellow [ˈfeləu] 1. *adj* ɗan'uwan... 2. *n* taliki
fellowship [ˈfeləuʃip] *n* zumunci
felony [ˈfeloni] *n* babban laifi
felt [felt] *duba wajen* **feel**
female [ˈfiːmeil] 1. *adj* ta-mace 2. *n* mace
feminine [ˈfemənin] *adj* tamata
femininity [ˌfeməˈniniti] *n* matuci
fence [fens] *n* shinge

fender [ˈfendə] (US) *n* mutagadi, (Nr) gardabu
fend off *v* ware
ferment [fəˈment] *v* ruɓa
fermentation [ˌfəːmənˈteiʃn] *n* ruɓawa
ferocity [fəˈrɔsəti] *n* tashin hankali
ferry [ˈferi] *n* jirgin fito
ferryboat [ˈferibəut] *n* jirgin fito
ferrying [ˈferijiŋ] *n* fito
fertile [ˈfəːtail] *adj* mai albarka
fertility [fəˈtiləti] *n* albarka
fertilize [ˈfəːtəlaiz] *v* zuzuzzuba taki
fertilizer [ˈfəːtəlaizə] *n* 1. taki 2. **chemical fertilizer** takin zamani
fervent [ˈfəːvənt] *adj* mai matsanancin ra'ayi
festival [ˈfestəvl] *n* 1. biki 2. (Islam.) idi
festive [ˈfestiv] *adj* na shagali
festivity [fesˈtivəti] *n* shagali
fetch [fetʃ] *v* nēmō
fetus [ˈfiːtəs] *n* ɗan tàyī
feud [fjuːd] *n* gàbā
fever [ˈfiːvə] *n* zazzaɓi
feverish [ˈfiːvəriʃ] *adj* mai jikin rawa
few, a few [fjuː] *adj* 1. kaɗan 2. waɗansu 3. **just a few** wasu 'yan 4. **a few days ago** kwanan baya
fiancè [fiˈɔnsei] *n* saurayi
fiancèe [fiˈɔnsei] *n* budurwa
fibre [ˈfaibə] *n* zare
fiction [ˈfikʃn] *n* ƙagaggen labari
field [fiːld] *n* 1. gona 2. (spor.) fili
fierce [fiəs] *adj* 1. mai ban tsoro 2. mai ƙarfi
fiery [ˈfaiəri] *adj* 1. mai gobara 2. muguwar zuciya

FIFA (Federation of International Football Associations) [ˈfiːfə] *n* Hukumar Kwallon Kafa ta Duniya

fifteen [ˌfifˈtiːn] *n/adj* goma sha biyar

fifteenth [ˌfifˈtiːnθ] *adj* na goma sha biyar

fifth [fifθ] *n* na biyar

fifty [ˈfifti] *n/adj* hamsin

fig [fig] *n* ɓaure

fight [fait] 1. *n* faɗà 2. *v* (fought) yi faɗà

fighting [ˈfaitiŋ] *n* faɗà

fighter [ˈfaitə] *n* mai faɗà

fighter-plane *n* jirgin saman yaƙi

figure [ˈfigə] *n* 1. siffa 2. adadi 3. ƙirà

figure out *v* gànè

file [fail] *n* 1. zarto 2. fayil, (Nr) dòsê

fill [fil] *v* cika

fill a form in/out *v* cike fom

filling [ˈfiliŋ] *n* (med.) cikò

filling station *n* gidan mai

film [film] 1. *n* yānā 2. fim, (Nr) filim 3. *v* yi fim

filter [ˈfiltə] 1. *n* filtà, (Nr) filtìř 2. *v* tace

filth [filθ] *n* auɗa

filthy [ˈfilθi] *adj* mai dauɗa

final [ˈfainl] 1. *adj* na ƙarshe 2. *n* wasan ƙarshe

finalize [ˈfainəlaiz] *v* zartar da

finally [ˈfainəli] *adv* daga ƙarshe

finance [ˈfainæns; fiˈnæns] 1. *n* sha'anin kuɗi 2. jari 3. *v* ba da kuɗi

finance markets *pl* kasuwannin hada-hadar kuɗi

financial [faiˈnænʃl] *adj* na sha'anin kuɗi

financial affairs *pl* hada-hadar kuɗi

financial losses *pl* asarar kuɗi

financial policy *n* manufofi na harkar kuɗi

Finance Secretary *n* (US) ma'aji, Sakataren Baitulmali

finances [ˈfainænsiz] *pl* al'amura na kuɗi

find [faind] *v* (found) 1. samu 2. tsinta

find out *v* gānō

findings [ˈfaindiŋz] *pl* bàyànai

fine [fain] 1. *adj* mai taushi 2. mai kyau 3. *n* tàrār kuɗi 4. *v* ci wa... tàrā 5. *adv* lafiya

finger [ˈfiŋgə] *n* yatsa

fingerprint [ˈfiŋgəprint] *n* zanen yatsa

finish [ˈfiniʃ] 1. *n* ƙarshe 2. *v* ƙare

fire [faiə] 1. *n* wuta 2. to set on fire ƙyasta 3. to catch fire kama gobara 4. *v* to fire a weapon buga bindiga 5. He has been fired. An kòre shì dàgà aikìn.

fire alarm *n* ƙararrawar hā-wuta

firearm [ˈfaiəraːm] *n* indiga

fire brigade *n* ma'aikatar kashe gobara

fire department *n* (US) ma'aikatar kashe gobara

fire engine *n* motar masu aikin kwana-kwana, (Nr) fiifā

fire escape, fire exit *n* hanyar fita, mafita in ta yi zafi

firefighter *n* ɗan kwana-kwana

firefighting *n* kwana-kwana

firefly [ˈfaiə,flai] *n* màƙèsū

fireman [ˈfaiəmən] *n* ɗan aikin kwana-kwana

fireplace [ˈfaiəpleis] *n* murhu

fire station *n* gidan 'yan kwana-kwana

firewood [ˈfaiwud] *n* ƙirare

fireworks [ˈfaiəwəːks] *pl* wasan wuta

firing squad *n* to execute by firing squad bindige

firm [fəːm] 1. *adj* mai kauri 2. **firm security measures** ƙwaranan matakai na tsaro 3. *n* kamfanin ciniki

first [fəːst] 1. *adj* na farko 2. **at first** da farko 3. **in the first place** da farko dai 4. *adv* tukuna

first aid *n* taimakon farko

first class *adj* 1. lambawan 2. fiskila

firstly [ˈfəːstli] *adv* da farko

first name *n* sunan rana

fiscal [ˈfiskəl] *adj* na kasafin kuɗi

fiscal year *n* shekarar kasafin kuɗi

fish [fiʃ] 1. *n* kifi 2. *v* yi su

fisherman [ˈfiʃəmən] *n* masunci

fishing [ˈfiʃiŋ] *n* su

fist [fist] *n* ɗunkulallen hannu

fit [fit] 1. *adj* mai lafiya 2. *n* (med.) farfaɗiya 3. *v* yi wa... daidai

fitness [ˈfitnis] *n* lafiya

five [faiv] *n/adj* biyar

fix [fiks] *v* 1. gyara 2. manna 3. shirya 4. ƙayyade 5. **to fix a date** sa rana

flag [flæg] *n* tuta

flake [fleik] *n* ɓarɓashi

flame [fleim] *n* harshe wuta

flap [flæp] *v* kaɗa

flash [flæʃ] *v* walƙa

flashlight [ˈflæʃlait] *n* tocilan, (Nr) cöcìlà

flask [flaːsk] *n* ƙarura

flat [flæt] 1. *adj* mai lebur 2. *n* gida 3. **flat tyre** fanca, (Nr) kirebe

flatter [ˈflætə] *v* làllamà

flavour [ˈfleivə] *n* daɗin danɗano

flaw [flɔː] *n* aibu

flay [flei] *v* feɗe

flea [fliː] *n* ƙuma

flee [fliː] *v* (**fled**) gudu

fleet [fliːt] *n* rundunar jirage

flesh [fleʃ] *n* tsôkā

flew [fluː] *duba wajen* **fly**

flexibility [ˌfleksəˈbiləti] *n* tànƙwàruwā

flexible [ˈfleksəbl] *adj* mai tànƙwàruwā

flight [flait] *n* 1. tashin sama 2. tafiyar sama 3. tsira 4. **a flight of stairs** matakala

fling [fliŋ] *v* (**flung**) watsar da

flip [flip] *v* jefa

flip open *v* buɗe

flirt [fləːt] *v* yi kwàřkwasà

float [fləut] *v* 1. taso kan ruwa 2. tashi

flock [flɔk] *n* garke

flood [flʌd] 1. *n* ambaliya 2. *v* yi ambaliya 3. **to flood the market** yi ambaliya a kasuwa

flooding [ˈflʌdiŋ] *n* ambaliya

floor [flɔː] *n* 1. dàɓē 2. bene

florist [ˈflɔrist] *n* mai sayar da fure

flour [ˈflauə] *n* gàři

flourish [ˈflʌriʃ] *v* yi yalwa

flourishing [ˈflʌriʃiŋ] *adj* mai yalwa

flout [flaut] *v* yi fatali da

flow [fləu] 1. *n* gùdànà 2. *v* gudana

flower [ˈflauə] *n* fure

flown [fləun] *duba wajen* **fly**

flow out *v* zube

flu (= **influenza**) [flu:] *n* mura

fluctuate [flʌktʃueit] *v* canza

fluctuation [ˌflʌktʃuˈeiʃn] *n* hawā da sauka

fluency [ˈfluːənsi] *n* jin harshe sosai

fluent [ˈfluːənt] *adj* ba gargada a harshe

fluid [ˈfluːid] 1. *adj* na ruwa 2. mai motsi 3. *n* ruwa

fluke [fləuk] *n* matsattsaku

fluorescent light bulb [flɔːˈresnt] *n* kyandir

flush [flʌʃ] *v* ja ruwa

flute [fluːt] *n* sarewa

fly [flai] 1. *n* (**flies**) ƙuda 2. *v* (**flew, flown**) tashi 3. **I flew to London.** Na tafi London cikin jirgin sama.

foal [fəul] *n* dùƙushī

foam [fəum] *n* kumfa

focus [ˈfəukəs] *v* mai da hankali (**on kan**)

fodder [ˈfɔdə] *n* harawà

foetus [ˈfiːtəs] *n* ɗan tàyi

fog [fɔg] *n* hazo, tuƙuƙin hazo

foil [fɔil] *v* tsare

fold [fəuld] *v* ninka

folder [ˈfəuldr] *n* fayil, (Nr) shamis

folk [fəuk] 1. *adj* na gargajiya 2. *n* mutane

folklore [ˈfəuklɔː] *n* ilimin hikimomin al'umma

folks [fəuks] *pl* iyaye

follow [ˈfɔləu] *v* 1. bi 2. gane

follower [ˈfɔləuə] *n* mabiyi

following [ˈfɔləuiŋ] 1. *adj* mai zuwa 2. *n* mabìyā

fond [fɔnd] *adj* **to be fond of** so

food [fuːd] *n* abinci

food production *n* yawan kayan abincin da a ke nomawa

food shortage *n* ƙarancin abinci

food subsidies *pl* kuɗin karya farashin kayayyakin abinci

foodstuffs [ˈfuːdstʌf] *pl* kayayyakin abinci

fool [fuːl] 1. *n* shashasha 2. *v* zàmbatà

foolish [ˈfuːliʃ] *adj* shashasha

foolproof [ˈfuːlpruːf] *adj* mai saukin fahimta

foot [fut] *n* (**feet**) 1. ƙafa 2. **to go on foot** tafi a ƙasa

football [ˈfutbɔːl] *n* wasan ƙwallo

football pools *pl* tambola

footballer [ˈfutbɔːlə] *n* mai wasan ƙwallon ƙafa

footprint [ˈfutprint] *n* sawu

footsoldier [ˈfutˌsəuldʒə] *n* dakare

footstep [ˈfutstep] *n* tākù

footwear [ˈfutweə] *n* tākalmà

for [fə; fɔː] *prep* 1. wà 2. gà 3. don 4. **He slept for eight hours.** Ya yi barci awa takwas. 5. **They fought for freedom.** Sun yi yaƙi don samun 'yanci.

foreseeable [ˌfɔːˈsiːəbl] *adj* gaba can

for example *duba wajen* e.g.

forbid [fəˈbid] *v* (**forbade, forbidden**) hana

forbidden [fəˈbidn] *adj* haram

force [fɔːs] 1. *n* ƙarfi 2. runduna 3. **military forces** sojoji 4. **to bring into force** wanzar da 5. **to come into force** fara aiki 6. **to take by force** ƙwace 7. *v* tilasta wa

forced [fɔːst] *adj* na dole

forced landing *v* saukar tilas

forced retirement *n* ritayar dōlè

forceful [ˈfɔːsfl] *adj* mai ƙarfi

forcefully [ˈfɔːsfəli] *adv* da ƙarfi

fore [fɔːd] *v* ƙetare

fore [fɔː] *n* to the fore a gaba

forearm [ˈfɔːraːm] *n* damtse

forecast [ˈfɔːkaːst] 1. *n* kìntàcē 2. *v* kìntātà

forefinger [ˈfɔːfiŋgə] *n* dan ali

forefront [ˈfɔːfrʌnt] *n* at the forefront kan gaba

foregone [ˈfɔːgɔn] *adj* These results are a foregone conclusion. Wannan sakamako abu ne da aka sani tun tuni

forehead [ˈfɔrid; ˈfɔːhed] *n* goshi

foreign [ˈfɔrən] *adj* na ƙasashen waje

foreign affairs *n* harkokin waje

foreign exchange *n* kudaden musaya na ƙetare

foreign exchange market *n* kasuwar musayar kudade

foreign minister *n* ministan harkokin waje

Foreign Office *n* (UK) ma'aikatar harkokin waje

foreign policy *n* manufar harkokin waje

foreign trade *n* cinikin ƙetare

foreigner [ˈfɔrənə] *n* bàƙō

foreman [ˈfɔːmən] *n* heluma

foremost [ˈfɔːməust] *adj* mafi shahara

foresee [fɔːˈsiː] *v* tsìnkàyà

foresight [ˈfɔːsait] *n* tsìnkàyā

forest [ˈfɔrist] *n* ƙungurmin daji

forest reserve *n* gandun dajì

forestalling [fɔːˈstɔːliŋ] *n* rige

forever [fəˈrevə] *adv* 1. har abada 2. kullum

foreword [ˈfɔːwəːd] *n* gabatarwa

forfeit [ˈfɔːfit] *v* yanke

forgave [fəˈgeiv] *duba wajen* forgive

forge [fɔːdʒ] *v* 1. ƙera 2. buga... na jabu

forged [fɔːdʒd] 1. forged documents takardun bogi 2. a forged cheque cak na jabu

forger [ˈfɔːdʒə] *n* dan katàfìs

forgery [ˈfɔːdʒəri] *n* jabu

forget [fəˈget] *v* (forgot, forgotten) manta

forgive [fəˈgiv] *v* (forgave, forgiven) yafe wa

forgive and forget a mai da kome ba kome ba

forgiveness [fəˈgivnis] *n* gafara

forgot, forgotten [fəˈgɔt; fəˈgɔtn] *duba wajen* forget

fork [fɔːk] *n* cokali mai yatsa

form [fɔːm] 1. *n* siffa 2. fam, (Nr) fish 3. (ed.) aji 4. *v* kafa

formal [ˈfɔːml] *adj* 1. na aiki 2. a rubuce

formal occasions *pl* bukūkuwa

formally [ˈfɔːməli] *adv* bisa manura

former [ˈfɔːmə] *adj* na da

formerly [ˈfɔːməli] *adv* a zamanin da

formidable [ˈfɔːmidəbl] *adj* gàgàrùmi

formula [ˈfɔːmjulə] *n* dabara

Formula One racing *n* gasar tsēren fìtattun direbobin mōtōcī

fort [fɔːt] *n* fadar soja

forth [fɔːθ] *adv* a gaba

forthcoming [ˌfɔːθˈkʌmiŋ] *adj* mai zuwa

fortify [ˈfɔːtifai] *v* ƙarfafa

fortnight [ˈfɔːtnait] *n* mako biyu

fortress [ˈfɔːtris] *duba wajen* **fort**

fortunate [ˈfɔːtʃənət] *adj* mài sã'à

fortunately [ˈfɔːtʃənətli] *adv* da yake an yi dace

fortune [ˈfɔːtʃuːn] *n* **1.** sa'a **2.** arziki

forty [ˈfɔːti] *n/adj* arba'in

forum [ˈfɔːrəm] *n* political forum dandalin sìyasa

forward [ˈfɔːwəd] **1.** *adv* gaba **2.** *v* tūrà

foster [ˈfɔstə] *v* ɗauki rènō

foster parents *pl* iyayen riƙo

fought [fɔːt] *duba wajen* **fight**

foul [faul] **1.** *adj* wāri **2.** *n* (spor.) fāwùl

found [faund] **1.** *v* kafà **2.** *duba wajen* **find**

foundation [faunˈdeiʃn] *n* **1.** harsashi **2.** tūshè

foundations [faunˈdeiʃn] *pl* harsashì

founder [ˈfaundə] *n* uba, uwa

fountain [ˈfauntin] *n* tubalin feshin ruwa

fountain pen *n* alƙalami, (Nr) istilo

four [fɔː] *n/adj* huɗu

four-wheel drive *n* landiroba

fourteen [ˌfɔːˈtiːn] *n/adj* goma sha huɗu

fourteenth [ˌfɔːˈtiːnθ] *adj* na goma sha huɗu

fourth [fɔːθ] **1.** *adj* na huɗu **2.** *n* rubu'i

fowl [faul] *n* su kàzā

fox [fɔks] *n* yanyawa

fraction [ˈfrækʃn] *n* **1.** ƙasarun adadi **2.** ɗan kaɗan

fracture [ˈfræktʃə] **1.** *n* kàrayà **2.** *v* karye

fragile [ˈfrædʒail] *adj* na aras

fragment [ˈfrægmənt] *n* gutsure

fragrance [ˈfreigrəns] *n* ƙamshi

fragrant [ˈfreigrənt] *adj* mai ƙamshi

frail [freil] *adj* mai rauni

frame [freim] *n* **1.** firam, (Nr) shashi **2.** katako

framework [ˈfreimwɔːk] *n* siga

franc [fræŋk] *n* tammā

France [frɑːns] *n* Faransa

franchise [ˈfræntʃaiz] *n* **1.** hakkin kaɗa ƙuri'a **2.** ikon amfani da sunan kamfani

francophone [ˈfræŋkəu,təun] *adj* **francophone countries** ƙasashen Afirka rènon Faransa

frankly [ˈfræŋkli] *adv* a fili

frantic [ˈfræntik] *adj* ruwa a jallo

fraternal [frəˈtəːnl] *adj* na 'yan'uwa

fraternity [frəˈtəːnəti] *n* zumunta

fraud [frɔːd] *n* zamba

fraudulent [ˈfrɔːdjulənt] *adj* mai zamba

free [friː] **1.** *adj* 'yantacce **2.** na kyauta **3. to be free** huta (**from** da) **4.** *v* 'yântà

freedom [ˈfriːdəm] *n* 'yanci

freedom of information *n* kwararar labarai,

freedom of speech *n* 'yancin faɗin albarkacin baki

freedom of the press *n* 'yancin jaridu

freedom struggle *n* yaƙin neman 'yanci

free elections *n* 'yantaccen zaɓe

free market competition *n* takarar harkokin kasuwanci

free of charge *adj* na kyauta

free trade *adj* cinikayya mara shinge

free trade zone *n* yankin cinikayyā mara shinge

freeze [friːz] *v* **(froze, frozen)** daskara

freight [freit] *n* sufurin kaya

freight car *n* wagunu

freighter ['freitə] *n* jirgin kaya

French [frentʃ] **1.** *adj* na Faransa **2.** *n* Bafaranshe **3.** Faransanci

Frenchman ['frentʃmən] *n* Bafaranshe

Frenchwoman ['frentʃ,wumən] *n* Bafaranshiya

frequency ['friːkwənsi] *n* mita

frequent ['friːkwənt] *adj* da yawa

frequently ['friːkwəntli] *adv* sau da yawa

fresh [freʃ] *adj* **1.** sabo **2.** ɗanye

fresh blood *n* sabon jini

freshwater ['freʃ,wɔːtə] *n* baƙin ruwa

fret [fret] *v* yi ƙōrafī

fretting ['fretiŋ] *n* ƙōrafī

friction ['frikʃn] *n* gògayyà

Friday ['fraidi] *n* ran Jumma'a

fridge [fridʒ] *n* firiji, (Nr) firigo

fried [fraid] *duba wajen* **fry**

friend [frend] *n* **1.** aboki **2.** ƙawa

friendliness ['frendlinis] *n* fara'a

friendly ['frendli] *adj* mai fara'a

friendly relations *n* zumunci

friendship ['frendʃip] *n* **1.** abokantaka **2.** **to strengthen the bonds of friendship** ƙara sada zumunci

fright [fait] *n* tsoro

frighten ['fraitn] *v* bayar da tsoro

frightened ['fraitənd] *adj* **to be frightened** ji tsoro

frightful ['fraitfl] *adj* mai ban tsoro

fro [frəu] *adv* **to and fro** kai-dà-kàwō

frog [frɔg] *n* kwaɗo

from [frɔm] *prep* **1.** daga **2.** daga gare **3.** tun daga **4.** **someone from the north** ɗan arewa

from now on *adv* daga yanzu

front [frʌnt] *n* **1.** gaba **2. in front** gaba **3. in front of** a gaban **4. to form a united front** yi babban shinge **5. war front** dāgā

front-line *n* bàkin dāgā

frontal attack ['frʌntl] *n* harì na gaba da gaba

frontier ['frʌntiə] *n* iyaka

frost [frɔst] *n* ƙanƙara

frosty ['frɔsti] *adj* mai ƙanƙara

froth [frɔθ] *n* kumfa

frown [fraun] *v* ɗaura gira

froze [frəuz] *duba wajen* **freeze**

frozen ['frəuzn] *adj* **1.** daskararre **2.** *duba wajen* **freeze**

fruit [fruːt] *n* 'ya'yan itace

fruitful ['fruːtfl] *adj* mai amfani

fruitless ['fruːtlis] *adj* **The talks were fruitless.** Shawarwari ba su haifar da kome ba.

frustrate [frʌ'streit] *v* ba da takâicī

frustrated [frʌ'streitid] *adj* **to be frustrated** ji takâicī

frustration [frʌ'streiʃn] *n* takâicī

fry [frai] *v* **(fried)** soya

frying-pan ['fraiiŋ,pæn] *n* kwanon tuya

ft. *duba wajen* **foot**

fuel ['fjuːəl] **1.** *n* makāmashī **2.** mâi **3.** *v* **This has fuelled demand for...** Wannan ya haɓaka bùkatun... **4. It has fuelled inflation.** Ya yi angizon hauhawar farashi.

fuel pump n famfòn mâi
fuel tank n tankìn mâi
fugitive [ˈfjuːdʒətiv] n magùjī
Fulani [fuːˈlaːni] 1. adj na Filani
2. n Bafilace 3. Fillanci
fulfil [fulˈfil] v cika
fulfilment [fulˈfilmənt] n biyan bukata
full [ful] adj cikakke
full stop n aya
fullness [ˈfulnis] n ƙòshī
fully fledged adj cìkakken shirì
fumes [fjuːm] pl 1. hayaƙi 2. wārī
fun [fʌn] n nishaɗi
function [ˈfʌnkʃn] 1. n aiki
2. social function biki 3. v yi aiki
functionary [ˈfʌnkʃənəri] n ma'aikaci
fund [fʌnd] n 1. asūsù 2. relief fund asusun agaji
fundamental [ˌfʌndəˈmentəl] adj muhimmi
fundamentalist [ˌfʌndəˈmentəlist] n 1. mai ra'ayin rìƙau 2. religious fundamentalist mai ra'ayin a koma wa addini na tsantsa

funding [ˈfʌndiŋ] n kuɗaɗè
funds [fʌndz] pl asūsù
funeral [ˈfjuːnərəl] n jana'iza
funnel [ˈfʌnl] n bututu
funny [ˈfʌni] adj 1. mai ban dariya 2. mai ban mamaki
fur [fəː] n gashin dabba
furious [ˈfjuəriəs] adj mai matsanancin fushi
furnace [ˈfəːnis] n wutar makera
furnish [ˈfəːniʃ] v sa kaya a daƙi
furniture [ˈfəːnitʃə] n kayan daƙi
further [ˈfəːðə] 1. n mafi nisa
2. wani kuma 3. v ciyar da... gaba
further details pl ƙarin bayani
furthermore [ˌfəːðəˈmɔː] adv bugu da ƙari
fury [ˈfjuəri] n matsanancin fushi
fuse [fjuːz] n fīs
fuss [fʌs] n kwàkwāzò
futile [ˈfjuːtail] adj a banza
future [ˈfjuːtʃə] 1. n gobe
2. adj na gaba 3. adv nan gaba
4. in the future zuwa gaba 5. in the near future nân gaba kaɗan

Gg

gadget [ˈgadʒit] n na'ura
gag [gæg] v sa takunkumi
gage *duba wajen* gauge
gag the press v tace labarai
gain [gein] 1. n riba 2. v samu
gale [geil] n ruwa da iska
gallant [ˈgælənt] *adj* jarumi
gallery [ˈgæləri] n 1. mazaunin
  'yan kallon muhawara 2. art
  gallery ma'adanin hotunan
  zane 3. gidan baje hotuna
gallon [ˈgælən] n galan
gallop [ˈgæləp] v yi sukuwa
gamble [ˈgæmbl] v yi caca
gambler [ˈgæmblə] n ɗan caca
gambling [ˈgæmbliŋ] n caca
gambling-house n gidan rēfùl
game [geim] n 1. wasa 2. namun
  daji
gang [gæŋ] n 1. gungù 2. 'yan
  iska
gangster [ˈgæŋstə] n ɗan iska
gap [gæp] n giɓi
garage [ˈgæra:ʒ; ˈgæridʒ] n 1.
  gārējì, (Nr) gàřâj 2. gidan mai
garbage [ˈga:bij] n shàřā
garbage can n garwař shàřā
garden [ˈga:dn] n lambu, (Nr)
  garkā
garden egg n gautā
gardener [ˈga:dnə] n gadina,
  (Nr) mai garka
gardening [ˈga:dniŋ] n aikin
  lambu
garlic [ˈga:lik] n tafarnuwa
garment [ˈga:mənt] n tufa
garrison [ˈgærisn] n barikin soja

gas [gæs] n 1. gâs 2. (US) fētùř,
  (Nr) isanshi
gasolene, gasoline [ˈgæsəli:n]
  (US) fētùř, (Nr) isanshi
gas station n (US) gidan mai
gate [geit] n ƙofa
gatecrasher n kūtsà
gather [ˈgæðə] v 1. taru 2. tara
gather together v tattara
gathering [ˈgæðəriŋ] n tarō
GATT (General Agreement
  on Tariffs and Trade) n
  Yarjejeniyar Cinikayya da
  Kuɗin Fito
gauge [geidʒ] 1. n gējì, (Nr)
  kwàntâř 2. v auna
gave [geiv] *duba wajen* give
gay [gei] *adj* 1. mai fara'a 2. ɗan
  lūɗù, 'yař māɗigō
gaze [geiz] v zuba ido (at wa)
gazelle [gəˈzel] n barewa
gazette [gəˈzet] n gazet
gear [giə] n giyà
gearbox [ˈgiəbɔks] n giyà bôs,
  (Nr) kàřtâř
geese [gi:s] *duba wajen* goose
gelignite [ˈdʒeligneit] n nakiya
gem [dʒem] n dutse
gendarme [dʒenˈda:m] n (Nr)
  jandařmà
gender [ˈdʒendə] n jinsi
genealogy [ˌdʒi:niˈalədʒi] n haifayya
general [ˈdʒenrəl] 1. *adj* na kowa
  2. n janar, (Nr) janaral 3. in
  general gālìbi
general assembly (UN) n
  taron babbar mashawarta

general election n babban zaɓe
generalise [ˈdʒenrəlaiz] v 1. yi na
mahaukaci 2. yi jam'i
generally [ˈdʒenrəli] adv gālìbī
generation [ˌdʒenəˈreiʃn] n 1.
sa'à 2. the younger
generation 'yan yau 3. the
older generation mazan jiya
4. the coming generations
zuriyar baya
generator [ˌdʒenəˈreitə] n
jànàrẽtò, (Nr) dìnàmô
generosity [ˌdʒenəˈrɔsəti] n halin
kyauta
generous [ˈdʒenərəs] adj mai
kyauta
genes [dʒiːnz] pl ƙwayoyin hali
genetics [dʒiˈnetiks] pl ilimin
ƙwayoyin hali
genial [ˈdʒiːniəl] adj mai kirki
genital [ˈdʒenitl] adj na al'aura
genitals [ˈdʒenitlz] n al'aura
genitive [ˈdʒenitiv] adj/n nasaba
genius [ˈdʒiːniəs] n ɗan baiwā
genocidal [ˈdʒenəsaidl] adj na
kisan ƙàrè-dangì
genocide [ˈdʒenəsaid] n kisan
ƙàrè-dangì
gentle [ˈdʒentl] adj 1. mai hankali
2. mai ladabi
gentleman [ˈdʒentlmən] n
(gentlemen) 1. dattijo 2.
mutum
gentleness [ˈdʒentlnis] n hankali
genuine [ˈdʒenjuin] adj na gaske
geography [dʒiˈɔgrəfi] n labarin
ƙasa
geologist [dʒiˈɔlədʒist] n mai
ilimin sanin ma'adinai
geology [dʒiˈɔlədʒi] n ilimin sanin
ma'adinai
geometry [dʒiˈɔmətri] n lissafi

germ [dʒəːm] n ƙwayar cuta
gesture [ˈdʒestʃə] n motsi
get [get; gɔt] v (got, gotten) 1.
samu 2. to get hurt ji ciwo
3. I got measles. Baƙon dauro
ya kama ni. 4. I will get
better. Zan sami sauƙi. 5. He
got a book from the library.
Ya ɗauko littafi daga laburare.
get along v yi shiri (with da)
get away v tsira
get back v dawo
get in v shiga
get off v sauka daga
get out v fita (of daga)
get ready v shirya
get to v ìsa
get through to v haɗu (with da)
get on well v gamsu
get up v tashi
ghastly [ˈgaːstli] adj ƙazami
ghetto [ˈgetəu] n unguwar
talakawa
ghost [gəust] n fatalwa
giant [ˈdʒaiənt] adj/n 1. ƙato
2. an economic giant gīwar
tattalin arzìkì
giddy [ˈgidi] adj mai jùwā
gift [gift] n kyauta
gifted [ˈgiftid] adj mai hazaƙa
gigantic [dʒaiˈgæntik] adj ƙato
giggle [ˈgigl] n ƙyalƙyàlà
gin [dʒin] n kōkinō
ginger [ˈdʒindʒə] n cìttař àhò
giraffe [giˈraːf] n raƙumin dawa
girl [gəːl] n yarinya
girlfriend [ˈgəːlfrend] n 1.
budurwa 2. ƙawa
give [giv] v (gave, given) 1. ba
2. bayar da
give away v 1. ba da 2. tona
wa... asiri

give back v mai da
give birth to v hàifà
give in v sakar (to wa)
give up v 1. sàdūdà 2. bari 3. daina
give way v ba da hanya
glacier ['glæsiə] adj kogin ƙanƙara
glad [glæd] adj mai farin ciki
gladden ['glædn] v faranta
gladly ['glædli] adv cikin murna
gladness ['glædnis] n murna
glance at [gla:ns] v ɗan dūbà
gland [glænd] n ɓangaren jiki mai aman abubuwan canja jiki
glass [gla:s] n 1. gilas 2. drinking glass gìlāshì, (Nr) ber
glasses ['gla:sìz] pl tabarau, (Nr) luleti
gleam [gli:m] v yi walƙiya
glide [glaid] v yi shawagi
glimpse [glimps] v hàngā
glitter ['glitə] v yi ƙyalƙyali
global ['gləubl] adj na duniya
globe [gləub] n 1. gulob, (Nr) gwàlâf 2. duniya
gloomy ['glu:mi] adj dùkū
glorious ['glɔ:riəs] adj mai girma
glory ['glɔ:ri] n yàbō
glossy ['glɔsi] 1. adj mai shèƙī 2. mujalla
glove [glʌv] n safar hannu
glow [gləu] v yi haskē
glue [glu:] 1. n gùlû, (Nr) kwâl 2. v liƙa
GNP duba wajen **gross national product**
go [gəu] v (**went, gone**) 1. je 2. tafi 3. tashi
go ahead v ci gaba
go ahead with v aiwatar da

goal [gəul] n 1. maƙasudi 2. (sport) gwâl, (Nr) bî 3. to score a goal ci gwal, (Nr) sa bi 4. duba wajen **goalpost**
goalkeeper ['gəulki:pə] n gōlà, (Nr) gòlê
goalpost ['gəulpəust] n gida
goat [gəut] n akwiya
go back v koma
go bad v ruɓe
go by v wuce
god [gɔd] n 1. Allah, Ubangiji 2. gulki
goddess ['gɔdis] n gunkiya
godless ['gɔdlis] adj kafiri
go down v 1. sauka 2. gangara
go far away v lūla
go fast v yi gudù
go in v shiga
going ['gəuiŋ] **to be going to** zâ...
gold [gəuld] 1. adj na zinari 2. n zinariya
golden ['gəuldn] adj na zinari
golf [gɔlf] n wasan golf
golf course n filin wasar golf
gone [gɔn] duba wajen **go**
gonorrhoea [,gonəri:ə] n ciwon sanyi
good [gud] 1. adj mai kyau 2. na kirki 3. mai amfani 4. n alheri 5. kirki 6. **for good** har abada 7. duba wajen **goods**
goodbye [,gud'bai] n 1. ban kwana 2. sai an jima!
good deed n alheri
good health n ƙoshin lafiya
good-looking adj kyakkyawa
good luck n sā'à
goodness ['gudnis] n nagarta
good quality n 1. kirki 2. of good quality nagari

good-tempered *adj* mai sanyin zuciya

goods [gʊdz] *n* 1. kaya 2. hājà

goods wagon *n* wagunu

goodwill [ˌgʊdˈwil] *n* fatan alhērì

go off *v* 1. tafi 2. ruɓe

go on *v* 1. ci gaba 2. gùdānà

goose [guːs] *n* (geese) dinya

go out *v* 1. fìta 2. mutu

go over *v* sākè

gorge [gɔːdʒ] *n* kwàzazzabò

gorgeous [ˈgɔːdʒəs] *adj* kyakkyawa

gorilla [gəˈrilə] *n* ƙaton biri wanda ba shi da wutsiya

gospel [ˈgɔspl] *n* Linjila

gossip [ˈgɔsip] 1. *n* jìta-jìta 2. *v* yi tsēgùmì

got [gɔt] *duba wajen* get

go through *v* kētà

go to sleep *v* yi barci

go towards *v* tìnkara

go up *v* tashi sama

gourd [gʊəd] *n* ƙwarya

govern [ˈgʌvn] *v* yi mulki

governing body [ˈguvəniŋ] *n* (acad.) hukūmar gudanarwa

government [ˈgʌvənmənt] *n* 1. gwamnati, (Nr) guhurnuma 2. mulkin ƙasa

government spokesman *n* kakakin gwamnatì

governor [ˈgʌvənə] *n* gwamna, (Nr) gwamnàn jahà

governor-general *n* gwamna janar

go with *v* dace da

gown [gaun] *n* riga

grab [græb] *v* (grabbed) ƙwace

grace [greis] *n* 1. albarkaci 2. alfarma

graceful [ˈgreisfl] *adj* mai alfarma

gracious [ˈgreiʃəs] *adj* mai albarkaci

grade [greid] *n* 1. daraja 2. (ed.) aji 3. maki 4. steepness grade gangare

gradual [ˈgrædjuəl] *adj* na yau da gobe

gradually [ˈgrædjuli] *adv* yau da gobe

graduate [ˈgrædjuət] *n* mai digiri, (Nr) mai difilam

graduate [ˈgrædjueit] *v* sami digiri

graft [graːft] 1. *n* hàndamā 2. *v* gwāmā

grain [grein] *n* 1. hatsi 2. ƙwaya

gram, gramme [græm] *n* giram

grammar [ˈgræmə] *n* nahawu

gramme [græm] *n* giram

gramophone [ˈgræməfəun] *n* garmahô

granary [ˈgrænəri] *n* rumbu

grand [grænd] *adj* 1. babba 2. muhimmi

grandchild [ˈgræntʃaild] *n* jika

granddaughter [ˈgræn,dɔːtə] *n* jika

grandfather [ˈgræn,faːðə] *n* kaka

grandmother [ˈgrænd,mʌðə] *n* kaka

grandson [ˈgrænsʌn] *n* jika

granite [ˈgrænit] *n* dutse

grant [graːnt] 1. *n* taimakon kuɗi 2. *v* ba da

grape(s) [greip] *n* inabi

grapefruit [ˈgreipfruːt] *n* garēhùl, (Nr) fanfalemus

grasp [graːsp] *v* laluba

grass [graːs] *n* ciyawa

grasshopper [ˈgraːshɔpə] *n* fārā

grateful [ˈgreitfl] *adj* mai jin godiya

gratis [ˈgraːtis] *adv* a banza
gratitude [ˈgrætitjuːd] *n* godiya
grave [greiv] **1.** *adj* mai nauyi **2.** *n* kabari
gravel [ˈgrævl] *n* tsakuwa
graveyard [ˈgreivjaːd] *n* makabarta
gravity [ˈgrævəti] *n* ƙarfin maganaɗisun ƙasa
gravy [ˈgreivi] *n* miya
gray [ˈgrei] *adj* toka-toka **2.** *duba wajen* **grey hair**
graze [greiz] *v* yi kiwo
grease [griːs] *n* **1.** maiƙo **2.** giris
greasy [ˈgriːsi] *adj* **1.** mai maiƙo **2.** mai giris
Great Britain [ˈgreitˈbritn] *n* Biritaniya
great [greit] *adj* **1.** babba **2.** muhimmi **3. a great deal** da yawa
great-grandchild [ˈgreitˈgræntʃaild] *n* tattaɓa-kunne
greatly [ˈgreitli] *adv* ƙwarai
greatness [ˈgreitnis] *n* daraja
greed [griːd] *n* haɗama
greedy [ˈgriːdi] *adj* mai haɗama
green [griːn] *adj* **1.** kore **2.** ɗanye **3.** (pol.) na lafiyar yanayin ƙasa
greengrocer [ˈgriːngrəusə] *n* mai kayan miya
greenhouse [ˈgriːnhaus] *n* gadinar rani
greens [griːnz] *pl* kayan lambu, (Nr) kayan garka
greet [griːt] *v* gayar da
greeting [ˈgriːtiŋ] *n* gaisuwa
grenade [grəˈneid] *n* gùrnât
grew [gruː] *duba wajen* **grow**
grey [grei] *adj* toka-toka
grey hair *n* fufura

grid [grid] *n* **1.** zanen yằwō **2.** gidajen wuta
grief [griːf] *n* tausayi
grieve [griːv] *v* yi baƙin ciki
grievous [ˈgriːvəs] *adj* mai tsanani
grill [gril] *v* gasa
grim [grim] *adj* mugu
grin [grin] *v* yi murmushi
grind [graind] *v* (**ground**) niƙa
grinder [ˈgraində] *n* injin niƙa, (Nr) màshîn kin niƙā
grip [grip] **1.** *n* riƙo **2.** *v* riƙe
groan [grəun] *v* yi gunaguni
grocer [ˈgrəusə] *n* mai kantin abinci iri-iri
groceries [ˈgrəusəriːz] *pl* kayan cefane
groin [grɔin] *n* kwankwaso
groom [gruːm] *n* **1.** ango **2.** ɗan barga
groove [gruːv] *n* tsāgì
gross earnings [grəus] *pl* albashi kashin ɗebe-ɗebe
gross national product (GNP) *n* kasafin da ƙasa ta tanada
ground [graund] *n* **1.** ƙasa **2.** *duba wajen* **grind, grounds**
groundnut [ˈgraundnʌt] *n* gyaɗa
grounds [graundz] *pl* **1.** fili **2.** dalili
groundwork [ˈgraundwəːk] *n* aikìn shìrye-shìrye
group [gruːp] **1.** *n* gungu **2.** ƙungiya **3.** *v* tara
grow [grəu] *v* (**grew, grown**) **1.** ƙaru **2.** yi girma **3.** noma **4.** (ec.) bunƙasa
grow up *v* balaga
grower [ˈgrəuə] *n* manomi
growl [graul] *v* yi gurnani

grown-up [grəunˈʌp] *adj/n* balagagge

growth [grəuθ] *n* 1. girma 2. ƙaruwa 3. (ec.) bunƙasa

growth-rate *n* 1. ƙarfin ƙaruwa 2. **negative economic growth rate** faɗuwar tattalin arziki

grudge [grʌdʒ] *n* **to hold a grudge against** ƙullataɗa

grumble [ˈgrʌmbl] *v* yi gunaguni

grumbling [ˈgrʌmbliŋ] *n* gunaguni

guarantee [ˌgærənˈtiː] 1. *n* garanti 2. *v* ba da tabbaci

guarantor [ˌgærənˈtɔː] *n* mai lamuni

guard [gaːd] 1. *n* mai gadi, (Nr) gardinye 2. **national guard** 'yan tsaron ƙasa, (Nr) gar-da-sarki 3. **presidential guard** sojoji masu tsaron lafiyar shugaban ƙasa 4. *v* tsare

guard duty *n* gadi

guardian [ˈgaːdiən] *n* mai riƙo

guerilla [gəˈrilə] *n* ɗan sari-ka-noƙè

guerilla warfare *n* yaƙin sari-ka-noƙè, yaƙin sunƙuru

guess [ges] 1. *n* cìntā 2. *v* cìntā

guesswork [ˈgeswəːk] *n* cìntā

guest [gest] *n* 1. bàƙō 2. **to be a guest of** bàƙuntà

guest house *n* gidan baƙi

guidance [ˈgaidəns] **to offer guidance** ja wa... gora

guide [gaid] 1. *n* ja-gora 2. *v* ja wa... gora

guidebook [ˈgaidbuk] *n* littafin ja-gora

guided missile [ˈgaidid] *n* harsashi mai linzami

guilt [gilt] *n* laifi

guilty [ˈgilti] *adj* 1. mai laifi 2. **to plead guilty** amsa laifi 3. **to find guilty** sami... da laifi

guinea-corn [ˈginikɔːn] *n* dāwà

guinea-fowl [ˈginifaul] *n* zabo

guise [gaiz] *n* siffa

guitar [giˈtaː] *n* garaya

gulf [gʌlf] *n* mashigin teku

gum [gʌm] *n* 1. danƙo 2. **chewing gum** cingam

gums [gʌmz] *pl* dasashi

gun [gʌn] *n* 1. bindiga 2. **to fire a gun** buga bindiga 3. **to load a gun** ɗura

gunman [ˈgʌnmən] *n* ɗan bindiga

gun powder *n* albarushi

gunrunner [ˈgʌnˌrʌnə] *n* ɗan sumogar makamai

gunrunning [ˈgʌnˌrʌniŋ] *n* sumogar makamai

gunship [ˈgʌnʃip] *n* jirgin rawan yaƙi

gush [gʌʃ] *v* bulbulo

guts [gʌts] *pl* 1. hanji 2. ƙarfin zuciya

gutter [ˈgʌtə] *n* mugunar ruwa

guy [gai] *n* mutum

gymnasium [dʒimˈneiziəm] *n* ɗakin motsa jiki

gymnastics [dʒimˈnæstiks] *n* wasannin motsa jiki

gynaecologist [ˌgainəˈkɔlɔdʒist] *n* likitan mata

gynaecology [ˌgainəˈkɔlɔdʒi] *n* ilimin kula da lafiyar mata

Hh

habit [ˈhæbit] *n* **1.** al'ada **2.** hali
habitable [ˈhæbitəbl] *adj* mai zaunuwa
habitat [ˈhæbitæt] *n* gida
habitation [həˌbiˈteiʃn] *n* mahalli
habitual [həbiˈtʃuːəl] *adj* na sabo
had [hæd] *duba wajen* have
haemorrhage [ˈheməridʒ] *v* zub da jini
haemorrhoids [ˈhemərɔidz] *n* bāsùr̃
hail [heil] **1.** *n* k̃ank̃ara **2.** *v* gayar da **3.** misalta
hair [heə] *n* **1.** gashi **2.** suma
hair-cut [ˈheəkʌt] *n* aski
hairbrush [ˈheəbrʌʃ] *n* buroshi
hairdresser [ˈheədresə] *n* makitsiya
hairdryer [ˈheədraiə] *n* mabushin gashi da lantarki
hairstyle [ˈheəstail] *n* ciko
hairy [ˈheəri] *adj* gàr̃gāsā
half [haːf; haːvz] *n* (*pl* **halves**) **1.** rabi **2. half past three** k̃arfe uku da rabi
half an hour *n* rabin awa
half-price *n* rabin kud̃i
half-time *n* (spor.) hutun rabin lokaci, haftayim
half-way *adv* tsakā-tsaki
hall [hɔːl] *n* babban d̃aki na taruwa
hallo [həˈləu] *duba wajen* hello
hallucinatory [həˌluːˈsiˈneitəri] *adj* mai sanya maye
halt [hɔːlt] *v* **1.** tsaya **2.** tsayar da **3. to come to a halt** dank̃wafe

halter [ˈhɔːltə] *n* ragama
halve [haːv] *v* raba biyu
halves [haːvz] *duba wajen* **half**
ham [hæm] *n* naman alade
hammer [ˈhæmə] **1.** *n* guduma, (Nr) marto **2.** buga
hamper [ˈhæmpə] *v* tsayar da
hand [hænd] **1.** *n* hannu **2. on the left hand** da hannun hagu **3. at/on hand** da ke akwai **4. on the one hand... and on the other** a wannan 6angare... a d̃aya 6angare kuma **5. on the other hand** amma dai **6.** *v* mik̃a
hand-made *adj* na aikin hannu
hand out *v* raba
hand over *v* mika
handbag [ˈhændbæg] *n* jakar mata, (Nr) såkwât
handball [ˈhændbɔːl] *n* k̃wallon hannu
handbrake [ˈhændbreik] *n* birkin hannu
handcuffs [ˈhændkʌfs] *pl* ankwa, (Nr) ankwar
handful [ˈhændful] *n* dintsì
hand-grenade [ˈhændgrəˌneid] *n* gùrnât
handicap [ˈhændikæp] *n* (spor.) rātā
handicapped [ˈhændikæpt] *adj* **1.** nàk̃àsasshē **2. mentally handicapped** taba66e
handkerchief [ˈhæŋkətʃif] *n* hankici, (Nr) musshawar
handle [ˈhændl] **1.** *n* marik̃i **2.** *v* tab̃a **3.** iya

handlebar [ˈhændlbaː] *n* hannun keke

handset [ˈhændset] *n* kan tarho

handshake [ˈhændʃeik] *n* musafaha

handsome [ˈhænsəm] *adj* kyakkyawa

handwriting [ˈhændˌraitiŋ] *n* rubutu

handy [ˈhændi] *adj* mai amfani

hang [hæŋ] *v* (**hung/hanged**) **1.** rataya **2.** rataye **3. to get the hang of** fara fahimtar

hanger-on *n* buwara

hang up *v* **1.** rataya **2.** ajiye tarho

hangar [ˈhæŋə] *n* rumfar ajiye jiragen sama

hanger [ˈhæŋə] *n* maratayi

hangman [ˈhæŋmən] *n* hauni

happen [ˈhæpən] *v* **1.** faru **2.** kasance

happily [ˈhæpili] *adv* cikin fara'a

happiness [ˈhæpinəs] *n* farin ciki

happy [ˈhæpi] *adj* mai farin ciki

harass [ˈhærəs] *v* matsa wa

harassment [ˈhærəsmənt] *n* matsawa, muzgunawa

harbour [ˈhaːbə] *n* tashar jiragen ruwa

hard [haːd] **1.** *adj* mai tauri **2.** mai wuya **3.** na cikin matsuwa **4.** *adv* ƙwarai

harden [ˈhaːdn] *v* ƙandare

hard hat *n* hular kwano

hard-hitting *adj* mai tsanani

hardly [ˈhaːdli] *adv* **1.** da ƙyar **2. Hardly anyone came.** Kusan ba wanda ya zo. **3. I hardly ever come here.** Ba safai na kan zo nan ba.

hardship [ˈhaːdʃip] *n* wahala

hardware [ˈhaːdweə] *n* injuna

hard work *n* ƙwàzō

hard-working *adj* mai aiki tuƙuru

hardy [ˈhaːdi] *adj* mai juriya

hare [heə] *n* zomo

harm [haːm] **1.** *n* cuta **2.** illa **3.** (leg.) lahani **4.** *v* yi wa... illa

harmattan [ˈhaːmətən] *n* hunturu

harmful [ˈhaːmfl] *adj* mai lahani

harmful effect *n* **to have a harmful effect** yi illa (**on** ga)

harmless [ˈhaːmlis] *adj* maras lahani

harmony [ˈhaːməni] *n* dàidàituwā

harness [ˈhaːnis] *n* kayan doki

harsh [haːʃ] *adj* matsananci

harvest [ˈhaːvist] **1.** *n* kaka **2.** *v* gìrbā

harvest time *n* kaka

has duba wàjen **have**

hassle [ˈhæsl] *n* màtsalà

haste [heist] *n* gaggāwā

hasten [ˈheisn] *v* gaggàutā

hasty [ˈheisti] *adj* mai gaggāwā

hat [hæt] *n* hula

hatch [hætʃ] *v* **1.** ƙyanƙyashe **2. to hatch a plot** yi ƙulli

hate [heit] **1.** *n* ƙiyayya **2.** *v* ƙi jinin...

hateful [ˌheitfl] *adj* mai ƙiyayya

hatred [ˈheitrid] *n* **1.** ƙiyayya **2. to feel hatred for** ƙi jinin...

haul [hɔːl] *v* ja

haunt [hɔːnt] *v* **1.** tayar da hankali **2.** duba wàjen **haunted**

haunted [hɔːntid] *adj* **a haunted house** gida mai fatalwa

Hausa [ˈhausə] **1.** *adj* na Hausa **2.** *n* Bahaushe **3.** Hausa

have [hæv] *v* (**had**) **1.** màllakà **2. I have a book.** Ina da

littafi. **3. We have returned.**
Mun dawo. **4. He has to come.**
Dole ya zo.
havoc [ˈhævək] *n* biji-biji
hawk [hɔːk] **1.** *n* shaho **2.** *v* yi
talla
hawker [ˈhɔːkə] *n* ɗan talla
hawking [ˈhɔːkiŋ] *n* tàllà
hay [hei] *n* ingirici
hay fever *n* haɓɓoje
hazard [ˈhæzəd] *n* haɗari
hazardous [ˈhæzədəs] *adj* mai
haɗari
haze [heiz] *n* hazo
he [hiː] *pro* **1.** shi **2.** ya
head [hed] **1.** *adj* babba **2.** *n* kai
3. shugaba **4.** *v* shugabanta
head for *v* nùfā
head pad *n* gammō
headphones [ˈhed,fəunz] *pl* belun
kunne
head towards *v* nùfā
headache [ˈhedeik] *n* ciwon kai
heading [ˈhediŋ] *n* kan bayani
headlight [ˈhedlait] *n* fitilar mota,
(Nr) idon mota
headline [ˈhedlain] *n* **1.** kanun
labari **2. to become headline
news** kasancē cikin kanun
labarai
headman [ˈhedmæn] *n* hēlùmà
(Nr) kwàntìr̃-mētìr̃
headmaster [ˈhedˈmaːstə] *n*
hedimasta
headmistress [ˈhedˈmistris] *n*
hedimistiris
headquarters [ˈhedˈkwɔːtəz] *n*
1. babban kamfani **2. police
headquarters** hedkwata, (Nr)
kwamseriya
headstart [hedˈstaːt] *n* rātā
heal [hiːl] *v* **1.** warkar da **2.** warke

health [helθ] *n* lafiya
health inspector *n* duba-gari
healthcare [ˈhelθkeə] *n*
hanyoyin kiwon lafiya
healthy [ˈhelθi] *adj* mai ƙoshin
lafiya
heap [hiːp] *n* tuli
hear [hiə] *v* (**heard**) **1.** ji
2. saurara
hearing [ˈhiəriŋ] *n* **1.** jî **2.** (leg.)
sauraron ƙara
heart [haːt] *n* **1.** zuciya **2. to
learn by heart** haddace
heart attack *v* ciwon zuciya
heartbeat [ˈhaːtbiːt] *n* bugun
zuciya
heartbreaking [ˈhaːt,breikiŋ] *adj*
mai ƙona zuciya
heartless [ˈhaːtləs] *adj* maras
tausayi
heart rate *n* saurin bugun
zuciya
heat [hiːt] **1.** *n* zafi **2.** *v* zafafa
heater [ˈhiːtə] *n* hītà
heated [ˈhiːtid] *adj* mai tsanani
heating [ˈhiːtiŋ] *n* ɗumama
heat stroke [ˈhiːtstrəuk] *n* (med.)
bugun rana
heatwave [ˈhiːtweiv] *n* ƙarin zafin
rana
heaven [ˈhevn] *n* **1.** sama
2. Aljanna
heavenly [ˈhevnli] *adj* na sama
heaviness [ˈhevinis] *n* nauyi
heavy [ˈhevi] *adj* mai nauyi
heavyweight [ˈheviweit] *adj* **1.**
zakara **2.** babba
Hebrew [ˈhiːbruː] *n* Yahūdancī
hectare [ˈhekteə] *n* sabuwar eka,
(Nr) eka
hectic [ˈhektik] *adj* mawùyàcī
hedge [hedʒ] *n* shinge

hedgehog [ˈhedʒhɔg] *n* bushiya
heed [hiːd] *v* kula da
heel [hiːl] *n* diddige
heifer [ˈhefə] *n* karsana
height [hait] *n* tsawo
heights [haits] *pl* tsaunuka
heir [eə] *n* magaji
heiress [ˈeəres] *n* magajiya
helicopter [ˈhelikɔptə] *n* jirgin sama mai saukar ungulu, helìkaftà, (Nr) èlìkàftâr̃
hell [hel] *n* Wuta
hello! [həˈləu] sannu!
helmet [ˈhelmit] *n* hular kwano
help [help] 1. *n* taimako 2. *v* tàimakà 3. I can't help doing... Na kāsà... 4. help! wayyo!
helper [ˈhelpə] *n* mataimaki
helpful [ˈhelpfl] *adj* mai taimako
helpless [ˈhelplis] *adj* mai rasa abin yi
hemisphere [ˈhemisfiə] *n* ɓangare
hemorrhage [ˈheməridʒ] *v* zub da jini
hemorrhoids [ˈhemərɔidz] *n* bāsùr̃
hen [hen] *n* kàzā
hence [hens] 1. *conj* saboda haka 2. *adv* nân dà
henceforth [hensˈfɔːθ] *adv* daga yau
her [həː] 1. ita 2. ta
herb [həːb] *n* ganye
herd [həːd] *n* garke
here [hiə] *adv* 1. nân 2. right here nân-nân
hereabouts [ˌhiərəˈbautz] *adv* nân kusa
hereditary [həˈreditri] *adj* na gàdò

heredity [həˈrediti] *n* gadon hali
heritage [ˈherətidʒ] *n* gādò
hero [ˈhiərəu] *n* (*pl* heroes) jarumi
heroin [ˈherəuin] *n* hōdàr̃ Ìblîs
heroine [ˈherəuin] *n* jaruma
heroism [ˈherəuizəm] *n* jarumtaka
hers [həːz] nàtà, tàtà
herself [həːˈself] kântà
hesitate [ˈheziteit] *v* They are hesitating. Suna duban bakin gatari.
hesitation [ˌheziˈteiʃn] *n* without hesitation bâ wata-wata
hiccough, hiccup [ˈhikʌp] 1. *n* shaƙuwa 2. *v* yi shaƙuwa
hidden [ˈhidn] *adj* damaluli
hide [haid] *v* 1. ɓuya 2. ɓoye
hide-and-seek [ˌhaidnˈsiːk] *n* wasan ɓuya
hideous [ˈhidiəs] *adj* mugu
hiding [ˈhaidiŋ] *n* to go into hiding shiga ɓūyā
hiding-place *n* maɓoya
high [hai] *adj* 1. mai tsawo 2. mai yawa 3. (sl.) to be high bugu
high commissioner *n* bàbban kwàmishinà
high court *n* babbar kotu
high jump *n* gasara tsalle
highlands [ˈhailəndz] *pl* tsaunuka
highlight [ˈhailait] 1. *n* mafi ban sha'awa 2. *v* haskaka 3. ba da ƙarin bayani
highly [ˈhaili] *adv* sosai
highness [ˈhainis] *n* mai martaba
highroad [ˈhairəud] *n* babbar hanya
high school [ˈhaiskuːl] *n* makarantar sakandare
highway [ˈhaiwei] *n* babbar hanya

highway code n dokar hanya
hijack [ˈhaidʒæk] v yi fashin jirgi
hijacker [ˈhaidʒækə] n ɗan fashìn jirgī
hijacking [ˈhaidʒækiŋ] n fashin jirgi
hike [haik] v yi yawo
hilarious [hiˈleəriəs] adj mai ban dariya ƙwarai
hill [hil] n tsauni
hilly [hili] adj mai tudu
him [him] shi
himself [himˈself] kânsà
hind [haind] adj na baya
hinder [ˈhində] v tauye
hindrance [ˈhindrəns] n tangaɽɗà
hinge [hindʒ] n hinji
hint [hint] 1. n habaici 2. **to drop a hint that** ba da haske game da cewa 3. v nuna
hip [hip] n ɗuwawu
hippopotamus [ˌhipəˈpɔtəməs] n dorina
hire [ˈhaiə] 1. n haya 2. v yi haya
hire-purchase n bashi da ruwa
hiring [ˈhaiəriŋ] n haya
his [hiz] nāsà, tāsà
hiss [his] v yi tsaki
historian [hiˈstɔːriən] n masanin tarihi
historical [hiˈstɔrikl] adj na tarihi
history [ˈhistri] n tarihi
hit [hit] v (**hit**) buga
hitch [hitʃ] n tangaɽɗà
hitch-hiking [ˈhitʃˌhaikiŋ] n neman rage hanya
hitherto [ˌhiðəˈtuː] adv à dâ
HIV virus n ƙwayoyin cuta na HIV
hive [haiv] n amya
hoard [hɔːd] v ɓoye
hoax [həuks] 1. adj na giri 2. n giri

hobble [ˈhɔbl] v dabaibàyē
hockey [ˈhɔki] n hoki
hoe [həu] 1. n fartanya 2. v yi noma
hog [hɔg] n alade
hold [həuld; held] v (**held**) 1. riƙe 2. ɗauka 3. **to hold a meeting** haɗar dà tārō 4. **to hold an inquiry** yi bincike 5. **to hold one's breath** ɗauke numfashi
hold back v 1. toge 2. tauye
holder [ˈhəuldə] n 1. mai akwai 2. mariƙi
hold office v 1. riƙe 2. muƙami
hold over v sâ à mālā
hold up 1. n fashi 2. v ɗaga 3. yi wa... fashi
hole [həul] n 1. huda 2. rami
holiday [ˈhɔlədei] n 1. ranar hutu, (Nr) raffo 2. (Isl.) Idi 3. **holidays** hutu, (Nr) bakans
hollow [ˈhɔləu] adj holoƙo
holocaust [ˈhɔləkɔːst] n kisan gilla
holy [ˈhəuli] adj mai tsarki
homage [ˈhɔmiʤ] n girmamawa
Home Office n (UK) ma'aikatar harkokin cikin gida
home [həum] n gida
homeland [ˈhəumlænd] n ƙasa
Homelands [ˈhəumlændz] pl yankuna na kabilun gargajiya
homeless [ˈhəumlis] n mai rashin matsuguni
home-made n na gida
home-sick adj **to be home-sick** yi kewar gida
home-sickness n kewar gida
hometown [ˈhəumtaun] n gari, garinmu
home trade n cinikin cikin gida
homework [ˈhəumwəːk] n aikin gida

homicide [ˈhɒmisaid] *n* kisan kai

homosexual [ˌhɒməˈsekʃuəl] *n* ɗan luɗu, 'yar maɗigo

homosexuality [ˌhɒməsekʃuˈælətɪ] *n* liwaɗi

honest [ˈɒnist] *adj* 1. mai ban gaskiya 2. (leg.) na halal

honestly [ˈɒnistli] *adv* da gaske

honesty [ˈɒnəsti] *n* gaskiya

honey [ˈhʌni] *n* zuma

honeymoon [ˈhʌnimuːn] *n* angwancì

honk [hɒŋk] *v* matsa ham, (Nr) yi oda

honour [ˈɒnə] 1. *n* girmamawa 2. in honour of na ban girma ga 3. *v* girmama 4. to honour a promise cika alkawari

honourable [ˈɒnərəbl] *adj* 1. mai mutunci 2. dattijo

hood [hud] *n* duba wajen bonnet

hoodwink [ˈhudwink] *v* yi wa... giri

hoof [huːf] *n* kofato

hook [huk] 1. *n* ƙugiya 2. *v* sarƙàfà (onto wa)

hooked [hukt] *adj* 1. mai lanƙwasa 2. He is hooked on drugs. Ya kamu da ƙwaya.

hookworm [ˈhukwəːm] *n* farar tsutsa

hooligan [ˈhuːligən] *n* ɗan bàngā

hoop [huːp] *n* ƙawanya

hoot [huːt] *v* matsa ham, (Nr) yi oda

hoover [ˈhuːvə] *n* hūbà

hop [hɒp] *v* yi tsalle

hope [həup] 1. *n* fata 2. *v* yi fata 3. to hope for yi fatan... 4. to give up hope fid da tsammani 5. to put one's hopes sa rai à (on a kan) 6. to hope for the best yi fatan alheri

hopeful [ˈhəupfl] *adj* mai fata

hopeless [ˈhəuplis] *adj* The situation is hopeless. Babu sauran sa rai.

horde [hɔːd] *n* cincirindo

horizon [həˈraizn] *n* sararin sama

horizontal [ˌhɒriˈzɒntl] *adj* a kwance

horn [hɔːn] *n* 1. ƙaho 2. ham, (Nr) oda 3. (mus.) kakaki

hornet [ˈhɔːnit] *n* rina

horrible [ˈhɒrəbl] *adj* 1. mugu 2. mai razanawa

horrid [ˈhɒrid] *adj* maƙetaci

horrify [ˈhɒrifai] *v* razana

horror [ˈhɒrə] *n* ràzanà

horse [hɔːs] *n* doki

horseback [ˈhɔːsbæk] *n/adv* on horseback a kan doki

horseman [ˈhɔːsmæn] *n* mai doki

horsepower [ˈhɔːspauə] *n* ƙarfin inji

horticulture [ˈhɔːtiˌkʌltʃə] *n* ilìmin shùke-shùke

hose [həuz] *n* mesa, (Nr) tiyo

hospital [ˈhɒspitl] *n* asibiti, (Nr) opital

hospitality [ˌhɒspiˈtælətɪ] *n* liyafa

host [həust] *n* 1. mai masauki 2. mai karɓi baƙunci 3. mai masaukin baƙi

hostage [ˈhɒstidʒ] *n* to take as hostage yi garkuwa da

hostel [ˈhɒstl] *n* ɗakunan kwanan ɗalibai

hostile [ˈhɒstail] *adj* mai adawa (to da)

hostility [hɒˈstilətɪ] *n* 1. gàbā 2. rikici

hot [hɒt] *adj* 1. mai zafi 2. mai yaji

hotel [həuˈtel] *n* hotel

hour [ˈauə] *n* **1.** awa **2.** **working hours** lokacin aiki

hourly [ˈauəli] *n* awa-awa

House of Commons *n* (UK) Majalisar Dokoki

House of Lords *n* (UK) Majalisar Dattijai

House of Representatives *n* (US) Majalisar Dokoki

house [haus] *n* **1.** gida **2.** soro

house arrest *n* **1.** ɗaurin talala **2. to put under house arrest** ɗora wa... ɗaurin talala

housebreaker [ˈhausbreikə] *n* ɓarawo

household [ˈhaushəuld] *n* **1.** iyali **2.** gida

householder [ˈhaushəuldə] *n* mai gida

housewife [ˈhauswaif] *n* uwargida

housing [ˈhauziŋ] *n* mahalli

hover [ˈhɔvə] *v* yi shawagi

hovering [ˈhɔvəriŋ] *n* shawagi

how [hau] **1.** yaya? **2.** haka **3. no matter how** ko ta halin ƙaƙa **4. How did Andrew do it?** Ta yaya Andrew ya yi haka? **5. I don't know how Andrew did it.** Ban ji yadda Andrew ya yi haka ba. **6. How are you?** Kana lafiya?

however [hauˈevə] **1.** *adv* ko yaya **2.** *conj* duk da haka

howl [haul] *v* yi kuka

how long? tun yaushe?

how many? nawa?

how much? How much is the book? Littafin nan kuɗinsa nawa ne?

how old? How old are you? Shekarunka nawa da haihuwa?

h.p. *duba wajen* **horse power**

hub [hʌb] *n* **1.** cibiya **2.** hôb

hubbub [ˈhʌbʌb] *n* rùɗami

hubcap [ˈhʌbkæp] *n* murfin wili, (Nr) anjalibar

huddle [ˈhʌdl] *v* tàkura

hug [hʌg] *v* rùngumà

huge [hjuːdʒ] *adj* ƙato

hull [hʌl] *n* gangar jiki ta jrgin ruwa

hum [hʌm] **1.** *n* amo **2.** *v.* yi waƙa

human [ˈhjuːmən] **1.** *adj* na 'yan Adam **2.** *n* ɗan Adam **3. the human race** jinsin ɗan Adam

human being *n* ɗan Adam

human error *n* laifin mutum

human nature *n* halin ɗan Adam

human rights *pl* hakkin ɗan Adam

humane [hjuːˈmein] *adj* mai mutunci

humanitarian [ˌhjuːˈmæniˈteəriən] *adj* na tausayin ɗan Adam

humanity [hjuːˈmænəti] *n* **1.** mutunci **2.** 'yan Adam

humble [ˈhʌmbl] *adj* mai tàwāliʼù

humid [ˈhjuːmid] *adj* mai laima

humidity [hjuːˈmidəti] *n* laima

humiliate [hjuːˈmilieit] *v* wulaƙantar da

humiliation [hjuːˌmiliˈeiʃn] *n* wulaƙanci

humility [hjuːˈmiləti] *n* tàwāliʼù

humorous [ˈhjuːmərəs] *adj* **1.** mai ban dariya **2.** mai barkwanci

humour [ˈhjuːmə] *n* ban dariya

hump [hʌmp] *n* tozo

hunch [hʌntʃ] *n* **to have a hunch** that kyautata zato cewa

hundred [ˈhʌndrəd] *n/adj* ɗari

hundredth [ˈhʌdrədθ] *adj* na ɗari

hundredweight [ˈhʌndrədweit] *n*
laba ɗari
hung [hʌŋ] *duba wajen* **hang**
hunger [ˈhʌŋgə] *n* yunwa
hungry [ˈhʌŋgri] **to be hungry** ji
yunwa
hunt [hʌnt] 1. *n* fàrautā 2. *v* yi
fàrautā 3. nema
hunting [ˈhʌntiŋ] fàrautā
hunter [ˈhʌntə] *n* mafarauci
hunting [ˈhʌntiŋ] *n* fàrautā
hurdles [ˈhəːdlz] *n* (spor.) gudun
tsallake shinge
hurl [həːl] *v* jefa
hurrah!, **hurray!** [huˈraː; huˈrei]
yawwa!
hurricane [ˈhʌrikən] *n* guguwar
iska mai ƙarfi
hurry [ˈhʌri] 1. *n* hanzari 2. **I am
in a hurry.** Ina sauri. 3. *v* yi
hanzari 4. **Hurry up!** Yi maza!
hurt [həːt] 1. *n* ciwo 2. *v* ji ciwo
3. ji wa... rauni
husband [ˈhʌzbənd] *n* miji
hush [hʌsk] *n* tsit

husk [hʌsk] *n* ɓuntu
hut [hʌt] *n* ɗaki
hydroelectric [ˌhaidrəuiˈlektrik]
adj na samar da wutar lantarki
hydroelectric dam *n* madatsar
ruwa ta samar da wutar lantarki
hyena [haiˈiːnə] *n* kura
hygiene [ˈhaidʒiːn] *n* kiwon lafiya
hygienic [haiˈdʒiːnik] *adj* na
kiwon lafiya
hymn [him] *n* (rel.) waƙe
hypertension [ˌhaipəːˈtenʃən] *n*
hauhuwar jini
hyphen [ˈhaifn] *n* gadà
hypnosis [hipˈnəusis] *n* kàu-dà-
idò
hypocrisy [hiˈpɔkrəsi] *n*
munafunci
hypocrite [ˈhipəkrit] *n* munafuki
hypocritical [ˌhipəˈkritikl] *adj*
mai fuska biyu
hypothesis [haiˈpɔθesis] *n*
hàsàshē
hysterical [hiˈsterikl] *adj* **to
become hysterical** haukace

Ii

I [ai] *pro* ni
Ibo [ˈiːbəu] *n* Ibo
ice [ais] *n* 1. ƙanƙara 2. ayis, (Nr) galas
iceberg [ˈaisbəːg] *n* tsibirin ƙanƙara
ice-cold *adj* ɗan karen sanyi
ice-cream [ˌaisˈkriːm] *n* aiskirim, (Nr) karamgalase
icy [ˈaisi] *adj* mai ƙanƙara
ID card [ˈaidiː ˌkaːd] *n* katin shaida, (Nr) kartidantite
idea [aiˈdiə] *n* 1. raˈayi 2. dabara
ideal [aiˈdiəl] 1. *adj* wanda ya dace 2. *n* aƙida
idealism [aiˈdiəlizəm] *n* hangen nesa
idealist [aiˈdiəlist] *n* mai hangen nesa
identical [aiˈdentikl] *adj* to be identical yi kunnen doki
identification [aiˌdentifiˈkeiʃn] *duba wajen* ID card
identify [aiˈdentifai] *v* 1. gane 2. tabbatar da
identity [aiˈdentəti] *n* asali
ideology [ˌaidiˈɔlədʒi] *n* manufa
idiot [ˈidiət] *n* wawa
idle [ˈaidl] *adj* na banza
idleness [ˈaidlnis] *n* ragwanci
idol [ˈaidl] *n* gunki
idolize [ˈaidəlaiz] *v* yi ƙaunā
i.e. (*id est* = *that is*) watau
if [if] *conj* 1. in, idan 2. dà 3. ko 4. **as if** sai ka ce 5. **even if** kō dà
if only *conj* dà mā

Igbo *n* Ibo
ignite [igˈnait] *v* kunna
ignition [igˈniʃn] *n* makunnin mota
ignorance [ˈignərəns] *n* jahilci
ignorant [ˈignərənt] *adj* jahili
ignore [igˈnɔː] *v* ƙyale
ill [il] *adj* mai rashin lafiya
ill-advised *adj* to be ill-advised yi kuskure
illegal [iˈliːgl] *adj* bà na hàlâk ba
illegally [iˈliːgəli] *adv* ba da izni ba
illegible [iˈledʒəbl] *adj* mai rashin cancanta
illegitimate [ˌiliˈdʒitimət] *adj* shege
illiteracy [iˈlitərəsi] *n* jahilci
illiterate [iˈlitərət] *adj* jahili
illness [ˈilnis] *n* ciwo
ills [ilz] *pl* economic ills taɓarɓarewar tattalin arziki
ill-treat *v* wulaƙanta
illuminate [iˈluːmineit] *v* haskaka
illumination [iˌluːmiˈneiʃn] *n* haske
illusion [iˈluːʒn] *n* shūcìn gizò
illusions [iˈluːʒnz] *pl* They have no illusions. Ba su da almara.
illustrate [ˈiləstreit] *v* 1. zana 2. misalta
illustration [ˌiləˈstreiʃn] *n* 1. zane 2. misali
image [ˈimidʒ] *n* 1. sura 2. suna
imaginary [iˌmædʒiˈneri] *adj* ba na gaskiya ba
imagination [iˌmædʒiˈneiʃn] *n* iya ƙaga

imagine [i'mædʒin] v 1. ƙaga 2. yi zato

imam [i'ma:m] n liman

IMF (International Monetary Fund) n Hukumar Kayyade Darajar Kudaden Duniya

imitate [·imiteit] v kwaikwaya

imitation [,imi'teiʃn] 1. adj jabu 2. n kwaikwayo

imitator [·imiteitə] n mai kwaikwayo

immeasurable [i'meʒərəbl] adj ba ya kimantuwa

immediate [i'mi:diət] adj da gaggawa

immediately [i'mi:diətli] adv 1. yanzu-yanzu 2. nan da nan

immense [i'mens] adj ƙato

immerse [·imə:s] v nitsar da

immigrant [·imigrənt] n 1. bàƙō, ɗan ci-rani 2. **illegal immigrant** bàƙon hàurē

immigrate [·imigreit] v ƙaura, tafi cin rani

immigration [,imi'greiʃn] n ci-rani

imminent [·iminənt] adj It is imminent. Aski ya kawo gaban goshi.

immoral [i'mɔrəl] adj 1. maras ɗa'a 2. (rel.) fasiƙi

immorality [,imɔ'ræliti] n 1. rashin ɗa'a 2. (rel.) fasiƙanci

immortal [i'mɔ:tl] adj mai ɗorewa

immune [i'mju:n] adj the human body's immune system ƙwayoyin da ke garkuwa da jikin mutum daga cututtuka

immunity [i'mju:nəti] n rigakafi

immunisation [,imjunai'zeiʃn] n lamba, (Nr) shasshawa

immunize [·imjunaiz] v yi wa... lamba

impact [·impækt] n to have an impact on shâfā

impair [im'peə] v hana

impart [im'pa:t] v bayar da

impartial [im'pa:ʃl] adj maras son kai

impartiality [im,pa:ʃi'aliti] n rashin son kai

impassable [im'pa:səbl] adj The road is impassable. Hanyar ba ta biyuwa.

impatience [im'peiʃns] n rashin haƙuri

impatient [im'peiʃnt] adj maras haƙuri

impeach [im'pi:tʃ] v tuɓe

impede [im'pi:d] v hana

impediment [im'pedimənt] n cikàs

impel [im'pel] v tilasta wa

impenetrable [im'penitrəbl] adj mai gàgàrà-shìgā

imperative [im'perətiv] adj wajibi

imperfect [im'pə:fikt] adj ba daidai ba

imperial [im'piəriəl] adj na mallaka

imperialism [im'piəriəlizəm] n mulkin mallaka

impersonate [im'pə:səneit] v yi sojan gona

impersonation [im,pə:sə'neiʃn] n yin sojan gona

impersonator [im'pə:səneitə] n sojan gona

impertinence [im'pə:tinəns] n tsiwà

impertinent [im'pə:tinənt] adj mài tsiwà

impetus [ˈimpitəs] *n* to give new
impetus bayar da sabon toho
(to ga)
implant [imˈplaːnt] *v* saka
implement [ˈimplimənt] **1.** *n*
kayan aiki **2.** *v* aiwatar da
implicate [ˈimplikeit] *v* aza wa...
laifi
implication [ˌimpliˈkeiʃn] *n* abin
nufi
implicitly [imˈplisitli] *adv* à
fàkàice
imply [imˈplai] *v* nuna a fakaice
impolite [ˌimpəˈlait] *adj* maras
ladabi
import [imˈpɔːt] **1.** *n* sayowa daga
ƙasashen waje **2.** *v* sayo daga
ƙasashen waje
import duties *pl* kuɗin fito
importance [imˈpɔːtns] *n* **1.**
muhimmanci **2.** girma
important [imˈpɔːtnt] *adj* **1.**
muhimmi **2.** babba **3.** the most
important mafî à'àlā
import-export business *n*
jigilar kaya da ƙasashen waje
importing [imˈpɔːtiŋ] *n* sayowa
daga ƙasashen waje
imports [ˈimpɔːts] *pl* kayan da
ake sayowa daga ƙasashen
waje
impose [imˈpəuz] *v* **1.** cusa (upon
wa) **2.** to impose a blockade
datse takunkumi **3.** to impose
a tax ɗora haraji (upon wa)
impossibility [imˌpɔsəˈbiləti] *n*
rashin yiwuwa
impossible [imˈpɔsəbl] *adj* maras
yiwuwa
impostor [imˈpɔstə] *n* sojan gona
impoverish [imˈpɔvəriʃ] *v* talàutā
impress [imˈpres] *v* ƙawatar da

impression [imˈpreʃn] *n* **1.** bùřgā
2. alama **3.** to be under the
impression ɗaukà (that cewa)
impressive [imˈpresiv] *adj* mai
cika fuska
imprison [imˈprizn] *v* ɗaure
imprisonment [imˈpriznmənt] *n*
1. ɗauri **2.** life imprisonment
ɗaurin rai da rai
improbable [imˈprɔbəbl] *adj* It is
improbable. Ba yâ yiwu ba.
improper [imˈprɔpə] *adj* maras
kyau
improve [imˈpruːv] *v* **1.** kyautata
2. gyara **3.** ìngantà **4.** (med.) ji
sauƙi
improvement [imˈpruːvmənt] *n* **1.**
kyàutàtuwā **2.** improvement in
relations ìngàntuwař dàngàntakâ
improvise [ˈimprəvaiz] *v*
kwàikwaiyà
imprudent [imˈpruːdənt] *adj*
That would be imprudent.
Wâuta ce a yi haka.
impudence [ˈimpjudəns] *n*
shegantaka
impudent [imˈpjudənt] *adj* shege
impulse [ˈimpʌls] *n* rashin tunani
impulsive [imˈpʌlsiv] *adj* jigìlì
impure [imˈpjuə] *adj* maras tsabta
impurity [imˈpjuriti] *n* gamî
in [in] *prep* **1.** in the room a cikin
ɗaki **2.** in the street cikin titi
3. in the hospital a asibiti **4.** in
the morning da safe **5.** He will
be back in a week. Bayan
mako guda zai dawo. **6.** He is
an expert in economics.
Gwani ne gurin ilimin tattalin
arziki. **7.** in English da Turanci
8. in my opinion a ganina
9. *duba wajen* into

in front *adv* a gaba

inability [ˈinəˈbiləti] *n* rashin iyawa

inaccessible [ˌinækˈsesəbl] *adj* The town is inaccessible. Garin ba ya shiguwa.

inaccurate [inˈækjərət] *adj* ba daidai ba

inaction [inˈækʃn] *n* rashin laka

inactive [inˈæktiv] *adj* mai

inadequate [inˈædikwət] *adj* inadequate housing rashin isasshen mahalli

inadvertently *adv* ba da gangan ba

inanimate [inˈænimət] *adj* maras rai

inappropriate *adj* to be inappropriate ba cancanta ba

inasmuch as [ˌinəzˈmʌtʃəz] *conj* tun da yake

inaudible [inˈɔːdəbl] *adj* wanda ba a ji

inaugurate [iˈnɔːgjureit] *v* naɗa

inauguration [iˌnɔːgjuˈreiʃn] *n* naɗi

incalculable [inˈkælkjuləbl] *adj* wanda ba a san iyakarsa ba

incapable [inˈkeipəbl] *adj* to be incapable of kasa

incendiary [inˈsendiəri] *adj* 1. mai gobara 2. mai ta da hankali

incense [ˈinsens] *n* turaren wuta

incense [inˈsens] *v* tunzura

incentive [inˈsentiv] *n* ihisānì

incessant [inˈsesnt] *adj* mai ɗorewa

incessantly [inˈsesntli] *adv* ba tsayawa

incest [ˈinsest] *n* jima'i da muharrami/muharrama

inch [intʃ] *n* inci

incident [ˈinsidənt] *n* 1. abin da ya faru 2. ɗan tashin hankali

incidentally *adv* af,...

incinerator [inˈsinəreitə] *n* bola

incision [inˈsiʒn] *n* yanka

incite [inˈsait] *v* hanzuga

inclination [ˌinkliˈneiʃn] *n* 1. sha'awa 2. ɗan tudu

incline [inˈklain] 1. *n* ɗan tudu 2. *v* yi tudu 3. *duba wajen* inclined

inclined [inˈklaind] *adj* to be inclined faye

include [inˈkluːd] *v* 1. haɗa da 2. ƙunsā

including [inˈkluːdiŋ] *prep* duk da

inclusive, inclusive of [inˈkluːsiv] *adj/adv* har zuwa

incoherent [ˌinkəuˈhiərənt] *adj* ba kai ba gindi

income [ˈinkʌm] *n* 1. albashi 2. gross income albashi gaba ɗaya

income tax *n* haraji

incomparable [inˈkɒmprəbl] *adj* to be incomparable wuce misali

incompatible [ˌinkəmˈpætəbl] *adj* mai gamin gàmbizà

incompetence [inˈkɒmpitəns] *n* rashin iya aiki

incompetent [inˈkɒmpitənt] *adj* sauna

incomplete [ˌinkəmˈpliːt] *adj* ba cikakke be

incomprehensible [inˌkɒmpriˈhensəbl] *adj* maras kai

inconceivable [ˌinkənˈsiːvəbl] *adj* ba ya yiwuwa

inconclusive [ˌinkənˈkluːsiv] *adj* They have held inconclusive discussions. An caɓa mahawara.

inconsiderate [ˌiŋkənˈsidərət] *adj*
maras kunya
inconsistent [ˌiŋkənˈsistənt] *adj*
to be inconsistent saɓa (**with**
da)
inconvenience [ˌiŋkənˈviːniəns] *n*
cikas
inconvenient [ˌiŋkənˈviːniənt] *adj*
to be inconvenient ƙuntata
(**for** wa)
incorporate [inˈkɔːpəreit] *v* ƙùnsā
incorrect [ˌiŋkəˈrekt] *adj* ba
daidai ba
increase [ˈinkriːs] **1.** *n* ƙari **2.** *v*
ƙara **3.** yawaita **4.** ƙaru
increased amount *n* ninki
incredible [inˈkredəbl] *adj* mai
wuce yarda
increment [ˈinkrimənt] *n* ƙari
incriminate [inˈkrimineit] *v* ɗora
laifi a kan...
incubate [ˈiŋkjubeit] *v* yi kwanci
incur [inˈkəː] *v* ci
incurable [inˈkjuərəbl] *adj* maras
magani
incursion [inˈkəːʃn] *n* (mil.)
katsalandan
indecency [inˈdiːsnsi] *n* tsiraici
indecent [inˈdiːsnt] *adj* maras
kunya
indecision [ˌindiˈsiʒn] *n* waswasi
indecisive [ˌindiˈsisiv] *adj* **to be
indecisive** yi waswasi
indeed [inˈdiːd] *adv* **1.** lalle
2. haba!
indefinitely [inˈdefinətli] *adv* sai
illa ma sha Allahu
indemnity [inˈdemnəti] *n* **war
indemnity** ramuwar diyya
independence [ˌindiˈpendəns] *n*
1. ʼyancin kai **2.** zaman kai
3. cin gashin kai

independent [ˌindiˈpendənt] *adj*
1. mai mulkin kai **2. an
independent newspaper**
jarida mai zaman kanta **3. of
independent means** mai cin
gashin kai
independent inquiry *n* bincike
da ba zai mara wa kowa baya
ba
indescribable [ˌindiˈskraibəbl]
adj maras misaltawa
indestructible [ˌindiˈstrʌktəbl]
adj **to be indestructible**
gàgarà
index [ˈindeks] *n* fihirisa
index finger *n* ɗan ali
indicate [ˈindikeit] *v* nuna
indicator [ˈindiˌkeitə] *n* sigina,
(Nr) kiliyotan
indict [inˈdait] *v* tùhumā̀
indictment [inˈdaitmənt] *n*
tuhuma
indifference [inˈdifrəns] *n* halin
kurum
indigenous [inˈdidʒinəs] *adj* na
asali
indigestion [ˌindiˈdʒestʃən] *n*
ɓacin ciki
indignant [inˈdignənt] *adj* **to be
indignant** ji takaici
indignation [ˌindigˈneiʃn] *n*
takaici
indigo [ˈindigəu] *n* shuni
indirect [indaiˈrekt] *adj* **1.**
kaikaitacce **2. to take an
indirect route** yi kewaye
indirectly [indaiˈrektli] *adv*
a fakaice
indiscipline [inˈdisiplin] *n* **1.**
rashin ɗaʼa **2. war on
indiscipline** yaƙi da rashin
ɗaʼa

indiscreet [ˌindiˈskriːt] *adj* maras asiri

indiscriminate [ˌindiˈskriminət] *adj* maras sabo

indispensable [ˌindiˈspensəbl] *adj* sai da shi

individual [ˌindiˈvidʒuəl] 1. *adj* ɗaya 2. *n* mutum

individualist [ˌindiˈvidʒuəlist] *adj* mai nuna son kai

individually [ˌindiˈvidʒuəli] *adv* ɗai-ɗai

indoctrinate [inˈdɔktrineit] *v* cusa wa

indoor [ˈindɔː] *adj* na cikin gida

indoors [ˈindɔːz] *adv* a cikin gida

induce [inˈdjuːs] *v* sa

indulge [inˈdʌldʒ] *v* shagwaɓar da

industrial [inˈdʌstriəl] *adj* na masana'antu

industrial exhibition *n* nunin kayan masana'antu

industrial products *pl* kayan da aka ƙera

industrial spy *n* mai leƙen asirin masana'antu

industrial tribunal *n* kotun sasantawa

industrial waste *n* sharar masana'antu mai illa

industrialize [inˈdʌstriəlaiz] *v* samar da masana'antu

industrialized [inˈdʌstriəlaizd] *adj* mai arzikin masana'antu

industries [ˈindəstriːz] *pl* 1. masana'antu 2. **service industries** kamfanonin ayyukan da ba na ƙère-ƙère ba

industrious [inˈdʌstriəs] *adj* mai himma wajen aiki

industry [ˈindəstri] *n* 1. ƙoƙari 2. masana'antu 3. **light industry** ƙananan sana'o'i 4. **heavy industry** manyan sana'o'i

ineffective [ˌiniˈfektiv] *adj* maras amfani

inefficient [ˌiniˈfiʃnt] *adj* maras aiki sosai

inequality [ˌiniˈkwɔləti] *n* rashin daidaito

inevitable [inˈevitəbl] *adj* It is inevitable that... Ba makawa sai...

inexcusable [ˌinikˈskjuːzəbl] *adj* maras dalili

inexhaustible [ˌinigˈzɔːstəbl] *adj* mai ɗorewa

inexpensive [ˌinikˈspensiv] *adj* mai araha

inexperience [ˌinikˈspiəriəns] *n* ɗanyantaka

inexperienced [ˌinikˈspiəriənst] *adj* ɗanye

inexplicable [ˌinikˈsplikəbl] *adj* maras bayani

in fact [inˈfækt] alhali

infallible [inˈfæləbl] *adj*

infamous [ˈinfəməs] *adj* riƙaƙƙe

infancy [ˈinfənsi] *n* jarintaka

infant [ˈinfənt] *n* jariri

infantry [ˈinfəntri] *n* dakaru

infatuation [inˌtætʃuˈeiʃn] *n* jaraba

infect [inˈfekt] *v* hàrɓā

infected [inˈfektid] *adj* **to be infected by a disease** kamu da cutā

infection [inˈfekʃn] *n* cuta

infectious [inˈfekʃəs] *adj* mai kamuwa

infectious disease *n* cuta mai kamuwa

infer [inˈtə] *v* ɗauka (**that** cewa)

inferior [inˈfiəriə] *adj* 1. maras aminci 2. ƙasa da

inferiority [inˌfiəriˈɔrəti] *n* ƙaskanci

infertile [inˈfəːtail] *adj* (med.) juya

infertile lands *pl* ƙasashe masu faƙo

infest [inˈfest] *v* hàřbā

infested [inˈfestid] *adj* to be infested harbu (with da)

infiltrate [ˈinfiltreit] *v* kurdàdà

infinite [ˈinfinət] *adj* bila haddin

infinity [inˈfinəti] *n* dàwwamà

infirm [inˈfəːm] *adj* kumama

infirmary [inˈfəːməri] *n* asibiti

infirmity [inˈfəːməti] *n* kumamanci

inflame [inˈfleim] *v* tunzura

inflamed [inˈfleimd] *adj* (med.) to be inflamed yi fushi

inflammable [ˈinflæməbl] *adj* 1. mai kamawa da wuta 2. mai rashin kamawa da wuta

inflammation [ˌinfləˈmeiʃn] *n* kumburi

inflammatory [inˈflæmətri] *adj* mai zuga mutane

inflate [inˈfleit] *v* 1. hura 2. (ec.) daga

inflation [inˈfleiʃn] *n* (ec.) hauhawar farashin kaya

inflexible [inˈfleksəbl] *adj* 1. maras lanƙwasuwa 2. to be inflexible tashi tsaye (about a kan)

inflict [inˈflikt] *v* to inflict harm ji wa... rauni

inflow [ˈinfləu] *n* capital inflow kuɗin jaura

influence [ˈinfluəns] 1. *n* tasiri 2. *v* yi wa.. tasiri

influenced to be influenced samo tasiri (by daga)

influential [ˌinfluˈenʃl] *adj* mài fàɗi à ji

influenza [ˌinfluˈenzə] *n* mura

influx [ˈinflʌks] *n* kwàřàřà

inform [inˈfɔːm] *v* sanar da

informal [inˈfɔːml] *adj* na wasa

information [ˌinfəˈmeiʃn] *n* 1. labari 2. bayani

information office *n* ofishin ba da labari

informed [inˈfɔːmd] *adj* sane (of da)

informer [inˈfɔːmə] *n* ɗan rahoto

infrastructure [ˈinfrəˌstrʌktʃə] *n* economic infrastructure tsarin da ake bukata domin tafiyar da tattalin arziki

infrequently [inˈfriːkwəntli] *adv* ba safai ba

infringe [inˈfrindʒ] *v* keta hakki

infuriate [inˈfjuːrieit] *v* tunzura

infusion [inˈfjuːʒn] *n* jiƙo

ingenious [inˈdʒiːniəs] *adj* mai fasaha

ingratitude [inˈgrætitjuːd] *n* rashin godiya

ingredients [inˈgriːdiənts] *pl* kayan miya

inhabited [inˈhæbit] *adj* The building is inhabited. Da mutane a gidan.

inhabitant [inˈhæbitənt] *n* mazauni

inhale [inˈheil] *v* zùƙà, shaƙa

inherit [inˈherit] *v* gàɗa

inheritance [inˈheritəns] *n* gàɗò

inhibit [inˈhibit] *v* hana

inhospitable [ˌinhɔˈspitəbl] *adj* rashin sakin fuska

inhuman [inˈhjuːmən] *adj* maras tausayi

inhumanity [ˌinhjuːˈmæniti] *n* rashin tausayi

initial [iˈniʃl] 1. *adj* na farko 2. *v* sa hannu

initiate [iˈniʃieit] *v* fara

initiative [iˈniʃətiv] *n* fasaha

inject [inˈdʒekt] *v* yi wa... allura

injection [inˈdʒekʃn] *n* 1. allura 2. yin allura

injunction [inˈdʒʌnkʃn] *n* (leg.) dokar dakatarwa

injure [ˈindʒə] *v* ji wa... rauni

injured [ˈindʒəd] *adj* to be injured yi rauni

injury [ˈindʒəri] *n* rauni

injustice [inˈdʒʌstis] *n* rashin adalci

ink [iŋk] *n* tawada

inland [ˈinlənd] *adj* cikin ƙasa

in-law [ˈinlɔː] *n* suruki, suruka

inmate [ˈinmeit] *n* fursuna

inn [in] *n* hotel

inner [ˈinə] *adj* na ciki

inner cabinet *n* manyan 'yan majalisar ministoci

inner city *n* cikin gari

inner tube *n* tif, (Nr) shambur

innocence [ˈinəsəns] *n* 1. rashin laifi 2. **to prove one's innocence** wanke kai

innocent [ˈinəsnt] *adj* maras laifi

innocent people *pl* mutane bayin Allah

innovation [ˌinəˈveiʃn] *n* sabon abu

innuendo [ˌinjuˈendəu] *n* habaici

innumerable [iˈnjuːmərəbl] *adj* to be innumerable ba lissaftuwa ba

inoculate [iˈnɔkjuleit] *v* yi wa.. lamba, (Nr) yi wa... shasshawa

inoculation [iˌnɔkjuˈleiʃn] *n* lamba, (Nr) shasshawa

inoffensive [ˌinəˈfensiv] *adj* maras lahani

input [ˈinput] 1. *n* bayanai 2. tofa albarkacin baki 3. *v* (input/inputted) shigar da bayanai

inquest [ˈiŋkwest] *n* binciken sanadin mutuwa

inquire [inˈkwaiə] *v* 1. tambaya 2. yi bincike

inquire at *v* tùntuɓà

inquire into *v* bincika

inquiry [inˈkwaiəri] *n* 1. tambaya 2. bincike 3. **an independent inquiry** bincike da ba zai mara wa kowa baya ba

inquisitive [inˈkwizətiv] *adj* mai ganin ƙwaf

inquisitiveness [inˈkwizətivnis] *n* shisshigi

inroad [ˈinrəud] *n* **to make inroads** ci gaba

insane [inˈsein] *adj* mahaukaci

insane asylum *n* gidan mahaukata

insanity [inˈsænəti] *n* hauka

inscription [inˈskripʃn] *n* rubutu

insect [ˈinsekt] *n* ƙwaro

insecticide [inˈsektisaid] *n* maganin kashe ƙwari

insecure [ˌinsiˈkjuə] *adj* to be insecure yi juyayi

inseparable [inˈseprəbl] *adj* mai rashin rabuwa

insert [ˈinsəːt] *v* sa

insertion [inˈsəːʃn] *n* 1. sakawa 2. sâ

inside [inˈsaid] 1. *n* ciki 2. *prep* a cikin 3. *adv* a ciki

inside-out *adj* bai-bai

insight [ˈinsait] *n* basira

insignia [inˈsignia] *n* lamba

insignificant [ˌinsigˈnifikənt] *adj* maras muhimmanci

insincere [ˌinsinˈsiə] *adj* mai romon baka

insincerity [ˌinsinˈseriti] *n* romon baka

insinuate [inˈsinjueit] *v* yi habaici (against wa)

insinuation [inˌsinjuˈeiʃn] *n* habaici

insist [inˈsist] *v* dage

insistent [inˈsistənt] *adj* mai naci

insolence [ˈinsələns] *n* tsaurin ido

insolent [ˈinsələnt] *adj* mai tsaurin ido

insolvency [inˈsɔlvənsi] *n* karayar arziki

insomnia [inˈsɔmniə] *n* rashin barci

insomniac [inˈsɔmniæk] *n* mai rashin barci

inspect [inˈspekt] *v* duba

inspection [inˈspekʃn] *n* dubawa

inspector [inˈspektə] *n* 1. health inspector duba-gari, (Nr) ɗan larwai 2. school inspector mai duba makarantu 3. police inspector sufeto

inspector-general *n* babban sufeton 'yan sanda

inspiration [ˌinspəˈreiʃn] *n* ilhama

inspire [inˈspaiə] *v* tsima

install [ˈinstɔːl] *v* 1. sa 2. naɗa

installation [ˌinstəˈleiʃn] *n* 1. sâ 2. abin da aka sa 3. naɗi

instalment [inˈstɔːlmənt] *n* 1. kashì 2. sâ

instance [ˈinstəns] *n* 1. for instance misalin 2. in the first instance da farko dai

instant [ˈinstənt] 1. *adj* nan take 2. *n* this very instant yanzu-yanzu 3. in an instant nan take

instantaneous [ˌinstənˈteiniəs] *adj* nan take

instantly [ˈinstəntli] *adv* nan take

instead [inˈsted] *adv* maimakon

instead of *prep/conj* a madadin

instigate [ˈinstigeit] *v* àngazà

instigation [ˌinstiˈgeiʃn] *n* at our instigation a bisa angazarmu

instinct [ˈinstiŋkt] *n* ilhami

instinctive [inˈstiŋktiv] *adj* It's instinctive. Ga jiki ya ke.

institute [ˈinstitjuːt] *n* cibiya

institute for strategic studies *n* cibiyar nazarin harkokin tsaro da makamai

institution [ˌinstitjuːʃn] *n* 1. babbar ƙungiya 2. al'ada 3. mental institution gidan mahaukata.

instruct [inˈstrʌkt] *v* 1. koya wa 2. umarta

instruction [inˈstrʌkʃn] *n* 1. umurni 2. koyarwa

instructions [inˈstrʌkʃnz] *pl* umurni

instruction book *n* ja-gora

instructive [inˈstrʌktiv] *adj* mai koyarwa

instructor [inˈstrʌktə] *n* malami

instrument [ˈinstrumənt] *n* 1. na'ura 2. kayan aiki 3. (mus.) kayan kiɗa

insubordinate [ˌinsəˈbɔːdinət] *adj* to be insubordinate ƙi bi

insubordination [ˌinsəˌbɔːdiˈneiʃn] *n* rashin biyayya

insufficient [ˌinsəˈfiʃnt] *adj* to be insufficient kasa

insulate [ˈinsjuleit] *v* rufe da

insulation [ˌinsjuˈleiʃn] *n* kuɓutarwa

insult [ˈinsʌlt] *n* zagi

insult [in·sʌlt] v zằgằ
insurance [in·ʃɔːrəns] n inshora,
(Nr) assirans
insurance agent n wakilin
kamfanin inshora
insure [in·ʃɔː] v yi wa... inshora
insurgence [in·səːdʒəns] n
tawaye
insurgent [in·səːdʒənt] n ɗan
tawaye
insurrection [,insə·rekʃn] n
tawaye
intact [in·tækt] adj 1. daidai
2. cif-cif
integral [·intigrəl] adj na game
integrate [·intigreit] v haɗe
integration [,inti·greiʃn] n 1.
haɗewar jama'a 2. racial
integration haɗewar al'ummomi
integrity [in·tegrəti] n mutunci
intellect [in·təlekt] n ilimi
intellectual [,inti·lektʃuəl] adj mai
ilimi
intelligence [in·telidʒəns] n 1.
hankali 2. hazaƙa 3. (mil.)
aikin leƙen asiri
intelligence agency/service n
sashen leƙen asiri
intelligent [in·telidʒənt] adj
haziƙi
intelligible [in·telidʒəbl] adj mai
fahimta
intend [in·tend] v nùfằ
intense [in·tens] adj 1. babba
2. mai tsanani
intensify [in·tensifai] v iza wuta
a...
intensity [in·tensəti] n tsanani
intensive [in·tensiv] adj mai
tsanani
intensive care n (med.) ɗakin
marasa lafiya sosai

intent, intention [in·tent;
in·tenʃn] n niyya
intentional [in·tenʃənl] adj mai
niyya
intentionally [in·tenʃənəli] adv
da gangan
interact [intər·ækt] v yi hulɗa
interactive [,intər·ækʃn] adj mai
hulɗace-hulɗace
intercede [,intə·siːd] v shiga
tsakani
intercept [,intə·sept] v dàtsằ
interchange [,intətʃeindʒ] n 1.
mararraba 2. musaya
intercourse [·intəkɔːs] n 1. hira
2. sexual intercourse jima'i
interdependence [,intədi·pendəns]
n dogaro da juna
interest [·intrəst] 1. n sha'awa
2. harka 3. one's own interest
son rai 4. in the public interest
don amfanin jama'a 5. (fin.)
kuɗin ruwa 6. v ba da sha'awa
interested [·intrəstid] adj to be
interested in yi sha'awar...
interest-free adj (fin.) maras
ruwa
interesting [·intrəstiŋ] adj mai
ban sha'awa
interface [·intəfeis] n 1. gami
2. musaya
interfere [,intə·fiə] v tsoma baki
(in cikin/ga)
interference [,intə·fiərəns] n 1.
shisshigi 2. transmission
interference tangarɗa
interim [·intərim] adj na wucin-
gadi
interim assembly n majalisar
wucin-gadi
interim government n
gwamnatin wucin gadi

interior [inˈtiəriə] **1.** *adj* na ciki
2. *n* ciki
interlude [ˈintəluːd] *n* ɗan hutu
intermediary [ˌintəˈmiːdiəri] *n* **1.**
wakili **2.** mai shiga tsakani
intermediate [ˌintəˈmiːdiət] *adj* **1.**
matsakaici **2.** madaidaici
intermission [ˌintəˈmiʃn] *n* ɗan
hutu
intermittent [ˌintəˈmitənt] *adj*
akai-akai
internal [intəːnl] *adj* na ciki
internal affairs *pl* harkokin
gida
international [ˌintəˈnæʃnəl] *adj*
na duniya
International Labour Organization *n* Kungiyar
Kwadago ta Duniya
international law *n* dokokin
ƙasashen duniya
International Monetary Fund (IMF) *n* Hukumar
Kayyade Darajar Kuɗi ta
Duniya
international news *n* labarun
duniya
international relations *pl*
hulɗoɗin ƙasashen duniya
international trade *n*
cinikayyar ƙasashen duniya
Internet [ˈintənet] *n* hanyoyin
sadarwa ta kwamfuta
interpret [inˈtəːprit] *v* **1.** yi tafinta
2. bayyana
interpretation [inˈtəːpriteiʃn] *n*
1. fassara **2.** ma'ana
interpreter [inˈtəːpritə] *n* tafinta,
(Nr) antamfereti
interrogate [inˈterəgeit] *v* tùhumtằ
interrogation [inˈterəˈgeiʃn] *n*
tuhuma

interrupt [ˌintərˈʌpt] *v* **1.** katse
wa
interrupt electricity *v* katse
wuta
interrupt talks *v* dakatar da
shawarwari
interruption [ˌintərˈʌpʃn] *n*
1. katsewa **2.** without
interruption babu fashi
intersection [ˌintəˈsekʃn] *n*
mahaɗa
intersperse [ˈintəspəːs] *v* tsarma
interval [ˈintəvl] *n* **1.** rabi **2.** at
intervals lokaci-lokaci
intervene [ˌintəˈviːn] *v* **1.** sa
baki **2.** (mil.) yi katsalandan
(in a)
intervention [ˌintəˈvenʃn] *n* **1.**
shisshigi **2.** (mil.) katsalandan
interview [ˈintəvjuː] **1.** *n* ganawa
2. intabiyu **3.** *v* gana da
intestines [ˈintesˌtainz] *pl* hanji
intimacy [ˈintiməsi] *n* shaƙuwa
intimate [ˈintimət] *adj* amini
intimidate [inˈtimideit] *v* ci wa...
da burga
intimidation [inˌtimiˈdeiʃn] *n*
kurari
into [ˈintu] *prep* **1.** a cikin **2.** to go
into shiga
intolerable [inˈtɔlərəbl] *adj* to be
intolerable ba ƙyalu ba
intolerance [inˈtɔlərəns] *n* rashin
girmamawa
intolerant [inˈtɔlərənt] *adj* mai
faɗin rai
intoxicated [inˈtɔksiˌkeitid] *adj*
bugagge
intoxication [inˈtɔksiˌkeiʃn] *n*
maye
intransigence [inˈtrænsidʒəns] *n*
taurin kai

intrepid [in·trepid] *adj* mai ƙarfin
zuciya
intricate [·intrikət] *adj* rikitacce
intrigue [in·tri:g] 1. *n* makirci 2. *v*
ƙayatar da
introduce [,intrə·dju:s] *v* 1. haɗa
(to da) 2. gabatar da
introduce a motion *v* (pol.)
gabatar da batu
introduction [,intrə·dʌkʃn] *n*
gabatarwa
intrude [in·tru:d] *v* shiga ba izini
intruder [in·tru:də] *n* ɓarawo
intrusive [in·tru:siv] *adj* mai
shisshigi
intrusion [in·tru:ʒn] *n* shisshigi
intuition [,intju:·iʃn] *n* ilhami
invade [in·veid] *v* màmayà
invader [in·veidə] *n* mamayi
invalid [in·vælid] *adj* maras ƙarfi
invalid [·invəlid] *n* naƙasasshe
invaluable [in·væljuəbl] *adj* mai
muhimmanci
invasion [in·veiʒn] *n* mamayewa
invent [in·vent] *v* 1. ƙaga
2. ƙirƙira
invention [in·venʃn] *n* 1. ƙirƙira
2. sabon abu
inventor [in·ventə] *n* mai
ƙirƙirowa
inventory [in·ventəri] *n* **to take
an inventory** ƙidaya kaya
invert [in·və:t] *v* kifa
invest [in·vest] *v* zuba jari (**in**
cikin)
investigate [in·vestigeit] *v* yi
bincike
investigation [in,vesti·geiʃn] *n*
bincike
investigator [in,vesti·geitə] *n* 1.
mai bincike 2. **private
investigator** ƙanshin gari

investment [in·vestmənt] *n* saka
jari
investor [in·vestə] *n* mai saka jari
invincible [in·vinsəbl] *adj* mai
nasara
invisible [in·vizəbl] *adj* **It is
invisible. Ba ya ganuwa.**
invitation [,invi·teiʃn] *n* gayya
invitation card *n* katin gayyata
invite [in·vait] *v* gàyyatà
invoice [·invɔis] *n* rasit
invoke [in·vəuk] *v* kirawo
involuntary [in·vɔləntri] *adj* na
tilas
involve [in·vɔlv] *v* shàfà
involvement [in·vɔlvmənt] *n* sa
kai
irascible [i·rasibl] *adj* mai saurin
fushi
Ireland [·aiələnd] *n* Ailan
iris [·airis] *n* ƙwayar ido
Irish [·aiəriʃ] *adj* ɗan Ailan
iron [·aiən] 1. *n* baƙin ƙarfe
2. ayan 3. **corrugated iron**
kwano 4. *v* goge
iron rule *n* (pol.) mulkìn
muzgùnâwà
ironic, ironical [ai·rɔnik; -əl] *adj*
It is ironic. Abin mamaki ne.
ironing [·aiəniŋ] *n* guga
irony [·aiərəni] *n* gatse
irradiate [i·reidieit] *v* haskaka
irrational [i·ræʃənl] *adj* mai
rashin tunani
irreconcilable [i,rekən·sailəbl]
adj hàihatàn-hàihatàn
irregular [i·regjulə] *adj* maras
tabbas
irregularity [i,regju·lærəti] *n*
rashin tabbas
irrelevant [i·reləvənt] *adj* maras
amfani

irreparable [i'repərəbl] *adj*
maras gyaruwa
irreplaceable [,iri'pleisəbl] *adj*
He is irreplaceable. Ba wanda
zai iya maye gurbinsa.
irresistible [,iri'zistəbl] *adj* maras
baruwa
irrespective of [,iri'spektiv] ko da...
irresponsibility [,iri,spɔnsə'biləti]
n rashin kamun kai
irresponsible [,iri'spɔnsəbl] *adj*
1. shawaraki 2. **an irresponsible
government** bàrà-gurbìn
gwamnatì
irrigate ['irigeit] *v* yi ban ruwa
irrigation [,iri'geiʃn] *n* ban ruwa
irrigation farming *n* noma na
ban ruwa
irritate ['iriteit] *v* 1. ba wa...
haushi 2. sa ƙaiƙayi
irritating ['iriteitiŋ] *adj* mai ban
haushi
irritation [,iri'teiʃn] *n* 1. haushi
2. ƙaiƙayi

is [iz] *duba wajen* **be**
Islam ['izla:m] *n* Musulunci
Islamic [iz'læmik] *adj* na
Musulunci
island ['ailənd] *n* tsibiri
isolate ['aisəleit] *v* ware
isolated ['aisəleitid] *adj* saniyar
ware
isolation [,aisə'leiʃn] *n* 1. kaɗaici
2. **in isolation** a kaɗaice
issue ['iʃu:] 1. *n* magana 2. *v* kafa
3. fito da
issue an order ba da umurni
it [it] *pro* 1. shi, ita 2. sa, ta
italics *pl* rubutun tafiyar tsutsa
itch [itʃ] 1. *n* ƙaiƙayi 2. *v* yi
ƙaiƙayi
itching ['itʃiŋ] *n* ƙaiƙayi
item ['aitəm] *n* abu
item by item *adv* fillà-fillà
itinerary [ai'tinərəri] *n* tafiya
its [its] nāsà, nātà
itself [it'self] kansa, kanta
ivory ['aivəri] *n* hauren giwa

Jj

jack [dʒæk] 1. n jâk, (Nr) kìr̃ìk
2. v ɗaga da jak
jackel [ˈdʒækl] n dila
jacket [ˈdʒækit] n jaket, (Nr) bês
jackpot [ˈdʒækpɔt] n ci zungure
jail [dʒeil] 1. n kurkuku, (Nr)
kaso 2. v ɗaure
jailer [ˈdʒeilə] n gânduɽ̃ôbà, (Nr)
mai gadin 'yan kaso
jalopy [dʒəˈlɔpi] n akwalà
jam [dʒæm] 1. n (UK) jam, (Nr)
kwanfitir 2. traffic jam
cunkoson motoci 3. v
(jammed) cunkusa 4. cije
jammed [dʒæmd] adj to become
jammed cije
January [ˈdʒænjuəri] n Janairu
jar [dʒaː] n kwalaba
jargon [ˈdʒaːgən] n sàr̃ā
jaundice [ˈdʒɔːndis] n ta jikà
javelin [ˈdʒævəlin] n (spor.) jifàn
māshì
jaw [dʒɔː] n muƙamuƙi
jazz [dʒæz] n waƙar 'jazz'
jealous [ˈdʒeləs] adj mai kishi
jealousy [ˈdʒeləsi] n kishi
jeans [dʒiːnz] pl jinz
jeep [dʒiːp] n jîf
jeer [dʒiːr] 1. n ihu 2. v yi ihu (at
wa)
jelly [ˈdʒeli] n (US) jam, (Nr)
kwanfitir
jeopardize [ˈdʒepədaiz] v ja
haɗari
jerk [dʒəːk] v karkaɗa
jersey [ˈdʒəːzi] n 1. suwaita
2. (spor.) jēsì

jet [dʒet] n 1. injin jirgin sama
2. jirgin sama 3. fighter jet
jirgin yaƙi
jet-lag [ˈdʒetlag] n gajiyar tafiya
jet-plane [ˈdʒetplein] n jirgin
sama
jetty [ˈdʒeti] n matsayar jirgi
Jew [dʒuː] n Bàyahūdè
jewel [ˈdʒuːəl] n jauhari
jeweller [ˈdʒuːələ] n sarkin ƙira
jewellery [ˈdʒuːəlri] n kayan ado
Jewish [ˈdʒuːiʃ] adj 1. na
Yahudawa 2. Bàyahūdè
job [dʒɔb] n 1. aiki 2. matsayi
jockey [ˈdʒɔki] n mahayin dokin
sukuwa
jog [dʒɔg] v yi ɗan guje-guje don
lafiya
jogging [ˈdʒɔgiŋ] n 'yan guje-
guje don lafiya
join [dʒɔin] 1. n haɗuwa 2. v haɗa
3. to join a club shiga ƙungiya
joint [dʒɔint] 1. adj na haɗin
gwiwa 2. n gaɓa 3. magami
4. joint of meat tsokar nama
joint commission n hukumar
haɗin gwiwa
jointly [ˈdʒɔintli] adv à hàɗe
joint statement n jawabin
haɗin gwiwa
joint-venture company n
kamfanin abokan zuba jari-
hujja
joke [dʒəuk] 1. n abin ba da
dariya 2. v yi barkwanci
joker [ˈdʒəukə] n mai barkwanci
joking [ˈdʒəukiŋ] n barkwanci

jolly [ˈdʒɔli] *adj* mai fara'a

jolt [dʒɔlt] *v* karkaɗa

journal [ˈdʒɔːnl] *n* **1.** mujalla
2. tarihi

journalism [ˈdʒɔːnəlizəm] *n* aikin jarida

journalist [ˈdʒɔːnəlist] *n* ɗan jarida

journalistic source [ˌdʒɔːnəˈlistik] *n* kafar labarai

journey [ˈdʒɔːni] **1.** *n* tafiya **2.** *v* yi tafiya

joy [dʒɔi] *n* murna

joy-ride [ˈdʒɔiraid] **1.** *n* daɗi-mota **2.** *v* yi tuƙin daɗi-mota

joyful [ˈdʒɔiful] *adj* mai jin murna

joyous [ˈdʒɔiəs] *adj* na murna

jubilee [ˈdʒuːbili] *n* biki

judge [dʒʌdʒ] **1.** *n* joji, (Nr) juju **2.** alƙali **3. chief judge** cif-joji **4.** *v* gani **5.** (leg.) yanke hukunci

judgement [ˈdʒʌdʒmənt] *n* **1.** hukunci **2. to pass judgement** yanke hukunci (**on** wa)

judicial [ˌdʒuːˈdiʃl] *adj* na shari'a

judo [ˈdʒuːdəu] *n* jido

jug [dʒʌg] *n* buta

juggle [ˈdʒʌgl] *v* yi wasa da ƙananan ƙwallaye

juggler [ˈdʒʌglə] *n* mai wasa da ƙananan ƙwallaye

juice [dʒuːs] *n* ruwan 'ya'yan itace

juicy [ˈdʒuːsi] *adj* mai ruwa-ruwa

juju [ˈdʒuːdʒuː] *n* juju

July [dʒuːˈlai] *n* Yuli

jumbled [ˌdʒʌmbəld] *adj* a barkatai

jump [dʒʌmp] **1.** *n* tsalle **2.** (spor.) **high jump** tsallen sama **3.** *v* yi tsalle

jump over *v* tsallake

jumper [ˈdʒʌmpə] *n* **1.** jamfa **2.** (spor.) wanda ya yi tsalle

jumping [ˈdʒʌmpiŋ] *n* tsallē

junction [ˈdʒʌŋkʃn] *n* mahaɗin hanya

June [dʒuːn] *n* Yuni

jungle [ˈdʒʌŋgl] *n* kurmin daji

junior [ˈdʒuːniə] *adj* ƙarami

junk [dʒʌŋk] *n* tàkàrcē

junta [ˈdʒʌntə] *n* mulkin soja

jurisdiction [ˌdʒuərisˈdikʃn] *n* iko

jurisprudence [ˌdʒuərisˈpruːdəns] *n* **1.** ilimin shari'a **2.** (Isl.) fiƙihu

juror [ˈdʒuərə] *n* ɗan shaidun kotu

jury [ˈdʒuəri] *n* shaidun kotu

just [dʒʌst] **1.** *adj* daidai **2. a just ruler** sarki mai adalci **3.** *adv* kawai **4. just now** ɗazu **5. just on time** daidai cikin lokaci **6. just so** daidai haka **7. I have just one brother.** Ina da ƙane guda kawai. **8. We just caught the train.** Da ƙyar muka sami jirgin ƙasa.

just as kamar yadda

just as if sai ka ce

just before a goshin

justice [ˈdʒʌstis] *n* **1.** adalci **2.** shari'a **3.** joji, (Nr) juju

justification [ˌdʒʌstifiˈkeiʃn] *n* hujja

justified [ˈdʒʌstifaid] *adj* mai hujja

justify [ˈdʒʌstifai] *v* ba da hujja

justly [ˈdʒʌstli] *adv* cikin adalci

juvenile [ˈdʒuːvənail] **1.** *adj* na yaro **2.** *n* yaro

juvenile delinquent *n* kangararre

Kk

Kanuri *adj/n* Kanuri
kapok [ˈkeipɔk] *n* audugar rimi
karate [kiˈbæb] *n* kร̃ร̃êt, (Nr) kร̃ร̃àtê
kebab [kiˈbæb] *n* tsire
keen [kiːn] *adj* 1. mai kaifi 2. mai himma 3. to be keen to ƙallafa rai
keep [kiːp] *n* 1. riƙe 2. ajiye 3. to keep doing riƙa 4. to keep the peace tsare zaman lafiya 5. to keep a promise cika alkawari
keep away *v* yi nesa (**from** da)
keep back *v* ja da baya
keep from *v* hana
keep on *v* riƙa
keep out *v* 1. kร̃rรจ 2. Keep out! Bâ shàgร̃!
keep quiet *v* yi shiru
keep to *v* dร̃gรจ kân
keeper [ˈkiːpə] *n* 1. marìƙi 2. *duba wajen* goalkeeper
keloid [ˈkiːlɔid] *n* tabo
kennel [ˈkenl] *n* gidan kare
kernel [ˈkəːnl] *n* ƙwaya
kerosene [ˈkerəsiːn] *n* kànànzîr, (Nr) fîtร̃rô
kerosene can *n* garwar kananzir
kettle [ˈketl] *n* 1. buta 2. electric kettle butar lantarki
key [kiː] 1. *adj* mafi muhimmanci 2. *n* mabuɗî, maƙulli, (Nr) lakile 3. madangwalin kwamfiyuta
key position *n* babban muƙami
keyhole [ˈkiːhəul] *n* kafar makulli
keyboard [ˈkiːbɔːd] *n* 1. tafintar

kwamfuta 2. (mus.) fiyano
kick [kik] 1. *n* harbi 2. *v* doka 3. hàrbร̃
kid [kid] *n* yaro, yarinya
kidding [ˈkidiŋ] *adj* No kidding! Bâ dร̃ma!
kidnap [ˈkidnæp] *v* sace
kidnapper [ˈkidnæpə] *n* masaci
kidney [ˈkidni] *n* ƙoda
kill [kil] *v* kashe
killer [ˈkilə] 1. *adj* mai kisa 2. *n* mai kisan kai
killer disease *n* cutar ajali
killing [ˈkiliŋ] *n* kisa
killjoy [ˈkildʒɔi] *n* ɗan bindiga-daɗi
kill time *v* yi zaman jiran lokaci
kiln [kiln] *n* huru
kilo, kilogramme [ˈkiːləu; ˈkiləgræm] *n* kilo, kilogiram
kilometre [kiˈlɔmitə] *n* kilomita, (Nr) kilometir
kin [kin] *n* dangi
kind [kaind] 1. *adj* mai kirki 2. *n* iri 3. to reply in kind mayar da martàni
kindergarten [ˈkindəgaːdn] *n* nasare, (Nr) matarnal
kind-hearted *adj* mai halin kirki
kindle [ˈkaindl] *v* kunna
kindness [ˈkaindnis] *n* 1. kirki 2. to do a kindness kyâutร̃ (**to** wa)
king [kiŋ] *n* sarki
kingdom [ˈkiŋdəm] *n* daula
kingship [ˈkiŋʃip] *n* sarauta

kinship [ˈkinʃip] *n* dangataka
kiosk [ˈkiːɔsk] *n* kiyas
kiss [kis] **1.** *n* sumba **2.** *v* sùmbatà
kit [kit] *n* kaya
kitchen [ˈkitʃin] *n* kicin, (Nr)
kizin
kite [kait] *n* fifilo
kitten [ˈkitn] *n* 'yar kyanwa
knack [næk] *n* baiwã
knead [niːd] *v* cuɗa
knee [niː] *n* gwiwa
knee-cap [ˈniːkæp] *n* ƙoƙon
gwiwa
kneel, kneel down [niːl] *v*
durƙusa
knew [njuː] *duba wajen* **know**
knickers [ˈnikəz] *n* kamfan mata
knife [naif] **1.** *n* (*pl* **knives**)wuƙa
2. soka wa... wuƙa
knight [nait] *n* barde
knit [nit] *v* saƙa
knives [naivz] *duba wajen* **knife**
knob [nɔb] *n* **1.** mariƙi
2. mamurɗi
knock [nɔk] *v* **1.** ƙwanƙwasa
2. buga
knock down *v* **1.** bankaɗe

2. banke **3.** rushe
knock out *v* buge har ƙasa
knock over *v* **1.** ɓarar da
2. *duba wajen* **knock down**
knocker [ˈnɔkə] *n* maƙwanƙwashi
knot [nɔt] **1.** *n* ƙulli **2.** *v* ƙulla
know [nəu] *v* (**knew, known**)
1. sani **2.** ji **3.** iya
know by heart *v* haddace
know-how [ˈnəuhau] *n* sanìn
makāmā/madafa
know how to *v* iya
knowledge [ˈnɔlidʒ] *n* **1.** sani
2. ilimi **3. branch of**
knowledge fanni
knowledgeable [ˈnɔlidʒəbl] *adj*
masàni
known [nəun] *adj* **1.** sananne
2. *duba wajen* **know**
knuckle [ˈnʌkl] *n* gaɓà
kobo [ˈkɔbɔ] *n* kwabo
kolanut [ˈkəulænʌt] *n* goro
Koran [kɔrˈaːn] *n* Alƙur'ani
kowtow [ˈkəutəuː ˈkautau] *v* yi
durƙusawa
k.p.h. (kilometres per hour)
kilomita cikin awa

Ll

label [ˈleibl] 1. *n* lamba 2. *v* laƙabtā

laboratory [ləˈbɔrətri] *n* ɗakin gwaje-gwaje

laborious [ləˈbɔːriəs] *adj* da wuya

labour [ˈleibə] 1. *n* aiki 2. ƙwadago **manual labour** leburanci 3. **seasonal farm labour** barema 4. (med.) **She is in labour.** Tana naƙuda. 5. *v* yi aiki

labourer [ˈleibərə] *n* lēbura

labour exchange, federal labour exchange *n* Hukumar Kwadago ta Tarayya

labour force *n* 'yan ƙwadago

Labour Party *n* Jam'iyyar Leba

labour union *n* ƙungiyar 'yan ƙwadago

lace [leis] *pl* **shoe laces** maɗaurin takalmi

lack [læk] 1. *n* rashi 2. *v* rasa

lad [læd] *n* yaro

ladder [ˈlædə] *n* tsani

ladle [ˈleidl] *n* ludayi

lady [ˈleidi] *n* misisi, (Nr) madan

lag [læg] 1. *v* **to lag behind** yi sanyin jiki 2. *see* **jet-lag**

lager [ˈlaːgə] *n* giya

lagoon [ləˈguːn] *n* tabki

laid [leid] *duba wajen* **lay**

lain [lein] *duba wajen* **lie**

lake [leik] *n* tabki

lamb [læm] *n* 1. ɗan tunkiya 2. naman ɗan tunkiya

lame [leim] 1. *n* gurgu 2. *v* gurgunta

lament [ləˈment] *v* yi kuka

lamentable [ləˈmentəbl] *adj* abin takaici

lamp [læmp] *n* fitila

lamp-post *n* càbê

lampshade [ˈlæmpʃeid] *n* murfin fitila

lance [laːns] *v* yanka

land [lænd] 1. *n* ƙasa 2. fili 3. *v* sauka 4. isa bakin ruwa

landholder [ˈlændˌhəuldə] *n* mai wuri

landing [ˈlændiŋ] *n* 1. sauka 2. **forced landing** saukar tilas

landlady [ˈlændleidi] *n* uwargida

landlord [ˈlændlɔːd] *n* 1. mai gida 2. maigidan haya

landmark [ˈlændmaːk] 1. *adj* babba 2. *n* alama

landscape [ˈlændskeip] *n* shimfiɗar wuri

landslide [ˈlændslaid] *n* gocewar ƙasa

lane [lein] *n* 1. lāyì 2. 'yar hanya

language [ˈlæŋgwidʒ] *n* 1. harshe 2. magana 3. **bad language** mugun baki

lantern [ˈlæntən] *n* fitila

lap [læp] 1. *n* cinya 2. (spor.) kewayen fili 3. *v* lashe

lapse [læps] *v* ƙare

laptop [ˈlæptɔp] *n* kwafutar tàfi-dà-gidankà

larder [laːdə] *n* kantar kicin

large [laːdʒ] *adj* babba

large-scale *adj* babba

laryngitis [ˌlærinˈdʒaitis] *n* shaƙewar murya

larynx [ˈlæriŋks] *n* màƙwallatò
laser [ˈleizə] *n* hasken wutar kimiyya
laser printer *n* babbar firinta
lash [læʃ] *v* 1.ɗaura 2. shauɗa wa bulala
lash out at *v* rāmà
lass [læs] *n* yarinya
last [laːst] 1. *adj* na ƙarshe 2. na dâ 3. **last night** jiya da dare 4. **last week** makon jiya 5. **last year** bàra 6. **in the last few months** a cikin watannin da suka gabata 7. **at the last minute** a lokacin da aski ya zo gaban goshi 8. **at last** a ƙarshē 9. *v* ɗore 10. yi ƙarƙo 11. **to last long** daɗe 12. **to last forever** dawwama 13. **to last till... kai zuwa...**
lasting [ˈlaːstiŋ] *adj* dawwamamme
lastly [ˈlaːstli] *adv* daga ƙarshe
latch [lætʃ] *n* sakata
late [leit] *adj* 1. mai makara 2. **the late Mr...** marìgàyi Màlàm... 3. **to be late** màkarà 4. yi latti
late-comer *n* makararre
lately [ˈleitli] *adv* kwanan nan
later [ˈleitə] 1. *adv* daga baya 2. bayan 3. **a little later** jim kaɗan 4. *duba wajen* **late**
latest [ˈleitist] *adj* 1. na daga yau-yau 2. **the latest news** labari mai ɗumi-ɗumi
lather [ˈlaːðə] *n* kumfa
Latin [ˈlætin] *n* Rumanci
latitude [ˈlætitjuːd] *n* layin da ya zagaye duniya
latter [ˈlætə] *adj* na ƙàrshên
latterly [ˈlætəli] *adv* kwanan nan
laugh [laːf] 1. *n* dariya 2. *v* yi dariya (at wa)

laughable [laːfəbl] *adj* mai sa dariya
laughter [ˈlaːftə] *n* 1. dariya 2. **to burst into laughter** bushe da dariya
launch [lɔːntʃ] *v* 1. gabatar da 2. saka jirgi a kan ruwa 3. harba roka
launch-pad *n* tashar harba roka
laundrette [ˌlɔːndəˈret] *n* ɗakin wanki
laundry [ˈlɔːndri] *n* 1. kayan wanki 2. ɗakin wanki
lava [ˈlaːvə] *n* aman wutar dutse
lavatory [ˈlævətri] *n* 1. bayan gida 2. **public lavatory** gidan wanka da bâ haya 3. **to go to the lavatory** kewaya 4. **to need to go to the lavatory** ji bayan gida
lavish [ˈlæviʃ] *adj* mai rawar gani
law [lɔː] *n* 1. shari'a 2. doka 3. **against the law** abîn ya zama ba ya bisa shari'a 4. **to break the law** karya doka 5. **to obey the law** bi doka 6. **to disobey the law** taka doka 7. **to implement a law** zartar da doka 8. *duba wajen* **jurisprudence**
law-court [ˈlɔːkɔːt] *n* kōtù, (Nr) jastis
lawful [ˈlɔːfl] *adj* 1. na doka 2. (Islam.) halal
lawn [lɔːn] *n* dausayi mai ciyawa
lawsuit [ˈlɔːsuːt] *n* 1. ƙara 2. **to file a lawsuit** kai ƙara
lawyer [ˈlɔːjə] *n* 1. lauya, (Nr) aboka 2. **defence lawyer** lauya mai kare wanda ake tuhuma 3. **prosecuting lawyer** lauyan gwamnati

lax [læks] *adj* mai rashin ɗa'a

laxative [ˈlæksətiv] *n* maganin wanke ciki

lay [lei] *v* **1.** ajiye **2. to lay an egg** saka ƙwai **3.** *duba wajen* **lie**

lay down *v* **1.** ajiye **2.** kafa

layer [ˈleiə] *n* kwanciya

layman [ˈleimən] *n* almajiri

lay off *v* sàllamà

lay on *v* ɗora

lay out *v* shimfiɗa

lay-out *n* tsari

laziness [ˈleizinis] *n* lalaci

lazy [ˈleizi] *adj* malalaci

lead [led] *n* darmā

lead [liːd] **1.** *n* alama **2.** *v* (**led**) ja wa... gora **3.** shugabanta **4.** bi **5. They are in the lead.** Su ne kan gaba.

leader [ˈliːdə] *n* shugaba

leadership [ˈliːdəʃip] *n* **1.** shugabanci **2. to assume leadership** amshi shugabanci **3. to take over leadership** karɓi jagoranci

leading [ˈliːdiŋ] *adj* **1.** shahararre **2. leading party figures** gâgga-gâggan wakilan jam'iyya

leaf [liːf] *n* (*pl* **leaves**) **1.** ganye **2.** warƙa

leaflet [ˈliːflit] *n* ƙasida

league [liːg] *n* (spor.) lîg-lîg

leak [liːk] **1.** *n* yayyo **2.** *v* yi yayyo

lean [liːn] **1.** *adj* siriri **2.** maras kitse **3.** *v* (**leant/ leaned**) dogara **4.** jingina **5.** karkace

lean against *v* jingina

leaned [liːnd] *duba wajen* **lean**

lean on *v* dogara

leanings [ˈliːniŋz] *pl* ra'ayi

leant [lent] *duba wajen* **lean**

leap [liːp] **1.** *n* tsalle **2.** *v* (**leapt/ leaped**) yi tsalle

leap over *v* tsallake

leap-year [ˈliːpjiə] *n* shekara mai kwana 366

learn [ləːn] *v* (**learnt/ learned**) **1.** koya **2.** ji **3. to learn by heart** haddace

learn of *v* gānō

learned [ˈləːnid] *adj* mai ilimi

learner [ləːnə] *n* ɗan koyo

learning [ˈləːniŋ] *n* ilimi

lease [liːs] **1.** *n* haya **2.** *v* ba da haya

least [liːst] *adj* **1.** mafi kaɗan duk **2. at least** aƙalla

leather [ˈleðə] *n* fātà

leather worker *n* baduku

leave [liːv] **1.** *n* izini **2.** lifi, (Nr) kwanje **3.** *v* (**left**) bari **4.** tashi **5.** rabu da **6.** *duba wajen* **left**

leave of absence *n* lifi, (Nr) farmaso

leave off *v* daina

leaves [liːvz] *duba wajen* **leaf**

lecture [ˈlektʃə] **1.** *n* lacca **2.** *v* ba da laccā

lecturer [ˈlektʃərə] *n* **1.** mai ba da lacca **2.** malamin jami'a

led [led] *duba wajen* **lead**

ledge [ledʒ] *n* kanta

ledger [ˈledʒə] *n* lajà

left [left] *adj* **1.** hagu **2. Not much is left.** Kaɗan ya rage. **3. There is little time left.** Lokaci ya ƙure. **4.** *duba wajen* **leave**

left-handed *adj* bahago

left over *adj* **to be left over** rage

left-wing *adj* (pol.) mai neman sauyi

left-winger *n* (pol.) mai neman
sauyi

leg [leg] *n* **1.** ƙafa **2.** (spor.) **first
leg** karo na farko **3. second leg**
karo na biyu

legacy [ˈlegəsi] *n* gādò

legal [ˈliːgl] *adj* **1.** na doka
2. (Isl.) halal

legal right *n* dama ta doka

legalization [ˌliːgəlaiˈzeiʃn] *n*
halattawa

legalize [ˈliːgəlaiz] *v* halàttā

legend [ˈledʒənd] *n* almara

legendary [ˈledʒəndri] *adj* na
almara

legible [ˈledʒəbl] *adj* mai
karantuwa

legion [ˈlidʒən] *n* **1.** ƙungiya
2. bataliya

legislate [ˈledʒisleit] *v* kafa doka

legislation [ledʒisˈleiʃn] *n* kafa
doka

legislative [ˈledʒislətiv] *adj* **1.** na
kafa doka **2.** na majalisa

legislative body *n* majalisa

legislator [ˈledʒisleitə] *n* mai
kafa doka

legitimacy [liˈdʒitiməsi] *n* **1.**
halak **2.** halaccì

legitimate [liˈdʒitimət] *adj* na
doka

leisure [ˈleʒə] *n* sukuni

leisurely [ˈleʒəli] *adj* sannu-
sannu

leisure time *n* lokacin
shaƙatawa

lemon [ˈlemən] *n* lemon tsami

lemonade [ˌleməˈneid] *n* ruwan
lemo, (Nr) limonat

lend [lend] *v* (**lent**) rântā wà

lend a hand *v* tayà

lender [ˈlendə] *n* mai ba da bashi

lending rate [ˈlendiŋ] *n* ƙa'idar
bashi

length [leŋθ] *n* **1.** tsawo **2. at
length** da daɗewa

lengthen [ˈleŋθən] *v* ƙara tsawo

lengthways [ˈleŋθweiz] *adv* a
tsaye

leniency [ˈliːniənsi] *n* afuwa

lenient [ˈliːniənt] *adj* mai afuwa

lens [lenz] *n* (*pl* **lenses**) ruwan
tabarau

lent [lent] *duba wajen* **lend**

leper [ˈlepə] *n* kuturu

leprosy [ˈleprəsi] *n* albaras

lesbian [ˈlezbiən] *n* 'yar maɗigo

lesbianism [ˈlezbiənizm] *n*
maɗigo

less [les] *adj* **1.** mafi kaɗan **2. to
do less** rage **3. more or less**
kusan

lessen [ˈlesn] *v* tsaigata

lesson [ˈlesn] *n* darasi

less than *prep* ƙasa da

lest [lest] *adv* don kada

let [let] *v* (**let**) **1.** bari **2.** ba da
gida/ɗaki haya

let alone 1. *conj* ballantana **2.** *v*
ƙyale

let down *v* bayar da

let go *v* **1.** saki **2.** sàllamà

let off *v* yafe wa

let out *v* sàkā

let up *v* tsagaita

letter [ˈletə] *n* **1.** wasiƙa, (Nr)
letar **2.** harafi

letter-box [ˈletəbɔks] *n* (UK)
akwatin wasiƙu

letter of the law ƙa'idojin doka

lettuce [ˈletis] *n* letas

level [ˈlevl] **1.** *n* tsawo **2.** yawa **3.**
adj mai lebur **4.** daidai **5. sea
level** tsagin ruwa **6.** *v* rusar da

level crossing n magama
lever [ˈliːvə] n liba
levy [ˈlevi] v sa haraji
lewd [ˈljuəd] adj na batsa
liability [ˌlaiəˈbiləti] n bashi
liable [ˈlaiəbl] adj 1. **He is liable for the damage**. Shi ke da alhakin gayra/biya. 2. **They're liable to come back**. Sâ dawo.
liar [ˈlaiə] n maƙaryaci
libel [ˈlaibl] 1. n sharri 2. v yi wa... sharri
liberal [ˈlibərəl] adj/n (pol.) mai sassaucin ra'ayi
liberality [libəˈræləti] n kyauta
liberalization [ˌlibərəlaiˈzeiʃn] **trade liberalization programme** shiri na sassauta harkokin ciniki
liberate [ˈlibəreit] v 'yanta (**from** da)
liberation [ˌlibəˈreiʃn] n ƙwaton 'yancì
liberation movement n ƙungiyar ƙwaton 'yanci
liberty [ˈlibəti] n 'yanci
librarian [laiˈbreəriən] n ma'aikacin laburare
library [ˈlaibrəri] n laburare, (Nr) bibilotek
lice [lais] duba wajen **louse**
licence [ˈlaisns] n 1. takardar izini, (Nr) lisans 2. **driving licence** lasin, (Nr) farmi
licence office n ofishin lasisi
licence plate n lambar mota, (Nr) limaron mota
license [ˈlaisns] v ba da lasisi
licensee [ˌlaisənˈsiː] n mai lasisi
lick [lik] v làsà
lid [lid] n murfi
lie [lai] 1. n ƙarya 2. v (**lay, lain**)

kwântā 3. (**lied**) yi ƙarya
lie down v yi kwanciya
lieu [ljuː] n **in lieu of** a maimakon
lieutenant [lefˈtenənt] n laftana, (Nr) itina
lieutenant-colonel [lefˈtenəntˈkɔːnl] n laftana-kanar
life [laif] n (pl **lives**) 1. rai 2. **way of life** rayuwa
life imprisonment n ɗaurìn râi da râi
life-belt n ɗamarar ceto
life-boat n jirgin ceto na ruwa
life insurance n inshorar kai
lifeless [ˈlaifls] adj maras rai
lifespan [ˈlaifspæn] n ajali
lifestyle [ˈlaifstail] n halin rayuwa
lifetime [ˈlaiftaim] n rayuwa
lift [lift] 1. n lifti 2. **to give a lift** ba da ɗani (**to zuwa**) 3. v ɗaga 3. **to lift subsidies** jânyè kuɗin cikò
ligament [ˈligəmənt] n jijiya
light [lait] 1. adj maras nauyi 2. mai haske 3. n fitila 4. haske 5. wuta 6. v (**lit**) kunna
lightbulb[ˈlaitbʌlb] n ƙwan lantarki
lighten [ˈlaitn] v 1. haskaka 2. rage nauyi
lighter [ˈlaitə] n ƙyastu, (Nr) birike
lighthouse [ˈlaithaus] n gidan fitila mai nuna hanya a teku
lightly [ˈlaitli] adv a hankali
lightness [ˈlaitnis] n rashin nauyi
lightning [ˈlaitniŋ] n walƙiya
lightning-strike n (pol.) ajiye kayan aiki
light switch n abin ɗana wuta
like [laik] 1. prep kamar 2. sai ka

ce 3. **to feel like doing** ji
4. **This looks like mine.**
Wannan shigen tawa. 5. **It
looks like rain.** Ga alama za a
yi ruwa. 6. *v* so
likelihood [ˈlaɪklɪhud] *n* alama
likely [ˈlaɪklɪ] *adj/adv* 1. mai
yiwuwa 2. ga alama
liken [ˈlaɪkn] *v* misalta
likeness [ˈlaɪknɪs] *n* shigĕ
likewise [ˈlaɪkwaɪz] *adv* kazalika
liking [ˈlaɪkɪŋ] *n* so
limb [lɪm] *n* 1. gaɓa 2. babban
reshe
lime [laɪm] *n* lemon tsami
limit [ˈlɪmɪt] 1. *n* iyaka 2. haddi
3. **age limit** yawan shekarun
da aka yanke 4. **speed limit**
ƙayyadadden yawan gudu
5. **to the limit of** iyakacin 6. *v*
iyakance
limitation [ˌlɪmɪˈteɪʃn] *n* haddi
limited [ˈlɪmɪtɪd] *adj* **to be
limited** yi ƙalilan
limited company *n* kamfanin
saka jari
limitless [ˈlɪmɪtləs] *adj* maras
iyaka
limp [lɪmp] 1. *adj* mai yaushi 2. *v*
yi ɗingishi
line [laɪn] *n* 1. layi 2. baiti
3. **telephone line** waya
lineage [ˈlɪnɪədʒ] *n* asali
line up *v* jera
linen [ˈlɪnɪn] *n* lilin
liner [ˈlaɪnə] *n* babban jirgin
ruwa
linger [ˈlɪŋgə] *v* yi shâwâgì
lingua franca [ˌlɪŋgwəˈfrænkə] *n*
harshen hulɗar ƙabilu
linguist[ˈlɪŋgwɪst] *n* masanin
harsuna

linguistic [lɪŋˈgwɪstɪk] *adj* mai
ilimin harsună
linguistics [lɪŋˈgwɪstɪks] *n* ilimin
harsună
lining [ˈlaɪnɪŋ] *n* shâfì
link [lɪŋk] 1. *n* hulɗa 2. haɗuwa
3. *v* haɗa
links [lɪŋks] *pl* 1. hulɗoɗi
2. dangantaka
lino, linoleum [ˈlaɪnəu; lɪˈnəuliəm]
n leda
lion [ˈlaɪən] *n* zaki
lioness [ˈlaɪənɪs] *n* zakanya
lip [lɪp] *n* leɓe
lip service *n* **to pay lip service**
yi magana ta fatar baka
lipstick [ˈlɪpstɪk] *n* jan-baki
liquefy [ˈlɪkwɪfaɪ] *v* mai da...
ruwa
liquid [ˈlɪkwɪd] 1. *adj* ruwa-ruwa
2. *n* ruwa
liquidate [ˈlɪkwɪdeɪt] *v* (fin.) yi
karayar arziki
liquidation [ˌlɪkwɪˈdeɪʃn] *n*
karayar arziki
liquor [ˈlɪkə] *n* barasa
list [lɪst] 1. *n* tsari 2. *v* lissafa
listen [ˈlɪsn] *v* sàuràrà
listen in *v* sauraro
listener [ˈlɪsnə] *n* 1. mai sauraro
2. **radio listeners** masu
sauraron rediyo
listings [ˈlɪstɪŋs] *n* jerin shirye-
shirye
listless [ˈlɪstlɪs] *adj* **to feel listless**
ji kasala
lit [lɪt] *duba wajen* **light**
liter [ˈlitə] (US) *n* lita, (Nr) litar
literacy [ˈlɪtərəsi] *n* karatu da
rubutu
literacy campaign *n* yaƙi da
jahilci, (Nr) kurdadi

literal [ˈlitərəl] *adj* na zahiri
literally [ˈlitərəli] *adv* ba habaici
ba
literate [ˈlitərəl] *n* masani
literature [ˈlitrətʃə] *n* adabi
litre [ˈlitə] *n* lita, (Nr) litar
litter [ˈlitə] *n* shārā
little [ˈlitl] **1.** *adj* ƙarami **2.** *adv*
kaɗan **3. a little** kaɗan
little by little *adv* **1.** à kwāna à
tāshì
live [laiv] *adj* **1.** mai rai **2.** mai
wuta **3. a raye 4. a live concert**
kana gani ana waƙa
live [liv] *v* **1.** yi rai **2.** zauna
livelihood [ˈlaivlihud] *n* gātā
lively [ˈlaivli] *adj* **1.** mai fara'a
2. mai ban sha'awa
liver [ˈlivə] *n* hanta
lives [laivz] *duba wajen* **life**
livestock [ˈlaivstɔk] *n* dabbobin
kiwo
livid [ˈlivid] *adj* **to be livid** hàsalà
living [ˈliviŋ] **1.** *adj* mai rai
2. *n* rayuwa **3. cost of living**
tsadar rayuwa **4. to make a
living** nemi abinci
living-room *n* falo
lizard [ˈlizəd] *n* ƙadangare
load [ləud] **1.** *n* nauyi **2.** kaya
3. *v* aza wa... kaya **4.** hau da
5. to load a gun ɗura
loading [ˈləudiŋ] *n* lodi
loaf [ləuf; ləuvz] *n* (*pl* **loaves**)
burodi
loan [ləun] **1.** *n* bashi **2. soft loan**
sassauƙan lamuni **3. to take
out a loan** ci bashi **4. to pay
back a loan** biya bashi
5. *v* rânta
loanword [ˈləunwəːd] *n* kalmar
aro

loathe [ləuð] *v* yi ƙyama
loathsome [ˈləuðsəm] *adj* mai
ƙyama
loaves [ləuvz] *duba wajen* **loaf**
lobby [ˈlɔbi] **1.** *n* (pol.) làllamà
2. hotel lobby haraba **3.** *v*
(pol.) làllamà
lobe [ləub] *n* fatar kunne
local [ˈləukl] *adj* **1.** na wuri ɗaya
2. na unguwa
local authority *n* hukumar gari
local council *n* gunduma,
hukumar gari
local government *n* ƙaramar
hukuma
locality [ləuˈkæləti] *n* haraba
localize [ˈləukəlaiz] *v* sarrafa
locate [ləuˈkeit] *v* **1.** gano
2. *duba wajen* **located**
located [ləuˈkeitid] *adj* **The town
is located in the north.** Garin
yana a arewa.
location *n* wuri
lock [lɔk] *n* **1.** *n* kuba **2.** *v* kulle
locked [lɔkt] *adj* a kulle
locksmith [ˈlɔksmiθ] *n* mai
makulli
locomotive [ˌləukəˈməutiv] *n*
tukunyar jirgi
locust [ˈləukəst] *n* fārā
lodge [lɔdʒ] **1.** *n* gida **2.** *v* saukar
da **3.** makàlē **4. to lodge a
complaint** kai ƙara
lodger [ˈlɔdʒə] *n* baƙo
lodgings [ˈlɔdʒiŋz] *n* masauki
loft [lɔft] *duba wajen* **attic**
lofty [ˈlɔfti] *adj* mai tsawo
log [lɔg] *n* gungume
log in *v* sa hannu
logic [ˈlɔdʒik] *n* **1.** hankali
2. (acad.) ilimin mandiki
logical [ˈlɔdʒikl] *adj* mai ma'ana

loins [lɔinz] *n* tsatsò
loiter [ˈlɔitə] *v* yi shàwāgì
loll about [lɔl] *v* shantàkē
lonely [ˈləunli] *adj* **1.** mai kaɗaici
  2. a kàɗaice
loneliness *n* kaɗaici
long [lɔŋ] **1.** mai tsawo **2.** dogo
  3. before long bằ dà daɗēwā
  ba **3.** in the long run a ƙarshe
  4. as long as matuƙar **6.** how
  long? tun yaushe? **7.** to last
  long daɗe **5.** *duba wajen* long
  for
long ago *adv* **1.** tun tuni **2.** not
  long ago nân bằ dà daɗēwā ba
long-distance call *n* wayar
  nesa
longer *duba wajen* long, no
  longer
long for *v* yi bege
longing [ˈlɔŋiŋ] *n* bege
longitude [ˈlɔŋgitjuːd] *n* layin da
  ya keta duniya
long-lasting *adj* mai danƙò
long-range weapons *pl*
  makamai masu cin dogon
  zango
long-sighted *adj* mai hangen
  nesa
long-term *adj* na dogon lokaci
look [luk] **1.** *n* kallo **2.** sifa
  3. *v* duba **4.** ba da alama
look after *v* kula da
look at *v* **1.** yi wa... kallō **2.** lura
  da
look back on *v* tuna da
look carefully after *v* ādànā
look for *v* nēmā
look forward to *v* sa ido ga
looking-glass [ˈlukiŋglaːs] *n* madubi
look into *v* bincika
look like *duba wajen* like

look-out *n* ɗauka
look out *v* **1.** mai da hankali
  2. look out! yi hankali!
look over *v* duba
look up *v* nēmā
look upon *v* yi là'akàrī
look up to *v* girmama
loop [luːp] *n* maɗauki
loophole [ˈluːphəul] *n* They found
  a loophole in the agreement.
  Sun sami kafar jure wa
  yarjejeniya.
loose [luːs] *adj* **1.** sako-sako
  2. to get loose sakì **3.** to let
  loose kwance
loosely [ˈluːsli] *adv* sako-sako
loosen [ˈluːsn] *v* sassauta
lopsided [ˌlɔpˈsaidid] *adj* to be
  lopsided karkace
loquacious [ləˈkweiʃəs] *adj* mai
  rùɗāmī
loquacity [ləˈkwæsəti] *n* rùɗāmī
lord [lɔːd] *n* **1.** mai sarauta
  2. (rel.) Our Lord Ubangiji
lorry [ˈlɔri] *n* (UK) babbar mota,
  (Nr) kamyo
lorry park *n* tashar mota
lose [luːz; lɔst] *v* (lost) **1.** ɓatar da
  2. I have lost my suitcase. Jaka
  ta ɓace mini. **3.** (spor.) We lost
  the game. An cinye mu a wasar.
lose face *v* He has lost face.
  Martabarsa ta zube.
lose hope *v* fid da rai
loser [ˈluːzə] *n* wanda bai ci ba
lose time *v* **1.** ɓata lokaci **2.** yi
  latti
loss [lɔs] *n* **1.** hasara **2.** fāɗuwa
  3. financial loss hasarar kuɗi
  4. loss of trust raguwar amana
  (in ga) **5.** to sell at a loss
  karyar da

lost [lɔst] *adj* **1.** to get/be lost ɓata hanya **2.** *duba wajen* **lose**
lot [lɔt] *n* **1.** fili **2.** rabo **3.** lots, a lot (of) da yawa **4.** quite a lot da ɗan dama
lotion [ˈləuʃn] *n* man shafawa
lots of [ˈlɔtsɔv] da yawa
lottery [ˈlɔtəri] *n* tambola
loud [laud] *adj* **1.** mai ƙarfi **2.** to read out loud karanta a fili
loudly [ˈlaudli] *adv* da ƙarfi
loudness [ˈlaudnəs] *n* ƙarfi
loudspeaker [ˌlaudˈspiːkə] *n* lasfika, (Nr) ofarlar
lounge [laundʒ] *n* falo
louse [laus; lais] *n* (*pl* **lice**) kwarkwa
love [lʌv] **1.** *n* soyayya **2.** *v* so **3.** ji daɗi **4.** to make love yi jima'i **5.** I have fallen in love. Na kamu.
lovely [ˈlʌvli] *adj* **1.** kyakkyawa **2.** mai kyau
lover [ˈlʌvə] *n* masoyi
love story *n* labarin soyayya
loving [ˈlʌviŋ] *adj* mai ƙauna
low [ləu] *adj* **1.** maras tsayi **2.** mai rahusa **3.** low voice murya mai taushi
low-key *adj* The party was low-key. Biki bai yi armashi ba.
Lower House [ˈləuə] *n* Majalisar Dōkōki
lower [ˈləuə] **1.** *adj* na ƙasa **2.** *v* saukar da **3.** rage **4.** to lower trade barriers kawar da kariyar ciniki
lowlands [ˈləulændz] *pl* kwari
loyal [ˈlɔiəl] *adj* mai biyayya
loyalty [ˈlɔiəlti] *n* biyayya
lp [elˈpiː] *n* (mus.) faifai
ltd *duba wajen* **limited**

lubricate [ˈluːbrikeit] *v* sa wa... giris
luck [lʌk] *n* **1.** sa'a **2.** gamon katari
luckily [ˈlʌkili] *adv* an yi sa'a...
lucky [ˈlʌki] *adj* **1.** mai sa'a **2.** mai gamon katari
lucrative [ˈluːkrətiv] *adj* mai tsoka
ludicrous [ˈluːdikrəs] *adj* na wofi
luggage [ˈlʌgidʒ] *n* kaya
lukewarm [ˌluːkˈwɔːm] *adj* **1.** mai ɗan ɗumi **2.** to be lukewarm towards yi sanyi-sanyi
lumber [ˈlʌmbə] *n* icen katako
luminous [ˈluːminəs] *adj* mai ƙyalli
lump [lʌmp] *n* **1.** guda **2.** ƙullutu
lump sum *n* to pay in a lump sum biya gaba ɗaya
lunacy [ˈluːnəsi] *n* hauka
lunar [ˈluːnə] *adj* na wata
lunatic [ˈluːnətik] *n* mahaukaci
lunch [lʌntʃ] abincin rana
luncheon, lunchtime [ˈlʌnʃən; ˈlʌntʃtaim] *n* abincin rana
lung [lʌŋ] *n* huhu
lure [luə] *v* jawo
lurk [ləːk] *v* laɓe
luscious [ˈlʌʃəs] *adj* mai daɗi
lust [ˈlʌst] *n* kwaɗayi
luxurious [ˈlʌgˈʒuəriəs] *adj* mai alatu
luxury [ˈlʌkʃəri] *n* alatu
luxury goods *pl* kayan ālātu
lying [ˈlajiŋ] *n* **1.** ƙarya **2.** *duba wajen* **lie**
lynch [lintʃ] *v* yi wà... kisàn àturè
lynch mob *n* 'yan kisàn àturè
lynch-law *n* dòkaŕ fiŕ'aunà, dòkaŕ àturè
lyrics [ˈliriks] *pl* rubutacciyar waƙa

Mm

MA (master's degree) *n* digiri na biyu

mac *duba wajen* **macintosh**

macabre [mə`ka:brə] *adj* mummuna

machine [mə`ʃi:n] *n* **1.** na'ura **2.** inji

machine-gun *n* bindigā mai ruwa

machinery [mə`ʃi:nəri] *n* injuna

machinist [mə`ʃi:nist] *n* afareta

macintosh [`mækintɔʃ] *n* **1.** (UK) rigar ruwa **2.** kwamfiyuta

mad [mæd] *adj* **1.** mahaukaci **2.** mai fushi **3.** He's mad about football. Yana masifar son kwallon kafa.

madam [`mædəm] *n* uwargida

madden [`mædn] *v* fusata

made [meid] *duba wajen* **make**

madhouse [`mædhaus] *n* gidan mahaukata

madman [`mædmən] *n* mahaukaci

madness [`mædnəs] *n* hauka

magazine [,mægə`zi:n] *n* mujalla

magic [`mædʒik] **1.** *adj* na dabo **2.** *n* dabo

magical [`mædʒikl] *adj* na sihiri

magician [mə`dʒiʃn] *n* mai dabo

magistrate [`mædʒistreit] *n* majistare, (Nr) majistara

magistrate's court *n* kotun majistare, (Nr) jastis

magnet [`mægnit] *n* maganadiso

magnificent [mæg`nifisnt] *adj* **1.** mai girma **2.** mai kyau **3.** mai ban mamaki

magnify [`mægnifai] *v* kara girma

magnifying glass [`mægnifaiŋ] *n* tabaron hangen nesa

magnitude [`mægnitju:d] *n* girma

mahogany [mə`hɔgəni] *n* icen madaci

maid [meid] *n* baranya

maiden [`meidn] *n* budurwa

maiden name *n* sunan yanka

mail [meil] **1.** *n* mel, (Nr) kure **2.** registered mail wasika ta gudu **3.** express mail wasika kar-ta-kwana **4.** *v* aika da

mail-bag [`meilbæg] *n* akwatin gidan waya

mailbox [`meilbɔks] *n* akwatin wasiku

mailman [`meilmæn] *n* masinjan gidan waya

mail-order [`meilɔdə] *n* cinikin gila/dillaliya

maim [meim] *v* lahanta

main [mein] *adj* babba

mainland [`meinlænd] *n* ketare

main road *n* babbar hanya

mainly [`meinli] *adv* galiban

mainstay [`meinstei] *n* bel

maintain [mein`tein] *v* **1.** rike **2.** kula da **3.** He is maintaining his position. Yana kan makaminsa.

maintenance [`meintənəns] *n* adani

maize [meiz] *n* masara

majestic [mə`dʒestik] *adj* mai alfarma

majesty [ˈmædʒəsti] *n* His Majesty Mai Alfarma

major [ˈmeidʒə] 1. *adj* muhimmi 2. *n* (mil.) manjo, (Nr) majar

major debtor nations *pl* ƙasashen da basussuka suka yi musu kanta

major powers *pl* (pol.) manyan ƙasashen duniya

major-general *n* (mil.) manjojanar

majority [məˈdʒɔrəti] *n* 1. mafi yawa 2. (pol.) masu rinjaye

majority rule *n* mulkin masu rinjaye

make [meik; meid] 1. *n* iri 2. *v* (made) yi 3. ƙera 4. naɗa 5. The guard made us wait outside. Mai gadi ya sa mu sauraro a waje.

make fun of *v* zòlayà

make love *v* yi jima'i

make out *v* gano

maker [ˌmeikə] *n* wanda ya yi

makeshift [ˈmeikʃift] *adj* na wucin-gadi

make-up *n* 1. kayan shafa 2. to put on make-up yi kwalliya

make up *v* 1. shirya 2. rama 3. ƙaga labari 4. yi kwalliya

make up one's mind *v* tsai da shawara

malady [ˈmælədi] *n* ciwo, (Nr) malati

malaria [məleəriə] *n* zazzaɓin cizon sauro, (Nr) zazzaɓin damina

male [meil] 1. *adj* namiji 2. *n* mutum

malice [ˈmælis] *n* mugun hali

malicious [məˈliʃəs] *adj* mamùgùncì

malign [məˈlain] *v* yi wa... sharri

malignant [məˈlignənt] *adj* mai yaɗuwa

mall [mɔl] *n* kantunan sai da kayan marmari

malnutreated [ˌmælnjuːˈtriːtid] *adj* mai rashin isasshen abinci

malnutrition [ˌmælnjuːˈtriʃn] *n* rashin isasshen abinci

malpractice [mælˈpraktis] *n* maguɗi

mammal [ˈmæml] *n* halitta mai ba-da-nono

man [mæn] *n* (*pl* men) mutum

manage [ˈmænidʒ] *v* 1. sarrafa 2. iya 3. We just managed to get it. Da ƙyar muka samu.

management [ˈmænidʒmənt] *n* 1. sarrafawa 2. gudanarwa 3. manajoji

manager [ˈmænidʒə] *n* manaja, (Nr) daraktar

managing director *n* manajan darakta

mandate [ˈmændeit] *n* 1. wakilci 2. (pol.) to cancel a mandate soke wakilci

mandatory [mænˈdeitəri] *adj* na dole

mane [mein] *n* geza

maneuver [məˈnuːvə] *duba* wajen **manoeuvre**

mango [ˌmæŋgəu] *n* magwaro

manhood [ˈmænhud] *n* mazakuta

mania [ˈmeiniə] *n* 1. hauka 2. jaraba

maniac [ˈmeiniæk] *n* mahaukaci

manicure [ˈmænikjuə] *v* yanka farce

manifest [ˈmænifest] *v* nuna

manifesto [ˌmæniˈfestəu] *n* 1. manufa 2. the Communist

Manifesto Manufofin Gurguzu

manioc [ˈmæniɔk] *n* rogo

manipulate [məˈnipjuleit] *v* **1.**
sarrafa **2.** mallaka

manipulation [mə,nipjuˈleiʃn] *n*
1. sarrafawa **2.** (pol.) maguɗi

mankind [mænˈkaind] *n* 'yan
Adam

man-made *adj* na ƙirar ɗan
Adam

mannequin [ˈmænikin] *n*
mutum-mutumi

manner [ˈmænə] *n* **1.** hanya
2. hali **3.** iri

manners [ˈmænəz] *pl* ladabi

mannerism [ˈmænərizm] *n*
ɗabi'a

manoeuvre [məˈnuːvə] **1.** *n*
noƙewa **2.** *v* yi kwana (around
wa) **3.** *duba wajen* **manoeuvres**

manoeuvres [məˈnuːvəz] *n*
(mil.) **1.** atasaye **2.** **land
manoeuvres** rawar daji **3.** **sea
manoeuvres** rawar daji a teku

manor [ˈmænə] *n* gidan gona

manpower [ˈmænpauə] *n* 'yan
ƙwadago

mansion [ˈmænʃn] *n* babban
gida

manslaughter [ˈmænslɔːtə] *n*
mutuwar ajali

mantle [ˈmæntl] *n* mantir

manual [ˌmænjuəl] **1.** *adj* na
hannu **2.** *n* littafin bayani

manufacture [ˌmænjuˈfæktʃə] **1.**
n ƙira **2.** ƙera

manufactured [ˌmænjuˈfæktʃəd]
adj ƙerarre

manufactured goods *pl* kayan
da aka ƙera

manufacturer [ˌmænjuˈfæktʃərə]
n kamfanin ƙira

manufacturing [ˌmænjuˈfæktʃəriŋ]
n ƙira

manure [məˈnjuə] *n* taki

manuscript [ˈmænjuskript] *n*
littafin da ba a buga ba

many [ˈmeni] *adj* **1.** da yawa **2.**
as many as ko nawa **3.** **how
many?** nawa?

map [mæp] *n* taswira

map out *v* tsara

mar [maː] *v* lalata

marathon [ˈmærəθən] *n* gudun
dogon zango

marble [ˈmaːbl] *n* marmara

march [maːtʃ] **1.** *n* zanga-zanga
2. *v* (mil.) yi maci, (Nr) yi
defile

March *n* Maris

mare [meə] *n* goɗiya

margarine [ˌmaːdʒəˈriːn] *n* bota

margin [ˈmaːdʒin] *n* gefe

marijuana [ˌmæriˈhwaːnə] *n*
wiwi

marine [məˈriːn] **1.** *adj* na teku
2. *n* soja na rundunar jiragen
ruwa

mariner [ˈmærinə] *n* ma'aikacin
jirgin ruwa

maritime [ˈmæritaim] *adj* na teku

mark [maːk] **1.** *n* alama **2.** aibi
3. (acad.) maki **4.** *v* sa alama
5. (acad.) gyara **6.** *duba wajen*
deutschmark

mark out *v* shata

market [ˈmaːkit] **1.** *adj* na
kawsuwa **2.** *n* kasuwa **3.** *duba
wajen* **black market**

market competition *n*
gogayyar kasuwanci

marketing [ˈmaːkitiŋ] *n* kasuwanci

marketing board hukumar
kasuwanci

marmalade [ˈmaːməleid] n (UK) jam

marriage [ˈmæridʒ] n aure

married [ˈmærid] adj wanda ya yi aure

marrow [ˈmærəu] n 1. kabushi 2. ɓargo

marry [ˈmæri] v 1. yi aure 2. ɗaura wa... aure

marsh [maːʃ] n fadama

marshal [ˈmaːʃl] n māshàl

marshy [ˈmaːʃi] adj mai laka

martial law [ˈmaːʃl] n dokar soja

martyr [ˈmaːtə] n shahidi

martyrdom [ˈmaːtədəm] n shahada

marvel [ˈmaːvl] v yi mamaki

marvellous [ˈmaːvələs] adj mai ban mamaki

Marxism [ˈmaːksizəm] n Makisanci

masculine [ˈmæskjulin] adj namiji

masculinity [ˌmæskjuˈliniti] n mazakuta

mash [mæʃ] v markaɗa

mask [maːsk] 1. n abin rufe fuska 2. v ɓoye

mason [ˈmeisn] n magini

mass [mæs] 1. n ɗimbi 2. (Chr.) hōlìmâs 3. v tara

mass meeting n tsaron jama'a

mass-circulation newspaper n jaridar da aka fi sayarwa

massacre [ˈmæsəkə] 1. n kisan gilla 2. v tarwatsa, yi wa... kisan gilla

massage [ˈmæsaːʒ] n/v tausa

massive [ˈmæsiv] adj 1. ƙato 2. **a massive campaign** gagarumin kamfe

mass media n kafofin watsa labarai

mast [maːst] n maratayin ƙaramin jirgi

master [ˈmaːstə] 1. n maigida 2. malami 3. v ƙware 4. duba wajen **schoolmaster**

Master's [ˈmaːstəz] n digiri na biyu

masterly [ˈmaːstəli] adj mai fasaha

masterpiece [ˈmaːstəpiːs] n fitaccen aiki

mastery [ˈmaːstəri] n fasaha

mat [mæt] n tabarma

match [mætʃ] 1. n ashana, (Nr) alimeti 2. (spor.) wasa 3. v dace da 4. yi daidai

match-box n gidan ashana

matchless [ˈmætʃlis] adj ba irinsa

mate [meit] 1. n aboki 2. v yi barbara

material [məˈtiəriəl] n 1. yadi 2. kaya 3. duba wajen **materials**

materialize [məˈtiəriəlaiz] v bàyyanà

materials [məˈtiəriəlz] pl 1. **building materials** kayan gini 2. **raw materials**

materiel [məˈtiəriəl] n **war materiel** kayan yaƙi

maternal [məˈtəːnl] adj na uwa

maternal aunt n inna

maternity [məˈtəːnəti] adj na haihuwa

maternity clinic n asibitin haihuwa

maternity leave n hutun jego

maths, mathematics [mæθs; ˌmæθəˈmætiks] n ilimin lissafi

matrimony [ˈmætriməni] n aure

matron [ˈmeitrən] n (med.) babbar sista, magajiya

matter [ˈmætə] **1.** n kaya
2. al'amari **3.** What's the
matter? Akwai wata matsala?
4. v It doesn't matter. Ba
kome.

mattress [ˈmætris] n katifa, (Nr)
matala

mature [məˈtjuə] **1.** adj
balagagge **2.** mai kamun kai
3. v bàlagà **4.** nũna

maturity [məˈtjuərəti] n halin
dattako

mausoleum [ˌmɔːsəˈliːəm] n
babban kushewa

maxim [ˈmæksim] n tãkẽ

maximum [ˈmæksiməm] adj/ n
iyaka

May [mei] n Mayu

may [mei] v (might) **1.** May I
come with you? Ìn rakà ka?
3. I may come with you. Nâ
rakà ka.

maybe [ˈmeibi] adv watakila

mayor [ˈmeə] n magajin gari,
(Nr) mer

MBA [embiːˈei] n babban digirin
kasuwanci

me [miː] pro ni

meadow [ˈmedəu] n dausayi

meagre [ˈmiːgə] adj ƙalilan

meal [miːl] n abinci

meal-time n kalaci

mean [miːn] **1.** adj marowaci
2. mugu **3.** matsaikaci **4.** v
(meant) nùfã **5.** yi niyya

meaning [ˈmiːniŋ] n **1.** ma'ana
2. maƙasudi

meaningful [ˈmiːniŋfəl] adj mai
ma'ana

meaningless [ˈmiːniŋləs] adj
maras ma'ana

means [miːnz] n **1.** hanya

2. zarafi **3.** means of living
sukuni **4.** means of support
madafa

meant [ment] duba wajen **mean**

meantime [ˈmiːntaim] n in the
meantime kafin nan

meanwhile [ˈmiːnwail] adv a wata
sabuwa kuma

measles [ˈmiːzlz] n ƙyanda

measurable [ˈmeʒərəbl] adj mai
misaltuwa

measure [ˈmeʒə] **1.** n ma'auni
2. v gwada **3.** duba wajen
measures

measurement [ˈmeʒəmənt] n awo

measures [ˈmeʒəz] pl to take
measures ɗauki waɗansu
matakai

meat [miːt] n nama

mechanic [miˈkænik] n makaniki,
(Nr) makanise

mechanical [miˈkænikl] adj na
inji

mechanics [miˈkæniks] n ilimin
inji

mechanism [ˈmekənizm] n **1.**
na'ura **2.** hanya

mechanize [ˈmekənaiz] v yi
amfani da inji

medal [ˈmedl] n lamba

meddle [ˈmedl] v yi shisshigi

media [ˈmiːdiə] n **1.** 'yan jarida
2. duba wajen **mass media**

mediate [ˈmiːdieit] v yi sulhu
tsakani

mediation [ˌmiːdiˈeiʃn] yin sulhu
tsakani

mediator [ˈmiːdieitə] n mai yin
sulhu tsakani

medical [ˈmedikl] adj na aikin likita

medicate [ˈmedikeit] v ba da
magani

medication [ˌmediˈkeiʃn] n
magani

medicinal [məˈdisinl] adj na
magani

medicine [ˈmedsn] n 1. ilimin
aikin likita 2. magani

medieval [ˌmediˈiːvl] adj na dâ

mediocre [ˌmiːdiˈəukə] adj makiri

mediocrity [ˌmiːdiˈɔkrəti] n
makirci

meditate [ˈmediteit] v yi tunani

meditation [ˌmediˈteiʃn] n tunani

Mediterranean Sea [ˌmeditəˈreiniən
ˈsiː] n Bahàř Rûm

medium [ˈmiːdiəm] 1. adj
matsakaici 2. n hanya

medium-range weapons pl
makamai masu cin matsakaicin
zango

medium-sized adj madaidaici

meek [miːk] adj mai tàwāli'ù

meekness [ˈmiːknis] n tàwāli'ù

meet [ˈmiːt] 1. n (spor.) karawa
2. v (met) gamu da 3. (spor.)
kara da juna

meeting [ˈmiːtiŋ] n 1. taro
2. alkawari 3. mitin, (Nr) ranyo

melancholic [ˈmeləŋkɔli] adj mai
baƙin ciki

melody [ˈmelədi] n karin waƙa

melon [ˈmelən] n kankana, (Nr)
malo

melt [melt] v narke

melted [ˈmeltid] adj narkakke

member [ˈmembə] n 1. ɗan
ƙungiya 2. **member of a**
political party ɗan jam'iyya 3.
member of legislature wakili

Member of Parliament n ɗan
majalisa

membership [ˈmembəʃip] n 'yan
ƙungiya

memo [ˈmeməu] duba wajen
memorandum

memorable [ˈmemərəbl] adj abin
tunawa

memorandum [ˌmeməˈrændəm]
n takardar bayani

memorial [məˈmɔːriəl] n 1. abin
tunawa 2. bikin tunawa

memorial service n bikin
tunawa

memorize [ˈmeməraiz] v haddace

memory [ˈmeməri] n 1. tunani
2. iya tunani

men [men] duba wajen **man**

menace [ˈmenəs] 1. n ban tsoro
2. v ba da tsoro

mend [mend] v gyara

menopause n **to reach**
menopause daina haila

menstruate [ˈmenstrueit] v yi
haila

menstruation [ˌmenstruˈeiʃn] n
haila

mental [ˈmentl] adj 1. na ƙwalwa
2. mahaukaci

mental home n gidan
mahaukata

mental health n hankali

mental hospital n asibitin
mahaukata

mentality [menˈtæləti] n hali

mention [ˈmenʃn] 1. n ambato
2. v àmbatà 2. **Don't mention**
it! Ba kome!

menu [ˈmenjuː] n tsarin abinci

mercantile [ˈməːkəntail] adj na
ciniki

Mercedes [məˈseidiz] n
Mansandi

mercenary [ˈməːsinəri] n sojan
haya

merchandise [ˈməːʃəndaiz] n haja

merchant [ˈməːtʃənt] *n* ɗan kasuwa

merciful [ˈməːsifl] *adj* mai tausayi

merciless [ˈməːsilis] *adj* maras tausayi

mercury [ˈməːkjuri] *n* zaiba

mercy [ˈməːsi] *n* tausayi

mere [ˈmiə] *adj* kawai

merely [ˈmiəli] *adv* kawai

merge [məːdʒ] *v* haɗe

merger [ˈməːdʒə] *n* haɗewa

meridian [məˈridiən] *n* babban layin taswira

merit [ˈmerit] **1.** *n* amfani **2.** *v* yi wa... amfani

merry [ˈmeri] *adj* mai fara'a

merry-making *n* shagali

mesh [meʃ] *n* raga

mess [mes] *n* **1.** rikici **2.** a barkatai **3.** *duba wajen* **mess up**

message [ˈmesidʒ] *n* saƙo

messenger [ˈmesindʒə] *n* masinja, (Nr) falanto

mess up *v* **1.** rikita **2.** dagula

messy [ˈmesi] *adj* kaca-kaca

met [met] *duba wajen* **meet**

metal [ˈmetl] **1.** *adj* na ƙarfe **2.** *n* ƙarfe

metallic [miˈtælik] *adj* na ƙarfe

metallurgy [meˈtælədʒi] *n* ilimin ƙarfe

metaphor [ˈmetəfɔː] *n* kàmàncē

meteorology [ˌmiːtiəˈrɔlədʒi] *n* ilimin yanayi

meteorologist [ˌmiːtiəˈrɔlədʒist] *n* mai ilimin yanayi

meter [ˈmiːtə] *n* **1.** mita, (Nr) kwantar **2.** (US) mita, (Nr) metir

method [ˈmeθəd] *n* hanya

methodical [miˈθɔdikl] *adj* mai fasali

meticulous [miˈtikjuləs] *adj* mai hankali

metre band *n* mita

metre [ˈmiːtə] *n* mita, (Nr) metir

metropolis [məˈtrɔpəlis] *n* alkarya

mice [mais] *duba wajen* **mouse**

microphone [ˈmaikrəfəun] *n* makarufo, (Nr) mikuro

microscope [ˈmikrəskəup] *n* madubin likita

midday [ˌmidˈdei] *n* tsakar rana, (Nr) midi

middle [ˈmidl] **1.** *adj* na tsakiya **2.** *n* tsakiya **3.** **in the middle of** a tsakar

middle-age *n* magidanci

middle-class *adj/n* ɗan boko

Middle East *n* Yankin Gabas ta Tsakiya

middleman [ˈmidlmæn] *n* ɗan baranda

middle school *n* midil, (Nr) se'eje

midget [ˈmidʒit] *n* wada

midnight [ˈmidnait] *n* tsakar dare, (Nr) munuwi

midst [midst] *n* **in the midst of** a tsakar

midway [ˌmidˈwei] *adv* tsakanin

midwife [ˈmidweif] *n* ungozoma

midwifery [midˈwiferi] *n* ungozanci

might [mait] **1.** *n* ƙarfi **2.** *duba wajen* **may**

might and main kamar ruwa a jallo

mighty [ˈmaiti] *adj* gago

migrant [ˈmaigrənt] *n* ɗan ƙaƙa gida

migrate [maiˈgreit] v ƙaura

migration [maiˈgreiʃən] n ƙaura

mild [maild] adj maras tsanani

mile [mail] n mil

mileage [ˈmailidʒ] n nisan miloli

militant [ˈmilitənt] n ɗan gā-ni-kashɛ̀-ni

militarily [ˌmiliˈterəli] adv a fannin soja

military [ˈmilitri] 1. n soja, (Nr) soji 2. adj na soja 3. by military means da ƙarfin soja

military affairs n sha'anin soja

military court n kotun soja

military expert n ƙwararre a fannin soja

military government n gwamnatin soja

military honours pl girmamawa irin ta sojoji

military might ƙarfin bindiga

military police n kurfau

military regime n mulkin soja

military rule n mulkin soja

military uniform n kayan soja

militia [miˈliʃə] n 'yan yaƙin sanƙara/sunƙuru

milk [milk] n 1. madara 2. baby's milk nono 3. dried milk garin madara 4. dried baby's milk nonon gwangwani

milkman [ˈmilkmən] n mai madara

milky [ˈmilki] adj madara-madara

mill [mil] n 1. ma'aikata 2. gidan niƙa

millennium [miˈleniəm] n ƙarni goma

millet [ˈmilit] n gero

million [ˈmiljən] n miliyan, (Nr) miliyo

millionaire [ˌmiljəˈneə] n miloniya

mime [maim] 1. n bɛ̀bàncɛ̌ 2. v bɛ̌bàncɛ̌

mimic [ˈmimik] 1. n ɗan kwaikwayo 2. v kwaikwaya

minaret [ˌminəˈret] n hasumiya

mince [mins] n yankakken nama

mind [maind] 1. n ƙwalwa 2. hankali 3. to change one's mind sake tunani 4. to keep in mind riƙe a zuciya 5. v kula da 6. damu da 7. Never mind! Ba kome! 8. Mind your own business! Yi kasafin gabanka!

mindful [ˈmaindfl] adj mai kula (of da)

mine [main] 1. nawa, tawa 2. n mahaƙa 3. (mil.) nakiya da ke haɗe da waya 4. sea mine nakiya da aka dasa a teku 5. v haƙo

miner [ˈmainə] n mai haƙan ma'adinai

mineral [ˈminərəl] 1. adj na ma'adini 2. n ma'adini

mineral water n 1. sōdǎ, (Nr) bùlbît

minerals [ˈminərəlz] pl ma'adinai

mingle [ˈmiŋgl] v shiga mutane

miniature [ˈminətʃə] n/adj dada

minibus [ˈminibʌs] n hayis

minimum [ˈminiməm] adj taƙaitacce

mining [ˈmainiŋ] n haƙan ma'adinai

minister [ˈministə] n 1. (pol.) minista, (Nr) ministir 2. (Chr.) fada

minister of state n ƙaramin minista

ministry [ˈministri] n ma'aikatar gwamnati

minor [ˈmainə] 1. *adj* ƙarami
2. *n* yaro, yarinya
minor issues *pl* ƙananan al'amura
minority [maiˈnɔrəti] *n* 1. tsirari
2. (pol.) marasa rinjaye
3. ethnic minority kabila
maras yawa
minority group *n* al'umma
maras rinjaye
minority rule *n* mulkin marasa
rinjaye
mint [mint] 1. *n* minti 2. *v* ƙera
kwabbai
minus [ˈmainəs] *prep* a ɗebe
minute [maiˈnjuːt] *adj* ɗan mitsili
minute [ˈminit] *n* minti
minutes [ˈminits] *pl* **minutes of a
meeting** minit
miracle [ˈmirəkl] *n* 1. abin
al'ajabi 2. mu'ujiza
miraculous [miˈrækjuləs] *adj*
abin al'ajabi
mirror [ˈmirə] *n* madubi
mirth [məːθ] *n* barkwanci
misadventure [ˌmisədˈventʃə] *n*
haɗari
misapply [ˈmisəˈplai] *v* kuskure
misapprehension [ˌmisapriˈhenʃn]
n rashin fahimta
misbehave [ˌmisbiˈheiv] *v* yi
rashin ladabi
misbehaviour [ˌmisbiˈheiviə] *n*
rashin ladabi
miscalculate [misˈkælkjuleit] *v* yi
kuskure
miscalculation [ˌmiskælkjuˈleiʃn]
n yin kuskure
miscarriage [ˈmiskæridʒ] *n*
to suffer a miscarriage yi ɓari
miscarriage of justice
[ˈmiskæridʒ] *n* rashin adalcin
kotu

miscarry [misˈkæri] *v* yi ɓari
miscellaneous [ˌmisəˈleiniəs] *adj*
na tarkace
mischance [misˈtʃaːns] *n* haɗari
mischief [ˈmistʃif] *n* fitina
mischievous [ˈmistʃivəs] *adj* mai
ta da zaune tsaye
misconduct [ˌmisˈkɔndʌkt] *n*
abin assha
misdeed [ˈmisˈdiːd] *n* aikin assha
misdemeanour [ˌmisdəmiːnə] *n*
ƙaramin laifi
miserly [ˈmaizəli] *adj* mai rowa
miserable [ˈmizrəbl] *adj* 1. mai
baƙin ciki 2. miskini
misery [ˈmizəri] *n* baƙin ciki
misfire [ˌmisˈfaiəd] *v* ci tirã/turã
misfortune [ˌmisˈfɔːtʃuːn] *n*
tsautsayi
misgivings [misˈgiviŋz] *pl* **to
have misgivings** yi da-na-sani
misguide [ˌmisˈgaid] *v* ɓatar da
mishap [ˈmishæp] *n* tsautsayi
mishear *v* yi jin kunne
misinterpret [ˌmisinˈtəːprit] *v*
kuskure
misjudge [ˌmisˈdʒʌdʒ] *v* rasa
fahimta
mislay [ˌmisˈlei] *v* ya da
mislead [ˌmisˈliːd] *v* (**misled**)
1. ɓatar da 2. rũɗã
misprint [ˈmisprint] *n* kuskuren
rubutu
misrule [ˌmisˈruːl] *n* rashin
adalcin gwamnati
miss [mis] 1. *n* kuskure 2. **Miss**
Malama 3. *v* kuskure 4. yi
kewa 5. yi saɓani 6. **They
missed the plane.** Sun rasa
jirgin sama.
misshapen [ˌmisˈʃeipən] *n*
naƙasasshe

missile [ˈmisail] *n* **1.** harsashi **2.** guided missile harsashi mai linzami

missile boat *n* kwale-kwalen faɗa

missing [ˈmisiŋ] *adj* to be missing 6ace

mission [ˈmiʃn] *n* **1.** ƙungiya **2.** (Chr.) mishan **3.** diplomatic mission manzanci **4.** to carry out a mission i da manzanci

missionary [ˈmiʃənri] *n* (Chr.) ɗan mishan

mist [mist] *n* hazo

misty [misti] *adj* mai hazo

mistake [miˈsteik] **1.** *n* kuskure **2.** by mistake bisa kuskure **3.** to make a mistake yi kuskure **4.** *v* (mistook, mistaken) yi wa... mummunar fahimta

mistaken [miˈsteikn] *adj* **1.** ba daidai ba **2.** *duba wajen* mistake

mister [mistə] *duba wajen* Mr

mistreat [misˈtriːt] *v* zàluntà

mistreatment [misˈtriːtmənt] *n* zalunci

mistress [mistris] *n* **1.** uwargida **2.** fàr̃kà **3.** *duba wajen* Mrs, schoolmistress

mistrust [ˌmisˈtrʌst] **1.** *n* ƙin amincewa **2.** *v* ƙi amincewa da

mistrustful [misˈtrʌstfl] *adj* mai ƙin amincewa

misunderstand [ˌmisʌndəˈstænd] *v* (misunderstood) ba ji ba sosai

misunderstanding [ˌmisʌndəˈstændiŋ] *n* **1.** rashin fahimta **2.** to avoid any misunderstanding kawar da duk wata gurguwar fahimta

misuse [ˌmisˈjuːz] *v* wulaƙanta

mitigate [ˈmitigeit] *v* sauƙaƙa

mix [miks] **1.** *n* haɗi **2.** *v* haɗa

mixed [mikst] *adj* to be mixed hàutsunà

mixed race *adj* mai ruwa biyu

mixed up *adj* **1.** rikice (about da) **2.** to be mixed up in shiga cikin sha'ani

mixer [ˈmiksə] *n* mahautsini

mixing [miksiŋ] *n* haɗi

mixture [ˈmikstʃə] *n* abin da aka gauraye

moan [məun] **1.** *n* nishi **2.** *v* yi nishi

mob [mɔb] *n* **1.** cincirindo **2.** 'yan zanga-zanga

mobile [məubail] *adj* na tafi-da-gidanka

mobile home *n* gidan tirela

mobile phone *n* oba-oba

mobility [məuˈbiləti] *n* tafi-da-gidanka

mobilise [məubilaiz] *v* **1.** to mobilise support nemi goyon baya **2.** to mobilise an army kira ga soja

mock [mɔk] *v* yi wa... ba'a

mockery [ˈmɔkəri] *n* ba'a

mode [məud] *n* hali

model [ˈmɔdl] **1.** *n* samfur, (Nr) modal **2.** yayi **3.** ƙira **4.** fashion model binta Sudan **5.** *v* ƙera

modem [məudem] *n* mōdèm

moderate [mɔdəret] **1.** *adj* madaidaici **2.** *n* (pol.) mai tsakaitaccen ra'ayi

moderate [mɔdəreit] *v* yi gwargwado

moderation [ˌmɔdəˈreiʃn] *n* in moderation kimà

modern [ˈmɔdn] *adj* na zamani

modernize [ˈmɔdənaiz] *v* sabunta

modest [ˈmɔdist] *adj* 1. mai kunya 2. madaidaici

modesty [ˈmɔdisti] *n* jin kunya

modification [ˌmɔdifiˈkeiʃn] *n* gyare-gyare

modify [ˈmɔdifai] *v* gyaggyara

moist [mɔist] *adj* mai laima

moisten [ˈmɔisn] *v* laimata

moisture [ˈmɔistʃə] *n* laima

molar, molar tooth [ˈməulə] *n* matauni

mold [məuld] *duba wajen* **mould**

mole [məul] *n* 1. tawadar Allah 2. jaɓa

molest [mɔˈlest] *v* lalata

moment [ˈməumənt] *n* 1. 'yar jim kaɗan 2. **at the moment** yanzu 3. **in a moment** in an jima

momentary [ˈməuməntri] *adj* na jim kaɗan

momentous [məuˈmentəs] *adj* muhimmi

momentum [məuˈmentum] *n* ruruwa

monarch [ˈmɔnək] *n* sarki, sarauniya

monarchy [ˈmɔnəki] *n* mulukiya

monastery [ˈmɔnəstri] *n* (rel.) gidan sufi

Monday [ˈmʌndi] *n* ran Litinin

monetary [ˈmʌnitri] *n* na kuɗi

monetary policy *n* manufar harkar kuɗi

money [ˈmʌni] *n* kuɗi

money-order *n* moni'oda

monk [mʌŋk] *n* (rel.) sufi

monkey [ˈmʌŋki] *n* biri

mono- [ˈmɔnəu] *adj* na ɗaya

monopolize [məˈnɔpəlaiz] *v* (ec.) yi babakere

monopoly [məˈnɔpəli] *n* (ec.) babakere

monotonous [məˈnɔtənəs] *adj* mai cin rai

monotony [məˈnɔtəni] *n* cin rai

monster [ˈmɔnstə] *n* dodo

monstrous [ˈmɔnstrəs] *adj* mugu

month [mʌnθ] *n* wata

monthly [ˈmʌnθli] *adj* wata-wata

monument [ˈmɔnjumənt] *n* abin tunawa

mood [muːd] *n* 1. **good mood** farin ciki 2. **bad mood** baƙin ciki 3. **to be in the mood for** ji yin

moon [muːn] *n* wata

moonlight [ˈmuːnlait] *n* farin wata

moonstruck [ˈmuːnstrʌk] *adj* taɓaɓɓe

moor [mɔː] *v* ɗaure

moral [ˈmɔrəl] *adj* 1. mai ɗa'a 2. *duba wajen* **morals**

morale [məˈræl] *n* ƙarfin gwiwa

morality [məˈræləti] *n* ɗa'a

morals [ˈmɔrəlz] *n* ɗa'a

morbid [ˈmɔːbid] *adj* na mugun tunani

more [mɔː] *adj/adv* 1. **the more... the more** 2. **Audu is more intelligent than Gambo.** Audu ya fi Gambo basira. 3. **There is no more food.** Babu sauran abinci. 4. **more or less** kusan 5. **I will try more.** Zan ƙara ƙoƙari.

more than 1. fiye da 2. **more than ever** fiye da na kowane lokaci

moreover [mɔːˈrəuvə] *conj* bugu da ƙari kuma

morning [ˈmɔːnɪŋ] *n* **1.** safiya **2. Good morning!** Barka da safiya!

morning sickness *n* laulayin ciki

morsel [ˈmɔːsl] *n* gutsure

mortal [ˈmɔːtl] *adj/n* mamaci

mortality [mɔːˈtæləti] *n* mace-mace

mortality rate *n* yawan mace-amce

mortar [ˈmɔːtə] *n* **1.** turmi **2.** kwaɓi (mil.) laimota

mortar fire *n* ruwan laimota

mortgage [ˈmɔːgidʒ] *n* jinginar gida

mortgagee [ˌmɔːgəˈdʒiː] *n* mai jinginar gida

mortuary [ˈmɔːtʃəri] *n* ɗakin ajiyar gawa

Moslem [ˈmʌzlim] *adj/n* musulmi

mosque [mɔsk] *n* masallaci

mosquito [mɔsˈkiːtəu] *n* sauro

mosquito net *n* gidan sauro

most [məust] *adj/adv* **1.** mafi yawa **2.** kusan duka **3.** most of all fiye da duka **4. for the most part** galiban **5. most guests** yawancin baƙi **6. most of them** mafi yawansu **7. The most beautiful flower.** Fure wanda ya fi duka kyau. **8. to make the most of** ci moriyar abu

mostly [ˈməustli] *adv* galiban

motel [məuˈtel] *n* masauki

moth [mɔθ] *n* faɗa-wuta

mother [ˈmʌðə] *n* uwa

mother-in-law *n* suruka

mother-tongue *n* harshen uwa

motherhood [ˈmʌðəhud] *n* haihuwa

motherland [ˈmʌðəlænd] *n* ƙasa

motherly [ˈmʌðəli] *adj* mai reno

motion [ˈməuʃn] *n* **1.** motsi **2.** (pol.) batu **3. to set in motion** tayar da

motionless [ˈməuʃnlis] *adj* tsit

motion sickness *n* tashin zuciya

motive [ˈməutiv] *n* dalili

motor [ˈməutə] *n* inji

motor boat *n* kwalekwale mai inji

motorbike [ˈməutəbaik] *n* mashin

motor bus *n* bas, (Nr) kar

motor car *n* mota

motorcycle [ˈməutəˌsaikl] *n* babur

motorcyle rider *n* mahayin babur

motoring [ˈməutəriŋ] *n* tuƙi

motorist [ˈməutərist] *n* direba

motor scooter *n* basfa

motorway [ˈməutəwei] *n* babbar hanya

motto [ˈmɔtəu] *n* take

mould [məuld] **1.** *n* zubi **2.** hunhuna **3.** *v* siganta

mouldy [ˈməuldi] *adj* mai hununa

mound [maund] *n* ɗan tudu

mount [maunt] **1.** *n* babban dutse **2.** *v* hau

mountain [ˈmauntin] *n* babban dutse

mountaineer [ˌmauntiˈniə] *n* mai hawan dutse

mountainous [ˈmauntinəs] *adj* mai duwatsu

mourn [mɔːn] *v* yi makoki

mourner [ˈmɔːnə] *n* mai zaman makoki

mourning [ˈmɔːnɪŋ] *n* **1.** makoki

2. zaman makoki **3. day of mourning** ranar juyayi

mouse [maus] n (pl **mice**) ɓera

moustache [məˈstaːʃ] n gashin baki

mouth [mauθ] n baki

mouth-wash n ruwan kurkurar baki

mouthful [ˈmauθful] n loma

mouthpiece [ˈmauθpiːs] duba wajen **spokesman**

movable [ˈmuːvəbl] adj mai ɗaukuwa

move [muːv] v **1.** yi motsi **2.** kau da **3.** ba da tausayi

move house v sake gida (**to zuwa**)

movement [ˈmuːvmənt] n **1.** motsi **2.** ra'ayi **3.** (pol.) ƙungiya

movie, movies [ˈmuːviː, ˈmuːviz] n fim

movie theatre n siliman

moving [ˈmuːviŋ] adj mai ban tausayi

mow [məu] v (**mowed, mown**) yanke ciyawa

MP (Member of Parliament) n wakili

m.p.h. (miles per hour) mil cikin awa

Mr (mister) [ˈmistə] Malam, (Nr) Mushe

Mrs (mistress) [ˈmisiz] Malama

Ms [məz; miz] Malama

MSc digirin kimiyya na biyu

Mt duba wajen **mount**

much [mʌtʃ] adj/adv **1.** mai yawa **2.** da yawa **3. much less** lalle **4. She eats too much.** Ta faye cin abinci. **5. how much?** nawa? **6. however much** ko nawa

mud [mʌd] n taɓo

muddle [ˈmʌdl] n rikici

muddy [ˈmʌdi] adj taɓa-taɓo

mudguard [ˈmʌdgaːd] n mutagadi, (Nr) gardabu

muezzin [muˈezin] n ladan

muffler [ˈmʌflə] n salansa, (Nr) shamfama

mug [mʌg] **1.** n moɗa **2.** v yi wa... fashi

mugger [ˈmʌgə] n ɗan fashi

mule [mjuːl] n alfadari

multi- [ˈmʌlti] adj mai yawa

multilingual [ˌmʌltiˈlingwəl] adj mai iya harsuna

multilingualism [ˌmʌltiˈlingwəlizm] n iya harsuna

multi-media [ˌmʌltiˈmiːdia] n surƙullen hanyoyin sadarwa

multinationals [ˌmʌltiˈnæʃnəlz] pl manyan kamfanoni

multiple [ˈmʌltipl] n ninki

multiplication [ˌmʌltipliˈkeiʃn] n sau

multiply [ˈmʌltiplai] v ninka

multiracial [ˌmʌltiˈreiʃl] adj mai gama jinsuna

multiracial organization n ƙungiyar da ta ƙunshi jinsuna da dama

multiracial society n al'ummar mai gama jinsuna

multitude [ˈmʌltitjuːd] n ɗimbi

mum [mʌm] n innà

mumble [ˈmʌmbl] v yi gunguni

mummy [ˈmʌmi] n innà

mumps [mʌmps] n hangum

municipal [mjuːˈnisipl] adj na birni

municipality [mjuːˌnisiˈpæləti] n birni

murder [ˈməːdə] **1.** n kisan kai **2.** v kashe

murderer [ˈməːdərə] *n* mai kisan kai

murderess [ˈməːdəris] *n* mai kisan kai

murmur [ˈməːmə] *v* yi gunguni

muscle [ˈmʌsl] *n* **1.** tsoka **2.** ƙarfi

muscular [ˈmʌskjulə] *adj* murɗeɗe

muse [mjuːz] *v* yi tunani

museum [ˈmjuːziəm] *n* gidan kayan gargajiya

mushroom [ˈmʌʃrum] *n* naman kaza

music [ˈmjuːzik] *n* kiɗa, waƙa

musical [ˈmjuːzikl] *adj* na kiɗa

musician [mjuːˈziʃn] *n* makaɗi

Muslim [ˈmʌzlim] *adj/n* musulmi

mussel [ˈmʌsl] *n* ƙumba

must [məst; mʌst] *v* **1.** I must go home now. Dole in tafi gida yanzu. **2.** You must not come! Kada ka zo! **3.** He must be at home. Lalle gida yake.

mutate [mjuːˈteit] *v* rikiɗa

mutation [mjuːˈteiʃn] *n* rikiɗa

mute [mjuːt] *adj/n* bebe

mutilate [ˈmjuːtileit] *v* naƙasa

mutilated [ˈmjuːtileitid] *adj* kaca-kaca

mutineer [ˌmjuːtiˈniə] *n* ɗan tawayen soja

mutiny [ˈmjuːtini] **1.** *n* tawayen soja **2.** *v* yi tawayen soja

mutter [ˈmʌtə] *v* yi bàdà-bàdà

mutton [ˈmʌtn] *n* naman tunkiya

mutual [ˈmjuːtʃuəl] *adj* na juna

muzzle [ˈmʌzl] **1.** *n* takunkumi **2.** *v* yi wa... takunkumi

my [mai] nawa, tawa

myself [maiˈself] kâinā

mysterious [miˈstiəriəs] *adj* mai ban mamaki

mystery [ˈmistəri] *n* **1.** abin mamaki **2.** labarin ɗan sandan ciki

mystic [ˈmistik] *n* sufi

mystify [ˈmistifai] *n* ɗaure wa... kai

myth [miθ] *n* hikayar mafari

mythical [ˈmiθikl] *adj* na hikayar mafari

Nn

nail [neil] 1. *n* farce 2. ƙusa
3. *v* kafa

naira [ˈnairə] *n* naira

naive [naiˈiːv] *adj* bagidaje

naivety [naiˈiːviti] *n* gidadanci

naked [ˈneikid] *adj* huntu

nakedness [ˈneikidnəs] *n* tsirara

name [neim] 1. *n* suna 2. **in the
name of...** da sunan... 3. *v* sa
wa... suna 4. naɗa

nameless [ˈneimlis] *adj* baƙo

namely [ˈneimli] *adv* watau

name-plate *n* lamba

namesake [ˈneimseik] *n* takwara

nanny [ˈnæni] *n* mai reno

nap [næp] *n* **to take a nap**
rintsa

napkin [ˈnæpkin] *n* hankici

nappy [ˈnæpi] *n* banten jinjiri

narcotic [naːˈkɔtik] *adj* na ƙwaya

narcotics [naːˈkɔtiks] *pl* ƙwaya

narrate [nəˈreit] *n* ba da labari

narration [nəˈreiʃn] *n* warwara

narrative [ˈnærətiv] *n* labari

narrator [nəˈreitə] *n* mai ba da
labari

narrow [ˈnærəu] *adj* 1. maras
faɗi 2. mai ƙunci

narrow-minded *adj* **They are
narrow-minded.** Ba sa karɓar
shawara.

narrows [ˈnærəuz] *pl* makurɗaɗa

nasty [ˈnaːsti] *adj* mai sa ƙyama

nation [ˈneiʃn] *n* al'umma

national [ˈnæʃnəl] 1. *adj* na
al'umma 2. *n* ɗan ƙasa

national anthem *n* take

national defence *n* tsaron
al'umma

national dress *n* kayan ƙasa

national guard 'yan tsaron
ƙasa, (Nr) gar-da-sarki

nationalism [ˈnæʃnəlizm] *n*
kishin ƙasa

nationalist [ˈnæʃnəlist] 1. *adj* na
kishin ƙasa 2. *n* ɗan kishin ƙasa

nationality [ˌnæʃənæliti] *n* ƙasa

nationalization [ˌnæʃnəlaiˈzeiʃn]
n zama ɗan ƙasa

nationalize [ˈnæʃnəlaiz] *v* mai
da... hannun 'yan ƙasa

national security *n* tsaron
lāfiyar al'umma

national service *n* ɗaukar
mutane a soja

nationwide [ˌneiʃnˈwaid] *adv* a
ƙasar gaba ɗaya

native [ˈneitiv] *adj/n* ɗan...

native country *n* ƙasa

native language *n* harshe

**NATO (North Atlantic Treaty
Organization)** [ˈneitəu] *n*
Ƙungiyar Tsaron Arewacin
Tekun Atlantika

natural [ˈnætʃrəl] *adj* 1. na
halitta 2. na hali

natural history *n* labarin
halitta

natural disaster *n* bala'i daga
indallahi

natural resources *pl* arzikin
ƙasa

naturalize [ˈnætʃrəlaiz] *v* zama
ɗan ƙasa

naturally [ˈnætʃrəli] *adv* **1.** da
hali **2.** dâ mā
nature [ˈneitʃə] *n* **1.** halitta
2. hali **3.** ainihi **4.** human
nature mutuntaka
nature reserve *n* gandun daji
naughty [ˈnɔːti] *adj* mai fitina
nausea [ˈnɔːsiə] *n* tashin zuciya
nauseous [ˈnɔːsiəs] *adj* mai jin
tashin zuciya
nautical [ˈnɔːtɪkl] *adj* na aikin
teku
naval [ˈneivl] *adj* na rundunar
jiragen ruwa
navel [ˈneivl] *n* cibiya
navigable [ˈnævigəbl] *adj* (ruwa)
mai zurfi
navigate [ˈnævigeit] *v* bi ruwa ta
jirgi
navigation [ˌnæviˈgeiʃn] *n* bin
ruwa ta jirgi
navigator [ˈnævigeitə] *n* mai
jirgi, abokin tuƙi
navy [ˈneivi] *n* rundunar jiragen
ruwa
nazi [ˈnaːtsi] *adj/n* ɗan bangar
nuna wariyar al'umma, ɗan
nāzì
near, near to [niə] *adj/adv*
1. kusa da **2.** to draw near
ƙarātō
nearby [ˈniəbai] *adv* nan kusa
Near East *n* ƙasashen Gabas ta
Tsakiya
nearly [ˈniəli] *adv* **1.** kusan
2. saura kaɗan
nearness [ˈniənis] *n* kusa
near-sighted *adj* She is near-
sighted. Ba ta ganin nesa.
neat [niːt] *adj* kintsattse
neatness [ˈniːtnis] *n* tsabta
necessarily *adv* lalle

necessary [ˈnesəsəri] *adj* **1.** na
dole **2.** if necessary idan ta
ɓaci
necessity [niˈsesəti] *n* **1.** dole
2. wajibi
neck [nek] *n* wuya
necklace [ˈneklis] *n* dutsen
wuya, saƙar wuya
necktie [ˈnektai] *n* taye
need [niːd] **1.** *n* bukata **2.** *v* yi
bukata **3.** You need to do it.
Ya kamata ku yi shi.
needful [ˈniːdfl] *adj* mai bukata
needle [ˈniːdl] *n* allura
needless [ˈniːdlis] *adj* needless to
say ba sai an faɗa ba
needs [niːdz] *pl* bukata
needy [ˈniːdi] *adj* miskini
negative [ˈnegətiv] **1.** *adj* kòrau
2. *n* dodon hoto, (Nr) kilishe
neglect [niˈglekt] **1.** *n* rashin kula
2. *v* ƙyale
negligence [ˈneglidʒəns] *n* sakaci
negligent [ˈneglidʒənt] *adj* mai
rashin kula (of da)
negotiable [niˈgəuʃiəbl] *adj* mai
sansantuwa
negotiate [niˈgəuʃieit] *v* **1.** yi
shawarwari **2.** yi jìngā
negotiating table [niˈgəuʃieitiŋ]
n teburin shawarwari
negotiation [ni,gəuʃˈeiʃn] *n* **1.**
shawarwari **2.** duba wajen
negotiations
negotiations [ni,gəuʃˈeiʃnz] *pl*
1. shawarwari **2.** peace
negotiations shawarwarin
lumana **3.** to break off
negotiations katse shawarwari
negotiator [ni,gəuʃˈeitə] *n* mai
shawarwari
neigh [nei] *v* yi haniniya

neighbour [ˈneibə] n maƙwabci
neighbourhood [ˈneibəhud] n
unguwa, (Nr) karce
neighbouring [ˈneibəriŋ] adj
kusa da
neither [ˈnaiðə; ˈniːðə] 1. babu
2. ba ko ɗaya
neither... nor ba... (ba) kuma
ba... (ba)
neo- [ˈniːəu] adj sabon fasalin...
neo-colonialism [ˈniːəukəˈləuniəlizəm]
n sabon fasalin mulkin
mallaka
neo-nazi [ˈniːəuˈnaːtsi] n ɗan
bangar nāzì
nephew [ˈnefjuː] n ɗan wa
nerve [nəːv] n 1. jijiya 2. jar
zuciya
nervous [ˈnəːvəs] adj to feel
nervous yi juyayi
nervousness [ˈnəːvəsnis] n juyayi
nest [nest] n sheƙa
net [net] n raga
netball [ˈnetbɔːl] n ƙwallon raga
network [ˈnetwəːk] 1. n sadarwa
2. communications network
hanyoyin sadarwa
neuralgia [njuəˈrældʒə] n ciwon
kai
neurosis [njuəˈrəusis] n taɓuwar
ƙwaƙwalwa
neurotic [njuəˈrɔtik] adj mai
taɓuwar ƙwaƙwalwa
neutral [ˈnjuːtrəl] adj (pol.) na
'yan ba-ruwanmu
neutral gear n firi
neutrality [njuːˈtræləti] n (pol.)
tsaka-tsakanci
neutralize [ˈnjuːtrəlaiz] v kawar
da matsala
never [ˈnevə] adv 1. ba daɗai ba
2. never mind! ba kome! 3.

I've never heard it. Ban taɓa
ji ba.
never-ending adj ba tsayawa
nevermore [ˈnevəˈmɔː] adv 1. har
inataha 2. sam!
nevertheless [ˌnevəðəˈles] conj
amma duk da haka
new [njuː] adj 1. sabo 2. brand
new sabo ful
newborn [ˈnjuːbɔn] adj jariri
newcomer [ˈnjuːˌkʌmə] n farin
shiga
newly [ˈnjuːli] 1. adj sabon...
2. adv kwanan baya
news [njuːz] n labari, (Nr) duge
news agency n ofishin watsa
labarai
newscast [ˈnjuːzcaːst] n watsin
labari
newscaster, newsreader
[ˈnjuːzcaːstə; -riːdə] n mai ba da
labarai
newsstand [ˈnjuːzstænd] n
rumfan jaridu
newspaper [ˈnjuːspeipə] n jarida
New Year [ˈnjuːˈjiːə] n Sabuwar
Shekara
New Year's Eve n Jajiberen
Sabuwar Shekara
New Zealand [njuːˈziːlənd] n
Niyù Zilân
next [nekst] 1. adj mai zuwa
2. na gaba 3. adv daga baya
next to prep kusa da
nib [nib] n kan alƙalami
nibble [ˈnibl] v gàigayà
nice [nais] adj 1. mai daɗi
2. mai kyau
niceness [ˈnaisnis] n daɗi
niche [niːʃ] n 1. àlkūkì 2. gurbi
nick [nik] in the nick of time
à kân karì

nickname [ˈnikneim] **1.** *n* laƙabi **2.** *v* laƙabta

niece [niːs] *n* 'yar wa

Niger [ˈnaidʒə] Nìjâr

Nigeria [naiˈdʒiəriə] *n* Nijeriya

Nigerian [naiˈdʒiəriən] **1.** *adj* na Nijeriya **2.** *n* ɗan Nijeriya

Nigerien 1. *adj* na Nijer **2.** *n* ɗan Nijer

night [nait] *n* **1.** dare **2.** at night da dare **3.** Good night! Mu kwan lafiya! **4.** to spend the night kwana

night-club *n* ba daɗai ba

nightly [ˈnaitli] *adv* kowane dare

nightmare [ˈnaitmeə] *n* mafarki mai ban tsoro

night watchman *n* mai gadi, (Nr) gardinye

nil [nil] *n* sifiri

Nile [nail] *n* kôgin Nilu

nine [nain] *n* /adj tara

nineteen [ˌnainˈtiːn] *n* /adj goma sha tara

nineteenth [ˌnainˈtiːnθ] *adj* na goma sha tara

ninetieth [ˈnaintiəθ] *adj* na tasa'in

ninety [ˈnainti] *n* /adj tasa'in, casa'in

ninth [nainθ] *adj* na tara

nip [nip] *v* ɗan cîzā

nipple [ˈnipl] *n* kan nono

no [nəu] **1.** a'a **2.** babu

Nobel Peace Prize [nəuˈbel] *n* lamba ta zaman lafiya ta Nòbêl

Nobel Prize *n* lambar girmamawa ta Nòbêl

noble [ˈnəubl] *adj* *adj* **1.** mai martaba **2.** na kirki

nobility [nəuˈbiləti] *n* sarakai

nobody [ˈnəubədi] **1.** ba kowa **2.** ba wanda

nod [nɔd] *v* gyaɗā

no-go area [ˌnəugəuˈeəriə] *n* wurin da aka haramtā wa... shìgā

noise [nɔiz] *n* **1.** ƙara **2.** amo

noiseless [ˈnɔizlis] *adj* mai shiru

noisy [ˈnɔizi] *adj* mai ƙara

no longer [nəuˈlɔngə] *adv* **They no longer live here.** Sun tashi daga nân.

nomad [ˈnəumæd] *n* makiyayi

nomadic [nəuˈmædik] *adj* makiyayi

no man's land *n* sansani ihunka banza

no matter what ko ta halin ƙaƙa.

nominate [ˈnɔmineit] *v* gabatar da

nomination [ˌnɔmiˈneiʃn] *n* gabatarwa

nominee [ˌnɔmiˈniː] *n* wanda aka gabatar

non- [nɔn] maras...

non-aggression pact *n* yarjejeniyar hana kai hari

non-alcoholic [ˌnɔnælkəˈhɔlik] *adj* maras sifirit

non-aligned nations [ˌnɔnəˈlaind] *pl* ƙasashen 'yan bâ-ruwanmu

non-alignment [ˌnɔnəˈlainmənt] *n* tsaka-tsakanci

non-Christian [ˌnɔnˈmʌzlim] *adj/n* wanda ba Kirista ba

non-commissioned officer [ˌnɔnkəˈmiʃnd] *n* ƙaramin hafsa

none [nʌn] **1.** ba ko ɗaya **2.** babu

nonetheless [ˌnʌnðəˈles] *adv* amma duk da haka

none whatsoever ko ƙyas

non-fiction [ˌnɔnˈfikʃn] *n* labari

non-intervention [ˈnɔnˌintəˈvenʃn] *n* rashin kàtsàlandàn

non-Muslim [ˌnɔnˈmʌzlim] *adj/n* wanda ba Musulmi ba

non-payment [ˌnɔnˈpeimənt] *n* rashin biya

nonplus [ˈnɔnˈplʌs] *v* ba da mamaki

nonsense [ˈnɔnsns] *n* 1. maganar banza 2. wauta

non-smoker [ˌnɔnˈsməukə] *n* mai ƙin shan taba

non-smoking *adj* na marasa shan taba

non-stop [ˌnɔnˈstɔp] *adj* ba tsayawa

noodles [ˈnuːdəlz] *n* taliya

noon [nuːn] *n* tsakar rana, (Nr) midi

no one [ˈnəuwʌn] 1. ba kowa 2. ba wanda

noose [nuːs] *n* zàrgē

nor [nɔː] *duba wajen* **neither... nor**

norm [nɔːm] *n* mizani

normal [ˈnɔːml] *adj* na kullum

normally [ˈnɔːməli] *adv* a bisa al'ada

north [nɔːθ] 1. *adj* na arewa 2. *n* arewa

North Africa *n* Afirka ta Arewa

north-east *n* arewa maso gabas

northern [ˈnɔːðən] *adj* na arewa

Northern Ireland *n* Ailan ta Arewa

northerner [ˈnɔːðənə] *n* ɗan arewa

northward(s) [ˈnɔːθwədz] *adv* arewa-arewa

north-west *n* arewa maso yamma

nose [nəuz] *n* 1. hanci 2. **to blow one's nose** fyace majina

nosebleed [ˈnəuz] *n* haɓo

nostalgia [nɔˈstældʒə] *n* bege

nostalgic [nɔˈstældʒik] *adj* **to be nostalgic about** yi begen...

nostril [ˈnɔstrəl] *n* kafar hanci

not [nɔt] 1. ba... (ba) 2. kada

notable [ˈnəutəbl] *adj* sananne

not at all 1. sam-sam 2. ba kome!

note [nəut] 1. *n* 'yar wasiƙa 2. (*mus.*) amo 3. *v* kula da 4. *duba wajen* **banknote**

notebook [ˈnəutbuk] *n* littafin rubutu, (Nr) kaye

noted [ˈnəutid] *adj* sananne

note down *v* rubuta

noteworthy [ˈnəutˌwəːði] *adj* abin lura

nothing [ˈnʌθiŋ] 1. ba kome 2. ba abin da 3. **for nothing** a banza

notice [ˈnəutis] *n* 1. sanarwa 2. **to give notice** ba da nōtìs 3. **until further notice** sai illa ma sha Allahu 4. *v* lura da 5. **to take notice of** kula da

notice-board *n* allon ba da sanarwa

noticeable [ˈnəutisəbl] *adj* na fili

notification [ˌnəutifiˈkeiʃn] *n* sanarwa

notify [ˈnəutifai] *v* sanar da

notion [ˈnəuʃn] *n* ra'ayi

not only... but also bà... ba kawai,... mā

notorious [nəuˈtɔːriəs] *adj* riƙaƙƙe

notwithstanding [ˌnɔtwiθˈstændiŋ] *prep* duk da

not yet *adv* (ba... ba) tukuna

nought [nɔːt] *n* sifiri

noun [naun] *n* suna
nourish ['nʌriʃ] *v* 1. ciyar da
2. gina jiki
nourishing ['nʌriʃin] *adj* na gina jiki
nourishment ['nʌriʃmənt] *n* abincin gina jiki
novel ['nɔvl] 1. *adj* sabo 2. *n* ƙagaggen littafi
novelist ['nɔvəlist] *n* marubuci
novelty ['nɔvlti] *n* sabon abu
November [nəu'vembə] *n* Nuwamba
novice ['nɔvis] *n* ɗan koyo
now [nau] 1. yanzu 2. just now ɗazu
nowadays ['nauədeiz] *adv* a zamanin yau
now and then *adv* lokaci-lokaci
nowhere ['nəuweə] 1. ba ko'ina 2. ba inda
now that *conj* tun da
noxious ['nɔkʃes] *adj* mai guba
nuclear ['nju:kliə] *adj* nukiliya
nuclear arms *pl* makaman nukiliya
nuclear deterrent *n* manufar yawan makaman nukiliya ƙarin zaman lafiya
nuclear energy *n* makamashin nukiliya
nuclear fallout *n* dùsař makamashin nukiliya
nuclear power *n* ƙarfin nukiliya
nuclear power station *n* tashar ƙarfin nukiliya
nuclear test *n* gwajin nukiliya
nuclear test site *n* sansanin gwajin nukiliya

nuclear warheads *pl* kawunan makaman nukiliya
nuclear waste *n* sharar nukiliya
nuclear weapons *pl* makaman nukiliya
nude [nju:d] *adj* mai tsirara
nudity ['nju:diti] *n* tsirara
nuisance ['nju:sns] *n* abin damuwa
null and void *adj* haramtacce
numb [nʌm] *adj* to be numb ƙage
number ['nʌmbə] *n* 1. alƙalami, (Nr) limaro 2. jimla 3. yawa 4. *v* kai
number-plate *n* (UK) *n* lambar mota, (Nr) limaron mota
numeral ['nju:mərəl] *n* alƙalami, (Nr) limaro
numerical [nju:'merikl] *adj* na lamba
numerous ['nju:mərəs] *adj* masu yawa
nun [nʌn] *n* (rel.) sista
nuptial ['nʌpʃəl] *adj* na aure
nurse [nə:s] 1. *n* (med.) nas 2. *v* shayar da 3. (med.) yi jiyya
nursery ['nə:səri] *n* nasare, (Nr) matarnal
nursing ['nə:sin] *n* 1. jego 2. (med.) aikin nas
nursing home *n* gidan kula da tsofaffi
nursing ['nə:sin] *n* jinya
nursing sister *n* sista
nut [nʌt] *n* ƙwaya
nutritious [nju:'triʃəs] *adj* na gina jiki
nylon ['nailɔn] *n* nailan

Oo

oar [ɔ:] *n* matuƙin jirgin ruwa

oasis [ˈəuˈeisis] (*pl* oases) zango

oath [əuθ] *n* 1. rantsuwa 2. to put under oath rantsar dà 3. to take an oath yi rantsuwa 4. to break an oath karya rantsuwa

OAU (Organization of African Unity) *n* Kungiyar Haɗa Kan Kasashen Afirka

obedience [əˈbi:diəns] *n* biyayya

obedient [əˈbi:diənt] *adj* mai biyayya

obey [əˈbei] *n* bi

obituary [əˈbitʃuəri] *n* sanarwar rasuwa/mutuwa

object [ˈɔbdʒikt] *n* 1. abu 2. manufa

object [əbˈdʒəkt] *v* ƙi

objection [əbˈdʒekʃn] *n* to have an objection to ƙi

objectionable [əbˈdəʒəkʃənəbl] *adj* abin ƙi

objective [əbˈdʒəktiv] *n* maƙasudi

obligation [ˌɔbliˈgeiʃn] *n* 1. wajibi 2. to fulfil one's obligation sake nauyi 3. (rel.) farilla

obligate [ˌɔbliˈgeit] *v* tilasta wa

obligatory [əˈbligətri] *adj* na dole

oblige [əˈblaidʒ] *v* tilasta wa

obliged [əˈblaidʒd] *adj* I was obliged to go. Tilas ya sa in tafi.

obliging [əˈblaidʒiŋ] *adj* mai yarda

oblique [əuˈbli:k] *adj* kaikaice

obliterate [əˈblitəreit] *v* halakar da

oblivious [əˈblivijəs] *adj* They were oblivious to the danger. Ba su farga da haɗarin ba.

oblong [ˈɔblɔŋ] *n* murabba'i mai dari

obnoxious [əbˈnɔkʃəs] *adj* mugu

obscene [ɔbˈsi:n] *adj* na batsa

obscenity [ɔbˈseniti] *n* batsa

obscure [əbˈskjuə] 1. *adj* ɓoyayye 2. *v* ɓoye

observant [əbˈzə:vənt] *adj* mai lura (of da)

observation [ˌɔbzəˈveiʃn] *n* lūr̃ā

observatory [əbˈzə:vətri] *n* mahangin taurari

observe [əbˈzə:v] *v* 1. duba 2. to observe the law kiyaye doka

observer [əbˈzə:və] *n* 1. ɗan kallo 2. political observer mai lura da harkokin siyasa

obsessed [əbˈses] *adj* He is obsessed with this. Abin yana cin ransa.

obsession [əbˈseʃn] *n* jaraba

obsolete [ˈɔbsəli:t] *adj*

obstacle [ˈɔbstəkl] *n* cikas

obstinate [ˈɔbstənət] *adj* 1. mai taurin kai 2. to be obstinate dāgè

obstruct [əbˈstrʌkt] *v* yi wà... bàbàkère

obstruction [əbˈstrʌktʃən] *n* 1. cikas 2. toshewa

obstructive [əbˈstrʌktiv] *adj* mai kawo cikas

obtain [əbˈtein] *v* samu

obtainable [əbˈteinəbl] *adj* mai samuwa

obvious [ˈɔbviəs] *adj* 1. a fili 2. zahiri

obviously [ˈɔbviəsli] *adv* tabbas

occasion [əˈkeiʒn] *n* lokaci

occasional [əˈkeiʒənl] *adj* na lokaci-lokaci

occasionally [əˈkeiʒənli] *adv* lokaci-lokaci

occidental [əksiˈdentl] *adj* na yamma

occupant [ˈɔkjupənt] *n* 1. wanda ke ciki 2. ɗan haya

occupation [ˌɔkjuˈpeiʃn] *n* 1. sana'a 2. (mil.) mamaya

occupational hazard [ˌɔkjuˈpeiʃənl ˈhæzəd] *n* haɗarin sana'a

occupied [ˈɔkjupaid] *adj* **to be occupied** shagala (**with** da)

occupy [ˈɔkjupai] *v* 1. yi aiki 2. zauna 3. (mil.) mamaye 4. **to occupy a position** riƙe maƙami

occupying forces *pl* sojojin mamaye

occur [əˈkəː] *v* (**occurred**) 1. auku 2. faɗo

occurrence [əˈkʌrəns] *n* abin da ya faru

ocean [ˈəuʃn] *n* babbar teku

o'clock [əuˈklɔk] *adv* ƙarfe

October [ɔkˈtəubə] *n* Oktoba

octopus [ˈɔktəpəs] *n* kifin teku mai ƙafa takwas

odd [ɔd] *adj* 1. mai ban mamaki 2. mai ban daidai ba 3. **odd number** mårå

ode [əud] *n* ƙasida

odious [ˈəudiəs] *n* mugu

odorous [ˈəudərəs] *adj* mai wari

odour [ˈəudə] *n* 1. **good odour** ƙamshi 2. **bad odour** wari

O E C D (**Organization of Economic Cooperation and Development**) *n* Kungiyar Haɗin Kan Tattalin Arziki da Ayyukan Raya Kasa

of [əv] *prep* na, ta

of course! i mana!

off [ɔf] 1. *prep* daga 2. *adv* **Lawal took his coat off.** Lawal ya tuɓe kwat ɗinsa. 3. **The travellers set off for York.** Sai matafiya suka tafi York. 4. **Did you switch off the light?** Kin kashe fitila?

offence [əˈfens] *n* laifi

offend [əˈfend] *v* bata wa... rai

offensive [əˈfensiv] *adj* mai rashin kunya

offer [ˈɔfə] 1. *n* tayi 2. *v* miƙa wa 3. ce 4. **to make an offer** taya

office [ˈɔfis] *n* 1. ofis, (Nr) biro 2. (pol.) **to hold office** riƙe muƙami

office hours *pl* lokacin aiki

officer [ˈɔfisə] *n* 1. ma'aikaci 2. (mil.) hafsa

official [əˈfiʃl] 1. *adj* na aiki 2. *n* ma'aikacin hukuma

official language *n* harshen gudunar da ayyuka

official statement *n* sanarwa ta hukuma

official talks *pl* tattaunawa ta musamman

official visit *n* ziyarar aiki

officially [əˈtiʃəli] *adv* bisa hukuma

offload [ˌɔfˈləud] *v* jibge

offshore [,ɔf·ʃɔ:] *adj* na cikin teku

offside [,ɔf·ʃaid] *adv* (spor.) ofsáyì

offspring [·ɔfspriŋ] *n* zuriya

often [·ɔfn; ·ɔftən] *adv* sau da yawa

oh! [əu] ashe!

oil [ɔil] *n* 1. mai 2. man fetur 3. baƙin mai

oil can *n* gwangwanin baƙin mai

oilfield [·ɔilfi:ld] *n* wurin haƙar ami

oil painting *n* zane

oil pipe-line *n* bututun mai

oil producing states *pl* ƙasashe mai haƙo mai

oil production *n* kwàsar mâi

oil refinery *n* matatar mai

oil rig *n* injin haƙar mai

oil rights *pl* hakkin haƙar fetur

oil spill, oil slick *n* zubewar man fetur

oil storage tank *n* rumbun ajiye man fetur

oil tanker *n* jirgin ruwa mai jigilar man fetur

oil well *n* rijiyar haƙar mâi

oily [·ɔili] *adj* mài mâi

ointment [·ɔintmənt] *n* liliman

okay, OK [,əu·kei] 1. ba laifi 2. to, (shi ke nan)

okra [·ɔkrə] *n* kuɓewa

old [əuld] *adj* 1. tsoho 2. na dâ 3. of old a zamanin dâ 4. *duba wajen* how old

old age *n* tsufa

old-fashioned *adj* na dâ

olden times *pl* gargajiya

olive [·ɔliv] *n* zaitun

olive oil *n* man zaitun

Olympics, Olympic games [ə·limpik] *pl* wasannin Oliyamfus

omelette [·ɔmlit] *n* wainar ƙwai

omen [·əumen] *n* ishara

ominous [·ɔminəs] *adj* mai ishara

omission [ə·miʃn] *n* kuskure

omit [ə·mit] *v* (omitted) 1. tsallake 2. rasa

omnibus [·ɔmnibəs] *n* 1. bas 2. sharhin ayyukan fasaha

on [ɔn] *prep* 1. a 2. kan 3. on his arrival... da isowarsa... 4. to get on a train shiga jirgin ƙasa 5. a book on Shakespeare littafi bisa kan Shakespeare 6. The book is on the table. Littafin bisa tebur ya ke. 7. I shall visit you on Sunday. Zan ziyarce ka ran Lahadi. 8. I put on my new shoes. Na sa sabon takalmi nawa. 9. Could you put the light on please? Don Alla, ka kunna fitila. 10. What's going on here? Me ake yi a nan?

on top of *prep* a kan

once [wʌns] *adv* 1. sau daya 2. at once yanzu-yanzu 3. all at once gaba ɗaya

one [wʌn] *n/adj* 1. ɗaya 2. guda 3. wani

one another *adv* juna

one by one *adv* ɗai-ɗai

one... the other wani... wani

one-party state *n* ƙasa mai bin tafarkin jam'iyya ɗaya

one-way street *n* wanwe

one-way ticket *n* tikitin zuwa

oneself [wʌn·self] 1. (a) kansa 2. mutum

onion(s) [·ʌniən] *n* albasa

onlooker [·ɔnlukə] *n* ɗan kallo

only [ˈəunli] adj/adv 1. kawai 2. kaɗai 3. an only son ɗan tilo 4. one only ɗaya tak 5. Only Christopher came. Sai Christopher ya zo. 6. if only... in dà...

only after conj sai da

onus of proof n (jur.) alhakin ba da shaida

onwards [ˈɔnwədz] adv gaba

ooze [uːz] v fito

opaque [əuˈpeik] adj mai baƙibaƙi

OPEC (Organization of Petroleum Exporting Countries) n Kungiyar Kasashe Masu Arzikin Man Fetur

open [ˈəupən] 1. adj/adv a buɗe 2. in the open air a sarari 3. v buɗe 4. to open an account buɗe ajiyar banki

opener[ˈəupənə] n mabuɗin gwangwani

opening [ˈəupniŋ] 1. adj na farko 2. n mashigi 3. dāmā 4. buɗewa

opening ceremony n bikin buɗewa

opening speech n jawabin buɗe taro

openly [ˈəupənli] adv a fili

openness [ˈəupənəs] n faɗin gaskiya

open space n fili

opera [ˈɔprə] n wasar kwaikwayo ta waƙa

opera house n gidan wasar kwaikwayo ta waƙa

operatic [ˌɔpəˈrætik] adj kama da wasar kwaikwayo ta waƙa

operate [ˈɔpəreit] v 1. sarrafa 2. (med.) yanke (on wa)

operating costs pl kuɗin aiki

operation [ˌɔpəˈreiʃn] n 1. sarrafawa 2. (med.) aiki, (Nr) opere 3. (mil.) ɗaukī

operative [ˈɔpərərətiv] n ma'aikaci

operator [ˈɔpərəitə] n afareta

ophthalmic [ɔpˈθælmik] adj na likitan ido

opinion [əˈpiniən] n 1. ra'ayi 2. in my opinion a ganina 3. a personal opinion ra'ayi na bayan rage 4. to have a high opinion of ƙaddara 5. to change one's opinion sake tunani

opinionated [əˈpiniə,neitid] adj 1. mai ra'ayi 2. mai girman kai

opinion poll n dandalin jin ra'ayin jama'a

opponent [əˈpəunənt] n 1. abokin gasa 2. (pol.) abokin hamayya

opportunity [ˌɔpəˈtjuːnəti] n dāmā

oppose [əˈpəuz] v 1. sòkā 2. (pol.) nuna adawa ga

opposing [əˈpəuziŋ] adj mai hamayya

opposite [ˈɔpəzit] adj/n 1. kishiya 2. opposite to daura da

opposition [ˌɔpəˈziʃn] n 1. hamayya 2. the opposition abokan hamayya 3. member of the opposition abokin adawa

opposition party n jam'iyyar adawa

oppress [əˈpres] v zàluntà

oppressed [əˈprest] adj/n wanda aka danne

oppression [əˈpreʃn] n zalunci

oppressive [ə'presiv] *adj* na danniya

oppressor [ə'presə] *n* àzzālùmì

optician [ɔp'tiʃn] *n* likitan ido

optics ['ɔptiks] *pl* **fibre optics** ƙananan wayoyin aika saƙo ta haske

optimism [,ɔpti'mizm] *n* kyakkyawan fata

optimistic [,ɔpti'mistik] *adj* **to be optimistic** sa rai (**about** a kan)

option ['ɔpʃn] *n* zaɓi

optional ['ɔpʃnəl] *adj* na ganin dama

options ['ɔpʃəns] *pl* hanyoyin da za a bi (**don** for)

opulence ['ɔpjuləns] *n* arziki

opulent ['ɔpjulənt] *adj* mai arziki

or [ɔ:] *conj* **1.** ko **2. either... or** ko... ko

oral ['ɔ:rəl] *adj* na baka

orange ['ɔrindʒ] **1.** *adj* mai ruwan lemon zaƙi **2.** *n* lemon zaƙi

orator ['ɔrətə] *n* mai zalaƙa

orbit ['ɔ:bit] **1.** *n* kewayewa **2.** *v* kewaye

orchard ['ɔ:tʃəd] *n* garka

orchestra ['ɔ:kistrə] *n* makaɗa

ordain [ɔ:'dein] *v* kafa doka

order ['ɔ:də] **1.** *n* umurni **2.** oda **3. law and order** doka **4. in order** bi da bi **5. to be in order** yi daidai **6. The lift is out of order.** Lif ba ya aiki. **7. in order to** domin **8. in order not to** domin kada **9. to put in order** tsara **10. to place an order** yi oda **11. to order a meal** faɗi abin da za ka ci **12. to give an order** ba da umurni **13. to follow an order**

bi umurni **14.** *v* umurta **15.** tsara

orderliness ['ɔ:dəlinəs] *n* fasali

orderly ['ɔ:dəli] **1.** *adj* mai tsari **2.** *n* (med.) ma'aikacin asibiti, (Nr) lakwataro **2.** (mil.) odale, (Nr) falanto

ordinarily ['ɔ:dənrəli] *adv* galiban

ordinary ['ɔ:dənri] *adj* na kullum

ore [ɔ:] *n* tamā

organ ['ɔ:gən] *n* **1.** zuciya da sauransu **2. sexual organ** gindi **3. church organ** fiyano na coci

organic [ɔ:'gænik] *adj* na halitta

organism ['ɔ:gənizəm] *n* halitta

organisation [,ɔ:gənai'zeiʃn] *n* **1.** ƙungiya **2.** shiri **3.** tsari

Organisation of African Unity (OAU) Kungiyar Haɗa Kan Kasashen Afirka

organise ['ɔ:gənaiz] *v* **1.** shirya **2.** tsara

organizer ['ɔ:gənaizə] *n* oganeza

orifice ['ɔ:rifis] *n* mashigi

orgasm ['ɔ:gæzm] *n* inzali

oriental [,ɔ:ri'entl] *adj* na gabas

origin ['ɔridʒin] *n* **1.** asali **2. country of origin** ƙasa ta gado

original [ə'ridʒənl] *adj* **1.** na asali **2.** na ainihi **3.** sabo

originality [ə,ridʒə'næliti] *n* azanci

originally [ə'ridʒənəli] *adv* dâ mā

originate [ə'ridʒineit] *v* yiwo asali (**from** daga)

originator [ə'ridʒineitə] *n* makaƙi

ornament ['ɔ:nəmənt] *n* **1.** ado **2.** abin ado

ornamental [ˌɔːnəˈmentl] *adj* na ado

orphan [ˈɔːfn] *n* maraya

orphanage [ˈɔːfənidʒ] *n* gidan marayu

orthodox [ˈɔːθədɔks] *adj* (Isl.) na sunna

orthography [ɔːˈθɔgrəfi] *n* ƙa'idojin rubutu

orthopaedic [ˌɔːθəˈpiːdik] *adj* na ƙashi

ostracize [ˈɔstrəsaiz] *v* tsàrgã

ostrich [ˈɔstritʃ] *n* jimina

other [ˈʌðə] *adj/n* 1. wancan 2. saura 3. some other wani dabam 4. each other juna 5. one... the other wani... wani 6. on the one hand..., and on the other a wannan ɓangare..., a ɗaya ɓangaren kuma

otherwise [ˈʌðəwaiz] *conj* in ba haka ba

otter [ˈɔtə] *n* karen ruwa

ought [ɔːt] *v* I ought to go now. Ya kamata in tafi yanzu.

ounce [auns] *n* oza

our [aː] namu, tamu

ourselves [aːˈselvz] kanmu

oust [aust] *v* hamɓarar da

ousted [ˈaustid] *adj* hamɓararre

out [aut] *adv* 1. waje 2. out of daga cikin 3. way out mafita 4. inside out bài-bâi 5. to be out of rasa 6. They went out of the classroom. Sun fito ɗakin karatu. 7. The fire went out. Wuta ta mutu. 8. This chair is made out of wood. Wannan kujera da ice ake yinta.

out and out *adj* ƙunƙà

outbid [ˌautˈbid] *v* fi sa suna

outbreak [ˈautbreik] *n* 1. ɓarkewa 2. outbreak of war tashin yaƙi

outburst [ˈautbəːst] *n* ɓarkewa

outcast [ˈautkaːst] *n* bâřē, tunkiyar ware

outcome [ˈautkʌm] *n* sakamako

outcry [ˈautkrai] *n* ƙara

outdistance [ˌautˈdistəns] *v* ba da tazarã

outdo [ˌautˈduː] *v* tsere wa

outdoors [ˌautˈdɔːz] *adv* a waje

outer [ˈautə] *adj* na daga waje

outer space *n* sararin samaniya

outermost [ˈautəməust] *adj* na can waje

outfit [ˈautfit] *n* kaya

outgoing [ˈautgəuiŋ] *adj* the outgoing leader shugaba mai barin aiki

outgrow [ˌautˈgrəu] *v* wuce da

outing [ˈautiŋ] *n* bàlàguřò

outlast [ˌautˈlaːst] *v* ga baya

outlaw [ˈautlɔː] 1. *n* mai laifi 2. *v* haramta

outlay [ˈautlei] *n* (fin.) kuɗin tsari

outlet [ˈautlet] *n* 1. mafitã 2. kanti

outline [ˈautlain] 1. *n* shaci 2. *v* shata

outlook [ˈautluk] *n* hange

outnumber [ˌautˈnʌmbə] *v* rìnjayà

out of date *adj* This tin is out of date. Gwangwanin ya tsufa.

output [ˈautput] *n* yi

outrage [ˈautreidʒ] *v* bakanta rai

outraged [ˈautreidʒd] *adj* to be outraged hàsalà

outrageous [autˈreidʒəs] *adj* mai baƙanta rai

outright ['autrait] *adj* kai tsaye

outrun [·aut'rʌn] *v* tsere wa

outside [,aut'said] 1. *n* baya
2. *adv* waje

outsider [,aut'saidə] *n* bằrē

outsize ['autsaiz] *adj* ƙato

outskirts ['autskə:ts] *pl* bayan gari

outsmart [,aut'sma:t] *v* yi wa... shiri

outspoken [,aut'spəukən] *adj* maras tsoro

outstanding [,aut'stændiŋ] *adj* 1. gằgārùmì 2. **issues outstanding** batutuwan da suka rage

outstrip [,aut'strip] *v* tsere wa

outward ['autwəd] *adj* zuwa waje

outwards ['autwədz] *adv* zuwa waje

outweigh [,aut'wei] *v* fi nauyi

outwit [,aut'wit] *v* yi wa... shiri

oval ['əuvl] *adj* mai siffar ƙwai

ovary [·əuvəri] *n* ƙwan mace

oven ['ʌvn] *n* ōbìn, (Nr) hūřừ

over ['əuvə] 1. *prep* bisa kan 2. ketaren 3. **a sign over the door** lamba bisa kan ƙofar 4. *adv* sama da 5. **over there** can nesa 6. **over the limit** fiye da yadda aka ƙayyade 7. **The cow jumped over the moon.** Shaniyar ta tsallake wata. 8. **There is some food left over.** Akwai ragowar abinci. 9. **The play is over.** An gama wasan kwaikwayo.

overall [,əuvər'ɔ:l] *adj* cikakke

over and above a baitakin wannan kuma

overcast [,əuvə'ka:st] *adj* **to be overcast** dushe

overcharge [,əuvə'tʃɔ:dʒ] *v* ƙwằrā

overcoat ['əuvəkəut] *n* abakwat, (Nr) kaffoti

overcome [,əuvə'kʌm] *v* 1. rìnjāyằ 2. **shawo kan**

overconfident [,əuvə'kɔnfidənt] *adj* **to be overconfident** nuna iya yi

overcrowded [,əuvə'kraud] *adj* **to be overcrowded** yi cìkōwằ

overcrowding [,əuvə'kraudiŋ] *n* cìkōwằ

overdo [,əuvə'du:] *v* yi fiye da kima

overdraft ['əuvədra:ft] *n* lamunin banki

overdrawn [,əuvə'drɔ:n] *adj* **My bank account is overdrawn.** Na ci bashi a banki.

overdue [,əuvə'dju:] *adj* **to be overdue** wuce lokaci

overeager [,əuvə'i:gə] *adj* mai ci-da-zuci

overeagerness [,əuvə'i:gənəs] *n* ci-da-zuci

overeat [,əuvə'i:t] *v* yi mugun ci

overflow [,əuvə'fləu] *v* 1. yi ambaliya 2. yi cìkōwằ

overgraze [,əuvə'greiz] *v* yawàità kiwồ

overgrown [,əuvə'grəun] *adj* **to be overgrown** sarƙe

overhaul [,əuvə'hɔ:l] 1. *n* garambuwal 2. *v* yi wa... garambuwal

overhead ['əuvəhed] *adj* sama

overheads ['əuvəhedz] *pl* bashi wajen tafiyar da ayyuka

overhear [,əuvə'hi:ə] *v* ji ƙishin-ƙishin (**that** cewa)

overheat [,əuvə'hi:t] *v* zafafa fiye da kima

overjoy(ᵈl [ˌəuvəˈdʒɔid] *adj* mai muma sosai

overlap [ˌəuvəˈlæp] *v* zoɓa

overload [ˌəuvəˈləud] *v* labta wa

overlook [ˌəuvəˈluk] *v* yafe wa

overnight [ˌəuvəˈnait] *adv* a dare ɗaya

overpower [ˌəuvəˈpauə] *v* ri̇njāyằ

overproduction [ˌəuvəprəˈdʌkʃn] *n* yi fiye da kima

overprotect [ˌəuvəprəuˈtekt] *v* yi fiye da tsaro

override [ˌəuvəˈraid] *v* màllakằ

overrule [ˌəuvəˈruːl] *v* soke hukunci

overrun [ˌəuvəˈrʌn] *v* mằmayằ

overseas [ˌəuvəˈsiːz] **1.** *adj* na ƙasashen ƙetare **2.** *adv* a ƙasashen ƙetare

overseer [ˌəuvəˈsiːə] *n* abasiya

oversight [ˈəuvəsait] *n* ri̇fkanằ

oversleep [ˌəuvəˈsliːp] *v* yi mugun barci

overstock [ˌəuvəˈstɔk] *v* sayo kaya fiye da kima

overstrain [ˌəuvəˈstrein] *v* girsa

overtake [ˌəuvəˈteik] *v* cim mà

overthrow [ˌəuvəˈθrəu] (pol.) **1.** *n* juyin mulki **2.** *v* hamɓarar da

overtime [ˈəuvətaim] *n* obataya

overtired [ˌəuvəˈtaiəd] *adj* **to be overtired** gaji tiɓis

overture [ˈəuvətjuə] *n* shigo-shigo

overturn [ˌəuvəˈtəːn] *v* **1.** kife **2.** kayar da

overvalue [ˌəuvəˈvæljuː] *v* daraja fiye da kima, fafata

overweight [ˌəuvəˈweit] *adj* **to be overweight** yi fiye da nauyi

overwhelm [ˌəuvəˈwelm] *v* **1.** fi ƙarfi **2.** mằmayè

overwhelming [ˌəuvəˈwelmiŋ] *adj* **with an overwhelming majority** tare da gagarumin rinjaye

overwork [ˌəuvəˈwəːk] *n* aiki da yawa

ovulate [ˈəuvjuleit] *v* yi saukar ƙwai

owe [əu] *v* bi bashi

owing [ˈəuiŋ] *adj* **owing to** saboda

owl [aul] *n* mujiya

own [əun] **1.** **on my own** ni da kaina **2.** **He has his own car.** Yana da tasa motar. **3.** *v* màllakằ

own up to *v* yarda

owner [ˈəunə] *n* mài...

ownership **private ownership** mallakar tajirai

oxygen [ˈɔksidʒən] *n* iskar shaƙa

oz. *duba* wajen **ounce**

ozone [ˈəuzəun] *n* lemar sararin samaniya

Pp

PA (personal assistant)
[ˌpiːˈai] *n* mataimaki

pace [peis] 1. *n* taki 2. *v* yi taki

pacifism [ˈpasiˌfizm] *n* aƙidar kwantar da yaƙi

pacifist [ˈpasifist] *n* ɗan gwagwarmayar hana yaƙi

pacify [ˈpæsifai] *v* kwantar da hankali

pack [pæk] 1. *n* fakiti, (Nr) fake 2. *v* kintsa 3. *duba wajen* packed

pack up *v* tattara

package [ˈpækidʒ] *n* fakiti, ƙunshi

packed *adj* to be packed cūshè (with da)

packet [ˈpækit] *n* fakiti, (Nr) fake

pact [pækt] *n* yarjejeniya

pad [pæd] 1. *n* gammo 2. paper pad littafin rubutu 3. *v* yi taki

padded [ˈpædid] *adj* mai soso

paddle [ˈpædl] 1. *n* matuƙi 2. *v* tuƙa

padlock [ˈpædlɔk] *n* kwaɗo

paediatrician [ˌpiːdijaˈtriʃn] *n* likitan yara

pagan [ˈpeign] *adj/n* arne

page [peidʒ] *n* shafi

pager [ˈpeidʒə] *n* wayar rubutu

paid [ˈpeid] *duba wajen* pay

pail [peil] *n* bokiti

pain [pein] 1. *n* zafi 2. to suffer pain sha zafi 3. *v* yi wa... zafi

painful [peinfl] *adj* mai ciwo

paint [peint] 1. *n* fenti, (Nr) fantir

2. *v* shafe da fenti 3. zana hoto

painter [ˈpeintə] *n* 1. fenta 2. mai zanen hoto

painting [ˈpeintiŋ] *n* zane, (Nr) fantir

pair [peə] *n* guda biyu

palace [ˈpælis] *n* fādà

palate [ˈpælət] *n* ganɗa

pale [peil] *adj* koɗaɗɗè

palm [paːm] *n* 1. tàfin hannu 2. goruba

palm oil [paːm ɔil] *n* mân jā

paltry [ˈpɔːltri] *adj* ƙyas

pamphlet [ˈpæmflit] *n* ƙasida

pan [pæn] *n* kwano

pancake [ˈpæŋkeik] *n* fanke

pancreas [ˈpæŋkreəs] *n* tumburkuma

pandemonium [ˌpændəˈməuniəm] *n* rikici

pane [pein] *n* gilashin taga

panel [ˈpænl] *n* 1. ɓangare 2. kwamiti

panic [ˈpænik] 1. *n* tsoro 2. *v* tsòratà

pant [pænt] *v* yi sàsshèƙà

panties [ˈpæntiz] *pl* duros na mata

pantry [ˈpæntri] *n* ɗakin abinci

pants [pænts] *pl* 1. kamfai 2. (US) wando

papal [ˈpaipl] *adj* na Paparoma

papaya [pəˈpaːyə] *n* gwanda

paper [ˈpeipə] *n* 1. takarda 2. jarida 3. (acad.) maƙala

paper mill *n* maʼaikatar takarda

par [paː] *n* to be on a par yi daidai (with da)

parachute [ˈpærəʃuːt] 1. *n* laima
2. yi saukar laima

parade [pəˈreid] *n* farētì, (Nr) defile

paradise [ˈpærədais] *n* Aljanna

paradox [ˈpærədɔks] *n* mawuyacin hali

paraffin [ˈpærəfin] *n* kananzir

paragraph [ˈpærəgraːf] *n* sakin layi

parallel [ˈpærəlel] *adj* a layi daya

paralyse [ˈpærəlaiz] *v* shânyē

paralysis [pəˈræləsis] *n* shânyêwař jìkī

paralytic [ˌpærəˈlitik] *adj* mài shânyêwař jìkī

paramount [ˈpærəmaunt] *adj* muhimmi

paraphrase [ˈpærəfreiz] *v* takaita bayani

parasite [ˈpærəsait] *n* kaska

paratrooper [ˈpærətruːpə] *n* sojan laima

paratroops [ˈpærətruːps] *pl* sojojin laima

parcel [ˈpaːsl] *n* kunshi, (Nr) kwali

pardon [ˈpaːdn] 1. *n* gafara
2. ahuwa 3. I beg your pardon! Gafara dai! 4. I beg your pardon? Ni ban ji ba!
5. *v* gafarta 6. yi wa... ahuwa

parent [ˈpeərənt] *n* mahaifi

parentage [ˈpeərəntidʒ] *n* asali

parental [pəˈrentl] *adj* na iyaye

parents [ˈpeərəntz] *pl* iyaye

parish [ˈpæriʃ] *n* unguwar coci

parity [ˈpæriti] *n* daidaito

park [paːk] 1. *n* wurin shakataw
2. carpark tashar mota
3. game park gandun daji 4. *v*

to park a car yi kiliya, (Nr) yi gare

parking [ˈpaːkiŋ] *n* kiliya, (Nr) gare

parking lot, parking space *n* filin ajiye motoci

parliament [ˈpaːləmənt] 1. *adj* na majalisar dokoki 2. *n* majalisar dokoki

parliamentary [ˌpaːləˈmentri] *adj* na majalisar dokoki

parody [ˈpærədi] *n* ba'à

parrot [ˈpærət] *n* aku

parson [ˈpaːsn] *n* (Chr.) fâdā

part [paːt] 1. *n* kashi 2. yanki
3. rukuni 4. for the most part galiban 5. as part of a sashin
6. to take part in shiga
7. *v* raba

partial [ˈpaːʃl] *adj* 1. kadan
2. to be partial to nuna bambanci 3. so

participant [paːˈtisipənt] *n* mai shiga

participate [paːˈtisipeit] *v* shiga

participation [paːˌtisiˈpeiʃn] *n* shiga

particle [ˈpaːtikl] *n* barbashi

particular [pəˈtikjulə] *adj* 1. na musamman 2. in particular musamman 3. *duba wajen* particulars

particularly [pəˈtikjuləli] *adv* 1. musamman 2. tun bà mā... bâ

particulars [pəˈtikjuləz] *pl* bayanai

partition [paːˈtiʃn] 1. *n* bangere
2. *v* raba

partly [ˈpaːtli] *adv* kadan

partner [ˈpaːtnə] *n* 1. abokin tarayya 2. miji, màtā 3. trading partner abokin ciniki

partnership [ˈpaːtnəʃip] *n* tarayya

part-time *adj* na ɗan lokaci

party [ˈpaːti] *n* **1.** biki **2.** ƙungiya **3.** (pol.) jam'iyya, (Nr) farti **4.** (leg.) abokin shari'a

party member *n* ɗan jam'iyya

party militant *n* ɗan gà-ni-kàshĕ-ni na jàm'iyyà

pass [paːs] **1.** *n* izini **2.** mountain pass wurin ƙetare duwatsu **3.** *v* wuce **4.** miƙa **5.** to pass the day wuni **6.** to pass an exam ci jarrabawa **7.** to pass a law kafa doka **8.** to pass a resolution zartar da ƙudiri

pass away *v* ràsu

passable [ˈpaːsəbl] *adj* mai ratsuwa

passage [ˈpæsidʒ] *n* **1.** tafiya **2.** wucewa **3.** hanya

pass by *v* shige ta

passenger [ˈpæsindʒə] *n* fasinja, (Nr) fasaje

passer-by *n* mai wucewa

passion [ˈpæʃn] *n* jaraba

passionate [ˈpæʃənət] *adj* mai jaraba

passive [ˈpæsiv] *adj* maras ƙoƙari

pass out *v* sūma

passport [ˈpaːspɔːt] *n* **1.** fasfo, (Nr) fazgo **2.** forged passport fàsfô na jàbu

pass through *v* ratsa

past [paːst] **1.** *adj* wanda ya wuce **2.** *n* zamanin dâ **3.** in the past a lokacin baya **4.** half past four ƙarfe huɗu da rabi **5.** *adv* to go past wuce

pasta [ˈpastə] *n* taliya

paste [peist] **1.** *n* liƙi **2.** *v* liƙa

pastime [ˈpaːstaim] *n* aikin sa kai

pastor [ˈpaːstə] *n* (Chris.) fasto

pastoral [ˈpaːstrəl] *adj* na daji

pastry [ˈpeistri] *n* cincin

pasture [ˈpaːstʃə] *n* makiyaya

pastureland [ˈpaːstʃələænd] *n* dausayi

pat [pæt] *v* dàddaɓà

patch [pætʃ] **1.** *n* faci **2.** *v* liƙe

patent [ˈpeitnt] *n* lambar ƙira

patented [ˈpeitəntid] *adj* mai lambar ƙira

patent office *n* ofishin ba da lambar ƙira

paternal [pəˈtəːnl] *adj* na uba

path [paːθ] *n* turba

pathetic [pəˈθetik] *adj* mai ban tausayi

pathway [ˈpaːθwei] *n* hanya

patience [ˈpeiʃns] *n* haƙuri

patient [ˈpeiʃnt] **1.** *adj* mai haƙuri **2.** *n* majiyyaci

patriot [ˈpætriət] *n* ɗan kishin ƙasa

patriotic [ˌpætriˈɔtik] *adj* mai kishin ƙasa

patriotism [ˈpætriətizəm] *n* kishin ƙasa

patrol [pəˈtrəul] **1.** *n* 'yan sintiri **2.** *v* yi sintiri

patron [ˈpeitrən] *n* **1.** maigida **2.** abokin ciniki

patronize [ˈpætrənaiz] *v* **1.** zuwa bi **2.** tallafa wa **3.** wulaƙanta

pattern [ˈpætn] *n* **1.** zane **2.** samfur

pause [pɔːz] **1.** *n* ɗan hutu **2.** *v* tsaya kaɗan

pavement [ˈpeivmənt] *n* (UK) gefen hanya

paw [pɔː] *n* dàgi

pawn [pɔːn] v dangànā
pawpaw [pɔː pɔː] n gwanda
pay [pei] 1. n albashi 2. v biya
pay a visit v kai wa... ziyara
pay attention v lura (to da)
pay back v 1. farke bashi
2. rama
payday n ranar biya
pay rise n ƙarin albashi
payable [ˈpeiəbl] adj a biya...
payee [peiˈiː] n mai kuɗi
payment [ˈpeimənt] n biyà
pc [piːˈsiː] n inji mai ƙwaƙwalwa
peas [piːz] pl waken Turawa
peace [piːs] n 1. zaman lafiya
2. kwanciyar hankali
peaceful [ˈpiːsfl] adj mai zaman
lafiya
peaceful competition n
gogayya ta lumana
peacefully [ˈpiːsfəli] adv to solve
a problem peacefully warware
batu cikin ruwan sanyi
peaceful means pl hanyoyin
lumana
peace talks pl shawarwarin
sulhu
peace treaty n yarjejeniyar
zaman lafiya
peach [piːtʃ] n wani irin 'ya'yan
zaƙi
peak [piːk] 1. adj iyaka 2. n
ƙololuwa 3. ganiya 4. v gàwuřtà
peak season n babban lokaci
peanut [ˈpiːnʌt] n gyaɗa
pearl [pəːl] n lu'ulu'u
peasant [ˈpeznt] n baƙauye
peat [piːt] n baƙar ƙasa
pebble [ˈpebl] n tsakuwa
peck [pek] v yi ƙòtō
peculiar [piˈkjuːliə] adj 1. ba na
kullum ba 2. mai ban mamaki

peculiarity [piˌkjuːliˈærəti] n abin
ba na kullum ba
pedal [ˈpedl] n feda
peddler [ˈpedlə] n ɗan jaura
pedestal [ˈpedistl] n ƙaramin
dandamali
pedestrian [piˈdestriən] n mai
tafiya a ƙafa
pediatrician [ˌpiːdjəˈtriʃn] n
likitan yara
pedigree [ˈpedigriː] n asali
pedlar [ˈpedlə] n ɗan jaura
peek [piːk] v leƙa
peel [piːl] 1. n ɓawo 2. v ɓare
peep [piːp] v leƙa
peer [piə] 1. n sa'à 2. saraki
3. v dudduba
peerage [ˈpiəridʒ] n sarauta
peerless [ˈpiəlis] adj ba kamarsa
peg [peg] n 1. fegi 2. maratayi
pelican [ˈpelikən] n kwasa-kwasa
pelt [pelt] v jèfà
pen [pen] n alƙalami, (Nr) istilo
penal [ˈpiːnl] adj na dokar horo
penalise [ˈpiːnəlaiz] v hòrā
penalty [ˈpenlti] n 1. horo
2. hukunci 3. (spor.) fanariti
penance [ˈpenəns] n shafe laifi
pence [pens] duba wajen **penny**
pencil [ˈpensl] n fensir, (Nr)
karaniyo
pencil sharpener n shafana
pendant [ˈpendənt] n abin wuya
pending [ˈpendiŋ] 1. adj wanda
ba a yanke ba tukuna 2. prep
har zuwa
penetrate [ˈpenitreit] v 1. huda
2. kutsa
penetrating [ˈpenitreitiŋ] adj 1.
mai dabara 2. mai ƙarfi
penetration [ˌpenitreiʃn] n 1.
huji 2. kutsawa

peninsula [pə'ninsjulə] *n* makurɗaɗa

penis ['pi:nis] *n* azzakari

penitent ['penitənt] *adj* mai tuba

penniless ['penilis] *adj* miskini

penny ['peni] *n* (*pl* pence/pennies) kwabo

pension ['penʃn] *n* fensho, (Nr) antare

pensioner ['penʃnə] *n* mai karɓar fensho, (Nr) ɗan antare

pensive ['pensiv] *adj* mai tunani

people ['pi:pl] *pl* 1. mutane 2. jama'a 3. the people al'umma

people's republic *n* jamhuriyar al'umma

people's revolutionary council *n* majalisar turu ta al'umma

pepper ['pepə] *n* 1. barkono 2. yaji

peppermint ['pepəmint] *n* minti

peptalk ['peptɔ:k] *n* maganar ba da ƙarfi

per [pə; pə:] *prep* How much do they pay per hour? Nawa ake biya awa guda?

perceive [pə'si:v] *v* gane

per cent [pə'sent] three per cent kashi uku cikin ɗari

percentage [pə'sentidʒ] *n* kashi cikin ɗari

perceptible [pə'septəbl] *adj* mai fahimtuwa

perception [pə'sepʃn] *n* fahimi

perceptive [pə'septiv] *adj* mai fahimi

percussion [pə'kʌʃn] *n* kiɗa

perestroika [,pere'strɔikə] *n* aƙidar yi wa kwaminisanci gyaran fuska

perfect ['pə:fikt] *n* 1. maras aibi 2. wanda ya dace

perfect [pə'fekt] *v* inganta

perfection [pə'fekʃn] *n* kammala

perfectly [pə'fektli] *adv* sosai

perforate ['pə:fəreit] *v* huda

perforation [,pə:fə'reiʃn] *n* huji

perform [pə'fɔ:m] *v* 1. aikata 2. to perform a play yi wasan kwaikwayo

performance [pə'fɔ:məns] *n* 1. aikatawa 2. wasan kwaikwayo, (Nr) tiyatir

perfume ['pə:fju:m] *n* turare

perhaps [pə'hæps] *adv* wataƙila

peril ['perəl] *n* haɗari

perilous ['perələs] *adj* mai haɗari

period ['piəriəd] *n* 1. lokaci 2. ajali 3. zamani 4. aya 5. haila 6. to miss a period yi ɓatan wata

periodic [,piəri'ɔdik] *adj* lokaci-lokaci

perish ['periʃ] *v* hàlakà

perishable ['periʃəbl] *adj* mai ruɓa

perjury ['pə:dʒəri] *n* 1. shaidar zur 2. to commit perjury yi shaidar zur

perm [pə:m] *n* ƙunar gashi

permanence ['pə:mənəns] *n* dindindin

permanent ['pəmənənt] *adj* na dindindin

permanent delegate *n* dawwamammen wakili, zaunannen wakili

permanently ['pəmənəntli] *adv* har abada

permanent seat *n* (pol.) zaunanniyar kujera

permanent secretary *n* (pol.) dawwamammen sakatare

permission [pə'miʃn] *n* izini

permit [ˈpəːmit] *n* takardar izini
permit [pəˈmit] *v* (**permitted**)
1. ba da izini 2. yarda
perpendicular [ˌpəːpənˈdikjulə] *adj* a tsaye
perpetrate [pəˈpetʃueit] *v* aikata laifi
perpetual [pəˈpetʃuəl] *adj* dawwamamme
perpetually [pəˈpetʃuəli] *adv* kullum
perpetuate [pəˈpetʃueit] *v* dawwama
perplex [pəˈpleks] *v* rikita
persecute [ˈpəːsikjuːt] *v* zàluntà
persecution [ˌpəːsiˈkjuːʃn] *n* zalunci
persecutor [ˈpəːsikjuːtə] *n* azzalumi
perseverance [ˌpəːsiˈviərəns] *n* daurewa
persevere [ˌpəːsiˈviə] *v* tashi tsaye
persist [pəˈsist] *v* dage
persistence [pəˈsistəns] *n* dagewa
persistent [pəˈsistənt] *adj* mai dagewa
person [ˈpəːsn] *n* 1. mutum, mutuniya 2. in person da kansa
personal [ˈpəːsənl] *adj* 1. na kansa 2. na bayan fage
personally [ˈpəːsənli] *adv* da kansa
personal opinion *n* ra'ayi na bayan fage
personal organiser *n* littafin tsarin lokaci, kalkuletar tsarin lokaci
personality [ˌpəːsəˈnæləti] *n* halin mutum

personnel [ˌpəːsəˈnel] *n* ma'àikàta
perspective [pəˈspektiv] *n* ra'ayi
perspiration [ˌpəːspəˈreiʃn] *n* gumi
perspire [pəˈspaiə] *v* yi gumi
persuade [pəˈsweid] *v* làllàsà
persuasion [pəˈsweiʒn] *n* lallashi
persuasive [pəˈsweisiv] *adj* mai lallashi
pertinent [ˈpəːtinənt] *adj* to be pertinent to shàfà
perusal [ˈpəruːzl] *n* dubawa
peruse [pəˈruːz] *v* duba
pervert [ˈpəːvəːt] *n* mugu mai abin assha
pervert [pəˈvəːt] *v* 6ata
pessimism [ˈpesimizəm] *n* mugun fata
pessimist [ˈpesimist] *n* mai mugun fata
pessimistic [ˌpesiˈmistik] *adj* to be pessimistic nuna shakku
pest [pest] *n* ƙwaro
pester [ˈpestə] *v* matsa wa
pestle [ˈpesl] *n* ta6arya
pet [pet] *n* dabbar gida
petal [ˈpetl] *n* kunnen fure
petition [pəˈtiʃn] 1. *n* takarda kai ƙara 2. *v* yi ƙara
petitioner [pəˈtiʃnə] *n* mai ƙara
petrol, petroleum [ˈpetrəl; pəˈtrəuliəm] *n* mâi, (Nr) isanshi
petrol pump *n* famfon man fetur
petrol station *n* gidan mai
petroleum [pəˈtrəuliəm] man fetur, (Nr) fitaro
petticoat [ˈpetikəut] *n* fatari
petty [ˈpeti] *adj* maras muhimmanci

petty cash n feti-kash
petty trading n jaura
phantom [ˈfæntəm] n fatalwa
pharmacologist [ˌfaːməˈkɔlɔdʒist] n mai ilimin harhaɗa magunguna
pharmacology [ˌfaːməˈkɔlɔdʒi] n ilimin harhaɗa magunguna
pharmacist [ˈfaːməsist] n kyamis, (Nr) hwarmashi
pharmacy [ˈfaːməsi] n kantin magani
PhD [ˌpiːeitʃˈdiː] n babban digirin karatu
phenomenon [fəˈnɔminən] n (pl **phenomena**) sabon abu
philosopher [fiˈlɔsəfə] n mai falsafa
philosophy [fiˈlɔsəfi] n ilimin falsafa
phlegm [flem] n kaki
phone [fəun] 1. n teliho 2. **car phone** tarhon mota 3. **cordless phone** woki-toki 4. **mobile phone** oba-oba 5. v buga wa... waya
phonetic [fəˈnetik] adj mai furucui
phonetics [fəˈnetiks] n ilimin furuci
phonology [fəˈnɔlɔdʒi] n ilimin tsarin sauti
photo [ˈfəutəu] 1. n hoto 2. v ɗauki hoto
photocopier [ˈfəutəukɔpiə] n majuyin takardu
photocopy [ˈfəutəukɔpi] 1. n kwafè, (Nr) kòpî 2. v yi kwafè, (Nr) yi kòpî
photograph [ˈfəutəgraːf] 1. n hoto 2. v ɗauki hoto
photographer [fəˈtɔgrəfə] n mai ɗaukar hoto

photography [fəˈtɔgrəfi] n ɗaukar hoto
phrase [freiz] n jimla
physical [ˈfiziklˌ] adj na jiki
physical education n ilimin motsa jiki
physician [fiˈziʃn] n likita, (Nr) daktar
physicist [ˈfizisist] n mai ilimin kimiyyar ƙere-ƙere
physics [ˈfiziks] n ilimin aikin ƙira
physiotherapist [ˌfiziəuˈθerəpist] n likitan gashì
physiotherapy [ˌfiziəuˈθerəpi] n gashì
piano, pianoforte [piˈænəuˌ piˌænəuˈfɔːti] n biyano
pick [pik] v 1. tsinta 2. zàɓā 3. cire 4. **to pick a pocket** yanke wa... aljihu 5. duba wajen **pickaxe**
pickaxe [ˈpikæks] n diga
picket [ˈpikit] 1. n zanga-zanga 2. v yi zaznga-zanga
pick on v zòlayà
pick out v 1. tsame (**from** daga) 2. zàɓā
pickpocket [ˈpikˌpɔkit] n ɗan sānè
pick-up n a-kori-kura
pick up v 1. ɗaga 2. ɗauka
picnic [ˈpiknik] n fikinik
pictorial [pikˈtɔːriəl] n mai hoto
picture [ˈpiktʃə] n 1. zane 2. hoto 3. sura
Pidgin English n Buroka
Pidgin French n (Nr) Faransanshin tsohon soji
pie [pai] n abincin Turai
piece [piːs] 1. gutsure 2. yanki 3. **to break into pieces** kakkarya

piece together v harhaɗa

piecework [ˈpiːswəːk] n gwargwadon aiki gwargwadon biya

pier [piə] n kwàtã

pierce [piəs] n sôkã

piercing [ˈpiəsiŋ] adj mai tsanani

pig [pig] n alade

pigeon [ˈpidʒin] n tattabara

pigeonhole [ˈpidʒinhəul] n tasar barin sako a ofis

piglet [ˈpiglit] n ɗan alade

pigsty [ˈpigstai] n 1. gidan alade 2. barktai

pile [pail] 1. n tari 2. v tara

piles [pailz] pl basur

pile up v tsiba

pilgrim [ˈpilgrim] n 1. mai ziyara 2. (Isl.) alhaji

pilgrimage [ˈpilgrimidʒ] 1. ziyara 2. (Isl.) haji

pill [pil] n 1. ƙwayar magani 2. the Pill ƙwayar hana haihuwa 3. to take a pill sha ƙwaya

pillar [ˈpilə] n ginshiƙi

pillar box n (UK) akwatin wasiƙu

pillow [ˈpiləu] n matashin kai

pilot [ˈpailət] 1. n matuƙin jirgi 2. v tuƙa jirgi

pimp [pimp] n kàwãlì

pimple [ˈpimpl] n ƙurji

pin [pin] n fil

pinch [pintʃ] v tsunkula

pineapple [ˈpainæpl] n abarba

ping-pong [ˈpiŋpɔŋ] n ƙwallon tebur

pink [piŋk] adj mai ruwan hoda

pinnacle [ˈpinəkl] n ganiya

pins and needles pl minjirya

pint [paint] n fayint

pioneer [ˌpaiəˈniə] n jagoran uba

pious [ˈpaiəs] adj mai tsoron Allah

pipe [pip] n 1. bututu 2. famfo 3. lofe

pipeline [ˈpaiplain] n oil pipeline bututun mâi

pirate [ˈpaiərət] n 1. ɗan fashi na teku 2. ɗan kantafis

pirated goods pl kayayyakin jabu

pistol [ˈpistl] n libarba, (Nr) fistole

piston [ˈpistən] n fistin, (Nr) fistan

pit [pit] n rami

pitch [pitʃ] 1. n kaifin sauti 2. (spor.) filin wasa 3. v to pitch a tent kafa laima

pitch black adj baƙi ƙirin

pitch dark adj duhu ƙirin

pitfall [ˈpitfɔːl] n cikas

pitiable [ˈpitiəbl] adj mai ban tausayi

pitiful [ˈpitifəl] adj mai ban tausayi

pitiless [ˈpitilis] adj maras tausayi

pity [ˈpiti] 1. n tausayi 2. what a pity! àsshã! 3. v ji ƙai

pivot [ˈpivət] n ginshiƙi

pizza [ˈpiːtsə] n fisa

placard [ˈplækaːd] n lamba

place [pleis] 1. n wuri 2. matsayi 3. in place of a madadin 4. out of place 5. in the first place da farko dai 6. to take place faru 7. to take someone's place zauna a matsayin 8. v sa

placenta [pləˈsentə] n uwar cibiya

place of residence n wurin zama

place of work *n* ma'aikata

place onto *v* ɗora kan

placid [ˈplæcid] *adj* mai kwanciyar hankali

plagiarism [pleidʒəˈrizm] *n* hankākancì

plague [pleig] *n* annoba

plain [plein] **1.** *adj* maras ado **2.** a fili **3.** *n* sararin ƙasa

plain-clothes police [ˈplein-klauɓz] *n* 'yan sandan farin kaya

plainly [ˈpleinli] *adv* a fili

plaintiff [ˈpleintif] *n* (leg.) mai ƙara

plait [plæt] **1.** *n* kitso **2.** *v* kitse

plan [plæn] **1.** *n* dabara **2.** shaci **3.** *v* **(planned)** shirya

plane [plein] *n* **1.** jirgin sama **2.** fili **3. by plane** a jirgin sama

planet [ˈplænit] *n* tauraro

plank [plæŋk] *n* katako

planning [ˈplæniŋ] *n* tanadi

plant [plaːnt] **1.** *n* tsiro **2.** ma'aikata **3.** *v* shuka

plantain [ˈplaːntein] *n* agade

plantation [plænˈteiʃn] *n* gandu

planting [ˈplaːntiŋ] *n* shuka

plants [plaːnts] *pl* tsìre-tsìre

plaster [ˈplaːstə] **1.** *n* shāfē **2.** (med.) filasta **3.** *v* shafa

plasterer [ˈplaːstərə] *n* mài shāfē

plastic [ˈplæstik] **1.** *adj* na roba **2.** *n* roba

plastic bag *n* leda

plate [pleit] *n* faranti

plateau [ˈplætəu] *n* tudu

platform [ˈplætfɔːm] *n* dandamali

play [plei] **1.** *n* wasan kwaikwayo **2.** *v* (spor.) yi wasa **3.** (mus.) yi kiɗa **4. They played**

against each other. Sun kara da juna a wasanni.

player [ˈpleiə] *n* (spor.) ɗan wasa

playground [ˈpleigraund] *n* filin wasa, fagen gaɗa

playing-field *n* filin wasa

plea [pliː] *n* rɔ̂ƙɔ̂

plead [pliːd] *v* rɔ̂ƙâ

pleasant [ˈpleznt] *adj* mai daɗi

pleasantness [ˈplezntnis] *n* dāɗì

please [pliːz] *v* **1.** faranta wa... rai **2. please!** don Allah!

pleased [pliːzd] *adj* **to be pleased** yi murna

pleasing [ˈpliːziŋ] *adj* mài fàràntà râi

pleasure [ˈpleʒə] *n* jin daɗi

plebiscite [ˈplebisait] *n* ƙuri'ar neman ra'ayi

pledge [pledʒ] **1.** *n* alwashi **2.** *v* ɗauki alwashi

plenary session [ˈpliːnəri] *n* taro mai cikakken iko

plentiful [ˈplentifl] *adj* da yawa

plenty [ˈplenti] *adj/adv* da yawa

pleurisy [ˈpləːrisi] *n* maɗaukai

pliers [ˈplaiəz] *pl* filaya, (Nr) fans

plight [plait] *n* matsala

plot [plɔt] **1.** (pol.) maƙarƙashiya **2. plot of land** fuloti **3. story plot** ƙàshi **4.** *v* ƙulla maƙarƙashiya (**against** wa)

plough [plau] **1.** *n* garma **2.** *v* yi kaftu

pluck [plʌk] *v* **1.** cire **2.** (mus.) buga

plug [plʌg] *n* **1.** matoshi **2. electric plug** kan lantarki, (Nr) fish **3. spark plug** fulogi, (Nr) buji

plug in *v* sa kan lantarki a soket

plug socket *n* soket, (Nr) firis

plum [plʌm] *n* ɗinya

plumber [ˈplʌmə] *n* mai aikin famfo

plumbing [ˈplʌmiŋ] *n* 1. aikin famfo 2. famfuna

plume [pluːm] *n* gashi

plump [plʌmp] *adj* mai ƙiba

plunder [ˈplʌndə] *v* washe

plunge [plʌndʒ] *v* 1. diro 2. sânyă

plural [ˌpluərəl] *adj/n* jam'i

plus [plʌs] *prep* 1. tara da 2. da

plus factor *n* to be a plus factor zàmanà wani tàimakō (for gà)

plush [plʌʃ] *adj* na alatu

plywood [ˈplaiwud] *n* fale-falen katako

p.m. (post meridiem) [ˌpiːˈem] da yamma

PMB (post mail bag) *n* jakar gidan waya

pneumonia [njuːˈməuniə] *n* namoniya

PO (post office) [ˌpiːˈəu] *n* gidan waya, (Nr) fas

poach [pəutʃ] *v* sace harbi

poacher [ˈpəutʃə] *n* masacin harbi

PO box *n* akwatin gidan waya

pocket [ˈpɔkit] *n* aljihu

pocket money *n* gùzuri̇

pocketful [ˈpɔkitful] *n* cike da aljihu

pod [pɔd] *n* kwafsa

poem [ˈpəuim] *n* waƙa

poet [ˈpəuit] *n* mawaƙi

poetic [pəuˈetik] *adj* na waƙa

poetry [ˈpəuitri] *n* waƙa

point [pɔint] 1. *n* ɗigo 2. maƙasudi 3. maki 4. (spor.) ci

5. **compass point** kusùrwă 6. **point of a needle** tsinin allura 7. **point of view** ra'àyi 8. **to adopt a point of view** ɗauki ra'ayi 9. **an unofficial point of view** ra'ayi na bayan fage 10. **what's the point of...?** ina fa'idar...? 11. **to be on the point of** gòshin 12. **from her point of view** ta fuskarta 13. **zero point three (0.3)** ɗigo uku na kashi ɗaya 14. *v* nuna 15. **to point a gun at** auna... da bindinga

pointed [ˈpɔintid] *adj* mai tsini

pointless [ˈpɔintləs] *adj* maras amfani

point out *v* nusar da

poise [pɔiz] *n* hankali kwance

poised [ˈpɔizd] *adj* to be poised to yi shiri

poison [ˈpɔizn] 1. *n* guba 2. *v* ba da guba

poison gas *n* gas mai guba

poisonous [ˈpɔizənəs] *adj* mai guba

poisonous waste *n* shàră mài illă

poke [pəuk] *v* tsokana

poker [ˈpəukə] *n* matsokani

pole [pəul] *n* 1. dogon sanda 2. **the North Pole** iyakacin duniya na arewa 3. **the South Pole** iyakacin duniya na kudu

pole vault *n* (spor.) tsallen gwangwala

police [pəˈliːs] *pl* 1. 'yan sanda, (Nr) falis 2. **secret police** 'yan sandan leƙen asiri 3. **military police** kùrfau, (Nr) falis militar

police force *n* ƙungiyar 'yan sanda

police inspector *n* sufeto, (Nr) ansfaktar
policeman, police officer [pə'li:smən] *n* ɗan sanda
police station *n* ofishin 'yan sanda
policewoman [pə'li:s,wumən] *n* 'yar sanda
policy ['pɔləsi] *n* 1. (pol.) manufa 2. **insurance policy** takardar inshora
polio ['pəuliəu] *n* ciwon inna
polish ['pɔliʃ] 1. *n* mâi 2. *v* goge
politburo [,pɔlit'bju:rəu] *n* kwàmitìn zartârwā
polite [pə'lait] *adj* mai ladabi
politeness [pə'laitnis] *n* ladabi
political [pə'litikl] *adj* na siyasa
political asylum *n* mafakar siyasa
political demands *pl* bukatu na siyasa
political institutions *pl* kafofin siyasa
political order *n* daula
political party *n* jam'iyya
political science *n* ilimin siyasa
political scientist *n* mai ilimin siyasa
politician [,pɔli'tiʃn] *n* ɗan siyasa
politics ['pɔlətiks] *n* siyasa
poll [pəul] 1. *n* zàɓē 2. **opinion poll** binciken ra'ayin jama'a 3. *v* bincike ra'ayin jama'a
polling ['pəuliŋ] *n* jefa ƙuri'a
polling booth *n* rumfar jefa ƙuri'a
polling day *n* ranar zàɓē
polls [pəulz] *n* zàɓē
poll tax *n* (UK) harajin kai
pollute [pə'lju:t] *v* gurɓata

pollution [pə'lu:ʃn] *n* gurɓacewa
polo ['pəuləu] *n* hōlò
polygamy [pə'ligəmi] *n* auren mace fiye da guda
polytechnic [,pɔli'teknik] *n* (ed.) kwalejin fasaha da sana'a
pompous ['pɔmpəs] *adj* mai girman kai
pond [pɔnd] *n* ɗan tabki
ponder ['pɔndə] *v* yi tunani
pony ['pəuni] *n* ƙuru
pool [pu:l] 1. *n* ɗan tabki 2. (fin.) àɗàshi 3. *v* to pool resources haɗa gwiwa 4. *duba* wajen **swimming-pool**
poor [pɔ:] *adj* 1. mataulaci 2. maras kyau
poorly ['pɔ:li] 1. *adj* maras lafiya 2. *adv* ba sosai ba
pop [pɔp] *v* fashe
pop in *v* ɗan zìyartà
pope [pəup] *n* Paparoma
popular ['pɔpjulə] *adj* 1. na al'umma 2. mai farin jini
popularity [,pɔpju'lærəti] *n* farin jini
popularize ['pɔpjuləraiz] *v* tallata, ya da
populate ['pɔpjuleit] *v* turara cikin
populated [,pɔpju'leitid] *adj* **The area is populated.** Mutane suna zama a wurin.
population [,pɔpju'leiʃn] *n* 1. al'umma 2. yawan jama'a
population control *n* yaƙin hana yaɗuwar al'umma
population explosion *n* ambaliyar jama'a
populous ['pɔpjuləs] *adj* mai jama'a
porcelain ['pɔ:səlin] *n* faɗi-ka-mutu

porch [pɔ:tʃ] *n* **1.** rumfa **2.** (US) baranda

pore over [pɔ:] *v* duba

porcupine [ˈpɔːkjupain] *n* beguwa

pork [pɔːk] *n* naman alade

porn [pɔːn] *duba wajen* pornography

pornographic [ˌpɔːnəˈgræfik] *adj* na batsa

pornography [pɔːˈnɔgrəfi] *n* batsa

porous [ˈpɔːrəs] *adj* mai ramuka

porridge [ˈpɔridʒ] *n* kunu

port [pɔːt] *n* tashar jiragen ruwa

portable [ˈpɔːtəbl] *adj* mai ɗaukuwa

porter [ˈpɔːtə] *n* **1.** ɗan dako **2.** ƙofa

portfolio [pɔːtˈfəuliəu] *n* **1.** fayil **2.** (pol.) matsayi **3.** **minister without portfolio** minista maras ma'aikata

portion [ˈpɔːʃn] *n* **1.** kashi **2.** rabo

portly [ˈpɔːtli] *adj* mai ƙiba

portrait [ˈpɔːtreit] *n* hoto

pose [pəuz] *v* shirya kai

pose a problem *v* zama matsala

pose a question *v* yi tambaya

position [pəˈziʃn] *n* **1.** matsayi **2.** wuri **3.** ra'ayi

positive [ˈpɔzətiv] *adj* **1.** tabbatacce **2.** mai faranta rai

positively [ˈpɔzətivli] *adv* ba shakka

possess [pəˈzes] *v* mallaka

possession(s) [pəˈzeʃn] *pl* dukiya

possessor [pəˈzesə] *n* mài...

possibility [ˌpɔsəˈbiləti] *n* dāmā

possible [ˈpɔsəbl] *adj* mai yiwuwa

possibly [ˈpɔsəbli] *adv* watakila

post [pəust] **1.** *n* matsayi **2.** turke **3.** mel **4.** *v* aika da **5.** kafa

postage [ˈpəustidʒ] *n* kuɗin sufurin wasiƙu

postage stamp *n* kan sarki, (Nr) tambur

postal order *n* fas'oda, (Nr) manda

postbox [ˈpəustbɔks] *n* akwatin gidan waya

postcard [ˈpəustkaːd] *n* katin gaisuwa

post code *n* (UK) lambar titi

poster [ˈpəustə] *n* talla

posterior [ˈpɔstiəriə] *adj* na baya

posterity [pɔˈsterəti] *n* don gaba

post mail bag *n* jakar gidan waya

postman [ˈpəustmən] *n* masinjan gidan waya

post office *n* gidan waya, (Nr) fas

post office box *n* akwatin gidan waya

postpone [pəˈspəun] *v* ɗaga

postponement [pəˈspəunmənt] *n* ɗagawa

posture [ˈpɔstʃə] *n* diri

post-war [ˌpɔstˈwɔː] *adj* bayan yaƙi

pot [pɔt] *n* tukunya

potato [pəˈteitəu] *n* (*pl* **potatoes**) dankalin Turawa, (Nr) kwambitar

potency [ˈpəutnsi] *n* ƙarfi

potent [ˈpəutnt] *adj* mai ƙarfi

potential [pəˈtenʃl] *n* **1.** iko **2.** dāmā

pot-hole [ˈpɔthəul] *n* ramin titi

potter [ˈpɔtə] *n* mai ginin tukwane

pottery [ˈpɔtəri] *n* 1. tukwane
2. ginin tukwane
potty [ˈpɔti] *n* sàkainaȓ kāshī
pouch [pautʃ] *n* 'yar jaka
poultry [ˈpəultri] *pl* kaji
pounce on [pauns] *v* fyauce
pound [paund] 1. *n* laba 2. (fin.)
fam 3. *v* daka
pounding [ˈpaundiŋ] *n* lùgùdē
pour [pɔ:] *v* zuba
pouring [pɔ:riŋ] *adj* It is
pouring. Ana ruwa.
pout [paut] *v* zungurō bāki
poverty [ˈpɔvəti] *n* talauci
poverty-stricken *adj* matalauci
powder [ˈpaudə] *n* hoda
power [ˈpauə] *n* 1. iko 2. ƙarfi
3. ƙarfin wutar lantarki
4. (pol.) **to take power** karɓi
mulki 5. **to seize power** yi
juyin mulki
power cut *n* kashe wuta
power plant, power station *n*
gidan wuta, (Nr) gidan inarji
power-sharing *n* rarràbà
màdàfan ikð
powerbook [ˈpauəbuk] *n* inji
mai ƙwaƙwalwa
powerful [ˈpauəfl] *adj* mai ƙarfi
powerless [ˈpauələs] *adj* maras
ƙarfi
PR [ˌpi:ˈa:] *duba wajen* **public**
relations
practical [ˈpræktikl] *adj* mai
amfani
practically [ˈpræktikli] *adv* kusan
practice [ˈpræktis] *n* 1. gwaji
2. faratis 3. aiki 4. **in practice**
à àikàce 5. **to put into practice**
yi tà'ammàlī dà
practise [ˈpræktis] *v* 1. gwada
2. yi faratis 3. aikata

practitioner [prækˈtiʃənə] *n*
ma'aikaci
praise [preiz] 1. *n* yabo 2. *v* yàbā
praise-singer *n* maroƙi
praiseworthy [ˈpreizwə:ði] *adj*
abin yabo
pram [præm] *n* firam
prank [præŋk] *n* wasa
pray [prei] *v* 1. yi addu'a
2. (Isl.) yi salla
prayer [preə] *n* 1. addu'a
2. (Isl.) salla
praying mantis [ˌpreijiŋˈmæntis]
n ƙoƙi-ƙoƙi
pre-empt [pri:ˈempt] *v* yi wa...
tarbon gaba
pre-war [pri:ˈwɔ:] *adj* kafin yaƙi
preach [pri:tʃ] *v* yi wa'azi
preacher [ˈpri:tʃə] *n* mai wa'azi
precarious [priˈkeəriəs] *adj* mai
haɗari
precaution [priˈkɔ:ʃn] *n* rigakafi
precautionary measure
[priˈkɔ:ʃənəri] *n* rigakafi
precede [priˈsi:d] *v* gabata
preceding [priˈsi:diŋ] *adj* **the**
preceding years shekarun da
suka wuce
precedence [ˈpresidəns] *n* fīfīkō
precedent [ˈpresidənt] *n*
kwatanci
precinct [ˈpri:siŋkt] *n* 1. (US)
unguwa, (Nr) karce 2. (UK)
shopping precinct babbar
kasuwa
precious [ˈpreʃəs] *adj* mai daraja
precise [priˈsais] *adj* 1. daidai
2. na ainihi
precisely [priˈsaisli] *adv* daidai
precision [priˈsiʒn] *n* daidaito
preconception [ˌpri:kənˈsepʃn] *n*
kudurta

precondition [ˌpriːkənˈdiʃn] *n*
without preconditions ba tare
da shimfiɗa ƙa'idoji ba

predecessor [ˈpriːdisesə] *n*
wanda aka gada

predicament [priˈdikəmənt] *n*
jidali

predict [priˈdikt] *v* tsìnkayà

prediction [priˈdikʃn] *n* tsìnkàyā

predominant [priˈdɔminənt] *adj*
to be predominant rìnjāyà

predominate [priˈdɔmineit] *v*
rìnjāyà

preface [ˈprefis] *n* gabātârwā

prefer [priˈfəː] *v* fi so

preferable [ˈprefrəbl] *adj* It is
preferable to... Zai fi dacewa
idan...

preference [ˈprefrəns] *n* fifiko

preferential trade area *n*
gamayyar kasuwanci

preferential treatment *n* ba
da fifiko

pregnant [ˈpregnənt] *adj* 1. mai
ciki 2. She is pregnant. Tana
da ciki.

prejudice [ˈpredʒudis] *n* 1. nuna
bambanci 2. racial prejudice
bambancin launin fata

prejudicial [ˌpredʒuˈdiʃl] *adj* mai
lahani

preliminary [priˈliminəri] *adj* na
shiri, na farko

premature [ˈpremətjuə] *adj* 1.
wanda bai kai ba 2. premature
baby bakwaini

premeditated [ˌpriːˈmediteitid]
adj da gangan

premeditated murder *n* kisan
kai da gangan

premier [ˈpremiə] *n* firimiya,
(Nr) firimar

premiere [ˈpremieə] *n* nunin
farko

premises [ˈpremisiz] *pl* 1. gini
2. haraba

premium [ˈpriːmiəm] *adj*
lambawan

preoccupation [ˌpriːɔkjuˈpeiʃn] *n*
kasàfî

preoccupied [priːˈɔkjupaid] *adj*
to be preoccupied shagaltu
(with da)

prepaid [ˈpriːpeid] *adj* da adibas

preparation [ˌprepəˈreiʃn] *n* shiri

preparatory [priˈpærətri] *adj* na
share fage

prepare [priˈpeə] *v* 1. shirya 2.
to prepare in advance tànadà

prepared [priˈpeəd] *adj* shiryayye

prescribe [priˈskraib] *v* ƙayyade

prescription [priˈskripʃn] *n*
takardar sayen magani

presence [ˈprezns] *n* 1. hàllařà
2. in the presence of gaban

present [ˈpreznt] 1. *adj* na yanzu
2. *n* kyauta 3. halin yanzu
4. at present a halin yanzu
5. to be present hàllařà

present [priˈzent] *v* 1. ba
2. gabatar da

presentation [ˌpreznˈteiʃn] *n* 1.
nuni 2. gabatarwa

present-day [ˈpreznuˈdei] *adj* na
yanzu

presenter *n* mai gabatarwa

presently [ˈprezntli] *adv* a yanzu

preservation [ˌprezəˈveiʃn] *n*
adani

preserve [priˈzəːv] *v* adana

preserves [priˈzəːvz] *pl* jam

preside [priˈzaid] *v* shùgàbantà

presidency [ˈprezidənsi] *n*
shugabanci

president [ˈprezidənt] *n* shugaba, (Nr) farzidan

president-elect *n* shugaba mai jiran gā̀dò̀

presidential [preziˈdənʃl] *n* na shugaba

presidential guard *n* sojojin masu tsaron lafiyar shugaban ƙasa

press [pres] **1.** *n* maɗaba'a **2. the press** ('yan) jaridu **3.** *v* danna

press censorship *n* tace labarai

press conference *n* taron manema labarai

pressing [ˈpresiŋ] *adj* na gaggawa

pressure [ˈpreʃə] *n* **1.** matsi **2.** ƙarfi **3. They are under pressure.** Suna cikin damuwa.

pressurize [ˈpreʃəraiz] *v* matsa wa

prestige [preˈstiːʒ] *n* martaba

prestigious [preˈstiːʒəs] *adj* mai kwarjini

presume [priˈzjuːm] *v* ɗauka (**that** cewa)

presumptuous [priˈzʌmptʃuəs] *adj* **to be presumptuous** sa rai

pretence [priˈtens] *n* fankama

pretend [priˈtend] *v* nuna kamar

pretension [priˈtenʃn] *n* iya yi

pretentious [priˈtenʃəʃ] *adj* mai iya yi

pretext [ˈpriːtekst] *n* uzuri

pretty [ˈpriti] *adj* kyakkyawa

prevail [priˈveil] *v* samu

prevalent [ˈprevələnt] *adj* na ruwan dare

prevent [priˈvent] *v* hana

prevention [priˈvenʃn] *n* rigakafi

preventive, preventative [priˈventiv; priˈventətiv] *adj* mai hanawa

previous [ˈpriːviəs] *adj* wanda ya riga

previously [ˈpriːviəsli] *adv* dâ

prey [prei] **1.** *n* kamu **2.** yi jewa

price [prais] **1.** *n* kuɗi **2. world price** farashi na kasuwannin duniya **3. to agree on a price** sallama **2.** *v* kimanta

priceless [ˈpraislis] *adj* mai daraja ƙwarai

prick [prik] *v* soke

prickly [ˈprikli] *adj* mai ƙaya

pride [praid] *n* **1.** alfahari **2.** girman kai

priest [priːst] *n* (Chris.) fada

primarily [praiˈmerili] *adv* yawanci

primary [ˈpraiməri] *adj* babba

primary education *n* ilimin firamare

primary elections *pl* zaɓen 'yan takara

primary school *n* firamare, (Nr) lakkwal

Prime Minister *n* firayim minista, (Nr) faram minista

prime [praim] *n* ganiya

primitive [ˈprimitiv] *adj* mai duhun kai

prince [prins] *n* ɗan sarki

princess [prinˈses] *n* 'yar sarki

principal [ˈprinsəpl] **1.** *adj* babba **2.** *n* (ed.) shugaban makaranta, shugabar makaranta

principality [ˌprinsiˈpæləti] *n* ƙaramar daula

principle [ˈprinsəpl] *n* **1.** ƙa'ida **2. in principle** bisa manufa

print [print] **1.** *n* rubutun keke **2.** hoto **3.** *v* buga **4.** wanke

printed [ˈprintid] *adj* na bugun dutse

printer [ˈprɪntə] *n* mai bugun dutse

printing [ˈprɪntɪŋ] *n* d̠ab'i

printing house *n* mad̠aba'a

printing press *n* mad̠aba'a

prior to [ˈpraɪə] *prep* gabannin

priority [praɪˈɔrəti] *n* fifiko

prison [ˈprɪzn] *n* kurkuku

prison riot *n* tarzomar kurkuku

prison sentence *n* d̠auri

prisoner [ˈprɪznə] *n* **1.** fursuna, (Nr) d̠an kaso **2. to take prisoner** dankè

privacy [ˈprɪvəsi] *n* keɓantawa

private [ˈpraɪvɪt] **1.** *adj* mai zaman kansa **2.** na asiri **3. in private** a asirce **4.** *n* (mil.) farabiti, (Nr) farmankalashi

private businessman *n* d̠an kasuwa mai zaman kansa

private discussion *n* gānàwā

private individual *n* mai zaman kansa

private investigator *n* ƙanshin gari

private ownership *n* mallakar tajirai

private parts *pl* al'aura

private territory *n* hàr̃àbà

private visit *n* ziyara ta radin kai

privately [ˈpraɪvɪtli] *adv* a kakkeɓe

privatization [ˌpraɪvətaɪˈzeɪʃn] *n* shirin sayar da ƙadarorin gwamnati

privatize [ˈpraɪvətaɪz] *v* sayar da ƙadarorin gwamnati

privilege [ˈprɪvəlɪdʒ] *n* gatanci

privileged [ˈprɪvəlɪdʒd] *adj* mai gatanci

prize [praɪz] *n* lambar girma

prize winner *n* mai samun lamba

prize-cup *n* kōfì

prize money *n* kud̠in gasa

probability [ˌprɔbəˈbɪləti] *n* yiwuwa

probable [ˈprɔbəbl] *adj* mai yiwuwa

probably [ˈprɔbəbli] *adv* watakila

problem [ˈprɔbləm] *n* **1.** matsala **2. to solve a problem** warware matsala **3. no problem!** ba damuwa!

procedure [prəˈsiːdʒə] *n* hanya

procedures [prəˈsiːdʒəz] *pl* màtàkai

proceed [prəˈsiːd] *v* ci gaba

proceedings [prəˈsiːdɪŋz] *n* (leg.) jin ƙara

process [ˈprəʊses] **1.** *n* hanya **2. in the process of** garin **3.** *v* sarrafa

processed food *n* abincin kwali

procession [prəˈseʃn] *n* jerin gwano

proclaim [prəˈkleɪm] *v* ayyana

proclamation [ˌprɔkləˈmeɪʃn] *n* shèlà

procrastinate [prəʊˈkræstɪneɪt] *v* jinkìrtā

procure [prəˈkjuə] *v* samu

prod [prɔd] *v* tsokana

produce [ˈprɔdjuːs] *n* kayan lambu

produce [prəˈdjuːs] *v* **1.** yi **2.** fito da **3.** ƙera **4.** haifar da

producer [prəˈdjuːsə] *n* mai ƙira

product [ˈprɔdʌkt] *n* samfur

production [prəˈdʌkʃn] *n* **1.** yi **2.** kayan da aka samar **3. movie production** had̠a fim

productive [prə'dʌktiv] *adj* mai albarka

profess [prə'fes] *v* haƙiƙanta

profession [prə'feʃn] *n* sana'a

professional [prə'teʃənl] *adj/n* 1. mai sana'a 2. mai fasaha

professor [prə'tesə] *n* shehun malami

proffer [prɔfə] *v* miƙa

proficiency [prə'fiʃnsi] *n* gwaninta

proficient [prə'fiʃnt] *adj* gwani

profile ['prəufail] *n* sura

profit ['prɔfit] 1. *n* riba 2. *v* ci riba

profitable ['prɔfitəbl] *adj* mai riba

profiteer [,prɔfi'tiə] *n* mai cin riba

profiteering [,prɔfi'tiəriŋ] *n* cin riba

profound [prə'faund] *adj* mai zurfi

profusion [prə'fju:ʒn] *n* in profusion caka-caka

programme, program ['prəugræm] *n* 1. shirye-shirye 2. takardar shiri 3. *v* shirya

progress ['prəugres] *n* 1. ci-gaba 2. to make progress ci gaba

progress [prə'gres] *v* ci gaba

progressive [prə'gresiv] *adj* mai neman sauyi

progressive party [prə'gresiv] *n* jam'iyyar neman sauyi

prohibit [prə'hibit] *v* hana

prohibition [,prəuhi'biʃn] *n* hani

project ['prɔdʒekt] *n* aiki

project [prə'dʒekt] *v* 1. gōtā 2. buga siliman

projection [prə'dʒekʃn] *n* tsìnkāyā

projector [prə'dʒektə] *n* majigi

proliferate [prə'lifəreit] *v* yaɗu

proliferation [prə,lifə'reiʃn] *n* yaɗuwa

prologue ['prəulɔg] *n* gabatarwa

prolong [prə'lɔŋ] *v* tsawaita

prominent ['prɔminənt] *adj* 1. mashahuri 2. babba

promise ['prɔmis] 1. *n* alkawari 2. *v* yi alkawari

promising ['prɔmisiŋ] *adj* da alamar rahama

promote [prə'məut] *v* 1. ciyar da 2. (ec.) yi kiran kasuwa

promotion [prə'məuʃn] *n* 1. ci-gaba 2. kiran kasuwa

prompt [prɔmpt] *adj* mai sauri

pronounce [prə'nauns] *v* faɗi

pronunciation [prə,nʌnsi'eiʃn] *n* lafazi

proof [pru:f] *n* 1. shaida 2. waterproof mai hana-ruwa-shiga

prop [prɔp] *v* tokare

prop against *v* jingina

propaganda [,prɔpə'gændɛ] *n* furofaganda

propeller [prə'pelə] *n* farfela

proper ['prɔpə] *adj* na daidai

properly ['prɔpəli] *adv* sosai

property ['prɔpəti] *n* 1. mallaki 2. dukiya 3. private property kadarar kai 4. government property kadarar gwamnati

property rights *pl* hakkin mallakar dukiyoyi

prophecy ['prɔfəsi] *n* duba

prophesy ['prɔfəsai] *v* yi duba

prophet ['prɔfit] *n* annabi

proportion [prə'pɔ:ʃn] *n* 1. gwargwado 2. rabo 3. in proportion to gwargwadon

proportional [prə'pɔːʃənl] *adj* na gwargwado

proportional representation *n* (pol.) tsarin da kowace jam'iyya za ta sami wakilai a majalisa gwargwadon yawan ƙuri'un da aka jefa mata

proportionate to [prə'pɔːʃən] *prep* gwargwadon

proposal [prə'pəuzl] *n* 1. shawara 2. **to defeat a proposal** shure shawara

propose [prə'pəuz] *v* kawo shawara

proposition [,prɔpə'ziʃn] *n* shawara

proprietor [prə'praətə] *n* mai...

prop up *v* 1. tokare 2. ɗaure wa... gindi

prose [prəuz] *n* adabi

prosecute ['prɔsikjuːt] *v* yi wa... shari'a

prosecution [,prɔsi·kjuːʃn] *n* 1. shari'a 2. lauyan gwamnati

prosecutor ['prɔsikjuːtə] *n* (leg.) lauyan gwamnati

prospect ['prɔspekt] *n* abin yiwuwa

prospect [prɔs'pekt] *v* nema

prospective [prə'spektiv] *adj* mai yiwuwa

prosper ['prɔspə] *v* yi albarka

prosperity [prɔ'sperəti] *n* albarka

prosperous ['prɔspərəs] *adj* mai albarka

prostitute ['prɔstitjuːt] *n* karuwa

prostitution [,prɔsti·tjuːʃn] *n* karuwanci

prostrate ['prɔstreit] *v* yi sujjada

protect [prə'tekt] *v* kare

protection [prə'tekʃn] *n* kariya

protectionism [prə'tekʃnizəm] *n* (ec.) kariyar ciniki

protective [prə'tektiv] *adj* na kariya

protector [prə'tektə] *n* 1. mai gadi 2. makari 3. ginshiƙi

protectorate [prə'tektərət] *n* ƙasa riƙon amana

protein ['prəutiːn] *n* furotin

protest ['prəutest] *n* 1. ƙara 2. zanga-zanga

protest [prə'test] *v* 1. yi ƙara 2. yi zanga-zanga

protest march *n* zanga-zangar nuna adawa

Protestant ['prɔtistənt] *n /adj* ɗan Furotesta

prototype ['prəutətaip] *n* ƙirar farko

protrude [prə'truːd] *v* gota

proud [praud] *adj* 1. mai alfarma 2. mai girman kai

prove [pruːv] *v* tabbatar da

proverb ['prɔvəːb] *n* karin magana

provide [prə'vaid] *v* samar da

provided that [prə'vaidid] *conj* muddin

provide for [prə'vaid] *v* 1. yi tanadi 2. tàllafà

province ['prɔvins] *n* lardi

provincial ['prɔvinʃəl] *adj* baƙauye

provincial council *n* majalisar lardi

provision [prə'viʒn] *n* 1. samarwa 2. **on the provision that** muddin

provisional [prə'viʒənl] *adj* na wucin gadi

provisions [prə'viʒnz] *n* guzuri

proviso [prə'vaizəu] *n* sìgà

provocative [prə'vɔkətiv] *adj* mai tsokana

provocation [ˌprɔvə'keɪʃn] *n* tsokana

provoke [prə'vəuk] *v* tsòkanà

proximity [prɔk'sɪmətɪ] *n* màƙwàbtakà

proxy ['prɔksi] *n* wakili

prudent ['pru:dnt] *adj* mai hankali

psalm(s) [sa:m] *n* zabura

pseudonym ['sju:dənim] *n* sunan ƙarya

psychiatrist [saɪ'kaɪətrɪst] *n* likitan halin taɓaɓɓu

psychiatry [saɪ'kaɪətrɪ] *n* ilimin halin taɓaɓɓu

psycho ['saɪkəu] *adj/n* mahàukàcī tubuřàn

psychological [ˌsaɪkə'lɔdʒɪkl] *adj* na halin ɗan Adam

psychologist ['saɪ'kɔlədʒɪst] *n* mai ilimin halin ɗan Adam

psychology ['saɪ'kɔlədʒɪ] *n* ilimin halin ɗan Adam

psychosis [saɪ'kəusis] *n* hauka

pub [pʌb] *n* (UK) mashaya

puberty ['pju:bətɪ] *n* **1.** bàlagà **2. to reach puberty** bàlagà

pubic hair [ˌpju:bɪk'heə] *n* gashin gaba

public ['pʌblɪk] **1.** *adj* na jama'a **2.** a fili **3.** *n* jama'a

public board *n* hùkùmà

public health *n* lafiyar jama'a

public holiday *n* ranar hutu

public house *duba* wajen **pub**

public relations *pl* dangantaka da jama'a

public servant *n* ma'aikacin hukuma

publication [ˌpʌblɪ'keɪʃn] *n* littafi, jarida

publicise ['pʌblɪsaɪz] *v* tallàtä

publicity [pʌb'lɪsətɪ] *n* talla

publicly ['pʌblɪklɪ] *adv* à bainàř jàma'à

publish ['pʌblɪʃ] *v* buga

publisher ['pʌblɪʃə] *n* mai buga littattafai

publishing ['pʌblɪʃɪŋ] *n* buga littattafai

publishing house *n* maɗaba'a

pudding ['pudɪŋ] *n* kayan zaƙi

puddle ['pʌdl] *n* makwancin ruwan sama

puff [pʌf] *v* busa

pull [pul] *v* **1.** ja **2. Don't pull my leg! Bař shàmmàtàtà!**

pull down *v* rushe

pulley ['pulɪ] *n* kura

pull out *v* cire

pull through *v* rayu

pullover ['puləuvə] *n* suwaita

pulp [pʌlp] *n* totuwa

pulsate [pʌl'seɪt] *v* yi zògī

pulse [pʌls] *n* bugun jini

pump [pʌmp] **1.** *n* famfo **2.** *v* yi famfo

pumpkin ['pʌmpkɪn] *n* kabewa

pun [pʌn] *n* wasan magana

punch [pʌntʃ] **1.** *n* naushi **2.** *v* kai wa... naushi

punctual ['pʌŋktʃuəl] *adj* cikin lokaci

punctuality [ˌpʌŋktʃu'ælətɪ] *n* cikin lokaci

punctuation [ˌpʌŋktʃu'eɪʃn] *n* alamomin rubutu

puncture ['pʌŋktʃə] **1.** *n* fanca **2.** *v* huda **3.** yi fanca

punish ['pʌnɪʃ] *v* **1.** hòrā **2.** (leg.) hukunta

punishable ['pʌnɪʃəbl] *adj* **This crime is punishable by**

death. Wannan laifi na ɗauke da horon kisa.

punishment [ˈpʌniʃmənt] *n* 1. horo 2. (leg.) hukunci 3. **capital punishment** hukuncin kisa

punitive measures [ˈpjuːnətiv] *pl* màtàkan hòrō

pupil [ˈpjuːpl] *n* ɗan makaranta

puppet [ˈpʌpit] *n* 1. 'yar tsana a rataye 2. (pol.) ɗan kòrā

puppet regime *n* (pol.) mulkìn jè-ka-nā-yi-kà

puppy [ˈpʌpi] *n* kwikwiyo

purchase [ˈpəːtʃəs] 1. *n* sayayya 2. *v* sàyā

purchaser [ˈpəːtʃəsə] *n* mài sàyē

purchasing power [ˈpəːtʃəsiŋ] *n* ƙarfin sàyē

purdah [ˈpəːdə] *n* kùllē

pure [pjuə] *adj* 1. mai tsabta 2. zalla

purely [pjuə] *adv* zalla

purge [ˈpəːdʒ] *v* (pol.) tankaɗe da rairaya

purify [ˈpjuərifai] *v* tsarkaka

purity [ˈpjuərəti] *n* tsarki

purple [ˈpəːpl] *adj* mai launin shuni

purpose [ˈpəːpəs] *n* 1. maƙasudi 2. **on purpose** da gangan

purposely [ˈpəːpəsli] *adv* da gangan

purr [pəː] *v* yi gurnani

purse [pəːs] *n* alabe

pursue [pəˈsjuː] *v* bi

pursuit [pəˈsjuːt] *n* bi

pus [pʌs] *n* mugunya

push [puʃ] *v* tura

push over *v* ture

push-button *adj* mai makunnai

push-chair *n* keken hannu

put [put] *v* (put) 1. sa 2. ajiye

put aside *v* 1. ajiye 2. sa a mala

put away *v* ajiye

put back *v* mayar da

put down *v* 1. ajiye 2. ci zarafi 4. kashe 3. (pol.) kwantar da

put off *v* ɗagà

put on *v* 1. sa 2. ɗora kan

put out *v* kashe

put up with *v* daure

putty [ˈpʌti] *n* foti

puzzle [ˈpʌzl] 1. *n* ɗaurin gwarmai 2. *v* ɗaure wa... kai

puzzling [ˌpʌzliŋ] *adj* mai ɗaure kai

pyjamas [pəˈdʒaːməz] *pl* fanjama

pyramid [ˈpirəmid] *n* dàlā

pyrotechnics [ˌpaiərəuˈtekniks] *pl* wasan wuta

python [ˈpaiθn] *n* mesa

Qq

quack [kwæk] **1.** *n* kukan
agwagwa **2.** *v* yi kukan
agwagwa

quadrangle [ˈkwɔdræŋgl] *n*
tsakar gida

quadruple [kwɔˈdruːpl] *v* ninka
sau huɗu

quadruplets [kwɔˈdruːplits] *pl*
'yan huɗu

quaint [kweint] *adj* baƙauye

quake [kweint] *v* **1.** girgiza
2. *duba wajen* **earthquake**

qualification [ˌkwɔlifiˈkeiʃn] *n*
ƙwarewa

qualified [ˈkwɔlifaid] *adj* ƙwararre

qualify [ˈkwɔlifai] *v* dace

quality [ˈkwɔləti] *n* **1.** iri **2.** ƙwari

quantity [ˈkwɔntəti] *n* yawa

quarantine [ˌkwɔrəntiːn] *n* **to put
in quarantine** keɓe

quarrel [ˈkwɔrəl] **1.** *n* hùsūmà
2. *v* yi faɗa (**with** da)

quarreling [ˈkwɔrəliŋ] rìgimà,
tankiyā

quarrelsome [ˈkwɔrəlsəm] *adj*
mài tsìyā

quarry [ˈkwɔrəl] *n* wurin haƙa

quarter [ˈkwɔːtə] *n* **1.** kwata,
(Nr) karce **2. a quarter of a
loaf** rubu'in burodi **3.** unguwa,
(Nr) karce

quarterly [ˈkwɔːtəli] *adv* sau
huɗu a shekara

quarters [ˈkɔːtəz] *pl* **1.** (mil.)
bariki **2. at close quarters** baki
da hanci

quay [kiː] *n* kwàtā

queen [kwiːn] *n* sarauniya

queer [kwiə] *adj* **1.** bàƙō **2.** ɗan
luɗu, 'yar maɗigo

quell [kwel] *v* kashe

quench [kwentʃ] *v* kashe

query [ˈkwiːri] **1.** *n* tambaya
2. *v* tambaya

question [ˈkwestʃən] **1.** *n*
tambaya **2.** magana **3. there's
no question** ba shakka (**about**
game da) **4.** *v* tùhumtà **5.** yi
shakka

questionable [ˈkwestʃənəbl] *adj*
mai ban shakka

question mark *n* alamar
tambaya

questionnaire [ˌkwestʃəˈneə] *n*
tsarin tambayoyi

queue [kjuː] **1.** *n* jerin gwano
2. *v* yi jerin gwano

quick [kwik] *adj* **1.** mai sauri
2. ɗan **3.** *duba wajen* **quickly**

quick-witted *adj* mai basira

quicken [ˈkwikn] *v* ƙara sauri

quickly [ˈkwikli] *adv* da sauri

quickness [ˈkwiknis] *n* sauri

quid [kwid] *n* (UK) fam

quiet [ˈkwaiət] **1.** *adj* mai shiru
2. maras ƙara **3.** *n* shiru

quieten down [ˈkwaiətn] *v*
làllasà

quietly [ˈkwaiətli] *adv* a hankali

quietness [ˈkwaiətnis] *n* shiru

quilt [kwilt] *n* bargo

quinine [kwiˈniːn] *n* kuni, (Nr)
kinin

quit [kwit] *v* **1.** daina **2.** bari

quite [kwaɪt] *adv* **1.** sosai **2.** da
  dāmā
quite a lot dà dāmā
quite so! nà'am!
quiz [kwɪz] **1.** *n* wasan
  ƙwaƙwalwa **2.** *v* tùhumtà
quorum [ˈkwɔːrəm] *n* yawan

isa shawara
quota [ˈkwəutə] *n* ƙa'ida, rabo
quotation [kwəuˈteiʃn] *n* ambato
quotation marks *pl* alamar
  zancen wani
quote [kwəut] **1.** *n* ambato **2.** *v*
  àmbatà

Rr

rabbi [ˈræbaɪ] *n* (rel.) fadan Yahudawa

rabbit [ˈræbit] *n* zomo

rabble [ˈræbl] *n* 'yan zanga-zanga

rabies [ˈreibiːz] *n* haukan kare

race [reis] 1. *n* jinsi 2. (spor.) tsere 3. **mixed race** mai ruwa biyu 4. *v* gaggàutā 5. (spor.) yi tsere

racecourse, racetrack [ˈreiskɔːs; ˈreistrak] *n* filin sukuwa

race horse *n* dokin sukuwa

race relations *pl* dangantakar al'ummomi

racial [ˈreiʃl] *adj* na al'umma

racial integration *n* haɗewar al'ummomi

racial prejudice *n* bambancin launin fata

racing [ˈreisiŋ] *n* **horse racing** sukuwa

racing car *n* motar tsere

racism [ˈreisizəm] *n* wariyar al'umma

racist [ˈreisist] 1. *adj* na wariyar al'umma 2. *n* ɗan wariyar al'umma

rack and ruin [ˌrækəndˈruːin] *n* **to go to rack and ruin** dukurkùcē

racket [ˈrækit] *n* 1. ƙara 2. zàmba 3. (spor.) raket

racketeer [ˌrækiˈtiə] *n* ɗan cuku-cuku

racketeering [ˌrækiˈtiəriŋ] *n* cuku-cuku

radar [ˈreidaː] *n* rada, (Nr) radar

radiant [ˈreidiənt] *adj* mai haske

radiate [ˈreidieit] *v* haskaka

radiation [ˌreidiˈeiʃn] *n* 1. iska mai guba 2. **nuclear radiation** iska mai guba ta nukiliya

radiator [ˈreidieitə] *n* lagireto

radical [ˈrædikl] 1. *adj* mai tsauri 2. *n* (pol.) ɗan tsagèrā

radical change *n* canji mai muhimmanci

radio [ˈreidiəu] *n* rediyo, (Nr) radiyo

radio programme *n* shirin rediyo

radio receiver *n* akwatin rediyo

radio station *n* gidan/tashar rediyo

radius [ˈreidiəs] *n* iyakar da'ira

raffle [ˈræfl] *n* tambola

raft [raːft] *n* gadon fito

rag [ræg] *n* tsûmmā

rage [reidʒ] *n* 1. babban fushi 2. **It's all the rage.** Sabon salo ne.

ragged [ˈrægid] *adj* cikin tsûmmā

raid [reid] 1. *n* hari 2. *v* kai wa... hari 3. màmayà

rail [reil] 1. *adj* na jirgin ƙasa 2. *n* dogo

railroad [ˈreilrəud] *n* (US) reluwe

railway [ˈreilwei] *n* reluwe

railway corporation *n* kamfanin reluwe

railway line [ˈreilwei] *n* hanyar reluwe

rain [rein] 1. *n* ruwan sama 2. *v* yi ruwan sama

rainbow ['reinbəu] *n* bakan gizo

rainclouds ['reinklaudz] *pl* hadari

raincoat ['reinkəut] *n* rigar ruwa

raindrop ['reindrɔp] *n* ɗigon ruwa

rainfall ['reinfɔːl] *n* yawan ruwan sama

rainy ['reini] *adj* **to be rainy** yi ta ruwa

rainy season *n* damina

raise [reiz] 1. *n* ƙarin albashi 2. *v* ta da 3. ɗaga 4. ƙara 5. **to raise an issue** ɗago

raise children *v* gòyā

raisin ['reizin] *n* zabibi

rally ['ræli] *n* 1. haɗuwa 2. (spor.) tseren mota

ram [ræm] *n* rago

Ramadan ['ræmədæn] *n* Ramalan

ramp [ræmp] *n* gangare

ran [ræn] *duba wajen* run

ranch [raːntʃ] *n* gonar kiwon shanu

random ['rændəm] *adj* **at random** dà ka

rang [ræŋ] *duba wajen* ring

range [reindʒ] *n* 1. zango 2. **mountain range** jeri 3. **shooting range** ranji 4. **with a range of...** mai iya lulawa har... 5. **medium-range weapons** makamai masu matsakaicin zango 6. **long-range weapons** makamai masu dogon zango

range of products *n* kaya iri-iri

rank [ræŋk] *n* 1. maƙami 2. martaba

ransack ['rænsæk] *v* washe

ransom ['rænsəm] 1. *n* kuɗin fansa 2. *v* fànsā

rap [ræp] *v* ƙwanƙwasa

rape [reip] 1. *n* fyàɗè 2. *v* yi wa... fyàɗè

rapid ['ræpid] *adj* mai sauri

rapidly ['ræpidli] *adv* da sauri

rapist ['reipist] *n* mafyàɗì

rapprochement [ræˈprɔʃmaː] *n* kusantar juna

rare [reə] *adj* 1. nadiri 2. mai wuyar samuwa

rarely ['reəli] *adv* da wuya

rarity ['reərəti] *n* nadiri

rash [ræʃ] 1. *adj* maras hankali 2. *n* ƙuraje

rat [ræt] *n* ɓera

rate [reit] 1. *n* yawa 2. kuɗi 3. **first rate** lambawan 4. **at any rate** ko ta yaya 5. **birth rate** yawan hayayyafa 6. **growth rate** ƙarfin ƙaruwa 7. **interest rate** yawan kuɗin ruwa 8. **lending rate** ƙa'idar bashi 9. **unemployment rate** yawan marasa aikin yi 10. *v* kimanta

rate of exchange *n* darajar musayar kuɗi

rather ['raːðə] *adv* 1. ɗan 2. **Amina would rather stay at home.** Amina ta fi so ta tsaya a gida.

ratification [ˌratifiˈkeiʃn] *n* tabbatarwa

ratify ['rætifai] *v* tabbatar dà

ratio ['reiʃjo] *n* rabo

ration ['ræʃn] *v* raba

ration card *n* katin karɓar rabo

rational ['ræʃnəl] *adj* mai basira

rattle ['rætl] *v* yi caccaka

ravage ['rævidʒ] *v* ɓarnatar da

rave [reiv] 1. *n* biki 2. *v* yi sambatu 3. fayè zàgwàɗì

raven ['reivn] *n* hankaka

ravine [rə'viːn] *n* kwazazzabo
raw [rɔ:] *adj* ɗanye
raw materials [rɔ:] *pl* albarkatun ƙasã
ray [rei] *n* 1. sun ray hasken rana 2. x-ray hoto
raze [reiz] *v* ragargaza
razor ['reizə] *n* reza, (Nr) razuwar
raor-blade *n* reza, (Nr) lam
re-elect [,riː'əlekt] *v* sake zaɓe
re-election [,riːə'lektʃən] *n* neman a sake zaɓe
re-enter [,riː'entə] *v* sake shiga
re-establish [,riː'estæbliʃ] *v* sake kafa...
re-organization [riː,ɔːgənai'zeiʃn] *n* tànkàɗè dà ràirayà
re-schedule debts [,riː'ʃedjul; ,riː'skedjul] *v* saka tsarin amsar bashi
reach [riːtʃ] *v* 1. isa 2. kai 3. miƙa
reach agreement *v* 1. yanke shawara 2. (pol.) ƙulla yarjejeniya
reach an aim *v* cim ma buri
reach out *v* miƙa
react [ri'ækt] *v* ɗauka
reaction [ri'ækʃn] *n* ɗauki
reactionary [ri'ækʃənri] *n* ɗan kòmà-bāya
read [riːd] *v* (read [red]) karanta
reader ['riːdə] *n* 1. mai karatu 2. littafin koyon karatu
readily ['redili] *adv* nan da nan
readiness ['redinis] *n* halin shiri
reading ['riːdiŋ] *n* karatu
readjust [,riːə'dʒʌst] *v* sake yi
ready ['redi] *adj* 1. a shirye 2. to be ready gama 3. to get ready shirya

ready-made [,redi'meid] *adj* shiryayye
reaffirm [,riːə'fəːm] *v* ƙarfafa magana
real [riəl] *adj* 1. na gaskiya 2. na ainihi 3. babba 4. the real problem ainihin matsalar
real estate *n* ƙasa
realistic [,riːə'listik] *adj* mai idon basira
realistically [,riːə'listikli] *adv* da idon basira
reality [ri'æləti] *n* 1. halin gaskiya 2. in reality a bisa gaskiya
realization [,riːəlai'zeiʃn] *n* farga
realize ['riːəlaiz] *v* 1. farga 2. cim ma
really ['riːəli] *adv* 1. da gaske 2. really? ashe?
realm [relm] *n* daula
realtor ['riːəltə] *n* mai sayar ƙasa
reap [riːp] *v* girba
reap the benefit of *v* ci moriyar
reappear [,riːə'piə] *v* sake fitowa
rear [riə] 1. *adj* na baya 2. *n* baya 3. *v* yi raino
rearrange [,riːə'reindʒ] *v* sake shiri
reason ['riːzn] *n* 1. hankali 2. dalili 3. for that reason saboda haka
reasonable ['riːznəbl] *adj* 1. mai hankali 2. mai kima
reassurance [,riːə'ʃɔːrəns] *n* goyon baya
reassure [,riːə'ʃɔ:] *v* goyi baya
rebel ['rebl] *n* ɗan tawaye
rebel [ri'bel] *v* 1. kàngarà 2. yi tawaye (against wa)
rebellion [ri'beliən] *n* tawaye

rebelliousness [rɪˈbeliəsnis] *n* bɔ̀ře

rebirth [ˌriːˈbəːθ] (ec.) sâkè farfaɗôwǎ

rebuff [rɪˈbʌf] *v* gwale

rebuild [ˌriːˈbild] *v* (ec.) tayar da

recall [rɪˈkɔːl] *v* 1. tuna da 2. koma da

recede [rɪˈsiːd] *v* jânyě

receipt [rɪˈsiːt] *n* rasit, (Nr) resi

receive [rɪˈsiːv] *v* 1. kàrɓǎ 2. to receive a message sadu da saƙo 3. to receive a radio signal kama tashi

receiver [rɪˈsiːvə] *n* 1. rediyo 2. kan tarho

recent [ˈriːsnt] *adj* na kwanan nan

recently [ˈriːsəntli] *adv* kwanan baya

receptacle [rɪˈseptəkl] *n* gwangwani

reception [rɪˈsepʃn] *n* 1. liyafa, (Nr) ambite (in honour of na ban girma ga) 2. state reception liyafar alfarma 3. to get good reception kama tashi sosai

receptionist [rɪˈsepʃnist] *n* sakatare

receptive [rɪˈseptiv] *adj* mai sauƙin kai

recess [rɪˈses] *n* 1. saƙo 2. ɗan hutu

recession [rɪˈseʃn] *n* (ec.) komabayan tattalin arziki

recipe [ˈresəpi] *n* girke-girke

reciprocate [rɪˈsiprəkeit] *v* saka wa

recite [rɪˈsait] *v* faɗi

reckless [ˈreklis] *adj* maras ganganci

recklessness [ˈreklisnəs] *n* ganganci

reckon [ˈrekən] *v* 1. yi zato 2. ƙidaya

reckoning [ˈrekənd] *n* lissafi

reclaim [rɪˈkleim] *v* samo

recline [rɪˈklain] *v* kishingiɗa

recognition [ˌrekəgˈniʃn] *n* 1. shâidâwǎ 2. (pol.) amincewa

recognize [ˈrekəgnaiz] *v* 1. gane 2. (pol.) amince da

recoil [rɪˈkɔil] *v* ja da baya

recollect [ˌrekəˈlekt] *v* tuna da

recollection [ˌrekəˈlekʃn] *n* tunani

recommend [ˌrekəˈmend] *v* yaba wa

recommend that *v* ba da goyon baya

recommendation [ˌrekəmenˈdeiʃn] 1. yabo 2. shawara 3. letter of recommendation takardar yabo

recompense [ˈrekəmpens] 1. *n* sàkayyǎ 2. *v* saka wa

reconcile [ˈrekənsail] *v* sasanta

reconciled [ˈrekənsaild] *adj* to be reconciled tàusasà

reconciliation [ˌrekənˌsiliˈeiʃn] *n* sulhu

reconnaissance [rɪˈkɔnisns] *n* bincike

reconnaissance plane *n* jirgin saman leƙen asiri

reconnoitre [ˌrekəˈnɔitə] *v* yi bincike

reconsider [ˌriːkənˈsidə] *v* sake duba

reconsideration [ˌriːkənˌsidəˈreiʃn] *n* sake duba

reconstruct [ˌriːkənˈstrʌkt] *v* sake yi

reconstruction [ˌriːkənˈstrʌktʃn] n maimaitawa

record [ˈrekɔːd] n 1. fayil, (Nr) dose 2. tarihi 3. (mus.) faifai 4. **official record** rajista, (Nr) girgam 5. **world record** bajintar duniya

record [rɪˈkɔːd] v 1. rubuta 2. ɗauka

record player n garmaho

recording [rɪˈkɔːd] n (mus.) 1. naɗi 2. ɗaukan sauti

recover [rɪˈkʌvə] v 1. warke 2. farfaɗo 3. gane

recovery [rɪˈkʌvəri] n 1. (ec./med.) farfaɗowa

recovery programme n shirin farfaɗo da ƙasa

recreation [ˌrekriˈeiʃn] n wasanni

recrimination [ˌrekrimiˈneiʃn] n tsiyã-tsiyã

recruit [reˈkruːt] 1. n (mil.) kurtu, (Nr) lakuru 2. v ɗauka ma'aikata

recruitment [rekruːˈtmənt] n ɗaukar ma'aikata

rectangle [ˈrektæŋgl] n mai kaman shan soro

rectify [ˈrektifai] v daidaita

rector [ˈrektə] n rekta

rectum [ˈrektəm] n dubura

recuperate [rɪˈkuːpəreit] v warke

recuperation [riˌkuːpəˈreiʃn] n warkewa

recur [rɪˈkəː] v sake aukuwa

recurrence [ˌrɪˈkʌrəns] n sake aukuwa

Red Cross [ˌredˈkrɔs] n Kungiyar Agaji ta Red Cross

red [red] adj ja

redecorate [ˌriːˈdekəreit] v sake yi wa... ado

redeem [rɪˈdiːm] v fànsã

redemption [rɪˈdempʃn] n (rel.) ceto

red-handed [ˌredˈhændid] adj dumu-dumu

red-hot adj mài zãfĩ jà-zĩr̃

red light n danja

redness [ˈrednis] n ja

red tape n matsalolin gudanarwa

reduce [rɪˈdjuːs] v rage

reduced [rɪˈdjuːst] adj at **reduced prices** bisa farashi mai rahusa

reduction [rɪˈdʌkʃn] n 1. ragi 2. rangwame 3. **arms reduction** rage makamai

reduplicate [rɪˈdjuplikeit] v ninka

reed [riːd] n tsaurẽ

reef [riːf] n dutsen teku

reel [riːl] n faifai

refer to [rɪˈfəː] v 1. yi magana 2. wàiwayà (about kan) 3. miƙa ga

referee [ˌrefəˈriː] n alƙalin wasa

reference [ˈrefərəns] n 1. zance 2. takardar yabo 3. **with reference to** game da

reference book n littafin ƙara sani

referendum [ˌrefəˈrendəm] n ƙuri'ar neman ra'ayin jama'a

refill [ˌriːˈfil] v sake cika...

refine [rɪˈfain] v tace

refined [rɪˈfaind] adj mai ladabi

refined oil n tàtaccen mâi

refinement [rɪˈfainmənt] n ladabi

refinery [rɪˈfainəri] n matata

refit [ˌriːˈfit] v 1. maye gurbi 2. yi kwàskwàrimà

reflect [rɪˈflekt] v 1. yi ƙyalli 2. yi tunani

reflection [rɪˈflekʃn] n 1. inuwa 2. tunani

reflex [ˈriːfleks] n zùmût
reform [riˈtɔːm] 1. n gyara
2. (rel.) tajadidi 3. political
reform programme shirin
sake tsarin harkokin siyasa
4. v gyara 5. (rel.) jaddada
reformation [ˌrefəˈmeiʃn] n (rel.)
tajadidi
reformer [riˈtɔːmə] n 1. mai
gyara 2. (rel.) mujaddadi
refrain [riˈtrein] n amshi
refrain from v bari
refresh [riˈtreʃ] v shaƙata
refreshments [riˈtreʃmənts] pl
abin sha
refrigerate [riˈtridʒəreit] v
sanyaya a firiji
refrigerator [riˈtridʒəreitə] n
firiji, (Nr) firshidan
refuel [ˌriːˈtjuəl] v ƙara shan mai
refuge [ˈretjuːdʒ] n mafaka
refugee [ˌretjuˈdʒiː] n ɗan gudun
hijira
refund [riˈtʌnd] 1. n ramuwa
2. v rama kuɗi
refurbish [ˌriːˈtəːbiʃ] v yi
kwàskwàrimà
refurbishment [ˌriːtəːbiʃmənt] n
kwàskwàrimà
refusal [riˈtjuːzl] n ƙi
refuse [ˈretjuːs] n shàrā
refuse [riˈtjuːz] v ƙi
refute [riˈtjuːt] v musanta
regain [riˈgein] v ƙwato
regard [riˈgaːd] 1. n gìrma
2. with regard to kan batun
3. v duba 4. ɗauka
regard as v yi wa... kallo
regarding [riˈgaːdiŋ] prep kan
batun
regardless of [riˈgaːdlis] prep ko
da kuwa

regards [riˈgaːdz] pl 1. gaisuwa
2. as regards kan batun
regenerate [riˈdʒenəreit] v
farfaɗo da
regeneration [riˌdʒenəˈreiʃn] n
farfaɗowa
regime [reiˈʒiːm] n gwamnati
regiment [ˈredʒimənt] n
rajimanti, (Nr) bataliya
region [ˈriːdʒən] n yanki
regionalism [ˈriːdʒən,lizm] n
batun yanki-yanki
register [ˈredʒistə] 1. n rajista
2. v yi rajista
registered [ˈredʒistə] adj na
rajista
registered letter n wasiƙa ta
rajista
registrar [ˌredʒiˈstraː] n rajistara
registration [ˌredʒiˈstreiʃn] n
1. lambar mota 2. yin rajista
regress [riˈgres] v koma da baya
regret [riˈgret] 1. n da-na-sani
2. baƙin ciki 3. v yi da-na-sani
4. nuna baƙin ciki
regretfully [riˈgretfuli] adv da
baƙin ciki
regrettable [riˈgretəbl] adj na
da-na-sani
regular [ˈregjulə] adj 1. na
kullum 2. na al'ada
regularity [ˌregjuˈlærəti] n
ɗorewa
regularly [ˈregjuləli] adv a kai a
kai
regulate [ˈregjuleit] v ƙayyade
regulation [ˌregjuˈleiʃn] n doka
regulations [ˌregjuˈleiʃnz] pl
dokoki
rehabilitation centre n
[ˌrihaˌbiliˈteiʃn] n gidan gajiyayyu
rehearsal [riˈhəːsl] n gwaji

rehearse [ri·həːs] v gwada
reign [rein] 1. n shekarun sarauta
2. v yi sarauta.
reimburse [ˌriːimˈbəːs] v mayar
da kuɗi
rein, reins [rein; -z] n kamazuru
reinforce [ˌriːinˈfɔːs] v ƙarfafa
reinforcement [ˌriːinˈfɔːsmənt] n
ƙarfafawa
reinforcements [ˌriːinˈfɔːsmənts]
pl (mil.) gudummawa
reins of power pl ragamar
mulki
reinsure [ˌriːinˈʃuə] v sake yi
wa... inshorà
reiterate [riːˈitəreit] v nānàtā
reject [riˈdʒekt] v ƙi karɓa
rejection [riˈdʒekʃn] n ƙin karɓa
rejoice [riˈdʒɔis] v yi murna
rejoin [riˈdʒɔin] v sake shiga
rejuvenate [riˈdʒuːvəneit] v
farfaɗo da
relapse [riˈlæps] n to suffer a
relapse sake kamuwa da
relate [riˈleit] v 1. faɗa 2. dàngantà
related [riˈleitid] adj to be related
dàngantà (to dà)
relation [riˈleiʃn] n 1. dangi
2. hadî 3. in relation to game
da 4. duba wajen relations
relations [riˈleiʃns] pl 1.
hulɗoɗi 2. friendly relations
abokantaka 3. diplomatic
relations hulɗar jakadanci
4. international relations
hulɗoɗin ƙasashen duniya
5. to establish relations ƙulla
hulɗa 6. to break off relations
katse hulɗa
relationship [riˈleiʃnʃip] n
1. dangantaka 2. zumunci
3. ƙàwàncē

relative [ˈrelətiv] n dangi
relatively [ˈrelətivli] adv da dama
relax [riˈlæks] v 1. huta 2. sassauta
relaxation [ˌriːlækˈseiʃn] n
shaƙatawa
relaxed [riˈlækst] adj mai
walwala
relay [ˈriːlei] v ba da
relay race n gudun ba da sanda
release [riˈliːs] 1. n saki 2. v sàkā
released [riˈliːs] adj à sàke
relegate [ˈreligeit] v mai da...
kafaɗa guda
relent [riˈlent] v ji tausayi
relentless [riˈlentlis] adj mài bâ jî
bâ ganî
relevance [ˈreləvəns] n tāsìrì
relevant [ˈreləvənt] adj to be
relevant to shàfā
reliability [riˌlaiəˈbiləti] n inganci
reliable [riˈlaiəbl] adj 1. tabbatacce
2. mai aminci 3. a reliable
source majiya mai tushe
reliance [reˈlaiəns] n aminci
relic [ˈrelik] n abin dâ
relief [riˈliːf] n sauƙi 2. agaji
3. to give relief to tàllafā
relief fund n asusun agaji
relief organisation n ƙungiyar
agaji
relieve [riˈliːv] v 1. sauƙaƙa
2. kwantar da 3. to relieve
from office tumɓuke
relieved [riˈliːvd] adj We were
relieved by the report. Labarin
ya kwantar da hankalinmu.
religion [riˈlidʒən] n addini
religious [riˈlidʒəs] adj 1. na
addini 2. mai ibada
religious fundamentalist n
mai ra'ayin a koma wa addini
na tsantsa

relinquish [riˈliŋkwiʃ] v bari
relish [ˈreliʃ] v more da
reluctance [riˈlʌktəns] n nàwă
reluctant [riˈlʌktənt] adj to be reluctant ji nauyi
rely [riˈlai] v dògarà (on da)
remain [riˈmein] v 1. zauna 2. saura
remainder [riˈmeində] n saura
remains [riˈmeinz] pl 1. kufai 2. human remains gawa
remake [ˌriːˈmeik] v sake yi
remark [riˈmaːk] 1. n magana 2. v furta
remarkable [riˈmaːkəbl] n abin lura
remedy [ˈremədi] n magani
remember [riˈmembə] v tuna da
remembrance [riˈmembrəns] n tunawa
remembrance ceremony n bikin tunawa
remind [riˈmaind] v tuna wa
reminder [riˈmaində] n matăshìyă
remnant [ˈremnənt] n guntu
remorse [riˈmɔːs] n nadama
remorseful [riˈmɔːsfl] adj mai nadama
remote [riˈməut] adj mai nisa
removal [riˈmuːvl] n kawarwa
remove [riˈmuːv] v 1. kau da 2. tuɓe 3. fitar da
renaissance [riˈneisəns] n farfaɗowa
render [ˈrendə] v sa
renege [riˈneg] v saɓa alkawari
renew [riˈnjuː] v 1. sabunta 2. sake
renewal [riˈnjuːwəl] n sabuntawa
renounce [riˈnauns] v yi wătsi da
renovate [ˈrenəveit] v sabunta

renown [riˈnaun] n shahara
renowned [riˈnaund] adj mashahuri
rent [rent] 1. n kuɗin haya 2. v yi haya 3. ba da haya
rented [ˈrentid] adj na haya
rent-free n hayar kyauta
renting [ˈrentiŋ] n haya
reopen [riːˈəupn] v sake buɗewa
reorganization [riːˌɔːgənaiˈzeiʃn] n yin garambawul
reorganize [riːˈɔːgənaiz] v yi garambawul ga
repair [riˈpeə] 1. n gyara 2. v gyarta
reparations [ˌrepəˈreiʃnz] pl diyya
repatriate [riːˈpætrieit] v cire... daga ƙasa
repatriation [riːˌpætriˈeiʃn] n cirewa daga ƙasa
repay [riːˈpei] v 1. mayar da 2. rama wa
repayment [riːˈpeimənt] n ramuwa
repeal [riˈpiːl] v soke
repeat [riˈpiːt] v maimaita
repeatedly [riˈpiːtidli] adv to do repeatedly nănătă
repel [riˈpel] v gùdă
repent [riˈpent] v tuba
repentance [riˈpentəns] n tuba
repetition [ˌrepiˈtiʃn] n maimaitawa
replace [riˈpleis] v 1. maye gurbi 2. sake
replacement [riˈpleismənt] n maimako
replenish [riˈpleniʃ] v cika
reply [riˈplai] 1. n amsa 2. v mayar da amsa
report [riˈpɔːt] 1. n labari 2. rahoto 3. **annual report**

rahoto na shekara-shekara 4. *v*
ba da labari 5. kai rahoto
reporter [riˈpɔːtə] *n* 1. mai ba da
labarai 2. ɗan jarida
repossess [riˈpəzes] *v* ƙwace wa
represent [ˌrepriˈzent] *v* 1.
wàkiltà 2. **to represent the
interests of...** kare mutuncin...
representation [ˌreprizenˈteiʃn] *n*
wakilci
representative [ˌrepriˈzentətiv]
1. *adj* mai wakilci 2. *n* wakili
3. (US) ɗan Majalisar Dokoki
4. *duba wajen* House of
Representatives, sales
representative
repress [riˈpres] *v* **to repress a
revolt** kwantar da bore
repression [riˈpreʃn] *n* zalunci
repressive [riˈpresiv] *adj* na
zalunci
reprieve [riˈpriːv] *v* soke wa...
hukunci
reprimand [ˈreprimaːnd] 1. *n*
tsâwā 2. *v* tsâwàtà wà
reprint [ˈriːˈprint] *v* sake bugawa
reproach [riˈprəutʃ] *v* zàrgā
reproachful [riˈprəutʃfl] *adj* mai
zargi
reproduce [ˌriːprəˈdjuːs] *v* 1.
hàifā 2. yi kwafi
reproduction [ˌriːprəˈdʌkʃn] *n*
1. haifuwa 2. yin kwafi
reptile [ˈreptail] *n* ja-jiki
republic [riˈpʌblik] *n* jamhuriya
republican [riˈpʌblikən] *n* 1. ɗan
salon mulkin jamhuriya 2. (US)
ɗan jamˈiyyar 'Republican'
republicanism [riˈpʌblikənizm] *n*
salon mulkin jamhuriya
republish [ˈriːˈpʌbliʃ] *v* sake
bugawa

repudiate [riˈpjuːdieit] *v* juya
wa... baya
repugnant [riˈpʌgnənt] *adj* mai
ƙyama
repulse [riˈpʌls] *v* 1. yi wa...
ƙyama 2. gùdā
repulsive [riˈpʌlsiv] *adj* mai
ƙyama
reputable [ˈrepjutəbl] *adj* mai
suna
reputation [ˌrepjuˈteiʃn] *n* 1. suna
2. **to have a reputation** yi
suna (for wajen)
repute [riˈpjuːt] *n* suna
request [riˈkwest] 1. *n* roƙo
2. *v* roƙa
require [riˈkwaiə] *v* 1. bukata
2. (leg.) ce
required [riˈkwaiəd] *adj* **to be
required to...** ya kama tilas...
requirement [riˈkwaiəmənt] *n* 1.
bukata 2. (leg.) ƙaˈida
resale [ˈriːˈseil] *n* sake sayarwa
reschedule a debt [riˈʃedjul;
riːˈskedjul] *v* sake tsarin amsar
bashi
rescue [ˈreskjuː] 1. *n* ceto 2. agaji
3. *v* cêtā (from daga) 4. àgazà
research [riˈsəːtʃ] 1. *n* bincike
2. *v* nàzartà
research into *v* bincika
researcher [riˈsəːtʃə] *n* mai
bincike
research programme *n* shirin
bincike
resell [ˈriːˈsel] *v* sake sayarwa
resemblance [riˈzembləns] *n*
kama
resemble [riˈzembl] *v* yi kama da
resent [riˈzent] *v* ta da ƙayar baya
resentful [riˈzentfl] *adj* mai
rashin jituwa

resentment [riˈzentmənt] *n*
1. rashin jituwa 2. to show
resentment ta da ƙayar baya

reservation [ˌrezəˈveiʃn] *n*
1. shakka 2. to make a hotel
reservation riƙe ɗaki a hotel

reserve [riˈzəːv] 1. *adj/n* nature
reserve gandun daji 2. *v* ajiye
3. keɓe 4. *duba wajen* military
reserves

reserve bank *n* bankin tsimi da
tanadi

reserved [riˈzəːvd] *adj* This table
is reserved. An keɓe wannan
tebur.

reserve funds *pl* ajiyar kuɗi

reserves [riˈsəːvz] *pl* 1. bank
reserves ajiyar kuɗi ta banki
2. oil reserves tarin albarakun
mâi 3. military reserves
sojojin sa kai

reset [riːˈset] *v* sake yi

reshuffle [ˈriːˈʃʌfl] *v* 1. tankaɗe
da rairaya 2. (pol.) yi wa...
garambawul

reside [riˈzaid] *v* zauna

residence [ˈrezidəns] *n* 1.
mazauni 2. country of
residence ƙasar zama

residence permit *n* ikon zama
cikin ƙasa

resident [ˈrezidənt] *n* mazâuni

residential quarters [ˌreziˈdenʃl]
pl mazaunai

resign [riˈzain] *v* bari

resignation [ˌrezigˈneiʃn] *n* barin
aiki

resigned [riˈzaind] *adj* to be
resigned dànganà (to ga)

resist [riˈzist] *v* 1. ƙi 2. daddage
wa

resistance [riˈzistəns] *n* dagiya

resistant [riˈzistənt] *adj* mai
dagiya

resolute [ˈrezəluːt] *adj* to be
resolute tashi tsaye a kan

resolution [ˌrezəˈluːʃn] *n* 1.
shawara 2. to adopt a
resolution karɓi zartawa

resolve [riˈzɔlv] 1. *n* ƙarfin zuciya
2. *v* shirya 3. dage (to kan)

resort [riˈzɔːt] 1. *n* wurin 'yan
yawon shaƙatawa 2. the last
resort mafitar ƙarshe 3. *v* to
resort to violence kai ga yin
ɓarna

resourceful [riˈsɔːsfl] *adj* mai
dabara

resources [riˈsɔːsis] *pl* 1.
albarkatu 2. to pool resources
haɗa gwiwa

respect [riˈspekt] 1. *n* ladabi
2. ban girma 3. with respect to
game da 4. to show respect to
girmama 5. to pay one's last
respects to bai wa... gaisuwar
girmamawa ta ƙarshe 6. *v*
girmama

respectability [riˌspektəˈbiləti] *n*
dattako

respectable [riˈspektəbl] *adj* mai
halin dattijo

respectful [riˈspektfl] *adj* mai
ladabi

respectively [riˈspektivli] *adv* a
jere

respects [riˈspekts] *pl* gaisuwa

respiration [ˌrespəˈreiʃn] *n*
numfashi

respite [ˈrespait] *n* sauƙi

respond [riˈspɔnd] *v* amsa

response [riˈspɔns] *n* amsa

responsibility [riˌspɔnsəˈbiləti] *n*
1. nauyi 2. (leg.) hukunci 3. to

accept responsibility ɗauki
nauyi

responsible [riˈspɔnsəbl] *adj* mai
nauyi

responsive [riˈspɔnsiv] *adj* mai
lallasuwa

rest [rest] 1. *n* hutu 2. saura
3. *v* huta

rest and recuperation (R&R)
n hutuwa da wartsakewa

restaurant [ˈrestrɔnt] *n* gidan
abinci

restitution [ˌrestiˈtjuːʃn] *n* biyan
ranko, ramuwa

restless [ˈrestlis] *adj* mai shìgi dà
fici

restlessness [ˈrestlisnis] *n* shìgi
dà fici

restoration [ˌrestəˈreiʃn] *n*
1. sabuntawa 2. mayarwa

restore [riˈstɔː] *v* 1. sabunta
2. mayar da 3. raya

restrain [riˈstrein] *v* tsare

restraint [riˈstreint] *n* 1. **wage
restraint** hana tashin albashi
2. **to exercise restraint** daure

restrict [riˈstrikt] *v* ƙayyade

restricted [riˈstriktid] *adj*
ƙayyadadde

result [riˈzʌlt] *n* 1. sakamako
2. **as a result of** saboda

result in *v* sa

resulting from [riˈzʌltiŋ]
a sanadiyyar

resume [riˈzjuːm] *v* ci gaba da

resume [ˌrezuˈmei] *n* taƙaitawa

resuscitate [riˈsʌsiteit] *v* farfaɗo
da

retail [ˈriːteil] *n* kiri

retailer [ˈriːteilə] *n* ɗan kiri

retail price [ˈriːteil] *n* farashin
kiri

retain [riˈtein] *v* riƙe

retaliate [riˈtælieit] *v* rãmã

retaliation [riˌtæliˈeiʃn] *n*
ramuwa

retard [reˈtaːd] *v* tauye

retarded [riˈtaːdid] *adj* **mentally
retarded** taɓaɓɓe

rethink [ˌriːˈθiŋk] *v* sauya rawa

retinue [ˈretinjuː] *n* mabìyã

retire [riˈtaiə] *v* 1. ja da baya
2. yi murabus **(from daga)**

retirement [riˈtaiəmənt] *n*
1. murabus 2. **voluntary
retirement** ritaya ta ganin
dama 3. **forced retirement**
ritaya ta dole

retrace [riːˈtreis] *v* bi diddigī

retract [riˈtrækt] *v* jânyē

retreat [riˈtriːt] 1. *n* kòmã-bãya
2. (rel.) taron addu'a 3. *v* koma
da baya

retrench [riˈtrentʃ] *v* rage yawa

retribution [ˌretriˈbjuːʃn] *n*
sakamako

retrieve [riˈtriːv] *v* ɗauko

retroactive [ˌretrəˈæktiv] *adj* mai
koma-baya

retrogression [ˌretrəˈgreʃn] *n*
kòmã-bãya

retrospective [ˌretrəˈspektiv] *adj*
mai hangen baya

return [riˈtəːn] 1. *n* dawowa
2. **in return for** saboda da
3. *v* dawo 4. koma 5. mayar da

return ticket *n* tikitin zuwa da
dawowa

reunion [riˈjuːnjən] *n* taro sada-
zumunta

Rev. [ˈrevərənd] *duba wajen*
Reverend

reveal [riˈviːl] *v* 1. bayyana
2. tona

revel [ˈrevl] v ci duniya

revelation [ˌrevəˈleiʃn] n 1. bayani 2. (rel.) wahayi

revenge [riˈvendʒ] n 1. ramuwa 2. to take revenge ɗauki fansa 3. v rama

revenue [ˈrevənjuː] n 1. kuɗaɗen shiga 2. Inland Revenue ofishin haraji

revere [riˈviə] v girmama

reverence [ˈrevərəns] n girmamawa

reverend [ˈrevərənd] n (rel.) fàdà

reversal [riˈvəːsl] n juyin waina

reverse [riˈvəːs] 1. n akasi 2. ribas 3. baya 4. v yi juyin waina 5. yi ribas 6. soke

reversible [riˈvəːsəbl] adj mai gyaruwa

revert [riˈvəːt] v koma

review [riˈvjuː] v 1. duba 2. yi bita 3. rubuta sharhi

reviewer [riˈvjuːə] n marubucin sharhi

revise [riˈvaiz] v yi bita

revision [riˈviʒn] n bita

revival [riˈvaivl] n farfaɗowa

revive [riˈvaiv] v 1. raya 2. farfaɗo

revoke [riˈvəuk] v soke

revolt [riˈvəult] 1. n tawaye 2. v yi tawaye 3. to crush a revolt murƙushe tawaye

revolution [ˌrevəˈluːʃn] n 1. juyi 2. juyin juya hali 3. (pol.) juyin mulki

revolutionary [ˌrevəˈluːʃənəri] adj/n mai neman sauyi

revolutionary government n gwamnatin juyin juya hali

revolutionize [ˌrevəˈluːʃənaiz] v yi wa... babban sauyi

revolve [riˈvɔlv] v kewaya

revolver [riˈvɔlvə] n libarba, (Nr) fistole

revulsion [riˈvʌlʃn] n ƙyama

reward [riˈwɔːd] 1. n lada 2. v ba da lada

rewind [ˌriːˈwaind] v yi baya kaɗan

rheumatism [ˈruːmətizəm] n amosanin ƙashi

rhinoceros [raiˈnɔsərəs] n karkanda

rhyme [raim] n 'yar waƙa

rhythm [ˈriðəm] n kari

rib [rib] n harƙarƙari

ribbon [ˈribən] n kirtani

rice [rais] n shinkafa

rich [ritʃ] adj 1. mai kuɗi 2. mai albarka

riches [ˈritʃiz] pl arziki

rid [rid] v/adj to get rid of rabu da

ridden [ˈridn] duba wajen ride

riddle [ˈridl] n ka-cinci-ka-cinci

ride [raid] 1. n tafiya 2. v (rode, ridden) hau 3. shiga jirgi

rider [ˈraidə] n mahayi

ridge [ridʒ] n 1. kan dutse 2. kunya

ridicule [ˈridikjuːl] 1. n ba'a 2. v yi wa... ba'a

ridiculous [riˈdikjuləs] adj 1. mai ban dariya 2. na banza

riding [ˈraidiŋ] n hawa

rifle [ˈraifl] n bindiga

rift [rift] n ɓaraka

rig [rig] duba wajen oil rig

rig an election v yi magudi a zaɓe

right [rait] 1. adj na dàma 2. daidai 3. na gaskiya 4. right away yanzu-yanzu 5. n dàma 6.

iko **7.** hakki **8. to have the
right to...** sami ikon... **9. to put
right** daidaita **10.** *v* daidaita
right to vote *n* damar ka da
ƙuri'a
right-hand man *n* mutum na
hannun dama
right-wing *adj* (pol.) mai
ra'ayin riƙau
right-winger *n* (pol.) mai
ra'ayin riƙau
righteous [ˈraitʃəs] *adj* mai
sanin gaskiya
rights [raits] *pl* **1.** hakki, hakkoki
2. human rights hakkin ɗan
Adam **3. legal rights** hakki na
doka **4. civil rights** 'yancin da
doka ta tanadar **5.
constitutional rights** hakkin
tsārìn mulki **6. oil rights**
hakkin haƙar mâi
rigid [ˈridʒid] *adj* ƙandararre
rigor mortis [ˌrigəˈmɔːtis] *n*
sanƙamewar jiki
rigorous [ˈrigərəs] *adj* mai
tsanani
rigour [ˈrigə] *n* tsanani
rim [rim] *n* baki
rind [raind] *n* ɓawo
ring [riŋ] **1.** *n* zobe **2. boxing
ring** filin dambe **3.** *v* (**rang,
rung**) kaɗa ƙararrawa **4.** yi
ƙara **5.** buga wa... waya
ring off *v* ajiye tarho
ring up *v* buga wa... waya
rink [riŋk] *n* **ice rink** wurin
wasannin ƙanƙara
rinse [rins] *v* ɗauraye
riot [ˈraiət] **1.** *n* tarzoma **2.** *v* yi
tarzoma
riot police *pl* 'yan sandan
kwantar da tarzoma

rioter [ˈraiətə] *n* ɗan tarzoma
rip [rip] **1.** *n* ɓaraka **2.** *v* ɓarke
ripe [raip] *n* nunanne
ripen [ˈraipən] *v* **1.** nùna **2.** nunar
da
ripeness [ˈraipnis] *n* nùnā
ripple [ˈripl] *n* 'yar igiyar ruwa
rise [raiz] **1.** *n* tudu **2.** (fin.)
hauhawa **3. pay rise** ƙarin
albashi **4. sunrise** fitowar rana
5. to give rise to haifar da **6.** *v*
(**rose, risen**) tashi **7.** hauhawa
8. ƙara
rising [ˈraiziŋ] *adj* mai hauhawa
risk [risk] **1.** *n* haɗari **2.** *v* yi ƙuru
risk control *n* hasashen
aukuwar haɗari
risky [ˈriski] *adj* mai haɗari
ritual [ˈritjul] **1.** *adj* na al'ada **2.** *n*
al'ada
rival [ˈraivl] *n* **1.** ɗan takara
2. (pol.) abokin hamayya
3. (spor.) abokin gasa
rivalry [ˈraivlri] *n* **1.** takara **2.**
(pol.) hamayya **3.** (spor.) gasa
river [ˈrivə] *n* kogi
river bank *n* gaɓa
river bed *n* ƙwaryar kogi
road [rəud] *n* **1.** hanya **2. by
road** a mota
road sign *n* alamar hanya
roadway [ˈrəudwei] *n* hanya
roam [rəum] *v* yi gantali
roar [rɔː] **1.** *n* ruri **2.** *v* yi ruri
roast [rəust] **1.** *adj* gasasshen,
(Nr) roti **2.** *v* gasa
rob [rɔb] *v* (**robbed**) yi wa...
fashi
robber [ˈrɔbə] *n* ɗan fashi
robbery [ˈrɔbəri] *n* **1.** fashi
2. armed robbery fashi da
makamai

robe [rəub] *n* riga

robot [ˈrəubɔt] *n* mutum-mutumin inji

robust [rəuˈbʌst] *adj* mai

rock [rɔk] **1.** *n* dutse **2.** *v* yi rawa

rocket [ˈrɔkit] *n* **1.** roka **2.** injin roka

rock'n'roll [ˌrɔkənˈrɔl] *n* (mus.) kiɗan 'rock and roll'

rocky [ˈrɔki] *adj* **1.** mai duwatsu **2.** mai rawa

rod [rɔd] *n* sanda

rode [rəud] *duba wajen* ride

rogue [rəug] *n* ɗan damfara

role [rəul] *n* **1.** aiki **2.** matsayi **3.** tauraron fim **4. America is playing a role...** Amirka tana da hannu... (**in** a cikin/wajen)

roll [rəul] **1.** *n* ƙaramin burodi **2.** abin naɗi **3.** *v* gara **4.** mirgina

roll call *n* kiran suna

roll over *v* mirgine

roll up *v* naɗa

romance [rəuˈmæns] *n* **1.** soyayya **2.** labarin soyayya

romantic [rəuˈmæntik] *adj* na soyayya

roof [ruːf] *n* rufi

room [ruːm; rum] *n* **1.** ɗaki **2.** wuri

roommate *n* abokin zama

rooster [ˈruːstə] *n* (US) zakara

root [ruːt] *n* **1.** sâiwā **2.** tushe **3. to take root** kànkāmà

roots [ruːts] *pl* asali

rope [rəup] *n* igiya

rose [rəuz] **1.** wardi **2.** *duba wajen* rise

rosy [ˈrəuzi] *adj* **a rosy future** gaba mai albarka

rot [rɔt] **1.** *n* ruɓewa **2.** *v* (**rotted**) ruɓe

rotary [ˈrəutəri] *adj* mai juyi

rotate [rəuˈteit] *v* **1.** juya **2.** sauya

rotation [rəuˈteiʃn] *n* **1.** juyi **2.** sauyi

rotten [ˈrɔtn] *adj* **1.** ruɓaɓɓe **2.** na banza

rough [rʌf] *adj* **1.** mai kaushi **2.** maras ɗa'a **3.** kimanin

roughly [ˈrʌfli] *adv* wajen

roughneck [ˈrʌfnek] *n* ɗan banga

round [raund] *adj* **1.** mai da'ira **2.** kewayayye **3.** (spor.) karawa **4. all year round** rani da damina **5. to go round** kewaya **6.** *duba wajen* **around**

roundabout [ˈraundəbaut] *n* rawul, (Nr) rampuwan

round-table conference *n* taron yin shawarwari

round trip *n* tafiya da dawowa

round up *v* tasō ƙēyà

rouse [rauz] *v* ta da

rout [raut] *v* fàtàttakà

route [ruːt; raut] *n* hanya

routed [ˈrautid] *adj* **to be routed** watse

routine [ruːˈtiːn] **1.** *adj* na yau da kullum **2.** *n* hanya

row [rau] *n* jayayya

row [rəu] **1.** *n* jeri **2.** sahu **3. in a row** a layi **4.** *v* tuƙa

rower [ˈrəuə] *n* matuƙi

rowing boat [ˈrəuiŋ] *n* kwale-kwale

royal [ˈrɔiəl] *adj* mai sarauta

royalty [ˈrɔiəlti] *n* **1.** sarauta **2.** sarakai **3.** kamasho

rub [rʌb] *v* goge

rubber [ˈrʌbə] *n* **1.** roba, (Nr) kaushu **2.** magogi

rubber band *n* maɗaurin roba

rubbish [ˈrʌbiʃ] **1.** *adj* na banza **2.** *n* shàra

rubbish bin *n* garwar shara
rubbish heap *n* juji
rude [ru:d] *adj* mai rashin kunya
rudeness [ˈru:dnis] *n* rashin kunya
rudimentary [ˌru:diˈmentri] *adj* na farko
rudiments [ˈru:diments] *pl* ƙa'idoji
rug [rʌg] *n* kafet
rugby [ˈrʌgbi] *n* ƙwallon zariruga
ruin [ˈru:in] **1.** *n* lalacewa **2.** kango **3.** *v* lalata **4.** *duba wajen* ruins
ruined [ˈru:ind] *adj* to be ruined lalace
ruins [ˈru:inz] *pl* **1.** kufai **2.** gidajen tarihi
rule [ru:l] **1.** *n* doka **2.** mulki **3.** military rule mulkin soja **4.** as a rule galiban **5.** *v* yi mulki
rule over *v* yi sarauta
ruler [ˈru:lə] *n* **1.** sarki **2.** mai iko **3.** rula, (Nr) regil
rules and regulations *pl* dokoki da ƙa'idoji
ruling [ˈru:liŋ] *n* (leg.) hukunci
rumble [ˈrʌmbl] *v* yi cida
rumour [ˈru:mə] *n* **1.** jita-jita **2.** to spread rumours yaɗa jita-jita
rump [rʌmp] *n* kuturi
run [rʌn] **1.** *n* gudu **2.** *v* (ran, run) yi gudu **3.** gudana **4.** zuba **5.** yi aiki **6.** gudanar da **7.** to run a business tafiyar da ciniki **8.** to run guns yi sumogar makamai **9.** to run for office shiga takarar zaɓe

run away *v* gudù
runaway [ˈrʌnəwei] *n* ɗan gudun hijira
run down *v* **1.** take **2.** lalata
run dry *v* ƙafe
run into *v* **1.** yi kìciɓìs dà **2.** yi karɓ dà
run out *v* ƙare
run over *v* **1.** take **2.** *duba wajen* overflow
run short *v* gabce
rung [rʌŋ] *duba wajen* ring
runner [ˈrʌnə] *n* maguji
runner-up [ˌrʌnəˈʌp] *n* na-biyu
running [ˈrʌniŋ] *adj/adv* four days running kwana huɗu a jere
running water *n* ruwan famfo
runway [ˈrʌnwei] *n* titin tashi na jiragen sama
rupture [ˈrʌptʃə] **1.** *n* ɓaraka **2.** *v* ɓarke
rural [ˈruərəl] *adj* na karkara
rural development [ˈruərəl] *n* raya karkara
rush [rʌʃ] **1.** *n* gaggawa **2.** *v* shēƙà dà gudù
rush hour *n* lokacin zuwa ko tashi daga aiki
rush through *v* (pol.) to rush through a bill gaggauta amincewa da doka
rust [rʌst] **1.** *n* tsatsa **2.** *v* yi tsatsa
rustic [ˈrʌstik] *adj/n* baƙauye
rusting [ˈrʌstiŋ] *adj* mai tsatsa
rusty [ˈrʌsti] *adj* mai tsatsa
rut [rʌt] *n* galan
ruthless [ˈru:θlis] *adj* maras tausayi

Ss

sabbath [ˈsæbəθ] n Sati
sabotage [ˈsæbətɑːʒ] 1. n
  maƙarƙashiya 2. v ɓarnatar da
sabre [ˈseibə] n takobi
sachet [ˈsæʃei] n ƙaramin fakiti
sack [sæk] 1. n buhu, (Nr) sak
  2. v sàllamà
sacred [ˈseikrid] adj mai tsarki
sacrifice [ˈsækrifais] 1. n
  sadaukarwa 2. (rel.) hadaya
  3. v sadaukarwa
sacrilege [ˈsækrilidʒ] n saɓo
sad [sæd] adj 1. mai baƙin ciki
  2. a sad story labari mai ban
  tausayi
sadden [ˈsædn] v ɓata wa rai
saddle [ˈsædl] n sirdi
sadism [ˈseidizm] n fir'aunanci
sadistic [səˈdistik] adj mai halin
  fir'auna
sadness [ˈsædnis] n baƙin ciki
safari [səˈfɑːri] n yawon
  shaƙatawa/safari
safe [seif] 1. adj mai lafiya 2. mai
  aminci 3. n sef, (Nr) asusu
safeguard [ˈseifgɑːd] v tsare
safely [ˈseifli] adv lafiya
safe sex n jima'in roba
safety [ˈseifti] n 1. lafiya 2. rashin
  hadari
safety regulations pl dokokin
  kiyaye hadari
safety pin n fil, (Nr) fangil
Sahara Desert [səˈhɑːrə] n
  Sàhàrà
sail [seil] 1. n filafili 2. v shiga
  jirgin ruwa 3. to set sail tashi

sailing-boat, sailing-ship
  [ˈseiliŋˌbəut; -ʃip] n jirgen ruwa
  mai filafili
sailor [ˈseilə] n ma'aikacin jirgin
  ruwa
saint [seint] n waliyi
sake [seik] n 1. for the sake of
  domin 2. for my (own) sake
  don (karin) kaina
salad [ˈsæləd] n salak, (Nr) salati
salary [ˈsæləri] n albashi
salary increase n ƙarin albashi
salary scale n tsarin albashi
sale [seil] n 1. sayarwa 2. gwanjo
  3. for sale na sayarwa
saleable [ˈseiləbl] adj mai
  sayarwa
sales [seilz] pl tallace-tallace
salesclerk [ˈseilzklɑːk] n mai jiran
  kanti, (Nr) kwami
salesman, salesperson
  [seilzmən; ˈseilzpəːsn] n 1. ɗan
  kamasho 2. mai jiran kanti,
  (Nr) kwami
sales representative n 1. ɗan
  kamasho 2. dilali
sales staff n 1. yaron kanti
  2. 'yan kamasho
saleswoman [ˈseilzwumən] duba
  wajen salesman
saline [ˈseilain] adj na gishiri
saliva [səˈlaivə] n miyau
Sallah [ˈsælə] n Salla
salmon [ˈsæmən] n kifi
saloon [səˈluːn] n 1. falo 2. mota
  3. (US) mashaya
salt [sɔːlt] n gishiri

salty [ˈsɔːlti] *adj* mai gishiri
salute [səˈluːt] 1. *n* jinjina
2. (mil.) sara, (Nr) gardabu
3. yi wa... gaisuwa 4. (mil.)
sara wa, (Nr) yi wa... gardabu
salvage [ˈsælvidʒ] *v* tsamo
salvation [sælˈveiʃn] *n* tsira
same [seim] *adj* 1. ɗaya 2. daidai
(as da) 3. all the same duk da
haka
sample [ˈsaːmpl] *n* samfur
sanction [ˈsæŋkʃn] 1. *n* (ec., leg.)
takunkumi 2. *v* tabbatar da
sanctuary [ˈsæŋktʃuəri] *n* 1.
mafaka 2. gandu
sand [sænd] *n* rairayi
sandal [ˈsændl] *n* sandal, (Nr)
samara
sandpaper [ˈsænd,peipə] *n*
samfefa
sandwich [ˈsænwidʒ] *n* sanwici,
(Nr) sanwic
sane [sein] *adj* mai hankali
sang [sæŋ] *duba wajen* sing
sanitary [ˈsænitri] *adj* mai tsabta
sanitary engineer *n* ma'aikacin
tsabta
sanitary towel *n* tawalin al'ada,
fâd
sanitation [,sæniˈteiʃn] *n* aikin
tsabta
sanitation department *n*
ma'aikatar tsabta
sanity [ˈsæniti] *n* hankali
sank [sæŋk] *duba wajen* sink
sap [sæp] *n* ruwan bishiya
sarcasm [ˈsaːkæzəm] *n* gatse
sarcastic [saːˈkæstik] *adj* mai
gatse
sardine [saːˈdiːn] *n* kifin
gwangwani
sat [sæt] *duba wajen* sit

Satan [ˈseitn] *n* Shaiɗan
satchel [ˈsætʃəl] *n* jaka
satellite [ˈsætəlait] *n* 1. kumbo
2. **communications satellite**
kumbon saƙo
satellite dish *n* faifan kamo
yashar tauraron ɗan Adam
satire [ˈsætaiə] *n* zambo
satirical [səˈtirikl] *adj* na zambo
satirist [ˈsætərist] *n* ɗan zambo
satisfaction [,sætisˈfækʃn] *n*
1. gamsuwa 2. alfahari 3. biyan
bukata
satisfactory [,sætiˈfæktəri] *adj*
mai gamsarwa
satisfied [ˈsætisfaid] *adj* 1. mai
gamsuwa 2. mai alfahari 3. **to
be satisfied** gamsu
satisfy [ˈsætisfai] *v* 1. gamsar da
2. **to satisfy one's curiosity**
kashe kwarkwatan idanu 3. **Our
expectations were satisfied.**
Mun sami biyan bukata.
saturate [ˈsætʃəreit] *v* jiƙe jagab
Saturday [ˈsætədi] *n* Sati, (Nr)
Samdi
sauce [sɔːs] *n* miya
saucepan [ˈsɔːspən] *n* tukunya
saucer [ˈsɔːsə] *n* faranti
sausage [ˈsɔsidʒ] *n* tsiran alade
savage [ˈsævidʒ] *adj* 1. maras
mutunci 2. mahaukaci
savannah [səˈvaːnə] *n* daji
save [seiv] *v* 1. tserar da
2. kiyaye 3. yi tanadi 4. **to save
money** ajiye kuɗi
saver [ˈseivə] *n* mai ajiye juɗi
savings [ˈseiviŋz] *pl* kuɗin ajiya
savings and loans *pl* ajiya da
ba-da-bashi
savings bank *n* bankin ajiyar
kuɗi

saviour ['seiviə] *n* mai ceto

savoir-faire ['sævwa:'feə] *n* sanin madafa

savour ['seivə] *v* more da

savoury ['seivəri] *adj* mai daɗi

saw [sɔ:] 1. *n* zarto 2. *v* (sawed, sawn/sawed) yanka da zarto 3. *duba wajen* see

sawdust ['sɔ:dʌst] *n* garin katako

sawmill ['sɔ:mil] *n* ma'aikatar katako

sawn [sɔ:n] *duba wajen* saw

say [sei; sed] *v* (said) 1. ce (to wa) 2. that is to say watau

saying ['seiiŋ] *n* karin magana

scab [skæb] *n* 1. ɓamɓaroki 2. (pol.) bàdùjalä

scaffold ['skæfɔld] *n* tsani

scald [skɔ:ld] *v* ƙone

scale [skeil] 1. *n* ma'auni 2. tsari 3. *v* hau

scales [skeilz] *pl* sikeli

scalpel ['skælpl] *n* aska

scan [skæn] 1. *n* hoto 2. *v* ɗan leƙa 3. jùyä

scandal ['skændl] *n* abin kunya

scandalize ['skændəlaiz] *v* kunyata

scandalous ['skændələs] *adj* mai ban kunya

scanner ['skænə] *n* injin ɗaukar hoton takardu

scanty ['skænti] *adj* da wuya

scapegoat ['skeipgəut] *n* à-laɓà-gà-sàbarà-à-hàrbi-bàrēwä

scar [ska:] *n* tabo

scarce [skeəs] *adj* da wuya

scarcely ['skeəsli] *adv* da ƙyar

scarcity ['skeəsəti] *n* ƙaranci

scare ['skeə] *v* tsorata

scarecrow ['skeəkrəu] *n* mutum-mutumi

scared ['skeəd] *adj* to be scared ji tsoro

scaremonger ['skeəmʌŋgə] *n* ɗan sharri

scarf [ska:f] *n* 1. adiko 2. ɗan kwali

scarlet ['ska:lət] *adj* ja wur

scarred [ska:d] *adj* mai tabo

scary ['skeəri] *adj* mai ban tsoro

scatter ['skætə] *v* 1. watsa 2. watsu

scattered ['skætəd] *adj/adv* a barkatai

scattering ['skætəriŋ] *n* wàtsi

scene [si:n] *n* 1. mahalli 2. sashen wasan kwaikwayo 3. behind the scenes a bayan shinge

scenery ['si:nəri] *n* 1. shimfiɗar wuri 2. kyan karkara

scent [sent] *n* 1. ƙamshi 2. turare

sceptic ['skeptik] *n* ɗan kushe

sceptical ['skeptikl] *adj* 1. mai shakka 2. mai kushe

scepticism ['skeptisizəm] *n* kushe

sceptre ['septə] *n* kandiri

schedule ['ʃedju:l] *n* jadawali

scheduled ['ʃedju:ld] *adj* a kan ƙa'ida

scheme [ski:m] 1. *n* dabara 2. tsari 3. *v* haɗa kai

scholar ['skɔlə] *n* masani

scholarship ['skɔləʃip] *n* 1. sukolashif, (Nr) burus 2. to award a scholarship bayar da sukolashif

school [sku:l] 1. *adj* na makaranta 2. *n* makaranta 3. (US) jami'a

school board *n* hukumar makaranta

schooldays ['sku:ldeiz] *pl* zaman makaranta

schooling ['sku:liŋ] *n* ilimi

school marks *pl* maki

schoolmaster *n* malamin makaranta

schoolmistress *n* malamar makaranta

school uniform *n* yằyin makarantă

school-leaving certificate *n* takardar shaida ta kammala karatu

science [ˈsaiəns] *n* kimiyya

science and technology *n* kimiyya da fasaha

scientific [ˌsaiənˈtifik] *adj* na ilimin kimiyya

scientist [ˈsaiəntist] *n* mai ilimin kimiyya

scissors [ˈsizəz] *pl* almakashi

scoff [skɔf] *v* wulaƙantar (at da)

scold [skəuld] *v* yi wa... tsawa

scoop [skuːp] **1.** *n* samun babban labari **2.** *v* ɗiba

scooter [ˈskuːtə] *n* babur, (Nr) basfa

scope [skəup] *n* faɗi

scorch [skɔːt] *n* ƙona

score [skɔː] **1.** (ed.) maki **2.** (spor.) yawan ci **3.** *v* ci

scorn [skɔːn] **1.** *n* raini **2.** *v* raina

scornful [skɔːnfl] *adj* mai raini

scorpion [ˈskɔːpiən] *n* kunama

scot-free [ˈskɔtˌfriː] *adj* **to let off scot-free** yi wa... ci da ceto

Scotch [skɔtʃ] *adj* na Sikotlan

scotch tape *n* salatif, (Nr) iskwac

Scotland [ˈskɔtlənd] *n* yankin Sikotlan

Scotsman [skɔtsmən] *n* ɗan Sikotlan

Scottish [ˈskɔtiʃ] *adj* **1.** na Sikotlan **2.** ɗan Sikotlan

scout [skaut] *duba wajen* **boy scout**

scrabble [ˈskræbl] *v* yi wasoso

scramble for [ˈskræmbl] *v* yi wasoso

scrambled eggs *pl* daƙashin ƙwai

scrap [skræp] *n* ragowa

scrape [skreip] *v* **1.** kuje **2.** kankare

scratch [skrætʃ] *v* **1.** sosa **2.** karce

scream [skriːm] **1.** *n* kururuwa **2.** *v* yi kururuwa

screen [skriːn] **1.** *n* kariya **2.** *v* kare

screw [skruː] **1.** *n* sukur, (Nr) bis **2.** *v* ɗaura sukur

screwdriver [ˈskruːˌdraivə] *n* sukundireba, (Nr) turnabis

scribble [ˈskribl] *v* rubuta

script [skript] *n* rubutu

scripture [ˈskriptʃə] *n* littafin addini

scrotum [ˈskrəutm] *n* jakar ƙwalatai

scrounger [ˈskraundʒə] *n* ɗan zaman kashe wando

scrub [skrʌb] *v* goge

scruples [ˈskruːplz] *pl* adalci

scrupulous [ˈskruːpjuləs] *adj* mai adalci

scrutinize [ˈskruːtinaiz] *v* duba

scrutiny [ˈskruːtini] *n* tsokaci

scuba-diver [ˈskuːbaˌdaivə] *n* ɗan sama jannatin ruwa

scuffle [ˈskʌfl] *n* ɗan rikici

sculpt [skʌlpt] *v* sassaƙa

sculptor [ˈskʌlptə] *n* masassaƙi

sculpture [ˈskʌlptʃə] *n* sassaƙa

scum [skʌm] *n* yānā

scythe [saið] *n* lauje

sea [siː] *n* teku

seafood [ˈsiːfuːd] *n* abincin teku

sea-level [ˈsiːlevl] *n* tsagin ruwa

seagull [ˈsiːgʌl] *n* balbelar teku

seal [siːl] 1. *n* hatimi 2. naman daji da ya zama a teku 3. *v* liƙe

seaman [ˈsiːmən] *n* ma'aikacin jirgin ruwa

search [səːtʃ] 1. *n* nema 2. police search cajewa 3. *v* caje 4. to search for nèmā

searchlight [ˈsəːtʃlait] *n* babbar fitila mai juyawa

search warrant *n* waranti, (Nr) manda

seasick [ˈsiːsik] *n* mai tashin zuciya na teku

seaside [ˈsiːsaid] *n* bakin teku

season [ˈsiːzn] *n* 1. lokacin shekara 2. all-season na rani da damina

season ticket *n* tikitin jirgi ta makwanni/watanni/shekara

seasoning [ˈsiːzəniŋ] *n* kayan yaji

seat [siːt] 1. *n* kujera 2. wurin zama 3. *v* zaunar da

seatbelt [ˈsiːtbelt] *n* bel

seated [ˈsiːtid] *adj* a zaune

seat of government *n* mazaunin gwamnati

seaweed [ˈsiːwiːd] *n* ciyawar teku

secede [səˈsiːd] *v* ɓalle

secession [səˈseʃn] *n* ɓallewa

secluded [siˈkluːdid] *adj* à kèɓe

second [ˈsekənd] 1. *adj* na biyu 2. daƙiƙa 3. (pol.) goyi baya

secondary [ˈsekəndri] *adj* maras muhimmancin gaske

secondary school *n* sakandare

second class *adj/n* sikinkila

second-hand *adj* kwàncē

second-rate *adj* maras nagarta

secrecy [ˈsiːkrəsi] *n* rùfā-rùfā

secret [ˈsiːkrit] 1. *adj* na asiri 2. *n* asiri 3. in secret à àsìr̄ce

secret agent ɗan leƙen asiri

secretariat [ˌsekrəˈteəriət] *n* sakateriya

secretary [ˈsekrətri] *n* sakatare

secretary general *n* 1. babban sakatare 2. shugaba

secretary of state *n* sakataren harkokin waje

secret police *pl* 'yan sandan leƙen asiri

secret service *n* ƙungiyar leƙen asiri

secret talks *pl* shawarwari a asirce

secretly [ˈsiːkritli] *adv* à àsìrce

sect [sekt] *n* ɗariƙa

section [ˈsekʃn] *n* sashe

sector [ˈsektə] *n* shiyya

sectors of the economy *pl* sâssā na harkokin tattalin arziki

secular [ˈsekjulə] *adj* na boko

secure [siˈkjuə] 1. *adj* tam 2. *v* ƙulla

securely [siˈkjuəli] *adv* tam

security [siˈkjuərəti] *n* 1. tsaro 2. national security tsaron ƙasa

Security Council *n* Kwamitin Sulhu

security forces *pl* sojojin tsaron ƙasa

sedative [ˈsədətiv] *n* maganin sa barci

sedentary [ˈsedntri] *adj* mai zaune

sediment [ˈsedimənt] *n* laka

sedition [siˈdiʃn] *n* bore

seduce [siˈdjuːs] *v* ɗauki hankali

seduction [siˈdʌktʃən] *n* karawanci

see [si:] v (**saw, seen**) gani
see through v gane
seed [si:d] n iri
seeing ['si:iŋ] n gani
seeing that conj ganin cewa
seek [si:k] v (**sought**) nema
seek opinion v tùntuɓà
seem [si:m] v ba da alama
seemingly ['si:miŋli] adv ga alama
seen [si:n] duba wajen see
see off v raka
segregate ['segrigeit] v ware
segregation [ˌsegri·geiʃn] n wariya
seize [si:z] v kama
seizure ['si:ʒə] n kamuwa
seldom ['seldəm] adv ba safai ba
select [si·lekt] v zàɓā
selection [si·lektʃn] n zaɓe
selective [si·lektiv] adj mai zaɓe
self [self] n (pl **selves**) kâi
self-awareness [ˌselfə·weənəs] n sanin ciwon kai
self-centred [ˌself·sentəd] adj mai son kai
self-confidence [ˌself·kɔnfindəns] n ji da kai
self-control [ˌselfkən·trəul] n kamun kai
self-criticism [ˌself·kritisizəm] n hisabin da a ke yi wa kansa
self-deception [ˌselfdi·sepʃn] n cutar kai
self-defence [ˌselfdi·fens] n tsaron kai
self-determination ['selfdi,tə:mi·neiʃn] n zaɓar wa kai makoma
self-governing [ˌself·gʌvniŋ] adj mai mulkin kai
self-government [ˌself·gʌvnmənt] n mulkin kai

self-interest [ˌself·intrist] n son kai
selfish ['selfiʃ] adj mai son kai
selfishness ['selfiʃnis] n son kai
self-reliance [ˌselfri·la:jəns] n dogara da kai
self-respect [ˌselfri·spekt] n mutunci
self-sufficient [ˌselfsə·fiʃənt] adj
1. **to be self-sufficient** wàdātà
2. **to be self-sufficient in food** noma wa kai isasshen abinci
self-supporting [ˌselfsə·pɔtiŋ] adj ci-da-kai
self-taught [ˌself·tɔ:t] adj **to be self-taught** koyar da kai
sell [sel] v (**sold**) sayar da
sell off v sayar da
seller ['selə] n 1. mai sayarwa 2. **best-seller** fitaccen littafi
selling ['seliŋ] n sayarwa
sellotape n salatif, (Nr) iskwac
semblance ['sembləns] n kama
semen ['si:mən] n maniyyi
semi- ['semi] adj rabi da rabi
semi-desert [ˌsemi·dezət] n faƙo
semi-final [ˌsemi·fainl] n wasan kusa da ƙarshe
senate ['senit] n majalisar dattijai
senator ['senətə] n dattijo
send [send] v (**sent**) aika da
senile ['si:nail] adj mai gigin-tsufa
senior ['si:niə] adj/n 1. mafi girma 2. na gaba
senior official n ƙusa
sensation [sen·seiʃn] n 1. ji 2. abin mamaki
sensational [sen·seiʃənl] adj mai ba da mamaki
sense [sens] 1. n ji 2. hankali 3. ma'ana 3. v ji

senseless ['senslis] *adj* 1. maras hankali 2. mai rashin ma'ana 3. sumamme

sensibility [,sensi'biləti] *n* hankali

sensible ['sensəbl] *n* mai hankali

sensitive ['sensətiv] *adj* mai mutunci

sensitivity [,sensə'tiviti] *n* mutunci

sensual ['senʃuəl] *adj* mai ta da gashin jiki

sent [sent] *duba wajen* **send**

sentence ['sentəns] 1. *n* jimla 2. (leg.) hukunci 3. **death sentence** hukuncin kisa 4. *v* (leg.) yanke wa... hukunci

sentiment ['sentimənt] *n* ra'ayi

sentinel ['sentinl] *duba wajen* **sentry**

sentry ['sentri] *n* ɗan sintiri, (Nr) santinal

separate ['seprət] *adj* 1. dabam 2. a rabe

separate ['sepəreit] *v* 1. raba 2. ware 3. rabu

separately ['sepəreitli] *adv* ɗai-ɗai

separation [,sepə'reiʃn] *n* rabuwa

separatism ['seprə,tizm] *n* ra'ayin ɓallewa

separatist ['seprə,tist] *adj/n* mai ra'ayin ɓallewa

separator ['sepəreitə] *n* marabi

September [sep'tembə] *n* Satumba

sequel ['si:kwəl] *n* mabiyi

sequence ['si:kwəns] *n* 1. jeri 2. **in sequence** bi da bi

sequential [si'kwenʃl] *adj* bi da bi

sequestrate [si'kwestreit] *v* ƙwace

serene [si'ri:n] *adj* mai hankali kwance

sergeant ['sa:dʒənt] *n* saja, (Nr) sarjan

sergeant-major [,sa:dʒənt 'meidʒə] *n* samanja, (Nr) shefu

serial ['siəriəl] *adj* na jeri

serial killer *n* makashin jama'a

series ['siəri:z] *n* 1. jeri 2. **tv series** jerin talabijin

serious ['siəriəs] *adj* 1. mai tsanani 2. babba 3. maràs gàràjē

seriously ['siəriəsli] *adv* 1. da gaske 2. **to take seriously** kula da

sermon ['sə:mən] *n* huɗuba

serpent ['sə:pənt] *n* maciji

serum ['siərəm] *n* magani

servant ['sə:vənt] *n* 1. bara, baranya 2. **civil servant** ma'aikacin gwamnati

serve [sə:v] *v* 1. yi wa... bauta 2. yi wa... hidima 3. kawo

service ['sə:vis] *n* 1. hidima 2. aikin sabis 3. (mil.) aikin soja 4. (rel.) du'a'i 5. **funeral service** jana'iza 6. **civil service** aikin gwamnati 7. **secret service** ƙungiyar leƙen asiri

serviceable ['sə:visəbl] *adj* mai gyaruwa

service industries *pl* kamfanonin ayyukan da ba na ƙere-ƙere ba

service station *n* gidan mai

session ['seʃn] *n* 1. zama 2. **joint session** haɗaɗɗen zama 3. **closed session** zaman ɓoye 4. **in session** cikin shawara

set [set] 1. *adj* a shirye 2. *n* tsari 3. **television set** talabijin 4. *v*

(set) sa **5.** daidaita **6. to set an
exam** tsara jarrabawa **7. to set
a time** yanke wa'adi **8.** *duba
wajen* **sunset**
set aside *v* keɓe
setback [ˈsetbæk] *n* kàrantsàyi
set down *v* sauke
set fire *v* sa wuta (**to** wa)
set free *v* 'yantar da
set off, set out *v* tashi
settee [seˈtiː] *n* dogon kujera
setting [ˈsetiŋ] *n* wuri
settle [ˈsetl] *v* **1.** zauna **2.** kwântā
3. shirya **4.** sulhunta **5.** biya
settle down *v* kwântā
set up *v* **1.** kafa **2.** yi wa... shiri
set up camp *v* ya da zango
settlement [ˈsetlmənt] *n* **1.**
yarjejeniya **2.** mazauni
settler [ˈsetlə] *n* ɗan kàkà-gidā
settle up *v* yi balas
seven [ˈsevn] *n/adj* bakwai
seventeen [ˌsevnˈtiːn] *n/adj* goma
sha bakwai
seventeenth [ˌsevnˈtiːnθ] *adj* na
goma sha bakwai
seventh [ˈsevnθ] *adj* na bakwai
seventy [ˈsevnti] *n/adj* saba'in
sever [ˈsevə] *v* yanke
several [ˈsevrəl] *adj* **1.** waɗansu
2. da dama
severe [siˈviə] *adj* mai tsanani
severity [siˈverəti] *n* tsanani
sew [səu] *v* (**sewed, sewn/sewed**)
ɗinka
sewer [ˈsuːə] *n* lambatu
sewing [ˈsəuiŋ] *n* ɗinki
sewing machine *n* keken ɗinki
sex [seks; ˈseksiz] *n* (*pl* **sexes**)
1. jinsi **2.** jima'i
sex education *n* ilimin jima'i
sexism [ˈseksizm] *n* wariyar jinsi

sexist [ˈseksist] *adj/n* ɗan wariyar
jinsi
sexual [ˈsekʃuəl] *adj* **1.** na jinsi
2. na jima'i
sexual desire *n* jaraba
sexual intercourse *n* jima'i
sexual relations *n* jima'i
sexy [ˈseksi] *adj* mai farin jini
shabby [ˈʃæbi] *adj* ƙazami
shade [ʃeid] *n* **1.** inuwa **2.**
a shade of green shigen kore
shadow [ˈʃædəu] *n* inuwa
shadowy [ˈʃædəui] *adj* mai inuwa
shady [ˈʃeidi] *adj* mai inuwa
shaft [ʃaːft] *n* ƙota
shaggy [ˈʃægi] *adj* buzu-buzu
shake [ʃeik] *v* (**shook, shaken**)
1. girgiza **2.** yi rawa
shake hands *v* yi musafaha
shaken [ˈʃeikən] *duba wajen*
shake
shake-up *n* tankaɗe da rairaya
shaking [ˈʃeikiŋ] **1.** gìřgizà
2. rawa
shaky [ˈʃeiki] *adj* **1.** mai rawa
2. maras tabbas
shall [ʃəl; ʃæl] *duba wajen* **be**
shallow [ˈʃæləu] *adj* maras zurfi
sham [ʃæm] *n* jabu
shame [ʃeim] **1.** *n* kunya **2. what
a shame!** kaico! **3.** *v* fallasa
shamefaced [ˈʃeimfeist] *adj* mai
kunya
shameful [ˈʃeimfəl] *adj* mai ba da
kunya
shameless [ˈʃeimlis] *adj* maras
kunya
shampoo [ʃæmˈpuː] *n* shamfu
shape [ʃeip] **1.** *n* siffa **2. to take
shape** tàbbàtà sòsai
shapeless [ˈʃeiplis] *adj* maras
siffa

shapely [ˈʃeiplɪ] *adj* kyakkyawa
share [ʃeə] 1. *n* rabo 2. (fin.) hannun jari 3. *v* raba
share out *v* rarràbā
shareholder [ˈʃeə,həuldə] *n* mai hannun jeri
shark [ʃaːk] *n* babban kifin teku
sharp [ʃaːp] *adj* 1. mai kaifi 2. mai tsanani
sharpen [ˈʃaːpən] *v* wāsā
sharpener [ˈʃaːpnə] *n* mawashi
sharply [ˈʃaːplɪ] *adv* sosai
sharpness [ˈʃaːpnɪs] *n* 1. kaifi 2. tsanani
shatter [ˈʃætə] *v* fasa
shattered [ˈʃætəd] *adj* fasasshe
shave [ʃeiv] *v* 1. yi aski 2. gyara fuska
shaving [ˈʃeiviŋ] *n* aski
shawl [ʃɔːl] *n* mayafi
she [ʃiː] *pro* 1. ita 2. ta
sheath [ʃiːθ] *n* gida
shed [ʃed] 1. *n* rumfa 2. *v* zubar da
sheep [ʃiːp] *n* (*pl* sheep) tunkiya
sheer [ʃiə] *adj* 1. matsananci 2. mai tsawo
sheet [ʃiːt] *n* 1. zanen gado 2. falle 3. a sheet of paper warka
shelf [ʃelf; ʃelvz] *n* (*pl* shelves) kanta
shell [ʃel] 1. *n* ɓawo 2. katantanwa 3. (mil.) harsashi 4. *v* (mil.) jefa bom
shellfish [ˈʃelfɪʃ] *n* ɓawon kifi
shelter [ˈʃeltə] 1. *n* rumfa 2. mahalli 3. mafaka 4. to take shelter fake 5. *v* kare
shelve [ʃelv] *v* keɓe
shelves [ʃelvz] *duba wajen* shelf
shepherd [ˈʃepəd] *n* makiyayi

sheriff [ˈʃerɪf] *n* (US) duba-gari, sarkin doka
shield [ʃiːld] 1. *n* garkuwa 2. *v* kare
shift [ʃɪft] *v* 1. kawar da 2. canja
shilling [ˈʃɪlɪŋ] *n* sule
shin [ʃɪn] *n* ƙwauri
shine [ʃain; ʃɔn] *v* (shone) 1. yi haske 2. yi ƙyalli
shiny [ˈʃaini] *adj* mai walƙiyai
ship [ʃɪp] 1. *n* jirgin ruwa 2. *v* aika da kaya
shipment [ˈʃɪpmənt] *n* kaya
shipping [ˈʃɪpiŋ] *n* 1. jirage 2. sufuri
shipwreck [ˈʃɪprek] *n* kifewar jirgi a ruwa
shipyard [ˈʃɪpjaːd] *n* tashar ƙera jiragen ruwa
shire [ˈʃaiə] *n* (UK) ƙaramar hukuma
shirt [ʃəːt] *n* taguwa
shit [ʃɪt] *n* (sl.) kashi
shiver [ˈʃivə] *n* yi rawar jiki
shivery [ˈʃivəri] *adj* mai rawar jiki
shock [ʃɔk] 1. *n* motsi 2. firgita 3. electric shock wutar lantarki 4. *n* firgitar da
shock absorber *n* cakosoba, (Nr) amartisar
shocked [ʃɔkt] *adj* to be shocked gigice
shocking [ˈʃɔkiŋ] *adj* mai gigitarwa
shoddy [ˈʃɔdi] *adj* mummunan aiki
shoe [ʃuː] *n* takalmi
shoelace [ˈʃuːleis] *n* maɗaurin takalmi
shoemaker [ˈʃuː,meikə] *n* shumeka

shoestring [ˈʃuːstriŋ] *n* (US)
maɗaurin takalmi

shone [ʃɔn] *duba wajen* **shine**

shook [ʃuk] *duba wajen* **shake**

shoot [ʃuːt] **1.** *n* tsiro **2.** *v* (**shot**)
harba

shoot down *v* harbe

shooting [ˈʃuːtiŋ] *n* harbi

shooting star *n* tauraruwa mai
wutsiya

shoot-out [ˈʃuːtaut] *n* musayar
wuta

shop [ʃɔp] **1.** *n* kanti **2.** *v* yi
sayayya

shopkeeper [ˈʃɔp,kiːpə] *n* mai
kanti

shoplifter [ˈʃɔp,liftə] *n* ɓarawo

shoplifting [ˈʃɔp,liftiŋ] *n* sata

shopping [ˈʃɔpiŋ] *n* cin kasuwa

**shopping centre, shopping
mall** *n* kantunan sai da kayan
marmari

shop window *n* tagar shago

shore [ʃɔː] *n* **1.** gaɓa **2.** baki

short [ʃɔːt] *adj* **1.** kaɗan **2.** gajere
3. to be short of kāsā **4.** in
short a takaice

shortage [ˈʃɔːtidʒ] *n* rashi

shortchange [,ʃɔːtˈtʃeindʒ] *v*
ƙwārā

short circuit [,ʃɔːtˈsəːkit] *n*
ƙonewa

shortcoming [ˈʃɔːtkʌmiŋ] *n* illa

short cut *n* yànke

shorten [ˈʃɔːtn] *v* taƙàitā

shorthand [ˈʃɔːthænd] *n* zàuràncē

shortly [ˈʃɔːtli] *adv* in an jima

shortness [ˈʃɔːtnis] *n* gajarci

shorts [ʃɔːts] *pl* **1.** (UK) gajeren
wando **2.** (US) *duba wajen*
underwear

short-sighted [,ʃɔːtˈsaitid] *adj*
She is short-sighted. Ba ta
ganin nesa.

short-term [,ʃɔːtˈtəːm] *adj* na
gajeren lokaci

short-wave [ˈʃɔːtweiv] *adj* mai
gajeren zango

shot [ʃɔt] **1.** *n* bugu **2.** (med.)
allura **3.** *duba wajen* **shoot**

should [ʃud] *v* ya kamata...

shoulder [ˈʃəuldə] *n* kafaɗa, (Nr)
kanhwala

shout [ʃaut] **1.** *n* ihu **2.** *v* yi ihu

shout about *v* yāyàtā

shout at *v* zāgā

shout out *v* yi kuwwa

shouting [ˈʃautiŋ] *n* ihu

shove [ʃʌv] *v* bangaje

shovel [ˈʃʌvl] *n* tebur, (Nr) felu

show [ʃəu] **1.** *n* nuni **2.** wasan
kwaikwayo/kiɗa **3.** *v* (**showed,
shown**) nuna **4.** bayyana

show how to *v* kwatanta

show off *v* yi taƙama

show out *v* raka

showcase [ˈʃəukeis] *v* yi nuni

shower [ˈʃauə] *n* **1.** shawa
2. yayyafi

shown [ʃəun] *duba wajen* **show**

showroom [ˈʃəurum] *n* shago

shrank [ʃræŋk] *duba wajen* **shrink**

shrewd [ʃruːd] *adj* mai wayo

shriek [ʃriːk] *v* yi ƙara

shrimp [ʃrimp] *n* jatan lande

shrine [ʃrain] *n* maziyarta

shrink [ʃriŋk] *v* (**shrank,
shrunk**) ɗage

shrivel [ˈʃrivl] *v* yànƙwanà

shroud [ʃraud] *n* likkafani

shrub [ʃrʌb] *n* ƙaramar bishiya

shrug [ʃrʌg] *v* ɗaga kafaɗa

shrunk [ʃrʌŋk] *duba wajen* **shrink**

shudder [ˈʃʌdə] *v* yi rawa

shuffle [ˈʃʌfl] v 1. tànkàɗẽ dà ràirayà 2. (pol.) yi wà... gàràmbawùl

shun [ʃʌn] v ƙaurace wa...

shunt [ʃʌnt] v kawar da

shut [ʃʌt] 1. adj a rufe 2. v (shut) rufe

shut down v kashe, rufe

shut up! v rufe mana baki!

shutter [ˈʃʌtə] n ƙyauren taga

shuttle [ˈʃʌtl] 1. n jirgin jigila 2. v yi jigila

shy [ʃai] adj mai kunya

shyness [ˈʃainis] n jin kunya

siblings [ˈsibliŋ] pl ’yan’uwa

sick [sik] adj 1. maras lafiya 2. to feel sick ji ciwo

sick of [ˈsik,ɔv] adj to be sick of gundura da

sicken [ˈsikən] v ji ciwo

sickle [ˈsikl] n lauje

sickle call anaemia n naƙasar ƙwayoyin jini

sickly [ˈsikli] adj maras lafiya

sickness [ˈsiknis] n ciwo

side [said] n 1. gefe 2. kwiɓi 3. waje 4. (pol.) ɓangare 5. (spor.) ƙungiya 6. side of the house jikin gida 7. side of the road bakin hanya

side-splitting [ˈsaid,splitiŋ] adj mai ban dariya ƙwarai

sideboard [ˈsaidbɔːd] n kanta

sideline [ˈsaidlain] v keɓe

sidewalk [ˈsaidwɔːk] n (US) gefen hanya

sideways [ˈsaidweiz] adv à kàikàice

siege [siːdʒ] n to set/lay siege kewaye

siesta [siːˈestə] n barcin rana

sieve [siv] 1. n rariya, (Nr) tame 2. v tace

sift [sift] v rairaye

sigh [sai] v yi ajiyar zuciya

sight [sait] 1. n gani 2. abin gani 3. v hàngã

sightless [ˈsaitlis] adj makaho

sightseeing [ˈsait,siːiŋ] n yawon shaƙatawa

sign [sain] 1. n alama 2. lamba 3. sanarwa 4. road sign alamar hanya, (Nr) fano 5. There is no sign of them. Ba a ji ɗuriyarsu ba. 6. v sa hannu

signal [ˈsignəl] 1. n sigina, (Nr) kiliyotan 2. yi sigina, (Nr) yi kiliyotan

signaller [ˈsignələ] n singila

signatory [ˈsignətri] n mai sa hannu

signature [ˈsignətʃə] n sa hannu, (Nr) sinye

signboard [ˈsainbɔːd] n sanarwa

significance [sigˈnifikəns] n 1. manufa 2. ma’ana 3. muhimmanci

significant [sigˈnifikənt] adj muhimmi

signify [ˈsignifai] v nùfã

signing ceremony n bikin sa hannu

signpost [ˈsainpəust] n alamar hanya, (Nr) fano

silence [ˈsailəns] n shiru

silencer [ˈsailənsə] n salansa, (Nr) shamfama

silent [ˈsailənt] adj mai shiru

silk [silk] n siliki

silken [ˈsilkn] adj na siliki

silliness [ˈsilinis] n wauta

silly [ˈsili] adj na wauta

silo [ˈsailəu] n rumbun tanadi

silver [ˈsilvə] 1. adj na azurfa 2. n azurfa

similar [ˈsimilə] *adj* mài kàmā
similarity [ˌsiməˈlærəti] *n* kàmā
simple [ˈsimpl] *adj* 1. mai sauƙi
2. kawai
simplicity [simˈplisəti] *n* sauƙi
simplify [ˈsimplifai] *v* sauƙaƙa
simply [ˈsimpli] *adv* kawai
simulate [ˈsimjuleit] *v* kwàikwayà
simulation [ˌsimjuˈleiʃn] *n* kwaikwaiyo
simultaneous [ˌsimlˈteiniəs] *adj* na lokaci guda
simultaneously [ˌsimlˈteiniəsli] *adv* a lokaci guda
sin [sin] *n* zunubi
since [sins] *prep/conj* 1. tun 2. tun da
sincere [sinˈsiə] *adj* sahihi
sincerely [sinˈserəti] *adv* da gaskiya
sincerity [sinˈserəti] *n* gaskiya
sing [siŋ] *v* (**sang, sung**) rera waƙa
singe [sindʒ] *v* babbaka
singer [ˈsiŋə] *n* mawaƙi
singing [ˈsiŋiŋ] *n* rera waƙa
single [ˈsiŋgl] 1. *adj* ɗaya tak 2. *n* wanda bai yi aure ba 3. (mus.) faifai
single out *v* ware
singular [ˈsiŋgjulə] *n* mufaradi
sinister [ˈsinistə] *adj* mugu
sink [siŋk] 1. *n* baho 2. *v* (**sank, sunk**) nitse 3. nitsar da 4. sauka
sinner [ˈsinə] *n* mai zunubi
sip [sip] *v* kùrɓā
sir [səː] *n* yallaɓai
siren [ˈsaiərən] *n* jiniya, (Nr) fifa
sister [ˈsistə] *n* 1. 'yar uwa 2. (med./rel.) sista
sister-in-law [ˈsistərinlɔː] *n* kanwa

sit [sit] *v* (**sat**) zauna
sit down *v* zauna
sit-down protest *n* zaman dàɓàrō
sit-in [ˈsit,in] *n* zaman dàɓàrō
site [sait] *n* wuri
sitting [ˈsitiŋ] *n* zama
sitting-room *n* falo
situated [ˈsitjueitid] *adj* **The theatre is situated in the town centre.** Gidan wasar yana a tsakiyar gari.
situation [ˌsitʃuˈeiʃn] *n* 1. hali 2. al'amari 3. **the present situation** halin da ake ciki yanzu
six [siks] *n/adj* shida
sixteen [sikˈstiːn] *n/adj* goma sha shida
sixteenth [sikˈstiːnθ] *adj* na goma sha shida
sixth [siksθ] *adj* na shida
sixty [ˈsiksti] *n/adj* sittin
size [saiz] *n* 1. girma 2. lamba
skate [skeit] *v* yi gudu kan ƙanƙara
skating-rink [ˈskeitiŋ,riŋk] *n* wurin wasan gudu kan ƙanƙara
skeleton [ˈskelitn] *n* ƙwarangwal
skeptic, skeptical, skepticism *duba wajen* **sceptic, sceptical, scepticism**
sketch [sketʃ] 1. *n* zane 2. *v* zana
ski [skiː] *v* yi gudun ƙanƙara
skid [skid] *v* zame
skier [ˈskiːə] *n* ɗan gudun ƙanƙara
skiing [ˈskiːiŋ] *n* gudun ƙanƙara
skilful [ˈskilfl] *adj* mai fasaha
skill [skil] *n* gwaninta
skilled [ˈskild] *adj* gwani
skim [skim] *v* yàɗà

skimmed milk [skiməd'milk] *n* tatattar madara

skin [skin] 1. *n* fātā 2. *v* feɗe

skin-deep *adj* samà-samà

skinny ['skini] *adj* ramamme

skip [skip] 1. *n* (UK) bola 2. *v* yi ɗan tsalle 3. yi fashi

skip over *v* tsallake

skirmish ['skə:miʃ] *n* 'yaɼ dāgā

skirt [skə:t] *n* siket, (Nr) jif

skull [skʌl] *n* ƙoƙon kai

sky [skai] *n* sama

sky-blue *adj* shūɗi bàu

skyscraper ['skai,skreipə] *n* babban bene

slab [slæb] *n* yanki

slack [slæk] *adj* 1. mài nàwā 2. sako-sako

slacken ['slækən] *v* sassauta

slacker ['slækə] *n* mài nàwā

slackness ['slæknis] *n* sassaucì

slain [slein] *duba wajen* **slay**

slam [slæm] *v* (**slammed**) rufe da ƙarfi

slander ['sla:ndə] 1. *n* cîn zaɼàfî 2. ci zaɼàfî

slanderer ['sla:ndərə] *n* mài cîn zaɼàfî

slanderous ['sla:ndrəs] *adj* na cîn zaɼàfî

slang [slæŋ] *n* sàrā

slant [sla:nt] 1. *n* gangara 2. *v* karkata

slanting ['sla:ntiŋ] *adj* mai gangara

slap [slæp] 1. *n* mari 2. *v* (**slapped**) màrā

slash [slæʃ] *v* yanke

slate [slæt] *n* allo

slaughter ['slɔ:tə] 1. *n* yanka 2. kisan gilla 3. *v* yanka 4. yi kisan gilla

slaughterhouse ['slɔ:təhaus] *n* mahauta

slave [sleiv] *n* bawa

slave trade *n* cinikin bayi

slavery ['sleivəri] *n* bauta

slay [slei] *v* (**slew, slain**) kashe

sled, sledge [sled; sledʒ] *n* keken tafiya a kan ƙanƙara

sleek [sli:k] *adj* siriri

sleep [sli:p] 1. *n* barci 2. (**slept**) yi barci 3. kwana

sleeper ['sli:pə] *duba wajen* **sleeper car**

sleepiness ['sli:pinis] *n* jin barci

sleeping bag *n* bargon shiga na barci

sleeping car *n* taragun mai gadon kwana

sleeping pill *n* maganin barci

sleeping sickness *n* ciwon barci

sleepless ['sli:plis] *adj* mai rashin barci

sleeplessness ['sli:plisnis] *n* rashin barci

sleepwalker ['sli:p,wɔ:kə] *n* matafiyi cikin barcinsa

sleep with *v* yi jima'i da

sleepy ['sli:pi] *adj* mai jin barci

sleet [sli:t] *n* sulɓin daskararriyar ƙanƙara

sleeve [sli:v] *n* hannun riga

sleigh [slei] *duba wajen* **sled**

slender ['slendə] *adj* siriri

slept [slept] *duba wajen* **sleep**

slew [slu:] *duba wajen* **slay**

slice [slais] 1. *n* yanki 2. *v* yanka

sliced [slaisd] *adj* mài yankā-yankā

slick [slik] *n* oil slick zubewar man fetur

slide [slaid] 1. *n* wajen zamiya 2. hoto 3. *v* (**slid**) zame

slight [slait] *adj* kaɗan
slightly [ˈslaitli] *adv* kaɗan-kaɗan
slim [slim] **1.** *adj* siriri **2.** *v* saɓè
slimy [ˈslaimi] *adj* mai yauƙi
sling [sliŋ] **1.** *n* rataya **2.** *v* jefa
slip [slip] **1.** *n* rasit, (Nr) resi **2. slip of paper** 'yar guntuwar takarda **3.** *v* (**slipped**) zame **4. Kande slipped.** Santsi ya kwashe Kande.
slip away *v* sulâlē
slip of the tongue *n* katoɓara
slip out *v* kuɓuce (**of** daga)
slipper [ˈslipə] *n* silifa
slippery [ˈslipəri] *adj* mai santsi
slit [slit] **1.** *n* tsaga **2.** *v* tsaga
slogan [ˈsləugən] *n* take
slope [sləup] *n* gangara
sloping [ˈsləupiŋ] *adj* mai gangara
sloppy [ˈslɔpi] *adj* **to be sloppy** yi garaje
slot [slɔt] *n* rami
slow [sləu] *adj* **1.** maras sauri **2. This clock is slow.** Wannan agogo ya yi latti. **3. to be slow to** yi sanyin jiki wajen
slow down *v* **1.** rage gudu **2.** dakusar da
slow-motion [sləuˈməuʃn] *n* **in slow motion** silo-moshin
slowly [ˈsləuli] *adv* **1.** sannu-sannu **2.** a hankali
slowness [ˈsləunis] *n* **1.** rashin sauri **2.** latti
slumber [ˈslʌmbə] **1.** *n* barci **2.** *v* yi barci
slump [slʌmp] **1.** *n* (ec.) komaɗar tattalin arziki **2.** *v* (ec.) ja da baya
slums [slʌmz] *pl* gidajen bayan gari
sly [slai] *adj* mai wayo

smack [smæk] **1.** *n* mari **2.** *v* yi mari
small [smɔːl] *adj* **1.** ƙarami **2.** kaɗan
small arms *pl* ƙananan makamai
small trader *n* ɗan koli
smallness [ˈsmɔːlnəs] *n* ƙankantà
smallpox [ˈsmɔːlpɔks] *n* agana
smart [smaːt] *adj* **1.** mai dabara **2.** mai iya ado
smash [smæʃ] *v* fasa
smashing [ˈsmæʃiŋ] *adj* (UK) da kyau ƙwarai
smear [smiə] *v* **1.** shafa **2.** ɓata wa... suna
smell [smel] **1.** *n* sansana **2. nice smell** ƙamshi **3. bad smell** wari **4.** *v* (**smelt/smelled**) sansana
smell bad *v* yi wari
smell good *v* yi ƙamshi
smelt [smelt] *v* **1.** narkar da **2.** *duba wajen* **smell**
smile [smail] **1.** *n* murmushi **2.** *v* yi murmushi
smith [smiθ] *n* maƙeri
smoke [sməuk] **1.** *n* hayaƙi **2.** *v* sha taba **3.** ƙyafe
smoker [ˈsməukə] *n* mai shan taba
smoking [ˈsməukiŋ] *n* **1.** shan taba **2. No smoking!** Ba a shan taba nan!
smoky [ˈsməuki] *adj* mai hayaƙi
smooth [smuːð] *adj* **1.** sumul **2.** mai laushi
smoothly [ˈsmuːðli] *adv* daidai
smoothness [ˈsmuːðnəs] *n* **1.** sulɓi **2.** laushi
smuggle [ˈsmʌgl] *v* yi fasa-ƙwauri

smuggler [ˈsmʌɡlə] *n* ɗan fasa-ƙwauri

smuggling [ˈsmʌɡliŋ] *n* fasa-ƙwauri

snack [snæk] *n* ƙwalama

snag [snæɡ] *n* tangarɗa

snail [sneil] *n* dodon koɗi

snake [sneik] *n* maciji

snap [snæp] *v* (**snapped**) karye

snapshot [ˈsnæpʃɔt] *n* hoto

snare [sneə] *v* zarge

snarl [snaːl] *v* yi gurnani

snatch [snætʃ] *v* fizgā

sneak [sniːk] *v* laɓaba

sneakers [ˈsniːkəz] *pl* (US) kambas

sneaky [ˈsniːki] *adj* mai cuku-cuku

sneer [sniə] *v* yi gatsine

sneeze [sniːz] *v* yi atishawa

sniff [snif] *v* 1. sansana 2. ja majina

snob [snɔb] *n* mài hūrà hancì

snobbery [ˈsnɔbəri] *n* hūrà hancì

snooze [snuːz] *v* yi ɗan barci

snore [snɔː] *v* yi minshari

snort [snɔːt] *v* ja majina

snow [snəu] 1. *n* ƙanƙara 2. *v* yi ƙanƙara

snow-flakes *pl* dusar ƙanƙara

snow-white *adj* fari fat

snub [snʌb] *v* gwale

snug [snʌɡ] *adj* mai daɗin zama

so [səu] *adv* 1. kamar haka 2. ƙwarai 3. **and so** ma 4. **even so** duk da haka 5. **that is so** haka ne

soak [səuk] *v* jiƙe

so-and-so [ˈsəuənˌsəu] *n* wānè, wāncè

soap [səup] *n* sabulu

soap opera *n* tatsuniyar kwaikwayo

soar [sɔː] *v* tashi

so as not to *conj* don gudun kada

sob [sɔb] *v* yi kuka sa shassheƙa

sober [ˈsəubə] *adj* 1. da hankali 2. mai nitsuwa

so-called [səuˈkɔːld] *adj* wanda ake kira...

soccer [ˈsɔkə] *n* wasan ƙwallon ƙafa

sociable [ˈsəuʃəbl] *adj* mai son mutane

social [ˈsəuʃl] *adj* na zaman jama'a

social-democrat *n* ɗan kishin dimokuraɗiyya

social science *n* ilimin rayuwar jama'a

social scientist *n* mai ilimin rayuwar jama'a

social security, social welfare *n* jin daɗin jama'a

socialism [ˈsəuʃəlizəm] *n* gurguzanci

socialist [ˈsəuʃəlist] 1. *adj* na gurguzu 2. *n* ɗan gurguzu

socialize [ˈsəuʃəlaiz] *v* yi hulɗa da jama'a

society [səˈsaiəti] *n* 1. zaman jama'a 2. ƙungiya

sociologist [ˌsəusiˈɔlɔdʒist] *n* mai ilimin halayyar zaman jama'a

sociology [ˌsəusiˈɔlɔdʒi] *n* ilimin halayyar zaman jama'a

sock [sɔk] *n* safa, (Nr) suseti

socket [ˈsɔkit] *n* 1. gurbi 2. **power socket** soket, (Nr) firis

soda water *n* soda

sofa [ˈsəufa] *n* babban kujera

so far *adv* kàwō yànzu

soft [sɔft] *adj* 1. mai taushi 2. maras karfi

soft drink *n* lemo
soft loan *n* sàssauƙan lāmùnì
soften [ˈsɔfn] *v* tausasa
softly [ˈsɔftli] *adv* sannu-sannu
softness [ˈsɔftnis] *n* taushi
soggy [ˈsɔgi] *adj* langaɓaɓɓe
soil [sɔil] **1.** *n* ƙasa **2.** *v* ɓata
solar [ˈsəulə] *adj* na rana
solar energy *n* makamashin
zafin rana
sold [səuld] *duba wajen* **sell**
sold out [səuldˈaut] *adj* **Sorry,**
we are sold out. Yi haƙuri,
mun sayar.
solder [ˈsəuldə] **1.** *n* soda, (Nr)
sode **2.** *v* yi soda, (Nr) yi sode
soldier [ˈsəuldʒə] *n* soja
sole [səul] **1.** *adj* tilo **2.** *n* tafin
ƙafa **3.** ƙasan takalmi
sole agent *n* wakilin tilo, babban
dillali
solely [ˈsəuli] *adv* zalla
solemn [ˈsɔləm] *adj* maras garaje
solicit [səˈlisit] *v* rôƙā
solicitor [səˈlisitə] *n* lauya, (Nr)
aboka
solid [ˈsɔlid] *adj/n* **1.** daskararre
2. mai ƙwari **3.** na haƙiƙa
solidarity [ˌsɔliˈdærəti] *n* zumunci
solidify [səˈlidifai] *v* daskare
solitary [ˈsɔlitri] *adj* **1.** mai
kaɗaici **2.** ɗaya tak
solitude [ˈsɔlitjuːd] *n* kaɗaici
so long as *conj* muddin
so long! sai an jima!
solution [səˈluːʃn] *n* **1.** magani
2. ruwa **3.** amsa
solve [sɔlv] *v* warware
solvency [ˈsəulvənsi] *n* mallakar
abin hannu
solvent [ˈsɔlvənt] *adj* mai abin
hannu

some [səm; sʌm] **1.** waɗansu
2. ɗan **3.** wani, wata
somebody [ˈsʌmbədi] **1.** wani,
wata **2.** wani mutum
someday [ˈsʌmdei] *adv* nan gaba
somehow [ˈsʌmhau] *adv* ko ta
yaya
someone [ˈsʌmwʌn] **1.** wani,
wata **2.** wani mutum
someplace [ˈsʌmpleis] *adv* wani
wuri
somersault [ˈsʌməsɔlt] **1.** *n*
alkahura **2.** *v* yi alkahura
something [ˈsʌmθiŋ] **1.** wani abu
2. abu
sometimes [ˈsʌmtaimz] *adv*
lokaci-lokaci
somewhat [ˈsʌmwɔt] *adv* da
dama-dama
somewhere [ˈsʌmweə] *adv* wani
wuri
son [sʌn] *n* ɗa
son-in-law [ˈsʌninlɔː] *n* suruki
song [sɔŋ] *n* waƙa
soon [suːn] *adv* **1.** jim kaɗan
2. as soon as da zarar
soon after *conj* tun jim kaɗan
bayan
soon afterwards *adv* jim kaɗan
sooner or later [ˈsuːnə] *adv* yau
da gobe
soothe [suːð] *v* kwantar da
hankali
sophisticated [səˈfistikeitid] *adj*
ɗan duniya
sophistication [sə,fistiˈkeiʃn] *n*
iya duniya
sorcerer [ˈsɔːsərə] *n* maye
sorcery [ˈsɔːsəri] *n* tsafi
sordid [ˈsɔːdid] *adj* maras daɗi
sore [sɔː] **1.** *n* gyambo **2.** *adj* mai
jin zafi

sore throat n ciwon maƙogwaro
soreness [ˈsɔːnis] n tsami
sorrow [ˈsɔrəu] n baƙin ciki
sorry [ˈsɔri] adj 1. mai tuba
2. **sorry!** gafara dai! 3. **to be sorry for**... ji tausayin...
sort [sɔːt] 1. n iri 2. v kasà
sort out 1. kasà 2. warware
SOS [ˌesəuˈes] n koke share hawaye
so-so [səu səu] adv haka-haka
so that conj 1. don 2. don haka
sought [sɔːt] duba wajen **seek**
soul [səul] n rai
sound [saund] 1. adj mai ƙwari 2. n amo 3. ƙara 4. v yi ƙara
sound wave n sauti
soundless [ˈsaundlis] adj mai shiru
soundness [ˈsaundnis] n ƙwari
soundproof [ˈsaundpruːf] adj hànà-sautì
soup [suːp] n romo
sour [ˈsauə] 1. adj mai tsami 2. mai barci 3. **to go sour** lalace 4. v yi tsami
source [sɔːs] n 1. mafari 2. tushe 3. idon ruwa 4. **journalistic source** kafar labarai
source of income n hanyar kuɗi
source of information n majiya
sourness [ˈsauənis] n tsami
south [sauθ] 1. adj na kudu 2. n kudu
South Africa n Afirka ta Kudu
southeast [ˈsauθˈiːst] adj/adv kudu maso gabas
southerly [ˈsʌðəli] adj kudu
southern [ˈsʌðən] adj na kudu

southerner [ˈsʌðənə] n bakudu
southwards [ˈsauθwəːds] adv kudu-kudu
southwest [ˈsauθˈwest] adj/adv kudu maso yamma
souvenir [ˌsuːvəˈniə] n tsaraba
sovereign [ˈsɔvrin] n sarki, sarauniya
sovereign state n ƙasa ta musamman
sovereignty [ˈsɔvrənti] n zaman kai
soviet [ˈsəuviət] adj ɗan sobiyet
sow [sau] n ta-macen alade
sow [səu] v (**sowed, sown**) shuka
spa [spaː] n wurin ɗima jiki
space [speis] n 1. fili 2. sarari 3. giɓi 4. wuri 5. **outer space** sararin samaniya
spacecraft [ˈspeiskraːft] n kumbo
spaceman [ˈspeismæn] n ɗan sama jannati
spaceship [ˈspeisʃip] n kumbo
space shuttle [ˈspeisʃʌtl] n jirgin jigila
spacious [ˈspeiʃes] adj mai fili
spade [speid] n shebur
spaghetti [spəˈgeti] n taliya
span [spæn] n 1. ɗani 2. **lifespan** ajali
spanner [ˈspænə] n sufana, (Nr) kile amulat
spare [speə] 1. adj safaya 2. v hutar da 3. **Do you have any tickets to spare?** Kana da sauran tikitin nan ko?
spare a life v yi wa... rai
spare parts pl kayayyakin gyara
spare time n lokacin hutawa
spare tyre n safaya, (Nr) fine sekur

spark [spɑːk] *n* tartsatsi
sparkle [ˈspɑːkl] *v* yi ƙyalƙyali
sparkling [ˈspɑːklɪŋ] *adj* mai ƙyalƙyali
sparkling water *n* ruwa garai-garai
sparkling wine *n* giya mai fartsatsi
spark plug *n* fulogi, (Nr) buji
sparrow [ˈspærəu] *n* gwarā
spasm [ˈspæzəm] *n* sūkǎ
spat [spæt] *duba wajen* spit
spate [speit] *n* cìkōwǎ
speak [spiːk] *v* (spoke, spoken) 1. yi magana 2. faɗi 3. yi lacca 4. to speak English ji Turanci
speaker [ˈspiːkə] 1. mai magana 2. (acad.) mai ba da lacca 3. *duba wajen* loudspeaker
Speaker of Parliament *n* (pol.) Shugaban Taron Majalisa
speak out *v* fito a fili
speak up *v* ɗaga murya
spear [spiə] *n* mashi
special [ˈspeʃl] *adj* na musamman
specialist [ˈspeʃəlist] *n* gwani
specialty, speciality [ˈspeʃəltiː, ˌspeʃiˈælətiː] *n* 1. aiki 2. (ac.) fanni
specialization [ˌspeʃəlaiˈzeiʃn] *n* ƙwarewa
specialize [ˈspeʃəlaiz] *v* ƙware (in a kan)
specialized [ˈspeʃəlaizd] *adj* ƙwararre (in a kan)
specially [ˈspeʃəli] *adv* musamman
species [ˈspiːʃiːz] *n* jinsi
specific [spəˈsifik] *adj* takamaimai
specifically [spəˈsifikli] *adv* takamaimai

specification [ˌspəsifiˈkeiʃn] *n* bayani dall-dalla
specify [ˈspesifai] *v* ƙayyade
specimen [ˈspesimən] *n* samfur
speck [spek] *n* ɗigo
specs [speks] *duba wajen* spectacles
spectacle [ˈspektəkl] *n* biki
spectacles [ˈspektəklz] *pl* tabarau, (Nr) luleti
spectator [spekˈteitə] *n* ɗan kallo
speculate [ˈspekjuleit] *v* 1. yi hasashe 2. (fin.) yi baranda
speculation [spekjuˈleiʃn] *n* 1. hasashe 2. (fin.) baranda
speculative [ˈspekjulətiv] *adj* (fin.) na baranda
speculator [ˈspekjuleitə] *n* (fin.) ɗan baràndà
speech [spiːtʃ] *n* 1. magana 2. jawabi 3. lafazi 4. to make a speech gabatar da jawabi
speechless [ˈspiːtʃlis] *adj* to be speechless kasa magana
speed [spiːd] 1. *n* sauri 2. at top speed da gudun gaske 3. *v* yi gudu
speeding [spiːdiŋ] *n* mugun gudu
speed limit *n* ƙayyadadden yawangudu
speedometer [spiːˈdɔmitə] *n* maleji, (Nr) kwantar
speed up *v* gaggauta
speedy [ˈspiːdi] *adj* mai sauri
spell [spel] 1. *n* lokaci 2. sihiri 3. *v* (spelt/spelled) iya ƙa'idojin rubutu
spellbound [ˈspelbaund] *adj* mai rasa ta cewa
spelling [ˈspeliŋ] *n* ƙa'idojin rubutu
spend [spend] *v* (spent) 1. kashe

kuɗi 2. yi lokaci 3. **to spend the day** wuni 4. **to spend the night** kwana

spendthrift [ˈspendθrift] *adj/n* almubazzari

sperm [spə:m] *n* maniyyi

sphere [sfiə] *n* 1. ƙwallo 2. fili

spice, spices [spais; ˈspaisiz] *n/pl* yaji

spider [ˈspaidə] *n* gizo-gizo

spike [spaik] *n* tsini

spill [spil] 1. *n* **oil spill** zubewar man fetur 2. *v* **(split/spilled)** zube 3. zubar da

spin [spin] *v* **(spun)** 1. juya 2. kaɗa

spinach [ˈspinidʒ] *n* alayyaho

spinal [ˈspainl] *adj* na ƙashin baya

spinal cord *n* laka

spine [spain] *n* 1. ƙaya 2. ƙashin baya

spinning [ˈspiniŋ] *n* kaɗi

spinster [ˈspinstə] *n* wadda bai yi aure ba

spiny [ˈspaini] *adj* mai ƙaya

spirit [ˈspirit] *n* 1. kurwa 2. ruhu 3. aljan 4. **spirit of the law** ainihin manufar doka

spirited [ˈspiritid] *adj* mai zuciya

spirits [ˈspirits] *pl* 1. barasa 2. aljanu 3. **high spirits** annashuwa

spiritual [ˈspiritʃuəl] *adj* na ibada

spit [spit] 1. *n* miyau 2. *v* ((UK) **spat/** (US) **spit**) tofa

spite [spait] 1. *n* hassada 2. **in spite of** duk da 3. *v* ɓata wa

spiteful [spaitfl] *adj* mai hassada

spit out *v* furza

spittle [ˈspitl] *n* miyau

splash [splæʃ] *v* fantsama

splendid [ˈsplendid] *adj* kyakkyawa

splendour [ˈsplendə] *n* alatu

splint [splint] *n* karan ɗori

splinter [ˈsplintə] *n* sartse

splinter group *n* ƙungiyar 'yan a ware

split [split] 1. *n* tsaga 2. *v* **(split)** tsage 3. raba

spoil [spɔil] *v* **(spoilt/spoiled)** 1. ɓata 2. ruɓe

spoil a child *v* shagwaɓa

spoiled [spɔild] *adj* **to be spoiled** lalace

spoils [spɔilz] *pl* ganima

spoilsport [ˈspɔilspɔ:t] *n* mai hana-ruwa-gudu

spoke, spoken [spəuk; ˈspəukən] *duba wajen* **speak**

spokesman, spokeswoman [ˈspəuksmən; -wumən] *n* kakaki

sponge [spʌndʒ] *n* soso

sponsor [ˈspɔnsə] 1. *n* uban tafiya 2. *v* tallafa wa

spontaneous [spɔnˈteiniəs] *adj* maras wata-wata

spool [spu:l] *n* kwařkwařõ

spoon [spu:n] *n* cokali

spoonful [ˈspu:nfl] *n* cokali guda

sport [spɔ:t] *n* wasa

sportsman [ˈspɔ:tsmən] *n* ɗan wasa

sportswear [ˈspɔ:tsweə] *n* kayan wasa

sportswoman [ˈspɔ:tswumən] *n* 'yar wasa

spot [spɔt] 1. wuri 2. ɗan aibi 3. ɗigo 4. ƙurji 5. **on the spot** nan tāke 6. *v* **(spotted)** hàngā

spotless [ˈspɔtlis] *adj* maras aibi

spotlight [ˈspɔtlait] *n* **to put in the spotlight** ƙura wa... ido

spouse [spaus] *n* miji, mata

spout [spaut] *n* baki

sprain [sprein] *v* gurɗe

sprang [spræŋ] *duba wajen* spring

sprawl [sprɔ:l] *v* shimfiɗa

spray [sprei] 1. *n* feshi 2. *v* fesa

spray-can *n* gwangwanin feshi

spray-gun *n* gwangwanin feshi

spraying [·sprejiŋ] *n* feshi

spread [spred] 1. *n* yaɗuwa 2. *v* (spread) yaɗa 3. shimfiɗa

spread out *v* baza

sprightly [·spraitli] *adj* mai zafin nama

spring [spriŋ] 1. *n* idon ruwa 2. bazara 3. **metal spring** sirifin, (Nr) resuwal 4. *v* (sprang, sprung) yi tsalle

spring up *v* 1. zâburà 2. auku

sprinkle [·spriŋkl] *v* yayyafa

sprinkler [·spriŋklə] *n* injin ban ruwa

sprint [sprint] *v* yi gudu

sprinter [·sprintə] *n* maguji

sprout [spraut] 1. *n* tsìrō 2. *v* tsirō

sprung [sprʌŋ] *duba wajen* spring

spur [spə:] *n* ƙaimi

spurn [spə:n] *v* ƙi

spurt [spə:t] *v* tsarto

spy [spai] 1. *n* ɗan leƙen asiri 2. **industrial spy** ɗan leƙen asirin masana'antu 3. *v* leƙa asiri

spying [·spa:jiŋ] *n* leƙen asiri

spy plane *n* jirgin sama na leƙen asiri

squadron [·skwɔdrən] *n* rundunar jirage

squalid [·skwɔlid] *adj* ƙazami

squalor [·skwɔlə] *n* ƙazanta

squander [·skwɔndə] *v* ɓatar da

square [skweə] 1. *adj* mai kaman shan soro 2. *n* murabba'i 3. **town square** dandali

square metre *n* murabba'in mita

square kilometre *n* murabba'in kilomita

squash [skwɔʃ] 1. lemo 2. kabewa 3. (spor.) wasan sikose 4. *v* latsa

squat [skwɔt] *v* tsuguna

squeak [skwi:k] *v* yi tsuwwa

squeeze [skwi:z] *v* matsa

squeeze through *v* kutsa

squint [·skwint] *v* rintsa ido

squirrel [·skwirəl] *n* kurege

squirt [skə:t] *v* tsarta

SS (= steamship) *n* jirgin ruwa

St. *duba wajen* **saint, street**

stab [stæb] *v* (stabbed) soka

stability [stə·biləti] *n* zaman lafiya

stabilization [ˌsteibəlai·zeiʃn] *n* ƙarfafawa

stabilize [·steibəlaiz] *v* ƙarfafa

stable [·steibl] 1. *adj* mai zaman lafiya 2. mai ƙarƙo 3. *n* barga

stable economy *n* tsayayyen tattalin arziki

stack [stæk] 1. *n* tari 2. *v* tara

stadium [·steidiəm] *n* filin wasa

staff [sta:f] *n* 1. sanda 2. ma'aikata 3. **diplomatic staff** ma'aikatan diflomaɗiyya

stage [steidʒ] 1. *n* dandamali 2. matsayi 3. *v* **to stage a walk-out** bar haraba

stage-managed [·steidʒˌmænedʒd] *adj* **stage-managed by...** a ƙarƙashin sa idon...

stagger [ˈstægə] v yi tangaɗi
stagnant [ˈstægnənt] adj (ec.)
  stagnant economic growth
  tsayawar tattalin arziki
stagnate [stægˈneit] v 1. gurɓace
  2. (ec.) taɓarɓare 3. His
  business has stagnated. Ya
  shiga ƙamfar ciniki.
stain [stein] 1. n tabo 2. v ɓata
  3. shafa
stainless [ˈsteinlis] adj maras aibi
stainless steel n baƙin ƙarfe
stair, stairs [steə; steəz] n
  matakala, (Nr) askaliye
staircase [ˈsteəkeis] n matakala,
  (Nr) askaliye
stairs, stairway [steəz;
  ˈsteəwei] duba wajen stair
stake [steik] n 1. fegi 2. da'awa
  3. at stake a hannu
stale [steil] adj ba sabo ba
stalemate [ˈsteilmeit] n aràngamà
stalk [stɔːk] 1. n kara 2. v fàrautà
stall [stɔːl] 1. n rumfa 2. v yi
  shiririta
stallion [ˈstæliən] n ingarma
stammer [ˈstæmə] 1. n i'ina 2. v
  yi i'ina
stamp [stæmp] 1. n hatimi
  2. postage stamp kan sarki,
  (Nr) tambur 3. v buga hatimi
stamp on v tattaka
stance [stæns] n matsayi
stand [stænd] 1. n rumfa 2. ra'ayi
  3. v (stood) tsaya 4. daure
standard [ˈstændəd] 1. adj
  daidaitacce 2. na kullum 3. n
  ƙa'ida 4. lamba
standardization [ˌstændədaiˈzeiʃn]
  n daidaitawa
standardize [ˈstændədaiz] v
  daidaita

stand-by [ˈstændbai] n ko-ta-
  kwana
stand by v 1. tsaya wa 2. saurara
  3. shirya
stand for v 1. nuna 2. amince
stand for election v tsaya a
  zaɓe
stand out v fito
stand up v miƙe tsaye
stand up for v ƙarfafa wa...
  gwiwa
standing [ˈstændiŋ] n mutunci
standpoint [ˈstændpɔint] n
  matsayi
standstill [ˈstændstil] n to come
  to a standstill tsaya cak
stank [stæŋk] duba wajen stink
staple [ˈsteipl] 1. adj na masarufi
  2. n kayan masarufi 3. fil
  4. v maƙale
stapler [ˈsteiplə] n sitefila
star [staː] n tauraro
starring in... [ˈstaːriŋ] adj
  cikin...
starch [staːtʃ] n sitati
stare [steə] v ƙura ido (at wa)
stars and stripes pl tutar
  Amirka
start [staːt] 1. n farko 2. from
  the start tun daga farko
  3. from the very start tun
  daga farkon farawa 4. head
  start rata 5. v fara 6. ta da
  7. firgità
start a fire v kunna
starter [ˈstaːtə] n sitata
starting point n mafari
startle [ˈstaːtl] v firgitar da
startled [ˈstaːtld] adj to be
  startled firgità
start up a business v kafa
  kamfani

starvation [sta:ˈveiʃn] *n*
matsananciyar yunwa
starve [sta:v] *v* ji matsananciyar
yunwa
State Department (US) *n*
(pol.) Ma'aikatar Harkokin
Waje
state [steit] 1. *adj* na ƙasa
2. na gwamnati 3. *n* ƙasa
4. gwamnati 5. halin zama
6. federal state jiha 7. *v* furta
(that cewa) 8. bayyana
state of play *n* matsayin wasa
state house *n* gidan gwamnati
stately home [ˈsteitli] *n* gidan
sarauta
statement [ˈsteitmənt] *n* 1. bayani
2. bank statement bayanin
ajiya, siteman 3. to make a
statement ba da bayani
state of emergency *n* zaman
dokar-ta-ɓaci
States [steits] *pl* the States
Amirka
statesman [ˈsteitsmən] *n* tsohon
ɗan siyasa
state visit *n* ziyarar aiki
station [ˈsteiʃn] 1. *n* tasha 2. ofis
3. gida 4. *v* tsayar da
station wagon *n* jalof
stationary [ˈsteiʃənri] *adj* a tsaye
stationer's [ˈsteiʃnəz] *n* shagon
littattafai
stationery [ˈsteiʃənri] *n* takarda
statistical [stəˈtistikl] *adj* na
ilimin ƙididdiga
statistician [ˌstætisˈtiʃn] *n* mai
ilimin ƙididdiga
statistics [stəˈtistiks] *pl* ilimin
ƙididdiga
statue [ˈstætʃu:] *n* mutum-
mutumi

stature [ˈstætʃə] *n* girma
status [ˈsteitəs] *n* 1. matsayi
2. muƙami
statute [ˈstætʃu:t] *n* doka
stay [stei] 1. *n* zama 2. *v* tsaya
3. zauna 4. sauka 5. The door
won't stay closed. Kofar ba ta
tsayawa a rufe.
stead [sted] *n* in his stead a
madadinsa
steadfast [ˈstedfəst] *adj* tsayayye
steadiness [ˈstedinis] *n* ƙwari
steady [ˈstedi] *adj* 1. mai ƙwari
2. na kullum
steak [steik] *n* yankin nama
steal [sti:l] *v* (stole, stolen) sàtā
stealing [ˈsti:liŋ] *n* sata
stealth [stelθ] *n* sanɗa
steam [sti:m] *n* tururi
steam engine *n* tukunyar jirgi
steamer, steamship [ˈsti:mə;
ˈsti:mʃip] *n* jirgin ruwa
steel [sti:l] *n* baƙin ƙarfe
steelmaking [ˈsti:lmeikiŋ] *n*
mulmula ƙarfe
steel mill *n* ma'aikatar mulmula
ƙarfe
steep [sti:p] *adj* mai tsawo
steeple [ˈsti:pl] *n* hasumiyar coci
steer [stiə] *v* tuƙa
steering [ˈstiəriŋ] *n* sitiyari, (Nr)
dirakso
steering committee *n* kwamitin
shirya aiki
steering wheel *n* sitiyari, (Nr)
bolan
stem [stem] *n* tushe
stench [stentʃ] *n* ɗoyi
stencil [ˈstensl] *n* takardar sitansil
step [step] 1. *n* taki 2. mataki
3. matakala 4. to take a step
forward kara turawa gaba 5.

step by step fillā-fillā **6.** *v*
(**stepped**) taka
step aside *v* kauce (**for** wa)
step down *v* **1.** sauka **2.** yi
murabus (**from** daga)
step forward *v* yi gaba
step on *v* taka
step-child [ˈsteptʃaild] *n* agola,
agoliya
stereo [ˈsteriəu] *n* **1.** sitiriyo
2. garmaho
sterile [ˈsterail] *adj* **1.** mai kashe
ƙwayoyi masu sa cuta **2.** juya
sterilization [ˌsterəlaiˈzeiʃn] *n*
1. kashe ƙwayoyi masu sa cuta
2. aikin hana haihuwa
sterilize [ˈsterəlaiz] *v* **1.** kashe
ƙwayoyi masu sa cuta **2.** hana
haihuwa
sterling [ˈstəːliŋ] *n* **1.** azurfa
2. (fin.) kuɗin Ingila
stern [stəːn] **1.** *adj* mai tsananin
hali **2.** *n* bayan jirgin ruwa
stethoscope [ˈsteθəskəup] *n*
na'urar auna sautin jiki
stew [stjuː] *n* miya
steward [ˈstjuəd] *n* boyi
stewardess [ˌstjuəˈdes] *n* mai tuwo
stick [stik] **1.** *n* sanda **2.** *v* (**stuck**)
soka (**into** wa) **3.** liƙa **4.** kafa
stick to *v* **to stick to a policy**
kiyaye manufa
stickiness [ˈstikinis] *n* danƙo
sticking-plaster [ˈstikiŋˌplaːstə]
n filasta, (Nr) isfaradara
stick out *v* ɓullo
sticky [ˈstiki] *adj* mai danƙo
stiff [stif] *adj* **to be stiff** ƙage
stiffen [ˈstifn] *v* ƙandare
still [stil] **1.** *adj* tsit **2.** maras shiru
3. *adv* har yanzu **4.** *conj* amma
duk da haka

stimulant [ˈstimjulənt] *n* abu mai
ƙara kuzari
stimulate [ˌstimjuˈleit] *v* ƙara
kuzari
stimulating [ˈstimjuleitiŋ] *adj* mai
ƙara kuzari
stimulation [ˌstimjuˈleiʃn] *n* ƙara
kuzari
sting [stiŋ] *v* (**stung**) hàrbā
stingy [ˈstindʒi] *adj* marowaci
stink [stiŋk;] **1.** *n* wari **2.** *v*
(**stank, stunk**) yi wari
stint [stint] *n* zaman wani lokaci
stipulate [ˈstipjuleit] *v* ƙayyade
stipulation [ˌstipjuˈleiʃn] *n* ƙa'ida
stir [stəː] *v* (**stirred**) **1.** tuƙa **2.** yi
ɗan motsi
stir up *v* **1.** gurɓace **2.** hanzuga
stirrup [ˈstirəp] *n* likkafa
stitch [stitʃ] *v* ɗinka
stock [stɔk] **1.** *n* baƙar haja
2. asali **3.** (fin.) hannun jari
4. *v* tara
stockbroker [ˈstɔkˌbrəukə] *n*
dillalin jari
stock exchange *n* kasuwar jari
stockholder [ˈstɔkhəuldə] *n* mai
hannun jari
stockings [ˈstɔkiŋ] *pl* safa
stock market *n* kasuwa ta
cinikin jari
stock-take [ˈstɔkˌteik] *n* bin
diddigin kaya
stocky [ˈstɔki] *adj* daɓarɓashi
stoke a fire *v* iza wuta
stole, stolen [ˈstəul; ˈstəulən]
duba wajen **steal**
stomach [ˈstʌmək] *n* ciki
stomach ache *n* ciwon ciki
stone [stəun] **1.** *n* dutse **2.** ƙwallo
3. *v* jefe
stoned [stəund] *adj* (sl.) bugagge

stonemason [ˈstəunˈmeisn] *n* mesin

stony [ˈstəuni] *adj* mai duwatsu

stood [stud] *duba wajen* **stand**

stool [stuːl] *n* kujera

stop [stɔp] 1. *n* bus-stop tashar bas 2. **to put a stop to** hana 3. *v* (**stopped**) tsaya 4. tsayar da 5. **Stop shouting!** Ka rage murya! 6. **Sara has stopped going to the library.** Sara ta daina zuwa laburare. 7. **The rain has stopped.** Ruwan sama ya ɗauke. 8. **The train stopped.** Jirgin ƙasar ya tsaya.

stop dead *v* tsaya cak

stop gap *n* wucin gadi

stop-over [ˈstɔpˌəuvə] *n* zango

stoppage [ˈstɔpidʒ] *n* dakatarwa

stopper [ˈstɔpə] *n* matoshi

stop up *v* toshe

stopwatch [ˈstɔpwɔtʃ] *n* agogon gudu

storage [ˈstɔːridʒ] *n* ajiya

storage tank *n* rumbun adani

store [stɔː] 1. *n* sito, (Nr) mangaza 2. kanti 3. *v* adana

storekeeper [ˈstɔːˌkiːpə] *n* mai kanti

storeroom [ˈstɔːrum] *n* sito, (Nr) mangaza

storey [ˈstɔːri] *n* (*pl* **storeys**) hawa

stork [stɔːk] *n* shamuwa

storm [stɔːm] 1. *n* hadari 2. *v* (mil.) kai farmaki ga

stormy [ˈstɔːmi] *adj* da hadari

story [ˈstɔːri] *n* 1. labari 2. tatsuniya 3. **to tell a story** ba da labari 4. *duba wajen* **storey**

stout [staut] *adj* mai jiki

stove [stəuv] *n* kuka, (Nr) resho

stowaway [ˈstəuəwei] *n* mai sacen shiga jirgin ruwa/sama

straight [streit] 1. *adj* mikakke 2. *adv* sak 3. sosai

straightaway [ˈstreitəˈwei] *adv* nan da nan

straighten [ˈstreitnd] *v* mikar da

straighten out *v* daidaita

straightforward [ˌstreitˈfɔːwəd] *adj* mai saukin ganewa

strain [strein] 1. *n* damuwa 2. *v* yunƙura 3. gurɗe 4. tace

strained [streind] *adj* **Relations are strained.** Harkoki sun dagule.

straits [streits] *n* mashigin teku

strand [strænd] *n* tùfkà

strange [streindʒ] *adj* 1. mai ban mamaki 2. sabo 3. baƙo

stranger [ˈstreindʒə] *n* baƙo

strangle [ˈstræŋgl] *v* shaƙe

strap [stræp] *n* maɗauri

strategic [strəˈtiːdʒik] *adj* na dabara

strategy [ˈstrætədʒi] *n* dabara

straw [strɔː] *n* 1. haki 2. tsinke

strawberry [ˈstrɔːbri] *n* sitoberi

stray [strei] *v* yi makuwa

streak [striːk] *n* ratsi

stream [striːm] 1. *n* rafi 2. *v* zubo

streamlined [ˈstriːmlaind] *adj* daidaitacce

street [striːt] *n* titi

streetlamp, streetlight *n* fitilar titi

streetsign *n* alamar titi

strength [streŋθ] *n* 1. ƙarfi 2. ƙwari

strengthen [ˈstreŋθən] *v* 1. ƙarfafa 2. **to strengthen one's position** kyautata matsayi

strenuous [ˈstrenjuəs] *adj* mai damuwa

stress [stres] 1. *n* damuwa 2. ƙarfi 3. *v* ƙarfafa

stretch [stretʃ] *v* 1. miƙa 2. miƙar da

stretch out *v* miƙa

stretcher [ˈstretʃə] *n* amuku

stricken [ˈstrikn] *adj* to be stricken kamu (**with** da)

strict [strikt] *adj* mai tsanani

stride [straid] 1. *n* taki 2. *v* yi taki

strike [straik] 1. *n* yajin aiki 2. (mil.) hari 3. *v* (struck) buga 4. yi yaji

strike a match *v* ƙyasta ashana

striker [ˈstraikə] *n* mai yajin aiki

striking [ˈstraikiŋ] *adj* 1. kyakkyawa 2. babba

string [striŋ] *n* kirtani

stringent [ˈstrindʒənt] *adj* tsattsaura

strip [strip] 1. *n* ƙwarya 2. tsiri 3. *v* tuɓe

stripe [straip] *n* ratsi

striped [straipt] *adj* mai ratsi-ratsi

strive [straiv] *v* dage

striving [ˈstraiviŋ] *n* fama

stroke [strəuk] 1. *n* bugu 2. (med.) shanyewar jiki 3. *v* shafa

stroll [strəul] 1. *n* yawo 2. *v* yi yawo

strong [strɔŋ] *adj* 1. mai ƙarfi 2. mai ƙarko

strongbox [ˈstrɔŋbɔks] *n* sef, (Nr) asusu

stronghold [ˈstrɔŋhəuld] *n* ramin kura

struck [strʌk] *duba wajen* **strike**

structural [ˈstrʌktʃərəl] *adj* mai shafuwar tushe

structural adjustment programme *n* shirin farfaɗo da tattalin arziki

structure [ˈstrʌktʃə] *n* siga

struggle [ˈstrʌgl] 1. *n* fama 2. daga 3. *v* yi fama 4. yi kokawa

strut [strʌt] 1. *n* madogara 2. *v* yi taƙama

stub [stʌb] *n* guntu

stubborn [ˈstʌbən] *adj* mai taurin kai

stubbornness [ˈstʌbənnis] *n* taurin kai

stuck [stʌk] *duba wajen* **stick**

stud [stʌd] *n* 1. ingarma 2. maɓalli

student [ˈstjuːdnt] *n* ɗalibi

studentship [ˈstjuːdntʃip] *n* ɗalibtà

studio [ˈstuːdiəu] *n* sutudiyo

study [ˈstʌdi] 1. *n* nazari 2. karatu 3. *v* duba 4. kòya 5. yi karatu

studying [ˈstʌdjiŋ] *n* karatu

stuff [stʌf] 1. *n* kaya 2. *v* cunkusa

stuff into *v* cusa

stuffed [stʌft] *adj* abin da ya cushe

stumble [ˈstʌmbl] *v* yi tuntuɓe

stumbling block *n* ƙarfen ƙafa

stump [stʌmp] *n* 1. dungu 2. tree stump kututture

stun [stʌn] *v* ba da mamaki

stung [stʌŋ] *duba wajen* **sting**

stunk [stʌŋk] *duba wajen* **stink**

stunt [stʌnt] *n* wasar taron aradu, tsallen batsalu

stunted [ˈstʌntid] *adj* to be stunted tsumbùrě

stupid [ˈstjuːpid] *adj* wawa

stupidity [stjuːˈpidəti] *n* wawanci

sturdy [ˈstəːdi] *adj* mai ƙarko

stutter [ˈstʌtə] **1.** *n* i'ina **2.** *v* yi i'ina

sty [stai] *n* gidan alade

style [stail] **1.** *n* hanya, salo **2.** *v* siganta

stylish [ˈstailiʃ] *adj* mai salo

sub-committee [ˈsʌbkə,miti] *n* ƙaramin kwamiti

subdivide [,sʌbdiˈvaid] *v* rarraba

subdivision [ˈsʌbdi,viʒn] *n* yanki

subdue [səbˈdjuː] *v* rìnjāyà

subject [ˈsʌbdʒikt] *n* **1.** mabiyi **2.** batu **3.** (acad.) fanni

subject [sʌbˈdʒikt] *v* gana wa

subjugate [ˈsʌbdʒəgeit] *v* biyar da

submachine gun [ˈsʌbməˈʃiːngʌn] *n* bindiga

submarine [,sʌbməˈriːn] **1.** *adj* ƙarƙashin ruwa **2.** *n* jirgin ƙarƙashin ruwa

submerge [səbmˈəːdʒ] *v* nitse

submission [səbˈmiʃn] *n* **1.** gabatarwa **2.** dangana

submissive [səbˈmisiv] *adj* to be submissive mika wuya

submit [səbmˈit] *v* **1.** gabatar da **2.** dangana da

submit candidature *v* miƙa takardun neman takara a zaɓe

subordinate [səˈbɔːdinət] *adj* naƙasasshe

subscribe [səbˈskraib] *v* shiga (to cikin)

subscriber [səbˈskraibə] *n* mamba

subscription [səbˈskripʃn] *n* kuɗin shiga

subsequent [ˈsʌbsikwənt] *adj* na gaba

subsequently [ˈsʌbsikwəntli] *adv* daga baya

subservient [ˈsʌbsəːvjənt] *adj* mai fadanci

subside [səbˈsaid] *v* **1.** fàɗà **2.** janye **3.** huce

subsidiary [səbˈsidiəri] *adj* **1.** mai bi **2.** ƙarami

subsidiary company *n* ƙaramin kamfani

subsidize [ˈsʌbsidaiz] *n* zuba rangwame

subsidy [ˈsʌbsidi] *n* rangwame

subsistence [səbˈsistəns] *n* at subsistence level hannu baka hannu ƙwarya

subsistence farming *n* salon noman hannu baka hannu ƙwarya

substance [ˈsʌbstəns] *n* **1.** abu **2.** gundari

substandard [ˈsʌb,stændəd] *adj* ba nagari ba

substantial [səbˈstænʃl] *adj* mai tsoka

substitute [ˈsʌbstitjuːt] **1.** *n* madadi **2.** as a substitute for a madadin **3.** *v* canza (for da)

subterfuge [ˈsʌbtəfjuːdʒ] *n* makirci

subterranean [,sʌbtəˈreiniən] *adj* na ƙarƙashin ƙasa

subtle [ˈsʌtl] *adj* a kaikaice

subtlety [ˈsʌtlti] *n* iya magana

subtract [səbˈtrækt] *v* deɓe

subtraction [səbˈtrækʃn] *n* ɗebewa

suburbs [ˈsʌbəːbs] *pl* ugnuwannin bayan gari

suburban [səˈbəːbən] *adj* na kewayen birni

subversion [səbˈvəːʒn] *n* maƙarƙashiya

subversive [səb·və:siv] *adj* na maƙarƙashiya

subversive activity *n* ayyukan maƙarƙashiya

subvert [sʌb·və:t] *v* yi yankan baya

subway [·sʌbwei] *n* 1. (UK) gadar ƙasa 2. (US) jirgin ƙarƙashin ƙasa

succeed [sək·si:d] *v* 1. ci nasara 2. gàdā

succeeding [sək·si:diŋ] *adj* 1. mai ci 2. mai zuwa

success [sək·ses] *n* nasara

successful [sək·sesfl] *adj* mai cin nasara

succession [sək·seʃn] *n* 1. gado 2. in succession à jère

successive [sək·sesiv] *adj* à jère

successor [sək·sesə] *n* magaji

succumb [sə·kʌm] *v* sakar wa

such [sʌtʃ] *adj* irin wannan

such and such *adj* kàzā

such as kamar

suck [sʌk] *v* tsotsa

suckle [·sʌkl] *v* shayar da

suction [·sʌkʃn] *n* jawowa

sudden [·sʌdn] *adj* ba-zata

suddenly [·sʌdnli] *adv* ba zato ba tsammani

sue [su:] *v* kai ƙara

suede [sweid] *n* fātā

suffer [·sʌfə] *v* sha wahala

suffer a defeat *v* sha kāyè

sufferer [·sʌfərə] *n* mai shan wahala

suffering [·sʌfəriŋ] *n* shan wahala

suffice [sə·fais] *v* wàdātà

suffice to say à tàkàice

sufficiency [sə·fiʃntli] *n* wadatuwa

sufficient [sə·fiʃnt] *adj* isasshe

suffocate [·sʌfəkeit] *v* shaƙe

suffrage [·sʌfridʒ] *n* 'yancin ka da ƙuri'a

sugar [·ʃugə] *n* sukari

sugar cane *n* rake

sugar cube *n* ƙwayar sukari

suggest [se·dʒest] *v* ba da shawara

suggestion [sə·dʒestʃən] *n* sabuwar shawara

suicide [·su:isaid] *n* 1. kisan kai 2. to commit suicide yi kisan kai

suit [su:t] 1. *n* kwat da wando 2. (leg.) ƙara 3. *v* yi wa... kyau 4. dace da

suitable [·su:təbl] *adj* to be suitable dace

suitcase [·su:tkeis] *n* jaka, (Nr) balis

suite [swi:t] *n* babban ɗaki na otel

suited [·su:tid] *adj* to be suited dace

sulk [sʌlk] *v* yi jùgum

sullen [·sʌlən] *adj* mai fushi

sum [sʌm] *n* jimla

summarize [·sʌməraiz] *v* taƙaita

summary [·sʌməri] *n* taƙaitawa

summary trial *n* shari'a ta ɗan taƙaitaccen lokaci

summer [·sʌmə] *n* bazara

summit [·sʌmit] *n* kololuwa

summit conference *n* taron ƙoli

summon [·sʌmən] *v* kirawo

summons [·sʌmənz] *n* sammaci, (Nr) kombukaso

sums [sʌmz] *pl* lissafi

sum up *v* taƙaita

sun [sʌn] *n* rana

sunbathe [·sʌnbeið] *v* shanya kai a rana

sunbeam [ˈsʌnbiːm] *n* hasken rana

sunburn [ˈsʌnbəːn] *n* ƙunar rana a jiki

sunburnt [ˈsʌnbəːnt] *adj* mai jin ƙunar rana a jiki

Sunday [ˈsʌndi] *n* ran Lahadi, (Nr) Dumashi

sundown [ˈsʌndaun] *n* faduwar ranas

sung [sʌŋ] *duba wajen* sing

sunglasses [ˈsʌn,glaːsiz] *pl* tabarau

sunk [ˈsʌŋk] *duba wajen* sink

sunken [ˈsʌŋkən] *adj* mai nutsewa

sunlight [ˈsʌnlait] *n* hasken rana

sunny [ˈsʌni] *adj* da rana

sunrise [ˈsʌnraiz] *n* fitowar rana

sunset [ˈsʌnset] *n* faɗuwar rana

sunshade [ˈsʌnʃeid] *n* laima

sunshine [ˈsʌnʃain] *n* hasken rana

super [ˈsuːpə] *adj* 1. na ƙwarai 2. mafi kyau 3. mafi girma

superb [suːˈpəːb] *adj* na ƙwarai

supercilious [suːpəsiljəs] *adj* mai ciccira

superficial [,suːpəˈfiʃl] *adj* sama-sama

superficiality [,suːpə,fiʃiˈaliti] *n* biri-boko

superficially [,suːpəˈfiʃəli] *adv* sama-sama

superfluous [suːˈpəːfluəs] *adj* sama-sama

superhighway [ˈsuːpəˈhaiwei] *n* (US) babbar hanya

superhuman [,suːpəˈhjuːmən] *adj* kinkwâ

superintendent [,suːpərinˈtendənt] *n* sufeto

superior [suːˈpiəriə] 1. *adj* mafifici 2. *n* magabaci

superiority [suː,piəriˈɔrəti] *n* fifiko

supermarket [ˈsuːpəmaːkit] *n* babban kanti

supernatural [ˈsuːpənætʃrəl] *adj* na gaibu

superpower [ˈsuːpəpauə] *n* babbar ƙasa

supersede [suːpəˈsiːd] *v* wuce

superstition [,suːpəˈstiʃn] *n* camfi

supervise [ˈsuːpəvaiz] *v* duba

supervision [,suːpəˈviʒn] *n* dubawa

supper [ˈsʌpə] *n* abincin dare

supplant [səˈplaːnt] *v* cànjâ

supple [ˈsʌpl] *adj* mai laushi

supplement [ˈsʌplimənt] 1. *n* ƙari 2. *v* ƙara

supplementary [,sʌpliˈmentri] *adj* ƙarin

supplier [səˈplaiə] *n* mai kaya

supplies [səˈplaiz] *pl* kaya

supply [səˈplai] 1. *n* bayarwa 2. yawa 3. *v* bayar da 4. samar da 5. *duba wajen* supplies

supply and demand *n* bayarwa da bukata

support [səˈpɔːt] 1. *n* madogari 2. goyon baya 3. **means of support** madâfâ 4. *v* tokare 5. gòyi bāyâ 6. ɗaure wa... gindi 7. ciyar da

supporter [səˈpɔːtə] *n* mai goyon baya

suppose [səˈpəuz] *v* 1. zàtā 2. **They are supposed to arrive tomorrow.** Ya kamata su iso gobe.

supposition [,sʌpəˈziʃn] *n* zato

suppress [sə'pres] *v* 1. kashe
2. danne
suppression [sə'preʃn] *n* 1.
zalunci 2. dannewa
supremacy [suː'preməsi] *n* 1.
fifiko 2. iko
supreme [suː'priːm] *adj* na ƙoli
supreme commander *n*
babban kwamandan sojoji
supreme court *n* kotun ƙoli
supreme council *n* majalisar
ƙoli
sure [ʃɔː] 1. *adj* tabbatacce 2. *adv*
haƙiƙa 3. **for sure** ba shakka
4. **to make sure that** tabbatar
da
surely ['ʃɔːli] *adv* tabbas
surety ['ʃɔrəti] *n* lamuni
surface ['səːfis] *n* 1. kai
2. **surface of the earth** bayan
ƙasa 3. **surface of the ocean**
saman teku
surface mail *n* wasiƙu ta
ƙasa/jirgin ruwa
surge [səːdʒ] *v* tashi
surgeon ['səːdʒən] *n* likitan fiɗa
surgery ['səːdʒəri] *n* 1. fiɗa
2. tiyata 3. ofishin likita
surmise ['səːmaiz] *v* yi hàsàshē
surname ['səːneim] *n* sunan
mahaifi
surpass [sə'paːs] *v* fi
surplus ['səːpləs] *n* rara
surprise [sə'praiz] 1. *n* mamaki
2. **by surprise** bà zàtā 3. *v* ba
da mamaki 4. shàmmàtà
surprising [sə'praiziŋ] *adj* mai
ban mamaki
surrender [sə'rendə] 1. *n*
sallamawa 2. **unconditional
surrender** miƙa wuya ba
sharaɗi 3. *v* sallama (**to wa**)

surround [sə'raund] *v* 1. kewaye
2. (mil.) ritsa
surroundings [sə'raundiŋz] *pl*
kewaye
survey [sə'vei] 1. *n* duba
2. safiyo 3. *v* duba 4. yi safiyo
surveyor [sə'veiə] *n* mai safiyo
survival [sə'vaivl] *n* tsira
survive [sə'vaiv] *v* tsira
survivor [sə'vaivə] *n* 1. wanda
ya tsira 2. **sole survivor** wanda
ya yi saura
susceptible [sə'septəbl] *adj* mai
sauƙin kamuwa (**to da**)
suspect ['sʌspekt] *n* wanda ake
tuhuma
suspect [sə'spekt] *v* tùhumtà (**of
da**)
suspend [sə'spend] *v* 1. rataya
2. (ed.) fitar da 3. (leg.) soke
4. **to suspend from duties**
dākatar da... daga aiki
suspense [sə'spens] *n* jiran
tsammani
suspension [sə'spenʃn] *n* 1.
rataya 2. (ed.) fitarwa 3. (leg.)
suka
suspicion [sə'spiʃn] *n* (leg.)
tuhuma
suspicious [sə'spiʃəs] *adj* 1. na
zargi 2. mai shakka
sustain [sə'stein] *v* riƙe
sustenance ['sʌstinəns] *n* abinci
swallow ['swɔləu] 1. *n* tsattsewa
2. *v* haɗiye
swam [swæm] *duba wajen* **swim**
swamp [swɔmp] *n* fadama
swan [swɔn] *n* tsuntsun ruwa mai
siffar balbela
swap [swɔp] *v* (**swapped**)
musaya
swarm [swɔːm] *n* tàrō

sway [swei] *v* **1.** yi tangaɗi
2. shawo kai
swear [sweə] *v* **1.** yi ashar
2. rantse
swearing ['sweəriŋ] *n* ashar
swear into office *v* rantsar da
swearword ['sweəwə:d] *n*
mugun baki
sweat [swet] **1.** *n* gumi **2.** *v* yi
gumi
sweater ['swetə] *n* suwaita
sweep [swi:p] *v* (**swept**) share
sweeper ['swi:pə] *n* mashari
sweepstake ['swi:psteik] *n* cacar
sukuwa
sweet [swi:t] **1.** *adj* mai zaƙi
2. *n* alewa, (Nr) bombo
sweeten ['swi:tn] *v* zaƙaka
sweetheart ['swi:tha:t] *n* saurayi,
budurwa
sweetness ['swi:tnis] *n* zaƙi
sweet potato [,swi:tpə'teitəu] *n*
dankali
sweets [swi:tz] *pl* alewa, (Nr)
bombo
swell [swəl] *v* (**swelled, swollen/
swelled**) kumbura
swelling ['sweliŋ] *n* kumburi
swept [swept] *duba wajen* **sweep**
swerve [swə:v] *v* goce
swift [swift] *adj* mai saurari
swiftness ['swiftnis] *n* saurari
swim [swim] *v* (**swam, swum**) yi
iyo
swimmer ['swimə] *n* mai iyo
swimming ['swimiŋ] *n* iyo
swimming-pool ['swimiŋpu:l] *n*
wurin waha
swimsuit ['swimsu:t] *n* banten iyo
swindle ['swindl] *v* zàmbatà
swindler ['swindlə] *n* mazambaci
swindling ['swindliŋ] *n* zamba

swine [swain] *pl* aladai
swing [swiŋ] **1.** *n* lilo **2.** *v* yi lilo
switch [switʃ] **1.** *n* makunni,
makashi **2.** *v* sauya
switch off *v* kashe
switch on *v* kunna
switch over *v* sauya (**from**
daga; **to** zuwa)
switchboard ['switʃbɔ:d] *n*
marabar wayar tarho
swollen ['swəulən] *adj* **1.** rudu-
rudu **2.** *duba wajen* **swell**
swoop [swu:p] *v* dira
sword [sɔ:d] *n* takobi
swum [swʌm] *duba wajen* **swim**
sycophancy ['sikəfansi] *n*
fadanci
sycophant ['sikəfant] *n* ɗan
fadanci
syllable ['siləbl] *n* gaɓa
syllabus ['siləbəs] *n* manhaja
symbol ['simbl] *n* alama
symbolic [sim'bɔlik] *adj* mai
alama
symmetrical [si'metrikl] *adj* mai
fasali
symmetry ['simətri] *n* fasali
sympathetic [,simpə'θetik] *adj*
mai juyayi
sympathize ['simpəθaiz] *v* yi
juyayi
sympathy ['simpəθi] *n* juyayi
symphony orchestra *n* taron
makaɗa
symptom ['simptəm] *n* **1.** alama
2. (med.) bayyanar cuta
synagogue ['sinəgɔg] *n*
ma'ibadar Yahudawa
synchronize ['siŋkrənaiz] *v*
daidaita
syndicate ['sindikət] *n* ƙungiyar
ƙunci

synonymous [si·nɔniməs] *adj* mai daidai (**with** da)

syntax [·sintæks] *n* ginin jimla

synthesis [·sinθəsis] *n* ƙira

synthesize [·sinθəsaiz] *v* ƙera

synthetic [sin·θetik] *adj* na roba

syphilis [·sifilis] *n* tunjere

syringe [si·rindʒ] *n* allura

syrup [·sirəp] *n* lemo

system [·sistəm] *n* 1. hanya 2. tsari 3. **to run a system** tafiyar da tsari

systematic [ˌsistə·mætik] *adj* mai tsari

systematically [ˌsistə·mætikli] *adv* a tsare

Tt

ta! [taː] (UK) na gode!

table [ˈteɪbl] **1.** *n* tebur, (Nr) tabili **2.** *v* **to table a motion** gabatar da

tablecloth [ˈteɪblklɔθ] *n* zanen tebur

tablespoon [ˈteɪblspuːn] *n* babban cokali

tablet [ˈtæblɪt] *n* ƙwaya

table tennis [ˈteɪblˌtenɪs] *n* ƙwallon tebur

tabloid [ˈtæblɔːɪd] **1.** *adj* na jarida **2.** *n* jarida

taboo [təˈbuː] *adj n* abin kunya

tacit [ˈtæsɪt] *adj* mai shiru-shiru

tack [tæk] *n* ƙaramar ƙusa

tackle [ˈtækl] (spor.) *v* sa ƙafa

tackle a problem *v* tìnkārà

tact [tækt] *n* kaf-kaf

tactful [ˈtæktfəl] *adj* **to be tactful** yi kaf-kaf (**with** da)

tactic [ˈtæktɪk] *n* dabara

tactical [ˈtæktɪkl] *adj* na dabara

tactical consideration *n* manufar dabara

tactical weapons *pl* makaman a filin daga

tactless [ˈtæktləs] *adj* **to be tactless** yi katoɓara

tadpole [ˈtædpəʊl] *n* talibambam

tag [tæg] **1.** *n* guntuwa **2.** *v* haɗa

tail [teɪl] *n* wutsiya

taillight [ˈteɪlaɪt] *n* danja

tailor [ˈteɪlə] *n* maɗinki

taint [teɪnt] *v* ɓata

take [teɪk] *v* (**took**, **taken**) **1.** ɗauka **2.** kai **3.** hau

take action *v* yi abu

takeaway [ˈteɪkəweɪ] *adj* (UK) sayi-nan-ci-gida

take away *v* **1.** kawar da **2.** ɗebe

take back *v* mayar da

take back one's word *v* toge

take care *v* yi hankali

take care of *v* kula da

take notice of *v* lura da

take off *v* **1.** tashi **2.** tuɓe **3.** sheƙa

take off time *v* shaƙata

take-out [ˈteɪkəweɪ] *adj* (US) sayi-nan-ci-gida

take out *v* fitar da

take over control *v* ƙwace mulki

take over leadership *v* karɓi jagoranci

take place *v* faru

take time *v* ci lokaci

take up *v* karɓa

tale [teɪl] *n* **1.** labari **2.** tatsuniya

talent [ˈtælənt] *n* gwaninta

talented [ˈtæləntɪd] *adj* gwani

talk [tɔːk] **1.** *n* magana **2.** lacca **3.** *v* yi magana

talk about *v* zântā

talk over *v* tattauna

talkative [ˈtɔːkətɪv] *adj* mai surutu

talking [ˈtɔːkɪŋ] *n* magana

talks [tɔːks] *pl* shawarari

tall [tɔːl] *adj* dogo

tame [teɪm] **1.** *adj* na gida **2.** *v* horar da

tampon [ˈtæmpɔn] *n* audugar al'ada, tamfàs

tan [tæn] 1. *n* sun tan 2. *v* jema
tangerine [tændʒəriːn] *n* tanjarin
tangible [ˈtændʒəbl] *adj* na à-zõ-
à-gani
tangle [ˈtæŋgl] *v* cukwikwiya
tank [tæŋk] *n* tanki
tanker [ˈtæŋkə] *n* 1. tankar mai
2. jirgin ruwa mai ɗaukan mai
tannery [ˈtænəri] *n* majema
tanning [ˈtæniŋ] *n* jima
tantalize [ˈtæntəlaiz] *v* burge
tantalizing [ˈtæntəlaiziŋ] *adj* mai
burgewa
tap [tæp] 1. *n* kan famfo 2. *v*
ƙwankwansa
tape [teip] 1. *n* tef 2. kaset 3. *v*
ɗauka a rakoda
tape-recorder [ˈteiprikɔːdə] *n*
rakoda, (Nr) manyeto
tapeworm [ˈteipwəːm] *n* tsila
tapestry [ˈtæpəstri] *n* saƙa
tar [taː] *n* kwalta, (Nr) gudoro
tardy [ˈtaːdi] *adj* to be tardy
màkarà
tare [teə] *n* tiya
target [ˈtaːgit] *n* 1. abin bara
2. buri
tariff [ˈtærif] *n* kuɗin fito
tarnish [ˈtaːniʃ] *v* dusashe
tart [taːt] *n* kyat, (Nr) gato
task [taːsk] *n* aikin da za a yi
taste [teist] 1. *n* ɗanɗani 2. *v* yi
ɗanɗani 3. ɗanɗana
tasteful [ˈteistfəl] *adj* 1. mai
ɗanɗano 2. mai daɗi
tasteless [ˈteistlis] *adj* mai lami
tasty [ˈteisti] *adj* mai mai daɗi
tattered [ˈtætəd] *adj* à làlàce
tatters [ˈtætəz] *pl* in tatters à
làlàce
tattoo [təˈtuː] 1. *n* jarfa 2. *v* yi
wa... jarfa

taught [tɔːt] *duba wajen* **teach**
taunt [tɔːnt] *v* tsòkanà
taut [tɔːt] *adj* mai tsauri
tavern [ˈtævən] *n* hotel
tax [tæks] 1. *n* (*pl* taxes) haraji,
(Nr) lanho 2. **value added tax**
(**VAT**) haraji na kayan saya
3. **to pay tax** biya haraji 4. *v* sa
haraji 5. gwada
tax collector *n* mai tara haraji
taxi [ˈtæksi] *n* taksi
taxi driver *n* ɗan taksi
tax register *n* daftarin haraji
TB [tiːbiː] *duba wajen* **tuberculosis**
tea [tiː] 1. shayi 2. ɗan abincin
yamma game da shan ti
teabag [ˈtiːbæg] *n* jakar shayi
teach [tiːtʃ] *v* (**taught**) 1. koya
wa 2. koyar da
teacher [ˈtiːtʃə] *n* malami
teacher training college *n*
makarantar horon malamai
teaching [ˈtiːtʃiŋ] *n* aikin malanta
team [tiːm] *n* 1. ƙungiya 2. (spor.)
tim
team-leader [tiːmˈliːdə] *n*
heluma
team-mate [ˈtiːmˌmeit] *n* ɗan
ƙungiya
teamwork [ˈtiːmwəːk] *n* aikin
gayya
teapot [ˈtiːpɔt] *n* butar shayi
tear [tiə] *n* ɗan hawaye
tear [teə] 1. *n* ɓaraka 2. *v* (tore,
torn) keta
tear apart *v* ciccira
tear down *v* rushe
tear gas [ˈtiəgas] *n* barkonon
tsohuwa
tear off *v* cire
tears [tiəz] *pl* hawaye
tear up *v* yayyaga

tease [tiːz] *v* zolaya

teasing [ˈtiːziŋ] *n* barkwanci

teaspoon [ˈtiːspuːn] *n* ƙaramin cokali

technical [ˈteknikl] *adj* 1. na sana'a 2. keɓaɓɓe

technical college *n* kwalejin sana'a

technical installations *pl* kafofin kimiyya da fasaha

technical instructions *pl* bayani

technician [tekˈniʃn] *n* mai gyara

technique [tekˈniːk] *n* dabara

technological [ˌteknəˈlɔdʒikl] *adj* na fasaha

technological production *n* kayan da aka sarrafa

technology [tekˈnɔlədʒi] *n* 1. fasaha 2. **sophisticated technology** ƙayyatacciyar fasaha

tedious [ˈtiːdiəs] *adj* mai cin rai

teenager [ˈtiːneidʒə] *n* matashi

teens [tiːnz] *pl* ƙuruciya

tee-shirt [ˈtiːʃəːt] *n* singileti

teeth [tiːθ] *duba wajen* **tooth**

telecommunications [ˌtelikəˌmjuːniˈkeiʃnz] *n* hanyar sadarwa ta wayar iska

telegram [ˈteligræm] *n* talgiram

telegraph pole [ˈteligraːf] *n* tangarahu

telephone [ˈtelifəun] 1. *n* teliho, (Nr) talho 2. *v* buga wa... waya

telephone call *n* waya

telescope [ˈteliskəup] *n* madubi mai hangen-nesa

teletext [ˈtelitekst] *n* rubutun talabijin

television [ˈteliviʒn] *n* 1. talabijin 2. **to watch television** yi kallon **talabijin**

television channel *n* tasha

telex [ˈteleks] *n* teleks

tell [tel] *v* (**told**) 1. faɗa (wa) 2. sanar da 3. rabe

teller [ˈtelə] *n* kashiya, (Nr) kyasiye

tell time *v* san lokaci

temp [temp] *duba wajen* **temporary worker**

temper [ˈtempə] *n* 1. **Lawal has a good temper.** Lawal mai lafiya ne. 2. **Lawan has a bad temper.** Lawan ya cika fushi. 3. **to lose one's temper** yi fushi

temperament [ˈtemprəmənt] *n* hali

temperate [ˈtempərət] *adj* madaidaici

temperature [ˈtemprətʃə] *n* 1. yawan zafi/sanyi 2. zazzaɓi

tempest [ˈtempist] *n* hadari

temple [ˈtempl] *n* 1. goshi 2. gidan ibada

temporary [ˈtemprəri] *adj* 1. ba na dindindin ba 2. na ɗan lokaci

temporary work *n* aiki na ɗan lokaci

temporary worker *n* ma'aikaci na ɗan lokaci

tempt [tempt] *v* riya wa

temptation [tempˈteiʃn] *n* gwadawa

ten [ten] *n/adj* goma

tenacious [tiˈneiʃəs] *adj* tsayayye

tenacity [tiˈnæsəti] *n* tsayayya

tenant [ˈtenənt] *n* ɗan haya

tend [tend] *v* 1. yi kiwo 2. faye

tendency [ˈtendənsi] *n* 1. hali 2. fifiko

tender [ˈtendə] 1. *adj* mai jin ƙai 2. mai taushi 3. mai jin ciwo 4. *n* tanda 5. *v* yi tanda

tenderness [ˈtendənis] n 1. jin ƙai 2. taushi

tenement [ˈtenəmənt] n sashen gidaje

tennis [ˈtenis] n tanis

tennis shoes pl kambas, (Nr) kiraf

tense [tens] 1. adj mai tsauri 2. mai damuwa 3. The situation is tense. Hali ya ƙazanta. 4. n lokaci

tension [ˈtenʃn] n 1. damuwa 2. tsauri 3. tashin hankali

tent [tent] n tanti

tenth [tenθ] adj na goma

tenuous [ˈtenjuəs] adj maras tabbas

tepid [ˈtepid] adj mai ɗan ɗumi

term [təːm] n 1. ajali 2. oda 3. (ed.) tam 4. **short-term** na gajeren lokaci 5. **long-term** na dogon lokaci 6. duba wajen **terms**

terminal [ˈtəːminl] 1. adj na ajali 2. n tasha

terminate [ˈtəːmineit] v ƙare

termination [ˌtəːmiˈneiʃn] n ƙarewa

terminology [ˌtəːmiˈnolodʒi] n keɓaɓɓun kalmomi

terminus [ˈtəːminəs] n tasha

termite [ˈtəːmait] n gara

terms [təːmz] pl 1. sharuɗɗa 2. **to be on good terms** jitu

terms of agreement pl sharuɗɗan yarjejeniya

terrace [ˈterəs] n 1. gidaje 2. gandu 3. baranda

terrible [ˈterəbl] adj 1. mai tsanani 2. mugu

terrific [təˈrifik] adj na ƙwarai da gaske

terrify [ˈterifai] v razana

terrifying [ˈterifajin] adj mai ban tsoro

territorial [ˌterəˈtɔːriəl] adj na yanki

territory [ˈterətri] n 1. ƙasa 2. yanki

terror [ˈterə] n 1. tsoro 2. **state of terror** hālin ɗar-ɗar

terrorism [ˈterərizəm] n 1. ta'addanci 2. **to commit terrorism** yi ta'adda

terrorist [ˈterərist] n ɗan ta'adda

test [test] 1. n gwaji 2. v gwada

test well n rijiyar gwajin neman mâi

testicle n golo

testify [ˈtestifai] v yi shaida

testimonial [ˌtestiˈməuniəl] n 1. shaidar hali 2. (spor.) wasan ban kwana

testimony [ˈtestiməni] n shaida

test-tube [ˈtestʃuːb] n ma'aunin dafa sinadarai

tetanus [ˈtetənəs] n sarƙewar haƙora

text [tekst] n abin da ke ciki

textbook [ˈteksbuk] n littafi

textile [ˈtekstail] n yadi

textile mill n masaƙa

texture [ˈtekstʃə] n laushi

than [ðən] conj 1. **Your sister is taller than you.** Yarka ta fi ki tsawo. 2. **less than** ƙasa da 3. **more than** fiye da

thank [θæŋk] v gode wa

thank you! na gode!

thankful [ˈθæŋkfl] adj mai godiya

thankless [ˈθæŋklis] adj maras godiya

thanks [ˈθæŋks] pl 1. godiya 2. na gode!

thanks to *prep* albarkacin
that [ðət; ðæt] **1.** (*pl* those)
  wancan/waccan **2.** wanda
  3. *adv* haka **4.** *conj* cewa **5.** so
  that/in order that don
thatch [θætʃ] *v* jinke
that is (i.e.) watau
thaw [θɔ:] *v* narke
the [ðə; ði; ði:] -n, -r, ɗin, kin
theatre [ˈθiətə] *n* **1.** gidan wasan
  kwaikwayo **2. movie theatre**
  silima **3. operating theatre**
  tiyata
theft [θeft] *n* sata
their [ðeə] nasu, tasu
theirs [ðeəz] nasu, tasu
them [ðəm; ðem] *pro* su
theme [θi:m] *n* jigo
themselves [ðəmˈselvz] kansu
then [ðen] **1.** *adv* sa'an nan **2.** a
  lokacin **3. now and then** lokaci-
  lokaci **4.** *conj* kana **5. in haka ne**
theologian [ˌθiəˈləudʒən] *n* mai
  ilimin sanin Allah
theology [θiˈɔlədʒi] *n* ilimin sanin
  Allah
theoretical [ˌθiəˈretikl] *adj* na
  nazariyya
theory [ˈθiəri] *n* **1.** nazariyya
  2. in theory à nàzàřce
therapy [ˈθerəpi] *n* **1.** gashi
  2. magani **3.** hanyoyin kwantar
  da hankali
there [ðeə] can
there is/are akwai
there isn't/aren't babu
thereafter [ˌðeərˈaːftə] *adv*
  bayan haka
therefore [ˈðeəfɔ:] *adv* saboda
  haka
thereupon [ˌðeərəˈpɔn] *adv* daga
  baya

thermometer [θəˈmɔmitə] *n*
  ma'aunin zafi da sanyi
these [ði:z] *duba wajen* this
thesis [ˈθi:sis] *n* **1.** manufa
  2. kundi
they [ðei] *pro* su
thick [θik] *adj* mai kauri
thicken [ˈθikən] *v* kauràrā
thicket [ˈθikit] *n* surƙuƙi
thickness [ˈθiknis] *n* kauri
thief [θi:f] *n* (*pl* thieves) ɓarawo
thieve [θi:v] *v* yi sata
thigh [θai] *n* cinya
thin [θin] *adj* **1.** siriri **2.** maras
  kauri
thing [θiŋ] *n* abu
think [θiŋk] *v* (thought) yi
  tsammani
thinking [ˈθiŋkiŋ] *n* tsammani
think of *v* tuna da
Third World countries *pl*
  ƙasashen masu tasowa
third [θə:d] **1.** *adj* na uku **2.** *n*
  sulusi
thirst [θə:st] *n* ƙishirwa
thirsty [ˈθə:sti] *adj* **to be thirsty**
  ji ƙishirwa
thirteen [ˌθə:ˈti:n] *n/adj* goma sha
  uku
thirteenth [ˌθə:ˈti:nθ] *adj* na
  goma sha uku
thirtieth [ˈθə:tiəθ] *adj* na talatin
thirty [ˈθə:ti] *n/adj* talatin
this [ðis] (*pl* these) wannan
thorn [θɔ:n] *n* ƙaya
thorny [ˈθɔ:ni] *adj* mai ƙaya
thorough [ˈθʌrə] *adj* na sosai
thoroughbred [ˈθʌrəbred] *n*
  ingarma
thoroughfare [ˈθʌrəfeə] *n* hanya
thoroughly [ˈθʌrəli] *adv* sosai
those [ðəuz] *duba wajen* that

though [ðəu] *adv* 1. ko da yake
2. as though sai ka ce

thought [θɔ:t] *n* 1. tunani
2. *duba wajen* think

thoughtful [ˈθɔ:tfl] *adj* mai kula

thoughtfully [ˈθɔ:tfuli] *adv* da hankali

thoughtfulness [ˈθɔ:tflnis] *n* hankali

thoughtless [ˈθɔ:tlis] *adj* maras hankali

thought-provoking *adj* mai bukatar tunani

thousand [ˈθauznd] *n/adj* dubu

thousandth [ˈθauznθ] *adj* na dubu

thrash [θræʃ] *v* ƙwala wa... duka

thread [θred] *n* zare

threat [θret] *n* 1. barazana
2. to pose a threat kawo barazana (to kan/ga)

threaten [ˈθretn] *v* yi wa... barazana

threatening [ˈθretniŋ] *adj* mai kawo barazana

three [θri:] *n/adj* uku

thresh [ˈθreʃ] *v* sussuka

threshold [ˈθreʃhəuld] *n* bakin ƙofa

threw [θru:] *duba wajen* **throw**

thrift [θrift] *n* tsimi

thrifty [ˈθrifti] *adj* mai tsimi

thrill [θril] 1. *n* ban sha'awa
2. *v* burge

thrive [θraiv] *v* yi albarka

throat [θrəut] *n* maƙogwaro

throb [θrɔb] *v* yi zogi

throne [θrəun] *n* gadon sarauta

throng [θrɔŋ] *n* ɗimbi

throttle [ˈθrɔtl] 1. *n* totur, (Nr) askilatar 2. *v* shaƙe

through [θru:] *prep* ta

throughout [θru:ˈaut] *adv* a duk

through to *prep* har

throw [θrəu] *v* (**throw, thrown**) jefa

throw away/out *v* ya da

throw up *v* yi amai

thrust [θrʌst] *v* ɗirka

thug [θʌg] *n* ɗan iska

thumb [θʌm] *n* babban ɗan yatsa

thump [θʌmp] *v* doka

thunder [ˈθʌndə] *n* tsawa

thunderstorm [ˈθʌndəstɔ:m] *n* hadari

Thursday [ˈθə:zdi] *n* Alhamis

thus [ðʌs] *adv* haka

thus far *adv* har yanzu

tick [tik] 1. *n* alamar gyara
2. kaska 3. *v* gyara, sa hannu
4. The clock is ticking. Agogo yana gudu.

ticket [ˈtikit] *n* tikiti

ticket inspector *n* sufeton tikiti

ticket office *n* ofishin tikiti

tickle [ˈtikl] *v* yi cakulkuli

tidal wave [ˈtaidl] *n* tsunami

tide [taid] *n* 1. kawowar ruwa
2. high tide cikar ruwa 3. low tide janyewar ruwa

tidings [ˈtaidiŋz] *pl* labari

tidy [ˈtaidi] 1. *adj* tsaf 2. daki-daki 3. *v* kintsa

tie [tai] 1. *n* taye 2. dangantaka
3. (spor.) canjaras 4. *v* ɗaura
5. (spor.) yi canjaras

tie up *v* ɗaure

tier [tiə] *n* 1. tsagi 2. bene

tiger [ˈtaigə] *n* damisa mai jikin ratsi-ratsi

tight [tait] *adj* mai tsauri

tighten [ˈtaitn] *v* ɗame

tighten up a law v tsananta
doka

tightly adv tam

tights [taits] pl safar mata

'til [til] duba wajen **until**

tile [tail] n 1. tayal 2. fale-falen
burki

till [til] 1. n cash till asusun kanti
2. v yi noma 3. duba wajen
until

tilt [tilt] v karkata

timber ['timbə] n timba

time [taim] 1. n lokaci 2. sau
3. zamani 4. ƙarfe 5. **spare time**
sukuni, lokacin hutawa 6. **the
present time** yanzu 7. **on time**
cikin lokaci 8. **time after time**
kullum-kullum 9. **from time to
time** lokaci-lokaci 10. **at the
same time** gaba ɗaya 11. **at
the same time as** daidai
lokacin da 12. v auna lokaci
13. **to take time** ci lokaci
14. **to waste time** ɓata lokaci
15. **to take a long time** daɗe
16. **to tell time** san lokaci
17. **to have a good time** yi
nishaɗi

time-consuming adj mai cin
lokaci

timekeeper ['taim,kiːpə] n tankifa

times [taimz] prep sau

timetable ['taim,teibl] n 1.
tamtebul 2. lokatan tafiya

timid ['timid] adj mai kawaici

tin [tin] n 1. gwangwani, (Nr)
kwankwani 2. **tin-ore** kuza

tin roof n rufin kwano

tin-opener ['tinəupnə] n mabuɗin
gwangwani, (Nr) ubirbwat

tinned food [tind] n abincin
gwangwani

tint [tint] 1. n kala 2. v yi wa... kala

tiny ['taini] adj ɗan mitsitsi

tip [tip] 1. n ƙarshe 2. dashi
3. **rubbish tip** juji 4. v kife
5. yi wa... dashi

tip over v kife

tiptoe ['tiptəu] 1. n ɗage 2. v yi
sanɗa

tip-off ['tipɔf] n shaida wa...

tipsy ['tipsi] adj bugagge

tire ['taiə] v 1. gajiyar da 2. duba
wajen **tyre**

tired ['taiəd] adj **to be tired**
1. gàji (of da) 2. gùndurà (of da)

tiresome ['taiəsəm] adj mai
gundura

tissue ['tiʃuː] n tsoka

tissue paper n ƙyallen takarda

title ['taitl] n 1. suna 2. sarauta

titled ['taitld] adj mai sarauta

to [tə; tu; tuː] prep 1. zuwa 2. **We
went to London.** Mun tafi
London. 3. **The time is ten to
five.** Ƙarfe biyar saura minti
goma ne. 4. **Please give this
present to your mother.** Don
Allah, ku ba uwarku wannan
kyauta. 5. conj don 6. **I want
to learn English.** Ina so in
koyi Turanci.

toad [təud] n kwaɗo

toast [təust] 1. n gasasshen
burodi 2. gà nākà! 3. v gasa
burodi 4. sha wa...

tobacco [təˈbækəu] n taba

tobacco company n kamfani
mai yin taba

tobacconist [təˈbækənist] n mai
sayar da taba

today [təˈdei] n/adv yau

today's [təˈdeiz] adj na yau

toe [təu] n yatsar ƙafa

toenail [ˈtəʊneil] *n* farce

toffee [ˈtɔfi] *n* cakulan, (Nr) tofi

together [təˈgeðə] *adv* 1. tare 2. all together gaba ɗaya

together with *adv* game da

toil [tɔil] 1. *n* aiki 2. *v* yi aiki

toilet [ˈtɔilit] *n* 1. bayan gida 2. public toilets gidan wanka da ba haya 3. to go to the toilet kewaya

token [ˈtəʊkən] *n* 1. lamba 2. madadi

told [təʊld] *duba wajen* **tell**

tolerable [ˈtɔlərəbl] *adj* mai juruwa

tolerance [ˈtɔlərəns] *n* 1. jimiri 2. girmamawa

tolerant [ˈtɔlərənt] *adj* mai haƙuri

tolerate [ˈtɔləreit] *v* 1. girmama 2. yi jimiri

toleration [ˌtɔləˈreiʃn] *n* girmamawa

toll [təʊl] 1. *n* kuɗin fito 2. death toll yawan hasarar rayuka 3. *v* kaɗa ƙararrawa

tomato [təˈmaːtəʊ] *n* (*pl* tomatoes) tumatir, (Nr) tumati

tomb [tuːm] *n* kushewa

tombstone [ˈtuːmstəʊn] *n* alamar kabari

tomorrow [təˈmɔrəʊ] *n*/*adv* 1. gobe 2. the day after tomorrow jibi

ton [tʌn] *n* ton, (Nr) tan

tonal language [ˈtəʊnəl] *n* harshe mai karin sauti

tone [təʊn] *n* 1. amo 2. karin sauti 3. high tone karin sauti mai hawa 4. low tone karin sauti mai sauka 5. falling tone karin sauti mai faɗuwa

tone mark *n* alamar karin sauti

tongs [tɔŋz] *pl* hantsaki

tongue [tʌŋ] *n* harshe

tonic [ˈtɔnik] *n* tonik

tonight [təˈnait] *n*/*adv* yau da dare

tonnage [ˈtʌnidʒ] *n* yawan ton

tonne [tʌn] *n* ton, (Nr) tan

too [tuː] *adv* 1. **Aminu's sister came too.** Kanwar Aminu ta zo ma. 2. **The tea is too sweet.** Shayi ya yi zaƙi.

took [tuk] *duba wajen* **take**

tool [tuːl] *n* abin aiki

tools [tuːlz] *pl* kayan aiki

tool kit *n* kayan aiki

tooth [tuːθ] *n* 1. haƙori 2. to brush one's teeth goge haƙora

toothache [ˈtuːθeik] *n* ciwon haƙori

toothbrush [ˈtuːθbrʌʃ] *n* buroshin haƙori

toothless [ˈtuːθlis] *adj* wawilo

toothpaste [ˈtuːθpeist] *n* man goge baki

top [tɔp] 1. *adj* na sama 2. *n* kai 3. ƙololuwa 4. murfi 5. on top of a kan 6. They are top of the league. Su ne a sahun gaba cikin lig-lig.

topic [ˈtɔpik] *n* batu

topical [ˈtɔpikl] *adj* abin magana

topple [ˈtɔpl] *v* hamɓarar da

topple over *v* tuntsure

torch [tɔːtʃ] *n* torcilan, (Nr) cocila

tore, torn [tɔː; tɔːn] *duba wajen* **tear**

torment [ˈtɔːment] 1. *n* azaba 2. *v* azabta

tornado [tɔːˈneidəʊ] *n* guguwa mai ƙarfi

torpedo [tɔːˈpiːdəu] *n* (*pl* **torpedoes**) makamashin bindigar ruwa

torrent [ˈtɔrənt] *n* ambaliya

tortoise [ˈtɔːtəs] *n* kunkuru

torture [ˈtɔːtʃə] 1. *n* azaba 2. *v* yi wa... azaba

toss [tɔs] *v* jefa

total [ˈtəutl] 1. *n* jimla 2. *v* yi jimla

total up *v* jimlata

totalitarian [ˌtəutæliˈtaːriən] *adj* na mulkin danniya

totalitarianism [ˌtəutæliˈtaːriənizm] *n* mulkin danniya

totter [ˈtɔtə] *v* yi tangaɗi

touch [tʌtʃ] 1. *n* taɓawa 2. *v* taɓa

touching [ˈtʌtʃiŋ] *adj* mai ban tausayi

tough [tʌf] *adj* 1. mai ban wahala 2. mai ƙarfi 3. mai tauri

toughness [ˈtʌfnis] *n* tsauri

tour [tuə] 1. *n* yawon shaƙatawa 2. **official tour** rangadi 3. *v* zaga (cikin)

touring [ˈtuəriŋ] *n* yawon shaƙatawa

tourism [ˈtuərizəm] *n* yawon shaƙatawa

tourist [ˈtuərist] *n* ɗan yawon shaƙatawa

tourist bureau *n* ofishin harkar yawon shaƙatawa

tourist industry *n* harkar yawon shaƙatawa

tourist season *n* kakar 'yan yawon shaƙatawa

tournament [ˈtɔːnəmənt] *n* gasa

tow [teu] *v* ja

tow away *v* jânyē

toward, towards [təˈwɔːd; -z] *prep* 1. zuwa (ga) 2. gab da

towel [ˈtauəl] *n* tawul, (Nr) sarbeti

tower [ˈtauə] *n* hasumiya

towering [ˈtauəriŋ] *adj* mai tsawo ƙwarai

town [taun] *n* gari

town council *n* hukumar gari

town hall *n* ma'aikatar magajin gari, (Nr) meri

town planning *n* shirin tsara gari

toxic [ˈtɔksik] *adj* mai guba

toy [tɔi] *n* abin wasa

trace [treis] 1. *n* ɓurɓushi 2. **There is no trace of them.** Ba a ji ɗuriyarsu ba. 3. *v* bi diddigi

track [træk] 1. *n* turba 2. sau 3. (spor.) fili 4. **railtrack** dogo 5. **to keep track** sa ido (**of** wa) 6. **to lose track** ɓace (**of** wa) 7. *v* bi diddigi

tractor [ˈtræktə] *n* tarakta, (Nr) jirgin danƙaro

trade [treid] 1. *n* ciniki 2. sana'a 3. **barter trade** musayar albarkatu 4. **foreign trade** cinikin ƙetare 5. **retail trade** kiri 6. **wholesale trade** sari 7. **free trade** ciniki ba tare da cikas ba 8. **balance of trade** rarar ciniki 9. **to lower trade barriers** kawar da kariyar ciniki 10. *v* yi ciniki

trade agreement *n* yarjejeniyar ciniki

trade barrier *n* kariyar ciniki

trade centre *n* cibiyar ciniki

trade embargo *n* takunkumin tattalin arziki

trade fair *n* nunin sana'o'i

trademark [ˈtreidmaːk] *n* tambari

trade protectionism *n* matakai na kariyar ciniki

trader [ˈtreidə] n ɗan kasuwa
trade relations pl huldar ciniki
trade sanctions pl takunkumin
tattalin arziki
trade surplus n rarar ciniki
trade union, trades union n
ƙungiyar ma'aikata, (Nr)
sandika
trading [ˈtreidiŋ] n ciniki
tradition [trəˈdiʃn] n al'adar
gargajiya
traditional [trəˈdiʃənl] adj na
gargajiya
traffic [ˈtræfik] 1. n tafiye-tafiye
2. motoci 3. v yi fasa-ƙwauri
traffic jam n cunkoson motoci
traffic lights pl wutar ba da
hanya
tragedy [ˈtrædʒədi] n 1. bala'i
2. labari mai ban tausayi
tragic [ˈtrædʒik] adj mai ban
tausayi
trail [treil] 1. n sau 2. tafarki
3. v bi diddigi
trailer [ˈtreilə] n tirela
train [trein] 1. n jirgin ƙasa
2. **underground train** jirgin
ƙarƙashin ƙasa 3. **by train** a
jirgi 4. v yi horo 5. horar da
trainer [ˈtreinə] n mai horo
trainers [ˈtreinəz] pl kambas,
(Nr) kiraf
training [ˈtreiniŋ] n horo
training-college n teacher
training centre titisi
train route n hanyar jirgi
trait [treit] n abin hali
traitor [ˈtreitə] n maci amanar
ƙasa
tram [træm] n motar dogo
tramp [træmp] n mài ràgaità
trample [ˈtræmpl] v tattaka

tramway [ˈtræmwei] n hanyar
motar dogo
trance [trɑːns] n **to go into a
trance** hau bori
tranquil [ˈtræŋkwil] adj mai
lumana
tranquillity [træŋˈkwiləti] n
lumana
tranquillizer [træŋˈkwilaizə] n
maganin kwantar da hankali
transaction [trænˈzækʃn] n
ma'amala
transcribe [trænˈskraib] v juya
transfer [trænsˈfəː] v 1. mayar da
2. fitar da
transferable [trænsˈfəːrəbl] adj
mai iya canza hannu
transform [trænsˈfɔːm] v mayar da
transformation [ˌtrænsfəˈmeiʃn]
n rikirkiɗa
transformed [trænsˈfɔːmd] adj
to be transformed rikiɗa
transformer [trænsˈfɔːmə] n
gidan wuta
transfusion [trænsˈfjuːʒn] n 1.
blood transfusion ƙarin jini
2. **to give a blood transfusion**
ɗura jini (**to wa**)
transient [ˈtrænziənt] adj mai
shuɗewa
transit [ˈtrænzit] n sufuri
transition [trænˈziʃn] n juyi
translate [trænzˈleit] v fassara
(**from** daga; **into** zuwa)
translation [trænzˈleiʃn] n
fassara
translator [trænzˈleitə] n mai
aikin fassara
transmission [trænzˈmiʃn] n watsi
transmit [trænzˈmit] v aika da
transmitter [trænzˈmitə] n tashar
watsa labarai

transparency [trænsˈpærənsi] *n*
fim, (Nr) kilishe

transparent [trænsˈpærənt] *adj*
bayananne

transpire [trænsˈpaiə] *v* faru

transplant [trænsˈplaːnt] 1. *n*
dashi 2. *v* dasa

transport [ˈtrænspɔːt] *n* sufuri

transport [trænsˈpɔːt] *v* kai

transportation [ˌtrænspɔːˈteiʃn] *n*
sufuri

transporter [trænsˈpɔːtə] *n* mai
jigila

transvestite [trænsˈvestait] *n* ɗan
daudu

trap [træp] 1. *n* tarko 2. *v*
(trapped) kama da tarko

trash [træʃ] *n* shara

trash can *n* garwar shara

travel [ˈtrævl] 1. *n* tafiya
2. *v* (travelled) yi tafiya

traveller [ˈtrævlə] *n* mai tafiya

travel sickness *n* tashin zuciya

trawler [ˈtrɔːlə] *n* babban jirgin
kamun kifi

tray [trei] *n* tire

treacherous [ˈtretʃərəs] *adj*
maci amana

treachery [ˈtretʃəri] *n* cin amana

tread [tred] 1. *n* zanen taya
2. *v* (trod, trodden) taka

tread on *v* take

treason [ˈtriːzn] *n* cin amanar ƙasa

treasure [ˈtreʒə] *n* dukiya

treasurer [ˈtreʒərə] *n* ma'aji

treasury [ˈtreʒəri] *n* baitulmali

treasury department *n*
ma'aikatar kuɗi

treasury secretary *n* sakataren
baitulmali

treat [triːt] *v* 1. gana wa 2. (med.)
yi jiyya

treatise [ˈtriːtiz] *n* kundi

treatment [ˈtriːtmənt] *n* 1. lura
2. (med.) jiyya 3. **bad
treatment** zalunci

treaty [ˈtriːti] *n* 1. yarjejeniya
2. **to sign a treaty** ƙulla
yarjejeniya 3. **to break a
treaty** soke yarjejeniya

treble [ˈtrebl] *v* ninka sau uku

tree [triː] *n* itace

tremble [ˈtrembl] *v* yi ɓari

trembling [ˈtremblŋ] *n* ɓari

tremendous [triˈmendəs] *adj*
gagarumi

tremor [ˈtremə] *n* girgiza

trench [trentʃ] *n* rami

trend [trend] *n* salo

trespass [ˈtrespəs] *v* keta haddi

trial [ˈtraiəl] *n* 1. gwaji 2. (leg.)
shari'a 3. **to bring to trial**
durƙusar da... gaban shari'a
4. **He is on trial.** Yana gaban
shari'a.

triangle [ˈtraiæŋgl] *n* mai kaman
shacin murhu

tribal [ˈtraibl] *adj* na kabila

tribalism [ˈtraibəlizəm] *n* kabilanci

tribalist [ˈtraibəlist] *adj/n* mai
nuna kabilanci

tribe [traib] *n* kabila

tribunal [traiˈbjuːnl] *n* 1. kotu
2. **industrial tribunal** kotun
sansanta rikicin ma'aikata

tribute [ˈtribjuːt] *n* **to pay tribute
to** yàbā

trick [trik] *n* 1. dabara 2. dabo
3. abin zamba 4. **to play a
trick** yi dabara (on wa) 5. *v*
zàmbatà

trickery [ˈtrikəri] *n* zamba

trickle [ˈtrikl] *v* zurara

tricky [ˈtriki] *adj* mai wuya

trigger [ˈtrigə] 1. *n* kunama
2. *v* jawo
trigger off *v* tayar da
trim [trim] *v* datsa
trip [trip] 1. *n* tafiya 2. balaguro
3. **business trip** ziyarar aiki
4. **round trip** tafiya zuwa da
dawowa 5. **to go on a trip** yi
balaguro 6. *v* (**tripped**) taɗe
trip up *v* taɗiye
triple [ˈtripl] *v* ninka sau uku
triplets [ˈtriplits] *pl* ukunni
triplicate [ˈtriplikət] *n* kwafi uku
tripod [ˈtraipɔd] *n* ƙafa
triumph [ˈtraiʌmf] 1. *n* nasara
2. *v* ci nasara
triumphant [traiˈʌmfnt] *n* mai
nasara
trod, trodden [trɔd; trɔdn] *duba*
wajen **tread**
troop [truːp] *n* ƙungiya
troops [truːps] *pl* rundunar soja
trophy [ˈtrəufi] *n* (spor.) kwaf,
(Nr) kuf
tropical [ˈtrɔpik] *adj* na wurare
masu zafi
tropical forest *n* kurmi
tropics [ˈtrɔpikl] *pl* ƙasashen
masu zafi
trot [trɔt] *v* yi kwakkwafa
trouble [ˈtrʌbl] 1. *n* wahala
2. **economic troubles** rikicin
tattalin arzikin ƙasa 3. **to**
have trouble sha wuya (**with**
wajen) 4. **to take the trouble**
ɗauki ɗawainiya 5. *v* dàmā
troublemaker [ˈtrʌbl,meikə] *n*
ɗan hargitsi
troublesome [ˈtrʌblsəm] *adj* mai
damuwa
trough [trɔf] *n* komi
trousers [ˈtrauzəz] *pl* wando

truant [ˈtruːənt] *adj/n* mashiririci
truce [truːs] *n* sulhu
truck [trʌk] *n* babbar mota, (Nr)
kamyo
true [truː] *adj* 1. na gaskiya
2. **to come true** tàbbatà
truly [ˈtruːli] *adv* da gaske
trumpet [ˈtrʌmpit] *n* kakaki
trunk [trʌŋk] *n* 1. babban akwati
2. jikin bishiya 3. hannun
gwiwa 4. but, (Nr) kyas
trunk call *n* wayar nesa
trust [trʌst] 1. *n* aminci
2. **breach of trust** saɓa
alkawari 3. **to betray a trust** ci
amana 4. (leg.) **to put in trust**
waƙafta 5. *v* amince da
trustee [trʌˈstiː] *n* (leg.) ɗan
wanka, na'ibi
trusting [ˈtrʌstiŋ] *adj* mai amana
trustworthy [ˈtrʌst,wəːði] *adj*
amintacce
truth [truːθ] *n* gaskiya
truthful [ˈtruːθfl] *adj* mai gaskiya
truthfully [ˈtruːθfuli] *adv* bisa
gaskiya
try [trai] *v* 1. yi ƙoƙari 2. gwada
3. (leg.) yi wa... shari'a
try on *v* gwada
trying [ˈtraiiŋ] *adj* mai tsanani
Tuareg [ˈtwaːreg] *n* 1. Buzu
2. Buzanci
tub [tʌb] *n* 1. kwano 2. **bathtub**
baho
tube [tjuːb] *n* 1. bututu 2. **inner**
tube tif, (Nr) shambur 3. (UK)
the Tube jirgin ƙarƙashin ƙasa
tuberculosis [tjuː,bəːkjuˈləusis] *n*
tibi
tuck [tʌk] *v* cūsà
Tuesday [ˈtjuːzdi] *n* ran Talata
tug [tʌg] *v* ja

tuition [tjuːˈiʃn] *n* aikin koyarwa

tumble [ˈtʌmbl] *v* faɗi

tumbler [ˈtʌmblə] *n* gilashi, (Nr) finjali

tumour [ˈtjuːmə] *n* ciwon daji

tumult [ˈtjuːmʌlt] *n* hayaniya

tune [tjuːn] **1.** *n* karin waƙa **2. to be out of tune** karya karin waƙa **3.** *v* daidaita

tune in *v* buɗa

tunnel [ˈtʌnl] *n* dogon rami

turban [ˈtəːbən] *n* rawani

turbine [ˈtəːbain] *n* inji mai farfela

turbulent [ˈtəːbjulənt] *adj* mai gargada

turf [təːf] *n* ciyawa

turkey [ˈtəːki] *n* (*pl* **turkeys**) talo-talo

turmoil [ˈtəːmɔil] *n* rikici

turn [təːn] **1.** *n* kwana **2. a good turn** alheri **3. It's my turn now.** Kamuna ke nan yanzu. **4. in turn** bi da bi **5. to take turns** sauya hannu **6.** *v* juya

turn against *v* juya wa... baya

turn around *v* jirkita

turn back *v* **1.** komo **2. to turn one's back** juya baya (**on** wa)

turn down *v* ƙi

turning [ˈtəːniŋ] *n* kwana

turning-point *n* harsashi, babban abu

turn into *v* **1.** zama **2.** mayar da

turn off *v* **1.** ratse **2.** rufe **3.** kashe

turn on *v* **1.** buɗe **2.** kunna

turn out *v* **1.** hàllaɍà **2.** zamanto **3.** kashe

turnover [ˈtəːnˌəuvə] *n* (fin.) yawan ciniki

turn round *duba wajen* **turn around**

turn up *v* **1.** iso **2.** ƙara

turtle [ˈtəːtl] *n* kififiya

tusk [tʌsk] *n* haure

tutor [ˈtjuːtə] *n* malami

twelfth [twelfθ] *adj* na goma sha biyu

twelve [twelv] *n/adj* goma sha biyu

twentieth [ˈtwentiəθ] *adj* na ashirin

twenty [ˈtwenti] *n/adj* ashirin

twice [twais] *adv* sau biyu

twig [twig] *n* ɗan ƙirare

twilight [ˈtwailait] *n* magariba

twin [twin] *n* ɗan tagwai

twinkle [ˈtwiŋkl] *v* yi ƙyalƙyali

twins [twinz] *pl* tagwaye

twist [twist] *v* **1.** murɗa **2.** tufka **3.** *duba wajen* **sprain**

two [tuː] *n/adj* biyu

two-faced [ˌtuːˈfeist] *adj* mai fuska biyu

two-party system *n* tsārìn jam'iyyu guda biyu

tycoon [taiˈkuːn] *n* babban attajiri

type [taip] **1.** *n* iri, nau'i **2.** *v* buga tafireta

typewriter [ˈtaipˌraitə] *n* tafireta, (Nr) mashin

typhoid [ˈtaifɔid] *n* zazzaɓin gudanawa

typhoon [taiˈfuːn] *n* hadari mai ƙarfi

typical [ˈtipikl] *adj* mai kama (**of** da)

typical [ˈtipikli] *adv* yawanci

typist [ˈtaipist] *n* mai bugun tafireta

tyranny [ˈtirəni] *n* zalunci

tyrant [ˈtaiərənt] *n* azzalumi

tyre [taiə] *n* taya, (Nr) fine

Uu

ugliness [ˈʌglinis] *n* muni

ugly [ˈʌgli] *adj* 1. mummuna 2. ƙazami

UK [ˌjuːˈkei] *duba wajen* United Kingdom

ulcer [ˈʌlsə] *n* gyambo

ulterior [ʌlˈtiəriə] *adj* to have an ulterior motive ci da ceto

ultimate [ˈʌltimət] *adj* na ƙarshe

ultimately [ˈʌltimətli] *adv* daga ƙarshe

ultimatum [ˌʌltiˈmeitəm] *n* wa'adi

ultra- [ˌʌltrə] *adj* matsanancin...

umbilical cord [ˈʌmbilikl.kɔːd] *n* cibiya

umbrella [ʌmˈbrelə] *n* laima

umbrella organisation *n* uwa-uba

umpire [ˈʌmpaiə] *n* alƙalin wasa

unable [ʌnˈeibl] *adj* to be unable kasa

unacceptable [ˌʌnəkˈseptəbl] *adj* maras karɓuwa

unaccompanied [ˌʌnəˈkʌmpənid] *adj* kaɗai

unaccustomed to [ˈʌnəˈkʌstəmd] *adj* mai rashin sabo da

unaffected [ˈʌnəˈfektid] *adj* unaffected by it wanda ba a shafe shi ba

unanimous [juːˈnæniməs] *adj* da baki ɗaya

unanimously [juːˈnæniməsli] *adv* gaba ɗaya

unappealing [ˈʌnəˈpiːliŋ] *adj* mai baƙin jini

unarmed [ˈʌnˈaːmd] *adj* maras bindinga

unattended [ˈʌnəˈtendid] *adj* 1. mai rashin kula 2. mai rashin halarta

unavailable [ˈʌnəˈveiləbl] *adj* rashin suhuni

unavoidable [ˌʌnəˈvɔidəbl] *adj* ba makara

unaware [ˈʌnəˈweə] *adj* They were unaware of the danger. Ba su farga da haɗari ba.

unawares [ˈʌnəˈweəz] *adj* to catch unawares shàmmàtà

unbearable [ʌnˈbeərəbl] *adj* na aza hannu a kai

unbelievable [ˌʌnbiˈliːvəbl] *adj* mai ban mamaki

unbroken [ˈʌnˈbrəukən] *adj* 1. mai ɗorewa 2. ba ɓararre ba

unbutton [ˈʌnˈbʌtn] *v* ɓalle

uncertain [ʌnˈsəːtn] *adj* maras tabbas

uncertainty [ʌnˈsəːtənti] *n* rashin tabbaci

uncle [ˈʌŋkl] *n* kawu

unclear [ˌʌnˈkliə] *adj* to be unclear 1. cākùɗè 2. ƙàzantà

uncleared land [ˌʌnˈkliəd] *n* sùnƙūrù

uncomfortable [ʌnˈkʌmftəbl] *adj* 1. maras jin daɗî 2. maras sauƙi

uncommon [ʌnˈkɔmən] *adj* nadiran

unconcerned [ˈʌnkənˈsəːnd] *adj* biris

unconditional surrender
[ˈʌnkən·diʃənl] *n* miƙa wuya ba sharaɗi

unconditionally [ˈʌnkən·diʃənli] *adv* ba sharaɗi

unconscious [ʌn·kɔnʃəs] *adj* sumamme

unconsciouly [ʌn·kɔnʃəsli] *adv* ba da gangan ba

unconstitutional [ˈʌn,kɔnstɪ·tjuːʃənl] *adj* This is unconstitutional. Wannan ya kauce wa tsarin mulkin ƙasar.

uncontrollable [,ʌnkən·trəuləbl] *adj* to be uncontrollable gàgarà

uncooperative [,ʌnkəu·ɔpərətiv] *adj* mai ƙuyuya

uncover [ʌn·kʌvə] *v* 1. buɗe 2. tona

undamaged [ʌn·dæmidʒd] *adj* mai kyau

undaunted [ˈʌn·dɔːntid] *adj* mai ƙarfin zuciya

undecided [ˈʌndi·saidid] *adj* to be undecided yi waswasi

undefeated [,ʌndi·fiːtid] *adj* We are undefeated. Ba a taɓa cinmu ba.

undeniable [,ʌndi·naiəbl] *adj* ba shakka

under [ˈʌndə] *prep* 1. under the table ƙarƙashin tebur 2. under twenty years old shekaru ba su kai ashirin ba

undercut [ˈʌndəkʌt] *v* (fin.) kashe wa... kasuwa

underdeveloped nations [ˈʌndədi·veləpt] *pl* ƙasashen masu tasowa

underestimate [,ʌndər·estimeit] *v* raina

undergo [ˈʌndə·gəu] *v* sha

undergraduate [ˈʌndə·grædʒuət] *n* ɗalibi

underground [ˈʌndəgraund] *adj/adv* 1. ƙarƙashin ƙasa 2. (UK) the Underground jirgin ƙarƙashin ƙasa

underground organization *n* ƙunci

underground train *n* jirgin ƙarƙashin ƙasa

undergrowth [ˈʌndəgrəuθ] *n* sarƙaƙƙiya

underhand, underhanded [ˈʌndəhænd; -id] *adj* na cuku-cuku

underline [,ʌndə·lain] *v* ja layi a ƙarƙashi

undermine [,ʌndə·main] *v* yi wa... yankan baya

undermine confidence *v* kawo rashin jituwa

underneath [ˈʌndə·niːθ] 1. *prep* ƙarƙashin 2. *adv* a ƙarƙashi

underpants, undershorts [ˈʌndəpænts; ˈʌndəʃɔːts] *pl* duros

underside [ˈʌndə·said] *n* ƙarƙashi

understand [,ʌndə·stænd] *v* 1. fahimta 2. ji

understandable [,ʌndə·stændəbl] *adj* mai jiwuwa

understanding 1. *adj* mai jin tausayi 2. *n* fahimta 3. to come to an understanding shirya

undertake [,ʌndə·teik] *v* ɗauka

under-the-counter [ˈʌndəθə·kauntə] *adj* na bayan gida

underway [ˈʌndə·wei] *adv* tàfe

underwear [ˈʌndəweə] *n* kamfai

undid [ˈʌnˈdid] *duba wajen* **undo**
undo [ˈʌnˈduː] *v* (**undid, undone**)
kwance
undoubtedly [ʌnˈdautidli] *adv*
tabbas
undress [ˈʌnˈdres] *v* tuɓe
uneasiness [ʌnˈiːzinis] *n* juyayi
uneasy [ʌnˈiːzi] *adj* **to be uneasy**
yi juyayi
uneducated [ˈʌnˈedjukeitid] *adj*
jahili
unemployed [ˈʌnimˈplɔid] *adj* 1.
mai zaman kashe-wando 2. the
unemployed marasa aiki
unemployment [ˈʌnimˈplɔimənt]
n rashin aikin yi
unequal [ˈʌnˈiːkwəl] *adj* ba daidai
ba
unequivocally [ˈʌniˈkwivəkəli]
adv a fili
UNESCO [juːˈneskəu] *n*
Kungiyar Kyautata Ilimi da
Kimiyya da Al'adu ta
Majalisar Ɗinkin Duniya
uneven [ˈʌnˈiːvn] *adj* kacau
unexpected [ˈʌnikˈspektid] *adj*
ba-zata
unexpectedly [ˈʌnikˈspektili] *adv*
ba zato ba tsammani
unfair [ˈʌnˈfeə] *adj* maras adalci
unfasten [ˈʌnˈfaːsn] *v* kwance
unfinished [ˈʌnˈfiniʃt] *adj* ba
cikakke ba
unfit [ˈʌnˈfit] *adj* 1. maras lafiya
2. maras kyau
unfold [ʌnˈfəuld] *v* buɗe
unfortunate [ʌnˈfɔːtʃənət] *adj*
maras sa'a
unfortunately [ʌnˈfɔːtʃənətli] *adv*
amma kash
unfriendly [ʌnˈfrendli] *adj* **to be**
unfriendly ƙi mutane

ungrateful [ʌnˈgreitfl] *adj* mai
rashin godiya
unhappiness [ʌnˈhæpinis] *n*
baƙin ciki
unhappy [ʌnˈhæpi] *adj* mai baƙin
ciki
unhealthy [ʌnˈhelθi] *adj* 1.
maras lafiya 2. maras kyau
3. mummuna
unhindered [ˈʌnˈhindəd] *adj* ba
tare da wani cikas ba
unhurt [ˈʌnˈhəːt] *adj* maras rauni
unification [ˌjuːnifiˈkeiʃn] *n* haɗin
kai
uniform [ˈjuːnifɔːm] 1. *adj* mai bai
ɗaya 2. *n* inifam 3. **school**
uniform kayan makaranta
uniformity [ˈjuːnifɔːmiti] *n*
daidaito
unify [ˈjuːnifai] *v* haɗe
unify a system *v* daidaita tsari
unilateral step [juːniˈlætrəl] *n*
matakin ƙashin kai
unimportant [ˈʌnimˈpɔːtənt] *adj*
maras muhimmanci
uninhabited [ˌʌninˈhæbitid] *adj*
an uninhabited building
gidan da ba kowa
uninjured [ˈʌnˈindʒəd] *adj* maras
rauni
unintentional [ˈʌninˈtenʃənl] *adj*
ba da gangan ba
uninteresting [ʌnˈintərestiŋ] *adj*
mai cin rai
uninterrupted [ˈʌnˌintəˈrʌptid]
adj babu fashi
union [ˈjuːnjən] *n* 1. kungiya
2. tarayya 3. **trade union**
ƙungiyar ma'aikata
Union Jack [ˈjuːnjənˈdʒæk] *n* tutar
Ingila
unique [juːˈniːk] *adj* farda

unit [ˈjuːnit] *n* 1. sashe 2. (mil.) rukuni

unite [juːˈnait] *v* 1. haɗe 2. haɗa kai

united [juːˈnaitid] *adj* 1. haɗaɗɗe 2. da baki ɗaya

United Kingdom [juːˌnaitid ˈkiŋdəm] *n* Ingila

United Nations (UN) *n* Majalisar Ɗinkin Duniya (MDD)

United States of America *n* Amirka

unity [ˈjuːnəti] *n* haɗin kai

universal [ˌjuːniˈvəːsl] *adj* ruwan dare

universally [ˌjuːniˈvəːsəli] *adv* a ko'ina

universe [ˈjuːnivəːs] *n* duniya

university [ˌjuːniˈvəːsəti] *n* jami'a

unjust [ʌnˈdʒʌst] *adj* maras adalci

unkind [ʌnˈkaind] *adj* maras kirki

unknown [ˌʌnˈnəun] 1. *adj* baƙo 2. **as yet unknown** wanda ba a tabbatar da kasancewarsa ba 3. *n* sanin gaibi

unlace [ʌnˈleis] *v* kwance

unlawful [ʌnˈlɔːfəl] *adj* 1. ba bisa doka ba 2. (Isl.) haram

unless [ənˈles] *conj* 1. in ba... ba 2. sai dai

unlike [ʌnˈlaik] *adj* dabam

unlikely [ʌnˈlaikli] *adv* ba ya yiwuwa

unlimited [ʌnˈlimitid] *adj/adv* bila haddin

unload [ʌnˈləud] *v* sauke kaya

unlock [ʌnˈlɔk] *v* buɗe da makulli

unlucky [ʌnˈlʌki] *adj* maras sa'a

unmanageable [ʌnˈmænidʒəbl] *adj* gagararre

unmarried [ʌnˈmærid] *adj* wanda bai yi aure ba

unnatural [ʌnˈnætʃrəl] *adj* 1. abin al'ajabi 2. abin kunya

unnecessary [ʌnˈnesəsri] *adj* ba dole ba

unofficial [ʌnəˈfiʃl] *adj* ba na hukuma ba

unpack [ʌnˈpæk] *v* kwance kaya

unpalatable [ʌnˈpælitəbl] *adj* maras daɗi

unpleasant [ʌnˈpleznt] *adj* maras daɗi

unpopular [ʌnˈpɔpjulə] *adj* mai baƙin jini

unpopularity [ʌnˌpɔpjuˈlærəti] *n* baƙin jini

unprecedented [ʌnˈpresidentid] *adj* wanda ba a taɓa gani ba

unpredictable [ʌnpriˈdiktəbl] *adj* 1. maras tabbas 2. miskili

unprepared [ʌnpriˈpeəd] *adj* ba a shirye ba

unprincipled [ʌnˈprinsipəld] *adj* maras aƙida

unravel [ʌnˈrævl] *v* warware

unreasonable [ʌnˈriːznəbl] *adj* maras kan gado

unrelated [ʌnriˈleitid] *adj* **They are unrelated.** 1. Ba su gama dangi da juna ba. 2. Ba abin da ya haɗa su.

unreliable [ˈʌnriˈlaiəbl] *adj* maras gaskiya

unrest [ʌnˈrest] *n* tashin hankali

unripe [ʌnˈraip] *adj* ɗanye

unroll [ʌnˈrɔl] *v* warware

unruly [ʌnˈruːli] *adj* gagararre

unsafe [ˈʌnˈseif] *adj* mai haɗari

unsatisfactory [ˈʌnˌsætisˈfæktri] *adj* maras kyau

unscrew [ˈʌnˈskruː] *v* kwance ƙusa

unscrupulous [ʌnˈskruːpjuləs] *adj* maras adalci

unseen [ˈʌnˈsiːn] *adj* a dunƙule

unselfish [ˈʌnˈselfiʃ] *adj* mai kyauta

unsettle [ˈʌnˈsetl] *v* dằmā

unskilled [ˈʌnˈskild] *adj* jahili

unsophisticated [ʌnsɔˈfistikeitid] *adj* bagidaje

unsteady [ˈʌnˈstedi] *adj* mai tangal-tangal

unsuccessful [ʌnsʌkˈsesfəl] *adj* They were unsuccessful. Ba su ci nasara ba.

unsuitable [ˈʌnˈsuːtəbl] *adj* to be unsuitable ba dace ba

unthinkable [ʌnˈθiŋkəbl] *adj* maras misaltuwa

untidy [ʌnˈtaidi] *adj* maras tsari

untie [ˈʌnˈtai] *v* kwance

until [ənˈtil] *prep/conj* 1. har 2. sai

untouched [ˈʌnˈtʌtʃt] *adj* mai lafiya

untrue [ˈʌnˈtruː] *adj* maras gaskiya

unusual [ʌnˈjuːʒl] *adj* 1. ba safai... ba 2. baƙo

unveil [ʌnˈveil] *v* 1. buɗe fuska 2. bayyana

unwelcome [ʌnˈwelkəm] *adj* mai ƙin karɓuwa

unwell [ʌnˈwel] *adj* maras lafiya

unwilling [ʌnˈwiliŋ] *adj* to be unwilling bijire

unwillingness [ʌnˈwiliŋnis] *n* nàwā

unwind [ʌnˈwaind] *v* warware

unwise [ʌnˈwaiz] *adj* mai rashin tunani

unworthy [ʌnˈwəːði] *adj* to be unworthy ba cancanta ba

unwrap [ʌnˈræp] *v* buɗe

up [ʌp] *adv* 1. sama 2. *duba* wajen **up to**

upbringing [ˈʌpbriŋiŋ] *n* tarbiyya

uphill [ʌpˈhil] *adj/adv* to go uphill yi hawa

uphold [ʌpˈhəuld] *v* kiyaye

upon [əˈpɔn] *prep* 1. bisa kan 2. da

upper [ˈʌpə] *adj* na sama

Upper House *n* Majalisar Dattijai

upright [ˈʌprait] 1. *adj* adali 2. *adv* a tsaye

uprising [ˈʌpreiziŋ] *n* tawaye

uproar [ˈʌprɔː] *n* hargagi

uproot [ˌʌpˈruːt] *v* tumɓuke

upset [ˌʌpˈset] 1. *adj* to be upset gigice 2. *v* (upset) kife 3. ba wa... haushi 4. ɓata

upside-down [ˌʌpsaidˈdaun] *adv* a kife

upstairs [ˌʌpˈsteəz] *adv* sama

upswing [ˈʌpswiŋ] *n* economic upswing ci gaban bunƙasar tattalin arziki

up to [ʌp] *prep* har

up-to-date [ˌʌptuˈdeit] *adj* na yau, na zamani

up to now *adv* har yanzu

up to then *adv* har wannan lokaci

upward, upwards [ˈʌpwəd; -z] *adv* zuwa sama

uranium [juəˈreinijəm] *n* yureniyam, (Nr) iraniyan

urban [ˈəːbən] *adj* na birni

urban development *n* raya birane

urge [əːdʒ] *v* 1. ƙarfafa wa 2. matsa wa

urgency [ˈɔːdʒənsi] *n* gaggawa
urgent [ˈɔːdʒənt] *adj* na gaggawa
urgently [ˈɔːdʒəntli] *adv* da
  gaggawa
urinate [ˈjuərineit] *v* yi fitsari
urine [ˈjuərin] *n* fitsari
us [əs; ʌs] mu
US, USA *duba wajen* **United**
  States (of America)
usage [ˈjuːsidʒ] *n* amfani
use [juːs] *n* 1. amfani 2. fa'ida
use [juːz] *v* 1. yi amfani da
  2. yi aiki da
used [juːzd] *adj* kwance
used to [ˈjuːstu] 1. to be used to
  saba da 2. **We used to live in**
  Zaria. Dâ Zariya muke da
  zama.
used up [juːzdˈʌp] *adj* to be used
  up ƙare

useful [ˈjuːsfl] *adj* mai amfani
usefulness [ˈjuːsfəlnis] *n* amfani
useless [ˈjuːslis] *adj* 1. maras
  amfani 2. na banza
uselessness [ˈjuːslisnis] *n* 1.
  rashin amfani 2. banza
user [ˈjuːzə] *n* mai amfani
user-friendly [ˈjuːzə,frendli] *adj*
  mai sauƙin ganewa
usual [ˈjuːʒl] *adj* na kullum
usually [ˈjuːʒəli] *adv* yawanci
use up *v* ƙare
uterus [ˈjuːtərəs] *n* mahaifa
utilize [ˈjuːtilaiz] *v* yi amfani da
utmost [ˈʌtməust] *n* 1. iyaka 2. **to**
  do your utmost yi bakin
  ƙoƙarinka
utter [ˈʌtə] 1. *adj* na innanaha
  2. *v* furta
utterance [ˈʌtərəns] *n* furuci

Vv

v. *duba wajen* **versus**

vacancy [ˈveikənsi] *n* gurbi

vacant [ˈveikənt] *adj* ba kowa a ciki

vacation [vəˈkeiʃn] *n* hutu, (Nr) kwanje

vaccinate [ˈvæksineit] *v* yi wa... allura, (Nr) yi wa... shasshawa

vaccination [ˌvæksiˈneiʃn] *n* allurar rigakafi, (Nr) shasshawa

vaccine [vækˈsiːn] *n* (med.) magani

vacuum [ˈvækjuəm] *n* rashin iska

vacuum cleaner *n* injin shara

vagabond [ˈvægəbɔnd] *n* mài rầgaità

vagina [vəˈdʒainə] *n* farji

vague [veig] *adj* maras tabbas

vain [vein] *adj* 1. mai girman kai 2. in vain a wofi

vale [veil] *n* kwari

valiant [ˈvæliənt] *adj* mai ƙarfin zuciya

valid [ˈvælid] *adj* 1. mai inganci 2. (leg.) a valid driving licence lasin wanda bai ƙare ba

validity [vəˈlidəti] *n* inganci

valley [ˈvæli] *n* kwari

valour [ˈvælə] *n* jaruntaka

valuable [ˈvæljuəbl] *adj* mai daraja

valuables [ˈvæljuəblz] *pl* dukiya mai daraja

value [ˈvæljuː] 1. *n* daraja 2. amfani 3. (ec.) kadari 4. *v* ɗauka da daraja

value-added tax (VAT) *n* haraji na kayan sàyā

valve [vælv] *n* bawul, (Nr) sufaf

van [væn] *n* a-kori-kura

vandal [ˈvændl] *n* ɗan ɓata gari

vandalism [ˈvændəlizm] *n* ɓarna

vanish [ˈvæniʃ] *v* ɓace (into cikin)

vanity [ˈvænəti] *n* girman kai

vaporize [ˈveipəraiz] *v* dafa

vapour [ˈveipə] *n* tururi

variable [ˈveəriəbl] *adj* mai canji

variation [ˌveəriˈeiʃn] *n* bambanci

varicose veins [ˌværikəus ˈveinz] *pl* nankařwā

variety [vəˈraiəti] *n* 1. iri 2. iri-iri

various [ˈveəriəs] *adj* iri-iri

varnish [ˈvaːniʃ] *n* shafa man katako

vary [ˈveəri] *v* 1. canja 2. yi dabam

vase [vaːz] *n* gilashin fure

vast [vaːst] *adj* makake

VAT *duba wajen* **value-added tax**

vault [vɔːlt] 1. *n* taska 2. *v* yi tsalle

veal [viːl] *n* naman maraƙi

vegetable(s) [ˈvedʒtəbl] *n* kayan lambu, (Nr) kayan garka

vegetarian [ˌvedʒiˈteəriən] 1. *adj* maras nama 2. *n* wanda ba ya cin nama

vegetation [ˌvedʒiˈteiʃn] *n* tsire-tsire

vehement [ˈviːəmənt] *adj* mai tsanani

vehicle [ˈviəkl] *n* jirgi

veil [veil] *n* hijabi

vein [vein] *n* jijiyar jini

velocity [viˈlɔsəti] *n* sauri

vendor [ˈvendə] *n* 1. mai talla 2. mai sayarwa

venereal disease [vəˈniəriəl] *n* ciwon sanyi

vengeance [ˈvendʒəns] *n* ramuwa

venom [ˈvenəm] *n* 1. dafi 2. ƙiyayya

venomous [ˈvenəməs] *adj* 1. mai dafi 2. mai ƙiyayya

ventilation [ˌventiˈleiʃn] *n* samun iska

ventilator [ˈventileitə] *n* injin shaƙar iska

venture [ˈventʃə] *n* 1. kamfani 2. shiri

veranda [vəˈrændə] *n* baranda

verb [vəːb] *n* fiˈili

verbal [ˈvəːbl] *adj* da baki

verdict [ˈvəːdikt] *n* hukunci

verge [vəːdʒ] *n* 1. **road verge** bakin hanya 2. **on the verge of** gab da

verify [ˈverifai] *v* gaskata

verification [ˌverifiˈkeiʃn] *n* gaskatawa

verse [vəːs] *n* 1. baiti 2. waƙoƙi

version [ˈvəːʃn] *n* siga

vertical [ˈvəːtikl] *adj* a tsaye

versus [ˈvəːsəs] (spor.) **Nigeria versus England** Nijeriya da Ingila

very [ˈveri] 1. *adj* na gaske 2. *adv* ƙwarai 3. da gaske

very much *adv* haiƙan

very much so *adv* ƙwarai da gaske

vessel [ˈvesl] *n* 1. tulu 2. jirgin ruwa 3. **blood vessel** jijiyar jini

vest [vest] *n* 1. singileti 2. (US) falmaran

vet [vet] *n* likitan dabbobi

veteran [ˈvetərən] *n* tsohon soja, (Nr) tsohon soji

veterinary [ˈvetineri] *adj* na dabbobi

veterinary clinic *n* bitinariya

veterinary surgeon *n* likitan dabbobi

veto [ˈviːtəu] *n* (*pl* **vetoes**) 1. *n* hawan kujèrař-nã-ƙi 2. *v* hau kujèrař-nã-ƙi (game da)

vexed [vekst] *adj* **to be vexed** ji haushi

via [ˈvaiə] *prep* ta

vibrate [vaiˈbreit] *v* yi rawa

vibration [vaiˈbreiʃn] *n* rawa

vicar [ˈvikə] *n* (Chris.) fãdã

vice [vais] 1. *n* mugunta 2. *adj* mataimaki

vice-chairman *n* mataimakin shugaba

vice-president *n* mataimakin shugaba

vice versa [ˌvaisiˈvəːsə] ko akasin haka

vicinity [viˈsinəti] *n* kusanci

vicious [ˈviʃəs] *adj* mugu

victim [ˈviktim] *n* wanda aka yi wa laifi

victor [ˈviktə] *n* mai nasara

victorious [vikˈtɔːriəs] *adj* **to be victorious** ci nasara

victory [ˈviktəri] *n* nasara

video [ˈvidiəu] 1. *n* bidiyo 2. *v* ɗauki hoto

view [vjuː] 1. *n* gani 2. ra'ayi 3. *v* dùbã

viewer [ˈvjuːə] *n* mai kallo

viewpoint [ˈvjuːpɔint] *n* ra'ayi

vigorous [ˈvigərəs] *adj* mai kuzari

vile [vail] *adj* mugu

village [ˈvilidʒ] *n* ƙauye

villager [ˈvilidʒə] *n* ɗan ƙauye

village square *n* dandali

villain [ˈvilən] *n* 1. mugun mutum 2. mai yin laifi

vindicated [ˈvindikeitid] *v* **He has been vindicated.** Yana da hujja.

vinegar [ˈvinigə] *n* bìningà, (Nr)
binegar

vintage [ˈvintidʒ] *adj* 1. na dâ
2. mai ƙarƙo

violate [ˈvaiəleit] *v* keta

violence [ˈvaiələns] *n* tashin
hankali

violent [ˈvaiələnt] *adj* mai ta da
hankali

violin [ˌvaiəˈlin] *n* goge

VIP [ˌviːaiˈpiː] *n* babban mutum

viper [ˈvaipə] *n* kùbūbuwà

virgin [ˈvəːdʒin] *n* budurwa

virility [viˈriləti] *n* mazakuta

virtual [ˈvəːtʃuəl] *adj* kusan

virtual reality *n* kama-da-wane

virtually [ˈvəːtʃuəli] *adv* kusan

virtue [ˈvəːtʃuː] *n* kirki

visa [ˈviːzə] *n* bisa, (Nr) biza

vis-à-vis [ˌviːzaˈviː] *prep* daidai da

visibility [ˌvizəˈbiləti] *n* gani

visible [ˈvizəbl] *adj* mai ganuwa

vision [ˈviʒn] *n* 1. gani 2. (rel.)
wahayi

visit [ˈvizit] 1. *n* ziyara 2. *v* ziyarta

visitor [ˈvizitə] *n* 1. baƙo
2. wanda ya yi ziyara

visual [ˈviʒuəl] *adj* na gani

vital [ˈvaitl] *adj* mai muhimmanci

vitality [vaiˈtæləti] *n* kuzari

vitamin [ˈvitəmin] *n* bitamin

vivid [ˈvivid] *adj* bayananne

vocabulary [vəuˈkæbjuləri] *n*
kalmomi

vocal [ˈvəukl] *adj* na murya

vocals [ˈvəuklz] *pl* (mus.) murya

vocation [vəuˈkeiʃn] *n* sana'a

vodka [ˈvodkə] *n* giyar 'vodka'

vogue [vəug] *n* in vogue sabon
yayi ne

voice [vɔis] *n* murya

volatile [ˈvɔlətail] *adj* na rashin

sanin tabbas

volatility [ˌvɔləˈtiləti] *n* rashin
sanin tabbas

volcano [vɔulˈkeinəu] *n* (*pl*
volcanoes) dutse mai aman wuta

volley [ˈvɔli] *n* bugun bindigogi

volleyball [ˈvɔlibɔːl] *n* wasan
ƙwallon raga

volt [vəult] *n* ƙarfin wuta

voltage [ˈvəultidʒ] *n* awon ƙarfin
wuta

volume [ˈvɔljuːm] *n* 1. girma
2. littafi 3. ƙarfin murya

voluntarily [ˌvɔlənˈtrəli] *adv* da
ganin dama

voluntary [ˈvɔləntri] *adj* na ganin
dama, na sa kai

voluntary organization *n*
ƙungiyar taimakon kai da kai

voluntary work *n* aikin
taimakon kai da kai

volunteer [vɔlənˈtiə] 1. *n* mai
taimako 2. *v* sa kai

vomit [ˈvɔmit] 1. *n* amai 2. *v* yi amai

vote [vəut] 1. *n* ƙuri'a 2. **to take
a vote** yi ƙuri'a (**on a kan**)
3. *v* jefa ƙuri'a

voter [ˈvəutə] *n* mai jefa ƙuri'a

voting-booth [ˈvəutiŋˌbuːθ] *n*
rumfar jefa ƙuri'a

vouch [vautʃ] *v* tabbata (**for** da)

voucher [ˈvautʃə] *n* bauca

vow [vau] 1. *n* 2. *v* làshi takòbi

vowel [ˈvauəl] *n* wasali

voyage [ˈvɔjidʒ] *n* tafiya

vs. *duba wajen* **versus**

vulgar [ˈvʌlgər] *adj* maras dâ'a

vulnerability [ˈvʌlnərəbiliti] *n*
yanayin shigewa

vulnerable [ˈvʌlnərəbl] *adj* mai
yanayin shigewa

vulture [ˈvultʃə] *n* ungulu

Ww

wad [wɔd] *n* ƙunshi
wade into [weid] *v* **1.** yi tafiya a cikin ruwa **2.** sa baki
wafer [weifə] *n* biskin
wag [wæg] *v* kaɗa
wage [weidʒ] *n* **1.** albashi **2.** *duba wajen* **wage war**
wage freeze *n* takunkumin ƙarin albashi
wage rise *n* ƙarin albashi
wage war *v* kai da yaƙi (**on** wa)
wage-earner *n* ɗan albashi
wages [ˈweidʒiz] *n* albashi
wagon [ˈwægən] *n* wagunu
wail [weil] *v* yi kuka
waist [weist] *n* ƙugu
waistcoat [ˈweiskəut] *n* falmaran
wait [weit] *v* dakata
wait for *v* jira
waiter [ˈweitə] *n* sabis, (Nr) sarbis
waiting-room [ˈweitiŋru:m] *n* ɗakin jira
waitress [ˈweitris] *n* sabis, (Nr) sarbis
waive [weiv] *v* ɗâukē sharàɗì
wake, wake up [weik] *v* (**woke/waked, woken/waked**) **1.** farka **2.** farkar da
waken [ˈweikən] *duba wajen* **wake**
Wales [weilz] *n* yankin Welz
walk [wɔ:k] **1.** *n* yawo **2.** *v* yi tafiya a ƙas
walking stick [ˈwɔ:kiŋstik] *n* kwajiri
walkman [ˈwɔ:kmən] *n* oba-oba
walk out (of) [ˈwɔ:kaut] *v* **1.** fita daga **2.** yi yaji
wall [wɔ:l] *n* **1.** bango **2.** katanga
wallet [ˈwɔlit] *n* walàt, (Nr) far̃tamāmì
wander [ˈwɔndə] *v* yi ràgaità
wanderer [ˈwɔndərə] *n* ràgaità
wane [wein] *v* dusàshē
want [wɔnt] **1.** *n* bukata **2.** rashi **3.** *v* so
war [wɔ:] *n* **1.** yaƙi **2. civil war** yaƙin basasa **3. holy war** jihadi **4.** *duba wajen* **wage war**
war camp *n* sansani
war indemnity *n* ramuwar diyya
war zone *n* fagen daga
ward [ˈwɔ:d] *n* **1.** ɗakin asibiti **2.** unguwa, (Nr) karce
warder [ˈwɔ:də] *n* gândur̃ōbà
ward off *v* kārè
wardrobe [ˈwɔ:drəub]
warehouse [ˈweəhaus] *n* sito, (Nr) mangaza
wares [weə] *pl* kayan ciniki
warfare [ˈwɔ:feə] *n* yaƙi
warhead [ˈwɔ:hed] *n* **nuclear warheads** kawunan makamai
warm [wɔ:m] *adj* mai ɗumi
warm up *v* ɗumama
warmth [wɔ:mθ] *n* ɗumi
warn [wɔ:n] *v* gargaɗa
warning [ˈwɔ:niŋ] *n* gargaɗi
warped [wɔ:p] *adj* **to be warped** banƙare
warrant [ˈwɔrənt] **1.** *n* takardar kamu, (Nr) manda daho **2.** *v* tabbata wa

warranty [ˈwɔrənti] *n* gàràntî
warrior [ˈwɔriə] *n* mayaƙi
was [wəz; wɔz] *duba wajen* **be**
wash [wɔʃ] *v* 1. wanke 2. yi
    wanka
washing [ˈwɔʃiŋ] *n* kayan wanki
washing machine *n* injin
    ɗauraya
washing powder *n* omo
washing up *n* wanke-wanke
washroom [ˈwɔʃrum] *n* bayan gida
wash up *v* yi wanke-wanke
wasp [wɔsp] *n* zanzaro
waste [weist] 1. *n* ɓarna
    2. **industrial waste** sharar
    masana'antu mai illa 3. *v* ɓata
wastebin [ˈweistbin] *n* kwandon
    shara
watch [wɔtʃ] 1. *n* agogo 2. *v* yi
    kallo
watchman [ˈwɔtʃmən] *n* mai
    gadi, (Nr) gardanye
water [ˈwɔːtə] 1. *n* ruwa 2. *v*
    shayar da
waterbottle [ˈwɔːtə,bɔtl] *n* jallo
water-buffalo [ˈwɔːtə,bʌfələu] *n*
    ɓauna
water-cannon [ˈwɔːtə,kænən] *n*
    mesar ruwa
waterfall [ˈwɔːtəfɔːl] *n*
    magangarar ruwa
watering can [ˈwɔːtəriŋkæn] *n*
    bututu, (Nr) arezuwar
watermelon [ˈwɔːtəmelən] *n*
    kankana
waterproof [ˈwɔːtəpruːf] *adj* mai
    hana ruwa
watertank [ˈwɔːtətæŋk] *n* tanki
watery [ˈwɔːtəri] *adj* mai ruwa-
    ruwa
wave [weiv] 1. *n* igiyar ruwa
    2. *v* kaɗa hannu

wavelength [ˈweivleŋθ] *n* zango,
    (Nr) gâm
waver [ˈweivə] *v* ja da baya
wax [wæks] *n* kakin zuma
way [wei] 1. hanya 2. ɗabi'a
    3. **way of life** zama 4. **by way
    of** ta 5. **this way** ta haka 6. **on
    the way/underway** a tafe 7. **by
    the way...** af... 8. **to find a way
    of...** sami kafar... 9. **to get
    underway** farfaɗo da 10. **to
    make way** ba da wuri (**for** wa)
way in *n* mashiga
way out *n* mafita
wayside [ˈweisaid] *n* bakin hanya
we [wiː] *pro* mu
weak [wiːk] *adj* 1. maras ƙarfi
    2. **to be weak** raunana
weaken [ˈwiːkən] *v* 1. raunàna
    2. (fin.) fàɗì
weakness [ˈwiːknis] *n* 1. rashin
    ƙarfi 2. illa
wealth [welθ] *n* 1. arziki
    2. **mineral wealth** albarkatu
wealthy [ˈwelθi] *adj* mai arziki
wean [wiːn] *v* yaye
weapon [ˈwepən] *n* makami
wear [weə] *v* (**wore, worn**) 1. sa
    2. *duba wajen* **wear out**
wear out *v* 1. mutu 2. gajiyar da
weary [ˈwiəri] *adj* gajiyayye
weather [ˈweðə] 1. *n* yanayi
    2. *v* zage
weather forecast *n* kìntàcen
    yanàyì
weave [wiːv] *v* (**wove, woven**) saƙa
web [web] *v* saƙar gizo
wed [wed] *v* àurā
wedding [ˈwediŋ] *n* bikin aure
wedding ring *n* zoben aure
wedge [wedʒ] 1. *n* wêjì, (Nr) kâl
    2. *v* ƙwafa

Wednesday [ˈwenzdi] *n* ran Laraba

weed(s) [wiːd] *n* ciyawa

week [wiːk] *n* mako

weekday [ˈwiːkdei] *n* ranar aiki

weekend [ˌwiːkˈend] *n* ƙarshen mako

weekly [ˈwiːkli] *adj* 1. mako-nako 2. **a weekly newspaper** jarida mai fitowa a kowane mako

weep [wiːp] *v* yi hawaye

weevil [wiːp] *n* màyā

weigh [wei] *v* 1. auna 2. faye nauyi

weight [weit] *n* 1. nauyi 2. **to put on weight** yi jiki 3. **to lose weight** zub da ciki

welcome [ˈwelkəm] 1. *n* maraba 2. *v* yi wa... maraba 3. nuna amincewa da

weld [weld] *v* yi wa... walda, (Nr) yi wa... sude

welder [weldə] *n* walda

welding [ˈweldiŋ] *n* waldi

welfare [ˈwelfeə] *n* 1. zaman lafiya 2. (US) jin daɗin jama'a

well [wel] 1. *adj* mai ƙoshin lafiya 2. *n* rijiya 3. **oil well** rijiyar haƙar mâi 4. *adv* da kyau 5. **as well as** har da 6. **very well!** to shi ke nan!

well-being [welˈbiːjiŋ] *n* halin zama

well-off [welˈɔf] *adj* mai hannu da shuni

well-known [welˈnəun] *adj* mashahuri

well-to-do [weltəˈduː] *adj* mai hannu da shuni

went [went] *duba wajen* **go**

were [wəː] *duba wajen* **be**

west [west] 1. *adj* na yamma 2. *n* yamma

West Africa *n* Afirka ta Yamma

western [ˈwestən] 1. *adj* na yamma 2. *n* fim dîn kaboyi

western countries *pl* ƙasashen yammacin duniya

westerner [ˈwestənə] *n* bàyâmmī

West Europe *n* ƙasashen Turai na Yamma

westward(s) [ˈwestwəd] *adv* yamma-yamma

wet [wet] 1. *adj* jiƙaƙƙe 2. *v* jiƙa

wet paint *n* sabon fenti

wet season *n* damina

whale [weil] *n* babbar dabba na teku

wharf [wɔːf] *n* matsayar jirgi

what [wɔt] 1. abin da 2. me? 3. wànè

whatever [wɔtˈevə] 1. kome 2. kōwànè

what for? don me?

whatsoever [ˌwɔtsəuˈevə] ko kaɗan

wheat [wiːt] *n* alkama

wheel [wiːl] *n* wili, (Nr) ƙafar mota

wheelbarrow [ˈwiːlˌbærəu] *n* bāřò, (Nr) bùřwētì

wheelchair [ˈwiːlˌtʃeə] *n* keken hannu

when [wen] 1. lokacin da 2. yaushe? 3. idan

whenever [wenˈevə] koyaushe

where [weə] 1. inda 2. ina?

whereabouts [ˈweərəbauts] *n* inda ake

whereas [ˌweərˈæz] *conj* kùwa

whereby [ˌweərˈbaːi] *conj* ta

whereupon [ˈweərəpɔn] *adv* sai

wherever [ˌweərˈevə] koˈina

whether [ˈweθə] *conj* ko

which [witʃ] 1. wànè 2. wànnē? 3. wanda

whichever [,witʃ'evə] 1. kōwànè 2. kōwànnē

while [wail] 1. n ɗan lokaci 2. lokacin da 3. garin 4. **after a while** jim kaɗan 5. **in a while** in an jima 6. **once in a while** sa'i-sa'i

whip [wip] 1. n bulala 2. v tsala wa... bulala

whirl [wəːl] 1. n His mind is in a whirl. Hankàlinsà ya ƙàzantà. 2. v jujjuya

whirlwind ['wəːlwind] n gùguwā̀

whisker ['wiskə] n gashi

whiskey ['wiski] n wuskì, (Nr) wùskî

whisper ['wispə] v raɗa

whispering ['wispriŋ] n raɗe-raɗe

whistle ['wisl] 1. n usur, (Nr) suhule 2. v yi fito

white [wait] adj fari

whiten ['waitn] v faranta

whitewash ['waitwɔʃ] 1. n farar ƙasa 2. v yi wa... farar ƙasa

WHO (World Health Organization) n Hukumar Kiwon Lafiya ta Duniya

who [huː] 1. wanda 2. wa?

whoever [huː'evə] kowa

whole [həul] adj 1. duk 2. cikakke 3. gàbā ɗaya 4. **the whole (of)** ɗaukacin 5. **on the whole** galibi

whole-heartedly [,həul'haːtidli] adv da zuciya ɗaya

wholesale ['həulseil] adj/adv 1. **to buy wholesale** sara 2. **to sell wholesale** sayar da

wholesaler ['həulseilə] n ɗan sari

wholesale trade ['həulseil] n sari

whom [huːm] duba wajen **who**

whooping cough ['huːpiŋkɔf] n tàrin shiƙà

whose [huːz] 1. na wanda 2. na wa?

whosoever [,huːsəu'evə] kowa

why [wai] 1. abin da ya sa 2. don me?

why not? me zai hana?

wicked ['wikid] adj mugu

wide [waid] adj mai faɗi

wide awake adj a farke

widen ['waidn] v faɗaɗa

widespread ['waidspred] adj **to be widespread** bàzu

widow ['widəu] n mace wadda mijinta ya mutu

widower ['widəuə] n mutum wanda matarsa ta mutu

width [widθ] n faɗi

wield [wiːld] v riƙe

wife [waif] n (pl **wives**) màtā

wild [waild] adj na daji

wild animal n naman daji

wilderness ['wildənis] n ƙungurmin daji

will [wil] 1. n so 2. son rai 3. niyya 4. wasiyya 5. duba wajen **be**

willing ['wiliŋ] adj mai yarda

willingness ['wiliŋnis] n rāɗî

willpower ['wilpauə] n ƙarfin hali

wilt [wilt] v yi yaushi

wimp [wimp] n ragon maza

win [win] v (**won**) ci nasara

wind [wind] n iska

wind [waind] v 1. naɗa 2. yi wa... wani

wind on v naɗa

window ['windəu] n taga

windowpane ['windəupein] n gìlāshìn wundò

windscreen ['windskriːn] n gilashin mota

windscreen wipers [ˈwindskriːn
ˌwaipəz] *n* waifa
windshield [ˈwindʃiːld] *n* (US)
gilashin mota
windy [ˈwindi] *adj* mai iska
wine [wain] *n* giyã, (Nr) duban
wing [wiŋ] *n* fiffike
wink [wiŋk] *v* ƙyifta ido
winner [ˈwinə] *n* wanda ya ci
winnow [ˈwinəu] *v* sheƙa
winter [ˈwintə] *n* lokacin ɗari
wipe [waip] *v* goge
wipe away *v* shafe
wipe out *v* kashe
wiper [ˈwaipə] *n* waifa
wire [waiə] *n* 1. waya, (Nr) fil
2. **barbed wire** waya mai
ƙaya
wisdom [ˈwizdəm] *n* hikima
wise [waiz] *n* mai hankali
wisecrack [ˈwaizkræk] *n* **to make
a wisecrack** yi barkwanci
wish [wiʃ] 1. *n* buri 2. fata 3. *v* so
4. yi fata
wit [wit] *n* 1. azanci 2. barkwanci
witch [witʃ] *n* mayya
witchcraft [ˈwitʃkraːft] *n* maita
with [wið] *prep* 1. da 2. tare da
3. **the man with the moustache**
mutumin mai gashin baki
withdraw [wiðˈdrɔː] *v* (**withdrew,
withdrawn**) 1. noƙe 2. jânyẽ
3. **to withdraw money** karɓo
kuɗi 4. **to withdraw from use**
kashè
withdrawal [wiðˈdrɔːəl] *n* 1. (fin.)
karɓar kuɗi 2. (mil.) ja da baya
withdrawn [wiðˈdrɔːən] *adj* mai
kawaici
wither [ˈwiðə] *v* yi yaushi
withhold [wiðˈhəuld] *v* riƙe
within [wiˈðin] *adv* 1. a ciki

2. cikin 3. **within one year**
kafin shekara ta kewayo
without [wiˈðaut] *prep* 1. ban da
2. ba tare da... ba 3. **without a
doubt** ba shakka 4. **without
fail** bâ makawã
withstand [wiðˈstænd] *v* daddage
wa
witness [ˈwitnis] 1. *n* mai shaida
2. **to bear witness** shâidã
3. *v* gani
witty [ˈwiti] *adj* 1. mai iya zance
2. mai barwanci
wives [waivz] *duba wajen* **wife**
wizard [ˈwizəd] *n* maye
wobble [ˈwɔbl] *v* yi rawa
woe [wəu] *n* **economic woes**
lâlâcêewar tattalin arzìki
woke, woken [wəuk; wəukn]
duba wajen **wake**
wolf [wulf] *n* (**wolves**) dilan Turai
woman [ˈwumən] *n* (*pl* **women**)
mace
womankind [wumənkaind] *n*
mãtã
womb [wuːm] *n* mahaifa
women [ˈwimin] *pl* 1. mãtã
2. *duba wajen* **woman**
won [wʌn] *duba wajen* **win**
wonder [ˈwʌndə] 1. *n* mamaki
2. abin al'ajabi 3. *v* yi mamaki
4. yi waswasi 5. **I wonder
whether she'll come.** Ko za ta
zo kuwa?
wonderful [ˈwʌndəfl] *adj* 1. mai
ban mamaki 2. mai ban al'ajabi
woo [wuː] *v* nèmã dà aurẽ
wood [wud] *n* 1. ice 2. kurmi
wooden [ˈwudn] *adj* na ice
woods [wudz] *n* kurmi
wool [wul] *n* ulu
woollen [ˈwulən] *adj* na ulu

word [wəːd] *n* **1.** kalma **2. in other words** watau **3. to have a word** gana (**with** da) **4. to keep one's word** cika alkawari

wore [wɔː] *duba wajen* wear

work [wəːk] **1.** *n* aiki **2.** *v* yi aiki **3.** yi amfani **4. He is out of work.** Ba shi da aiki.

workable [ˈwəːkəbl] *adj* **to be workable** tsåru

workday [ˈwəːkdei] *n* ranar aiki

worker [ˈwəːkə] *n* ma'aikaci

working [ˈwəːkiŋ] *adj* **in working order**

workman [ˈwəːkmən] *n* ma'aikaci

workmanship [ˈwəːkmənʃip] *n* fasaha

work off *v* rage

work out *v* **1.** tsara shiri **2.** motsa jiki **3.** ci

workplace [ˈwəːkpleis] *n* gurbin aiki

workshop [ˈwəːkʃɔp] *n* **1.** ma'aikata **2.** bita, (Nr) istaji

work to rule *v* yi ƙayyadajjen aiki

world [wəːld] **1.** *adj* na duniya **2.** *n* duniya

World Bank *n* Bankin Duniya

World Cup *n* Bikin Kofin Duniya na Kwallon Kafa

World Health Organization *n* Hukumar Kiwon Lafiya ta Duniya

world market *n* kasuwannin duniya

world market prices *pl* farashin kasuwannin duniya

World Muslim Congress *n* Kungiyar Musulman Duniya

world power *n* ƙasa mai ikon faɗa-a-ji

world record, world title *n* bajintar duniya (**in wajen**)

World War One *n* Yaƙin Duniya na Farko

World War Two *n* Yaƙin Duniya na Biyu

worldwide [wəːldˈwaid] *adv* a duniya gaba ɗaya

worm [wəːm] *n* tsutsa

worn [wɔːn] *duba wajen* wear

worn out *adj* **to be worn out** **1.** gaji **2.** sha jiki

worried [ˈwʌrid] *adj* **to be worried** damu

worry [ˈwʌri] **1.** *n* abin damuwa **2.** (fin.) matsuwa sha jiki **3.** *v* dåmå **4.** damu

worrying [ˈwʌriiŋ] **1.** *adj* mai damuwa **2.** *n* damuwa

worse [wəːs] *adj* mafi muni

worsen [ˈwəːsn] *v* ta'azzara

worship [ˈwəːʃip] **1.** *n* ibada **2.** *v* bâutã

worst [wəːst] *adj* mafi muni duk

worth [wəːθ] **1.** *adj* mai amfani **2.** *n* daraja **3.** ƙima

worthless [ˈwəːθlis] *adj* na banza

worthwhile [wəːθˈwail] *adj* mai muhimmanci

worthy [ˈwəːði] *adj* mai daraja

would [wud] *duba wajen* will

wound [waund] *duba wajen* wind

wound [wuːnd] **1.** *n* rauni, (Nr) balshe **2.** *v* yi wa... rauni

wounded [ˈwuːndid] *adj* mai rauni

wove, woven [wəuv; wəuvn] *duba wajen* weave

wrangling [ˈræŋgliŋ] *n* cacar baki

wrap [ræp] *v* **1.** ƙunshe **2.** yafa

wrap round *v* naɗa

wrapper [ˈræpə] *n* zane
wreath [riːθ] *n* furannin jana'iza
wreck [rek] **1.** *n* **car wreck** matacciyar mota **2.** *v* ragargaza
wrench [rentʃ] **1.** *n* sufana, (Nr) kile amulat **2.** *v* fizge
wrestle [ˈresl] *v* yi kokawa
wrestler [ˈreslə] *n* ɗan kokawa
wrestling [ˈresliŋ] *n* kokawa
wretched [ˈretʃid] *adj* miskini
wriggle [ˈrigl] *v* yi watsal-watsal
wrinkle [ˈriŋkl] *n* ɗan tamoji
wrist [rist] *n* wuyan hannu

wrist watch [ˈristwɔtʃ] *n* agogon hannu
writ [rit] *n* (leg.) ƙara
write [rait] *v* (wrote, written) rubuta
writer [ˈraitə] *n* marubuci
writing [ˈraitiŋ] *n* rubutu
written [ˈritn] *adj* **1.** à rùbùce **2.** *duba wajen* **write**
wrong [rɔŋ] **1.** *adj* ba daidai ba **2.** *n* lâifî **3.** saɓa wa
wrongdoing [ˈrɔŋduːiŋ] *n* saɓo
wrote [rəut] *duba wajen* **write**

Xx

xenophobia [ˌzenəˈfəubjə] *n*
halin ƙyamar baƙi

xenophobic [ˌzenəˈfəubik] *adj*
mai ganin ƙyamar baƙi

xerox [ˈzerɔks] **1.** *n* kwafè,
(Nr) kòpî **2.** *v* yi kwafè, yi
kòpî

Xmas [ˈeksməs] *n* Kirsimati, (Nr)
Nòwâl

X-ray [ˈeksrei] *n* hoto, (Nr)
radiyo **2. to take an x-ray**
ɗauki hoto

X-ray room [ˈeksrei,rum] *n*
ɗakin hoto

Yy

yacht [jɔt] *n* jirgin ruwa mai filafili

yam [jæm] *n* doya

yank [jænk] *v* fizge

yard [jɑːd] *n* **1.** yadi **2.** farfajiya **3.** lambu, (US) garka

yawn [jɔːn] **1.** *n* hamma **2.** *v* yi hamma

year [jiə] *n* **1.** shekara **2. the year before last** bàra wàccan **3. last year** bàra **4. this year** bana **5. next year** bàɗi **6. the year after next** bàɗi wàccan **7. all year round** rānì dà dàminā

yearly [ˈjiəli] *adj* na shekara-shekara

yearning [ˈjəːniŋ] *n* bege

yeast [jiːst] *n* yîs

yell [jel] **1.** *n* kuwwa **2.** *v* yi kuwwa

yellow [ˈjeləu] *adj* rawaya

yellow fever *n* shāwařà

yes [jes] **1.** i **2.** na'am

yes-man [ˈjesmæn] *n* ɗan kan zagi

yesterday [ˈjestədei] *n/adv* **1.** jiya **2. the day before yesterday** shekaranjiya

yesterday's [ˈjestədeiz] *adj* na jiya

yet [jet] *adv* **1.** tukuna **2.** duk da haka

yield [jiːld] **1.** *n* yawa **2.** *v* sakar da

yoghurt [ˈjɔgət] *n* kindirmo

yolk [jəuk] *n* gwaiduwa

Yoruba [ˈjɔrubə] *n* **1.** Bayarabe **2.** Yarabanci

you [juː] *pro* kai, ke, ku

young [jʌŋ] *adj* **1.** ƙarami **2.** sabo

your, yours [jɔː; jɔːz] naka, naki, naku

yourself [jɔːˈself] kanka, kanki

yourselves [jɔːˈselvz] kanku

youth [juːθ] **1.** *adj* na ƙuruciya **2.** *n* matashi

youthful [ˈjuːθfl] *adj* mai ƙuruciya

Zz

zany [ˈzeɪnɪ] *adj* mai ban dariya
zap [zæp] *v* haɓè
zeal [ziːəl] *n* himma
zealous [ˈzeləs] *adj* mai himma
zebra [ˈzebrə] *n* jakin dawa
zenith [ˈzenɪθ] *n* ganiya
zero [ˈzɪərəu] *n* sifiri
zigzag [ˈzɪgzæg] *adj* mai wandar-
   wandar
zinc [zɪŋk] *n* kwano
zip [zɪp] *n* zik, (Nr) zi
zip code [ˈzɪpkəud] (US) *n* lambar
   titi

zipper [ˈzɪpə] *duba wajen* zip
zip up *v* ja zik
zodiac [ˈzəudiæk] *n* falaki
zone [zəun] *n* ɓangare
zoo [zuː] *n* gidan zu
zoologist [zuːˈɔlədʒɪst] *n* mai
   ilimin sanin dabbobi
zoological [ˌzuːɔˈlɔdʒɪkl] *adj* na
   ilimin sanin dabbobi
zoological gardens *n* gidan zu
zoology [zuːˈɔlədʒɪ] *n* ilimin sanin
   dabbobi
zoom [zuːm] *v* yi gudu

Appendices

Appendix 1:

ENGLISH IRREGULAR VERBS

Infinitive	Past tense	Past participle
arise *(tashi)*	arose	arisen
awake *(farka)*	awoke	awoken
be *(kasance)*	was/were	been
bear *(ɗauka)*	bore	borne
beat *(buga)*	beat	beaten
become *(zama)*	became	become
begin *(fara)*	began	begun
bend *(lankwasa)*	bent	bent
bet *(yi caca)*	bet, betted	bet, betted
bid *(sa kudî)*	bid, bade	bid, bidden
bind *(daure)*	bound	bound
bite *(ciza)*	bit	bitten
bleed *(yi jini)*	bled	bled
blow *(busa)*	blew	blown
break *(karya)*	broke	broken
breed *(haifar da)*	bred	bred
bring *(kawo)*	brought	brought
build *(gina)*	built	built
burn *(ƙona)*	burnt, burned	burnt, burned
burst *(fashe)*	burst	burst
buy *(saya)*	bought	bought
cast *(jefa)*	cast	cast
catch *(kama)*	caught	caught
choose *(zaɓa)*	chose	chosen
cling *(ɗafe)*	clung	clung
come *(zo)*	came	come
cost *(ci kudî)*	cost	cost
creep *(yi sanɗa)*	crept	crept
cut *(yanka)*	cut	cut
deal *(yi ciniki)*	dealt	dealt
dig *(haƙa)*	dug	dug
dive *(yi alkahura)*	dived; (US) dove	dived
do *(yi)*	did	done
draw *(ja)*	drew	drawn

dream *(yi mafarki)*	dreamt, dreamed	dreamt, dreamed
drink *(sha)*	drank	drunk
drive *(tuka)*	drove	driven
dwell *(zauna)*	dwelt, dwelled	dwelt, dwelled
eat *(ci)*	ate	eaten
fall *(fadi)*	fell	fallen
feed *(ci da)*	fed	fed
feel *(ji)*	felt	felt
fight *(yi fada)*	fought	fought
find *(samu)*	found	found
flee *(gudu)*	fled	fled
fling *(watsar da)*	flung	flung
fly *(tashi sama)*	flew	flown
forbid *(hana)*	forbade, forbad	forbade, forbad
forecast *(yi hasashe)*	forecast, forecasted	forecast, forecasted
forget *(manta)*	forgot	forgotten
freeze *(kame)*	froze	frozen
get *(samu)*	got	got; (US) gotten
give *(ba)*	gave	given
go *(je)*	went	gone
grind *(nika)*	ground	ground
grow *(girma)*	grew	grown
hang *(rataya)*	hung, hanged	hung, hanged
have *(mallaka)*	had	had
hear *(ji)*	heard	heard
hide *(boye)*	hid	hidden
hit *(buga)*	hit	hit
hold *(rike)*	held	held
hurt *(ji rauni)*	hurt	hurt
input *(sa)*	input, inputted	input, inputted
keep *(adana)*	kept	kept
kneel *(durkusa)*	knelt, kneeled	knelt, kneeled
know *(sani)*	knew	known
lay *(ajiya)*	laid	laid
lead *(yi wa ja-gora)*	led	led
lean *(jingina)*	leant, leaned	leant, leaned
leap *(tsallake)*	leapt, leaped	leapt, leaped
learn *(koya)*	learnt, leaned	learnt, leaned
leave *(bari)*	left	left
lend *(ranta)*	lent	lent
let *(bari)*	let	let
lie *(kwanta)*	lay	lain

light *(kunna)*	lit, lighted	lit, lighted
lose *(rasa)*	lost	lost
make *(ƙera)*	made	made
mean *(nuna alama)*	meant	meant
meet *(gamu da)*	met	met
misunderstand *(rasa fahimta)*	misunderstood	misunderstood
mow *(yanke ciyawa)*	mowed	mown, mowed
overthrow *(hamɓarar da)*	overthrew	overthrown
pay *(biya)*	paid	paid
prove *(tabbatar da)*	proved	proved; (US) proven
put *(sa)*	put	put
quit *(daina)*	quit, quitted	quit, quitted
read *(karanta)*	read [red]	read [red]
rend *(ɓarka)*	rent	rent
rid *(ya da)*	rid	rid
ride *(hau)*	rode	ridden
ring *(kaɗa kararrawa)*	rang	rung
rise *(tashi)*	rose	risen
run *(yi gudu)*	ran	run
saw *(yanka da zarto)*	sawed	sawn; (US) sawed
say *(ce)*	said	said
see *(gani)*	saw	seen
seek *(nema)*	sought	sought
sell *(sayar da)*	sold	sold
send *(aika da)*	sent	sent
set *(ajiye)*	set	set
sew *(dinka)*	sewed	sewn, sewed
shake *(kaɗa)*	shook	shaken
shed *(zub da)*	shed	shed
shear *(yanke gashi)*	sheared	shorn, sheared
shine *(yi haske)*	shone	shone
shoot *(harba)*	shot	shot
show *(nuna)*	showed	shown, showed
shrink *(ɗage)*	shrank, shrunk	shrunk
shut *(rufe)*	shut	shut
sing *(rera waka)*	sang	sung
sink *(nitse)*	sank	sunk
sit *(zauna)*	sat	sat
sleep *(yi barci)*	slept	slept
slide *(zame)*	slit	slit

sling *(jefa)*	slung	slung
slit *(tsaga)*	slit	slit
smell *(sansana)*	smelt, smelled	smelt, smelled
sow *(shuka)*	sowed	sown, sowed
speak *(yi magana)*	spoke	spoken
speed *(yi sauri)*	sped, speeded	sped, speeded
spell *(rubuta kalma)*	spelt, spelled	spelt, spelled
spend *(kashe kuɗi)*	spent	spent
spill *(zub da)*	split, spilled	spilt, spilled
spin *(juya)*	spun	spun
spit *(tofa)*	spat; (US) spit	spat; (US) spit
split *(tsaga)*	split	split
spoil *(ɓata)*	spoilt, spoiled	spoilt, spoiled
spread *(yaɗa)*	spread	spread
spring *(yi tsalle)*	sprang	sprung
stand *(tsaya)*	stood	stood
steal *(yi sata)*	stole	stolen
stick *(liƙa)*	stuck	stuck
sting *(harba)*	stung	stung
stink *(yi wari)*	stank, stunk	stunk
strike *(doka)*	struck	struck
strive *(yi ƙoƙari)*	strove	striven
swear *(rantse)*	swore	sworn
sweep *(shara)*	swept	swept
swell *(kumbura)*	swelled	swollen, swelled
swim *(yi iyo)*	swam	swum
swing *(yi lilo)*	swung	swung
take *(ɗauka)*	took	taken
teach *(koya wa)*	taught	taught
tear *(kece)*	tore	torn
tell *(faɗa)*	told	told
think *(yi tsammani)*	thought	thought
thrive *(yi albarka)*	thrived, throve	thrived
throw *(jefa)*	threw	thrown
thrust *(dirka)*	thrust	thrust
tread *(taka)*	trod	trodden, trod
undergo *(ɗanɗana)*	underwent	undergone
understand *(fahimta)*	understood	understood
undertake *(ɗauki nauyi)*	undertook	undertaken
undo *(kwance)*	undid	undone
wake *(farkar da)*	woke, waked	woken, waked
wear *(sa tufafi)*	wore	worn

weave *(saƙa)*	wove	woven
weep *(yi kuka)*	wept	wept
wet *(jiƙa)*	wet, wetted	wet, wetted
win *(ci nasara)*	won	won
wind *(naɗa)*	wound	wound
wring *(matsa)*	wrung	wrung
write *(rubuta)*	wrote	written

Appendix 2:

HAUSA VERBS

v1 – TRANSITIVE AND INTRANSITIVE

2-SYLLABLES: kāmà *'to take'*

Without object	**nā kāmà** – *'I took'*
Plus pronoun object	**nā kāmà shi** – *'I took it'*
Plus noun object	**nā kāmà r̄ēdiyò** – *'I took the gown'*
Plus indirect object	*a)* **nā kāmà matà r̄ēdiyò** – *'I took the radio for her'*
	b) **nā kāmà wà Mar̄yàm r̄ēdiyò** – *'I took the gown for Maryam'*

IMPERATIVES

Without object	**kàmā!** – *'take!'*
Plus pronoun object	**kàmā shi!** – *'take it!'*
Plus noun object	**kàma r̄ēdiyò!** – *'take the radio!'*
and, occasionally:	**kàmà r̄ēdiyò!**
Plus indirect object	*a)* **kàmā matà r̄ēdiyò!** – *'take the radio for her!'*
	b) **kàmā wà Mar̄yàm r̄ēdiyò!** – *'take the gown for Maryam!'*

3-SYLLABLES: kar̄àntā – *'to read'*

| *Without object* | **nā kar̄àntā** – *'I read'* |
| *Plus pronoun object* | **nā kar̄àntā shi** – *'I read it'* |

Note the non-polar pronouns – they are always **high.**

Plus noun object	**nā kaȓàntà lìttāfī** – *'I read the book'.*
Plus indirect object	*a)* **nā kaȓàntā matà lìttāfī** – *'I read the book for her'.*
	b) **nā kaȓàntā wà Maȓyàm lìttāfī** – *'I read the book for Maryam'.*

IMPERATIVES

Without object	**kàȓàntā!** – *'read!'*
Plus pronoun object	**kàȓàntā shì!** – *'read it!'*

Direct object pronouns here are **always** *high.*

Plus noun object	**kàȓàntà lìttāfī!** – *'read the book!'*
Plus indirect object	*a)* **kàȓàntā matà lìttāfī!** – *'read the book for her!'*
	b) **kàȓàntā wà Maȓyàm lìttāfī!** – *'read the book for Maryam!'*

VERBAL NOUNS

Weak:

kāmà	→	**kāmàwā**
kaȓàntā	→	**kaȓantàwā**

Strong:

This Grade permits some commonly-used verbs to form strong verbal nouns, none of which can be predicted, and most of these verbs can also form weak verbal nouns regularly, e.g. **kāmà** *also has the strong verbal noun* **kāmù,** *and* **kaȓàntā** *has also* **kàȓàtū.** *Often there is a difference in meaning between the two, the weak representing the CONTINUOUS action of the verb, and the strong, the COMPLETED action and, often, the ABSTRACT meaning of a verb.*

v2 – TRANSITIVE

2-SYLLABLES: sàyā – *'to buy'*

Without object	**nā sàyā** – *'I bought'*
Plus pronoun object	**nā sàyē tà** – *'I bought it'.*
Plus noun object	**nā sàyi fìȓjì** – *'I bought the fridge'.*
Plus indirect object	*There is no Plus indirect object for this Grade.*

Plus indirect objects from other grades, however, are borrowed and used normally. This is not predictable. The grades borrowed from are:

a) **Grade 1** *e.g.* **nā sayà matà fìȓjì, nā sayà wà Maȓyàm fìȓjì** *(for Grade 2* **sàyā***).*

b) Grade 2 e.g. nă sōkam matà Iliyă *or* nă sōkaŕ matà Iliyă – *'I stabbed Iliya for her' (for Grade 2* sōkă – *'to stab').*

c) Grade 4 (rare) e.g. nă săcě matà fīŕjì – *'I stole the fridge for her' (for Grade 2* sătă – *'to steal').*

IMPERATIVES

Without object	sàyi! – *'buy!'*
Plus pronoun object	sàyè shi! – *'buy it!'*
Plus noun object	sàyi fīŕjì! – *'buy the fridge!'*
Plus indirect object	sàyam matà fīŕjì! – *'buy the fridge for her!'*
	etc.

The imperative in the Plus indirect object is borrowed from Grades 1, 5 or 4, depending on the verb. Here sàyă *borrows from Grade 5.*

3-SYLLABLES: tàmbayà – *'to ask'*

Without object	nă tàmbayà – *'I asked'*
Plus pronoun object	nă tàmbàyē shì – *'I asked him'*
Plus noun object	nă tàmbàyi Maŕyàm – *'I asked Maryam'*
Plus indirect object	*see note above for 2-syllables*

IMPERATIVES

Without object	tàmbàyă! – *'ask!'*
Plus pronoun object	tàmbàyè ta! – *'ask her!'*
Plus noun object	tàmbàyi Maŕyàm! – *'ask Maryam!'*
Plus indirect object	*see note above for 2-syllables*

VERBAL NOUNS

No weak verbal noun pattern exists for Grade 2 verbs. The basic (strong) verbal noun pattern is to make a feminine noun from the Without object verb itself – e.g. tàmbayà *(f) is the verbal noun of* tàmbayà, hàrbā *(f) is the verbal noun of* hàrbā – *'to shoot'. Many verbs in this grade, though, form strong verbal nouns irregularly, e.g.* sàyè *gives* sayè *(m) as its verbal noun – etc. These are not predictable.*

v3 – INTRANSITIVE

2-SYLLABLE VERBS: fìta – *'to go out'*

Without object	nă fìta – *'I went out'.*
Plus indirect object	*see the notes for Grade 2*

IMPERATIVES
Without object   **fíta!** – *'get out!'*
Plus indirect object   *see the notes for Grade 2*

3-SYLLABLES: kàmmalà – *'to be finished'*

Without object   **yā kàmmalà** – *'it is finished'*
Plus indirect object   *See the notes for 2-syllable Plus indirect*
    object Imperatives.

IMPERATIVES
Without object   **kàmmàla!** – *'be finished!'*
Plus indirect object   *See the notes for 2-syllable Plus indirect*
    object Imperatives.

VERBAL NOUNS
   fíta   →   fítā
   kàmmalà →   kàmmalā

v4 – TRANSITIVE AND INTRANSITIVE

2-SYLLABLE VERBS: rìƙè – *'to hold'*

Without object   **nā rìƙè** – *'I held'*
Plus pronoun object   **nā rìƙè shi** – *'I held it'*
Plus noun object   **nā rìƙè fēdiyò** – *'I held the radio'*
Plus indirect object   *a)* **nā rìƙè matà fēdiyò** – *'I held the radio for*
    her'
    b) **nā rìƙè wà Kànde fēdiyò** – *'I held the*
    radio for Kande'

IMPERATIVES
Without object   **rìƙē!** – *'hold!'*
Plus pronoun object   **rìƙē shi!** – *'hold it!'*
Direct object pronouns are always high in tone.
Plus noun object   **rìƙe fēdiyò!** – *'hold the radio!'*
and, occasionally: **rìƙè fēdiyò!**
Plus indirect object   *a)* **rìƙē minì fēdiyò!** – *'hold the radio for*
    me!'
    b) **rìƙē wà Maryàm fēdiyò!** – *'hold the radio*
    for Maryam!'

3-SYLLABLES: danƙàrē – *'to pack down'*

Without object	**nā danƙàrē** – *'I packed down'*
Plus pronoun object	**nā danƙàrē shì** – *'I packed it down'*

Direct object pronouns are always **high** *in tone.*

Plus noun object	**nā danƙàrè kāyā** – *'I packed the stuff down'*
Plus indirect object	**nā danƙàrē musù kāyā** – *'I packed the stuff down for them'*

IMPERATIVES

Without object	**dànƙàrē!** – *'pack down!'*
Plus pronoun object	**dànƙàrē shì!** – *'pack it down!'*

Direct object pronouns are always **high** *in tone.*

Plus noun object	**dànƙàre kāyā!** – *'pack the stuff down!'*
Plus indirect object	**dànƙàrē musù kāyā!** – *'pack the stuff down for them!'*

VERBAL NOUNS

Grade 4 verbal nouns are weak

riƙè	→	**riƙèwā**
danƙàrē	→	**danƙàrêwā**

v5 – TRANSITIVE

2-SYLLABLES: cìyař dà – *'to feed'*

Without object	**nā cìyař** – *'I fed (someone/something)'*
Plus pronoun object	**nā cìyař dà sū** – *'I fed them'*
Plus noun object	**nā cìyař dà yârā** – *'I fed the kids'*
Plus indirect object	*a)* **nā cìyař matà (dà) yârā** – *'I fed the kids for her'*
dà *is optional*	
	b) **nā cìyař wà Mařyàm (dà) yârā** – *'I fed the kids for Maryam'*

IMPERATIVE

Without object	**cìyař!** – *'feed (someone or something)!'*
Plus pronoun object	**cìyař dà sū!** – *'feed them!'*
Plus noun object	**cìyař dà yârā!** – *'feed the kids!'*
Plus indirect object	*a)* **cìyař matà (dà) yârā!** – *'feed the kids for her!'*

Note that dà is optional

> b) cìyaȓ wà Maȓyàm (dà) yârā! – *'feed the children for Maryam!'*

3-SYLLABLES: tabbataȓ dà – *'to confirm'*

Without object	nā tabbataȓ – *'I confirmed'*
Plus pronoun object	nā tabbataȓ dà ita – *'I confirmed it'*
Plus noun object	nā tabbataȓ dà mà'ànā – *'I confirmed the meaning'*
Plus indirect object	a) nā tabbataȓ masà (dà) mà'ànā – *'I confirmed the meaning for him'*
	b) nā tabbataȓ wà Iliyā (dà) mà'ànā – *'I confirmed the meaning for Iliya'*

IMPERATIVE

Without object	tàbbàtaȓ! – *'confirm!'*
Plus pronoun object	tàbbàtaȓ dà ita! – *'confirm it!'*
Plus noun object	tàbbàtaȓ dà mà'ànā! – *'confirm the meaning!'*
Plus indirect object	a) tàbbàtaȓ masà (dà) mà'ànā! – *'confirm the meaning for him!'*
	b) tàbbàtaȓ wà Audù (dà) mà'ànā! – *'confirm the meaning for him!'*

Note that tàbbàtad dà for tàbbàtaȓ dà is also used

VERBAL NOUNS (weak)

ciyaȓ dà	→	ciyâȓwā (*also* ciyâswā)
tabbataȓ dà	→	tabbatâȓwā (*also* tabbatâswā)

SHORT FORMS

As well as being found in their long forms (see above), a limited number of commonly used Grade 5 2-SYLLABLE verbs can be found in a truncated, or contracted, form. This appearance of this form is related mainly to the fact that these verbs tend to have a final 'weak' consonant, -y-, in their root (e.g. maYaȓ dà, 'to put back' → maI dà), or a -t- which will assimilate to d, e.g. fīTaȓ dà, 'to extract' → fīTaD dà → fīD dà). This form is used with a DIRECT OBJECT, e.g.

mai dà – *'to put back' (from* mayaȓ dà*).*

Without object	[nā mayaȓ]

Plus pronoun object	nā mai dà ita – *'I put it back'*
Plus noun object	nā mai dà fĕdiyò – *'I put the radio back'*
Plus indirect object	[nā mayaf masà *(dà)* fĕdiyò / nā mayaf wà Mafyàm fĕdiyò]

IMPERATIVE

Without object	[màyaf!]
Plus pronoun object	mài dà ita! – *'put it back!'*
Plus noun object	mài dà fĕdiyò! – *'put the radio back!'*
Plus indirect object	[màyaf masà *(dà)* fĕdiyò! / màyaf wà Mafyàm fĕdiyò!]

NOTE:
*In the Plus pronoun object of this short form, some verbs add the suffix
-shē instead of dà. The resulting form makes a DIRECTLY TRANSITIVE
GRADE 5 verb form. This means that this new form will use DIRECT
OBJECT PRONOUNS instead of the independent pronouns used in the
other two Grade 5 verb forms as required by the dà preposition that
occurs in both, e.g.* gayaf dà *('to greet with' – i.e. 'to greet'
(transitive))* → gai dà → gaishē *(trans), e.g.* mun gaishē tà – *'we
greeted her' (=* mun gai dà ita = mun gayaf dà ita*). The final -T/-D of
verbs like* fitaf dà/fid dà *will assimilate once again for this form, this
time to SH under the influence of the -shē suffix, e.g.* fid dà *becomes*
fiSshē *(transitive). These forms always occur with a direct object
pronoun. The imperative simply follows the standard LOW-HIGH tone
pattern, e.g.* gàishē tà! – *'greet her!',* fìsshē tà! – *'take it out!'.*

V6 – TRANSITIVE AND INTRANSITIVE

2-SYLLABLE VERBS: kāwō – *'to bring'*

Without object	nā kāwō – *'I brought'*
Plus pronoun object	nā kāwō tà – *'I brought it'*
Plus noun object	nā kāwō mōtà – *'I brought the car'*
Plus indirect object	*a)* nā kāwō matà mōtà – *'I brought the car for her'*
	b) nā kāwō wà Mafyàm mōtà – *'I brought the car for Maryam'*

IMPERATIVE:

| *Without object* | kàwō! – *'bring!'* |

Plus pronoun object	**kàwō tà!** – *'bring it!'*
Plus noun object	**kàwō mōtà!** – *'bring the car!'*
Plus indirect object	*a)* **kàwō matà mōtà!** – *'bring the car for her!'*
	b) **kàwō wà Maryàm mōtà!** – *'bring the car for Maryam!'*

3-SYLLABLES: kirāwō – *'to call'*

Without object	**nā kirāwō** – *'I called'*
Plus pronoun object	**nā kirāwō shì** – *'I called him'*
Plus noun object	**nā kirāwo Iliyā** – *'I called Iliya'*
Plus indirect object	*a)* **nā kirāwō matà Iliyā** – *'I called Iliya for her'*
	b) **nā kirāwō wà Maryàm Iliyā** – *'I called Iliya for Maryam'*

IMPERATIVE

Without object	**kìràwō!** – *'call!'*
Plus pronoun object	**kìràwō shì!** – *'call him!'*
Plus noun object	**kìràwo Iliyā!** – *'call Iliya!'*
Plus indirect object	*a)* **kìràwō matà Iliyā!** – *'call Iliya for her!'*
	b) **kìràwō wà Maryàm Iliyā!** – *'call Iliya for Maryam!'*

Note that a long final **-ō** *may also be heard in all the Plus noun object forms above.*

VERBAL NOUNS (weak)

kāwō	→	**kāwôwā**
kirāwō	→	**kirāwôwā**

v7 – INTRANSITIVE

2-SYLLABLES: kàmu – *'to get captured'*

Without object	**nā kàmu** – *'I was captured'*
Plus indirect object	*No grade 7 form exists – however, grade 7*

behaves like grades 2 and 3 in that it borrows from corresponding forms in grades 1, 5 or 4.

IMPERATIVE
Without object   **kàmu!** – *'get captured!'*
Plus indirect object   *See Grade 2 Imperative notes.*

3-SYLLABLES: dàddàmu – *'to fret'*

Without object   **nā dàddàmu** – *'I fretted'*
Plus indirect object   *See notes to 2-syllable verbs.*

IMPERATIVE
Without object   **dàddàmu!** – *'fret!'*
Plus indirect object   *See notes to 2-syllable imperatives.*

VERBAL NOUN (weak)
  kàmu   →   **kàmūwā**
  dàddàmu →   **dàddàmūwā**

Appendix 3:

HAUSA PRONOUNS

1. INDEPENDENT PRONOUNS

nì	I
kai	you *masculine*
kē	you *feminine*
shì	he
ita	she
mū	we
kū	you *plural*
sū	they

2. OBJECT PRONOUNS
DIRECT OBJECT

ni/nì	mu/mù
ka/kà	ku/kù
ki/kì	su/sù
shi/shì	
ta/tà	

INDIRECT OBJECT

minì (mîn)	manà
makà (mã, mâ)	mukù
mikì	musù
masà	
matà	

3. POSSESSIVE PRONOUNS

ATTACHED

Masculine

-nã	-nmù
-nkà	-nkù
-nkì	-nsù
-nsà	
-ntà	

Feminine

-tã	-r̄mù
-r̄kà	-r̄kù
-r̄kì	-r̄sù
-r̄sà	
-r̄tà	

INDEPENDENT

Masculine

nàwa	nãmù
nãkà	nãkù
nãkì	nãsù
nãsà	
nãtà	

Feminine

tàwa	tãmù
tãkà	tãkù
tãkì	tãsù
tãsà	
tãtà	

4. SUBJECT PRONOUNS

COMPLETIVE

nã	mun
kã	kun

kin	sun
yā	
tā	
an	

RELATIVE COMPLETIVE

na	mukà
ka	kukà
kikà	sukà
ya	
ta	
akà	

NEGATIVE COMPLETIVE

bàn... ba	bà mù... ba
bà kà... ba	bà kù... ba
bà kì... ba	bà sù... ba
bài... ba	
bà tà... ba	
bà à... ba	

CONTINUOUS

inà	munà
kanà	kunà
kinà	sunà
yanà	
tanà	
anà	

RELATIVE CONTINUOUS

nakè	mukè
kakè	kukè
kikè	sukè
yakè	
takè	
akè	*(Note:* **nakè** *etc. with non-verbal predicates)*

NEGATIVE CONTINUOUS

bā nà	bā mà
bā kà	bā kwà
bā kyà	bā swà
bā yà	

bǎ tǎ
bǎ ǎ

FUTURE

zân	zǎ mù
zǎ kà	zǎ kù
zǎ kì	zǎ sù
zâí	
zǎ tǎ	
zǎ à	

NEGATIVE FUTURE
bà zân... ba
etc.

INDEFINITE FUTURE

nâ	mâ
kâ	kwâ
kyâ	sâ
yâ	
tâ	
â	

NEGATIVE INDEFINITE FUTURE
bà nâ... ba
etc.

SUBJUNCTIVE

ìn	mù
kà	sù
kì	kù
yà	
à	

NEGATIVE SUBJUNCTIVE
kadà ìn
etc.

HABITUAL

nakàn	mukàn
kakàn	kukàn
kikàn	sukàn

yakàn
takàn
akàn

NEGATIVE HABITUAL
(Use negative continuous)

'HAVE'

inà dà	munà dà
kanà dà	kunà dà
kinà dà	sunà dà
yanà dà	
tanà dà	
anà dà	

NEGATIVE 'HAVE'

bâ ni dà	bâ mu dà
bâ ka dà	bâ ku dà
bâ ki dà	bâ su dà
bâ shi dà	
bâ ta dà	
bâ a dà	

Appendix 4:

USEFUL PHRASES AND VOCABULARY

good morning	barka da safe
response:	barka kadai
good day	barka da rana
response:	barka kadai
good afternoon	barka da yamma
response:	barka kadai
good evening	barka da yamma
response:	barka kadai
good night	mu kwana lafiya

response:	**mu kwana lafiya**
hello	**sannu**
response:	**yauwa sannu / sannu kadai**
goodbye	**sai an jima**
response:	**sai an jima / to, sai an jima**
till tomorrow	**sai gobe**
till another time	**sai wani lokaci**
response:	**Allah ya kai mu**
excuse me!	**gafara (dai)!**
I don't understand.	**ban ji ba**
help!	**zo ku taimake ni!**
stop!	**tsaya!**
how much?	**nawa ne?**
how much each?	**nawa nawa ne?**
yes	**i**
no	**a'a**
please	**don Allah**
thank you	**na gode**
ladies	**mata**
gentlemen	**maza**
toilet	**bayan gida**
sir	**Allah shi gafarta Malam**
madam	**Allah shi gafarta Malama**

I do not speak Hausa.	**Ban iya Hausa ba.**
I only speak a little Hausa.	**Ina jin Hausa amma ba sosai ba.**
Do you speak English?	**Shin, ka/kin/kun ji Turanci?**
Please speak more clearly.	**Don Allah, yi magana a hankali.**
I do not understand	**Ban gane ba.**

Can you give me a lift to...?	**Don Allah, ka kai ni....**
I am in a hurry.	**Ina sauri.**
Thank you very much.	**Na gode ƙwarai.**
What is your name?	**Yaya sunanka/ki?**
My name is....	**Sunana...**
It is free of charge.	**Na kyauta ne.**
Bon voyage!	**A sauka lafiya!**

CARDINAL NUMBERS

one	1	ɗaya
two	2	biyu
three	3	uku
four	4	huɗu
five	5	biyar
six	6	shida
seven	7	bakwai
eight	8	takwas
nine	9	tara
ten	10	goma
eleven	11	goma sha ɗaya
twelve	12	goma sha biyu
thirteen	13	goma sha uku
fourteen	14	goma sha huɗu
fifteen	15	goma sha biyar
sixteen	16	goma sha shida
seventeen	17	goma sha bakwai
eighteen	18	goma sha takwas
nineteen	19	goma sha tara
twenty	20	ashirin
twenty one	21	ashirin da ɗaya
twenty two	22	ashirin da biyu
thirty	30	talatin
forty	40	arba'in
fifty	50	hamsin
sixty	60	sittin
seventy	70	saba'in
eighty	80	tamanin
ninety	90	tasa'in, casa'in
hundred	100	ɗari
one hundred and twenty one	121	ashirin da ɗaya da ɗari
two hundred	200	metin, metan, ɗari biyu
three hundred	300	ɗari uku
four hundred	400	arbaminya, ɗari huɗu
five hundred	500	hamsaminya, ɗari biyar
six hundred	600	ɗari shida
seven hundred	700	ɗari bakwai
eight hundred	800	ɗari takwas
nine hundred	900	ɗari tara

thousand	1,000	dubu, alif
ten thousand	10,000	dubu goma
one hundred thousand	100,000	dubu ɗari
million	1,000,000	miliyan

ORDINAL NUMBERS

first	1st	na farko
second	2nd	na biyu
third	3rd	na uku
fourth	4th	na huɗu
fifth	5th	na biyar
sixth	6th	na shida
seventh	7th	na bakwai
eighth	8th	na takwas
ninth	9th	na tara
tenth	10th	na goma

once	sau ɗaya
twice	sau biyu
three times, thrice	sau uku

one half	rabi
one quarter	rubu'i
one third	sulusi

WEIGHTS AND MEASURES

kilometre	kilomita
metre	mita
mile	mil
foot	ƙafa
yard	yadi

| gallon | galan |
| litre | lita |

kilogramme	kilo
gramme	giram
pound	laba
ounce	oza

TIME

second	**daƙiƙa**
minute	**minti**
hour	**awa, sa'a**
day (24 hours)	**kwana**
week	**mako, sati**
fortnight	**mako biyu**
month	**wata**
year	**shekara**
century	**ƙarni**

the year before last	**bara waccan**
last year	**bara**
this year	**bana**
next year	**baɗi**
the year after next	**baɗi waccan**

three days before	**shekaranjiya ban da jiya**
the day before yesterday	**shekaranjiya**
yesterday	**jiya**
today	**yau**
tomorrow	**gobe**
the day after tomorrow	**jibi**
three days hence	**gata**
four days hence	**citta**

DAYS OF THE WEEK

Monday	**Lahadi**
Tuesday	**Litinin**
Wednesday	**Talata**
Thursday	**Laraba**
Friday	**Alhamis**
Saturday	**Jumma'a**
Sunday	**Asabar, Sati**

MONTHS OF THE YEAR

January	**Janairu**
February	**Fabrairu**
March	**Maris**

April	**Afrilu**
May	**Mayu**
June	**Yuni**
July	**Yuli**
August	**Agusta**
September	**Satumba**
October	**Oktoba**
November	**Nuwamba**
December	**Disamba**

ISLAMIC MONTHS

Muharram
Safar
Rabi'u Lawwal
Rabi'u Lahir
Jimada Lawwal
Jimada Lahir
Rajab
Sha'aban
Ramalan, Ramazan
Shawwal
Zulƙida
Zulhajji

PRAYER TIMES

1. asuba
2. azahar
3. la'asar
4. magariba
5. lisha

Appendix 5:

AJAMI (Hausa written in Arabic script)

CONSONANTS *in order of the Arabic alphabet*

Boko	Hausa name	Arabic name	Ajami character			
			isolate	*final*	*medial*	*initial*
a, '	alif	*alif*	ا	ـا	—	—
b, ɓ	ba	*bā'*	ب	ـب	ـبـ	بـ
t	ta	*tā'*	ت	ـت	ـتـ	تـ
c	ca	*thā'*	ث	ـث	ـثـ	ثـ
j	jim	*jīm*	ج	ـج	ـجـ	جـ
h	ha ƙarami	*ḥā'*	ح	ـح	ـحـ	حـ
h	ha mai ruwa	*khā'*	خ	ـخ	ـخـ	خـ
d	dal	*dāl*	د	ـد	—	—
z	zal	*dhāl*	ذ	ـذ	—	—
r	ra	*rā'*	ر	ـر	—	—
z	zaira	*zā'*	ز	ـز	—	—
s	sin	*sīn*	س	ـس	ـسـ	سـ
sh	shin	*shīn*	ش	ـش	ـشـ	شـ
s	sodi	*ṣād*	ص	ـص	ـصـ	صـ
l	lodi	*ḍād*	ض	ـض	ـضـ	ضـ
ɗ	ɗa mai hannu	*ṭā'*	ط	ط	ط	ط
z	zadi	*ẓā'*	ظ	ظ	ظ	ظ

			isolate	final	medial	initial
ts	tsa	—	ظ	ظ	ظ	ظ
'	ain	'ain	ع	ع	ع	ع
g	angai	ghain	غ	غ	غ	غ
f	fa	fā'	ڢ	ڡ	ڡ	ڡ
ƙ	ƙaf mai ruwa, ƙaf wau	qāf	ف	ڡ	ڧ	ڧ
k	kaf	kāf	ک	ک	ک	ک
l	lam	lām	ل	ل	ل	ا
m	mim	mīm	م	م	م	م
n	nun	nūn	ن	ن ں	ن	ن
h	ha kuri, ha babba	hā'	ه	ه	ه	ھ
w	wau	wāw	و	و	—	—
y	ya	yā'	ی يکے	ی ي	ی	ی

Other consonants

| ' | hamza | hamza | ء |

(Hamza can be found isolate or riding on the following: (ئ ؤ إ أ)

| | | tā' marbūṭa | ة | ة | — | — |

(A feminine ending found in Arabic words, transcribed as -a, -ah, or -at)

Standard forms used in the Arab world

	fā'	ف	ف	ف	ف
	qāf	ق	ق	ق	ق
	kāf	ك	ك	ك	ك

VOWELS

Boko	Hausa name	Arabic name	Ajami character
a	wasali bisa	*fatḥa*	....
ā	alif	*alif*	....ا..(....آ...ىَ....)
i	wasali ƙasa	*kasra*	....
ī	ya	*yāʾ*	........ـِىـ.........
u	rufuʾa	*ḍamma*	........ُو..........
o, ō, ū	wau	*wāw*	..........ُو........
e	guda ƙasa	—	....
ē	guda ƙasa da imala	—	....ـى..ب..ا....

DIPTHONGS

| au | | | ....ـَوْ.... |
| ai | | | ....ـَىْ.... |

OTHER SIGNS

			ْ
	ɗauri	*sukūn*	....

(Indicates that no vowel follows the consonant on which it is placed)

			ّ
	shadda	*shadda, tashdīd*	....

(Indicates that the consonant on which it is placed is doubled)

Vowel signs used in Arabic words

| -un | ....ٌو........ | -in | ....ٍ........ | -an | ....ً.أَ.... |

CPSIA information can be obtained at www.ICGtesting.com
Printed in the USA
LVOW040215100512

281144LV00009B/4/P